WHERE TO WATCH BIRDS IN
NORTHERN & EASTERN SPAIN

THIRD EDITION

ERNEST GARCIA AND MICHAEL REBANE

B L O O M S B U R Y

LONDON · NEW DELHI · NEW YORK · SYDNEY

Acknowledgements

Valuable assistance or advice on parts of the text were provided by Juanjo Aja, Philip Croft, Juan Antonio Gonzalez Morales, Hugh Harrop, Daniel Lopez, Andy Paterson and Victor Vasquez. We particularly wish to thank the following who gave us the benefit of their extensive local experience in their thorough comments on the province accounts: Luis Carrera (Asturias), Ignacio Diez (Valencia), Felipe Gonzalez (Cantabria), Gorka Gorospe (Navarra), Ricard Gutiérrez (Cataluña), Eduardo de Juana (Aragón, Castilla y León, Castilla–La Mancha, Madrid and La Rioja), Antonio Sandoval, Cesar Vidal, Rafael Salvadores and Tito Salvadores (Galicia). We also thank our editor Katie Read for ably steering this work to completion.

Christopher Helm
An imprint of Bloomsbury Publishing Plc
50 Bedford Square
London
WC1B 3DP
UK

www.bloomsbury.com

BLOOMSBURY, CHRISTOPHER HELM and the Helm logo are trademarks of Bloomsbury Publishing Plc

First published 2017

A catalogue record for this book is available from the British Library.

Library of Congress Cataloguing-in-Publication data has been applied for.

ISBN: PB: 978-1-4729-3675-2
       ePDF: 978-1-4729-3676-9
       ePub: 978-1-4729-3674-5

2 4 6 8 10 9 7 5 3

Design by Jocelyn Lucas
Illustrations by Stephen Message / Maps by Brian Southern

Printed and bound in India by Replika Press Pvt. Ltd.

MIX
Paper from responsible sources
FSC
www.fsc.org   FSC® C016779

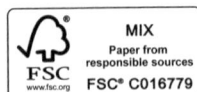

Front cover (top): Dupont's Lark © Alejandro Torés Sánchez; (bottom): Pin-tailed Sandgrouse © Alejandro Torés Sánchez. Spine. Back cover (left): Bearded Vulture © ESCOCIA/Shutterstock; (middle): Azure-winged Magpie © Jesus Giraldo Gutierrez/Shutterstock; (right): Audouin's Gull © erni/Shutterstock

CONTENTS

FOREWORD

Spain is a huge country, much larger than most first-time visitors ever imagine. Its vastness supports many spectacular and important wildlife habitats that in turn hold some of the most diverse bird communities in Europe. Some of these habitats remain under threat from human activities. Of all land uses, it is 'modern' farming practices that have been the most destructive and caused the greatest losses. Agricultural intensification, driven by funding from the European Union's Common Agricultural Policy continues to have a significant impact on farming, despite the introduction of some mitigation measures. Increased use of artificial fertilisers and pesticides, cropland irrigation, the introduction of new crop types, loss of fallow land and moves away from traditional forms of livestock farming have led to substantial declines in many species, in particular those of open country. Those hit hardest include the Lesser Kestrel, Little and Great Bustards, Black-bellied and Pin-tailed Sandgrouse and many lark species.

Land-use changes have not always been bad news. The expansion of rice cultivation has created new wetlands that harbour sometimes huge numbers of waterbirds, especially on passage and in winter. The increased planting of alfalfa (lucerne) as animal fodder has also benefited Little Bustards and sandgrouse, which eat the plants. However, in the main it is the more extensive traditional methods of food production that have created habitats and landscapes rich in wildlife. The black Iberian pigs continue to graze the open wooded dehesas, enabling the production of the renowned air-dried hams of Spain, the Jamones Ibéricos and Serranos. Remarkable cheeses of high quality are still produced from the milk of sheep and cattle which graze the alpine and valley meadows of the mountains. Unfortunately such farming practices as the widespread growing of fruits and vegetables 'under plastic' and the cultivation of strawberries, have focused on high-input production which has caused severe environmental problems, including the over-exploitation of scarce water resources.

The Mediterranean countries still do not have a good name in conservation circles. However, in Spain at least there have been great improvements over recent years accompanied by a widespread increase in interest and awareness among the Spaniards themselves. These trends are reflected in the ever-growing membership of conservation bodies in Spain and by the increase in protected areas, many of them featuring often splendid information centres and hides.

We hope that this book will encourage you to explore the vastness of Spain and to discover new landscapes and their wildlife. The spectacle of Great Bustards stalking the cereal fields, the effortless flight of squadrons of Griffon Vultures drifting across deep gorges and the remarkable sight and sound of thousands of Cranes flying to their wetland roosts, are but a few of the unforgettable experiences to savour.

We are all fortunate that there is still a great deal left to conserve in Spain. Conservation, though, has its price and the case for preserving important areas is strengthened if they can be seen to attract tourists as well. We hope that this book will continue to contribute to conservation of Spanish birds and their habitats by encouraging visits to protected areas and to other locations that deserve to be protected. Do tell hoteliers and other local people why you are visiting. By doing so you will be helping to ensure that Spanish wildlife remains the spectacle that it is.

A key driving force in encouraging interest in birds in Spain and in bringing about their conservation is the Spanish Ornithological Society and Birdlife partner, the Sociedad Española de Ornitología (SEO/Birdlife). We urge you to contribute to their efforts by joining the Society. You will find that their quarterly magazine 'Aves y Naturaleza' is a dynamic and informative update on anything to do with birds in Spain, including recent observations and some wonderful photographs. They also publish the scientific journal *Ardeola*, most of which is in English. You can contact them via their website seo.org.

This book has been written to help you to get the most out of your birding in Spain, whether you are a visitor or a longer-term resident. We hope you find it useful. Please let us know if it is or if it isn't! Your comments and suggestions will be most welcome and will of course be acknowledged in any future editions.

¡ *Buen viaje* !

Ernest Garcia & Michael Rebane   *2016*

INTRODUCTION TO THE THIRD EDITION

This book was first published in 1999, under the title 'Where to watch birds in North and East Spain'. It complements the sister volume, 'Where to watch birds in Southern and Western Spain', by Ernest Garcia and Andrew Paterson (3rd edition 2008), which covers Andalucía and Extremadura, as well as Gibraltar. The first edition was written by Michael Rebane and was revised and updated in 2008 by Michael Rebane and Ernest Garcia. This third edition has been updated by Ernest Garcia, drawing on his continuing association with the Iberian Peninsula and its avifauna. The text and maps have been fully revised. Many of the original locations, especially the most important ones, have received expanded treatment and an additional 14 sites have been highlighted as worth visiting.

The 17 years since the appearance of the first edition have seen further and ongoing changes in the Spanish natural environment and its wildlife. Some are developments of conservation significance, both positive and negative, and others have involved changes in numbers and geographical distribution of certain species.

Conservation Issues

The good news remains very real, notwithstanding a shortage of funds in recent years arising from the wider financial problems of the Spanish economy and the eurozone. Interest in Spanish birds and wildlife, and in the environment generally, continues to grow as evidenced by the rising membership of the Sociedád Española de Ornitología (Spanish Ornithological Society – also known as SEO/Birdlife) and other organisations. When SEO/Birdlife was founded in 1954 the number of Spaniards with a serious interest in birds (hunting excluded) probably did not exceed a couple of dozen. Now, over 60 years later, there are many thousands and it is perfectly normal to meet numbers of Spanish birders at key sites and in the wider countryside. School parties are taken routinely to visit places where there are information centres and suitable facilities: you will hear such groups before you see them, since Spanish children tend towards voluble exuberance, but do tolerate them patiently. It is vital that younger generations develop a sympathy for their natural heritage.

There has been welcome expansion in the network of local wildlife groups, in particular the provincial and regional groups of the SEO who undertake much survey work, which has already included two breeding bird atlasses (1997 and 2003), a winter atlas (2012), national censuses of a wide range of species and much more. The various local authorities have taken note of this interest by establishing Visitors' Centres, often with impressive infrastructure, in many key places and by producing a great deal of printed informative material, for the benefit of both the Spanish public and also of the ever-increasing number of foreign visitors who come to northern and eastern Spain in search of its rich natural heritage. Eco-tourism is well established as an important dimension to Spain's all-important and massive tourist industry.

The network of protected areas established and maintained by official bodies and, to a lesser extent, by voluntary organisations, has continued to expand, especially under the encouragement of the European Union. An increasingly extensive network of Important Bird Areas (IBAs), or ZEPAs (Zonas de Especial Protección para las Aves) as they are known in Spain, is now in place across the entire country. The ZEPAs identify key regions and provide a basic level of regulation of the land use there and are invaluable in providing essential protection to key habitats and their species. Many of the ZEPAs are also included in the broader network of Special Protection Areas or SPAs (LICs: Lugares de Importancia Comunitaria in Spain), which was set up under the Natura 2000 initiative and provides some protection of the full range of biodiversity, not just birds. All these EU-inspired measures, together especially with recent improvements to the Common Agricultural Policy, go some way to reduce and perhaps eventually reverse the harmful effects of initial EU policies on the natural environment. Designating a site as protected is, of course, very far from ensuring its conservation, but it is an essential first step.

Many of the ZEPAs/LICs enjoy higher levels of security under the Spanish network of protected areas. There are four principal categories of these, defined as follows:

Reserva Natural (Nature Reserve)   The lowest level of protection. Nature Reserves are intended to protect specific ecosystems or communities, but the degree to which they do this depends partly on security of tenure or ownership. These are mainly small sites, many of them lagoons. The organisation responsible for management varies, as happens in the UK. Normally only activities compatible with the conservation of the sites are permitted there. Visitors are typically encouraged to visit these areas (although access to parts of sites may be restricted) and consequently information centres and hides can be provided.

Paraje Natural (Natural Locality)   A similar status to Nature Reserve and protects mainly restricted areas of general scenic or biological interest. Traditional activities (not hunting) may be permitted to continue.

Parque Natural (Natural Park)   An extensive area, often of sierras and woodlands, which offers well-preserved natural or semi-natural habitats. The designation protects the area from further unsuitable development, while still allowing compatible traditional activities to continue. A feature of a Natural Park is that it aims to provide educational and recreational facilities for the general public. The protection of traditional architecture and cultural aspects is included. Many have information centres that offer factsheets, maps, displays and other information about the region.

Parque Nacional (National Park)   A National Park enjoys the highest level of protection. The designation protects extensive areas of international importance within which all human activities are strictly controlled. Access too may be limited where this is in the interests of the fauna and flora. There are 15 National Parks in Spain and its islands, seven of them in the region covered by this book. These seven are the Islas Atlánticas de Galicia (site GA3), Picos de Europa (AS7), Ordesa y Monte Perdido (AR4), Aigüestortes I Estany de

Sant Maurici (CAT1), Sierra de Guadarrama (M1), Cabañeros (CM13) and the Tablas de Daimiel (CM12).

All this notwithstanding, the natural environment remains under grave threat from a diversity of causes. Changes in land use often have implications for the environment that give cause for concern. Loss of steppelands to afforestation or to irrigated crops is a particularly serious problem affecting bustards and other open-country species especially. Recent changes to the Common Agricultural Policy may go some way to limit or correct damage caused by insensitive changes in land use but the problem is likely to remain severe for the foreseeable future.

The loss of green land to such developments as urban expansion – especially to tourist apartments and villas on the coasts – and new motorways and roads has had serious effects in many places. The expansion of ski facilities in the Pyrenees and elsewhere is also potentially damaging to mountain habitats and their wildlife. Among other infrastructures, wind-farms are a controversial, intrusive and increasingly widespread feature of our area. It remains imperative that they should be sited sensitively and only if validated by environmental impact assessments. Spain is well placed to exploit solar power, using solar panels and mirror power plants; these too have proliferated but also need to be sited sensitively.

Climate change may itself be having a broader impact on the regional ecology but, as elsewhere, the picture is very unclear. One of the most serious potential consequences would be water shortage. Much of southern and eastern Spain is relatively arid, with very dry years occurring from time to time. Indeed, 2005 saw the most severe drought in the region for 125 years, with many wetlands drying up completely for much longer than the usual midsummer period and forest fires becoming exceptionally widespread and damaging. The competing demands for ever-increasing quantities of water from tourism (think swimming pools and golf courses), agriculture, horticulture and direct human consumption put great pressure on the water supplies available for such places as natural wetlands. The overall response of the authorities has been to build more reservoirs but water problems are likely to continue and could become more acute.

A number of other problems deserve mention. The disturbance of the countryside by noisy visitors has reached new heights in some areas where quad-bikes have become popular, allowing people access to formerly quiet and remote forest tracks. Such vehicles are prohibited from many protected places but the law is very poorly enforced. Sundays are worst, indeed the people involved are known locally as 'domingueros': the Sunday-trippers, a point to bear in mind when planning your birding trips.

More insidious and pervasive is the effect of poison baits laid for the control of foxes and other 'vermin', especially on large estates where the practice is hard to detect. These, and the effects of some poorly designed electricity pylons which electrocute birds, have had severe impacts on the populations of many raptors. SEO/Birdlife has campaigned actively against both threats, with very considerable success. Many of the worst pylons have been rendered safe and there have been exemplary prosecutions of those responsible for poisoning raptors. However, such dangers are far from over.

Carrion-eaters have suffered locally from a variety of causes, other than the consumption of poison baits. EU regulations to close the 'muladares':

sites where farmers dump livestock carcases for prompt, free disposal by vultures, were promulgated for hygiene reasons. Such closures led to starvation of Griffon Vultures in some parts of Spain, especially in the north-east, but did not have a wider impact since the regulations were widely ignored. The possible legalised use of diclofenac for veterinary purposes is a new and more insidious threat, given that diclofenac has been responsible for the near extirpation of the vultures of the Indian sub-continent.

Changes in the Avifauna

The bird populations of such a large country as Spain are bound to fluctuate in the long term but significant recent changes have occurred and will continue to appear, as a consequence of habitat changes, climatic influences and conservation measures, among others.

The very large and rapid increase in the population of White Storks seen during the last 35 years has continued. The Spanish stork population was at an all-time low of 6,753 pairs in 1984 but the 2004 census found a record 33,217 pairs, with large increases in the traditional core areas of Extremadura and western Andalucía and in the south-west of our area. The population has continued to increase in some areas and the birds are well established in the Ebro valley. However, they are still absent from much of eastern Spain, which is probably too arid for them. White Storks continue to benefit from the food hand-outs at landfill garbage dumps, to the extent that many have become virtually resident in Spain and no longer risk the hazards of the annual return trip to Africa.

The Griffon Vulture population burgeoned from 3,240 pairs in 1979 to over 17,000 pairs in 1999 and had increased further to 25,000 pairs by 2008. The population has remained at least stable within our area since then. Vultures, like White Storks, are also beneficiaries of the sloppiness of human waste-disposal but they have also benefited from a reduction of direct persecution, now that raptor-shooting is universally prohibited in Spain. Many of the key colonies are directly protected. Black Vultures too have increased greatly in Spain, from 365 pairs in 1986 to some 2,400 pairs in 2006 and this species has never been easier to find nor more abundant, in its regular haunts. The Lammergeier maintains a slowly increasing population in the Pyrenees, where there were some 250 mature individuals and a similar number of immature birds in 2010, and is showing signs of return to the Cordillera Cantábrica, where there is a reintroduction programme.

A particularly welcome development in recent years has been the ongoing recovery of the Spanish Imperial Eagle, whose population declined to only 131 pairs in 1999 but numbered 365 pairs in 2012. It has continued to increase steadily since then, with some former haunts and new locations becoming occupied. Specific conservation measures coordinated by SEO, including agreements with landowners and the remedying of unsafe pylons, have played a large part in making this welcome trend possible.

Campaigns against the unsafe use of poison baits to control foxes in particular have begun to pay dividends. The breeding populations of the Red Kite, Egyptian Vulture and Raven have shown some recovery after suffering severe declines from poisoning in the past. Bonelli's Eagle has declined in the north of our area and has abandoned some former haunts there, but has increased in the south of its Iberian range. The Lesser Kestrel too has shown some considerable recovery in numbers locally, after a marked decline.

Other breeding species showing significant and ongoing increases in numbers and, in some cases, geographical spread within our area include Cormorant, Great White Egret, Grey Heron, Black Stork, Glossy Ibis, Black-shouldered Kite, Marsh and Montagu's Harriers, Short-toed, Booted and Golden Eagles, Purple Swamphen, Black-headed Gull, Yellow-legged Gull (alas!), Black Woodpecker and Red-rumped Swallow.

There is a debit list too, unfortunately. Significant declines within our area, associated with habitat loss especially, have been shown by Marbled Duck, Capercaillie, Grey Partridge, Little Bustard, Black-bellied and Pin-tailed Sandgrouse, Dupont's Lark and Moustached Warbler. Among these, the plight of the Little Bustard is especially worrying; although Spain remains a global stronghold of this species at least half the population has disappeared since the 1990s. Unfortunately also, the Galician outpost populations of two seabirds, the kittiwake and the guillemot, now seem to have disappeared after a long period of steady decline. The Lesser Grey Shrike too is practically extinct within its sole Iberian haunts in Catalunya, following the contraction of its Western European range.

Changes in Classification Status and Names

The whole issue of bird names and, especially the defining of species-boundaries, remains highly controversial. Some stability may be provided, in due course and for a while, by the studies that underlie the *Illustrated checklist of the birds of the World* (del Hoyo & Collar 2014). For the time being, however, the taxonomic decisions, names and sequence adopted by the most recent version of the Western Palearctic List of the Association of European Records and Rarities Committees (Crochet & Joynt 2015) have been followed here. These names will be familiar to all users and also correspond with those used in the regional avifauna, *The Birds of the Iberian Peninsula* (De Juana & Garcia 2015) and in the most recent List of the Birds of Spain (Gutiérrez *et al.* 2012). Qualifiers (e.g. 'Common') are given in the species accounts only for species such as coots, cuckoos and swallows that are represented in the area by more than one species. The full English, Spanish and scientific names are given for all species in the Status List chapter.

HOW TO USE THIS BOOK

The core of the book is the Site Accounts but we hope that you will find the preliminary chapters helpful in planning your visits. They describe the area and its birds. The Species List (Pages 333–369) gives the status of all those that occur with any regularity in the region as well as records of rarities. It is the principal reference to those widespread species that are seldom mentioned in the Site Accounts. The Species Index is cross-referenced with the Site Accounts to help you to track down those species that are likely to be of particular interest to you. For example, to see Lammergeiers you can look up that species in the Species Index and find a list of all those sites where they regularly occur. The Site Index will help you locate particular site accounts.

In many ways, all of Spain is one big birding site. Certainly you do not have to travel far to find a great deal of interest, especially if the region is new to you. A striking feature is the sheer numbers of larks, finches, sparrows, buntings and other common birds in the countryside, a welcome contrast with some more northern countries where farmland especially is impoverished birdwise. Birds of prey are everywhere: Montagu's Harriers quarter the fields and soaring Griffon Vultures and other large raptors are omnipresent. The towns and cities offer hordes of screaming swifts in spring and summer which share the rooftops, especially in the west, with White Storks and Lesser Kestrels. Still, there is a lot more to see: in the woodlands, forests, coasts, wetlands and mountains, and we have tried to provide a dossier of the principal sites of the area, selecting those that we know are accessible and can be relied upon to provide the main regional specialities. We also suggest areas that are likely to repay closer investigation but for which there is less available information. Spain is both fun and rewarding to explore and there remains a great deal of scope for birding in little-known corners, especially in the central regions.

LANGUAGES

Strictly speaking, there is no such language as Spanish. The official state language is properly called Castilian (Castellano) and it is spoken and understood throughout Spain. Nevertheless, there are a number of regional languages of long-standing and these have enjoyed a brisk – and in some cases aggressive – resurgence in recent years. These languages are spoken by a significant proportion of local people and often appear alongside (or instead of) 'Spanish' equivalents in public places and on road signs. Regional languages are a prominent feature of Galicia (Gallego), Asturias (Asturiano), the Basque Country (Euskera), Cataluña (Catalán) and Valencia (Valencià: a dialect of Catalán). All of these are intelligible to speakers of Castellano, at least when written down, with the conspicuous exception of the Basque language, which is completely distinct from any other European language.

We have tended to favour Castellano ('Spanish') for site names and place names, but we have diverged from this on occasion where a local name would be more useful to visitors. Non-polyglot birders will find that English is widely spoken on the east coast and at all major hotels and other tourist facilities

BAY of BISCAY

Santander Bilbao

FRANCE

Asturias Cantabria País Vasco Navarra

Galicia

La Rioja

Castilla y León

Cataluña

Barcelona

ATLANTIC OCEAN

Aragón

Madrid

PORTUGAL Extremadura

Castilla La Mancha

Comunidad Valenciana

Alicante

N

Murcia

Andalucía

MEDITERRANEAN SEA

Gibraltar

Map 1

Autonomous regions covered by this book

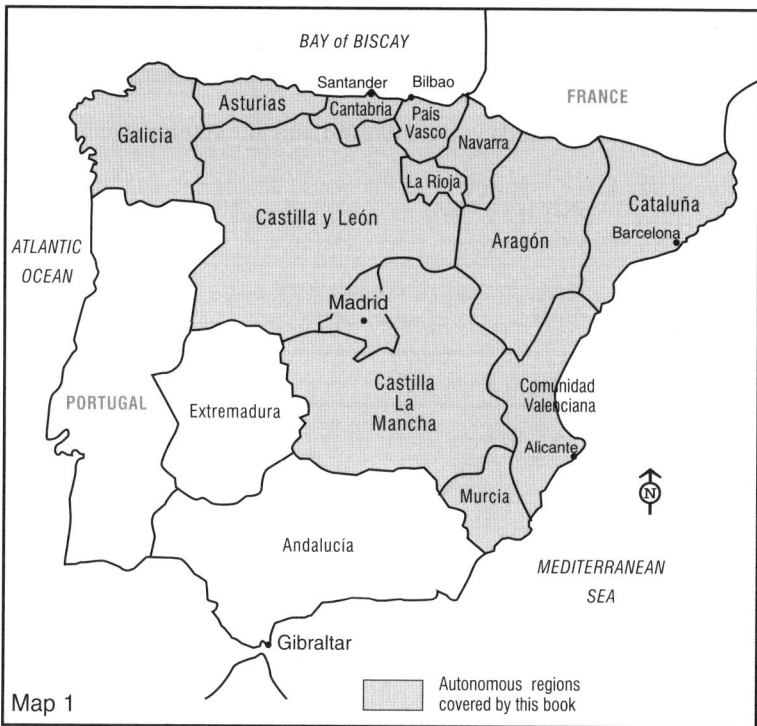

Map 1. Autonomous regions of Northern and Eastern Spain.

throughout the region, but it is not understood widely in rural areas in the north and inland. However, nearly all young people in Spain study English at school so if you find yourself needing to ask for directions in English somewhere inland you are far more likely to be able to communicate with a young person than with an elderly one.

REGIONAL CHAPTERS

The Spanish state is divided into regions, each of which has its own administration and a high degree of autonomy. Site accounts are grouped by autonomous regions into 13 chapters. Each Regional Chapter has an introductory section giving, in turn, a brief description of the region, a list of the sites with their code numbers, general information and an outline of access to the region. A regional map shows the position of individual sites within the province, in relation to main towns and access roads, for ease of location.

The sites themselves are coded by letters and numbers. The former are abbreviations for the autonomous regions, as follows; AR Aragón, AS Asturias, CAN Cantabria, CAT Cataluña, CLM Castilla–La Mancha, CyL Castilla y León, GA Galicia, MU Murcia, M Madrid, N Navarra, PV País Vasco, R La Rioja, V Valencia.

Map 1 shows the locations of the autonomous regions and national boundaries of the Iberian peninsula, indicating the area covered by this book.

SITE ACCOUNTS

Each site account gives the following information:

Site name (with Province in parentheses) and Site reference number

Status   The conservation status of the site, including the official names of any protected areas where these differ from the site name. The latter are useful when seeking further information from websites.

Site map   Showing the main features of the site and the access roads and paths. The map scales should be noted carefully. The smaller wetland sites have smaller-scale maps. The extensive sites covering the plains and mountains (sierras) are necessarily drawn on a larger scale.

Site description   The principal structural and botanical features of the area.

Species   The major bird species typical of the site. Species of other wildlife are also mentioned briefly where appropriate.

Timing   The best times of year to visit and any other factors to consider.

Access   How to get to, enter and explore the site. Directions are usually given from the nearest large town. Visitors' centres and their opening hours are mentioned for major sites especially; in general such centres (but not the sites themselves) are often closed on one day per week (often Mondays) and close for an afternoon lunchbreak (often 14.00–16.00 hrs) and on Sunday afternoons.

Calendar   The main bird species are listed under all or some of the following headings: All year, Breeding season, Winter, Passage periods. 'All Year' often means 'Resident' but for some species (Red Kite, Crag Martin etc.) there is actually a great deal of turnover among the populations involved. The lists are sometimes extensive but they are not exhaustive. In particular, they usually omit species such as Barn Swallow, Stonechat and Corn Bunting, which are widespread and common throughout Spain. Common species are included where they help to define the ornithological flavour of a site.

KEY TO SITE MAPS

town / village		marsh	
motorway or major road		reeds	
secondary road		sierra	
minor road		bridge	
track		viewpoint	
path		monastery / church	
regional boundary		mountain refuge	
railtrack		information centre	
river		hide	
lake		car park	
extent of reserve		lighthouse	
major peaks			

VISITING NORTHERN AND EASTERN SPAIN

PLANNING YOUR VISIT

This book can be used in a variety of ways, depending on the nature of your visit or, indeed, whether you live in the region. As far as visitors are concerned, there are two main options:

Touring

This is the best option for a birding holiday. Most touring birders fly to a suitable airport (see below) and then travel widely in a hired car, staying at a variety of hotels. Clearly, the amount of time available will dictate what is feasible.

Barcelona is a good starting point for a circular trip that can take in the Ebro delta, the Ebro valley including the steppes at Belchite, returning via the Pyrenees. The route can be 'done' in a week but two weeks would be more productive and less hectic. Late May and June would be the best time but summer is also a good season to choose, especially for visiting the mountains.

The coastal wetlands are the main attractions for visits starting at Valencia or Alicante, from where you can also head inland to visit sites in Aragón, Castilla –La Mancha and perhaps Madrid.

Arriving at Madrid puts you in easy reach of the very varied habitats of that region, from where you can go on to visit the key steppe areas of Castilla y León to the north-west and/or the wetlands and sierras of western Castilla–La Mancha, among other possibilities.

Asturias (Oviedo) airport in the centre of the north coast is strategically placed for visiting Galicia, Asturias and Cantabria. The emphasis will be on seabirds and shorebirds along the shoreline – including vagrants in autumn and winter especially – and on the birds of the Cantabrian mountains: including the Picos de Europa. Santander and Bilbao also give good access to the north coast, all of which is served by the west/east A-8 motorway, and are also handy for visiting the southern flanks of the Cantabrian mountains, in Castilla y León. They also provide good access to the Basque country itself, the adjacent region of La Rioja and the north-western sector of the Pyrenees in Navarra.

Many other possible routes will suggest themselves when you consult the introductions to the regional chapters.

Centre-based visits

This is the option for those who have a family in tow or who simply don't want to drive very far. Most typical family holidays will be based on the resorts on the Mediterranean coast but many of these are well placed for visiting a wide range of sites, as our maps of Catalonia, Valencia and Murcia will confirm. The north coast also has plenty to offer traditional sea-and-sand holidaymakers and yet offers superb seawatching and is within easy access of the Cantabrian mountains including the Picos de Europa.

It is obviously possible to establish a base-camp at any of the inland localities but none of these would prove a good choice for family holidays.

Access by birders with disabilities

Very few of the sites are conveniently accessible by public transport so birders with disabilities will need to have the use of a car. We are well aware that disability takes very many forms and that only a small minority of disabled birders are confined to wheelchairs. The information on 'Access' in the site accounts should allow those who have limited mobility to gauge the suitability or otherwise of particular sites. In general, hides and other watchpoints have parking fairly close by. Modern visitors' centres are generally designed with the needs of all visitors in mind and so are many of the hides: and the situation is improving.

Many sites in open country, for example in the steppelands of Castilla y León, involve scanning large areas from quiet roadsides: such places should be accessible to all. It is really only the rougher and steeper trails which may prove an insurmountable hurdle to some birders: including, as we have noticed, many people who are not actually disabled! However, there are always plenty of other easy-to-reach wonderful places to visit instead.

INTERNET BIRDING IN NORTHERN & EASTERN SPAIN

Websites have proliferated to the extent that a search for any of the locations in this book will provide a selection of 'hits', some of which are useful for last-minute information such as the appearances of rarities. The majority of sites and reserves have their own websites, generally giving details of access, species lists, opening hours of visitors' centres and maps. It is a good idea to google those sites that you are likely to visit. Most are in Spanish but the major ones often feature an English version. The following general websites are often useful:

Rare birds in Spain (rarebirdspain.net/home). Essential reading for news and often excellent photographs of recent rarities from throughout Spain. In English and updated weekly, usually on Mondays. One to check before visiting the region to ensure that you don't miss anything special. The site also offers, under 'Files' the latest version of the Spanish national bird list, complete with A, B ,C, D and E categories and both Spanish and English names, as well as English and Spanish language versions of the form for submitting descriptions of rarities. Former rarities committee member Ricard Gutiérrez maintains this site.

Sociedad Española de Ornitología / SEO/Birdlife (seo.org). The website of the Spanish Ornithological Society provides a great deal of information about the Society and its activities as well as links to kindred organisations and to its own local groups. Some entries are bilingual, Spanish/English. The postal address of the society is SEO/Birdlife, C/Melquiades Biencinto 34, 28053, Madrid. (Email: seo@seo.org). Particularly useful pages on this site, under Sobre nosotros/Grupos de Trabajo (About us/Workgroups), include:

> **'Comité de Rarezas'; the Rarities committee site:**
> including the proforma '*esta ficha*' (at the bottom of the

title page) for submitting details of rare birds. Such reports may be posted but are best submitted online to rarezas@ seo.org. The English equivalent of the rarities form is acceptable. Both forms are also available on the 'Rare birds in Spain' website.'

Grupos Locales; SEO Local Groups

Click on the map for further details of local groups in those regions where they exist (most of them). Some groups have their own websites and these are an excellent source of local information.

MAPS

In general our own maps are sufficient to guide you to the various sites. You will need to inspect the provincial header map, at the start of each chapter, ideally in conjunction with a published road map, to establish the exact location of the sites covered. A large-scale road map (Firestone, Michelin or equivalents) is essential to give an overview of your journey. Best of all is the annual 1:300,000 (1cm = 3km) official road atlas – Mapa Oficial de Carreteras published by the Spanish Ministry of Information. The latest version (see the Ministry of Information website: fomento.es) can be purchased from any bookshop (Librería), motorway service station or large newsagent anywhere in Spain. It costs around €25, including an interactive DVD. The atlas maps are excellent and up to date and there are legends in English and French. The atlas includes street maps of all the provincial capitals.

WHEN TO COME

All times of year are of interest but it is necessary to remember that the interior can be uncomfortably hot in summer and that the major mountain areas are heavily snowed-up in winter. Most regions are best visited in spring or autumn but early summer is the best time for birding high in the mountains and is always pleasant on the north coast. Winter visits will be especially productive on and near the coasts but many wintering species, notably the Crane, congregate inland.

Spring (March–May) is generally best for seeing a wide range of species. Visits in early spring (March–April) allow you to find many of the wintering species as well as some of the arriving migrants but will be too early for birding in the higher mountains. The attractions of springtime include the birdsong: which can be spectacular and also makes it much easier to find passerines, the aerial displays of raptors: which make species such as Goshawks much more visible than usual, and the truly splendid displays of wild flowers.

Summer (June–August) has the disadvantages of high temperatures, dried-up lakes and large numbers of tourists along the coasts but there is still plenty to see at many sites. This is a good time to be on the high tops of the major mountain ranges, with montane flora and butterflies to enjoy as well as the birds.

Autumn (September–November) is a pleasant season inland and on the east coast, especially once the rains arrive. There are plenty of birds, including migrants, although these are not generally as visible as in spring. The northern coastlands are very good in autumn, when seabird passage offshore is often spectacular and when there is a good chance of finding rare migrants, especially American waterfowl, gulls and waders. This is also a good season for rarities on the east coast.

Winter (December–February) has the attraction of the wintering species; including great numbers of waterfowl, seabirds, raptors, waders and Cranes. Summer visitors are naturally then absent but there is always a scattering of scarce and rare species to give added interest. The season is very mild along the Mediterranean coast, especially in Valencia and Murcia, but even the north coast is more wet than cold in winter. Inland, the northern Meseta is often very cold indeed, with periods of snow. The Ebro valley can also be very cold at this season but is relatively dry. The high mountain ranges are heavily affected by snow, which often closes many passes and renders large areas inaccessible, except at ski resorts.

The amount of daylight available varies significantly according to the season and is of obvious importance. The whole of Spain is on Central European Time; GMT plus one hour in winter and GMT plus two hours in summer. In summer, birding is possible from about 06.00–22.00 hours local time. In winter the days are noticeably longer than in northern Europe; birding is possible from about 08.00–18.00 hours local time at the solstice.

WHAT TO WEAR

Visitors in summer will get away with light clothing, although warmer clothing is useful when seawatching and is an essential precaution, along with windproof and waterproof garments, when visiting high mountains. At other times of year it is necessary to pack some warm clothing, especially when visiting inland and mountain sites. Winter can be very cold, with frost and snow in many areas away from the coast. Hence, warm clothing with waterproof and windproof outer garments will be necessary, not least because the cooler times of year are often very wet as well. In general, you can rely on hot weather anywhere in the lowlands between June and September but you should be prepared for something cooler at other times of year there and must be able to cope with demanding conditions in the higher mountain ranges at any season.

GETTING THERE

By air
Many visitors travel by air, either to take advantage of one of the many relatively inexpensive one-centre package holidays or as a preliminary to touring the country in a hire car. Package holidays are mainly centred on the Mediterranean coast, with flights to Girona, Barcelona, Alicante and Murcia among others. Scheduled flights are also available to these destinations as well as to Madrid, itself a handy starting point for a visit to central Spain, and most regional capitals. Flights to Madrid and Barcelona originate from many parts of Europe, including

from all the main British airports, and link with the comprehensive internal flight network. Between them the various airlines serve A Coruña, Alicante, Asturias, Barcelona, Bilbao, Girona, Madrid, Murcia, Santander, Santiago de Compostela, Valencia, Vallodolid and Zaragoza, among others.

By car

A car is not absolutely essential for enjoying Spain; you can spend enjoyable visits at coastal resorts or on trekking holidays, for example. It is, however, impossible to visit many of the sites in this book without using a vehicle and you would be severely limited in your options without one.

Flying-out and hiring a car is probably the best strategy for the short-term visitor. Car-hire is available at all the airports and resorts but it is advisable and usually cheaper to make arrangements beforehand through a travel agency or your airline. Unlimited-mileage rental is the norm and is essential; you will probably cover many hundreds of miles in a week or so. Hiring a car avoids the cost of travelling to Spain by road and saves your own vehicle from the undoubted wear-and-tear of a birding holiday. British visitors will also avoid the inconvenience of driving a right-hand drive car on the Continent.

By sea

If you do come in your own vehicle, several choices are on offer. Travellers from Britain will find that the easiest option is to take the ferries from Plymouth to Santander or from Portsmouth to Bilbao or Santander. Brittany Ferries was the sole operator in 2016. These crossings take up to 30 hours but there are excellent opportunities for seeing seabirds and cetaceans during the journey, especially during the summer and autumn. Otherwise you can drive down through France, taking in the Pyrenees on the way if desired.

DRIVING

Major cities apart, much of our area offers pleasant and varied driving on often traffic-free roads. A few words of caution, however.

Roads

These are often excellent. Nowadays, even most minor roads have been very much improved, often with the assistance of extravagant EU funding. However, since we are often guiding you off the beaten track, it is as well to be aware that such roads are often not at all good and driving on the dirt tracks mentioned in many of our site accounts is an acquired art. Common sense should suffice but remember that unsurfaced roads are gritty and slippery, needing great care when braking or cornering. Speeds should be kept down on such roads, not least because of the dust cloud which you will otherwise raise. Dirt roads are best avoided altogether in wet weather unless you have an all-terrain vehicle.

All the sites mentioned in this book are safely accessible, given reasonable care, but we naturally cannot accept any liability for any mishaps that may occur.

Road numbers

Road numbers have undergone a series of changes over a number of years and pre-2007 maps are now out of date in this respect. We have used the numbers given by the Official road atlas (Mapa Oficial de Carreteras), 2015 edition. Many major roads have two or three numbers, often shown together, e.g. E-15/A-7/N-340. In particular, a road often carries an E-number under the EU scheme alongside a national designation: e.g. E-902/N-323.

We have chosen to ignore all the 'E-' numbers for the sake of simplicity. 'N-' roads (Carreteras Nacionales) are major trunk roads, often dual carriageway. 'A-' roads are usually (but not always!) motorways (Autovías). 'AP' roads are toll motorways (Autopistas de Peáje), the best choice where available for getting from A to B since they are largely avoided by lorries and carry relatively light traffic: the Mediterranean coastal motorway is an unfortunate exception.

Kilometre posts

Irrespective of the vagaries resulting from official tampering with road numbers, main roads (N- & A- roads generally) benefit from marker posts. These indicate kilometres from the point of origin chosen for the numbering (and so read 'backwards' if you are going the other way). They are separated by numbered 100m posts or, on motorways, by unmarked 500m posts. This system is a very good one for indicating locations and turn-offs with some precision and we have made use of it where it seems helpful. References in the site accounts to km-'X' accordingly refer to the roadside marker posts.

Traffic densities

Traffic is refreshingly light by the sorry standards of northern Europe and south-east England in particular. Nevertheless, cities and their outskirts are often busy at peak periods and trunk roads may become painfully congested at holiday times, notably during the four days (Thursday–Sunday) of the Easter weekend, at Christmas, at New Year and at weekends during the summer months (July–September). The holiday travel periods, when Spaniards flock en masse to and from the coasts, are also best avoided: they comprise the middle of July and the beginning and end of August especially. Traffic problems occur along the main trunk roads; country roads are not greatly affected but congestion occurs around particular towns and villages during their local festivals (fiestas).

Signs

The following are likely to be noticed during a birding holiday:

Entrada Prohibida/Paso Prohibido	No Entry
Incendio Prohibido	No Fires
Basura Prohibida	No dumping of rubbish
Privado/Particular	Private
Camino Privado/Particular	Private Road (i.e. Keep Out)
Coto Privado de Caza	Hunting Rights Reserved – usually also indicated by little rectangular signs, diagonally split black and white.
Ganado Bravo	Fighting Cattle (see below).

Protected areas generally have green signs headed C.M.A or A.M.A (Consejería or Agencia de Medio Ambiente – environment agency) and giving the status of the site, e.g. Reserva Natural.

NATURAL HAZARDS

The Spanish countryside is a great deal wilder than that of northern Europe and certain hazards need to be kept in mind.

Bulls. Although south-west Andalucía and parts of Extremadura are the traditional land of the fighting bull there are plenty of ranches in central Spain, and more locally elsewhere, so it is always best to treat bovines with extreme discretion. These bulls are killers and they will kill you if they catch you. Never enter fenced fields containing cattle, especially if there are 'GANADO BRAVO' signs. Quite a few of the local varieties of 'ordinary'cattle also have impressive horns and should also be treated with respect, especially if they are with their calves.

Mosquitoes. These are present in many areas throughout the whole year and can be a nuisance. Fortunately malaria is not a hazard in Spain. If you are susceptible to insect bites you would be well advised to come equipped with your favourite repellent and anti-histamine cream. Anti-mosquito 'plugs', which fit into an electrical socket and burn a repellent tablet, are also helpful.

Dogs. The sheep flocks in the mountains are sometimes accompanied by large sheep dogs, some of which seem to be particularly unfriendly but most of them just enjoy barking at you. In some regions they wear spiked collars, apparently to protect them from wolves. Elsewhere the numerous strays are generally too emaciated to pose any direct threat but they are a definite menace on the roads. They show a total lack of road sense and have a suicidal knack of turning up in the middle of the carriageway even on the busiest stretches. Drivers beware! Main roads are littered with dog corpses in various stages of mummification but there always seem to be some live ones left.

Sunburn. Sunny Spain often lives up to its name, even in mid winter. Always wear a hat and use a good sunblock to prevent sunburn or worse. Remember that the cooling effect of coastal sea-breezes may well disguise the onset of sunburn; the painful reckoning will come later. Sunglasses are a boon when driving, in snowy conditions, when birding near water and, especially, when scanning high clouds for raptors.

GEOGRAPHY, HABITATS AND BIRDS

What follows is a brief introduction to the topography and the main wildlife habitats in northern and eastern Spain. It provides some guidance for seeking out the specialities and planning your visit. The Species List (Pages 333–369) provides basic information on all the bird species that have been recorded in these parts of Spain and, in particular, indicates whether they are residents, winter or summer visitors, passage migrants or vagrants. The Species Index (Pages 376–384) guides you to sites recommended for finding particular species. Many common and widely distributed birds enliven any visit to Spain. They are the inhabitants of the towns and cities and of traditionally managed olive and citrus groves, vineyards and extensively managed farmland. These ubiquitous species include the White Stork, Common Swift, Bee-eater, Crested Lark, Barn Swallow, House Martin, Stonechat, Woodchat Shrike, Spotless Starling, House Sparrow, Goldfinch, Corn Bunting and quite a few others that receive only limited mention in the site accounts.

Map 2 shows the location of the principal mountain ranges and rivers of Iberia.

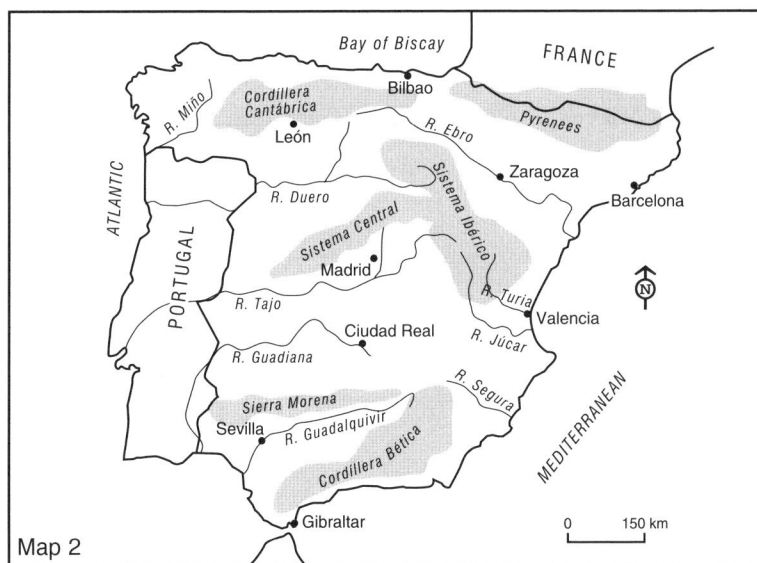

Map 2

THE MOUNTAINS AND FORESTS

Apart from Switzerland, Spain is the highest country in Europe, with a mean altitude of 600m. The principal mountain ranges include the Betic Cordillera in the far south, which is almost entirely within Andalucía and includes the highest peak in mainland Spain, Mulhacén in the Sierra Nevada (3,487m). Within our area the key mountain blocks are the following:

The Pyrenees (Pirineo) The imposing mountainous barrier separating Spain and France, a region with many peaks over 2,000m. The loftiest summit is Pico de Posets (3,375m). These are rugged mountains with many jagged out-crops, deep glacial valleys and alpine meadowlands at the higher levels. The largest natural forests remaining in the Pyrenees are in Navarra. Here the vast beech and Silver Fir forests of Irati and Quinto Real hold an extremely rich woodland bird fauna that includes seven woodpecker species.

The Cordillera Cantábrica The mountain barrier that runs west/east across the top of Spain between eastern Galicia and the Basque country, separat-ing a narrow strip of coastal lowlands from the central Spanish plateau, the Meseta. Some sectors, notably the Picos de Europa, are as dramatic as the Pyrenees. The range includes some notable forests among which the Bosque de Muniellos in Asturias is one of the largest mixed oakwoods in Spain and one of the finest in Europe.

The Sistema Ibérico This range runs roughly north-west/south-east to the west of the Ebro basin and forms the western boundaries of La Rioja, Navarra and Aragón.

The Sistema Central A rocky barrier across central Spain, splitting the Meseta into its northern and southern sectors. The range includes the Sierra de Gredos to the north of Extremadura and the Sierra de Guadarrama to the west and north of Madrid.

The Sierra Morena A comparatively gentle range, characterised by rounded summits and well-wooded hillsides, dividing the southern Meseta and Andalucía.

Smaller mountain blocks, still of considerable altitude and extent, include the Maestrazgo range: fringing Valencia, Cataluña and Aragón, the Montes de León: in the north-west of Castilla y León, the Montes de Toledo: to the south of Toledo in Castilla–La Mancha, and the Serrania de Cuenca: in the east of Castilla–La Mancha.

All of these mountain areas are characterised by more than high peaks and bare rock and comprise an intricate mosaic of crags, cliffs, gorges, rivers and streams, cultivated valleys, hay meadows and alpine grasslands, scrub and woodlands.

Pedunculate Oak and Sweet Chestnut forests are well developed in the Cantabrian mountains, although the beech is the dominant forest tree both there and in the Pyrenees. The Silver Fir forms the highest forest zone in the more humid north-facing valleys of the Pyrenees but, in contrast, is missing from the drier areas where the highest forests are of Scots Pine, with Black and Mountain Pines.

For the greatest variety of montane bird species, you should head for either the Pyrenees or the Cordillera Cantábrica. Both have a similar avifauna and species found in both include the Yellow-billed Chough, Snowfinch, Capercaillie, Black and Middle Spotted Woodpeckers and Wallcreeper. However, the Cordillera Cantábrica lacks four species that breed in the Pyrenees: the Lammergeier (which is being introduced), the Ptarmigan, the Boreal (Tengmalm's) Owl: which is found mainly in the eastern Pyrenees, especially Cataluña and the White-backed Woodpecker (found in Navarra). The other upland areas in

Northern and Eastern Spain, apart from the top end of the Sistema Ibérico (La Demanda) generally lack all these species. However, all the higher mountain areas have breeding Citril Finches, Water Pipits, Alpine Accentors and Goldcrests. One mountain species that is absent from the Pyrenees but is found in the western and central part of the Cordillera Cantábrica and in the Sistema Central is the Bluethroat: the Sierra de Gredos is a good place to find it.

A number of additional species breed widely only in the north of Spain. They are not specifically confined to the mountains but typically occur in the associated habitats of the Pyrenean and Cantabrian uplands, their woodlands, scrub and valleys. These include the Grey Partridge, Woodcock, Whinchat, Eurasian Treecreeper, Red-backed Shrike, Marsh Tit, Bullfinch and Yellowhammer.

STEPPES AND CEREAL PLAINS

The mountain ranges are separated by three main areas of plains.

The Valle del Ebro   The plains in the Ebro valley are mainly in Aragón, the most extensive areas being Los Monegros and Belchite, but spill over into neighbouring Navarra and Cataluña.

The Meseta Norte   Almost entirely within Castilla y León, fringed by the Sistema Central in the south and the Cordillera Cantábrica in the north.

The Meseta Sur   Almost entirely within Castilla–La Mancha, fringed by the Sistema Central in the north and the Sierra Morena in the south.

The Spanish plains, especially those of the Meseta, are vast expanses of flat or gently undulating territory. They are semi-arid and thus have a steppe-like natural vegetation of dwarf shrub species. Enormous areas are now given over to pasture and to the cultivation of non-irrigated crops, notably cereals. The latter are grown as part of a rotation including fallow periods, which produce areas (barbechos) of great birding interest. This complex mosaic supports some of the most threatened birds in Europe including the Quail, Montagu's Harrier, Lesser Kestrel, Great and Little Bustards, Pin-tailed and Black-bellied Sandgrouse and Dupont's Lark. The Stone-curlew, Greater Short-toed and Thekla Larks, Black-eared Wheatear and Spectacled Warbler are also widespread there as breeding species.

Not all the sites hold the full complement of breeding species and some are more common than others in particular areas. The Meseta Norte in Castilla y León is excellent for Great Bustards, while Little Bustards are relatively common in Castilla–La Mancha. For Dupont's Larks it is best to go to the Ebro Valley (particularly Aragón) where the densest population occurs. This is also one of the best areas in our regions for Black-bellied Sandgrouse, Calandra Lark and Lesser Short-toed Lark.

Outside the three main areas some steppe species also occur in Murcia: including Dupont's Lark, and in the saltpans of south Valencia: notably Stone-curlew, Greater Short-toed Lark and Lesser Short-toed Lark.

The plains are also very interesting in winter. Bustards and sandgrouse occur in sizeable flocks at this season. Very large numbers of wintering Lapwings, Golden Plovers, larks, pipits and finches are widespread as well as Hen Harriers, Merlins, Common Buzzards and other predators.

WETLANDS AND THE COAST

Much of the Spanish coastline is closely fringed by mountains. The Mediterranean coast is sandier, fairly straight and without major inlets. The lie of the much rockier north coast is also straight but it is deeply dissected by a series of beautiful fjord-like estuaries, the Rías, especially in Galicia. The Atlantic and Mediterranean coasts also differ conspicuously in their bird faunas. Seabirds are a particular attraction all year round on both coasts: advice on seabirding is given on pages 32–35.

The Mediterranean coast generally has a much richer bird fauna, inhabiting a diversity of internationally important coastal lagoons, marshes and saltpans. Most of the Spanish Moustached Warbler population occurs here. It is this coast, which includes the Costa Brava and Costa Blanca, that is so well known to millions of British holidaymakers. However, many natural coastal wetlands were lost to tourist developments in the 20th century. Conversion to rice paddies has had a major impact on the landscape of the Ebro delta and around the Albufera de Valencia especially. Nonetheless, such areas provide highly attractive feeding grounds for large numbers of waterbirds.

The most significant Mediterranean coastal sites include the Ebro Delta: one of the most important wetlands in Europe, housing a large Audouin's Gull colony, five breeding tern species, up to 4,000 pairs of Red-crested Pochards, a few hundred pairs of Slender-billed Gulls and Spain's northernmost Collared Pratincole colony, large numbers of passage and wintering waders and wildfowl, and much more besides; and the Albufera de Valencia, which has large breeding, passage and wintering populations of herons, gulls, terns, waders and waterfowl.

There are a number of other important coastal sites, for example the Mar Menor in Murcia, the largest coastal lagoon in Spain. Other wetlands in south Valencia have a breeding presence of two globally threatened duck species, the White-headed and Marbled Ducks. El Hondo is an important site for the latter and it is also a regular wintering site of the Greater Spotted Eagle. The saltpans in this area are also good for species typically associated with wetlands in dry inland steppes. They include the Stone-curlew, Avocet, Black-winged Stilt, Kentish Plover and Lesser Short-toed Lark.

The Atlantic coastline has southerly outpost breeding populations of some species that are widespread further north in Europe, including the Oystercatcher, Great and Lesser Black-backed Gulls and Grasshopper Warbler. Galicia has the majority of the Spanish Shag population. The northern coast-line attracts a good range of wintering birds and passage migrants, including an annual 'quota' of trans-Atlantic vagrants. The Galician and Asturian rías are excellent for passage and wintering waders. The Marismas de Santoña in Cantabria is a major wetland attracting large numbers of waders and also water-fowl, including wintering divers and Slavonian and other grebes. Santoña is also important as a staging post for migrant Spoonbills.

Many of the inland wetlands are reservoirs (embalses) and these are generally poor in birdlife, offering only the occasional Great Crested Grebe and little else. There are some notable exceptions, however, as you will find in the Regional chapters. The best natural wetlands include the large group of small lagoons in the centre of the Castilla–La Mancha, known as La Mancha Húmeda, the best known being Las Tablas de Daimiel. This group of wetlands has important breeding populations of Black-necked Grebes and Marsh Harriers, together with a diverse mix of other species including the White-headed Duck,

Whiskered and Gull-billed Terns and Bearded Tit. Daimiel is also very important for wintering waterfowl in wet years. Worth a special mention in its own
right is the Laguna de Gallocanta, a large natural lake in the far south-west of
Aragón renowned not only for large numbers of wintering duck but especially
as a major passage and wintering site for tens of thousands of Cranes.

THE RIVERS

There are nine major rivers in Spain. Of these the Segura (325km), the Júcar
(498km), the Turia (280km) and the Ebro (910km) drain into the Mediterranean
and the Miño (310km), the Duero (895km), the Tajo (Tagus, 1,007km), the
Guadiana (778km) and the Guadalquivir (657km) all empty into the Atlantic.
With the exception of the Ebro, which is sometimes swollen with snowmelt,
many of the rivers, even the major ones, have a very modest flow as they drain
away only rainwater and rainfall is scarce and irregular in some regions.

Much of the birdlife associated with the rivers inhabits the riverine woodlands (sotos), where there are breeding populations of Little Bitterns, Night and
Purple Herons, Penduline Tits and Golden Orioles. The Ebro basin has some
especially fine examples of this very rare habitat: the area around Zaragoza in
Aragón is particularly good. The Tajo and Tiétar valleys to the west of Toledo
have some large heronries, notably of Cattle Egrets, and also form part of an
important wintering area for Cranes. The other major habitat associated with
rivers is the deep gorges for which Spain is renowned, with their typical bird
fauna of Griffon and Egyptian Vultures, Golden and Bonelli's Eagles, Peregrine
Falcons, Eagle Owls, Alpine Swifts, Crag Martins, Blue Rock Thrushes and
Black Wheatears. Such gorges are widespread. There are some particularly fine
examples in the Pyrenean foothills, notably the Foz de Arbayún in Navarra.
Gorges are also well represented in Castilla y León: such as those of the Hoces
del Río Duratón. The Río Duero has some very impressive high river cliffs
where it forms the western boundary with Portugal.

DEHESAS AND PASTURES

The dehesas are the ancient grazing woodlands, unique to Iberia. They consist
of a savanna-like scattering of Iberian Holm Oaks (encinas) or, less typically,
Cork Oaks, interspersed by grassland or cereal cultivation. Some of tree branches
are cut periodically to provide fodder for browsing animals. The availability
of acorns in the autumn and winter supports both pigs and large numbers
of wintering birds including most of the western European Common Crane
population. The habitat also has important breeding populations of globally
threatened birds such as the Spanish Imperial Eagle and Black Vulture. It is a
characteristic habitat for Black-shouldered Kites and Azure-winged Magpies and
for a considerable diversity of insectivorous birds including Bee-eaters, Hoopoes,
Common Redstarts, Orphean Warblers, Southern Grey and Woodchat Shrikes
and Rock Sparrows. Many birders visit Extremadura to sample this particular
habitat but there are both extensive and good examples in the west of our area
in Madrid and Castilla y León. The dehesa at Cabañeros in Castilla–La Mancha
is home to some of the largest Black Vulture colonies in Spain.

WATCHING SEABIRDS IN NORTHERN AND EASTERN SPAIN

No birding visit to Spain is really complete without taking in the seabird activity on the coasts. Both the northern coasts and the east coast have plenty to offer at all times of year. The southern coasts and the Strait of Gibraltar are also excellent and are covered in *Where to Watch Birds in Southern & Western Spain* (3rd edition, Garcia & Paterson, 2008).

Seabirds in Spain are the concern of the Iberian Seabird Group, the Grupo Ibérico de Aves Marinas (GIAM), who produce an interesting on-line bulletin (in Spanish). See the SEO/Birdlife website (seo.org) and click on 'Sobre nosotros', again on 'Grupos de trabajo' and finally on 'GIAM'. GIAM seems latterly to have been eclipsed by the Iberian Seabird Network, Red de Aves Marinas (RAM) which organises coordinated watches for seabirds and cetaceans around the entire periphery of Iberia. Their website is informative: see redavesmarinas.blogspot.com.

Birding from the UK/Bay of Biscay ferries.

Many British visitors begin their birding trip to Spain from the moment they leave the UK, by making use of the car ferries linking Portsmouth to Bilbao and Santander and Plymouth to Santander. There are always plenty of seabirds around and the voyages are notable for sightings of cetaceans. The most interesting seabirds are seen in late summer and autumn and this is also the best time to find the whales and dolphins that then congregate in the Bay of Biscay. Both British and Spanish birders (and whale-watchers) organise trips to see and record birds and cetaceans from the ferries in August and September particularly.

The only company serving these routes currently (in 2016) is Brittany Ferries (brittany-ferries.co.uk), who run Portsmouth/Bilbao, Portsmouth/Santander and Plymouth/Santander services year-round. Crossings take 20–30 hours, depending on the route. Fares and schedule details are available from the company website and from ferry booking agencies online: just search for the desired route.

The ferries on these routes are large, comfortable vessels, equipped with stabilisers that dampen the worst effects of the notoriously choppy Bay of Biscay. You may have a crossing in flat calm conditions (good for spotting whales but not so good for seabirds, which tend to sit on the water then) but otherwise you may find the journey a little challenging if you are very prone to seasickness.

Watching from a ferry requires taking up a position up-forward, where you are best placed to scan for birds ahead and to see those which are flushed from the water by the vessel or slip around the bow. The wake is rarely productive. Windproof clothing is essential at any time of year and you will need to be well protected in cold or wet weather.

All of the seabirds of the North Atlantic may put in an appearance. The autumn passage period sees the greatest species-diversity, with Great and Sooty Shearwaters often numerous then. Cory's, Manx and Balearic Shearwaters are also common and there are quite frequent sightings of Macaronesian (Little)

Shearwaters. Wilson's Storm-petrels, Long-tailed Skuas and Sabine's Gulls are among the regular highlights at this time, alongside a wide range of commoner seabird species. Real rarities are always a possibility, but it will take a lot to beat the Masked Booby that flew alongside the southbound *Pride of Bilbao* in French waters on 3 September 2003 and then landed on the forward rail, where it remained overnight and all the way to Bilbao, to the delight of the large number of birders who happened to be on board.

Seabirds on the northern coasts.

The rugged Atlantic coasts of the north-west corner of Spain in Galicia, and the Biscayan coasts of Galicia, Asturias, Cantabria and the País Vasco, offer excellent opportunities for seabird watching. They also harbour significant breeding populations of Shags and Yellow-legged Gulls, with European Storm-petrels nesting on many of the offshore islets. Galicia has small local colonies of Lesser Black-backed Gulls. Common Terns breed locally in Cantabria. It is, however, the seabird migration, the wintering seabird populations and the annual occurrence of rare or vagrant species which makes this coast so interesting.

Seabird passage chiefly involves birds from northern Europe and the Arctic travelling to and from winter quarters in the central and southern Atlantic and the Mediterranean. In spring and autumn many seabirds pass off the western shore of Galicia and may be seen from strategic points on land, especially during or just after periods of strong onshore (westerly) winds. Some migrants may be seen in spring (March–May) along the Biscay coast, particularly if storm-driven, but most northward passage does not enter the Bay of Biscay. The autumn passage (August–October) is much more observable and reaches spectacular proportions at times. Many migrants, including large numbers of Cory's, Great, Sooty, Manx and Balearic Shearwaters, feed in the waters of the Bay in late summer and early autumn and may be seen moving west offshore as they return to the Atlantic. In addition, westerly gales repeatedly drive great numbers of southbound seabirds into the Bay from the Atlantic: these continue southwards and then turn west to follow the Biscay coast to regain their original heading. It is these westerly movements, of scoters, petrels, shearwaters, Gannets, skuas, gulls, terns and auks which provide most of the interest at suitable headlands all along the coast.

The key seabird migration watchpoint on the north coast is the Estaca de Bares (GA10), closely rivalled further west by Punta de la Vaca on the Cabo Peñas peninsula (AS5). Both these sites are excellent in autumn because they jut out from the line of the north coast and intercept the streams of westbound seabirds, which pass round the capes (*cabos*) close inshore. Other good places on the Biscay coast to watch seabird movements include, from west to east: Cabo Ortegal (GA9), Ribadeo and Tapia (AS1), Llanes (AS9), Cabo de Oyambre (CAN1), the Santander headlands (CAN5), Monte Buciero lighthouse (CAN7), Cabo Matxitxako (PV1) and Cabo Higer (PV10). Productive sites on the west coast of Galicia include Cabo Corrubedo (GA1), the Baiona coast (GA4), Cabo Laxe (GA11), Cabo Vilán (GA13) and Cabo Touriñan (GA15).

The principal species to be found off the north and north-west coasts in late summer and on passage include Red-breasted Merganser, Common Scoter; Cory's, Great (autumn only), Sooty (autumn only), Manx and Balearic Shearwaters; European, Leach's and Wilson's Storm-petrels, Gannet, Cormorant, Shag; Pomarine, Arctic, Long-tailed and Great Skuas; Mediterranean, Little, Sabine's, Black-headed, Lesser Black-backed, Yellow-legged and Great Black-backed Gulls, Kittiwake; Sandwich, Common, Arctic, Little and Black Terns, Common Guillemot, Razorbill and Puffin. Fea's/Zino's Petrels have been reported annually from Cape Bares in recent autumns. Vagrant seabirds seen there and elsewhere on the north coast have included Pacific Diver, Red-billed Tropicbird, Masked and Brown Boobies, Magnificent Frigatebird and South Polar Skua.

Inshore boat trips to watch seabirds are often organised by SEO in late summer and early autumn, sailing from Santander and sometimes Santoña. See the SEO/Cantabria website (seocantabria.blogspot.com) in season for more information. Pelagic boat trips off Galicia are organised by a private company, Chasula Aves: their website (chasulaaves.wordpress.com) gives full details.

Wintering seabirds are abundant all along the coast, although the pelagic species may only be visible from land in hard weather. At this season such species as divers, grebes and gulls may also be especially prominent within the major estuarine inlets or Rías and within bays and harbours. Interesting species may turn up almost anywhere but key sites to visit, listed south to north in Galicia and then west, include: the Río Miño estuary (GA5), Baiona coast and bay (GA4), the Ría de Vigo (GA14), Ría de Pontevedra and O Grove inlet (GA2), Ría de Corme y Laxe and Ensenada de A Insua (GA11), Ría de Coruña, Ría de Ortigueira (GA9), Ría del Eo (AS1), Ría de Avilés, Zeluán and Gijón Bay (AS5), Ría de Villaviciosa (AS6), Ribadesella (AS11), Ría de San Vicente (CAN1), Ría de Mogro (CAN4), Santander Bay (CAN5), Marismas de Santoña (CAN7), Bilbao Bay, Ría de Gernika (PV1) and San Sebastián. Any of the fishing ports may attract interesting gulls and all the migration watchpoints listed above can see seabird movements, especially in the aftermath of winter gales.

The wintering species include Red-breasted Merganser, Common and Velvet Scoters; Red-throated, Black-throated and Great Northern Divers, Red-necked and Slavonian Grebes, Leach's Storm-petrel, Gannet, Cormorant, Shag, Great Skua; Mediterranean, Little, Black-headed, Common, Lesser Black-backed, Herring, Yellow-legged and Great Black-backed Gulls, Kittiwake, Sandwich Tern, Common Guillemot, Razorbill and Puffin. A few Iceland and Glaucous Gulls and Little Auks also appear annually.

Seabirds on the east coast.

The long Mediterranean coast south from the French border to the boundary of our region with Almería has a very different character from the largely rugged north coast. Long sandy stretches predominate, interrupted by occasional saline lagoons and rocky headlands. A great deal of the coastline is intensively developed with tourism infrastructure and construction of further hotels, golf courses and retirement villas continues apace. Nevertheless, the various wetland reserves and saltpans especially have important seabird colonies. Seabird passage is also interesting and there are large numbers of wintering seabirds to see as well.

Arguably the flagship species of the coast is Audouin's Gull, whose colony at the Ebro Delta (CAT9) was only founded in 1981 but in recent years has sometimes numbered over 16,000 breeding pairs, comprising some three-quarters of the global population of this formerly rare species. Audouin's Gulls also now have sizeable breeding colonies in the Comunidad Valenciana at the Laguna de Torrevieja (V11), Castellón harbour, on the Columbretes islands off Castellón and at the Albufera (V4) as well as on the Isla Grosa off the Mar Menor in Murcia (MU2) and the Llobregat Delta in Catalonia (CAT6). Slender-billed Gulls also nest locally at the Ebro Delta (250–600 pairs), the

Albufera de Valencia (V4: up to 100 pairs), the Laguna de Torrevieja (V11) and sometimes at the Salinas de Santa Pola (V10). A handful of Mediterranean Gulls have bred at these localities in some years, alongside the much more numerous Yellow-legged and Black-headed Gulls. The Ebro Delta also offers breeding Gull-billed, Sandwich, Common, Little and Whiskered Terns, as well as a pair or two of Lesser Crested Terns in some years: Black Terns have nested there on rare occasions too. The first five tern species also breed at the Albufera de Valencia and Elegant Lesser Crested Terns have also nested there. Gull-billed Terns nest on the Murcia coast (MU2). Common, Little and Whiskered Terns breed at the Marjal de Moros (V3) and Salinas de Santa Pola (V10) among other wetlands on the coasts of Valencia and Murcia. Cory's (Scopoli's) Shearwaters nest very locally on the Columbretes islands and also on a few islets off Murcia, alongside European Storm-petrels: which also breed on the islet of Benidorm and other islands off Valencia. The only other breeding seabird of the region is the Shag, which has very small populations on the coast of northern Cataluña, on the Columbretes islands off Valencia and on Isla Grossa off Murcia.

Seabird migration has received relatively little attention on the east coast, except at Cabo de Creus (CAT3), Cabo Cullera (Valencia), Cabo de La Nao (V19) and Cabo de Palos (MU2). The movements of shearwaters attract attention but are not fully understood. Cory's (Scopoli's)* Shearwaters are reported offshore during most of the year, but are scarce in winter. Balearic Shearwaters are frequent from early summer onwards, when many coast south towards the Strait of Gibraltar and the Atlantic, returning from late autumn into spring. Levantine Shearwaters occur offshore, especially off Cataluña, in autumn and winter. Seabird movements may also involve numbers of Gannets, Cormorants, Arctic and Great Skuas; Mediterranean, Little, Black-headed, Slender-billed, Audouin's and Lesser Black-backed Gulls; Gull-billed, Sandwich, Common, Little, Whiskered and Black Terns, Razorbills and Puffins.

The east coast holds very large numbers of gulls in winter, the local Yellow-legged Gulls being joined by numerous Mediterranean, Little, Black-headed and Lesser Black-backed Gulls. Some Audouin's and Slender-billed Gulls remain in winter, mainly in the south, and Kittiwakes occur in some seasons. Sandwich Terns are common in winter and a few Common and Whiskered Terns may remain at favoured locations. Razorbills winter commonly along the coast but Puffins are rarely seen, tending to be pelagic. Common Scoters, Gannets and Great Skuas are also present offshore in winter. Red-breasted Mergansers winter locally: the Mar Menor (MU2) is a favoured site for them. A few Common Eiders are sometimes present in winter off the northern coasts of Cataluña. Divers and grebes are scarce, except for Black-necked Grebes which are common in winter at many coastal sites.

Wintering and passage seabirds may be found at all the principal coastal wetlands, including, from south to north, the Mar Menor (MU2), Lagunas de La Mata y Torrevieja (V11), Salinas de Santa Pola (V10), Salinas de Calpe (V8), Albufera de Valencia (V4), Torreblanca (V2), Delta del Ebro (CAT9), Delta del Llobregat (CAT6) and the Aiguamolls de L'Empordà (CAT4). Good coastal watchpoints also include Cabo de Palos (MU2), Cabo de La Nao (V19), Cabo de San Antoni (V6) and Cabo de Creus (CAT3). All the east coast ports, notably the harbours of Castellón and Tarragona, attract wintering gulls, in particular of course where fish are landed, and it is always worth scanning the flocks for something interesting.

ARAGÓN

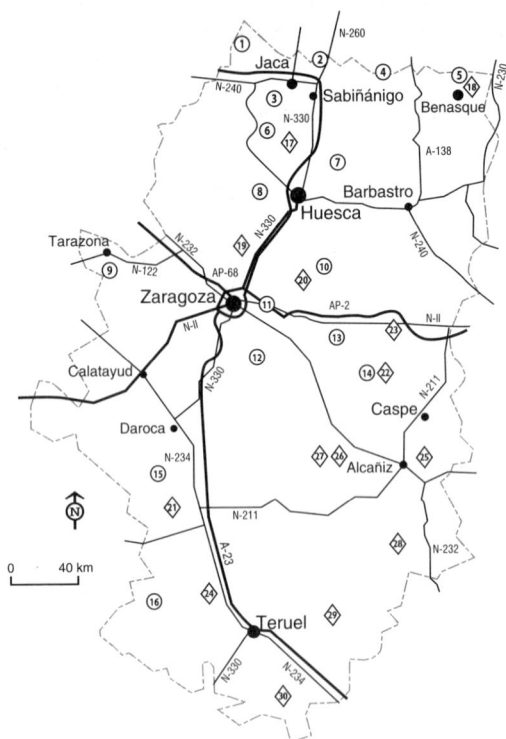

Main sites

AR1	Foz de Biniés and Valles de Ansó y Hecho
AR2	High Valleys and Passes of the Central Pyrenees
AR3	San Juan de la Peña
AR4	Parque Nacional de Ordesa y Monte Perdido
AR5	Valle de Benasque and Parque Posets–Maladeta
AR6	Los Mallos de Riglos
AR7	Sierra y Cañones de Guara
AR8	Embalse de La Sotonera
AR9	Sierra del Moncayo
AR10	Laguna de Sariñena
AR11	Los Galachos del Ebro
AR12	Las Estepas de Belchite
AR13	Los Monegros
AR14	Saladas de Chiprana
AR15	Laguna de Gallocanta
AR16	Serranía de Albarracín

Other sites worth visiting

AR17	Castillo de Loarre
AR18	El Turbón
AR19	Montes de Zuera
AR20	Sierra de Alcubierre
AR21	Estepas de Blancas
AR22	Laguna de La Estanca
AR23	Laguna de Candasnos
AR24	Laguna del Cañizar
AR25	Saladas de Alcañiz
AR26	Río Martín valley at Ariño
AR27	Alacón vulture restaurant
AR28	Río Guadalope
AR29	El Maestrazgo
AR30	Sierra de Javalambre

Both the mountains and steppe landscapes in equal measure draw birders to Aragón. This is the region to head for if you have only limited time to sample the Pyrenees. The mountains here are remarkably unspoilt, much less exploited than further east in Cataluña or across the border in France. Jaca is the only town of any real size in the mountains and is a good base from which to explore the higher ground and foothills. The region is best known for the Parque Nacional de Ordesa (AR4), a spectacular introduction to the birds and scenery of the Spanish Pyrenees. But there is much more to the Pyrenees than just this National Park. It is not only birds that draw people here, as the mountains are a major attraction to everyone interested in climbing, walking, alpine flowers and bears. However, the bear population is very small, fewer than 50 individuals, despite reinforcement by introductions from Slovenia: the western Cantabrian population is much healthier (see AS4).

The peaks are lowest in the west but slowly increase in height as you move eastwards, topping out at Aneto (3,404m). The high-level mountains of the Pyrenees are well known not only for their raptors: especially Lammergeiers and Golden Eagles, but also for their specialist upland birds such as Ptarmigan, Water Pipits, Alpine Accentors, the elusive Wallcreepers, Yellow-billed Choughs and Snowfinches. Lammergeier numbers have increased steadily in the Pyrenees: by 2010 there were some 120 pairs in Spain plus some 250 immature or non-breeding birds, as well as a further 35 pairs on the French side of the range. The core of the Pyrenean population is in Aragón, where the birds are easy to see. Other species of particular interest in the Pyrenees include the Honey-buzzard, Capercaillie, Boreal (Tengmalm's) and Eagle Owls, Grey Partridge, Black Woodpecker and Citril Finch. The distributions of Capercaillies and Boreal Owls are very restricted, both favouring open coniferous forests. Both species are at the south-western end of their European range here but whereas Capercaillies are also found in the Cordillera Cantábrica, Boreal Owls are restricted to the eastern part of the Pyrenees and favour the higher-altitude forests. There are only around 200 pairs of Boreal Owls in Spain, most of them in neighbouring Cataluña. Black Woodpeckers are always exciting to find and are relatively common in the right habitat across the Pyrenees, unlike White-backed Woodpeckers, which used to occur marginally in Aragón: the latter should be sought in Navarra. Grey Partridges in Spain only occur at some altitude, mainly above 1,500 metres, where they frequent mosaics of pasture and scrub; unlike in the UK where they inhabit lowland farmland.

A number of other species that are relatively common further north in Europe are also found in the Pyrenees and here they are near the southern limit of their breeding ranges. These include the Woodcock, Eurasian Treecreeper, Marsh Tit, Bullfinch and Yellowhammer.

The lower valleys and towering gorges are a very appealing distraction from the Pyrenees proper and the Ansó and Hecho valleys (AR1) are two of the most attractive in the whole mountain range. In addition to good numbers of Red-backed Shrikes and Wrynecks, the healthy raptor populations are again most impressive, these including Black and Red Kites and large colonies of Griffon Vultures. Egyptian Vultures have one of their Iberian strongholds in the Pyrenean foothills.

The Pyrenees are hardly awash with visitors yet much of the rest of Aragón is definitely overlooked and seldom visited by birders: fortunately so for those who prefer quiet and solitude. Its isolated and beautiful villages: for example in the district of El Maestrazgo (AR25), southern mountain ranges, long river gorges, wetlands, woodlands and meadows, and the River Ebro valley deserve closer attention.

Not only does Aragón lack tourists but it also has few inhabitants, being the least populated region in Spain. The countryside has become even emptier since half of the population now lives in the centrally located capital, Zaragoza. The city is on the Ebro, one of Spain's greatest rivers, which bisects Aragón into north and south. Zaragoza airport is very conveniently placed for exploring both the south and north of the region. Ryanair flies there from London Stansted.

The Ebro Valley is more populated and cultivated, and best known for its steppe areas. Most birders interested in steppe birds head for Extremadura and miss out on the attraction of Los Monegros (AR13) and the nature reserves of La Lomaza and El Planerón (AR12) on the plains of Belchite. This is an area of low rainfall and open impressive landscapes which are the habitat for a number of threatened species including Montagu's Harrier, Great and Little Bustards, Pin-tailed and Black-bellied Sandgrouse, Stone-curlew, Tawny Pipit and up to eight species of larks. It is especially important for its sandgrouse populations and is one of the best areas in Spain for seeing Dupont's Larks, Aragón having nearly half of the Spanish population. Greater Short-toed Larks, which have suffered some dramatic declines in some parts of Spain, also reach very high densities here, alongside Lesser Short-toed and Calandra Larks. Intensification of agriculture through irrigation, however, still poses a serious threat to these important habitats and birds. At the same time, rural depopulation and the associated decline in livestock, notably sheep, has affected the landscape, as dwarf shrub steppes are replaced by taller scrub, to the detriment of Dupont's Lark, among others.

While of immense importance for birds, there is much more to the Ebro Valley than its steppes and its cliffs, woods and wetlands are well worth exploring. The River Ebro itself supports a range of wetland species including Little Bitterns, Night Herons and Purple Herons. The oxbow lakes near Zaragoza (AR11) are especially worth a visit.

South of the Pyrenees the sierras then become the dominant landscape feature, the most impressive and famous – for landscape, climbing and birds – being the huge towering sandstone pillars of Los Mallos de Riglos (AR6), one of the most northerly localities in inland Spain for Black Wheatears and Sardinian Warblers.

Two mountainous regions in southern Aragón are also of interest for their great diversity of species. They are not quite as rich as the Pyrenees but they offer a considerable variety of upland habitats that are largely unexplored territory for birders. West of Teruel, the Serranía de Albarracín (AR16) and part of the Montes Universales have some excellent walking. To the east is the isolated and remote region of El Maestrazgo (AR25), offering some striking landscapes of stark peaks, deep ravines and colourful and lush meadows.

Gallocanta (AR15), a large natural lake in the far south-west, merits special mention. It is important not only for large numbers of wintering waterfowl but also as a major passage and wintering site for Common Cranes: with counts of over 70,000 on record!

FOZ DE BINIÉS AND VALLES   AR1
DE ANSÓ Y HECHO (Huesca)

Status: The western part of the Parque Natural de los Valles Occidentales (34,000ha) which is also a ZEPA.

Site description

These are two of the most beautiful and spectacular valleys in the whole of the Pyrenees. The Río Veral winds its way down from the high Pyrenees to join the Río Aragón to the west of Berdún, where the Ansó valley opens out into a broad plain. The valley can be narrow in places, especially so in its section through the rocky gorge and towering limestone cliffs of the impressive Foz de Biniés. A large part of the valley is covered in pine and beech woodland, or mixed oak scrub. Higher up the valley the composition of the woodland changes, with more Silver Fir, set amongst the alpine pastures above the village of Zuriza. The lower part of the Ansó valley, below the hilltop village of Berdún, is also very attractive, with the village perched above a mosaic of cultivated land, riverside woodland and eroded slopes.

The Valle del Hecho is also a very attractive Pyrenean valley running parallel but to the east of the Valle de Ansó. It has a similar landscape and range of habitats and species, and the higher elevations are one of the best known areas in the Spanish Pyrenees for seeing breeding Wallcreepers.

Species

A diversity of raptors are regularly seen over the valleys and the village of Berdún itself. They include Lammergeiers, Griffon and Egyptian Vultures, Red and Black Kites and Short-toed Eagles. There is a good chance of finding Montagu's Harriers and Quails in the cereal fields around Berdún and the lower parts of the Hecho valley. The riverside woodlands hold Golden Orioles, Nightingales and Wrynecks. The Foz de Biniés gorge begins at the first tunnel or arch, and for the next 3–4km you may expect a range of cliff-nesting birds such as Alpine Swifts, House and Crag Martins, Blue Rock Thrushes, Rock Sparrows and Rock Buntings, with Dippers and Grey Wagtails in the fast-flowing Río Veral below. Eagle Owls breed here and a colony of Griffon Vultures inhabits the high cliffs above and in the side valleys. Spotted Flycatchers, Firecrests and Bonelli's Warblers are common in the mixed and deciduous woodlands. Red-backed Shrikes are widespread where the landscape opens out higher up the valleys.

The woods and alpine pastures of the higher valleys offer a diverse range of species including Grey Partridge, Black Woodpecker and Citril Finch, with Rufous-tailed Rock Thrush, Wallcreeper and Snowfinch in the rocky terrain.

Many birders are particularly attracted to the higher parts of the Hecho valley to see breeding Wallcreepers, although the well-known site at the Boca del Infierno (Hell's Mouth), north of Siresa, is no longer a 'certainty'. However, it is easily accessible, being on the roadside, and so always worth checking out. A more reliable and regular site now appears to be on the crags above the Gabardito refuge, again north of Siresa.

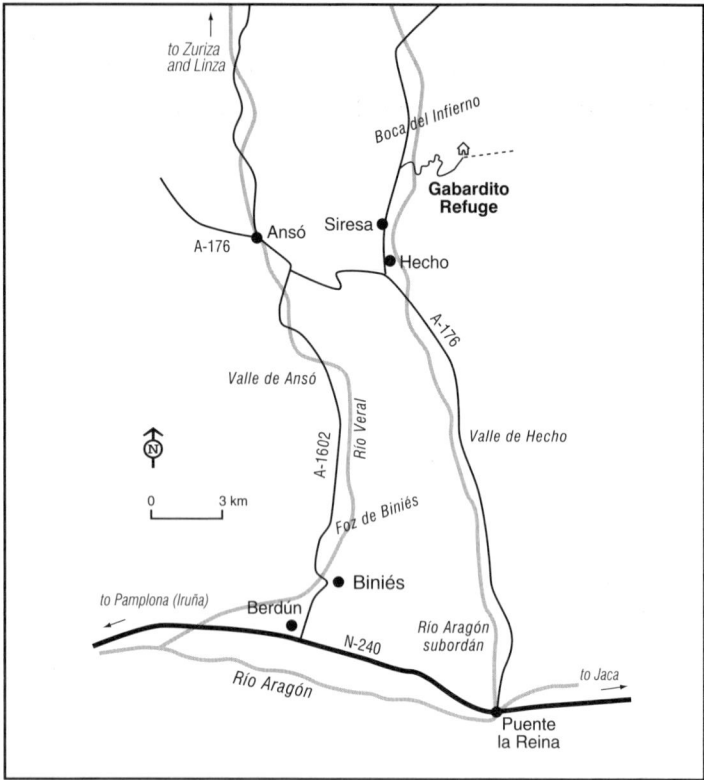

Both Yellow-billed and Red-billed Choughs are abundant in both valleys and there are several pairs of Golden Eagles and Lammergeiers. This is near the western limit in the Pyrenees for a number of species including Ptarmigan and Ring Ouzel, which are found above Zuriza in the Ansó valley, and Siresa in the Hecho valley. A number of mammals typical of high altitudes occur, the most interesting being the Brown Bear.

Timing
Late spring through into summer: May–July, can be particularly productive. Take care with late snowfalls in the highest area. Thunderstorms can also occur from time to time in summer.

Access
Take the N-240 from Pamplona for 70km eastwards towards Jaca. For the Ansó valley, at the hilltop village of Berdún turn north off the N-240 on to the A-1602 minor road towards the villages of Biniés and Ansó. An Information Centre in Ansó (Tel. 974 370 215) is open daily in summer and otherwise at weekends. There is much of interest in the whole length of the valley, with the options of visiting the lower reaches between Berdún and Biniés before exploring the gorges and valley higher up. Parking in the Foz de Biniés is not easy and care should be taken when birding from the roadside. It is easy

to park by the roadside along the valley between the Foz, Ansó and Zuriza. From Zuriza a track leads out into woodlands and finally to alpine pastures: it is drivable for part of the way. The Linza refuge (refugiodelinza.com), at the top of the Ansó valley, offers ready access to representative habitats; the refuge itself has accommodation and a restaurant and is open year-round.

From Zuriza you can retrace the road back to Ansó and then back to Berdún, or head east across the hillside to the Hecho Valley. Alternatively you can head westwards from Zuriza to join the Esca valley from Roncal (NA-137) and continue over into France.

The Hecho valley can also be reached off the main N-240 at Puente la Reina, where you take the A-176 minor road for Hecho and Siresa. The Gabardito refuge (Tel. 974 375 387) lies between Siresa and the Boca del Infierno. A few kilometres north of Siresa take a signposted right turn up a winding road to the refuge, where you can park. Walk up the track to the right of the refuge, through the forest, emerging below crags where Wallcreepers nest. Refreshments and accommodation are available at the refuge. For the Boca del Infierno, return to the main road and turn north (right) for another few kilometres.

CALENDAR

All year: Ptarmigan, Grey Partridge, Red Kite, Lammergeier, Griffon Vulture, Goshawk, Common Buzzard, Golden Eagle, Peregrine Falcon, Rock Dove; Scops, Eagle and Little Owls, Black Woodpecker, Water Pipit, Grey Wagtail, Dipper, Alpine Accentor, Blue Rock Thrush, Cetti's and Dartford Warblers, Firecrest, Wallcreeper, Yellow-billed and Red-billed Choughs, Raven, Spotless Starling, Rock Sparrow, Snowfinch, Citril Finch, Rock Bunting.

Breeding season: Quail, Honey-buzzard, Black Kite, Egyptian Vulture, Short-toed Eagle, Montagu's Harrier, Booted Eagle, Alpine Swift, Bee-eater, Wryneck, Crag and House Martins, Nightingale, Rufous-tailed Rock Thrush, Ring Ouzel, Subalpine and Orphean Warblers, Spotted Flycatcher, Golden Oriole, Red-backed Shrike.

HIGH VALLEYS AND PASSES OF   AR2
THE CENTRAL PYRENEES (Huesca)

Status: Monumentos Naturales de los Glaciares Pirenaicos. Partly within the Ordesa–Viñamala Biosphere Reserve (30,000ha).

Site description

This extensive area stretches from the highest cols on the French border down through alpine meadows, pine forests, mixed woodlands, hay meadows and river valleys. The area between the Aragón and Tena valleys and the adjoining mountain ranges lies towards the central part of the Pyrenees. This large expanse includes not only superb scenery but also a considerable wealth of bird habitats, some of which are very important. This is a very high mountain area with extremely rugged scenery including several glaciers. Alpine meadows occur higher up on either side of the France/Spain border and intersperse the mosaic of mixed and coniferous woodland.

The Valle de Canfranc, occupied by the Río Aragón, leads to a high mountain area where the steep valley sides are covered with pinewoods, giving way to alpine pastures at higher altitudes, where there are many rock outcrops.

The Valle de Tena, occupied by the Río Gállego, offers beech, oak, Silver Fir and pine forests, with hay meadows and pastures, rocky cliffs and tarns. The surrounding mountains rise to over 3,000m. The side valleys are picturesque and there are thermal springs at Panticosa.

A high limestone mountain range with alpine pastures separates the Aragón and Gállego rivers. The area to the east of the Tena Valley is included within the Ordesa–Viñamala Biosphere Reserve (AR4). This is another high elevation region with both limestone and granite rocks, numerous small glacial lakes (ibones) and pinewoods giving way to mountain pastures at higher levels.

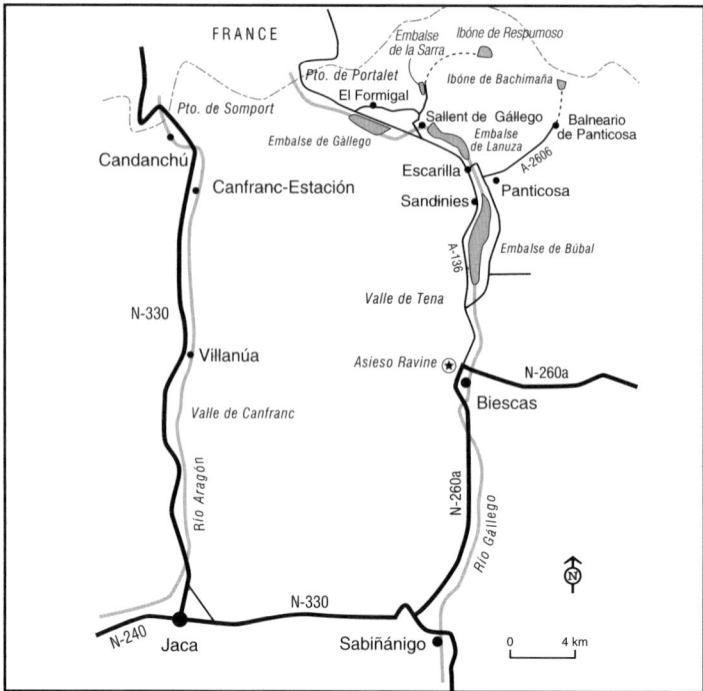

Species

Several pairs of Lammergeiers and Golden Eagles frequent both valleys. The international border areas, with their alpine meadows and rock outcrops at the Col de Somport and El Portalet, can be good for Rufous-tailed Rock Thrushes, Yellow-billed Choughs, Alpine Accentors, Water Pipits, Snowfinches and Citril Finches, as well as Marmots and Chamois. Lammergeiers can sometimes be seen soaring between Spain and France here. Small numbers of Ptarmigan and Ring Ouzels are also present.

You may be tempted to spend some time exploring rock faces for Wallcreepers, especially if you are of an optimistic nature. Boulder scree is also a favoured Wallcreeper habitat. Quarry faces are worth checking, for example at the well-known Wallcreeper site a few kilometres north of Villanúa near the km-66.2 post on the left-hand side of the N-330. This is mainly used irregularly outside the breeding season, however. It is worth spending time in the woodlands and meadows looking for Capercaillie, Grey Partridges, Honeybuzzards, Black Woodpeckers, Tree Pipits, Whinchats and Ring Ouzels. Red-backed Shrikes are common at lower altitudes.

Timing
The best time for visiting is mid-spring and summer. Road signs will indicate whether the roads are closed by snow, which is possible in the early part of this season.

Access
Access by road is possible to the highest areas.

Valle de Canfranc   Take the N-330 out of Jaca towards Villanúa, the Canfranc ski resort and the border with France at Somport. Various minor roads and tracks occur all the way up the valley and walking is easy across the alpine meadows at the border.

Valle de Tena   The N-260a/A-136 run the entire length of the Tena Valley, covering 44km between the small town of Sabiñánigo and El Portalet on the French border. There are a number of possible stopping points worth exploring before you reach El Formigal and El Portalet, including the Asieso Ravine: a wooded valley just to the north of Biescas, and Escarra Forest: near Escarrilla. Much of the main interest, however, is in the higher areas around El Formigal and El Portalet pass, where there is a car park next to some shops and cafes. There is easy walking in flower-rich meadows all around the border point. A track leads off to the left, around 200m before the shops, and passes disused mine workings which can be good for Yellow-billed Choughs.

Various paths occur around Sallent de Gállego. From La Sarra reservoir above Sallent there is a well-marked path to reach the Ibón de Respumoso, a small lake. The spa of Panticosa is reached via the A-136 towards Sandiniés, from where you take the minor road to Panticosa and the Balneario (spa), which is around 10km from the turning on the A-2606. Various tracks lead off from the spa: including a popular route to the lakes at Bachimaña, but there are many others.

CALENDAR

All year: Ptarmigan, Capercaillie, Grey Partridge, Red Kite, Lammergeier, Griffon Vulture, Goshawk, Golden Eagle, Peregrine Falcon, Woodcock, Rock Dove, Eagle and Tawny Owls, Black Woodpecker, Crag Martin, Blue Rock Thrush, Dartford Warbler, Dipper, Alpine Accentor, Crested and Marsh Tits, Wallcreeper, Eurasian Treecreeper, Yellow-billed and Red-billed Choughs, Rock Sparrow, Snowfinch, Citril Finch, Bullfinch, Yellowhammer, Cirl and Rock Buntings.

Breeding season: Honey-buzzard, Egyptian Vulture, Montagu's Harrier, Black Kite, Short-toed and Booted Eagles, Alpine Swift, Hoopoe, Tree and Water Pipits, Rufous-tailed Rock Thrush, Ring Ouzel, Whinchat, Melodious and Subalpine Warblers, Spotted Flycatcher, Red-backed Shrike, Ortolan Bunting.

SAN JUAN DE LA PEÑA (Huesca)   AR3

Status: ZEPA (including the nearby Peña Oroel) and Espacio Natural Protegido (310ha).

Site description

Essentially a flat-topped ridge covered in a pine plantation, with cliff faces and ridges giving spectacular views and panoramas and with steep wooded slopes. This is the site of two grand monasteries, both now museums. The lower and older (12th century) of the two is tucked under an impressive cliff overhang whilst the larger and more recent monastery (17th century) of San Juan is on top of the plateau, in a large grassy clearing on the edge of the pines. The surrounding area is well known for raptors and many species can be seen from the ridges.

Species

Despite the apparent lack of large old trees, Black Woodpeckers are found in the plantation and woodland and these are also good for Short-toed Treecreepers, Nuthatches, Crossbills and Crested Tits. The lower monastery has Alpine Swifts and Crag Martins, while both have Red-billed Choughs. The open areas around the new monastery attract Mistle Thrushes, Rock Sparrows and Citril Finches.

Viewpoints from the ridges and on the journey up to the monasteries provide opportunities for scanning for Lammergeiers, Griffon and Egyptian Vultures, Short-toed Eagles, Honey-buzzards and other raptors. Blue Rock Thrushes and Cirl and Rock Buntings are in the scrub and rock faces around. Alpine Accentors and Wallcreepers winter in the area.

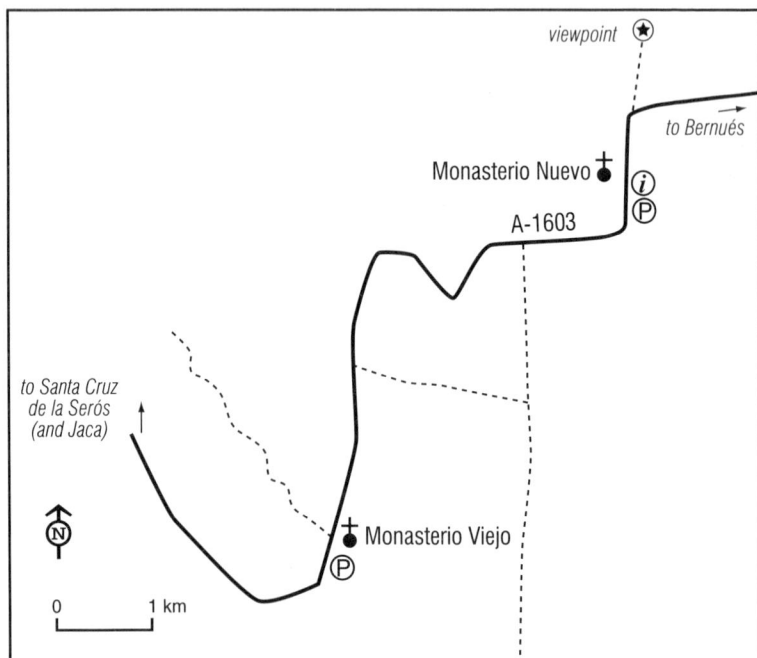

Timing

Spring is by far the most productive, particularly mid May to mid June. Early morning visits are recommended as the site can attract large numbers of visitors, including school parties. Most, however, stay within the open grassy area around the upper monastery.

Access

The site is signposted southwards off the N-240 from Pamplona to Jaca, around 9km west of Jaca. The A-1603 secondary road climbs up for 12km, passing through the attractive village of Santa Cruz de la Serós and on to the Monasterios de San Juan. Expect coaches on this road. It is well worth stopping between the village and the first monastery as there are several lay-bys from which to scan the cliff faces and skies for raptors. If you have time you can follow the footpath from the village of Santa Cruz up to the monastery but it is a steady and steep climb. There is plenty of car parking at the new monastery at the top of the ridge where most time should be spent. An Interpretation Centre (Tel. 974 361 476) at San Indalecio, next to the monastery, is open daily. There are various roads and tracks through the plantation, with a spectacular viewing area ideal for raptor-scanning close to the eastern end of the new monastery. In addition a track on the left, before the descent back down the road towards the old monastery, takes you through woodland out on to a ridge towards a communications tower and provides stunning views on two sides: again this can be very good for seeing birds of prey.

CALENDAR

All year: Red Kite, Lammergeier, Griffon Vulture, Goshawk, Golden Eagle, Peregrine Falcon, Black and Great Spotted Woodpeckers, Black Redstart, Goldcrest, Firecrest, Blue Rock and Mistle Thrushes, Crested and Coal Tits, Nuthatch, Short-toed Treecreeper, Jay, Red-billed Chough, Rock Sparrow, Citril Finch, Crossbill, Bullfinch, Cirl and Rock Buntings.

Breeding season: Honey-buzzard, Black Kite, Short-toed and Booted Eagles, Alpine Swift, Crag Martin, Common Chiffchaff, Bonelli's Warbler, Spotted Flycatcher.

Winter: Alpine Accentor, Wallcreeper.

PARQUE NACIONAL DE ORDESA   AR4
Y MONTE PERDIDO (Huesca)

Status: Parque Nacional (15,608ha). Also part of the Ordesa–Viñamala Biosphere Reserve (30,000ha) and ZEPA.

Site description

Ordesa was the first of the 15 Spanish National Parks to be established, in 1918, primarily to protect the Pyrenean subspecies of the Spanish Ibex, the *bucardo*. Sad to say the last remaining *bucardo* died in 2000 and this particular subspecies is now extinct. Fortunately the Park preserves much else of interest.

When first established the park only comprised the Ordesa Valley itself, after which it is named. In 1982 it was extended to include the spectacular Añisclo and Pineta valleys, the Escuaín (Escoaín) gorge, and the high peak of Monte Perdido (3,355m): which has one of the few remaining glaciers in the Pyrenees. This famous and important park now covers over 15,600ha. As one might imagine in a park of this size, a great variety of habitats occur, the most important being the high mountain tops themselves with their extensive grassy alpine pastures. Lower slopes are clothed in forests of Scots Pine, Black Pine, beech and Silver Fir. The rivers carve their way through a series of impressive valleys and gorges. The valleys of the four principal rivers each have their own individual characteristics: they are the Río Arazas (Ordesa Valley), the Río Bellos (Añisclo Valley and ravine), the Río Yaga (Tella Valley and Escuaín Gorge) and the Río Cinca (Pineta Valley).

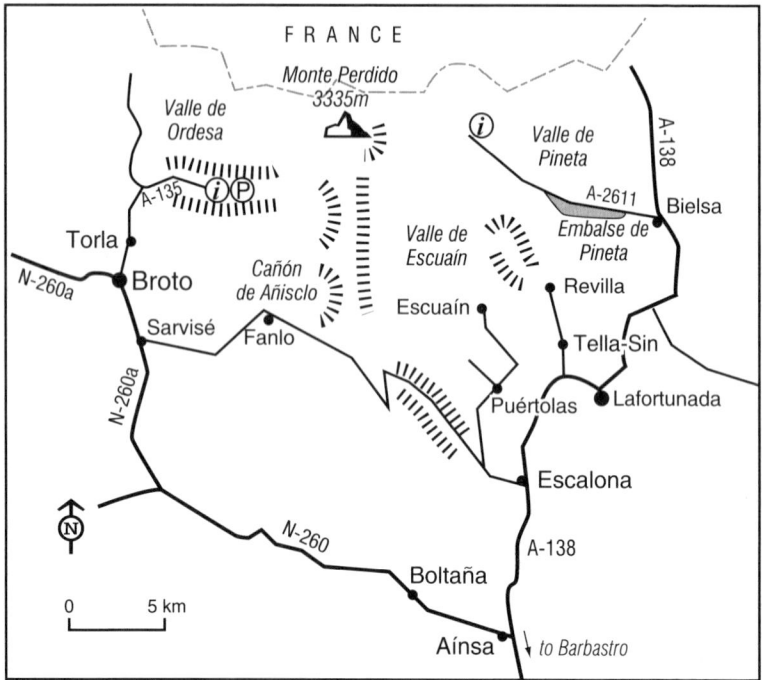

Species

The alpine meadows and rocky outcrops at the highest levels have Alpine Accentors, Snowfinches (particularly around the screes) and Water Pipits. Rocky areas also support Rufous-tailed Rock Thrushes, Northern Wheatears and Black Redstarts. Ring Ouzels are characteristic of open Black Pine stands around the treeline, which are also popular with Black Woodpeckers and Boreal Owls. Dunnocks frequent areas of scrub. Ptarmigan occur above 2,000m but have been steadily declining and there are no recent breeding records here.

Cliffs and rock faces are widespread throughout the park and support

Lammergeier

Golden Eagles, Lammergeiers, Peregrine Falcons, Alpine Swifts, Crag Martins, Wallcreepers, Yellow-billed and Red-billed Choughs and Ravens. Egyptian Vultures breed at the lower altitudes.

The mixed woodlands of beech, Silver Fir and pine hold Goshawks, Sparrowhawks, Black Woodpeckers, Crossbills, Crested Tits and Goldcrests. Grey Partridges and Citril Finches are found in the more open areas. Siskins, which are very local nesters in Spain, breed in these woods but Capercaillie are very scarce and no longer breed in the park.

Chamois are abundant in the National Park and it is also home to Genets, Polecats, Pine Martens, Wild Boars and Otters.

Timing

May and June are most productive, but avoid high summer, weekends and public holidays whenever possible as parts of the park, such as the Añisclo gorge, can get very busy during holiday periods. There are quieter areas if you avoid the main access points to the mountain. Roads can be blocked by snow.

Access

There are several points of access to the National Park and the general mountain area, including the four main river valleys. There are also numerous tracks and routes into the mountains, but some can be very difficult.

Ordesa Valley (main park entrance) The focus of most visits to the park is the Ordesa Valley, which is the main access point. The Visitors' Centre of El Parador (not to be confused with the Parador Nacional) is sited here and is open daily, April to October. There is a large car park and a number of trails, including the main one which starts off in the lower river valley of the Ordesa, climbs up through beech, Silver Fir and pine forests and finally into the high alpine pastures. This trail leads eventually to Gavarnie on the French side of the border, although you would take many hours to get that far. Take the

N-330 east out of Jaca, or north from Huesca as far as Sabiñánigo, then turn northwards towards France on the N-260a as far as Biescas. Turn right here and continue for some 25km along the N-260a to just north of Broto, where you should take the A-135 to Torla, Ordesa and the park entrance. There is also an information centre in Torla (Tel. 974 486 472).

Añisclo Valley and Gorge From the main park entrance return to Torla and take the N-260 south through Broto and Boltaña to Aínsa. If travelling from the south take the N-123 northwards from Barbastro, which is on the N-240 between Huesca and Lleida. After 8km turn north on the A-138 to Aínsa and continue north towards Bielsa and the French border. At the village of Escalona take a left turning for Ereta de Biés and the Ermita de San Urbez, where there is a car park and from where you can walk along the gorge. Wallcreepers and other species of rocky terrain occur here.

Escuaín Gorge and the Tella Valley Travel as directed above to Escalona. For Escuaín Gorge, take the same left turn here but shortly afterwards turn right along a minor road to Escuaín. Tracks lead from the village.

For the Tella Valley do not turn off at Escalona but carry on along the A-138 for a further 10km taking a left turn shortly after San Juste. If you reach the village of Lafortunada you will have missed the turn! This minor road leads to the village of Revilla from which a short track takes you up the Tella Valley. There is a spectacular viewpoint at Revilla from where you can regularly see Lammergeiers.

Pineta Valley From Aínsa continue on the A-138 north as far as Bielsa. From Bielsa turn left on to the A-2611, a quiet drive of 12km ending at the Parador Nacional de Monte Perdido at the head the valley. As well as the Parador there is an information kiosk and a number of walks lead from nearby, including one to the Valle de Lalarri through beechwoods and out on to alpine meadows. Lammergeiers may often be seen soaring along the ridges and the beechwoods are popular with Black Woodpeckers.

CALENDAR

All year: Ptarmigan, Capercaillie, Grey Partridge, Lammergeier, Griffon Vulture, Goshawk, Sparrowhawk, Common Buzzard, Golden Eagle, Common Kestrel, Peregrine Falcon, Woodcock, Common Sandpiper, Rock Dove, Woodpigeon; Boreal, Eagle and Tawny Owls, Black and Great Spotted Woodpeckers, Water Pipit, Sky Lark, Grey Wagtail, Dipper, Dunnock, Alpine Accentor, Robin, Black Redstart, Goldcrest, Firecrest, Long-tailed Tit, Marsh Tit, Wallcreeper, Short-toed and Eurasian Treecreepers, Jay, Yellow-billed and Red-billed Choughs, Raven, Snowfinch, Siskin, Crossbill, Common Bullfinch.

Breeding season: Egyptian Vulture, Alpine Swift, Crag and House Martins, Northern Wheatear, Rufous-tailed Rock Thrush, Ring Ouzel, Garden and Bonelli's Warblers, Whitethroat, Blackcap, Common Chiffchaff, Spotted Flycatcher, Red-backed Shrike, Citril Finch, Yellowhammer, Ortolan Bunting.

VALLE DE BENASQUE AND PARQUE NATURAL POSETS–MALADETA (Huesca)

AR5

Status: Parque Natural (33,267ha). Also part of the Reserva Nacional de Caza de Benasque (50,000ha) and a ZEPA.

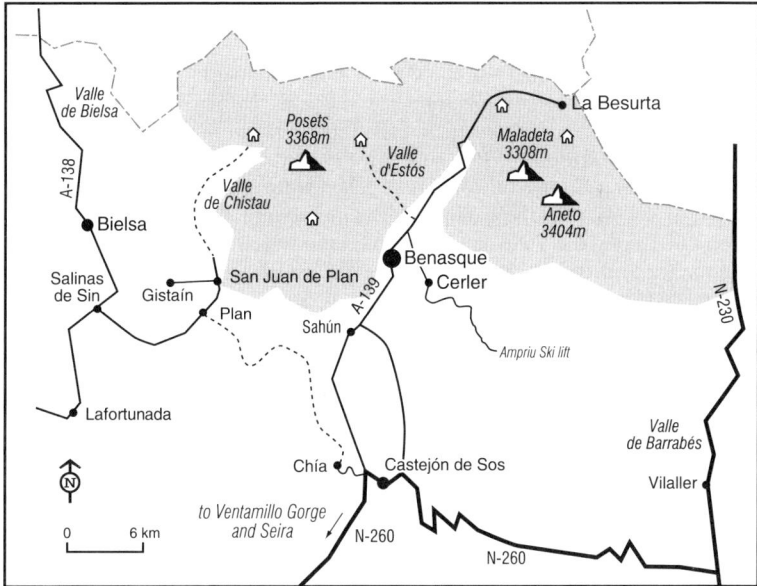

Site description

The Benasque Valley lies between the massifs of Posets and Maladeta, the locations of the highest summits in the Pyrenees, the Pico de Aneto (3,404m) and the Pico de Posets (3,375m). Peaks apart, extensive tracts lie at over 3,000m and feature small glaciers, numerous mountain lakes and many rocky areas. The interest is not restricted to the high mountains and, as with many other valleys, there is much to see between the summits and the foot of the valley at around 1,500m. The wide range of habitats includes hayfields, woods of birch and Silver Fir and large pine forests extending up to 2,200m. Habitats change above the treeline, giving way to alpine meadows, rock fields, lakes and some glacial cirques. The forests of Vallibierna and Artiga de Lin-Portillón are exceptional and include the best Black Pine forests in Aragón.

Species

As you would expect this site has high-mountain bird communities including Ptarmigan, Lammergeiers, Golden Eagles, Water Pipits, Alpine Accentors, Yellow-billed Choughs and Snowfinches. This is one of the best areas in the Pyrenees for Capercaillies, and the forest has very good numbers of Black

Woodpeckers and Boreal Owls. Areas of extensive woodland also have Honey-buzzards, Goshawks, Marsh Tits and Crossbills. In the more open woodland and in pastures and rocky slopes are Grey Partridges, Ring Ouzels, Rufous-tailed Rock Thrushes, Whinchats and Red-billed Choughs. A number of side valleys, for example the Estós Valley, have some huge rocky cliffs, attractive to raptors and Wallcreepers. Brown Bears, Marmots and Chamois also occur.

Timing
May to early July is the best period. Access becomes difficult during periods of heavy snowfall late in winter.

Access
Benasque can be reached via the A-139 from the south where it joins the N-260 and is the main focal point for the area, particularly so for serious climbers and walkers. The Natural Park Interpretation Centre (Tel. 974 552 066) is located 1km out of Benasque on the road to Anciles. It is open daily throughout the summer but only at weekends for the rest of the year. The Benasque Valley splits the park in half. The western arm of the area can be approached along the Valle de Chistau (Gistaín) which itself can be reached via a minor road off the A-138 at Salinas de Sin, or from the east via Chia along a minor road off the N-260 near Castejón de Sos.

There are numerous options for exploring the area in search of birds. Many mountain and hill routes are identified on the ground with coloured markers. Details of these routes can be found in the villages but particularly at the Centre in Benasque. There are five mountain refuges and numerous routes up many of the side valleys and from any of the villages along the A-139. The Estós valley to the north of Benasque offers a three-hour walk to the Estós refuge, with parking at a campsite after crossing the River Ésera. Another option is to take the road to Cerler and the Ampriu ski-lift, where there is a possibility of high-altitude birds including Snowfinches. In any case it is worth following the A-139 above Benasque for some 14km all the way up to La Besurta, the starting point for several alpine trails. This scenic road offers plenty of opportunities for exploring the fringing forests and scanning the ridges for raptors. There are also diverse trails linking the villages of the Valle de Chistau. The minor road from Plan to Chía and Castejón de Sos, signposted Puerto de Sahún, is good for Woodcock, Black Woodpeckers and Boreal Owls.

The Ventamillo gorge (Congosto de Ventamilla) on the N-260 just south of Castejón de Sos is one of the most accessible sites for breeding Wallcreepers in the Spanish Pyrenees. It is a busy road but a small but useful lay-by for cars is immediately after the tunnel when you approach the gorge from Seira.

CALENDAR

All year: Ptarmigan, Capercaillie, Red Kite, Griffon Vulture, Lammergeier, Goshawk, Golden Eagle, Peregrine Falcon, Rock Dove, Long-eared and Boreal Owls, Black Woodpecker, Crag Martin, Dipper, Alpine Accentor, Blue Rock Thrush, Marsh and Crested Tits, Wallcreeper, Yellow-billed and Red-billed Choughs, Raven, Rock Sparrow, Snowfinch, Citril Finch, Crossbill, Bullfinch, Yellowhammer, Rock Bunting.

Breeding season: Honey-buzzard, Black Kite, Short-toed Eagle, Woodcock, Alpine Swift, Water Pipit, Whinchat, Rufous-tailed Rock Thrush, Ring Ouzel, Red-backed Shrike, Ortolan Bunting.

LOS MALLOS DE RIGLOS (Huesca)   AR6

Status: Unprotected.

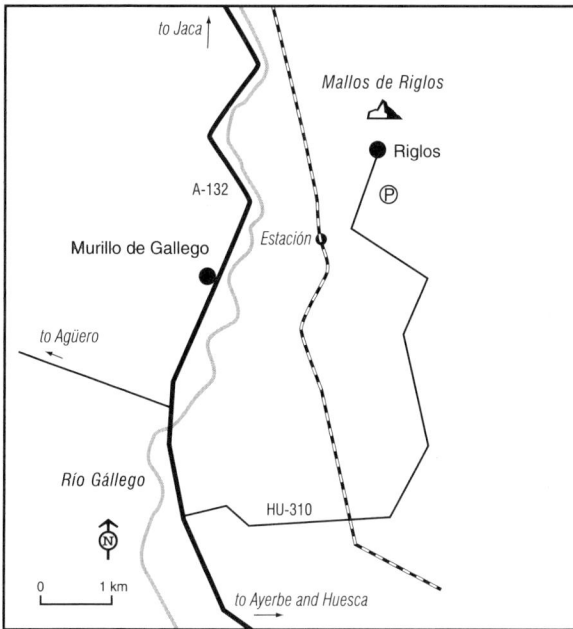

Site description
Los Mallos de Riglos, a popular rock climbing site, are part of the Sierra de Santo Domingo, a range that includes the spectacular red sandstone rock formations immediately behind and dominating the village of Riglos. The site consists of towering perpendicular cliffs, Los Mallos, with a rocky scree base. Vegetation is sparse to non-existent on the scree, with pockets of scrub in the gulleys, and more scrub, a river and cultivated land below the cliffs, scree and village. The local climate is noticeably much warmer and drier compared to other Pyrenean foothills further north. A number of other areas in the general area around Riglos, including similarly impressive sandstone cliffs above the nearby village of Agüero, are worth exploring.

Species
This is a well-known site for Black Wheatears, here at their northern limit in Spain. They nest amongst the boulder-scree at the cliff base but can be elusive, especially on windy days. Black Redstarts are very common here, and Rock Sparrows can be found around the church. The cliffs also support a good colony of Griffon Vultures and a range of other cliff-nesting birds such as Egyptian Vultures, Crag Martins and Peregrine Falcons, all despite disturbance from rock climbers. Although it is worth concentrating on the scree and cliff habitats, it can also be fruitful to search the scrub immediately below for

Dartford, Spectacled, Subalpine and Sardinian Warblers. The varied countryside below the cliffs and the river has Orphean Warblers, Woodchat Shrikes
and Golden Orioles, and the mountain areas around have Lammergeiers and
Golden and Booted Eagles.

Crag Martins

Timing

This site is good all year round but best in April and May. It also deserves a
winter visit for Wallcreepers and Alpine Accentors. The cliffs are very popular
with climbers and so are best avoided at weekends.

Access

Take the A-132 south from the N-240 Pamplona/Jaca road at the bridge of
Puente de Reina. As you travel south you will see Riglos and the cliffs on
your left after about 30km but will need to cross the river south of Murillo
de Gállego and then, at km-35, take the minor road north back to the village.
Visitors must park in the car park provided outside the village. Walk up the
village to the church at its highest point and then continue along the foot of
the cliffs on the scree. Blustery winds affect the cliff bases at times so you will
need to be careful on the unstable slopes. A track leading south-east from
Riglos crosses orchards and gives access to less disturbed cliffs, frequented by
nesting vultures.

CALENDAR

All year: Red Kite, Lammergeier, Griffon
Vulture, Golden Eagle, Peregrine Falcon,
Rock Dove, Eagle Owl, Blue Rock Thrush,
Black Redstart, Black Wheatear, Dartford
and Sardinian Warblers, Red-billed Chough,
Raven, Rock Sparrow.

Breeding season: Black Kite, Egyptian
Vulture, Short-toed and Booted Eagles, Alpine

Swift, Crag Martin, Tawny Pipit, Rufous-tailed
Rock Thrush; Spectacled, Subalpine and
Orphean Warblers, Golden Oriole.

Winter: Wallcreeper, Alpine Accentor,
Redwing, Ring Ouzel.

SIERRA Y CAÑONES DE GUARA   AR7
(Huesca)

Status: Parque Natural (47,450ha) and ZEPA.

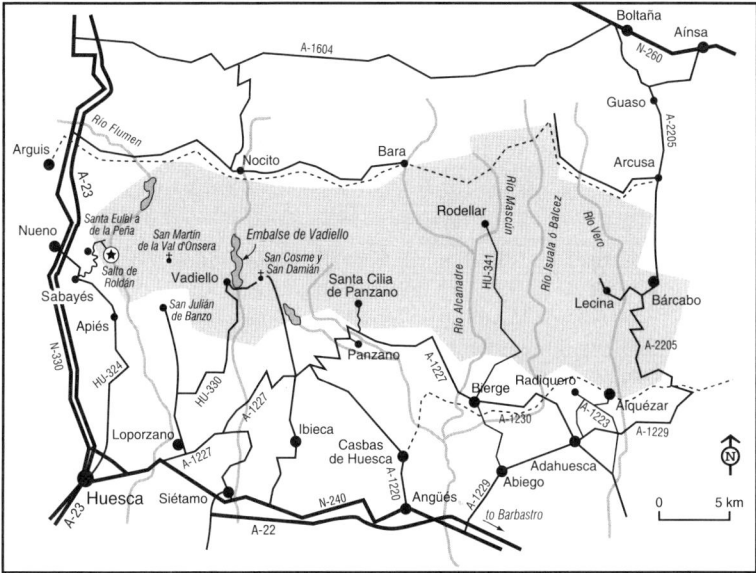

Site description

This is the largest of the 'pre-Pyrenean' ranges, a huge upland limestone massif north-east of the city of Huesca, at the southern edge of the Pyrenees, and stretching for 40km west/east. The limestone terrain is cut through by rivers which have produced many deep, steep-walled gorges that dissect the massif into 'mini-sierras'.

The altitude within the park ranges from 430m along the Río Alcanadre to 2,077m at the highest point, Tozal (or Puntón) de Guara. This is a sparsely populated area with many abandoned small villages. The limestone ravines have flowing torrents in winter but are mainly dry during the summer months. Extensive areas of grassland and oak and juniper scrub cover the park, among mixed oakwoods and woodlands of beech, pine and Yew.

Species

Extremely important for birds of prey, with around ten pairs of Lammergeiers, hundreds of pairs of Griffon Vultures and smaller numbers of Egyptian Vultures. Red Kites, Honey-buzzards and Peregrine Falcons are fairly widespread and there are small numbers of Short-toed Eagles, Golden Eagles and Eagle Owls. Bonelli's Eagles have a marginal presence here. The woodlands also support Sparrowhawks, Goshawks, Long-eared Owls, Black Woodpeckers and Hawfinches, with Wrynecks in the more open areas. Black Wheatears, at the northern edge of their range, and Blue Rock Thrushes are scattered throughout the open rocky areas.

The grassy and scrubby areas have Red-backed Shrikes and Cirl and Ortolan Buntings, with Montagu's Harriers also present hunting over these habitats as well as across the olive groves and cereal fields.

Wallcreepers, Alpine Accentors and Citril Finches occur in the higher parts of the gorges and surrounding land in winter.

Timing

Winters are not as severe here as in the high Pyrenees but spring does arrive relatively late. April–June are the best months, with May onwards being especially good. Some species, notably raptors, can be found throughout the year and high-altitude birds such as Wallcreepers and Alpine Accentors winter in the park.

Access

A network of small roads leads north from the N-240 Huesca/Barbastro road, or south from the A-1604, which links two major roads, the N-330 in the west and the N-260 (and A-23 motorway) in the east. Many lead to monasteries and chapels, which are interesting in their own right – San Martín and San Cosme y San Damián are particularly noteworthy – as well as good points of access to the wilder parts of the Guara. Numerous small roads and forest tracks lead into the inner parts of the park. The principal visitors' centre is situated in Bierge (Tel. 974 318 238) and is open daily in the summer, but only at weekends during the rest of the year. The Boletas Birdwatching Centre in Loporzano (Tel. 974 262 027, boletas.org) provides a focal point for birders as well as accommodation and guided tours.

Salto de Roldán A spectacular ravine offering excellent views of raptors, although access to the summit involves a metal ladder! Turn off the N-240 north of Huesca northwards on the HU-324 for 8km to the village of Apiés and continue north-west towards Sabayés. On reaching the edge of Sabayés take the right turn to Santa Eulalia de la Peña but park 4.5km after the turning in a wide open area at the end of this stretch of road (before you reach Santa Eulalia). Walk to the right of the large crag and follow the path to the cliff face or take the path on to the summit for further views. Care should be taken!

San Martín de la Val d'Onsera Take the N-240 from Huesca towards Barbastro. After 7km turn left on to the minor road for Loporzano, and left again to Barluengo and San Julián de Banzo. A signposted forestry road leads to a path that takes you up to the ravine, waterfall and chapel of San Martín de la Val d'Onsera.

Embalse de Vadiello Proceed as above as far as Loporzano and from there turn right after about 3km on to the HU-330 towards Sasa del Abadiado, Castilsabás and finally to the Embalse de Vadiello. A track from the far side of the dam of the reservoir goes to the Chapel of San Cosme, through oak scrub woodland climbing towards the Huevo de San Cosme, a rocky outcrop. Yet another excellent site for vultures and other rupestral species. Other possibilities include a track which starts at the last road tunnel, across a ravine, the Barranco del Diablo, along the bank of the reservoir to Nocito.

Santa Cilia de Panzano A view of a vulture feeding station, that attracts Lammergeiers among others, is available from a *mirador* (viewpoint) at the top of the village of Santa Cilia. La Casa de los Buitres (vulture house), an information centre in the old church bell-tower there, mainly opens at weekends. Take the N-240 from Huesca towards Barbastro. After 7km turn left on to the A-1227 minor road and after approximately 23km take a left turn to Santa Cilia de Panzano.

Alcanadre and Mascún Gorge From Huesca take the N-240 towards Barbastro. After some 30km, just after the bridge over the Río Alcanadre, turn left on to the A-1229 and A-1227 minor roads taking you to Abiego and Bierge. At Bierge continue north for 18km on the HU-341 to Rodellar. From Rodellar a path goes to Mascún Gorge, probably the most spectacular of all the gorges in the Natural Park, and it is possible to climb up to the source of the Río Mascún.

Sierra de Sevil and Balcés Gorge Access is as for Mascún above but continue at the village of Abiego to Adahuesca on the A-1229. Alternatively, in Barbastro take the A-1232 minor road towards Alquézar and, once through the village of Huerta de Vero, turn left for Adahuesca. In this village take the A-1233 to Radiquero and on to San Pelegrín. From San Pelegrín a track leads up to the high point of Mesón de Sivil (1,273m) and along Balcés Gorge for about 8km, ending at Sarsa de Surta.

River Vero and Forests at Bárcabo Take the A-1232 out of Barbastro for Castillazuelo, and from there continue to Alquézar. From the square in the village follow the base of Vero Gorge to look for cliff-nesting species. To reach other routes, 3km before Alquézar take the A-2205 to Colungo, Lecina and Bárcabo, from where there are numerous forest tracks suitable for seeking woodland species. Try also the road from Naval through Suelves to Bárcabo.

There are further tracks worth exploring at Santa Eulalia de la Peña and the Embalse de Belsué, the Barranco de la Pillera near Nocito, and near Lecina. Long-distance trails are also possible to the north and south of the main massif.

CALENDAR

All year: Lammergeier, Griffon Vulture, Red Kite, Goshawk, Sparrowhawk, Golden and Bonelli's Eagles, Peregrine Falcon, Stock Dove, Long-eared and Eagle Owls, Woodcock, Green and Black Woodpeckers, Crag Martin, Dipper, Black Redstart, Black Wheatear, Blue Rock Thrush, Red-billed Chough, Raven, Hawfinch, Cirl and Rock Buntings.

Short-toed and Booted Eagles, Hobby, Great Spotted Cuckoo, Bee-eater, Hoopoe, Wryneck, Alpine Swift, Red-rumped Swallow, Tawny Pipit, Common Redstart, Northern and Black-eared Wheatears, Rufous-tailed Rock Thrush; Orphean, Bonelli's, Subalpine and Melodious Warblers, Spotted Flycatcher, Woodchat and Red-backed Shrikes, Ortolan Bunting.

Breeding season: Egyptian Vulture, Black Kite, Honey-buzzard, Montagu's Harrier,

Winter: Wallcreeper, Alpine Accentor, Citril Finch.

EMBALSE DE LA SOTONERA   AR8
(Huesca)

Status: Unprotected.

Site description
This large reservoir, created by damming the Río Gállego, has a shallow indented shoreline and stands of tamarisk and willow intermixed with areas of reed and marsh. The north-west corner has the best developed and greatest expanse of marsh. During the year, considerable changes in water level occur, which can flood nests and drown vegetation but at other times can also leave considerable areas of mud exposed.

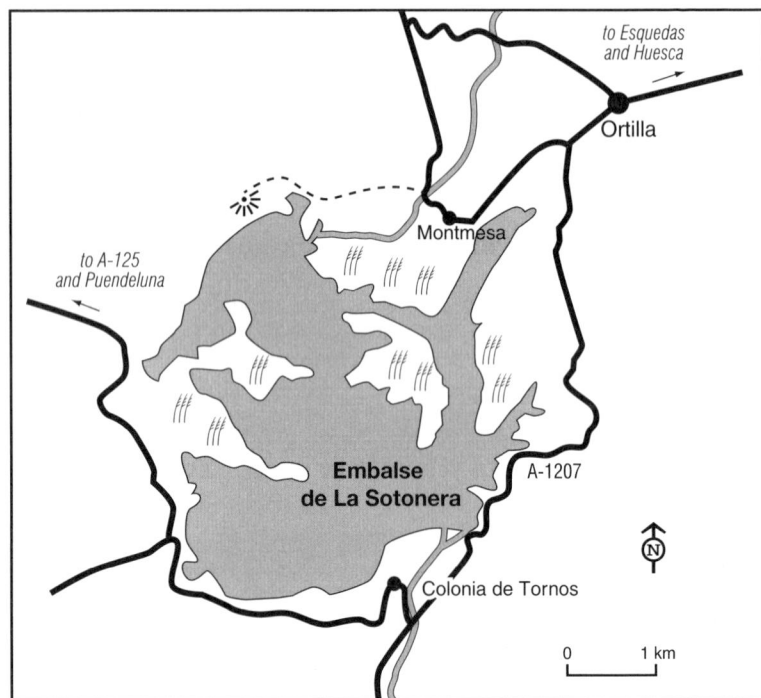

Species
The marshes are especially worth visiting and are of great bird interest, with Purple Herons, Spotted Crakes, Water Rails, Great Reed Warblers and a variety of waders and warblers occurring, especially during the spring and autumn. Large numbers of waterfowl winter on the reservoir. However, the site's real claim to fame is as a staging point for Cranes during their northward migration: it rivals Gallocanta (AR15) in some seasons, with up to 50,000 birds recorded.

The surrounding areas offer steppe birds, in particular Black-bellied and

Pin-tailed Sandgrouse, Little Bustards, Stone-curlews, Calandra Larks and, occasionally, Great Bustards.

Timing
Winter for wildfowl and Cranes (February–March), and spring and autumn for passage migrants, waders, warblers and terns. Heat haze can be a particular problem in summer.

Access
The reservoir can be reached off the A-132 out of Huesca, north-west towards Ayerbe. After around 15km turn left 1km past the village of Esquedas towards Lupiñén and Montmesa on the A-1207. From Montmesa a track to the north of the reservoir takes you to an observation point across the wetland. The area between the northern track and the reservoir, where well-developed marsh vegetation now occupies the site of a former reservoir, can be the most productive. There are also roads around the periphery of most of the site, although views across the wetland can be difficult.

CALENDAR

All year: Mallard, Little and Great Crested Grebes, Marsh Harrier, Water Rail, Moorhen, Common Coot, Little and Great Bustards, Stone-curlew, Kentish Plover, Lapwing, Common Redshank, Black-headed Gull, Black-bellied and Pin-tailed Sandgrouse, Little Owl, Calandra Lark, Cetti's and Dartford Warblers, Zitting Cisticola, Corn Bunting.

Breeding season: Purple Heron, Black Kite, Spotted Crake, Black-winged Stilt, Little Ringed Plover, Common Sandpiper, Bee-eater, Yellow Wagtail; Reed, Great Reed and Melodious Warblers, Woodchat Shrike.

Winter: Wigeon, Teal, Pintail, Shoveler, Tufted Duck, Golden Plover.

Passage: Red-crested Pochard, Garganey, Little Egret, Grey Heron, Osprey, Crane, Avocet, Ruff, Black-tailed Godwit, Whimbrel, Spotted Redshank, Black Tern.

SIERRA DEL MONCAYO (Zaragoza) AR9

Status: Parque Natural 'Dehesa del Moncayo' (10,000ha). The Sierra itself covers some 45,000ha.

Site description
An isolated massif in the far north-west of the region, part of the Sistema Ibérico. It ranges in altitude from 800m to the peak of Cerro de San Miguel (2,316m), the highest mountain in Aragón south of the Pyrenees. There are impressive limestone crags and gorges in the south, between the villages of Calcena and Purujosa on the CV-630. The area is sparsely forested but it includes one of the most southerly beechwoods in Europe, on the northern slopes, and relict oakwoods together with some fine Scots Pines in the pinewoods, as well as expanses of alpine pasture and scrub.

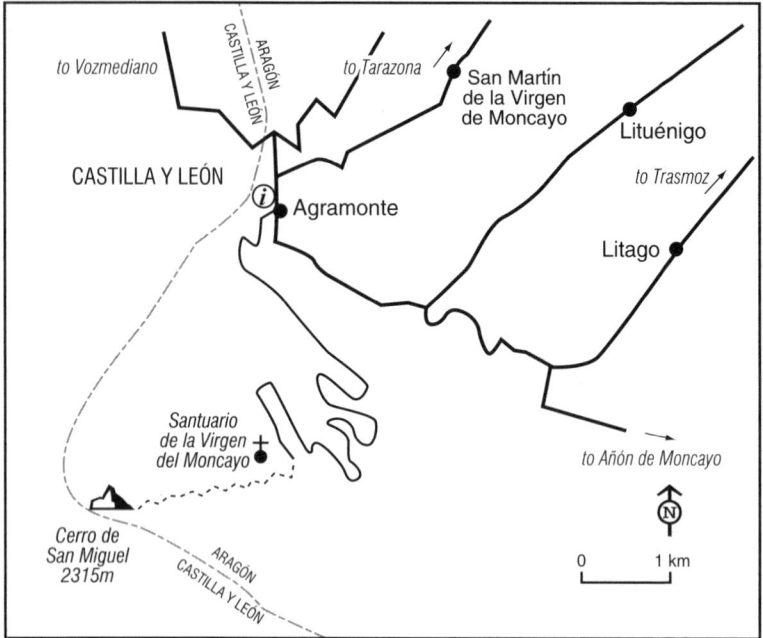

Species

The highest ground around the Santuario del Moncayo provides spectacular views of the Pyrenees, Iberian Range and the Ebro depression on clear days. The open ground of pasture, scrub and rock houses an outpost southern population of the Grey Partridge and also offers Rufous-tailed and Blue Rock Thrushes, Rock Sparrows, Water Pipits, Red-billed Choughs and Citril Finches. Griffon Vultures have a sizeable local population and Eagle Owls are present.

Crested Tit

The oakwoods have Short-toed Eagles, Honey-buzzards, Tree Pipits and Bonelli's Warblers with Turtle Doves, European Nightjars, Bee-eaters, Subalpine Warblers and Dartford Warblers in the lower scrubby and more open wooded areas. Goldcrests, Crested Tits and Crossbills breed in the pinewoods.

Timing
May and June are the best times to visit.

Access
Access is via Agramonte, which is reached by heading southwards from the N-122 Soria/Zaragoza road, that joins the AP-68 motorway west of Zaragoza, at junction 19. At Tarazona on the N-122 take the minor road south-west for the village of Santa Cruz de Moncayo and follow signs to San Martín de Moncayo and then Agramonte, where there are car parks and an information centre. From Agramonte a road climbs up the hillside to the Santuario de la Virgen del Moncayo, passing a number of springs on the way and a mountain refuge. A path leads from the sanctuary through pinewoods and areas of scree to the San Miguel peak. It is well marked and relatively easy to follow; allow 90 minutes each way.

CALENDAR

All year: Grey Partridge, Goshawk, Sparrowhawk, Golden Eagle, Woodcock, Eagle and Long-eared Owls, Wood Lark, Grey Wagtail, Dipper, Dunnock, Blue Rock and Song Thrushes, Common Chiffchaff, Firecrest, Goldcrest, Crested and Great Tits, Nuthatch, Short-toed Treecreeper, Red-billed Chough, Raven, Rock Sparrow, Citril Finch, Crossbill, Serin, Cirl Bunting.

Breeding season: Honey-buzzard, Short-toed and Booted Eagles, European Nightjar, Crag Martin, Tree and Water Pipits, Rufous-tailed Rock Thrush; Subalpine, Garden, Orphean and Bonelli's Warblers, Red-backed Shrike, Ortolan Bunting.

LAGUNA DE SARIÑENA (Huesca)   AR10

Status: Refugio de Fauna Silvestre and ZEPA (604ha).

Site description
A large shallow lake with a well-developed fringe of marsh vegetation situated in a steppe area between the valleys of the Ríos Alcanadre and Flumen. It is one of the most important wetlands in Aragón. Although the lake was formerly a saline lagoon, developed through evaporation during periods of high summer temperatures, it is now mainly freshwater as it is supplied by run-off from adjoining irrigation. A great deal of the area immediately around the lake has been given over to irrigated farmland, including rice paddies.

Species
Especially important for its heron populations. The lagoon is one of the few

Spanish locations where the Great Bittern nests with any regularity; it may be heard booming in spring. Purple Herons have a significant population here and there are also breeding Little Bitterns, Cattle and Little Egrets, Night Herons and Purple Herons. The Great White Egret has bred recently and Squacco Herons occasionally appear on passage. Marsh Harriers breed and over 100 may be present in winter. Purple Swamphens breed. Penduline Tits, and sometimes Bearded Tits, occur, mainly in winter. Moustached Warblers have bred here but are more frequently recorded in winter. A diversity of water-fowl, waders, and passerines occur on passage at the lake and in the adjacent ricefields. The lake itself can hold over 10,000 wildfowl over winter, Common Teal being especially numerous.

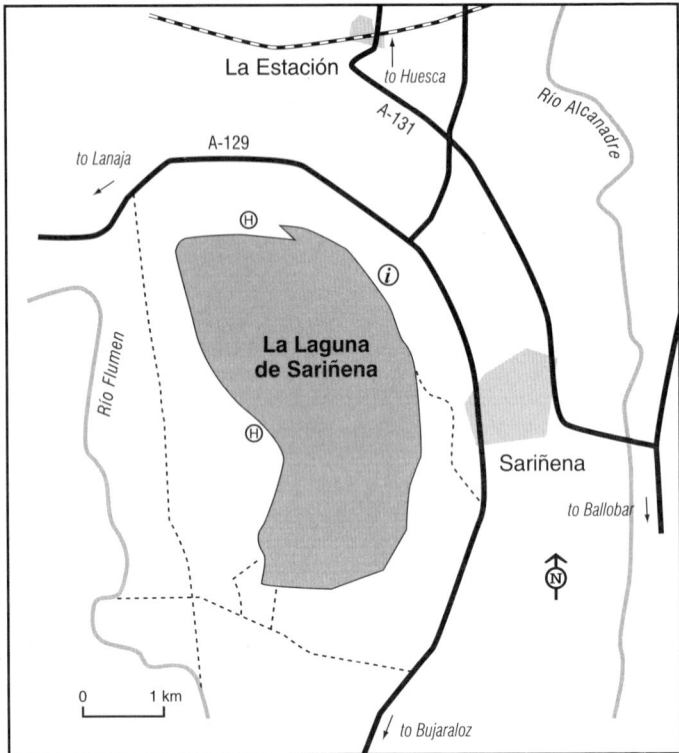

Timing
Spring and autumn, but winter also produces large numbers of wildfowl.

Access
The lake is immediately west of the town of Sariñena, around 70km north-east from Zaragoza along the A-129, or south from Huesca on the A-131. The lake is signposted from the town and a track leads up to the edge. An interpretative centre (Tel. 976 405 041), usually open only at weekends, is by the A-129 just before you reach Sariñena from the Zaragoza direction.

Paths follow much of the shore, although care is necessary when crossing the irrigation channels. Viewing over the reed fringe to the lake can sometimes be difficult but there are several main observation areas around the perimeter. The northernmost shore, where there is a tower hide, is the best place for waders.

CALENDAR

All year: Little, Great Crested, and Black-necked Grebes, Great Bittern, Cattle Egret, Grey Heron, Marsh Harrier, Purple Swamphen, Water Rail, Northern Lapwing, Black-headed Gull, Kingfisher, Cetti's Warbler.

Breeding season: Little Bittern, Night and Purple Herons, Little Egret, Black-winged Stilt, Little Ringed and Kentish Plovers, Common Redshank, Great Spotted Cuckoo, Roller, Sand Martin, Reed and Great Reed Warblers.

Winter: Greylag Goose, Common Shelduck, Wigeon, Teal, Mallard, Pintail, Shoveler, Cormorant, Grey Plover, Dunlin, Common Snipe, Moustached Warbler, Bearded Tit, Penduline Tit, Reed Bunting.

Passage periods: Garganey, Squacco Heron, Osprey, Crane, Little Stint, Curlew Sandpiper, Ruff, Spotted Redshank, Greenshank, Alpine Swift, hirundines.

LOS GALACHOS DEL EBRO (Zaragoza)   AR11

Status: Reserva Natural and ZEPA (800ha).

Site description
These oxbow lakes or *galachos* are situated in the Ebro valley near Zaragoza. The Galacho de Juslibol is north-west of the city. Three others lie 12km downstream of Zaragoza between Pastriz and Pina de Ebro. The largest and best conserved of these, the Galacho de La Alfranca, lies north of the Ebro and the other two, the Galachos de La Cartuja and El Burgo de Ebro, are south of the river. All are now unconnected with the river and fed entirely from underground supplies. Much of the area has been planted with poplars in recent years but there is also well-established associated fringe vegetation and extensive scrub.

Species
The lakes have small breeding populations of Little Bitterns, Night Herons, Little Egrets and Purple Herons as well as Marsh Harriers. The fringing poplar plantations and *sotos* are important for riparian species such Black Kites, Nightingales, Penduline Tits and Golden Orioles as well as Wrynecks and Woodchat Shrikes. Lesser Spotted Woodpeckers are a possibility here. Migrant passerines, including hirundines, warblers and flycatchers, may be numerous in spring and autumn.

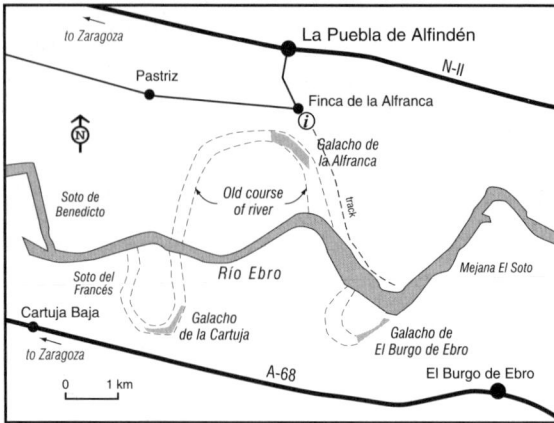

Timing

March–May and September–October can be outstanding for small migrants and roosting hirundines and wagtails.

Access

For the *galachos* to the south-east of Zaragoza take the N-II eastwards from Zaragoza towards Bujaraloz. Turn right at the village of La Puebla de Alfindén to Finca de la Alfranca, where there is an interpretative centre (Tel. 976 105 840). This is open daily and offers free guided tours at weekends, which allow wider access than at other times. It is also possible to reach the area along a minor road off the N-II, immediately right after the road crosses over the River Gállego, to Pastriz. A track from the Centre leads to the Galacho de La Alfranca and continues through riparian woodlands along the Ebro to a point opposite the Galacho de El Burgo de Ebro.

Another visitors' centre (Tel. 650 576 526), at the Galacho de Juslibol, is also open mainly at weekends. Parking is at the village of Juslibol, and visiting the centre and *galachos* beyond involves a walk of some 2–3km. Finding your way out of Zaragoza can be difficult and at weekends a good alternative is to take the *El Carrizal* tourist train to Juslibol: it departs from Calle María Zambrano, in front of the Carrefour supermarket, all year except mid November–February. A circular trail leads around the Galacho, nearby gravelpits and some open country.

CALENDAR

All year: Little and Great Crested Grebes, Little Egret, White Stork, Marsh Harrier, Water Rail, Common Coot, Kingfisher, Green and Lesser Spotted Woodpeckers, Penduline Tit, Cetti's and Sardinian Warblers, Zitting Cisticola.

Breeding season: Little Bittern, Night and Purple Herons, Black Kite, Scops Owl, Bee-eater, Wryneck, Sand Martin, Nightingale, Great Reed and Melodious Warblers, Spotted Flycatcher, Golden Oriole, Woodchat Shrike.

Winter: Water Pipit, Bluethroat, Reed Bunting.

Passage periods: Grey Heron, Booted Eagle, Barn Swallow, House Martin, Willow Warbler, Spotted and Pied Flycatchers.

LAS ESTEPAS DE BELCHITE AR12 (Zaragoza)

Status: Mostly unprotected (40,000ha), although part of the area is a ZEPA and there are two important reserves: the Refugio de Fauna Silvestre de la Lomaza de Belchite (961ha), administered by the regional government, and La Reserva Ornitológica El Planerón (600ha), run by SEO/Birdlife.

Site description

The area to the south and south-east of Zaragoza forms one of the most important steppe landscapes, not only in the Ebro Valley, but in the whole of Spain. Sad to say, substantial areas of steppe have been destroyed through ploughing and cultivation. Thus, the low hills and plains of the Ebro Valley and associated valleys are now a mosaic of steppe, cereal fields and irrigated areas with occasional wooded hillocks, and gullies and cliffs formed by the local rivers.

The area of interest is extensive but very fragmented. It stretches from west of Muel to Azaila in the east. Most is unprotected and the focus of attention is the two reserves of La Lomaza and El Planerón, although there are other areas worth visiting including the steppe area lying either side of the road running from Belchite to Azaila and known as El Saso.

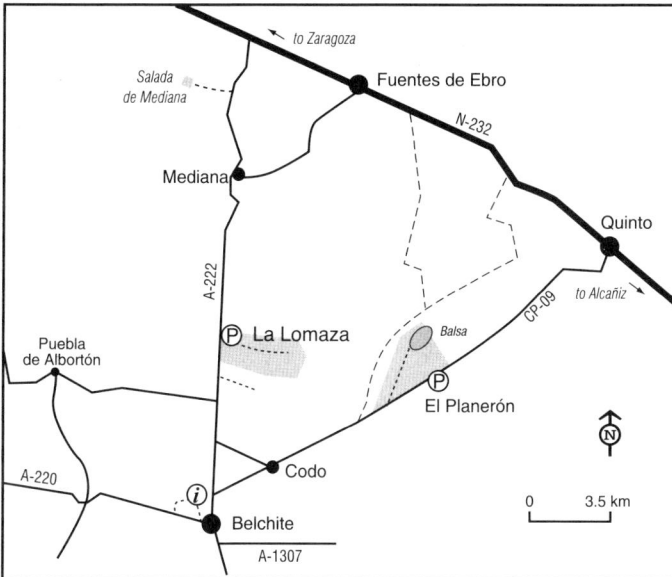

Species

The whole area is of great importance for steppe birds and is probably the best place in Spain to see Dupont's Larks, which number several hundred pairs. It is also a key region for both Black-bellied Sandgrouse and Pin-tailed Sandgrouse. Great Bustards seldom occur and there are only small numbers of Little Bustards. Other birds typical of steppe communities present here include around 150 pairs of Stone-curlews and several thousand pairs of Lesser Short-toed Larks, as well as Tawny Pipits, Calandra and Greater Short-toed Larks and Black-eared Wheatears.

Another species of note is the Dotterel, which can be found on passage at certain areas on the plain. It most commonly encountered at El Saso, in small flocks from late August to the end of October. Raptors likely to be encountered include Golden and Short-toed Eagles, and Hen Harriers in winter.

Black-bellied Sangrouse

Timing

Spring is the best season for steppe birds, early autumn for Dotterels. The evening and, particularly, the morning are good times to visit any pools to view sandgrouse coming down to drink. Dupont's Larks are best sought at dawn in spring: previous familiarity with the song, which is also given at night, will be helpful.

Access

Belchite town is on the A-222. From Zaragoza take the A-68/N-232 south-east towards Alcañiz and after 20km turn right on to the A-222. Continue past Mediana and the reserve of La Lomaza de Belchite lies 11km north of Belchite, on the left-hand (east) side of the road. There is a car park off the A-222 just before a windsock. Strictly speaking, visits to La Lomaza require a permit, which can be obtained from INAGA, the Environmental Management Institute of Aragón, based in Zaragoza (Tel. 976 716 633).

The El Planerón reserve is freely accessible. It can be reached from Belchite or by continuing along the N-232 out of Zaragoza until you reach Quinto. Turn right here on to the CP-09 minor road for Codo and Belchite. At Belchite there is an information centre, Centro de Informacion 'Estepas del Valle del Ebro' (Tel. 679 552 090/976 830 771) run by SEO/Birdlife, where you can obtain additional information. The Centre is open at weekends in spring and autumn. Coming from Belchite, El Planerón is on the left-hand (north) side about halfway between Belchite and Quinto. The best option is to descend into the valley floor and explore the good gravel tracks that provide several kilometres of access by car to the best sites. Signposted entrances to the tracks from the CP-09 are available 3.7km and 5.4km north of Codo. The central track passes a small, tamarisk-fringed pool, La Balsa de El Planerón, which attracts waterbirds in wet seasons but is often dry. A car park giving panoramic views of the reserve and with interpretative boards showing the trail network is 8.8km north of Codo. Sandgrouse and other species may be scanned for here. Please do not leave the marked trails anywhere in the Reserve.

CALENDAR

All year: White Stork, Golden Eagle, Peregrine Falcon, Little Bustard, Stone-curlew, Black-bellied and Pin-tailed Sandgrouse, Eagle Owl; Dupont's, Calandra, Lesser Short-toed and Thekla Larks, Black Wheatear, Blue Rock Thrush, Sardinian Warbler, Southern Grey Shrike, Rock Sparrow.

Breeding season: Black Kite, Short-toed Eagle, Egyptian Vulture, Montagu's Harrier, Lesser Kestrel, Bee-eater, Roller, Red-necked Nightjar, Greater Short-toed Lark, Tawny Pipit, Black-eared Wheatear, Spectacled Warbler, Woodchat Shrike.

Winter: Hen Harrier, Merlin, Sky Lark, Meadow Pipit.

Passage periods: Dotterel.

LOS MONEGROS (Huesca/Zaragoza)   AR13

Status: Four separate ZEPAs covering more than 100,000ha within a region of over 250,000ha.

Site description

Los Monegros is a huge semi-desert region, some 2,750km² in extent. It occupies the driest area in the whole Ebro Valley, lying north of the Ebro itself and stretching from Zaragoza eastwards almost as far as Lleida. It is one of the best-known steppe areas in Western Europe. The main area of interest lies north of the AP-2 motorway from Zaragoza and Lleida, although it extends south as far as Sástago and north to Alcolea de Cinca.

As with Belchite, these huge plains are now only a mosaic of steppe with sparse vegetation, hillsides, cereal fields, deep gullies, cliffs and land under irrigation. This last is not a new threat as irrigation has destroyed much steppe-land over the last 80 years but at least the importance of the region is now recognised through designation as ZEPAs.

The main differences from Belchite are the surviving areas of juniper and pine woodland and the seasonal brackish lagoons, *saladas*, which contain extremely saline water due to high evaporation rates but are bone dry in summer. The saladas are mainly concentrated between Sástago and Bujaraloz, the largest and most important being the Laguna de la Playa. A tendency for dry winters has emptied the saladas in some recent years.

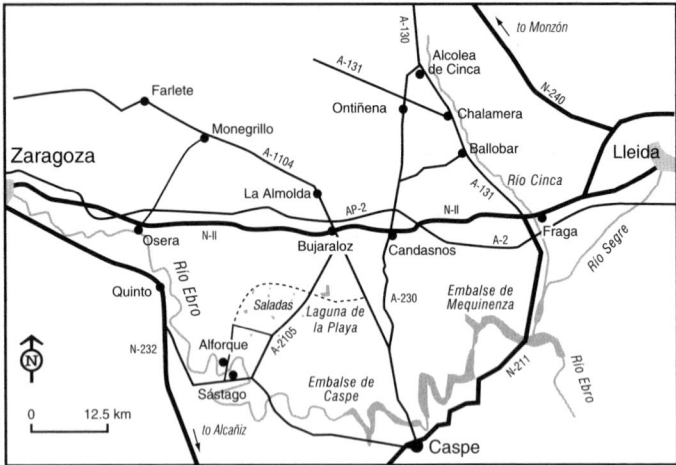

Species
The whole area is important for steppe birds but it is sometimes difficult to locate certain species since they are spread over a very wide expanse. Little Bustards, Stone-curlews, Pin-tailed and Black-bellied Sandgrouse, Dupont's and Lesser Short-toed Larks are all relatively common. Spectacled and Dartford Warblers are also widespread as are Black-eared Wheatears. Lesser Kestrels have sharply increased after a long period of decline and are now common nesting in the many abandoned farm houses (*mases*), often in company of the also rather abundant Red-billed Choughs.

There are numerous small brackish lagoons between Bujaraloz and Sástago, and the largest of the lakes, the Laguna de la Playa, can hold wildfowl in winter, water-permitting. The area around La Playa can be good for bustards, sandgrouse, Lesser Short-toed Larks, and for Dotterel on passage. The area north of Osera is well known for Dupont's Larks.

Raptors and other birds associated with cliffs and rocky faces, such as Egyptian Vultures, Peregrine Falcons, Alpine Swifts, Crag Martins and Rock Sparrows are present and are found near or alongside watercourses such as the Ebro at Alforque and Sástago, or the Río Cinca between Alcolea de Cinca and Fraga. White Storks nest in many of the villages.

Timing
There is much of interest from autumn through to spring, although the winters can be bitterly cold. Later in the season birding becomes much more difficult as the heat haze can be dramatic and the crop and vegetation height can make picking out ground birds such as larks very difficult. As elsewhere, Dupont's Larks are best sought at dawn in spring: previous familiarity with the song will be helpful. Late August to November can be good for Dotterel passage, which peaks towards the end of September. Great Bustards can also be seen through the autumn into spring.

Dupont's Lark

Access

Much of Los Monegros is sparsely populated but the region is crossed by good roads, including the AP-2 and N-II, which link Zaragoza and Lleida west/east. Three main areas deserve particular attention.

Osera de Ebro/Monegrillo/Farlete/La Almolda Take the N-II towards Lleida and at Osera turn left and north-eastwards on the CV-8 towards Monegrillo into an area of steppe. The landscape is very impressive, comprising undulating steppe countryside with the backdrop of the Sierra de Alcubierre. The southern 8km of the Osera/Monegrillo tract is sometimes good for Little Bustards, Pin-tailed Sandgrouse, Stone-curlews and Lesser Short-toed Larks and is probably the best-known area for Dupont's Larks in Los Monegros. Montagu's Harriers, and Booted Eagles from the nearby Sierra, also occur. Stop and scan along this road and the A-1104 between Farlete, Monegrillo and La Almolda. A good option to stretch your legs is around La Ermita de San Martín which is up a track on the west side of the CV-8 around 3km out of Osera.

Steppes and brackish lagoons south of Bujaraloz Bujaraloz is just under 70km from Zaragoza on the N-II. From Bujaraloz turn south on to the A-230 towards Caspe and shortly afterwards turn right on to a minor road (A-2105) for the village of Sástago. Numerous tracks off this road should be explored. In particular, the area of steppe immediately south of Bujaraloz, to either side of the A-2105 to Sástago as far as the turn-off to the Laguna de la Playa, is often particularly productive. This general area can be good for Dotterel in the autumn and Great Bustards occur through the autumn to early spring. Black-bellied Sandgrouse are fairly common and more numerous than Pin-tailed Sandgrouse which also occur here. The Laguna de La Playa is the largest of the lagoons of the area and is reached by a short track on the left(west) side 7.5km south of the A-2105/A-230 junction; the disused saltworks buildings are conspicuous. Other areas of steppe and saline pools along the A-2015 and the CV-411, from Bujaraloz south to the Ebro at Alforque and Sástago, and the riverine cliffs there, are worth exploring. Tracks off these roads allow wider exploration and the roads themselves are very quiet.

Candasnos/Ballobar/Ontiñena   Continue along the N-II from Zaragoza through Bujaraloz as far as Candasnos. Turn left on the A-2214 northwards towards Ontiñena which is around 20km to the north. Turn right to Ballobar after about 9km. The best places to search are the Ontiñena road north of the junction with the Ballobar road, the Ballobar road (HU-V-8601) itself and any seasonal ponds and saline steppe. The best known saline pool, although mainly dry, is El Baso. This is about halfway between the Ballobar turning and Ballobar itself, around 6km from the turning, where a track on the left opposite a cereal silo takes you to El Baso 'lagoon'. Both Black-bellied and Pin-tailed Sandgrouse are relatively common in all these areas, and Little Bustards, Dupont's Larks and Lesser Short-toed Larks also occur. Huge sandstone cliffs with Egyptian Vultures and other cliff-nesting species occur along the road between Alcolea de Cinca and Chalamera (HU-V-8611). The A-131 provides easy access to/from this area and the Laguna de Sariñena (AR10).

The nearby Laguna de Candasnos (AR23) offers a wide range of waterfowl and is well worth visiting.

CALENDAR

All year: White Stork, Golden Eagle, Peregrine Falcon, Little and Great Bustards, Stone-curlew, Black-bellied and Pin-tailed Sandgrouse; Dupont's, Calandra, Lesser Short-toed, Crested and Thekla Larks, Black Wheatear, Blue Rock Thrush, Rock Sparrow.

Breeding season: Egyptian Vulture, Montagu's Harrier, Lesser Kestrel, Great Spotted Cuckoo, Red-necked Nightjar, Bee-eater, Roller, Hoopoe, Greater Short-toed Lark, Tawny Pipit, Black-eared Wheatear, Spectacled Warbler.

Passage periods: Dotterel and other waders.

Winter: Hen Harrier, Merlin, Sky Lark, Meadow Pipit. Waterfowl at Candasnos.

SALADAS DE CHIPRANA   AR14
(Zaragoza)

Status: Ramsar site (162ha). Reserva Natural and LIC.

Site description
A complex of small natural lagoons in the Ebro Valley south of the river and west of the town of Caspe. The lakes have only limited shoreline fringes of reeds and other emergent vegetation. They are surrounded by scattered Tamarisks and other shrubs and are set in a landscape of low scrub, with some cereal fields and olive groves. The Salada Grande, the largest lake, and the nearby Salada de Roces have permanent water, the former being particularly deep, up to 5.6m. Smaller pools that form in other depressions are seasonal. A nearby but very different permanent freshwater lake is also worth visiting (See AR22).

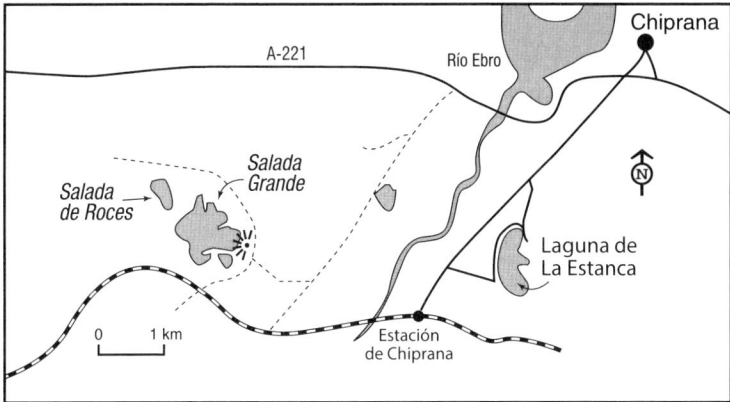

Timing

Spring is best for herons and for a wide range of both wetland and open-country species. Winter for wildfowl. Summer can be very hot and heat haze can be a problem from late morning well into the afternoon, even in spring.

Access

Caspe is 25km north of Alcañiz and the lagoons are west of the town and south of the A-221. From Caspe take the A-221 west for 12km towards Chiprana and continue towards Escatrón. At km-43.9, shortly after crossing a small reservoir on the Regallo river, turn left on to a tarmac road. Continue on this road for 3.9km, ignoring tracks off it. The track swings round by a farm before the railway line, where there is a parking area and an information board. It is better to take the right track from here and park at a larger car park that overlooks the Salada Grande. A marked circular trail leads around the main lake and also gives access to the other pools.

CALENDAR

All year: Mallard, Red-crested Pochard, Little and Black-necked Grebes, Marsh Harrier, Black-headed Gull, Sardinian Warbler.

Breeding season: Common Shelduck, Little Bittern, Purple Heron, Black-winged Stilt, Kentish Plover, Common Cuckoo, Great Spotted Cuckoo, Bee-eater, Black-eared Wheatear, Reed and Great Reed Warblers, Woodchat Shrike.

Passage periods: Ringed and Little Ringed Plovers, Little Stint, Dunlin, Ruff, Common Redshank, Greenshank, Common Sandpiper, Black and Whiskered Terns.

Winter: Teal, Pintail, Shoveler, Common Pochard, Great Crested Grebe, Red Kite, Lapwing.

LAGUNA DE GALLOCANTA   AR15
(Zaragoza/Teruel)

Status: Refugio de Fauna Silvestre, Ramsar site and ZEPA (6,720ha).

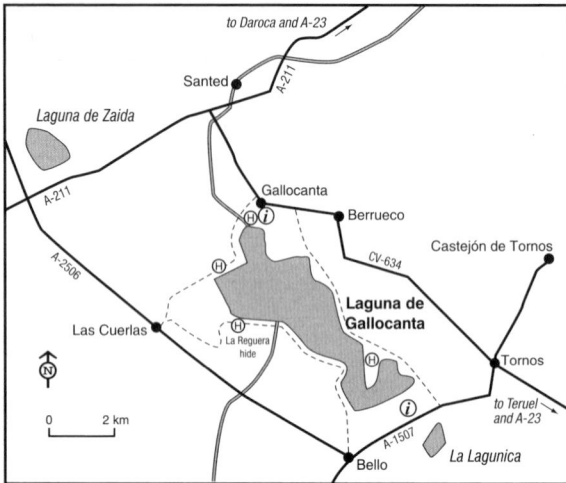

Site description
The largest natural lake in Spain, covering around 1,500ha of open water within a total protected area of some 6,720ha. The lake is fed mainly by rainwater, giving rise to dramatic changes in water level from year to year. In wet years the lake can be vast. In dry ones it dries out completely during the hot summers and it has been largely dry in some recent low-rainfall winters. The lake is at an altitude of 1,000m and temperatures can be low in winter when frosts are frequent. Gallocanta is the most important saline lake in western Europe but freshwater springs allow for localised patches of reeds and reedmace. The surrounding fields are steppe-like in character, although large areas are under cultivation, mainly of cereals.

Species
Common Cranes from Fennoscandia, the Baltic states and Germany take the west European migration route to their wintering grounds. The source populations have increased since the 1980s and the numbers wintering in Iberia now exceed 150,000 birds, most of them wintering in the west, chiefly in Extremadura. Gallocanta is a key staging post for Cranes both entering and leaving Spain and very large numbers use the lake and surrounding land to feed and rest for varying periods before continuing their journey. Up to 20,000 Cranes may be seen there regularly and concentrations of over 70,000 have been recorded in recent years, these being among the largest Crane gatherings to be seen anywhere in western Europe. Spring sees the largest concentrations of birds, which provide one of the great ornithological sights and sounds of

Europe as the clamouring flocks fill the sky. An increasing number of Cranes, 10,000–20,000 birds, now also remain to winter at and around the lagoon.

Huge numbers of other species of wildfowl use Gallocanta in wet years, with maximum counts of 3,000 Gadwall, 80,000 Common Pochards and 40,000 Common Coots, for example. Red-crested Pochards bred formerly in small numbers and were abundant in winter but have largely abandoned the lake since the late 1980s.

Around 220 species have been recorded here and over 90 breed. The latter include Black-winged Stilt, Lapwing, Avocet, Kentish Plover, Whiskered Tern and Gull-billed Tern at the lake itself and a number of steppe species, including both Pin-tailed and Black-bellied Sandgrouse and Stone-curlew, in the surrounding area. The Estepas de Blanca to the south-east of Gallocanta (see AR21) support good numbers of Dupont's Larks as well as a few Great and Little Bustards.

Cranes

Timing

There is much of interest all year round, although high summer is to be avoided as there can be little water and the heat haze is formidable. For Cranes and wildfowl the best times are early spring, autumn and winter. Weekends can be busy with human visitors, especially during the Crane passage periods.

The autumn Crane movements occur from the end of October into early December, peaking in November. The return migration northwards runs through February into March and peaks at the end of February, or occasionally in early March, and it is then that the largest concentrations occur. The Cranes disperse during the day to feed in the surrounding fields but they roost at the lake and fly in during the evening, often in spectacular numbers.

Access

The Laguna de Gallocanta lies some 100km south-west of Zaragoza beyond Daroca. From Zaragoza take the N-330 as far as Daroca, and here turn right on to the A-211 towards Cillas and Molina de Aragón. After 18km from Daroca turn left on to the minor road (CV-633) leading to Gallocanta village, on the north side of the lake. It may also be approached readily from the south; it is a three-hour drive from Valencia (Sagunt) on the A-23; leave at km-185 and head west for 12km on the A-1507. The lake is signposted.

Minor roads follow the periphery of the site and there are many good drivable tracks across the area and several hides. Among the best of these is the tower hide on the south-western shore (Observatorio de La Reguera), which is reached by driving northwards from Las Cuerlas; the entrance to the track is on the village side of the pedestrian crossing on the A-2506 through road. The information centre (Tel. 978 734 031) south of the lake on the A-1507 between Bello and Tornos offers only distant views but there are reservable restricted-access hides by the waterside for photographers here. During the crane months users need to be in place from before dawn until after sunset, making their own arrangements for survival. Guided birding tours may also be arranged here. The Centre is open every day in November and February during Crane migration, but only at weekends for the rest of the year. There is a second information centre (Tel. 976 803 069) immediately south of Gallocanta village, with displays and a boardwalk access to a lakeside hide. In Gallocanta village good accommodation and meals are on offer at the Albergue Allucant (C/S Vicente s/n, 50373 Gallocanta: Tel. 976 803 137) which acts as an informal meeting place for birders.

In addition to the Estepas de Blancas (AR21), steppe species may be sought along the A-2506 between Las Cuerlas and Cubel. The Laguna de La Zaida, just west of the A-2506 and some 3km from the A-211 crossroads, is a seasonal lagoon that holds waterbirds in some winters.

CALENDAR

All year: Common Shelduck, Mallard, Gadwall, Common Pochard, Great Crested and Little Grebes, Marsh Harrier, Common Coot, Little and Great Bustards, Stone-curlew, Lapwing, Black-headed Gull, Black-bellied and Pin-tailed Sandgrouse; Dupont's, Calandra, Lesser Short-toed and Thekla Larks, Spotless Starling, Rock Sparrow.

Breeding season: Black-necked Grebe, Black Kite, Short-toed Eagle, Montagu's Harrier, Lesser Kestrel, Little Bustard, Black-winged Stilt, Avocet, Little Ringed and Kentish Plovers, Collared Pratincole, Gull-billed Tern, Red-necked Nightjar, Bee-eater, Greater Short-toed Lark, Tawny Pipit, Yellow Wagtail, Northern Wheatear; Savi's, Reed and Great Reed Warblers.

Winter: Wigeon, Teal, Pintail, Shoveler, Tufted Duck, Red Kite, Hen Harrier, Merlin, Crane, Short-eared Owl, Linnet, Common Starling.

Passage: Greylag Goose, Spotted Crake, Crane, Avocet, Ringed Plover, Knot, Sanderling, Curlew Sandpiper, Ruff, Black-tailed and Bar-tailed Godwits, Whimbrel, Greenshank; Marsh, Green, Wood and Common Sandpipers; Common, Whiskered and Black Terns, Sand Martin, Red-throated Pipit, Aquatic Warbler.

SERRANÍA DE ALBARRACÍN　　　AR16
(Teruel)

Status: Part of the Montes Universales Reserva Nacional de Caza (59,260 ha).

Site description

This is a large mountainous area, the summits approaching 2,000m, tucked into the far south-west corner of Aragón, bordering Cuenca province in Castilla–La Mancha. It is covered by substantial areas of ancient pine forest, oak forest and juniper scrub, along with broom, mixed oak scrub and many meadows, pastures and gorges. The Serrania runs north-west/south-east and is made up of a number of isolated massifs or *muelas* with valleys between. The mountain complex consists of high limestone plateaux at 1,500–1,800m, such as Los Llanos de Pozondón, Ródenas and Monterde in the north of the Sierra and Los Llanos de Villar del Cobo Griegos in the south. The quaking bogs of the Sierra del Tremedal are also worthy of mention.

Especially outstanding are the forests at the mountain passes of Noguera, Orihuela and Bronchales which also have a number of natural meadows. In addition to normal forest management practices there is a tradition of collecting aromatic plants, mushrooms and truffles. The area is also famous for its Levantine-style cave paintings. The town of Albarracín, a well-preserved medieval walled city, deserves a visit.

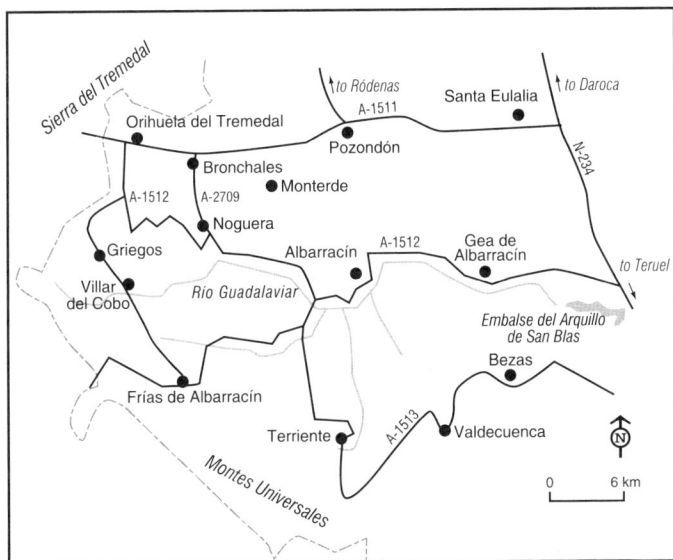

Species

The massif and its woodlands support a diverse raptor community that includes Griffon and Egyptian Vultures; Golden, Booted and Short-toed Eagles,

Sparrowhawks, Goshawks, Common Buzzards, Peregrine Falcons and Eagle Owls. Pied Flycatchers, Crested Tits and Bonelli's Warblers also breed.

Among the mammals, both Otters and Wild Cats occur together with Ibex, Beech Martens, Polecats, deer and Red Squirrels.

Timing
All year but at its best from April through to late June.

Access
The sierra is about 35km north-west of Teruel. Take the N-234 north out of Teruel and after 10km turn left on to the A-1512 towards Albarracín. There are many roads and forest tracks throughout the area. One of many possibilities includes taking the road (A-2709) towards the passes at Noguera, Bronchales and Orihuela del Tremedal, all of which have excellent areas of woodland and pasture.

CALENDAR

All year: Griffon Vulture, Goshawk, Common Buzzard, Golden Eagle, Peregrine Falcon, Eagle and Tawny Owls, Blue Rock Thrush, Black Redstart, Crested Tit, Southern Grey Shrike, Raven, Rock Sparrow, Rock Bunting.

Breeding season: Honey-buzzard, Black Kite, Egyptian Vulture, Short-toed and Booted Eagles, Hoopoe, Red-rumped Swallow, Black-eared Wheatear, Rufous-tailed Rock Thrush, Bonelli's Warbler, Woodchat Shrike.

OTHER SITES WORTH VISITING

AR17 CASTILLO DE LOARRE (HUESCA)
Worth a visit for its castle alone, one of the finest in Spain. The surrounding area offers a rich mixture of habitats, including pine forest, scrub, rocky areas and pasture. It is good for raptors and a diversity of other species, including Hoopoe, Wood Lark and Rock Bunting. Take the A-132 north-westwards to Ayerbe from Huesca then the A-1206 to Loarre. The castle is above the village.

AR18 EL TURBÓN (HUESCA)
A limestone mountain area in the Pyrenees with Lammergeiers, Golden Eagles and high-altitude birds including Alpine Accentors and Wallcreepers. Take the N-240 east from Huesca, turning left at Barbastro on the N-123, and then take the A-139 to Graus and towards Benasque. Take the minor road right at Campo to Vilas del Turbón.

AR19 MONTES DE ZUERA (ZARAGOZA)
Pine woods and juniper scrub on hillsides in the Ebro Valley with Short-toed Eagles, Orphean Warblers, Firecrests and Ortolan Buntings. Take the N-330/A-23 north out of Zaragoza towards Huesca and Zuera. Turn left after 22km at Zuera on to the A-124 towards Las Pedrosas. There are various tracks

off this road.

AR20 SIERRA DE ALCUBIERRE (ZARAGOZA)

A mountain area with pine woods, juniper scrub and cliffs. Raptors, Red-necked Nightjars, Black and Black-eared Wheatears and Rock Sparrows are characteristic. Take A-129 north-east to Alcubierre from Zaragoza. Forestry tracks lead into the sierra.

AR21 ESTEPAS DE BLANCAS (ZARAGOZA)

A high-level steppe area to the south of the Laguna de Gallocanta (AR15) with Little Bustards, Stone-curlews, Black-bellied Sandgrouse and Dupont's Larks. From Bello follow the minor road (TE-V-4307) to Odón (8km) and continue south-eastwards to Blancas, viewing the area to the north of that village.

AR22 LAGUNA DE LA ESTANCA (ZARAGOZA)

A freshwater, reed-fringed lake on private land near Chiprana. A visit can easily be combined with one to the Saladas nearby (AR14). Used for wild-fowl hunting in winter but otherwise quiet. Breeding species include Marsh Harrier, Little Bittern and Purple Heron. Waterfowl and waders occur in winter and on passage. Take the turn-off for Chiprana from the A-221 and loop back at the roundabout to pass under that road, heading for the railway station (Estación de Chiprana). After some 3km and shortly before the station take a track on the left marked Camino Privado and take the left fork at a pink house and continue past a yellow, red-tiled house to an elevated viewpoint next to the lake.

AR23 LAGUNA DE CANDASNOS (ZARAGOZA)

A readily accessible freshwater lake with reedbeds. Waterfowl are often numerous in winter and breeding species include Marsh Harrier and Red-crested Pochard. The lake is immediately south-west of Candasnos on the west side of the A-2410, where there is a car park and a short track to a hide.

AR24 LAGUNA DEL CAÑIZAR (TERUEL)

A partially restored lake on the site of an historical wetland that extended over some 10km² prior to its drainage in the 18th century. Its restoration has met with some resistance from farmers but if ultimately successful this will be a very interesting location for waterfowl, passage waders and other wetland species. Take the Villarquemado exit from the A-23, 21km north of Teruel. Follow signs from the town to the lake. There is an information centre and a hide.

AR25 SALADAS DE ALCAÑIZ (TERUEL)

Seasonal brackish lagoons in a steppe area. The pools attract passage waders and Cranes and wintering waterfowl. Steppe birds present include sand-grouse, Little Bustards, Lesser Short-toed Larks, Tawny Pipits and Spectacled Warblers. Short-eared Owls occur in winter and have nested here. The lagoons are immediately west of Alcañiz on either side of the N-232 at km-145. The Estanca, a permanent lagoon, is viewable on the north side from a roadside layby. A sandy track on the south side, opposite the camping site access road, leads to the Saladas proper.

AR26 RÍO MARTÍN VALLEY AT ARIÑO (TERUEL)

The cliffs of the Sierra de Arcos north of Ariño, west of Alcañiz, have a large colony of Griffon Vultures and also Egyptian Vultures, wild Rock Doves, Blue Rock Thrushes and Red-billed Choughs. Riparian woodland attracts passerines. The A-1401, linking the A-222 at Muniesa with the A-223 provides access, with good views of the sierra and woodlands and a walking trail, at the bridge north of Ariño.

AR27 ALACÓN VULTURE RESTAURANT

A fenced hilltop is used sporadically as a carcass dump that attracts Griffon and Egyptian Vultures, kites and others, which may be viewed from a nearby hide. It is signposted (Comedero de aves carroñeras) from the approach roads to Alacón village. Take the A-222 south to Muniesa and continue eastwards from there on the A-1401 for 8km to reach the northern approach road. The entrance track is on the right, 1.3km from the A-1401, leading to a car park near the hide.

AR28 RÍO GUADALOPE (TERUEL)

A river gorge with vultures, Bonelli's Eagles, Alpine Swifts and Dippers. Take the N-211 south from the N-232 3km west of Alcañiz and at Calanda take the A226 for Mas de las Matas and Castellote. From here take the road along the west shore of reservoir (Embalse de Santolea) and beyond to the village of Ladruñán from where there are walking trails beyond.

AR29 EL MAESTRAZGO (TERUEL)

A series of sierras, greatly eroded by rivers, with tall cliffs and needle-shaped rocks. This unspoilt and beautiful area is little visited but offers vultures, other raptors, Otters and Ibex. Take the A-226 eastwards from Teruel to Allepuz (46km), then continue on the same road to the heart of the area and Cantavieja.

AR30 SIERRA DE JAVALAMBRE (TERUEL)

A high mountain massif with pine and beech woods, pastures and many valleys and ravines. Breeding species include Honey-buzzard, Goshawk, Booted Eagle, Eagle Owl and Dartford and Subalpine Warblers. Take the N-234/A-23 south-east from Teruel and turn right after Sarrión towards Manzanera and Torrijas along the A-1514.

ASTURIAS

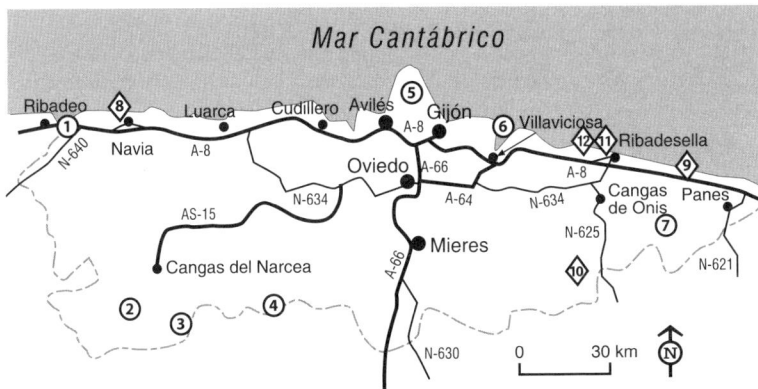

Main sites

AS1	Ría del Eo (Ribadeo)
AS2	Bosque de Muniellos
AS3	Degaña–Hermo
AS4	Somiedo
AS5	Cabo Peñas peninsula
AS6	Ría de Villaviciosa (Ría de la Villa)
AS7	Picos de Europa

Other sites worth visiting

AS8	Río Barayo
AS9	Llanes coast
AS10	Parque Natural de Redes
AS11	Ribadesella
AS12	Playa de La Vega

The Principality of Asturias is one of the four regions, together with Galicia, Cantabria and Euskadi (País Vasco), that make up España Verde – Green Spain — or, if you are spending a holiday on the coast, the Costa Verde. Most of Asturias is mountainous, including the central sector of the Cordillera Cantábrica (Cantabrian mountains), which forms a spectacular backdrop to the coastal lowlands. The coastal areas of this remarkably lush northern part of the Iberian peninsula enjoy mild temperatures throughout the year and are pleasantly warm, not hot, in the summer months: a southern European equivalent of Cornwall or the Lake District and very attractive to those who find the heat of the Mediterranean coasts a little too much. The mountains are another matter, however, especially in winter when temperatures fall very low and there is considerable snowfall. Warm, windproof layers are even needed in summer if visiting the highest peaks, which rise well over 2,000m. The weather anywhere in Asturias is notoriously changeable and a waterproof outer layer should always be carried.

The most visited and best known of the natural attractions of Asturias is the Picos de Europa National Park (AS7), a highly rugged sector of the Cantabrian mountains whose jagged peaks soar to 2,650m. The Picos are in the east, but the ranges of central and western Asturias (AS2, AS3, AS4, AS10) are at least as interesting birdwise. Moreover, they hold most of the Spanish population of Brown Bears and considerable numbers of Wolves as well as many other natural attractions, including an impressive diversity of orchids and alpine flowers. The Asturian mountains are a region of swift-flowing rivers, deep gorges and narrow valleys. The gentler slopes are densely wooded, with very extensive beech forests on the north-facing gradients especially and oaks and pines elsewhere. Subalpine pastures cover large tracts above the tree line.

The high cliffs support a good population of Wallcreepers, unarguably one of the most spectacular of all bird species, here at the westernmost part of a range that extends east to China. Both Red-billed and Yellow-billed Choughs, Alpine Accentors, Rufous-tailed Rock Thrushes, Water Pipits and Snowfinches are also typical of the high tops in summer. The scrub and heathland habitats above the treeline support Grey Partridges, and Ortolan Buntings and Bluethroats on the south-facing slopes. The mountain forests have a diverse bird community. Here the main attractions for many are the Black and Middle Spotted Woodpeckers, which are widely but sparsely distributed in the beechwoods and oakwoods respectively. The forests and woodlands also support Capercaillies (declining), Eurasian Treecreepers, Marsh Tits and Goldcrests, with Red-backed Shrikes, Bullfinches and Yellowhammers in the valley hedgerows: a range of species familiar to northern birders but all of which are largely absent from central and southern Iberia. Breeding raptors include healthy populations of Griffon and Egyptian Vultures and Golden Eagles. The Lammergeier is being reintroduced to the Picos de Europa.

The farmlands and coastal lowlands are dominated by smallholdings, with hay meadows, pastures and small fields of maize and beans, the latter the key ingredient of the 'fabada', the signature dish of Asturian cuisine, a very substantial bean stew laced with sausage – not recommended if you have an active day ahead. The red-roofed villages are picturesque, each home with its distinctive 'hórreo', an ornate and wooden produce store elevated on four stone or wooden legs, to protect the contents from rodents and damp. Apple orchards abound, providing the raw material for the ubiquitous local cider (sidra). Small mixed woodlands remain but the large areas of eucalyptus plantations on the coastal hillsides are an unwelcome landscape feature here, many of them having been planted on what used to be heathland. Large tracts of Common Gorse and heather survive nonetheless, especially near the sea. The coastline (AS1, AS5, AS6, AS8, AS9, AS11) itself is very rugged, but with small sandy beaches in the many coves. Small rocky islets are frequent offshore, where they support significant colonies of European Storm-petrels and Shags. A succession of large, fjord-like, tidal inlets, the 'rías' (AS1, AS5, AS6), interrupt the shoreline. All provide important habitat for waterfowl, gulls and waders especially.

The farming areas and associated woodlands are home to a wide range of breeding species, most of them familiar birds of temperate Europe and with a notable absence of typical Mediterranean species, most of which do not extend north of the Cantabrian range. Common Buzzards are abundant and characteristic. Honey-buzzards, Black Kites, Hen Harriers and Goshawks breed more locally. Peregrines are common on the coast especially. Other characteristic breeding birds typical of northern Spain include Dunnocks, Common Redstarts, Song Thrushes, Grasshopper and Melodious Warblers and Common Starlings. Winter sees the arrival of large flocks of Sky Larks, Meadow Pipits, Song Thrushes, Redwings, White Wagtails, Goldfinches and Chaffinches. The whole coastal area is very important during migration periods when falls of migrant passerines, including chats and warblers, occur periodically, especially in autumn. Some montane birds, notably Water Pipits and Rock Buntings but even a few Wallcreepers, descend to coastal locations in winter. The rías have influxes of passage and wintering waders and waterfowl. Seabird passage offshore is notable and sometimes spectacular, especially in autumn. The whole coastal strip is a Spanish hotspot for rare birds. Such birds as Sabine's Gulls, Pectoral and Buff-breasted Sandpipers and Richard's Pipits occur regularly and a series of even rarer vagrant species turn up every year, especially in autumn and winter.

Records of all observations in Asturias, not just the rarities, are welcomed by the compilers of the regional bird report 'El Draque' and may be submitted by email to anuario@coa.org.es

RÍA DEL EO (RIBADEO)   AS1

Status: Reserva Natural, ZEPA and Ramsar site (1,740 ha).

Site description
This is one of the most important coastal wetlands in the north of Spain. The fjord-like inlet, with only a narrow opening to the sea, is in the far west of Asturias straddling the regional boundary with Galicia. The estuary is mostly shallow, supporting underwater beds of Eelgrass, and large areas of mudflats and

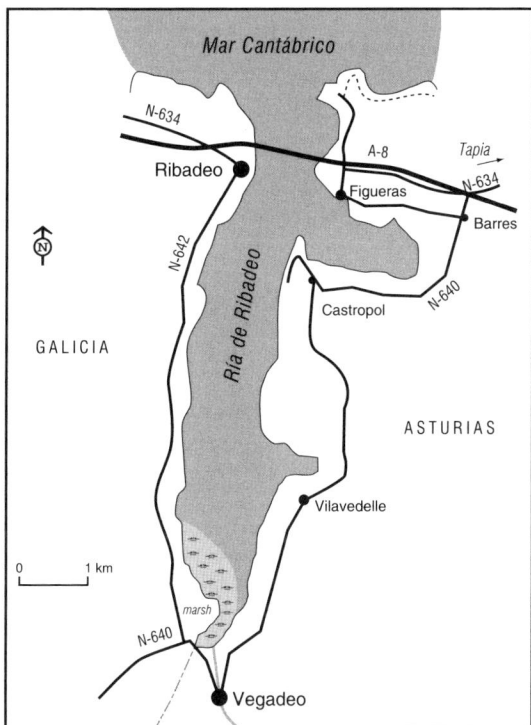

sandbanks are exposed at low water. There are peripheral areas of saltmarsh, with reedbeds and wet meadows in the upper reaches. The flanking headlands and rocky coast are covered with coastal heath and rough pastureland.

Species
The estuary is one of the most important sites on the north coast for passage and wintering waterfowl, sometimes holding over 5,000 ducks, including up to 1,000 Pintail and up to 4,000 Wigeon, as well as Shoveler, Teal and Common Shelducks. However, numbers have been lower in recent years following greater activity in the port of Ribadeo. The estuary also attracts numbers of passage and wintering waders, including Lapwings, Golden Plovers, Common Snipe, Common Redshanks and Curlews. Spoonbills occur occasionally. Ospreys are regular on passage, generally in autumn when individuals may linger locally. Seabird passage is often noteworthy offshore. Scarce and vagrant species occur annually, especially in winter, and are worth searching for especially among flocks of ducks, gulls and waders. Records have included American Wigeon, Goldeneye and Smew. The coastal meadows between Tapia and Figueras are excellent for wintering and migrant passerines; small flocks of Richard's Pipits have been regular here in recent winters, especially near Tapia. Otters occur in the estuary.

Timing
The largest concentrations of wildfowl occur in winter but the area can hold interesting birds all year round, and is particularly good in the spring and autumn passage periods.

Access
The estuary is best viewed from its eastern shore since the N-642 along the western side has fast traffic and few stopping places. The eastern side is reached via the N-640. From here the jetty and fishing port below Castropol are served by a quiet narrow road and offer excellent views of the main channel and the principal eastern inlet, and their mudflats. The upper estuary and salt marshes may be viewed from a wharf just north of Vilavedelle: waders roost on the marshes at high tide. It is also possible to stop at Vegadeo and walk along the roadsides to view the marshes and grasslands flanking the N-642. Elevated views of the entire estuary are available from Ribadeo itself, notably from the road that descends to the port from the N-642 immediately south of the town: a telescope is advisable.

The mouth of the estuary can be good in the winter when ducks, divers and auks seek shelter in the calmer waters. It is best reached by taking the minor seaward road north from the A-8 at the sliproad immediately east of the bridge across the estuary (km-501, Figueras turn-off). Park and walk once you reach the sea: it is possible to drive along the coastal tracks but you will miss the chance to search the pastures and scrub for passerines. The headland just east of the estuary is good for seawatching during onshore winds but at such times the best watchpoint is at Tapia de Casariego, north of the N-634 7km east of Ribadeo. Park in the village and walk down to the harbour and across the sea wall to the front of the lighthouse, from where there are excellent elevated views.

CALENDAR

All year: Mallard, Water Rail, Moorhen, Oystercatcher, Yellow-legged Gull, Barn Owl, Kingfisher, Green Woodpecker, Crested Lark (scarce), Grey and White Wagtails, Cetti's Warbler, Zitting Cisticola, Southern Grey Shrike (occasional), Carrion Crow, Rock Sparrow (scarce).

Breeding season: Hobby, Turtle Dove, Common Swift, House Martin, Yellow Wagtail; Grasshopper, Reed and Melodious Warblers, Whitethroat, Red-backed Shrike.

Winter: Greylag Goose, Wigeon, Pintail, Shoveler, Teal, Tufted Duck, Common Scoter, Red-breasted Merganser, Great Northern Diver (occasional), Gannet, Cormorant, Little Egret, Grey Heron, Merlin, Lapwing, Golden

Plover, Knot, Purple Sandpiper (Tapia), Dunlin, Common Snipe, Curlew, Common Redshank, Common and Great Black-backed Gulls, Guillemot, Razorbill, Puffin, Richard's Pipit, Fieldfare, Redwing, Brambling, Snow Bunting, vagrants.

Passage periods: Cory's and Balearic Shearwaters, Gannet, Little Bittern, Night and Squacco Herons, Spoonbill, Osprey, Ringed Plover, Dunlin, Ruff, Black-tailed and Bar-tailed Godwits, Whimbrel, Curlew, Spotted Redshank, Greenshank; Green, Wood and Common Sandpipers, Little Gull; Sandwich, Common and Black Terns, Tawny Pipit, Whinchat, Northern Wheatear, Willow Warbler, vagrants.

BOSQUE DE MUNIELLOS · AS2

Status: Reserva Natural, UNESCO Biosphere Reserve and ZEPA (5,644 ha). The whole area also lies within the Parque Natural 'Fuentes del Narcea, Degaña y Ibias'.

Site description

A mountainous area with extensive, near-virgin deciduous woodland, including the Bosque de Muniellos one of the most important and largest mixed oakwoods in Spain, and one of the finest in Europe. The area is in the western interior of Asturias within the Cordillera Cantábrica. Most of the forest is made up of ancient stands of Sessile and Pedunculate Oak, and areas of beech. The reserve lies at some altitude, from around 675m in the valley bottom to almost 1,700m at its highest point. Silver Birch becomes abundant at around 1,300m while in the valleys Hazel, Maple, Ash, Holly, Alder, Rowan and Yew also comprise the woodland complex. Muniellos is especially rich in fungi, mosses, liverworts and lichens, with over 1,000 species present. The area is very well watered by frequent rainfall and receives considerable winter snowfall.

Species

An excellent forest for its woodland bird communities which include breeding Black, Great Spotted, Middle Spotted, Lesser Spotted and Green Woodpeckers, as well as Wrynecks and Golden Orioles. The Willow Warbler, a very rare and local breeding species in Spain, has been proved to nest here and may do so regularly, alongside Iberian Chiffchaffs and Bonelli's Warblers. Breeding raptors include Golden, Short-toed and Booted Eagles, Honey-buzzards and Goshawks. The reserve is a key refuge for the Capercaillie, with perhaps some

30 males present, but even here the species is declining. The forest is the best place in Asturias for breeding Woodcock.

The area is also good for the larger mammals with Chamois, Wild Boar, Roe Deer, Wildcats, Otters, Wolves and Brown Bears all present, although the dense forest cover makes seeing the more elusive species even less likely than usual. Pyrenean Desmans occur in the valley streams. Some 500 species of moth and butterfly have also been recorded.

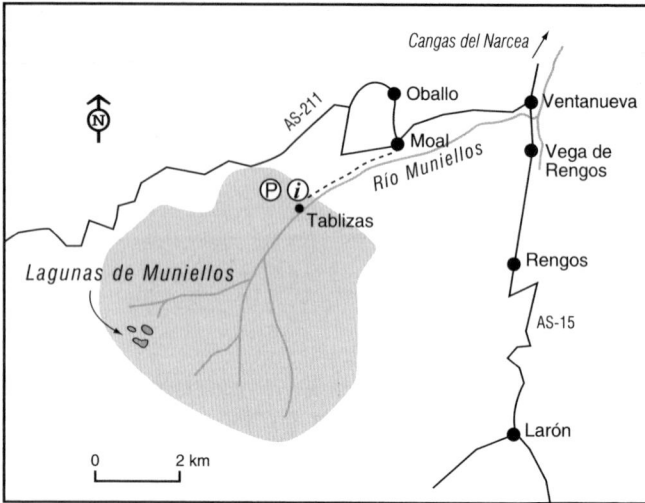

Timing
Spring and summer are best, although the colours and scenery in October and November can be spectacular.

Access
This is the most protected site in Asturias and can only be visited with prior permission, with a maximum of 20 people per day allowed. It is all but essential to apply early and to confirm your intended visit not less than two weeks beforehand. An on-line application form (muniellos.es/reserva.) allows available dates to be identified. You can also apply by telephone (Tel. 985 279 100) to the Asturian Environment Agency (Consejería de Medio Ambiente). The peak demand is in summer and autumn, as well as at weekends during public holidays, for which reservations may be needed a year in advance. Reservations for the following calendar year open annually on 15 December. You may be able to enter if you turn up on a day when the quota has not been filled, but this is unlikely at popular times.

Take the AS-15 from Cangas del Narcea south to Ventanueva. At Ventanueva turn right along the AS-211(AS-348) towards the village of Moal, from where a track takes you to the warden's post and car park 4km away at Tablizas, where your permit will be requested. The Information Centre for Muniellos and Degaña-Hermo (AS3) is at Oballo (Tel. 607 839 670), just north of Moal and signposted from the AS-211; open daily except Mondays, mainly 0900–1400 hrs. Several marked trails are signposted from Tablizas, the longest loop trail to the mountain lakes (Lagunas de Muniellos) covering 13.5km, for which you should allow a minimum of six hours. Shorter visits are of course possible and allow access to representative areas of the forest.

CALENDAR

All year: Capercaillie, Grey Partridge, Goshawk, Sparrowhawk, Common Buzzard, Golden Eagle, Woodcock; Scops, Tawny and Long-eared Owls, Wryneck; Green, Black, Great Spotted, Middle Spotted and Lesser Spotted Woodpeckers, Water Pipit, Dipper, Goldcrest, Firecrest, Dartford Warbler, Eurasian Treecreeper, Marsh and Crested Tits, Raven, Bullfinch.

Breeding season: Honey-buzzard, Hen Harrier, Short-toed and Booted Eagles, Hobby, European Nightjar, Tree Pipit, Common Redstart, Whinchat, Bonelli's and Willow Warblers, Iberian Chiffchaff, Pied Flycatcher, Golden Oriole.

DEGAÑA–HERMO   AS3

Status: Reserva Nacional de Caza and part of the Parque Natural 'Fuentes del Narcea, Degaña y Ibias' (55,500ha). Biosphere reserve. ZEPA (11,659 ha).

Site description
This section of the Cordillera Cantábrica, adjacent to Somiedo (AS4) offers the largest beechwood in Asturias: 1,500ha around the Monasterio de Hermo. beech and oakwoods predominate throughout the region, with birch at the higher elevations and Holly, Hazel, Yew, Ash and Alder in the valleys. The high tops include pastures, peat bogs and rocky terrain, the summits reaching over 1,800m.

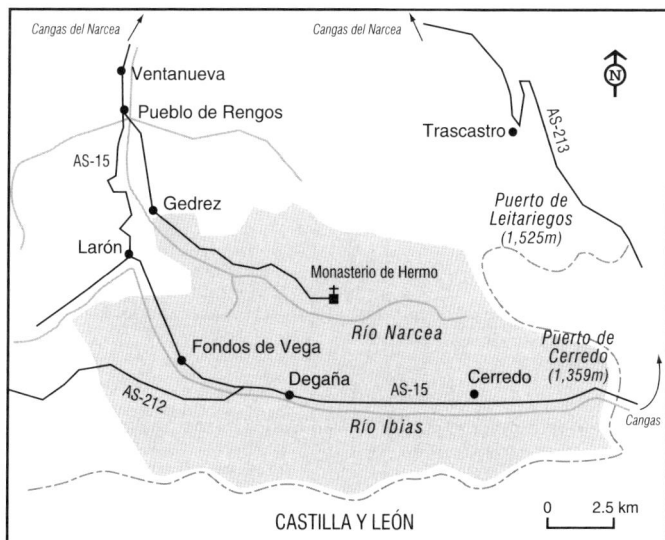

Species

A key reserve for the critically endangered Cantabrian race of the Capercaillie, which nonetheless has declined considerably, to fewer than 25 males, despite habitat conservation and a captive-breeding programme. They are unlikely to be encountered by casual visitors. Other breeding birds include Grey Partridges, Black and Middle Spotted Woodpeckers, Bluethroats and Ortolan Buntings. The mammal diversity is also considerable: Wolves are present and there are populations of Red and Roe Deer, Otters, Wild Cats, Beech and Pine Martens and Pyrenean Desmans. The Brown Bear has one of its healthiest populations here.

Timing

Late spring and early summer, when birds are most vocal, are best.

Access

Take the AS-15 south from Cangas del Narcea to Pueblo de Rengos. A local road follows the Narcea Valley eastwards from Rengos through Gedrez to the beech forests of Degaña and the Monasterio de Hermo. It is also worth continuing on the AS-15 towards the pass at Puerto Cerredo (1,359m), where Bluethroats may be sought in the low scrub around the high pastures. Marked walking trails are available from Fondos de Vega and Cerredo on the AS-15.

A viewpoint (Mirador del Oso) has been constructed at Fondos de Vega for observing bears but you are likely to see only crowds of people there at weekends. Visits away from holiday periods, and in spring when the bears have emerged from hibernation, are most likely to be successful. A guided tour is the best strategy for bear and wolf watching. For details of these and other information on the park you should visit the Visitors' Centre for the Parque Natural at Oballo (see AS2) or the Tourist Office in Cangas del Narcea (Palacio de Omaña, Plaza La Oliva. Tel. 985 811 498).

CALENDAR

All year: Capercaillie, Grey Partridge, Griffon Vulture, Golden Eagle, Goshawk, Peregrine Falcon, Woodcock, Eagle Owl, Black and Middle Spotted Woodpeckers, Crag Martin, Blue Rock Thrush, Crested Tit, Red-billed Chough, Crossbill, Bullfinch, Rock Sparrow, Cirl and Rock Buntings.

Breeding season: Honey-buzzard, Short-toed Eagle, Common Snipe, Hoopoe, Water Pipit, Melodious and Bonelli's Warblers, Bluethroat, Rufous-tailed Rock Thrush, Red-backed Shrike, Ortolan Bunting.

SOMIEDO   AS4

Status: Parque Natural and ZEPA (29,164ha). UNESCO Biosphere Reserve.

Site description

Somiedo occupies a large sector of the Cordillera Cantábrica south-west of

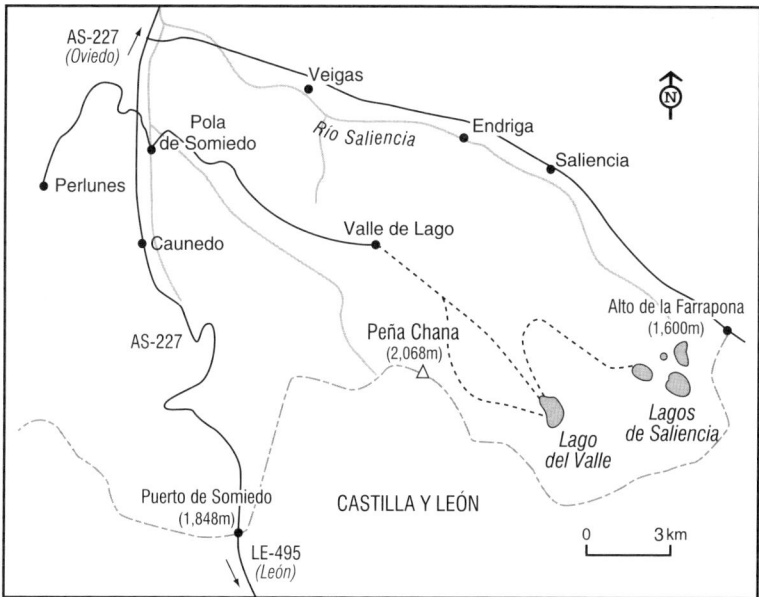

Oviedo. The reserve comprises a series of narrow valleys, flanked by forests of beech, oak and birch. Some 38 small villages are scattered in the valley bottoms, where there are stone-walled fields and riverine vegetation along the many mountain streams. The principal traditional land use is cattle grazing, especially on the high pastures (brañas), which are dotted with stone cabins and broom-thatched shelters. The mountains themsleves are rugged, rising to over 2,000m, with numerous sheer cliffs, areas of scree and subalpine grasslands at the summits. There are a number of picturesque glacial lakes, notably the Lago del Valle and the Lagos de Saliencia, at 1,500–1,700m.

Species

Somiedo has an important population of Capercaillies but, as elsewhere in the Cantabrian range, these are in severe decline and unlikely to be encountered. It is especially renowned as the principal refuge for Brown Bears in Spain. The western Asturian bear population of some 250 individuals, is increasing by about 10% a year after decades of decline. The bears are, as ever, highly elusive but Somiedo offers many other, more accessible natural attractions. These include some 120 bird species, as well as over 40 mammals and over 1,000 vascular plants, these last including 65 tree and shrub species.

Raptors are often conspicuous, particularly Egyptian and Griffon Vultures and Common Buzzards. Other breeding raptors include Golden and Short-toed Eagles and Honey-buzzards. Grey Partridges occur on the upper woodland edges. The woodlands themselves have sparse populations of both Black and Middle Spotted Woodpeckers and a diversity of passerines. Water Pipits are abundant on the pastures. Wallcreepers and Snowfinches occur at the highest levels, descending into the valleys in winter. Ortolan Buntings and a few Ring Ouzels breed around the Puerto de Somiedo.

Among the mammals, Chamois are readily visible on the ridges and scree

Capercaillie

slopes. Red and Roe Deer support a population of Wolves. Wild Boar, Otters, Wildcats, Pine Martens and Pyrenean Desmans are all present.

Timing
Late spring and summer tend to be most productive. The pass (Puerto de Somiedo) may be closed by snow for up to three months in some winters.

Access
From Oviedo take the N-634 west past Grado. Before reaching Cornellana turn left inland on the AS-15 for around 10km, then left again on the AS-227 towards the border with Castilla y León. The AS-16 links the A-8 coast motorway just west of Asturias airport with the AS-15. From the south, approach along A-66 motorway from León, take the Villablino exit on to the CL-626 and continue westwards as far as Piedrafita de Babia; then turn right towards the Puerto de Somiedo on the LE-495.

Your first stop should be the Visitors' Centre in Pola de Somiedo (Tel. 985 763 758, somiedo.es), where very useful trail maps of the dozen signposted trails are available. It would be a pity to visit Somiedo and not walk along at least one of these. Perhaps the most worthwhile for an initial visit is the track to the Lago del Valle, a glacial lake at the end of a spectacular cliff-lined valley fringed by peaks of 1,700–2,000m. The trail passes through pastureland and the fringes of beech forest. The cliffs themselves may produce Wallcreepers, especially in autumn and winter. The return distance is some 12km for which you should allow at least three hours. Most of the going is easy but the final kilometre or so is a stiff uphill climb to the Lago and since the lake itself has no birding interest you may prefer to visit the beechwoods instead. The trail begins near the village of Valle de Lago, reached via a minor road from Pola de Somiedo: drive through the village and park in one of the car parks before the hamlet of L'Autiero, and walk on up the valley. Brown Bears are sometimes seen in this valley at dawn and dusk.

Those with the time (allow six hours) and the energy may continue beyond the Lago del Valle to the Lagos de Saliencia, crossing alpine meadows and scree. The latter are more easily reached by taking the turning west to Saliencia from the AS-227, 3km north of Pola de Somiedo. This minor road (SD-1) leads to Saliencia and beyond to the pass at Alto de la Farrapona (1,600m), from where it is a short walk to the lakes. Wallcreepers and other high mountain species may be sought here.

The Somiedo pass (Puerto de Somiedo, 1,848m) is also worth visiting, giving access to wide expanses of the subalpine grassland and scrub, offering Grey Partridges, Water Pipits, Alpine Accentors, Northern Wheatears, Ring Ouzels, Snowfinches and Ortolan Buntings, with Citril Finches along the woodland edges.

CALENDAR

All year: Capercaillie, Grey Partridge, Griffon Vulture, Peregrine Falcon, Black and Middle Spotted Woodpeckers, Water Pipit, Alpine Accentor, Black Redstart, Blue Rock and Song Thrushes, Marsh Tit, Wallcreeper, Yellow-billed and Red-billed Choughs, Raven, Snowfinch, Citril Finch, Bullfinch, Yellowhammer, Rock Bunting.

Breeding season: Honey-buzzard, Black Kite, Egyptian Vulture, Hen Harrier, Short-toed and Booted Eagles, Eagle Owl, Alpine Swift, Wryneck, Crag Martin, Tawny and Tree Pipits, Whinchat, Northern Wheatear, Rufous-tailed Rock Thrush, Ring Ouzel, Bonelli's and Garden Warblers, Spotted Flycatcher, Red-backed Shrike, Ortolan Bunting.

CABO PEÑAS PROMONTORY   AS5

Status: Paisaje protegido (protected landscape: coastal strip only).

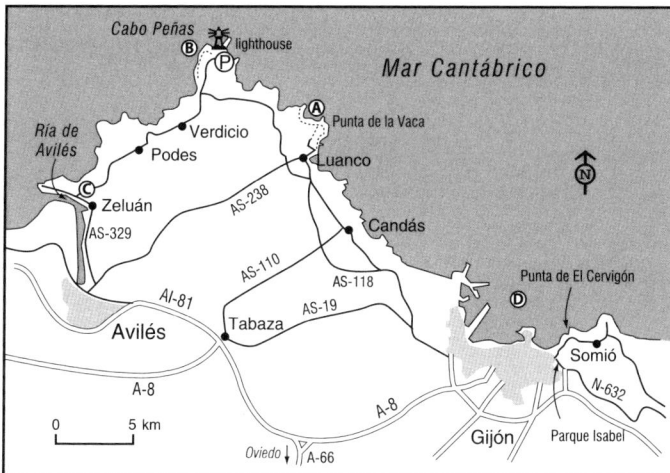

Site description

This broad triangular peninsula, which juts out very conspicuously from the coastline, comprises the northernmost point of Asturias. The terrain is stone-walled grassy fields chiefly but large expanses of coastal heath have been preserved. The tip of the promontory is flanked by steep cliffs offering dramatic sea views. There are large sandy beaches on the western side, some with extensive dune systems. The Ría de Aviles at Zeluán in the west and Gijón Bay to the east are important birding sites within the region.

Species

The peninsula offers the best seawatching in Asturias, from Punta de la Vaca. Probably its chief claim to fame though is as a migrant hotspot, one of the best in Iberia and comparable with the Strait of Gibraltar and the Catalonian coast for the diversity of species which occur on passage and for the frequent presence of otherwise scarce or vagrant species. In recent years these have included Black-shouldered Kite, Pallid Harrier, Richard's Pipit, Siberian Stonechat, Radde's Warbler and Lapland and Snow Buntings. The islets offshore have significant breeding colonies of Yellow-legged Gulls, European Shags and European Storm-petrels.

Timing

The area is always rewarding to visit but passage periods are the most productive, particularly the autumn from mid-August to October.

Access

From the west leave the A-8 at Avilés and follow the AS-238 to Luanco. From the east leave the A-8 to skirt Gijón on the AS-19 and continue to Luanco on the AS-118.

A. Punta de la Vaca Drive through Luanco and to the beachside promenade and turn left into the road (El Fuerte) serving the villas on the hillside overlooking the bay. Continue upwards and take the first left (Molino del Viento) and then right (La Atalaya). Drive to the end of this road where there is a small car park. Continue on foot along the short muddy track leading onwards from the car park, crossing a grassy area to reach the coastal footpath, which bears right to lead out to the Point. The walking distance is some 500m in all. The coastal heaths and pinewoods are often alive with migrants during passage periods when they should be checked carefully. Telescope essential. The best seawatching occurs during north-westerly winds in autumn, when a constant stream of birds passes westwards close offshore.

B. Cabo Peñas Well signposted everywhere. Park at the lighthouse (faro) or continue 200m to the clifftop cafe and restaurant – a useful 'watering hole'. The tip of the Cape is inaccessible and the stacks offshore conspire to divert seabird passage further away than desirable. However, the boardwalk west from the cafe gives good views of the cliffs and islets and their seabirds. The chief interest is the heathland and fields just inland. Follow the lighthouse fence inland and you reach a large expanse of coastal heath, criss-crossed by paths and with scattered ephemeral pools. The area is excellent for migrants, including such notable species as Dotterel (September) and Richard's Pipit (October and winter). Stubble fields nearby attract flocks of Sky Larks from October onwards and these often include Lapland and Snow Buntings. Anything may turn up here.

C. Zeluán   Access is from the AS-329 which branches off the AS-238 near Avilés, at km-2. The chief attraction here is the estuary, the Ría de Avilés, which attracts large numbers of gulls and a selection of waders. There are mudflats and a sandy spit at Zeluán. Drive into Zeluán to the waterfront promenade. Park by the boat sheds on the seaward side and walk out on the spit, where there is a hide. Alternatively, and perhaps better, view the mudflats from the roadside just north of Zeluán.

D. Gijón Bay (Bahía de Gijón)   Excellent views are available across both the Bay and harbour and the adjacent Bahía de San Lorenzo from the promontory of Cimadevilla, which divides the city waterfront. Views to seaward are also available from the coastal footpath at Punta de El Cervigón. The Bay has a reputation for attracting seaduck, divers and grebes in winter but these have been less evident in recent years, probably partly because of dredging work that was carried out to improve the port of El Musel. Such species as Common Eider, Great Northern Diver and Slavonian Grebe may still occur in some years, however.

The gull flocks on San Lorenzo beach should be checked, especially in winter, for scarce species such as Glaucous and Iceland Gulls but the area no longer attracts Ring-billed Gulls, which formerly occurred there regularly.

The small freshwater lakes in the adjacent **Parque de Isabel la Católica** sometimes attract waterfowl and gulls, as well as passerine migrants. Red Squirrels are an obvious feature here. Access to the Park is straightforward. Follow signs in the city to the waterfront (Playas) and park in one of the underground car parks there. Walk out and around the Cimadevilla promontory and along the beach promenade immediately to the east. The park is at the south-east corner of the beach, next to the Parador and football stadium. Pallid Swifts have recently colonised the older buildings at Cimadevilla; they should be looked for during April–October and are especially noticeable from early September onwards, when the much more numerous Common Swifts have departed.

CALENDAR

All year: Cormorant, Shag, Peregrine Falcon, Yellow-legged Gull, Black Redstart, Stonechat, Zitting Cisticola, Dartford Warbler, Raven.

Breeding season: European Storm-petrel, Pallid Swift.

Winter: Common Eider, Common Scoter, Red-throated and Great Northern Divers, Red-necked and Slavonian Grebes, Purple Sandpiper, Turnstone; Mediterranean, Black-headed, Common, Lesser Black-backed, Herring, Glaucous and Great Black-backed Gulls, Kittiwake, Sky Lark, Rock and Meadow Pipits, Common Chiffchaff, Snow Bunting, rarities.

Passage periods: Red-breasted Merganser, Common and Velvet Scoters; Cory's, Great (summer/autumn only), Sooty (summer/autumn only), Manx and Balearic Shearwaters, Leach's Storm-petrel, Gannet, Mediterranean, Little and Sabine's Gulls, Kittiwake; Sandwich, Common, Arctic, Little and Black Terns, Guillemot, Razorbill, Puffin, Merlin, Dotterel, Common Snipe, Wryneck, Richard's and Tree Pipits, Yellow Wagtail, Robin, Common Redstart, Whinchat, Northern Wheatear, Fieldfare, Song Thrush, Redwing, Whitethroat, Blackcap, Garden and Willow Warblers, Common Chiffchaff, Spotted and Pied Flycatchers, Red-backed Shrike, Lapland Bunting, rarities.

RÍA DE VILLAVICIOSA AS6 (RÍA DE LA VILLA)

Status: Reserva Natural and ZEPA (1,000ha).

Site description

This compact and accessible estuary, some 7km long, is one of the best wetlands in Asturias, offering a good range of habitats. The Ría is comparatively undisturbed, except by occasional bait-diggers and canoeists, and has an attractive backdrop of low wooded hills. Expanses of mudflats and sandbanks are exposed at low tide and there are areas of saltmarsh and a number of vegetated islands, which are important as roosts for waders and gulls at high tide. Extensive damp meadows (*porreos*), reclaimed long ago from the sea, occupy much of the eastern flanks and the upper estuary. They include patches of freshwater marsh, with flooded ditches, reedbeds and sedgebeds, and so attract a wide diversity of species.

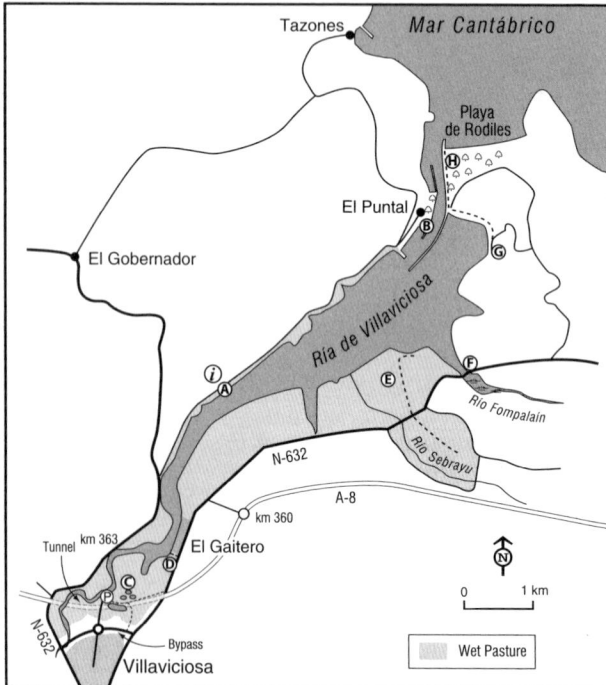

Species

This is an especially rewarding site to visit during migration periods and also in winter, when the species diversity is high. At these times a considerable range of waterfowl, gulls, terns, waders and passerines is annually enhanced by a sprinkling of rarities. These last have recently included Green-winged Teal, American Black Duck, Black Scoter, Pied-billed Grebe; Pectoral, Sharp-tailed, Buff-breasted and Solitary Sandpipers, and Long-billed Dowitcher. Garganey occur regularly on passage, especially in early spring. One or two Ospreys linger annually for long periods, particularly in autumn, when they can often be seen perched on posts or dead trees or fishing in the creeks; some have overwintered. A small flock of Cattle Egrets may accompany the cows on the *porreos*: they are a relatively recent arrival in Asturias, breeding on an offshore islet near Llanes. Peregrines also frequently hunt the estuary. Peak winter counts of 100 Wigeon, 600 Teal, 3,000 Golden Plovers, 7,500 Lapwings, 1,000 Dunlins, 600 Common Snipe and 250 Curlews have been recorded but numbers are generally modest. Occasional Common Eiders, Great Northern Divers and Black-necked Grebes occur in winter, as well as a few Brent Geese and Common Shelducks in some years.

Breeding species include Water Rails. Grasshopper Warblers and Reed Buntings also breed locally.

Timing
Passage periods and winter are most productive. The autumn passage (August–October) is generally better than the spring (March–May). The largest concentrations of ducks, waders and gulls tend to be in January. Visits at high tide are best for waders and waterfowl on the *porreos*, and for waterfowl on the creeks. Intermediate tide levels are best for seeing feeding waders on the mudflats.

Access
Take the Villaviciosa exits from the A-8 motorway at either km-360 for the east side of the estuary or km-363 for the west side. Afterwards you can avoid the town centre when crossing from one side of the Ría to the other: the signs to the Mercadona supermarket mark a bypass short-cut. The estuary and its hinterland are easily accessible from a number of points. A telescope is advisable.

West side (km-363)
The road follows the main creek closely and there are plenty of stopping places on the waterside verge, which are obvious if you drive slowly. This is the best side for viewing birds on the water.

A. Visitors' Centre The centre car park is on the left, halfway along the west shore. The display is interesting and a good map of the Ría is available free. View the creek and mudflats from the lay-by opposite.

B. El Puntal Park by the marina here and walk around the harbour, to where a promenade flanks the west side of the estuary.

East side (km-360)
This is the best for waders, especially at high tide when roosts form, and for access to the water meadows. Key sites are indicated by a blue 'binoculars' sign at the roadside.

C. Porreo del Salín A key site, with tamarisk-fringed pools backed by wet meadows. A hide overlooks the pools but the best birds are often to be seen on the meadows, which should be scanned carefully by telescope from the access road. The area is particularly attractive to freshwater waders but other species from the estuary may roost there at high tide. Take the bypass north of the town and take the northern exit from the roundabout adjacent to the Guardia Civil (police) station, which is a dead end leading to a car park overlooking the central creek. Footpaths lead eastwards from here to a dirt road from which there are good views over the Porreo. A number of pools, fringed by low scrub, have been constructed here to attract waders; Black-winged Stilts have nested here and a diversity of waders, especially freshwater species, and water-fowl occur at high tide especially. A hide provides an elevated viewpoint. The scrubby vegetation attracts a diversity of passerines, including migrant warblers in spring and autumn and Bluethroats and Water Pipits in winter.

D. El Gaitero   A cider factory, occupying a large building complex on the creekside by the N-632, 0.5km north of the A-8. A short broad drivable track just south of the factory leads to the creek edge where there are close views of mudflats.

E. Porreos de Arriba (de Sebrayu) and de Abajo   The wet meadows flanking the Río Sebrayu are accessible by footpaths to either side of the N-632 at km-37. Park by the binoculars sign and follow the track east to the Porreo de Arriba. A track on the opposite side of the road gives access to the Porreo de Abajo and the central creek of the Ría.

F. Bridge across the Río Fompalaín   This is on the road to Playa de Rodiles. Park in the lay-by at the north end of bridge. The pool and sedgebed on the right attracts Water Rails, Moorhens and possibly other rallids. A broad tidal creek and mudflats are on the left.

G. Playa de Misiegu   This beach is signposted on the left before Rodiles. Good views of the shallow bay and the central island of El Bornizal, an important wader roost, are available. A footpath follows the bay northwards round to Rodiles.

H. Playa de Rodiles   The good sandy beach is east of the mouth of the Ría but the main interest is the boardwalk along the east side of the estuary mouth.

CALENDAR

All year: Mallard, Little Egret, Grey Heron, Moorhen, Coot, Water Rail, Common Sandpiper, Yellow-legged Gull, Kingfisher, Grey Wagtail, Stonechat, Zitting Cisticola, Common and Spotless Starlings. Mediterranean, Black-headed, Lesser Black-backed, Herring and Great Black-backed Gulls, Water Pipit.

Breeding season: Hobby, Black-winged Stilt, Turtle Dove, Common Cuckoo, Yellow Wagtail, Grasshopper Warbler, Reed Bunting.

Winter: Greylag and Brent Geese, Wigeon, Pintail, Shoveler, Common Shelduck, Pochard, Eider, Great Northern Diver, Black-necked Grebe, Cormorant, Cattle Egret, Guillemot, Razorbill, Hen Harrier, Peregrine Falcon, Oystercatcher, Golden and Grey Plovers, Lapwing, Dunlin, Common Snipe, Curlew, Common Redshank, Turnstone,

Passage periods: Teal, Garganey, Spoonbill, Marsh Harrier, Osprey, Peregrine Falcon, Avocet; Ringed, Little Ringed and Kentish Plovers, Little and Temminck's Stints, Knot, Sanderling, Ruff, Bar-tailed and Black-tailed Godwits, Whimbrel, Spotted Redshank, Greenshank; Green, Wood and Curlew Sandpipers; Sandwich, Common and Black Terns, Common Swift, Sand Martin, Yellow Wagtail, Bluethroat, Northern Wheatear, Willow Warbler, Red-backed Shrike, vagrants: especially waterfowl and waders.

PICOS DE EUROPA   AS7

* *

*Status: Parque Nacional (64,660ha) including the Montaña de Covadonga
ZEPA (16,925ha); 24,560ha of the national park is in Asturias. The Castilla·
y León sector of the National Park forms part of the even larger Picos de
Europa regional park (120,760ha).*

Site description

The Picos de Europa is the most impressive, breathtaking and rugged part of
the Cordillera Cantábrica, the mountain chain that runs parallel to the whole
length of the coast of northern Spain from the Basque Country (Euskadi) to
Galicia. The National Park is immense. It originally covered almost 17,000ha,
when the Montaña de Covadonga was designated as the first national park in
Spain in 1918. Now it extends over 64,660ha, almost 650km², making it the
second-largest Spanish national park (after the Sierra Nevada in Andalucía). The
park is shared between three regions: Asturias, Cantabria and Castilla y León.

The spectacular core of the Picos includes numerous peaks above 2,400m,
the highest being Torre Cerredo (2,648m). Erosion of the limestone massif
has produced the dramatic peaks, jagged rock formations, immense cliff faces,
numerous caves and, especially, the deep river gorges which make these
mountains so impressive. Hay meadows in the wider valleys have a diverse
flora that includes over 40 orchid species. The gentler slopes below about
1,700m have extensive deciduous forests, of oak, beech and birch. Subalpine
pastures, with areas of mountain heath and juniper scrub, extend above the
tree line to about 2,000m. The highest peaks are largely bare rock, although
with an interesting herbaceous alpine flora, including a number of endemics.
There are a few glacial lakes, the two most famous being Lago Enol and Lago
Ercina above Covadonga.

The National Park has been carved into three separate regions by the Ríos
Sella, Cares, Duje and Deva, which flow through very deep and narrow
gorges. The Cornión, or the western massif, in Asturias and Castilla y León,
lies west of the famous Cares Gorge, its highest peak being Peña Santa
(2,596m). The central massif, Los Urrieles, is divided between Cantabria,
Asturias and Castilla y León and brings together the highest summits including
the legendary Naranjo de Bulnes (2,519 m), known locally as Picu Urriellu.
The eastern massif, Ándara, situated between the Deva and Duje rivers, falls
almost entirely within Cantabria where the high summits rise sharply above
the Liébana Valley.

A large part of the attractiveness of the Picos is the relative ease with which
you can reach and explore many areas above 2,000m, with their mountain
flora and fauna. The altitude makes for unpredictable and at times hazardous
weather conditions and all the sensible precautions for mountain trekking
must be taken. In particular, windproof and waterproof clothing must be
carried and special care is needed when there is fog, snow or ice. Several
fatalities have occurred in recent winters. The Picos receive over 2,000mm
of precipitation annually, chiefly as snow in winter, but mists and rain often
occur at other times.

Species

The Picos hold most of the montane specialities of the Pyrenees but in many cases they are far more accessible here. Three high-altitude specialists, the Wallcreeper, Snowfinch and Alpine Accentor, are widespread together with other mountain birds such Rufous-tailed Rock Thrushes, Red-billed and Yellow-billed Choughs and Water Pipits. Griffon Vultures are often numerous overhead and Golden, Short-toed and Booted Eagles, Egyptian Vultures, Goshawks, Sparrowhawks, Common Kestrels and Peregrines are all widespread. Crag Martins, Alpine Swifts, Black Redstarts and cliff-nesting raptors are characteristic of the gorges, with Dippers and Grey Wagtails on the rivers below.

The Lammergeier, that most emblematic of mountain raptors, was exterminated in the Picos early in the 20th century but the increasing Pyrenean population has encouraged dispersal to the Cantabrian mountains in recent years. Sightings in the Picos were frequent enough to suggest eventual recolonisation but this is being accelerated by the release of captive-reared birds; the first two of these were set free in the Picos in 2010.

Both Black and Middle Spotted Woodpeckers are not uncommon in the beech and oak woodlands respectively but they can be elusive. Grey Partridges occur on the upland woodland fringes but Capercaillies have declined almost to extinction within the park. Red-backed Shrikes, Wrynecks and Pied Flycatchers are among the birds of the valleys, together with Bee-eaters and Golden Orioles in the warmer southern and eastern sectors of the Picos.

The mammal population includes a thriving Chamois population on the high tops, with Wild Boar and Roe Deer in the forests and a wide range of mainly small carnivores, including Beech and Pine Martens. Wolves are present but Brown Bears only occasionally visit the park. The diversity of butterflies is enormous: over a third of all European species have been recorded here.

Snowfinches

Timing

Late May to early July is an ideal time to visit since many bird species are then most visible and vocal as they settle to breed. Access to the high tops is then straightforward, although snow may linger as low as 2,000m into June in some years. August can also be good but some areas receive a lot of visitors then. Indeed, Fuente Dé, the Desfiladero de la Hermida, Cares Gorge and the Covadonga lakes are best avoided at weekends and throughout July and (especially) August, when the roads may be congested with coaches and accommodation can be very hard to find without prior booking. September is often excellent, often with warm weather and relatively few visitors. The high tops can be rewarding, weather permitting, anytime between April and October. However, the winter months are still a good period to visit the gorges and lower valleys since Wallcreepers and Snowfinches descend then to lower altitudes.

Access
Most visitors enter the park from the north via the A-8 coastal motorway but there are several access points from the south, notably the N-625 and N-621 from León.

Eastern approach (Map A)
Leave the coastal motorway at Unquera, where the Picos de Europa is signposted, following the N-621 to Potes via Panes.

A. *Desfiladero de la Hermida* This narrow, steep-walled limestone gorge, cut by the Río Deva is 19km long and 600m deep in places. It extends from Panes into the Liébana Valley proper. Cliff-nesters including Griffon Vultures, Golden Eagles, Crag Martins, Red-billed Choughs and Alpine Swifts may be seen in and near the gorge. Unfortunately, this is the main access route to the Picos and the town of Potes and often busy with traffic. The winding road offers few safe stopping points other than a *mirador* on the east side halfway along which is clearly marked by a statue of a salmon on a plinth.

B. *Cantabrian Visitors' Centre of the Picos de Europa* This is a large building, resembling a sports hall, on the western (right-hand) side of the N-621 at the entrance to Potes. The centre offers interesting displays and useful maps of walking trails.

C. *Argüébanes oakwoods* Take the CA-185 west from Potes and turn right after 1km on to a minor road (CA-886) leading for 3km to the village of Argüébanes. Park and walk through the village, continuing uphill into the oakwoods. Middle Spotted Woodpeckers are quite often seen here.

D. *Fuente Dé* Take the CA-185 west from Potes for 20km to reach Fuente Dé and the bottom station of the cable car (*teleférico*), which provides quick access to easy montane birding on the high tops. The cable car is often busy, especially at weekends and in summer, and you may have to wait an hour or more if you are beaten to it by a couple of coaches. It is best to arrive early, which is most easily done by staying in the adjacent Parador de Fuente Dé or in Espinama. The five-minute trip 800m up the remarkably sheer cable is breathtaking. The top station, at the Mirador del Cable (1,800m) offers stunning and panoramic views of the Picos de Europa and the Cantabrian mountains. Yellow-billed Choughs are generally in the area but you will usually need to walk on to find the other montane species. Check the time of the last cable car down (often 18.00 hrs) if you intend to return on it; it is a long walk if you miss it.

a. Follow the stony track upwards from the *mirador* towards the massive cliffs on the left. A level track leads west just before you reach a col, following the foot of a scree slope. Follow this track for about 1km until you reach a fork, where the track divides opposite an expanse of boulder scree, the left fork following the base of a low cliff. The cliff and the scree are both a reliable haunt of Wallcreepers but be prepared to wait for an hour or so before assuming that they are not around. The Wallcreepers often descend to the boulders and disappear into the nooks and crannies underneath, to search for invertebrates. While you are waiting you should be able to find Alpine Accentors in the vicinity and vultures, other raptors and choughs are often overhead. Wallcreepers may also be sought by taking the right fork and following the steep track up to the cliffs and col of Horcados Rojos.

b. Continuing along the left fork for 1km or so will bring you to a series of stony platforms on the left and a deep valley on the right. Chamois are often on the ridges here and Alpine Accentors, Northern Wheatears, Rufous-tailed Rock Thrushes and Black Redstarts breed in the area.

c. Return to the main track at the col above the *mirador* and go over the col, to descend into a large area of subalpine pastures. Water Pipits breed here and flocks of both Red-billed and Yellow-billed Choughs may be seen foraging. Snowfinches should also be looked for. You have the option of staying here at the small Hotel Refugio de Áliva, which is open from June to mid-October. Prebooking is advisable (Tel. 942 730 999). Otherwise you will need to return to the cable car or descend to the valley on foot.

d. The descent to the valley follows a dirt road down to the main road at Espinama, from where there is a 3km walk uphill back to Fuente Dé. The way down passes through woodland and bushy areas, offering possible sightings of Middle Spotted Woodpeckers as well as Red-backed Shrikes and other passerines.

North-central approach (Map A)

E. *Desfiladero del Cares* Take the AS-114, eastwards from Cangas de Onís or westwards from Panes, to Arenas de Cabrales where you turn south into the mountains on the AS-264 to Puente Poncebos. From here a track goes down to the most spectacular gorge in the Picos de Europa. Cares Gorge, or the Garganta Divina as it is locally known, was formed by the fast-flowing Río Cares, and has sheer walls rising in places to over 2,000m. This is one of the most famous walks in the Picos de Europa, 12km (24km if you return!) along a narrow mule track that has been carved from the wall of the gorge and which eventually emerges at the village of Caín at its head. Be alert to the possibility of falling rocks. The gorge is a traditional site for Wallcreepers, especially in winter. Other more easily encountered species include Alpine Swifts, Crag Martins, Red-billed and Yellow-billed Choughs, Blue Rock Thrushes and Rock Buntings.

There are a number of other walking trails in the area, all offering opportunities to spend a few hours looking for montane species of flora and fauna. A funicular railway from Puente Poncebos provides the only vehicular access to

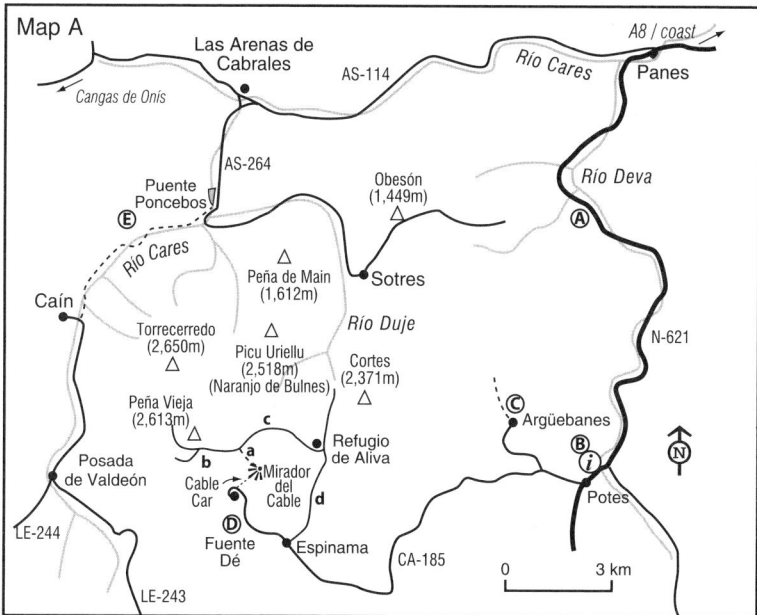

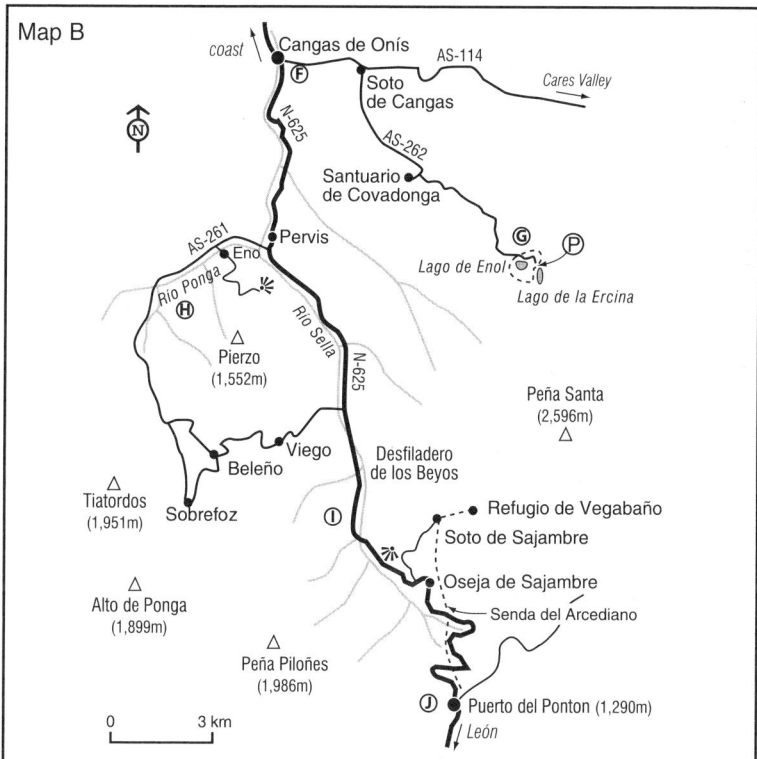

the village of Bulnes, at the foot of Picu Urrielu, from where you can explore the hinterland. It is also worth continuing on the AS-264 to the village of Sotres. Park along the track that leads down to the valley at the point where the road begins to climb up to Sotres, which is then visible on the ridge to the left. Continue on foot along this track and take the left fork which leads to meadows in the valley bottom. The right fork offers a climb through woodland, pastures and rocky outcrops to a narrow col, and beyond.

Western approach (Map B)

Leave the coastal motorway at the eastern exit for Ribadesella, where the Picos de Europa is signposted, following the N-634 to Arriondas and then the N-625 to Cangas de Onís.

F. Asturian Visitors' Centre of the Picos de Europa This is in Cangas (Casa Dago, Avda. de Covadonga 43, 33550 Cangas de Onís : Tel. 985 848 614) and provides the usual maps and other information.

G. Lagos de Covadonga   Take the AS-114 eastwards to Soto continuing on the AS-262 to the Santuario at Covadonga and then beyond for 14km on the CO-4 to the lakes of Enol and La Ercina. The road climbs through beech forests to upland heaths and pastures, with views to the sea and the high peaks. It is worth stopping at the information centre at Lago Enol, where information on walking trails is available. From here it is a short drive to a car park and cafe at the top lake, Lago Ercina, but it can get busy at weekends. Fortunately many visitors go no further than here. A variety of walks are possible, including a circular route of about 6km: for this, follow the left-hand bank of Lago Ercina and bear right round the back of the rocky peak (Pico el Mosquital) to reach Lago Enol, from where the path takes you back to the starting point. Water Pipits, Red-billed and Yellow-billed Choughs, Griffon Vultures, Black Redstarts, Crag Martins and possibly Rufous-tailed Rock Thrushes may be expected. Teal may be on the water; this is one of the few Spanish sites where they breed with any regularity.

H. Ponga This peaceful area on the western fringe of the Picos is well worth a visit. Take the N-625 from Cangas de Onís up the Río Sella valley to Pervis and take the next right turn on to the AS-261, which ascends the Río Ponga valley. This is a quiet scenic route passing through a series of gorges and with spectacular views of a varied landscape, with alternating pastures and beech and chestnut woodlands. An interesting circular route follows the AS-261 from the Río Sella valley to Beleño, with worthwhile diversions to a scenic viewpoint above Eno and to Sobrefoz, returning to the N-625 on the AS-261 via Viego. Woodland and cliff birds may be expected, including Golden Eagles, Yellow-billed Choughs, possibly Wallcreepers in winter, Black Woodpeckers and such northern Spanish specialities as Marsh Tits and Yellowhammers. Dippers are frequent on the river and Chamois are visible on the ridgetops. Several signposted walking trails are on offer.

I. Upper Sella valley Take the N-625 southwards to follow a long, deep gorge, the Desfiladero de los Beyos. The road is twisting but in good repair. Best of all it is fairly quiet so it is easy to stop to view the rock faces, the river and the woodlands along the upper reaches. Shortly after the road enters Castilla y León it is worth taking a minor road on the right which ascends 4km to the village of Soto de Sajambre. The Mirador de Vistalegre below the village is a good watchpoint for raptors and overlooks beech and oak woods. Continue to the village and drive up it and park. Four marked footpaths are signposted from here, including a convenient loop trail to Vegabaño (2 hours) which gives access to beech and oak forest, scrub and pastureland. The left (northern) entrance to loop gives quick access to the full range of habitats and is the best option for a short visit. There is some chance of finding Capercaillies here. Other characteristic species include Black Woodpeckers, Golden Eagles and Water Pipits.

J. Puerto del Pontón The N-625 climbs for 13km south from Oseja de Sajambre to the pass at Puerto del Pontón (1,290m), passing through great tracts of beech forest. A wide drove road, the Senda del Arcediano, is clearly marked at the pass and leads through the woodlands back to Soto de Sajambre. This is an excellent area to search for beech woodland species, including Black Woodpeckers. Ortolan Buntings (scarce) and Citril Finches may sometimes be present at the woodland edges around the pass.

CALENDAR

All year: Capercaillie, Grey Partridge, Mallard, Little Grebe, Griffon Vulture, Goshawk, Sparrowhawk, Common Buzzard, Golden Eagle, Peregrine Falcon, Common Kestrel, Woodcock, Tawny and Eagle Owls; Green, Black, Great Spotted and Middle Spotted Woodpeckers, Crag Martin, Sky and Wood Larks, Blue Rock Thrush, Stonechat, Crested Tit, Goldcrest, Firecrest, Dipper, Wren, Dunnock, Alpine Accentor, Nuthatch, Wallcreeper, Eurasian Treecreeper, Jay, Red-billed and Yellow-billed Choughs, Raven, Rock Sparrow, Snowfinch, Citril Finch, Siskin, Linnet, Crossbill, Bullfinch, Cirl and Rock Buntings.

Breeding season: Teal, White Stork, Black Kite, Honey-buzzard, Egyptian Vulture, Short-toed and Booted Eagles, European Nightjar, Alpine Swift, Bee-eater, Hoopoe, Wryneck, Tree and Water Pipits, Rufous-tailed Rock Thrush; Melodious, Subalpine, Garden and Bonelli's Warblers, Whitethroat, Blackcap, Spotted and Pied Flycatchers, Red-backed Shrike, Ortolan Bunting.

OTHER SITES WORTH VISITING

AS8 RÍO BARAYO

This small estuary with beach, dunes, extensive reedbeds and woods can attract a variety of wintering and passage birds, especially waders, herons and passerines. The coastal meadows are also interesting, especially in winter when Richard's Pipits are sometimes present. Take the coastal N-634 east from Navia and 2km after Villapedre take a left turn to Vigo village.

AS9 LLANES COAST

The coastal town of Llanes in central Asturias has an excellent seawall (Paseo de San Pedro) which offers an ideal elevation for seawatching and an 180° view. Seabird passage just offshore can be intense during suitable winds, especially with north-westerlies in autumn. The regular but scarce Wallcreeper may be sought on the coastal cliffs in winter. The coastal meadows of La Talá, at the western end of the Paseo de San Pedro, between Llanes and Póo, are a good place to find migrant passerines (mainly pipits, warblers & finches) both in spring and autumn (September–October). Breeding species here include Red-backed Shrikes, Zitting Cisticolas, Grasshopper and Melodious Warblers and Red-billed Choughs. Coastal scrub here and further west has both Dartford and Sardinian Warblers. The hinterland of Playa Torimbia, an attractive sheltered sandy cove west of Niembro village (7km west from Llanes) is a regular site for Richard's Pipits in autumn and winter. Inland, the LLN-7 road from Llanes climbs to the Alto de La Tornería pass (470m) and beyond; the roadside cliffs offer Griffon Vultures and other raptors and are also worth searching for Wallcreepers in winter.

AS10 PARQUE NATURAL DE REDES

A wilderness area on the western fringes of the Picos de Europa, centred on the Río Nalón valley. The AS-17 runs through the valley, passing through spectacular rocky gorges and tracts of beech forest, most notably between Campo de Caso and the Tarna pass (Puerto de Tarna 1,490m). Open heathland covers large expanses of the tops at and beyond the Tarna pass. The visitors' centre Campo de Caso can provide details of the many walking trails available. Woodland and upland birds occur, including Black and Middle Spotted Woodpeckers, Rufous-tailed Rock Thrushes, Wallcreepers and Snowfinches.

AS 11 RIBADESELLA

The village and port of Ribadesella straddle the Río Sella estuary. The river attracts gulls and some waders, especially during passage periods and in winter. View the estuary from the promenade on the east bank, which also gives views of several quite large mudbanks and reedy islands. The west bank is also interesting for herons, ducks and passerines, especially the damp meadows of La Mediana: take the RS-2 road from Ribadesella, park near the Tito Bustillo caves and walk beside the river bank for 1–2km. Good seawatching is possible in favourable winds (especially north-westerlies) from the seaward side of Ribadesella itself or from the hermitage at the top of the rocky promontory that comprises the eastern side of the estuary; follow the waterfront round to where a marked footpath leads up to the top.

AS 12 PLAYA DE VEGA

A broad sandy beach and a small estuary, with a hinterland of coastal meadowland, woodland and scrubby hillsides. A good location for migrant passerines, especially in autumn. Leave the AS-8 at km-330 (westbound)/km-337 (eastbound) on to the N-632 eastwards through Berbes and on to Vega. Follow signs to the beach (*Playa*).

CANTABRIA

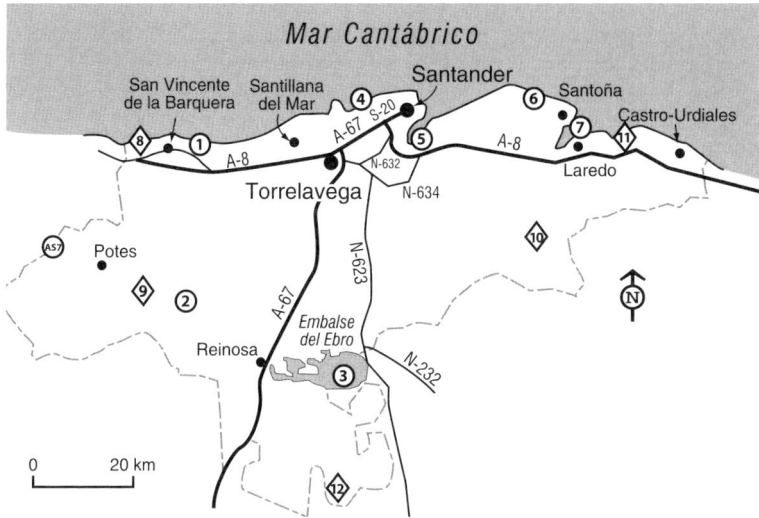

Main sites

CAN1   Oyambre
CAN2   Saja valley
CAN3   Embalse del Ebro
CAN4   Dunas de Liencres
CAN5   Bahía de Santander
CAN6   Marismas del Joyel y de la Victoria
CAN7   Marismas de Santoña

Other sites worth visiting

CAN8   Tina Mayor and Tina Menor Estuaries
CAN9   Nansa Valley
CAN10   Sierra del Hornijo
CAN11   Oriñón Estuary
CAN12   Valderrible

Cantabria is one of the smaller Spanish autonomous regions, lying on the north coast between Asturias to the west and the Basque country (País Vasco/ Euskadi) to the east. In common with Asturias, Cantabria is dominated by the east/west chain of the Cordillera Cantábrica, fronted by a narrow belt of coastal lowlands. The mountains are somewhat lower than in Asturias, except in the west where the eastern reaches of the Picos de Europa, including the popular site of Fuente Dé, fall within Cantabria. This sector of the range nonetheless still offers some rugged terrain and forests of beech and oak. The mountains are traversed by river valleys, providing access to the forests and to the upland pastures at the passes, as at Saja (CAN2) and Nansa (CAN9) and, of course, in the Picos themselves (AS7).

The mountain forests support good populations of Black and Middle Spotted Woodpeckers as well as such northern Spanish specialities as Goldcrests, Marsh Tits and Eurasian Treecreepers. Capercaillies survive here too but their population has declined to an alarming extent and they are hard to find. Grey Partridges are commoner in the upland scrub and the high tops are an excellent region to search for Yellow-billed and Red-billed Choughs, Alpine Accentors, Wallcreepers, Snowfinches and other mountain birds. The other wildlife here includes a great diversity of flowering plants and butterflies and some spectacular mammals, including Wolves. Chamois are abundant on the high tops, their kids being a favourite prey of Golden Eagles. There are a few Brown Bears here too but their principal and thriving population is in Asturias.

The coastal region is green and humid, although somewhat less wet than in Asturias. The mountains are relatively cool in summer and cold in winter, when there are heavy falls of snow on the peaks. The summer climate is warmer south of the Cordillera, where Mediterranean species such as Calandra Larks and Subalpine and Spectacled Warblers have a presence. The Embalse del Ebro (CAN3), one of the largest artificial wetlands in Spain, falls within this region. It is a major wintering site for waterfowl and an important refuge for Red-crested Pochards during their post-breeding moult.

The coastline itself is long and attractive, with magnificent sandy beaches, rocky coves, sea cliffs, extensive sand dunes and a number of large estuarine inlets. These last include the major wetland of Santoña (CAN6, CAN7), the most important site on the Spanish north coast for wintering and passage waders and an essential staging post for Spoonbills migrating between northern Europe and their southern winter quarters. Santoña is also the best site in Spain to see Slavonian Grebes and it regularly accommodates divers and scarce waterfowl in winter. Other major wetlands along the coast include Santander Bay (CAN5), the Ría de San Vicente (CAN1) and those associated with the Ría at Liencres (CAN4), which also boasts the most extensive sand dunes in northern Spain. The entire coastline provides outstanding opportunities to observe seabird and passerine migration, especially in autumn, when passerine falls are regular and the westward flow of seabirds just offshore is often spectacular.

Records of all observations in Cantabria, not just the rarities, are welcomed by SEO/BirdLife Cantabria. They may be emailed to cantabria@seo.org.

Yellow-billed and Red-billed Choughs

OYAMBRE   CAN1

Status: Parque Natural (5,758ha).

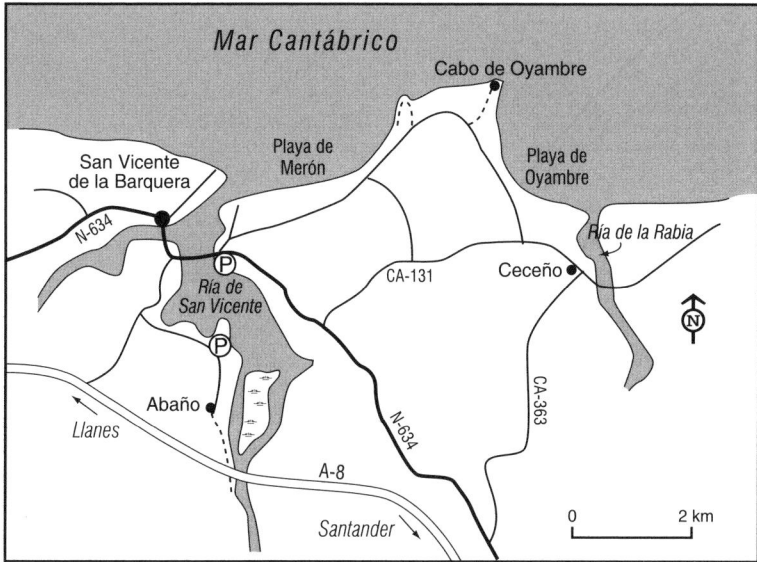

Site description

A complex of coastal habitats between, and including, two estuaries: the relatively small Ría de la Rabia to the east and the larger Ría de San Vicente to the west. Both estuaries have well-developed saltmarsh, mudflats and sandbanks with some reedbeds in their upper reaches. The coastline between the estuaries has cliffs, sand dunes and magnificent sandy beaches, backing on to pastures and areas of coastal scrub, with some mixed woodlands as well as eucalyptus and pine plantations. The headland of Cabo de Oyambre provides an excellent seawatching site.

Species

The Rías, especially San Vicente, are important for their waterfowl and waders, particularly in autumn and winter. Wintering ducks include mainly small flocks of Gadwall, Wigeon, Teal and Shoveler, with a few Common Pochards, Red-crested Pochards and Tufted Ducks. Curlews, Dunlins and Common Redshanks are the most obvious waders but many other species occur. Large flocks of gulls rest on the sandbanks at low tide and should be scrutinised for Mediterranean Gulls and other less common species. Divers, auks and other seabirds may be seen close inshore and in the estuaries during periods of rough weather in winter. Short-toed and Booted Eagles breed in the general area and Peregrines nest along the coast. Ospreys occur regularly on passage and may linger for some time in the Ría de San Vicente especially. The whole area receives numbers of passerine migrants, especially in autumn when large flocks of Sky Larks, Meadow Pipits, Yellow Wagtails and White Wagtails are conspicuous in the pastures, with chats and warblers in the taller coastal vegetation.

Timing

The area can be rewarding throughout the year, although many tourists are drawn in summer to San Vicente village and the beaches are busy then. The whole area can be excellent during migration, especially in autumn, and for wintering birds. Seawatching from Cabo de Oyambre is most productive in autumn during onshore winds.

Access

Oyambre is in the far west of Cantabria. The Ría de San Vicente includes the attractive fishing village of San Vicente de la Barquera, which is clearly sign-posted from the A-8. The two estuaries are linked by the CA-131. To reach Cabo de Oyambre follow the coastal loop road from this road serving the beaches (Playa de Merón and Playa de Oyambre) and take the road northwards from the top of the loop to approach the Cape. The road ends at a cluster of farms and chalets. Tracks to either side of these lead near the Cape and adjacent headland, which are approached by short footpaths.

The estuary at San Vicente can be viewed from a number of locations. The causeway is one of the best and the small car park at its eastern end is well placed for scanning both the inner and outer estuary. Parking is also easiest at the eastern end during holiday periods, when the village gets rather crowded. The inner estuary, which has many islands in the salt marshes where waders roost at high tide, is readily inspected from the road to Abaño, which leads eastwards from the motorway link road 1km before San Vicente. A tarmac track 0.9km from the entrance leads to a walled, part-tiled building (the village cemetery). Park here and view the adjacent estuary from the fringing meadows. You can also drive past Abaño and follow a dirt track to the river. The CA-131 also crosses the Ría de la Rabia: park at a lay-by on the west side, from where an elevated footpath gives excellent views from the western and southern banks. The direct distance between the two estuaries is around 6km.

CALENDAR

All year: Mallard, Little Grebe, Shag, Little Egret, Grey Heron, Peregrine Falcon, Common Sandpiper, Yellow-legged Gull, Barn Owl, Kingfisher, Green Woodpecker, Grey and White Wagtails, Stonechat, Common Chiffchaff, Spotless Starling, Southern Grey Shrike, Serin, Cirl Bunting.

Breeding season: Black Kite, Short-toed and Booted Eagles, Hobby, Cuckoo, Zitting Cisticola, Garden Warbler, Red-backed Shrike.

Winter: Greylag Goose, Gadwall, Wigeon, Teal, Shoveler, Great Northern Diver, Cormorant, Little and Great White Egrets, Oystercatcher; Ringed, Golden and Grey Plovers, Lapwing, Knot, Sanderling, Dunlin, Curlew, Common Redshank, Great Skua, Guillemot, Razorbill, Fieldfare, Redwing, Brambling.

Passage periods: Cory's, Great (summer/autumn), Sooty (summer/autumn), Manx and Balearic Shearwaters, Gannet, Spoonbill, Marsh Harrier, Osprey, Avocet, Little Stint, Curlew Sandpiper, Ruff, Whimbrel, Greenshank; Mediterranean, Little and Sabine's Gulls, Kittiwake, Guillemot, Razorbill, Yellow Wagtail.

SAJA VALLEY   CAN2

Status: Parque Natural Saja-Besaya (24,500ha). Also forms part of the
Reserva Nacional de Caza del Saja (180,186ha). ZEPA.

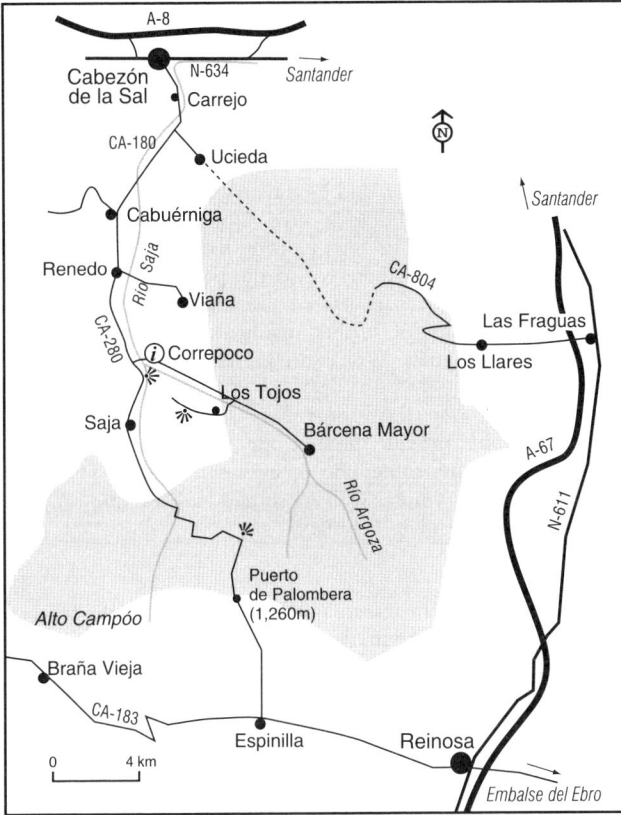

Site description

A mountainous area with extensive deciduous forests, among the largest
in Spain. The Parque Natural forms only part of the immense Saja Game
Reserve, an area which extends from the Besaya river to the Picos de Europa
thus covering practically the whole of the western half of Cantabria. Hunting
in the Game Reserve is controlled by permit, Red and Roe Deer, Chamois
and Wild Boar being the larger quarry.

The Parque Natural itself includes the valleys of the Saja and Besaya rivers
and the ridges between. Large expanses of oak and beech woodland clothe
the slopes, grading into birch woodland, scrub and seasonal pastures (brañas)
at higher altitudes. These last are inhabited in summer by herds of the small
native breed of beef cattle, the Tudancas, which you often meet on the road
itself if you ascend to the pass at Puerto de Palombera. They are attractive, grey

or chestnut animals, with distinctive white-fringed muzzles. Almost 70% of the total area is woodland. The beech forest is normally found in shaded valleys from 500–1,300m. The oak forest lies at a height of 600–700m. Mixed forest along the riverbanks includes a diversity of species, the most important being Ash, Elm, Blackthorn, Lime and Willow. The beech forest of the Monte de Saja and the oak forest of the Monte de Ucieda are the most important wooded areas. Bárcena Major is an historical enclave, a restored example of a typical Cantabrian mountain village.

Species

This is a good area in which to observe the breeding raptors of Cantabria, with many viewpoints available over the mountain slopes and woodlands. They include Golden, Short-toed and Booted Eagles, Honey-buzzards, Goshawks, Sparrowhawks and both Griffon and Egyptian Vultures. The woodland community includes Black and Middle Spotted Woodpeckers. Alpine Accentors occur in the upper reaches. The high pastures have Water Pipits, Whinchats and Northern Wheatears and there is also the possibility of Bluethroats and Ortolan Buntings here. The park has a considerable population of Red and Roe Deer and a diversity of smaller mammals including Badgers, Beech Martens, Polecats, and Genets. Wolves are present in good numbers.

Timing

Late spring and summer provide the best opportunity to see a wide range of species but there is always something of interest available. The pass can be blocked by snow in the winter. Walkers should exercise due caution during the hunting period (September–February).

Access

A representative transect of the reserve involves driving along the relatively quiet Saja valley. The Besaya valley to the east accommodates the A-67 motorway and is not comparable. From Santander head west along the A-8 as far as Cabezón de la Sal. Turn inland here along the CA-180 as far as Cabuérniga, from where the upper reaches are served by the CA-280, which runs along the length of the Saja valley up to the Palombera pass (Puerto de Palombera, 1,260m).

There are a number of routes into the different parts of the park and very many walking trails. The main points of access to the heart of the park are via Ucieda or Bárcena Mayor. The bridge across the Saja at the start of the approach road to Bárcena offers good views of the river. An information centre on this road at Correpoco provides maps of walking trails throughout the area. Just before Bárcena the road passes through meadowland, with oakwoods on the northern side of the valley and beeches on the facing slopes, giving good opportunities to search for woodland species. There is a campsite about 1km from Bárcena Mayor and from there a track follows the course of the Argoza river for 7km through ancient oak and beech forest to La Arbencia pool.

There are also various places to pull off the road between Saja and the Palombera pass. A viewpoint at km-9.5 by the Peña Colsa bar overlooks the canopy of oak woodland and is opposite a rocky escarpment which has a small Griffon Vulture colony. Ravens also nest nearby. The pass provides easy access to extensive pastureland, heavily overgrazed by cattle and horses, with patches of heath. Park at the pass and explore on foot. Another alternative is to continue over the pass down to Espinilla and then west along the CA-183, to the ski resort at Braña Vieja in the Alto Campóo.

The Cantabrian Nature Museum (Museo de la Naturaleza de Cantabria), an attractive exposition of the region's ecosystems, is at the beautiful village of Carrejo, about 2km south of Cabezón de la Sal. It is generally open from 10.00–15.00hrs; until 19.00 hrs mid April–September but closed on Mondays. It has excellent disabled access.

CALENDAR

All year: Grey Partridge, Griffon Vulture, Goshawk, Sparrowhawk, Golden Eagle, Tawny Owl, Black and Middle Spotted Woodpeckers, Crag Martin, Dipper, Alpine Accentor, Robin, Goldcrest, Marsh Tit, Eurasian Treecreeper, Red-billed and Yellow-billed Choughs, Raven, Bullfinch, Yellowhammer.

Breeding season: Honey-buzzard, Egyptian Vulture, Short-toed and Booted Eagles, Wryneck, Tree and Water Pipits, Bluethroat, Whinchat, Northern Wheatear, Rufous-tailed Rock Thrush, Bonelli's Warbler, Spotted and Pied Flycatchers, Red-backed Shrike, Ortolan Bunting.

EMBALSE DEL EBRO   CAN3

Status: ZEPA: Reserva Nacional de Aves Acuáticas (6,200ha). Hunting is prohibited.

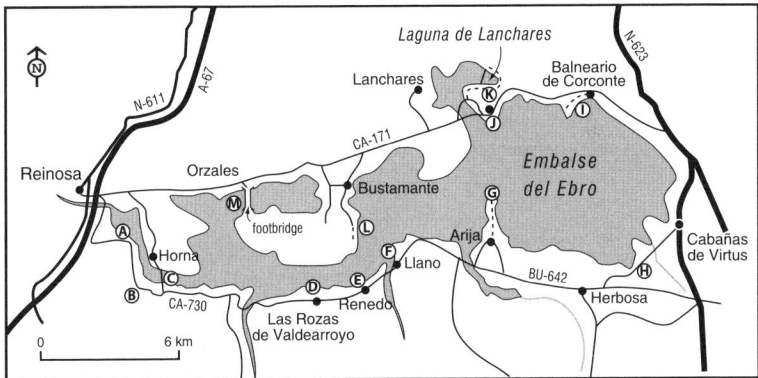

Site description

A large reservoir situated on a plain and sandwiched between mountain ranges in the south of Cantabria. Its south-eastern corner lies in Castilla y León. The longest river in Spain, the Ebro, has its source close by at Fontibre, and eventually finds its way into the Mediterranean after a journey across the breadth of Spain. At this point the Ebro is a modest stream, yet to be swelled by the Pyrenean meltwaters. However, the river and its tributaries suffice to feed a long, narrow lake which is the largest freshwater site in Cantabria and one of the largest in Spain with a surface area of roughly 6,000ha when full. The reservoir is about 20km long and 4km wide at the broadest part, with a perimeter of 90km. It was built in 1945 amid considerable controversy since it required the abandonment and submergence of several villages. The lake is quite shallow and its water levels fluctuate considerably, exposing often large islands and sandbars. Nevertheless it has well-developed aquatic vegetation and marshland locally, especially around the feeder streams. The shoreline is mainly heavily grazed pasture, with scrub and some significant areas of mixed woodland nearby.

Species

The shallow waters and the shores provide attractive roosting and feeding areas for waterfowl. It is an important site for Red-crested Pochards attracting a post-breeding population of up to 700, numbers peaking in July. Several hundred pairs of Great Crested Grebes and over 50 pairs of Gadwall breed. It is an important wintering site for Greylag Geese, Wigeon, Gadwall, Common Teal and other wildfowl. Ospreys occur regularly on passage. The general area holds the only significant White Stork population in Cantabria (135 pairs in 2006). Honey-buzzards, Black Kites and Short-toed Eagles breed in the area and Griffon Vultures are frequently overhead. Merlins are regular in winter, attracted by the wintering flocks of Sky Larks, Meadow Pipits and finches.

Timing

Waterfowl are present all year round but the largest numbers occur from late summer onwards and into early spring.

Access

The A-67 links the A-8 Cantabrian coast motorway at Torrelavega with the A-231 which connects Burgos and León. The N-611 follows the same route. These roads pass through Reinosa, which is the access point to the western end of the reservoir. The N-623, linking Burgos and Santander skirts the eastern end. The perimeter drive is over 40km long but makes for a worthwhile daytrip, involving stops at the recommended points. The south shore is better than the northern one since it gives closest access to areas of deeper water, the light is always in your favour and the road is very quiet. The sites below are listed as encountered during an anticlockwise circuit but the route may, of course, be taken in reverse.

South shore

Take the CA-730 west from Reinosa. A hide below a lay-by at km-3 (A) overlooks the westernmost end of the reservoir, which is often dry so that the river and adjacent grazing land are exposed: Wigeon may be numerous on the pastures here. The road passes through a large expanse of mixed oak/beech woodland (B) between km-4 and km-8, where there is access to search for woodland species. The bridge at Horna (C) gives good views of the western arm. Six rafts offshore at km-12 have been installed to provide nest sites for Great Crested Grebes and other waterfowl.

Another viewpoint is available at Las Rozas de Valdearroyo (D), next to a partly submerged church tower. A road by a picnic spot at Renedo, at km-16.4, leads down under a railway line to the lakeside (E) where access to the shoreline and excellent views are available by a disused church. Next it is worth stopping at Llano, where a bridge cuts across a minor arm of the lake

(F) and large sand spits are often exposed opposite: these attract gulls, terns and waders. The promontory at Arija (G) includes an area of pools and scrub, attractive respectively to Red-crested Pochard and passerines: drive through the village and past the campsite on the right.

Continuing east into the Castilla-Léon sector the road becomes the BU-642 and is too far from the shore but a useful shortcut to Cabañas de Virtus (H) passes through extensive pastures and areas of freshwater marsh in the south-east of the reservoir: waterfowl and waders occur here and Marsh Harriers are present regularly. The shortcut entrance is some 2km east of Herbosa, where a wide track descends to cross a railway line and then bears right, at a small marsh which is itself interesting.

North shore

The CA-171 is much busier than the southern road but provides access to several good sites. The north-east pastures and shoreline are accessible near the Balneario (Spa) de Corconte: park by the hotel and follow the track just west of it (I). Continuing west, good views are available from the village of La Población (J).

A large inlet of the reservoir west of the village often attracts geese, ducks and waders. It includes the Laguna de Lanchares bird reserve, where a dam preserves water levels. This lagoon is overlooked by two hides that are joined by the perimeter track (K). The aquatic vegetation attracts waterbirds although it is overgrazed. Take the road northwards just west of La Población, cross the narrow bridge and take the first road left. Stay on this road, which becomes a gravel track, for 0.8km to reach an information board where you should park and walk to the hides.

Excellent access to the lakeshore, and views of spits and islands offshore, is provided by the Bustamante peninsula. Bear left at the village of Bustamante and follow the road to the Estación de Bombeo (pumping station) (L). The stone footbridge to the Bustamante promontory at Orzales (M) is another useful stopping place. The entrance is from a lay-by just east of Orzales. Shore access and good views are available at both ends and from the bridge itself.

CALENDAR

All year: Gadwall, Mallard, Pochard, Red-legged Partridge, Little Grebe, Great Crested Grebe, Red Kite, Griffon Vulture, Marsh and Hen Harriers, Common Buzzard, Common Kestrel, Moorhen, Common Coot, Little Owl, White Wagtail, Cetti's and Dartford Warblers, Rock Sparrow.

Breeding season: Red-crested Pochard, Quail, White Stork, Honey-buzzard, Black Kite, Egyptian Vulture, Short-toed and Booted Eagles, Hobby, Little Ringed and Kentish Plovers, Common Sandpiper, Yellow-legged Gull, Common Cuckoo, European Nightjar, Hoopoe, Yellow Wagtail, Whinchat; Great Reed, Reed and Melodious Warblers, Whitethroat.

Winter: Greylag Goose, Wigeon, Teal, Pintail, Shoveler, Tufted Duck, Black-necked Grebe, Grey Heron, Merlin, Lapwing, Golden Plover, Curlew, Sky Lark, Meadow Pipit.

Passage periods: Greylag Goose, Spoonbill, Osprey, Little Stint, Ruff, Black-tailed and Bar-tailed Godwits, Common Redshank, Common Tern, Black Tern.

DUNAS DE LIENCRES   CAN4

Status: Parque Natural (194.5 ha).

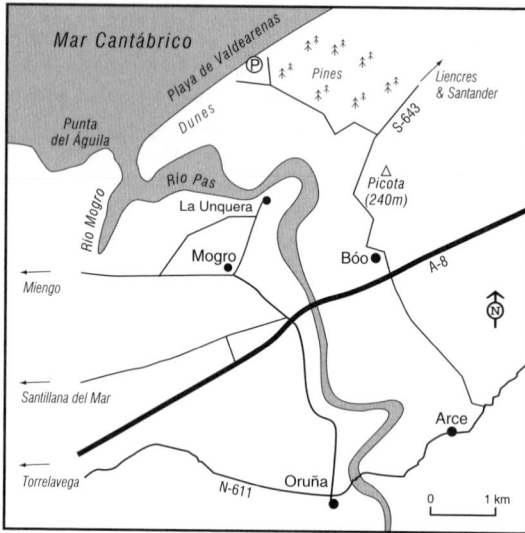

Site description
These are the most extensive sand dunes on Spain's northern coast, behind the Playas de Valdearenas and Canallave. The Ría de Mogro, including the estuary of the Río Pas, forms the western boundary. Maritime Pines were planted in 1949 to stabilise the dunes.

Species
This is a very good site for passage waders and passerines and also for seabirds, the latter especially in winter when auks, divers and sea-ducks may be present. Snow Buntings have been recorded in some winters. Breeding birds include Hobbies, Zitting Cisticolas and Red-backed Shrikes.

Timing
The site is interesting all year round although least so in summer, when the beaches may be busy. The dunes, pine plantations, deciduous woodlands and scrub are worth searching for migrant passerines in spring and autumn. Waders are most abundant on passage and in winter. Winter is also best for seabirds and waterfowl. The nearby hill of Picota can be popular with paragliders and mountain-bikers at weekends.

Access
The site is only 15km west of Santander. The most agreeable approach is to take the local road (S-463) to Liencres via Soto de la Marina. Carry on through Liencres and turn right to the Playa de Valdearenas, where there is a large car park. The popular hill of Picota offers excellent views over the park and estuaries and can be reached by a track from the car park. You can also leave the

A-8 motorway at Bóo and approach Liencres from the south, turning left for the beach which is signposted. The dunes offer good seaward views. Follow the beach south-westwards to the spit across the mouth of the Ría, to view the estuary. Views of the Ría are also available from the western side at La Unquera golf course or from the headland of Punta del Águila.

CALENDAR

All year: Shag, Sparrowhawk, Common Buzzard, Peregrine Falcon, Common Kestrel, Common Sandpiper, Kingfisher, Stonechat, Zitting Cisticola, Crested Tit, Short-toed Treecreeper, Serin, Cirl Bunting.

Breeding season: Hen Harrier, Hobby, Little Ringed Plover, Whinchat, Spotted Flycatcher, Golden Oriole, Red-backed Shrike.

Winter: Common Eider, Common and Velvet Scoters, Red-breasted Merganser, Great Northern Diver, Cory's and Balearic Shearwaters, Cormorant, Little Egret, Grey Heron, Grey and Golden Plovers, Sanderling, Curlew, Common Redshank, Guillemot, Razorbill, Snow Bunting (occasional).

Passage periods: Greylag Goose, Great and Sooty Shearwaters (summer/autumn), Gannet, Little Bittern, Osprey, Marsh Harrier, Kentish Plover, Knot, Sanderling, Dunlin, Whimbrel, Turnstone, Short-eared Owl, Tawny and Tree Pipits, Northern Wheatear; Grasshopper, Sedge and Wood Warblers, Woodchat Shrike.

BAHÍA DE SANTANDER (SANTANDER BAY) CAN5

Status: No special protection.

Site description

Santander, the capital of Cantabria, dominates the western side of a large bay. This attractive city is also a ferry port, a point of arrival for visitors from Britain travelling from Portsmouth and Plymouth. The city waterfront offers the prospect of a pleasant walk, starting at the wooded promontory of La Magdalena and continuing north to two capes, Cabo Menor and Cabo Mayor offering seaward views. Several rivers empty into the bay via two large inlets. The Ría del Astillero in the south receives the Ríos Solía, San Salvador and Bóo and the Ría de Cubas in the west is fed by the Río Miera. The bay proper stretches from Cabo Mayor in the west to Punta Langre in the east. Much of it is quite shallow and it offers extensive sandbanks and areas of mudflats with varying amounts of saltmarsh and intertidal vegetation, especially within the Rías and along the southern and eastern shores. There are sand dunes at the eastern mouth of the bay at the Playa de El Puntal and Playa de Somo.

Several small but interesting freshwater and tidal wetlands have been created or restored south-west of the bay near the airport, offering reedbeds and lagoons. They include the marismas de Alday, de Parayas, Negras and Blancas and a former mineworking, the Pozón de la Dolores. All are protected municipal areas. In addition, the Marismas Negras and Blancas are a reserve of SEO/Birdlife and the Marismas de Alday and de Parayas have been restored by La Fundación Naturaleza y Hombre.

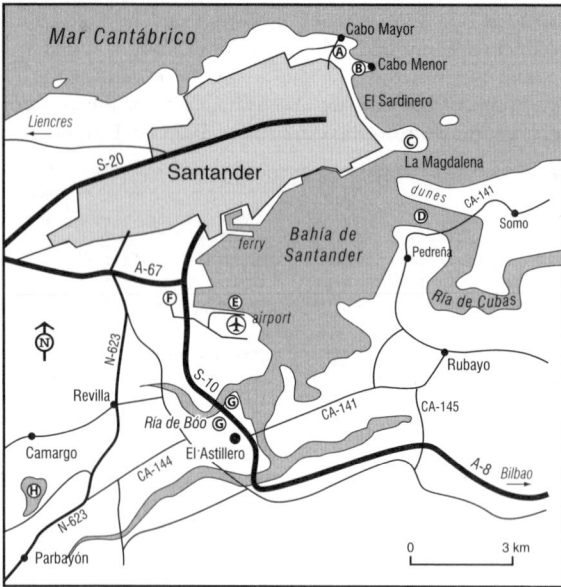

Species

The bay and coastline are most important for waders during passage periods and in winter. Waders can also be seen, often closely, at the Marismas Negras especially. Seabird passage offshore is often noteworthy in autumn especially. Wintering seabirds in inshore waters include a few divers, numbers of Black-necked Grebes and large flocks of gulls, as well as scoters, Cormorants, skuas and auks. European Storm-petrels, Shags and Yellow-legged Gulls nest on the rocky islets offshore. Small numbers of Common Terns nest on wrecks within the bay: their sole breeding site in northern Spain. Peregrines breed nearby and often hunt over the bay and city. The freshwater lagoons attract numbers of wintering ducks, especially Common Pochard, Shoveler and Teal, and have nesting Great Crested and Little Grebes, Little Bitterns, Water Rails, Reed Warblers and Reed Buntings among others. The whole area receives falls of passerine migrants, particularly in autumn, when interesting birds recorded at the lakes have included Aquatic Warblers.

Timing

The region is of greatest interest during passage periods, especially in autumn, and in winter. The lakes have interesting birds all year round. SEO/Cantabria organise pelagic seabirding trips regularly from Santander in late summer and autumn. See their website (seo.org/?cantabria) for more information.

Access

Views seaward and across the bay are available from the headlands of Cabo Mayor (A) and Cabo Menor (B). Cabo Menor lies off the waterfront road at the north end of El Sardinero, a shallow inlet with sandy beaches which is prominently signposted. Cabo Mayor and its lighthouse (*Faro*) are reached by continuing northwards from here. The peninsula of La Magdalena (C) projects into the bay at the south end of El Sardinero: park at the entrance car park and continue on foot. The woodlands and scrub at La Magdalena and at the two capes can be excellent for passage migrants at times. The best mudflats and Eelgrass beds are found on the eastern side, notably in the Ría de Cubas (D). Take the dual carriageway (S-10) out of the city towards Bilbao, turning off at El Astillero (8km from Santander) to follow the eastern shores of the bay towards Pedreña and across a bridge over the mouth of the Ría to Somo.

The airport itself has a marshy area, the Marismas de Parayas (E), including a reedy lake (La Charca de Raos), within its northern boundary, which is visible from the perimeter road. Follow signs to the airport and drive round to the marina on the eastern side. The lake attracts waterfowl and the rough grassland of the airport itself sometimes holds wintering Stone-curlews.

The Marismas de Alday (F) also have a hide and an observation platform. Driving south from the city take the airport exit from the S-10 motorway and the second exit from the roundabout at the top of the slip-road. Drive down this steep road and take the first right, to follow the bumpy tarmac road which skirts a shopping centre (Centro Comercial Valle Real). Park at the corner at the end, adjacent to the screens protecting the reserve.

The Marismas Negras and Blancas (G) straddle the S-10 motorway: take the Astillero exit and head south (right if coming from Santander) to the first roundabout. The regional headquarters of SEO/Birdlife is here alongside the Marismas Negras and offers a small car park and information centre. The reserve has perimeter trails and offers views over the mudflats of the Ría de Bóo. The Marismas Negras and Blancas are linked by a walkway passing below the motorway and railway line, alongside the Ría. The Marismas Blancas are also accessible directly by turning north from the Astillero exit, where parking is also available at the south-eastern corner. Waders are the principal attraction at the Marismas Negras and the permanent freshwater lake of the Marismas Blancas holds waterfowl, herons and other wetland birds.

The Pozón de la Dolores (H) is adjacent to a minor road which loops north of the N-623 near Parbayón.

CALENDAR

All year: Shag, Little Grebe, Great Crested Grebe, Common Buzzard, Peregrine Falcon, Yellow-legged Gull, Collared Dove, Kingfisher, White Wagtail, Cetti's Warbler, Zitting Cisticola, Reed Bunting. Egrets, Grey Heron, Merlin, Grey Plover, Oystercatcher, Curlew, Dunlin, Common Redshank, Purple Sandpiper, Guillemot, Razorbill.

Breeding season: Mallard, Common Pochard, European Storm-petrel, Oystercatcher, Little Ringed Plover, Common Tern, Common Swift, Reed and Great Reed Warblers.

Winter: Greylag Goose, Gadwall, Common Teal, Pintail, Shoveler, Common Pochard, Tufted Duck, Common Scoter, Red-breasted Merganser, Great Northern Diver, Black-necked Grebe, Cormorant, Cattle and Little

Passage periods: Red-breasted Merganser; Cory's, Great (summer/autumn), Sooty (summer/autumn), Manx and Balearic Shearwaters, Gannet; Pomarine, Arctic and Great Skuas, Grey Heron, Purple Heron, Spoonbill, Marsh Harrier, Dunlin, Curlew Sandpiper, Ruff, Whimbrel, Greenshank; Mediterranean, Little and Sabine's Gulls, Kittiwake; Sandwich, Common, Arctic, Little and Black Terns, Guillemot, Razorbill, Hoopoe, Sand Martin, Tree Pipit, Northern Wheatear, Red-backed Shrike, warblers.

MARISMAS DEL JOYEL Y DE LA VICTORIA   CAN6

Status: Protected as part of the Marismas de Santoña reserve (CAN7).

Site description

A north-western outpost of Santoña comprising two small wetlands flanked by hay meadows. There are coastal cliffs nearby at Cabo de Quejo. The Marisma del Joyel comprises rough grass, rushes, reedbeds, brackish lagoons and salt-marsh within a small estuary, the Ría de Cabo Quejo. The Marisma de la Victoria has a much larger area of reedbed surrounding a small freshwater lake.

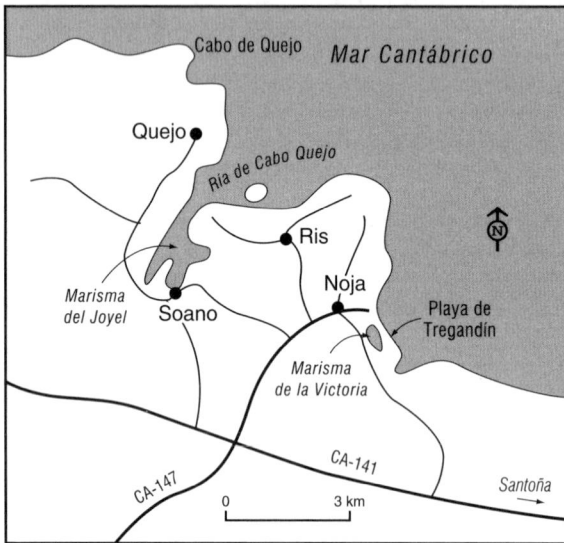

Species

The diversity of habitats makes for a good range of species. The reedbeds and pools attract breeding Little Grebes, Little Bitterns, Purple Herons, Marsh Harriers and Cetti's and Great Reed Warblers. Waterfowl, waders and Spoonbills frequent the pools, especially during passage periods and in winter. Tawny Pipits and Zitting Cisticolas breed in the area as well as Sardinian Warblers. Black Kites also breed in the area and Peregrines, Red-billed Choughs and Ravens nest on the cliffs.

Timing

Interesting throughout the year but best from September through to June.

Access

A visit here can usefully be combined with a visit to Santoña proper. Leave Santoña westwards on the CA-141 and turn right after 5km towards the village of Noja. The Marismas de la Victoria are south-east of Noja at the Playa de Tregandín. Drive west from Noja for 1km to reach the head of the Ría at

Soano. View the reedbeds and pools comprising the Marisma del Joyel here from the footpaths which skirt the estuary. Cabo de Quejo may be reached by driving north up the west side of the estuary to Quejo.

CALENDAR

All year: Little Grebe, Cormorant, Grey Heron, Marsh Harrier, Peregrine Falcon, Water Rail, Scops Owl, Kingfisher, Crag Martin, Black Redstart, Zitting Cisticola; Cetti's, Dartford and Sardinian Warblers, Firecrest, Red-billed Chough, Raven, Spotless Starling, Serin, Cirl Bunting.

Breeding season: Little Bittern, Purple Heron, Black Kite, Tawny Pipit; Great Reed, Grasshopper and Melodious Warblers.

Winter: Wigeon, Pintail, Gadwall, Red-breasted Merganser, Black-necked Grebe, Grey Heron, Common Snipe, Curlew, Razorbill.

Passage periods: Grey Heron, Spoonbill, Hobby, Spotted Crake, Common and Spotted Redshanks, Common Redstart, Orphean Warbler, Pied Flycatcher, Red-backed Shrike.

MARISMAS DE SANTOÑA   CAN7

Status: Reserva Natural, ZEPA and Ramsar site (6,907ha). Includes the Marismas del Joyel y de la Victoria (CAN6).

Spoonbills

Site description

The most important coastal wetland on the north coast of Spain. The large, very shallow tidal inlet is sheltered by a tall, rocky hill, Monte Buciero, (376m) and has only a narrow opening to the sea. The principal habitats are tidal mud-flats with Eelgrass beds and fringing salt marshes. There are also sand dunes and sand bars, and stony breakwaters. The southern flanks of Monte Buciero are well wooded with Iberian Holm Oaks (Encinas) and dense scrub, with sheer cliffs to seaward.

The inlet was threatened by reclamation projects but conservation efforts saved the site, which was designated a reserve in 1992, although some damage had already been done by then, notably the construction of the causeway road across the western salt marshes.

Traditional activities such as shellfish harvesting and fishing take place within the reserve although they are subject to controls. It is also worth visiting the remains of the traditional tidal watermills conserved in the area, notably the Jado mill in Argoños and the Santa Olalla mill in the Joyel marshland (CAN6).

Species

This is an important wintering site for waterfowl and waders, with thousands of birds including over 6,000 Wigeon and over 3,000 Dunlin using the inlet. The wintering bird community is very diverse and regularly includes such species as Brent Geese, Common Eiders; Great Northern, Red-throated and Black-throated Divers and Red-necked and Slavonian Grebes, all of which are uncommon or rare in northern Spain. It is also an important staging area for migrant waterfowl and waders, and most notably for Spoonbills, which are especially numerous in autumn (mid-August–October), when 2,000 or more may be present. Colour ringing has shown many or most of these Spoonbills to be of Dutch origin. Breeding birds include Common Shelducks, recent arrivals which have added Santoña to the short but expanding list of breeding sites for this species in Spain. The scrub on Monte Buciero is a regional stronghold of the Sardinian Warbler, a very local species in Cantabria.

The reserve has notched up an impressive list of rarities, the most notorious being the young White-tailed Eagle that spent the 2003/2004 winter here, feeding on Grey Herons among other prey. Another exceptional find here was a Pacific Diver, in 2009.

Timing

Some good birds may be found here all year round but the best time to visit is between September and June. Wintering wildfowl arrive in late October and stay until March. A telescope is all but essential. Many of the best viewpoints are on the west side of the Bay where therefore afternoon and evening visits are preferable on sunny days. Visits at mid-tide are most productive for observing waders since these roost at high tide and are widely dispersed at low tide.

Access

The reserve lies around 50km east of Santander and 75km west of Bilbao and is easily reached via the A-8 motorway which skirts the Bay. Leave the motorway at Colindres and take the N-634 west for 4km where the CA-241(S-401) heads north towards Santoña village. A dirt track on the right immediately before the CA-241 junction leads across a level crossing to a fish cannery, where you should park and continue on foot to view the saltings (A). Return to the main road and take the CA-241 northwards. Shortly after crossing a creek take the road off to the left heading for Escalante and stop and look where the road overlooks the saltmarshes on the right (B). You should return from here to the CA-241, turn left and shortly afterwards turn right into a sandy track leading to the Monasterio de Montehano, where you can park and view the adjacent creeks and saltings (C).

Continue northwards for 2km from here towards Santoña and you will see a lay-by on the right serving a very large elevated hide, the Observatorio de Aves de La Arenilla (D). This gives excellent views across the Bay, and of the sandbars and mudflats at low tide: Spoonbills are often present here. You can also view the saltmarsh and creeks from a footpath fringing the Bay which extends north all the way from here to Santoña village and some way southwards as well. The wharfside on the right at the entrance to Santoña itself is also a useful vantage point (E), especially at high tide in winter when divers, grebes and ducks may be present offshore.

Monte Buciero is accessible via the road to the lighthouse, the Faro del Pescador: take the CA-148 north-west out of Santoña and after 2km follow the coast road westwards to the lighthouse. This is an excellent seawatching point (F). A second lighthouse, the Faro del Caballo, is reached via a walking trail which leads uphill through the scrub from the coastal fort at the west end of Santoña village waterfront (G).

The eastern side of the Bay may be viewed from several points. Stop in Colindres and walk down to the central creek (Ría de Treto), where there are good views of the mudflats and also of a stony dyke which attracts gulls, terns and roosting waders (H). Continue on the N-634 from Colindres to Laredo and follow signs north to the Club Náutico/Puerto Deportivo (marina) which is on the sandspit at the southern entrance to the inlet (I). There are good views from the jetties here or you can walk down the eastern shoreline (Playa de Regatón). Birding boat trips within the Bay are sometimes on offer and are a very good way to get closer to the birds. Trips may be arranged with Aves Cantábricas SL (see avescantabricas.com). Inshore seabirding trips also leave from here in summer and autumn (see seo.org/?cantabria).

CALENDAR

All year: Common Shelduck, Gadwall, Mallard, Common Pochard, Little Grebe, Red Kite, Common Buzzard, Marsh Harrier, Goshawk, Peregrine Falcon, Common Coot, Yellow-legged Gull, Kingfisher, Stonechat, Song Thrush, Zitting Cisticola; Cetti's, Sardinian and Dartford Warblers, Firecrest, Southern Grey Shrike, Raven, Serin, Cirl and Reed Buntings.

Breeding season: Shag, Little Egret, Purple Heron, Black Kite, Honey-buzzard, Short-toed Eagle, Hobby, Little Ringed Plover, Sand Martin, Yellow Wagtail, Tree Pipit, Whinchat.

Winter: Greylag and Brent Geese, Wigeon, Teal, Pintail, Shoveler, Eider, Common and Velvet Scoters, Red-breasted Merganser; Red-throated, Black-throated and Great Northern Divers; Great Crested, Red-necked,

Slavonian and Black-necked Grebes, Little and Great White Egrets, Grey Heron, Glossy Ibis (irregular), Spoonbill, Hen Harrier, Oystercatcher; Ringed, Grey and Golden Plovers, Lapwing, Knot, Dunlin, Common Snipe, Black-tailed and Bar-tailed Godwits, Curlew, Whimbrel, Common Redshank, Greenshank; Mediterranean, Black-headed, Common, Lesser Black-backed and Great Black-backed Gulls, Sandwich Tern, Razorbill, Guillemot, Snow Bunting (occasional), rarities.

Passage periods: Garganey, Osprey, Spoonbill, Avocet, Knot, Sanderling, Curlew Sandpiper, Purple Sandpiper, Black-tailed Godwit, Ruff, Whimbrel, Common and Spotted Redshanks, Greenshank, Turnstone; Caspian, Common, Little and Black Terns, Hoopoe, Wryneck, Golden Oriole, Red-backed Shrike, rarities.

OTHER SITES

CAN8 RÍAS DE TINA MAYOR AND TINA MENOR
These two small attractive estuaries are in the far west of Cantabria, bordering Asturias. They attract a good range of waders, passerines and very large flocks of gulls. Both may be visited via the Pechón coast road, which loops northwards from the N-634 at Unquera. The coast road is best followed westwards, where you will be on the same side as the various lay-bys. Tina Menor is more accessible and easily viewed from a lay-by at the eastern entrance/exit to the Pechón road. A viewpoint at km-2 gives elevated views of the Tina Menor entrance and the coast may be reached on foot from here.

The west side of Tina Mayor is reached by driving north from Unquera, passing under the A-8 motorway. Take the local road to El Curtido. This side has extensive reedbeds mixed with pastures. Breeding species here include Grasshopper, Great Reed and Reed Warblers and Red-backed Shrikes. Water Pipits, Rock Buntings and Reed Buntings occur in winter.

CAN9 NANSA VALLEY
A rugged and beautiful valley, well wooded with oak and beech, but little visited by tourists. Black Woodpeckers are present. From the main coast road (A-8) near Pesués, around km-270, take the CA-181 south to Puentenansa and continue into the mountains along the CA-281.

CAN10 SIERRA DEL HORNIJO

A limestone massif with world-famous caves. This is an area of limestone crags with some outstanding woods and pastures, good for raptors and woodland species. Leave the A-8 motorway at km-200 (Solares) and head for La Cavada on the CA-161 continuing to Arredondo on the CA-261 and on to Asón on the CA-265.

CAN11 ORIÑON ESTUARY

The beautiful estuary lies below the two limestone massifs of Candina and Cerreda. The whole area is worth exploring. Monte Candina to the western side of the estuary supports the only sea cliff Griffon Vulture colony in Spain. The estuary is in the far east of Cantabria off the A-8 coast road at km-160 next to the village of Oriñón.

CAN12 VALDERRIBLE

This area lies in southernmost Cantabria, some 25km south of the Embalse del Ebro (CAN3). It is adjacent to the Hoces del Ebro (CyL 17). The main attraction here, and in the adjacent sector of Burgos, Castilla y León, is the mix of Mediterranean and northern species. Take the A-67 south past Reinosa and take the km-122 exit (Polientes/Arroyal). Follow the CA-272 to the village of Polientes. North from here, a narrow local road climbs to the high pastures and oak woodlands at Salcedo (1,000m): breeding birds include Subalpine Warblers, Marsh Tits and Citril Finches. Also starting from Polientes it is worth ascending to the Páramo de La Lora plateau (1,100m). Take the road south to Rocamundo and continue beyond to Sargentes de La Lora (Burgos). The La Lora steppes were the northernmost limit of Dupont's Lark in Iberia but there are no recent records. However, breeding birds include Stone-curlews, Little Bustards, Montagu's Harriers, Great Spotted Cuckoos, Calandra and Greater Short-toed Larks, Tawny Pipits, Subalpine and Spectacled Warblers and Rock Sparrows.

CASTILLA–LA MANCHA

Main sites

CLM1   Upper Tiétar Valley
CLM2   Llanos de Oropesa
CLM3   Embalse de Azután
CLM4   Embalse de Castrejón
CLM5   Sierra de Ayllón
CLM6   Río Dulce
CLM7   Alto Tajo
CLM8   La Alcarria
CLM9   Serranía de Cuenca
CLM10 Lagunas de Ruidera
CLM11 Lagunas de La Mancha Húmeda
CLM12 Tablas de Daimiel
CLM13 Cabañeros
CLM14 Sierra de los Canalizos
CLM15 Valle de Alcudia
CLM16 Sierra Madrona

Other sites worth visiting

CLM17 Montes de Toledo
CLM18 Laguna de Pozuelo de Calatrava
CLM19 La Guardia/Tembleque/El Romeral
CLM20 Embalse de Almoguera
CLM21 Paramera de Maranchón, Embid y Molina
CLM22 Laguna de El Hito
CLM23 Llanos de Valdelobos
CLM24 Valeria, Guadazaón and Moya
CLM25 Hoces del Río Cabriel
CLM26 Llanos de Montiel
CLM27 Sierra de Alcázar y Alto Segura
CLM28 Hoces del Río Mundo y Río Segura
CLM29 Saladares de Cordovilla
CLM30 Llanos de Chincilla/Almansa
CLM31 Lagunas de Pétrola and Salobralejo

Castilla–La Mancha is a huge autonomous region, the third most extensive in Spain at nearly 80,000km², comprised by five large provinces: Toledo, Ciudad Real, Guadalajara, Cuenca and Albacete. Although enclosed and surrounded by mountains, the region is most famous for the huge plateau that covers much of the central part of this dry inland part of Spain: the 'sun-baked Arabic wilderness'. This, the most extensive plain in Spain, has changed much since the times of Miguel Cervantes, no longer wilderness but a landscape of castles, cereal fields, vines and the windmills that most visitors closely associate with Don Quixote and his companion Sancho Panza. The tourist agencies make the most of that connection and you will certainly pass the Ruta de Don Quixote, if indeed you are not on the road itself.

La Mancha is yet another part of Spain that is little visited by birders from the UK and northern Europe, most of whom favour the adjoining region of Extremadura. For those who do visit the region, the plains and the dehesas – the open grazing woodlands – are the focus of attention. Most of the steppe specialities: Great and Little Bustards, Black-bellied and Pin-tailed Sandgrouse, Stone-curlews, Montagu's Harriers and Quails are in evidence, as well as Calandra and Greater Short-toed Larks. Dupont's Larks also breed in La Mancha but they are scarce and more easily located in Aragón and the Ebro Valley. Although Little Bustards have declined in many parts of Spain they are still relatively common here. The plains also have a number of common breeding birds, such as Tree Sparrows and Corn Buntings, that now have a fragmented distribution in the UK and northern Europe.

Head westwards from Toledo and south-west past Ciudad Real and you encounter further steppe areas, but this time with a backdrop of low hills and Holm Oak (Encina) dehesa woodland. These areas should figure on any itin-erary, having many of the species that bring birders to Spain. In addition to the steppe species there are also Spanish Imperial Eagles, some of the largest Black Vulture colonies in Spain: such as at Cabañeros (CLM13) and the Sierra de los Canalizos (CLM14), Black Storks, Lesser Kestrels, Azure-winged Magpies, Black-shouldered Kites and Spanish Sparrows. These typical birds of Extremadura are widespread in western Castilla–La Mancha as well.

The area west of Toledo has the added attraction of river valleys, reservoirs and marshes with some large heron colonies, especially of Night Herons and Cattle Egrets, at the Valle del Tiétar (CLM1), Embalse de Azután (CLM3) and Embalse de Castrejón (CLM4). These wetlands also have a population of Purple Swamphens, which are continuing to expand their range in Spain. The general area also sees large concentrations of wintering Cranes, which spend their days foraging on the cereal fields or searching for acorns in the dehesa and then fly in the evenings to roost around the reservoirs. The reservoirs east of Madrid, such as the Embalse de Buendía (CLM8), are regular staging sites for Cranes on their way to and from winter quarters further west.

It is La Mancha Húmeda (CLM11), however, that is the focus of attention for wetland sites. The baking afternoon heat of the arid Castilian plains can get a little too much sometimes, even for the most avid birders, especially after spending a long and dusty morning searching for Great Bustards and Black-bellied Sandgrouse. This is the time to have a siesta and consider the next day's birding itinerary, perhaps by planning a visit to the wetlands and marshes along the Cigüela and Guadiana valleys. Large-scale water abstraction for irrigating crops means that the wetlands are nowhere near as extensive as they once

were. Nevertheless, this group of more than 100 seasonal lagoons is still potentially one of the most important wetlands in Spain and it still provides some
excellent birding opportunities. In addition to some more widespread species,
the wetland complex has one of the largest breeding populations of Black-
necked Grebes in Europe: up to 500 pairs may nest in wet years. It is also a
good area for breeding Red-crested Pochards, White-headed Ducks and Savi's
Warblers and, especially, for Bearded and Penduline Tits. Whiskered and Gull-
billed Terns breed in wet years, generally in small numbers. Marsh Harriers are
common and increasing. The lagoons are of interest throughout much of the
year although many are dry throughout the summer. Two of the best to visit
are the Laguna de Manjavacas and Laguna de Pedro Muñoz.

Part of La Mancha Húmeda, but physically separated from the majority
of the lagoons, are Las Tablas de Daimiel (CLM12): the most famous of all
wetlands in the region and a National Park: the smallest in Spain. Daimiel
has suffered grievously from water abstraction for irrigation but is still of great
importance for its breeding birds; which include Moustached Warblers, for
migrants and for wintering waterfowl.

Returning to the mountains, the wooded limestone ground to the east of
the region in the Serranía de Cuenca, the Tagus (Tajo) gorges and the sparsely
populated Sierra Morena in the south-west are all of interest. Griffon and
Egyptian Vultures, Golden and Bonelli's Eagles, Eagle Owls, Alpine Swifts,
Crag Martins and Rufous-tailed Rock Thrushes are all present.

UPPER TIÉTAR VALLEY (Toledo)   CLM1

*Status: Reserva Natural. ZEPA 'Valle del Tiétar y Embalses de Rosarito y
Navalcán' (53,167ha).*

Site description
The Río Tiétar here marks the border between Castilla–La Mancha and
Castilla y León, flowing west eventually to join the Río Tajo (Tagus) at
Monfragüe in Extremadura. The often snowy peaks of the Sierra de Gredos
(CyL8) form a spectacular backdrop to the north.

The river and its tributaries have been dammed to produce a series of
reservoirs, including the Embalses de Rosarito and Navalcán to the north
of Oropesa. The diverse valley habitats include excellent dehesas extending
towards Toledo as well as pastures, cereal croplands and expanses of
Mediterranean scrub. The river itself has quite steep banks in places and Alder
and willow woods along some tracts. The protected area includes the Sierra
de San Vicente to the east. The sites considered here are immediately north of
the Llanos de Oropesa (CLM2).

Species
This diversity of habitats provides an opportunity to see a long and varied
list of species in a day's birding at any time of year. Breeding raptors include
several pairs of Black-shouldered Kites. Griffon and Black Vultures are often
overhead. Short-toed and Booted Eagles breed and both Bonelli's and Spanish

Imperial Eagles have a foothold in the area. Both Black and Red Kites breed and large numbers of the latter are present in winter. Black and White Storks breed and both species form post-breeding accumulations at the reservoirs, with some individuals remaining to winter.

The reservoirs attract numbers of wintering waterfowl: including Wigeon, Pintail, Shoveler and Common Pochards and roosting Lesser Black-backed and Black-headed Gulls, but also support a range of breeding aquatic species including Cormorants at the Embalse de Navalcán: one of the pioneer Spanish colonies of this rapidly increasing species. Little Terns and a few pairs of Night Herons breed and Ospreys occur regularly on passage. Baillon's Crakes have been reported in the valley and may breed. Bee-eaters certainly do so, excavating their nests in the riverbanks. The riparian woodlands offer breeding Golden Orioles and Melodious Warblers.

The dehesas have a conspicuous population of Azure-winged Magpies among a wide range of breeding passerines, including Orphean and Subalpine Warblers, Crested Tits and Rock Sparrows. Several thousand Cranes winter in the area and forage for acorns in the dehesas. Red-necked Nightjars breed locally in pinewoods.

Stone-curlews and Little Bustards breed in the open country and Great Bustards and Black-bellied Sandgrouse occur at least occasionally, chiefly in winter, when large flocks of Lapwings and Golden Plovers are also present. Spanish Sparrows are common.

Resident mammals include Otters and Wild Cats.

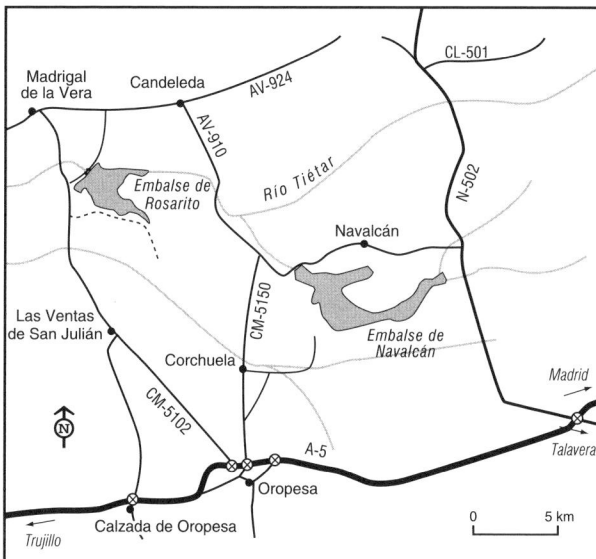

Timing

The area is always interesting but birds are most numerous in winter (November–February) which is a good time for raptors, Cranes, and waterfowl. The Rosarito reservoir can be very popular with visitors in summer and at weekends, when disturbance may be a problem.

Access

Leave the A-5 Madrid/Extremadura motorway at Oropesa. The two roads running north from here are both interesting and can be visited on a circular route via Candeleda.

The CM-5150 crosses open country to Corchuela, where minor roads provide worthwhile access to riverine woodland and the dehesas east of the village: a eucalyptus clump on the west side of the CM-5150 2km south of Corchuela is a traditional Red Kite winter roost site. Continue north to reach the Embalse de Navalcán, turning right to view the reservoir from the dam and its environs. Return to the main road and continue north through the dehesas, crossing the Río Tiétar and on to Candeleda. Turn west here and follow the AV-924/CL-501 for 7km towards Madrigal de La Vera, before turning south towards the Embalse de Rosarito. The reservoir may be viewed from the dam and also from tracks leading to the west and southern shores from the CM-5102. The pinewoods north of the dam have breeding Red-necked Nightjars.

The CM-5102 south of the Rosarito reservoir passes through areas of open country which hold steppe species and other farmland birds. The better areas are south of Las Ventas de San Julián, both along the CM-5102 and along the minor road heading south from that village to Calzada de Oropesa.

Eastern parts of the area can be explored by taking a variety of roads northwards from Talavera de la Reina. Alternatively, take the CL-501, a minor road which follows the route of the river through the foothills of the southern slopes of the Sierra de Gredos (CyL8) in Castilla y León: a diversion into these mountains is recommended for another day.

CALENDAR

All year: Gadwall, Mallard, Great Crested and Little Grebes, Cormorant, Cattle Egret, Grey Heron, Black-shouldered and Red Kites, Griffon and Black Vultures, Goshawk, Spanish Imperial and Bonelli's Eagles, Little Bustard, Stone-curlew, Eagle and Long-eared Owls, Hoopoe, Lesser Spotted Woodpecker, Crag Martin, Dartford Warbler, Firecrest, Crested Tit, Azure-winged Magpie, Spanish and Rock Sparrows, Cirl Bunting.

Breeding season: Night Heron, Little Egret, Black Stork, White Stork, Honey-buzzard, Black Kite, Egyptian Vulture, Short-toed and Booted Eagles, Montagu's Harrier, Hobby, Baillon's Crake, Black-winged Stilt, Common Sandpiper, Little Ringed Plover, Little Tern, Great Spotted Cuckoo, Red-necked Nightjar, Bee-eater, Roller, Melodious, Subalpine, Orphean and Bonelli's Warblers, Woodchat Shrike, Golden Oriole.

Winter: Greylag Goose, Wigeon, Teal, Pintail, Shoveler, Common Pochard, Hen Harrier, Merlin, Crane, Great Bustard, Golden Plover, Lapwing, Snipe, Lesser Black-backed and Black-headed Gulls, Black-bellied Sandgrouse, Water Pipit, Rock Bunting.

Passage periods: Purple Heron, Spoonbill, Osprey, waders, Black Tern.

LLANOS DE OROPESA (Toledo)   CLM2

Status: Reserva Nacional de Caza (44,000ha). Includes ZEPA 'Llanuras de Oropesa, Lagartera y Calera y Chozas' (14,948ha).

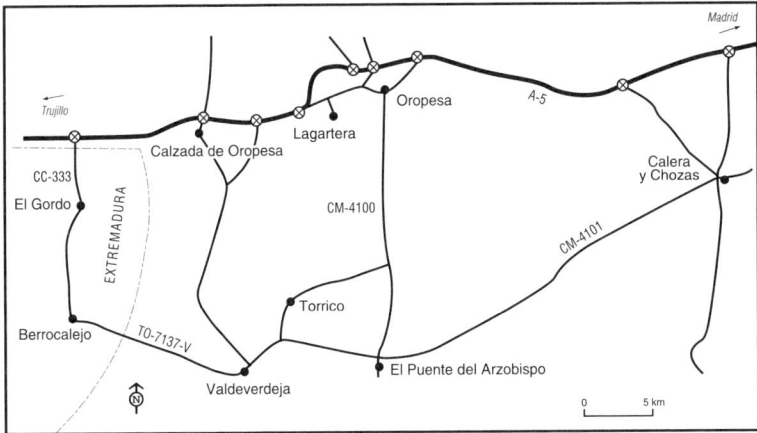

Site description
The sparsely populated plains of the Tajo Valley west of Talavera de la Reina are largely devoted to cereal crops and pasture but also offer large and important expanses of mature dehesas of Encinas and Cork Oaks. Parts of the area frequently flood in winter.

Species
The plains are of great ornithological significance because of their steppe bird community. Little Bustards are relatively numerous and other characteristic birds include Great Bustards, Black-bellied Sandgrouse and Stone-curlews. Calandra, Short-toed and Thekla Larks enliven the pastures. Montagu's Harriers have a good breeding population: as usual they are replaced by Hen Harriers in winter. White Storks and Lesser Kestrels nest in the towns and villages: the 14th-century castle that houses the Parador at Oropesa accommodates a well-known Lesser Kestrel colony. Griffon and Black Vultures are often overhead and Red Kites are frequent in winter. Characteristic inhabitants of the dehesas include Black Storks, Short-toed and Booted Eagles, Great

Lesser Kestrels

Spotted Cuckoos and Azure-winged Magpies. Cranes often feed in the dehesas in winter, roosting at nearby reservoirs.

Depending on the amount of winter rain, small seasonally flooded areas can occur scattered throughout the plain and attract many species. Some hold concentrations of waders, including large numbers of Golden Plovers and Lapwings.

Timing
The steppe and dehesa birds provide year-round interest. As ever the activity of nesting birds makes spring visits particularly rewarding but there is plenty to see in winter.

Access
Leave the A-5 Madrid/Extremadura motorway at Oropesa. The sector of the plains lying north of the motorway is described in CLM1. Much of the area is privately owned farmland but the quieter roads and the many tracks provide ample opportunities to view the main habitats.

A good circular route to take is the CM-4100 south from Oropesa crossing the dehesas to El Puente del Arzobispo, where you turn left along the CM-4101 through open country to Calera y Chozas, returning to the A-5 via the minor road heading north-west from the latter town. An alternative longer loop follows the A-5 west from Oropesa for 23km, leaving the motorway southwards on the CC-333 to El Gordo, passing through good steppeland. Continue south to Berrocalejo and then east to El Puente del Arzobispo and on to Calera y Chozas.

CALENDAR

All year: Cattle Egret, Black Stork, Black-shouldered Kite, Black and Griffon Vultures, Spanish Imperial Eagle, Little and Great Bustards, Stone-curlew, Black-bellied Sandgrouse, Barn and Little Owls; Calandra, Crested and Thekla Larks, Dartford Warbler, Southern Grey Shrike, Azure-winged Magpie, Raven, Spotless Starling, Spanish Sparrow.

Breeding season: White Stork, Egyptian Vulture, Short-toed and Booted Eagles,

Montagu's Harrier, Lesser Kestrel, Hobby, Turtle Dove, Great Spotted and Common Cuckoos, Red-necked Nightjar, Bee-eater, Roller, Hoopoe, Greater Short-toed Lark, Red-rumped Swallow, Black-eared Wheatear, Spotted Flycatcher, Woodchat Shrike.

Winter: Cormorant, Red Kite, Hen Harrier, Merlin, Lapwing, Golden Plover, Short-eared Owl, Fieldfare.

EMBALSE DE AZUTÁN (Toledo)   CLM3

Status: Reserva Nacional de Caza. Part of the ZEPA 'Río Tajo en Castrejón, Islas de Malpica de Tajo y Azután' (1,960ha).

Site description
The stretch of the Río Tajo (Tagus) between Talavera de la Reina and El Puente del Arzobispo was dammed in 1969 to form the sinuous Azután reser-

voir. The lake margins have developed good marshland, with some significant reedbeds and sedgebeds. There are also some important riverside woods, including a juniper wood, the 'Enebrales de Talavera', and stretches of riparian tamarisks, willows and poplars. Wooded islands in the lake are important for roosting and nesting waterbirds.

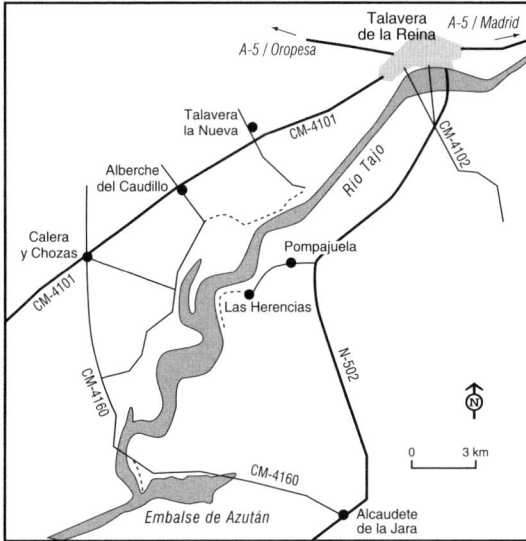

Species

The reservoir islands in the central sector, west of Las Herencias, support a mixed heronry with around 100 pairs of Night Herons and over 2,000 pairs of Cattle Egrets, as well as some Little Egrets, Grey Herons and Little Bitterns. Purple Herons, Purple Swamphens and both Reed and Great Reed Warblers nest in the marshes and both Great Bitterns and Spoonbills have nested here. The Great White Egret first nested in 2009. Red Avadavats occur increasingly frequently. Marsh Harriers breed and may often be seen quartering the marshes and surrounding farmland all year round. The riparian vegetation has breeding Penduline Tits and Scops Owls. Ospreys occur on passage and often in winter. Large numbers of Cormorants and Cattle Egrets roost at the reservoir in winter. A diversity of waterfowl also use the reservoir in winter especially.

Timing

The reservoir is of interest all year round but heat haze can be a problem in summer. The heronry is used throughout the year by breeding and roosting birds.

Access

Leave the A-5 Madrid/Extremadura motorway at Talavera and turn south at the town on to the N-502. That part of the reservoir closest to Talavera itself has well-developed fringing vegetation, bankside trees and wooded islands with heron colonies, including one close to the old bridge in the town.

Continue south for 9km on the N-502 and turn right on to a minor road to Las Herencias. From here you can continue on foot to the lake margins for elevated views over the reservoir and the heronries. Continue southwards on the N-502 to Alcaudete de la Jara and take the CM-4160 westwards. This road passes close to another arm of the reservoir, with well-vegetated margins, and crosses the Tajo on a bridge, the Puente de Silos, from where good views are also available. The road linking Alberche del Caudillo to the CM-4160 offers access to the western side of the reservoir.

CALENDAR

All year: Gadwall, Mallard, Cattle Egret, Grey Heron, Marsh Harrier, Water Rail, Purple Swamphen, Stone-curlew, Cetti's Warbler, Zitting Cisticola, Penduline Tit,

Breeding season: Little Bittern, Night and Purple Herons, Little and Great White Egrets, White Stork, Scops Owl, Roller, Sand Martin, Nightingale; Savi's, Reed, Great Reed and Melodious Warblers, Woodchat Shrike, Golden Oriole.

Winter: Greylag Goose, Wigeon, Pintail, Shoveler, Great Crested Grebe, Cormorant, Snipe, Black-headed and Lesser Black-backed Gulls.

Passage periods: Osprey, Crane, Black-winged Stilt, Avocet, Ruff, Black-tailed Godwit, Wood Sandpiper, Reed Bunting.

EMBALSE DE CASTREJÓN (Toledo)   CLM4

Status: Reserva Natural (1,900ha). Part of the ZEPA 'Río Tajo en Castrejón, Islas de Malpica de Tajo y Azután'.

Site description
This medium-sized reservoir lies on the Río Tajo some 25km downstream from the city of Toledo, providing water for irrigating much of the adjoining farmland, although there remain good areas of pasture and steppe vegetation to the north. The river winds through a series of old alluvial riverine meanders between steep sandstone banks, especially around the northern loop: an area of cliffs known as 'Las Barrancas'. The margins have areas of marshland and riparian woodland. There are several small islands within the reservoir.

Species
The reservoir has a breeding colony of around 100 pairs of Night Herons, 75 pairs of Cattle Egrets and small numbers of Little Egrets. Purple Herons and Purple Swamphens and Bearded Tits also breed here. Cormorants and a diversity of waterfowl occur in winter, these last sometimes in large numbers. The reservoir is used on passage by a range of waders including Avocets. The water-side passerines include Savi's, Reed and Great Reed Warblers and Penduline Tits. The surrounding area hosts a diversity of breeding and wintering raptors,

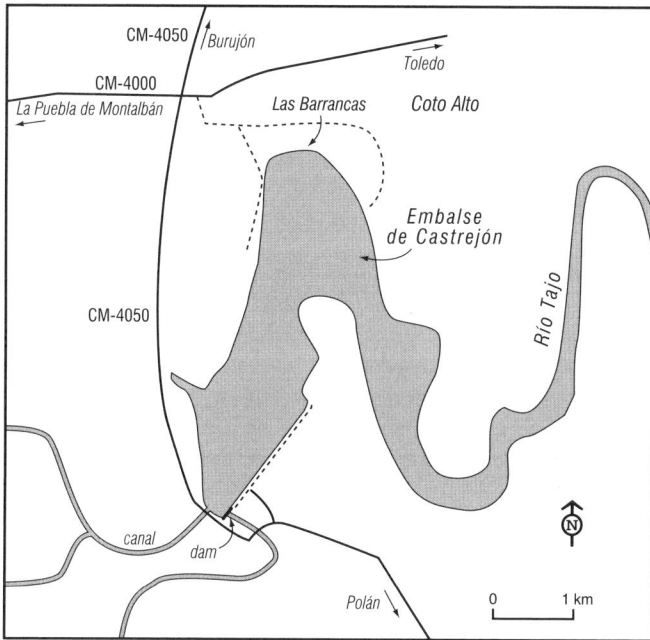

the former including Short-toed, Booted and Bonelli's Eagles, Peregrines and also Eagle Owls. Lesser Kestrels frequently hunt throughout the area. The dry farmlands support a diversity of steppe birds, including Little and Great Bustards, Stone-curlews, Black-bellied Sandgrouse and Calandra Larks.

Timing

Interesting species are present all year round but summer temperatures can be uncomfortably high.

Night Heron

Access

Take the CM-4000 west from Toledo towards La Puebla de Montalbán. Turn left (south) at km-166 on to the track leading to Las Barrancas. The track crosses cereal fields and pastures where you may find Little Bustards, Stone-curlews and Black-bellied Sandgrouse. Good views are available across the reservoir from the cliffs and from the tracks skirting the northern margins.

Return to the main road and take the CM-4050 south to the dam and the bridge beyond, from where a track leads to the lakeshore and footpaths permit further access to the lake margin.

It is also worth exploring to the north of the CM-4000 and the mapped area, where the pastures offer further opportunities to find steppe species. Take the CM-4050 north to Burujón and Gerindote, returning to the CM-4000 16km west of Toledo via Albarreal de Tajo.

CALENDAR

All year: Cattle Egret, Grey Heron, Marsh Harrier, Bonelli's Eagle, Water Rail, Purple Swamphen, Great and Little Bustards, Stone-curlew, Black-bellied Sandgrouse, Eagle Owl, Calandra and Crested Larks, Blue Rock Thrush, Cetti's Warbler, Zitting Cisticola, Bearded and Penduline Tits, Southern Grey Shrike, Raven, Spotless Starling, Spanish Sparrow, Red Avadavat.

Breeding season: Night and Purple Herons, Little Egret, Montagu's Harrier, Short-toed and Booted Eagles, Lesser Kestrel, Great Spotted Cuckoo, Bee-eater, Roller, Greater

Short-toed Lark, Red-rumped Swallow, Nightingale; Savi's, Reed and Great Reed Warblers, Woodchat Shrike.

Winter: Greylag Goose, Wigeon, Teal, Mallard, Common Pochard, Tufted Duck, Cormorant, Lesser Black-backed Gull, Short-eared Owl, Meadow Pipit.

Passage periods: Osprey, Black-winged Stilt, Avocet, Golden Plover, Lapwing, Little Stint, Sand Martin, Yellow Wagtail, Spotted Flycatcher.

SIERRA DE AYLLÓN   CLM5
(Guadalajara, Segovia, Madrid)

Status: ZEPA (91,537ha): including, in part, the Parque Natural 'Sierra Norte de Guadalajara, Hayedo de Tejera Negra' (125,772ha).

Site description

The Sierra de Ayllón lies well south of the medieval walled city of Ayllón (Castilla y León). This massif, at the eastern end of the Sistema Central mountain range, lies in the far north of Castilla–La Mancha and rises to 2,270m at its highest point, Pico del Lobo. It is really an eastward extension of the Sierra de Guadarrama (M1). The mountains are very eroded in places, offering cliffs and gorges, for example those along the Ríos Tiermes and Caracena in the north-east of the area. Spectacular waterfalls are common, especially around Valverde de los Arroyos. Small Holm Oak woodlands are characteristic along with extensive pine plantations. The uplands have juniper woods. The area

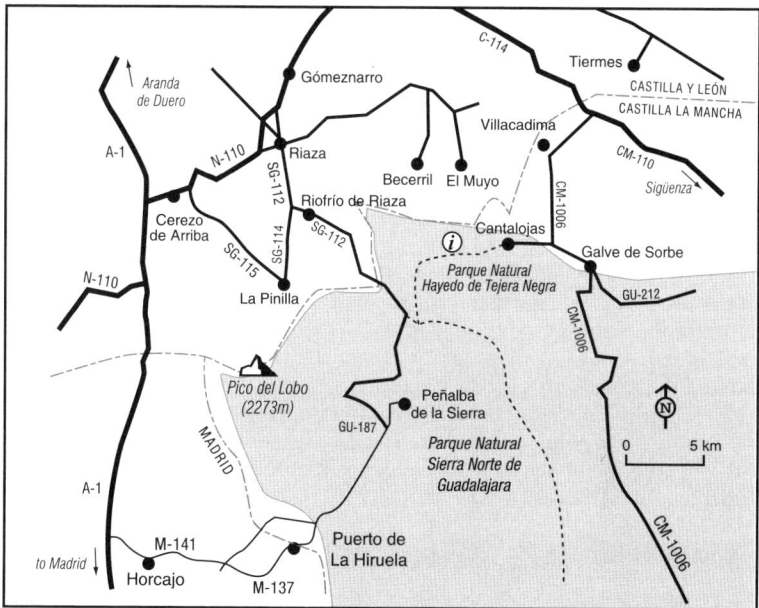

also has some of the southernmost beechwoods (*hayedos*) in Europe, the one at Tejera Negra being especially important, although there are others in the same range: the Hayedo de Puerto de la Quesera and the Hayedo de Montejo de la Sierra. Large tracts are covered with *Cistus* scrub. The area is sparsely populated, with many abandoned small villages and a limited amount of livestock grazing.

Species

Breeding raptors in the sierra include Honey-buzzards; Short-toed, Booted, Bonelli's Eagles and Golden Eagles, Peregrine Falcons and Eagle Owls. Red Kites and Goshawks frequent the beech forests. The riparian gorges east of Ayllón are important for Griffon and Egyptian Vultures. Montane passerines include Water Pipits, Bluethroats and Rufous-tailed Rock Thrushes.

Roe Deer, Wild Boars, Beech Martens and Otters are present and Wolves have recolonised the area. The Pyrenean Desman is thought to occur.

Timing

Visits are worthwhile throughout the year but spring is best. The high tops can be among the coldest places in Spain during the winter but the lower slopes are relatively mild.

Access

The best part of the park is at the junction of three regions, Castilla–La Mancha, Castilla y León and Madrid, although the eastern side is quite difficult to reach, and some areas have only forest tracks. Take the A-1 north out of Madrid and turn east at km-85 on to the M-141, continuing past Horcajo de La Sierra to the M-137 which leads to the Puerto de La Hiruela (1,477m) and beyond into the southern foothills.

Other options include turning right off the A-1 at km-104 on to the N-110 towards El Burgo de Osma. Turn right again after 12km to Riaza and follow the SG-112 towards Riofrío and the Hayedo de Tejera Negra. La Pinilla, at the foot of Pico del Lobo, where skiing takes place in the winter, is also approached via Riaza.

The beechwood of Tejera Negra can also be approached from the east via the village of Cantalojas 3km west from the CM-1006. A forest road leads from Cantalojas some 12km from the village: this can be impassable after heavy rain or snow. There is a car park and an information centre immediately before the beechwood.

The river valleys and gorges of the Ríos Tiermes and Carcena, to the north of the mapped area, should also be explored. If travelling north on the N-110 continue for 4km past the turning to Ayllón and take the SO-135 on the right to Torraño, Cuevas, Liceras and Montejo de Tiermes. From here you can explore the gorges of the Río Caracena, a tributary of the Duero, between Hoz de Arriba and Hoz de Abajo. Another option is 6km east of Montejo de Tiermes, at a gorge on the Río Tiermes, where there is an easily viewed Griffon Vulture colony close to the car park at the ruins of the pre-Roman settlement of Termancia.

CALENDAR

All year: Red Kite, Griffon Vulture, Goshawk, Common Buzzard, Golden and Bonelli's Eagles, Peregrine Falcon, Eagle and Long-eared Owls, Black Wheatear, Blue Rock Thrush, Crested Tit, Southern Grey Shrike, Red-billed Chough, Rock Sparrow, Rock Bunting.

Breeding season: White Stork, Honey-buzzard, Black Kite, Egyptian Vulture, Short-toed and Booted Eagles, Hoopoe, Red-rumped Swallow, Tree and Water Pipits, Bluethroat, Common Redstart, Black-eared Wheatear, Rufous-tailed Rock Thrush, Melodious and Bonelli's Warblers, Red-backed and Woodchat Shrikes, Ortolan Bunting.

Winter: Black Vulture, Spanish Imperial Eagle, Alpine Accentor.

Passage periods: Ring Ouzel.

BARRANCO DEL RÍO DULCE   CLM6 (Guadalajara)

Status: ZEPA 'Barranco del Río Dulce' (6,361ha) and Parque Natural (8,348ha).

Site description
From its source in the Sierra Ministra, the Río Dulce has cut its way through limestone rocks over the centuries to produce a series of spectacular ravines and gorges. The walls of the gorges vary considerably in height and oak and juniper woodland has become established where the cliff and valley sides are less steep. From time to time the valley opens out into cultivated land, with occasional belts of riverine woodland on the banks. The river and its gorges, the bankside

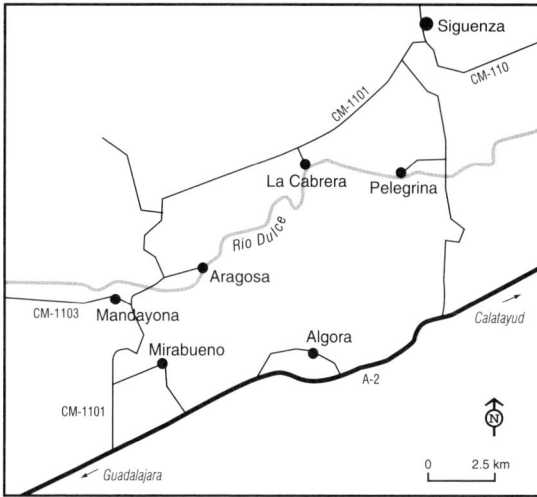

woodland, the mixed land use and varied vegetation cover provide a considerable diversity of habitats.

Species

The focus of interest is the gorge areas. Griffon and Egyptian Vultures, Bonelli's Eagles and Peregrine Falcons all breed here. However, there is also much to explore elsewhere along the valley. The bankside woodlands have breeding Goshawks, Common Buzzards and Golden Orioles and the open valley bottoms and mosaic of cultivated areas are likely to produce Quails, Southern Grey and Woodchat Shrikes, Common Cuckoos and Black-eared Wheatears. Dippers and Grey Wagtails occur on the river itself.

Wild cats, Otters and the rare Pyrenean Desman are all present.

Timing

Late spring and early summer are the best times to visit.

Access

The gorges are north of the A-2 about 50km north-east of Guadalajara. Turn towards Sigüenza at km-104 on to the CM-1101. The gorge and river are to the right of this road and can be reached most easily by taking one of a number of right turns to one of the villages along the valley: Aragosa (after 9km), La Cabrera or Pelegrina. An 11km riverside trail links all three villages.

CALENDAR

All year: Griffon Vulture, Goshawk, Common Buzzard, Golden and Bonelli's Eagles, Peregrine Falcon, Barn Owl, Kingfisher, Green Woodpecker, Grey Wagtail, Dipper, Blue Rock Thrush, Southern Grey Shrike, Red-billed Chough, Rock Sparrow, Cirl and Rock Buntings.

Breeding season: Egyptian Vulture, Quail, Common Cuckoo, Alpine Swift, Crag and House Martins, Nightingale, Black-eared Wheatear, Melodious Warbler, Woodchat Shrike, Golden Oriole.

ALTO TAJO (Guadalajara)   CLM7

Status: Parque Natural (174,545ha) and ZEPA 'Alto Tajo' (125,285ha).

Site description

The Alto Tajo is a huge and sparsely populated area. The distance from most towns, along with limited access has been the area's main protection, until its designation as a natural park named after the headwaters of the Tajo (Tagus), the longest river in the Iberian Peninsula. The Río Tajo and its tributaries pass through a stunning landscape of gorges, pine forests and juniper woods. The deep gorges with their high cliffs, carved by the waters of the Tajo, are some 80km long. Where the sides are less steep, the slopes are covered by pinewoods mixed in with stands of oak and some scrub maquis, but there is little true riverside woodland.

This was the ancient route of the 'gancheros' or loggers who until the 1950s rode their pine logs down the river, sometimes as far as Aranjuez. The loggers have now been replaced by canoeists and this 'wild river of Iberia', as it is known in canoeing circles, is now famous throughout Europe as a venue for this sport.

Species

The gorges are very important for cliff-nesting birds, particularly Griffon and Egyptian Vultures and Golden Eagles as well as several pairs of Bonelli's Eagles and Eagle Owls, together with Red-billed Choughs, Ravens, Jackdaws and Crag Martins. The high level pinewoods have Citril Finches and the fruiting junipers attract Ring Ouzels and other thrushes in winter.

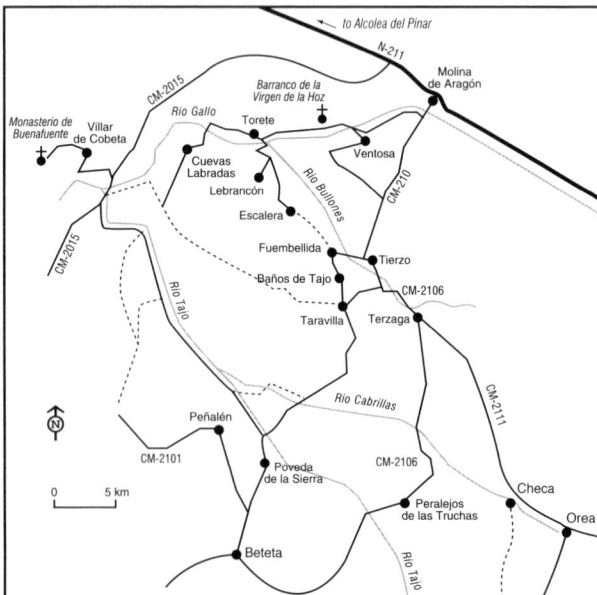

Mammals include Wild Boars, Otters, Genets, Beech Martens and Pyrenean Desmans.

Timing

Late spring and early summer are the best times to visit.

Access

Molina de Aragón on the N-211 north-east of the Parque Natural is a natural point of entry. The tourist office in the town (Tel. 949 832 098, open five days a week) has details of recommended walking and other routes in the park. A number of roads cross the rivers and gorges in the park, providing good views. From Molina take the CM-210 southwards towards Taravilla and Poveda de la Sierra. After passing over the Río Tajo there is a good dirt road on the right that follows the river for 20km up to the next main crossing point on the CM-2015. There are ample opportunities to stop and view rupestral and forest birds.

Another possibility is to explore the gorge over the River Gallo at Barranco de la Virgen de la Hoz, 12km west from Molina. The monastery that gives its name to this particular gorge is perched at the summit from where there are superb views over the surrounding countryside.

Peralejos de las Truchas is a good place to start exploration of the southern part of the area. From Molina take the CM-210 and CM-2111 south towards Terzaga and the CM-2106 to Peralejos. Access to the upper reaches (parameras) of the park, with their pine and juniper woods and montane passerines, is readily available along a 27km triangular route taking a dirt road south of the CM-2111 at Checa and returning to the CM-2111 on a tarmac road to Orea.

CALENDAR

All year: Griffon Vulture, Goshawk, Sparrowhawk, Common Buzzard, Golden and Bonelli's Eagles, Peregrine Falcon, Eagle and Tawny Owls, Hoopoe, Grey Wagtail, Dipper, Dartford Warbler, Common Chiffchaff, Crested Tit, Short-toed Treecreeper, Southern Grey Shrike, Jay, Red-billed Chough, Raven, Rock Sparrow, Citril Finch, Common Crossbill, Cirl and Rock Buntings.

Breeding season: Black Kite, Booted and Short-toed Eagles, Egyptian Vulture, Hobby, Bee-eater, Crag Martin, Northern Wheatear, Reed and Subalpine Warblers, Ortolan Bunting.

Winter: Alpine Accentor, Ring Ouzel, Fieldfare, Redwing.

LA ALCARRIA   CLM8
(Guadalajara/Cuenca)

Status: ZEPA 'Sierra de Altomira' (29,018ha).

Site description

The region of La Alcarria rises up to around 1,200m and is crossed by the Tajo and Guadiela rivers. There are numerous limestone cliffs along with dense areas of mixed oak scrub and pinewoods. Some of the plateau areas are now under cereal crops. There is also riverside woodland in the valley bottoms. The Río Tajo has reed margins as well as poplar and elm riverine woodlands in the valley bottoms, and a number of reservoirs. The Alcocén pinewoods, above the Entrepeñas reservoir, are the only remaining Mediterranean pines in Guadalajara.

The Tajo and Guadiela rivers were dammed in the 1960s to create a number of reservoirs, the two largest being the Embalses de Entrepeñas and de Buendía. Several other smaller reservoirs were also created further down the valley, including the one at Bolarque.

Buendía reservoir, on the Guadiela just upstream of its confluence with the Tajo, flooded a large area of this part of La Alcarria. Although many rich riverine habitats were lost, fortunately thousands of wildfowl have found the wetland attractive and now winter here.

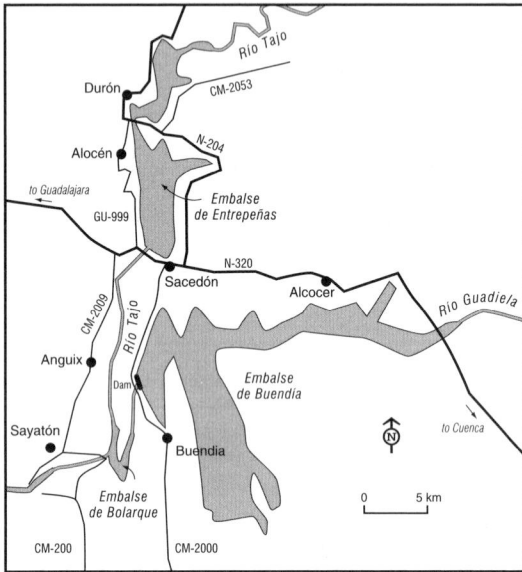

Species

The area is renowned for many breeding birds of prey, particularly cliff-nesters such as Golden and Bonelli's Eagles, Peregrine Falcons and Eagle Owls, and also Crag Martins, Red-billed Choughs and other species of rocky habitats.

Buendía reservoir is an important feeding and roosting site for Common Cranes and is used by thousands on migration. Moustached Warblers have nested here. It is strategically located between the Laguna de Gallocanta (AR15) in Aragón and the main Crane wintering areas in Extremadura and Castilla–La Mancha.

Timing

Spring visits are recommended for birds of prey and other breeding species. November is best for passage of Common Cranes and November–February for wintering wildfowl.

Access

Take the N-320 out of Guadalajara towards Cuenca until you reach Sacedón, which is in the heart of the area. Take the CM-2000 south from Sacedón to the dam of the Embalse de Buendía, from where good views of the lake are available. You can also scan the surrounding countryside for raptors from here. The Embalse de Entrepeñas, immediately north of Sacedón, is also worth inspecting for waterfowl in winter. Another worthwhile reservoir, the Embalse de Bolarque, can be reached by taking the CM-2009 turning off the N-320 towards Sayatón.

CALENDAR

All year: Great Crested Grebe, Marsh Harrier, Common Buzzard, Golden and Bonelli's Eagles, Peregrine Falcon, Eagle Owl, Thekla Lark, Crag Martin, Blue Rock Thrush, Cetti's and Dartford Warblers, Red-billed Chough, Rock Sparrow, Serin, Linnet, Rock Bunting.

Breeding season: Little Ringed Plover, Alpine Swift, Bee-eater, Nightingale, Black-eared Wheatear, Subalpine and Orphean Warblers, Woodchat Shrike, Golden Oriole.

Winter: Wigeon, Pintail, Red-crested Pochard, Common Pochard, Tufted Duck, Cormorant, Grey Heron, Alpine Accentor, Wallcreeper.

Passage periods: Crane, Osprey, Avocet, Black-winged Stilt, Sand Martin.

SERRANÍA DE CUENCA (Cuenca)   CLM9

Status: ZEPA 'Serranía de Cuenca' (128,345ha) and Parque Natural (73,726 ha). Includes the Monumento Natural 'Ciudad Encantada' (250ha).

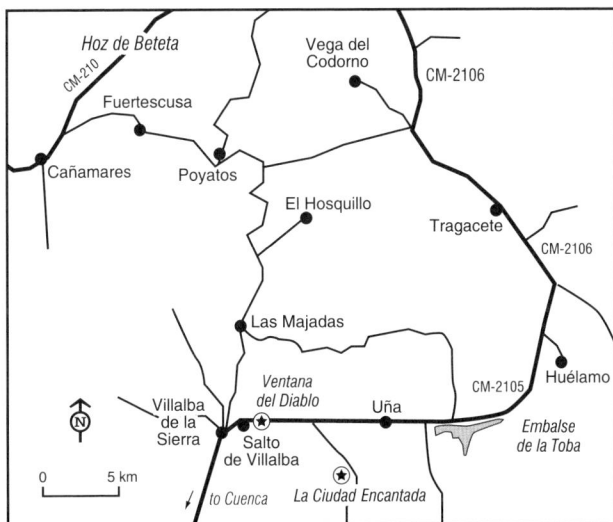

Site description

The peaks of the Serranía de Cuenca, a chain of mountains occupying the north-east corner of Cuenca province, rise high above the headwaters of the Río Tajo. The highest summit is the Cerro de San Felipe (1,839m) near Tragacete. The hills and rocky cliffs are full of surprises with hot springs, caves, cliff-hanging villages and an 'enchanted city', the Ciudad Encantada, a strange limestone landscape where huge rocks have acquired curious mushroom-like forms through erosion.

Much of the ground is covered by pine forests and juniper woods and it is one of the most important wooded limestone areas in Spain. The hills are crossed by three major rivers: the Ríos Cuervo and Escabas, which flow into the Tajo, and the Río Júcar, which flows into the Mediterranean in Valencia and whose upper reaches go through one of the least spoiled parts of the Serranía de Cuenca.

Species

The region is very important for raptors, including Griffon and Egyptian Vultures; Short-toed, Golden, Booted and Bonelli's Eagles, Peregrine Falcons and Eagle Owls. Citril Finches, Crossbills and sometimes Siskins breed in the pinewoods. The juniper woods attract Ring Ouzels and other thrushes in winter. The area is also rich in orchids and butterflies.

Timing

Late spring and early summer visits are best.

Access

The mountains lie east of Madrid and can be approached from a number of directions including from Guadalajara, Priego, Molina de Aragón and Cuenca.

Many of the paths traversing the Serranía are not marked but access is relatively easy, particularly through the pine forests. For views across the River Júcar and its gorges take the CM-2105 out of Cuenca through Salto de Villalba, Uña and Huélamo to Tragacete. Along this road, a popular spectacular viewpoint, towering over the 100m deep Júcar Gorge, is the Ventana del Diablo about 23km north of Cuenca. For the less-visited parts turn left at Villalba de la Sierra. In a triangle between Las Majadas, Fuertescusa and Vega del Codorno, the Escabas river crosses country of remarkable beauty and this is one of the most productive areas for vultures and birds of prey. Numerous forest tracks cross the pinewoods of these hills and they are generally in good condition except after heavy rains.

Other sites worth visiting, but not specifically for birds, are the rock formations of the Ciudad Encantada, north of Cuenca and, to the east and south of Cuenca, the geological formations known as torcas: natural depressions often containing water, found for example at Palancares and Cañada del Hoyo.

CALENDAR

All year: Griffon Vulture; Booted, Golden and Bonelli's Eagles, Peregrine Falcon, Great Spotted Woodpecker, Blue Rock Thrush, Crested and Coal Tits, Nuthatch, Southern Grey Shrike, Red-billed Chough, Raven, Rock Sparrow, Serin, Citril Finch, Crossbill, Cirl Bunting.

Breeding season: Egyptian Vulture, Alpine Swift, Crag Martin, Barn Swallow, Common Redstart, Northern Wheatear, Rufous-tailed Rock Thrush, Bonelli's Warbler, Siskin.

Winter: Ring Ouzel, Fieldfare, Redwing, Goldcrest.

LAGUNAS DE RUIDERA   CLM10
(Ciudad Real/Albacete)

Status: Part of 'La Mancha Húmeda' Biosphere Reserve. Parque Natural (3,772ha).

Site description

An unusual series of interconnected lagoons mentioned by Cervantes in the novel *Don Quixote*. Ruidera comes from the Spanish for noise (*ruido*), and the village and lakes were perhaps named after the sound made by the water running from lake to lake. They are separated from each other by natural barriers but occasionally linked by spectacular waterfalls.

The difference in altitude from the uppermost lake to the bottom is some 25m. The lakes comprise the Lagunas Cenagosa, Coladilla, Cueva Morenilla, Del Rey, Colgada, Batana, Santo Morcillo, Salvadora, Lengua (one of the deepest), Redondilla, San Pedro, Tinaja, Tomilla and Conceja. The Embalse de Peñarroya, whilst not a natural lake, is sometimes regarded as part of the system. The two largest natural lakes, the Lagunas Del Rey and Colgada, are not far from the sleepy village of Ruidera. The protected area also includes the tributary valley of San Pedro and the cave of Montesinos.

The lagoons are permanent although vulnerable to excessive water abstraction, being fed by underground springs. Many are reed-fringed and so provide cover for waterfowl, rails and herons. The surroundings are chiefly scrub, with occasional poplars, Holm Oaks and Black Pines.

Species

The main interest focuses on the lakes, which offer breeding Water Rails, Marsh Harriers, Red-crested Pochards and Bearded Tits, among others, as well as herons and Ospreys on passage. The immediate surroundings are rich in typical Mediterranean species including Bee-eater, Roller and Southern Grey Shrike.

Timing

Spring is the best season, although there is some interest all year round.

Access

From Ciudad Real take the A-43 or N-430 eastwards via Daimiel to Manzanares (59km) and then the N-430 to Ruidera (55km). Most of the lagoons are south of Ruidera, although there are some to the north including the Embalse de Peñarroya. The road south from Ruidera follows the lagoons and gradually ascends from one lake to the next. Several small lakes: the Lagunas Batana, Santo Morcillo and Salvadora, are followed by Laguna Lengua: which is very popular with fishermen. This lagoon is fed by small waterfalls that pour into it from the next lake, Laguna Redondilla. This in turn receives water from Laguna San Pedro whose shores are partly developed with houses and plant nurseries. The highest and least visited lake, Laguna Conceja, has a marshy shoreline and wooded surrounding hills and is worth exploring.

An information centre in Ruidera (Tel. 926 528 116) is open daily in summer and Wednesday–Sunday in winter. There are various nature trails in the park.

CALENDAR

All year: Northern Shoveler, Red-crested and Common Pochards, Little and Great Crested Grebes, Marsh Harrier, Common Buzzard, Common Kestrel, Water Rail, Little Owl, Kingfisher, Grey Wagtail, Cetti's Warbler, Bearded Tit, Southern Grey Shrike, Corn Bunting.

Breeding season: White Stork, Hobby, Little Ringed Plover, Lapwing, Turtle Dove, Common Cuckoo, Scops Owl, Bee-eater, Roller, Barn Swallow, Nightingale; Reed, Great Reed and Melodious Warblers.

Winter: Wigeon. Grey Heron,

Passage periods: Marbled Duck, Purple Heron, Booted Eagle, Osprey, Spotted Crake, Common and Whiskered Terns, Sand Martin.

LAGUNAS DE LA MANCHA   CLM11
HÚMEDA (Toledo/Ciudad Real/Cuenca)

Status: The whole area is a Biosphere reserve 'La Mancha Húmeda' (418,000 ha) and a ZEPA 'Humedales de la Mancha' (14,613ha).

The following lagoons have the stated additional designations:
Alcázar de San Juan lagoons: Ramsar site. Reserva natural.
Pedro Muñoz lagoons: Ramsar site (Laguna de la Vega del Pueblo).
*   Reserva natural.*

Laguna de Manjavacas: Ramsar site. Reserva natural.
Los Charcones de Miguel Esteban: SEO/Birdlife reserve.

Site description

In the very heart of the great plains of La Mancha is a complex of over 100 seasonal lagoons: temporary bodies of water of varying sizes, fed by a combination of rivers, springs and rainfall. Most have no outlet and extreme evaporation resulting from high summer temperatures has left saline soils and muds: many of these waterbodies become salt-encrusted early in the summer. Most of the lagoons are very small but collectively they are a wetland of considerable importance. Another very famous site and National Park, Las Tablas de Daimiel (CLM12), while geographically separated from these lagoons, also lies in 'La Mancha Húmeda' and has much in common with these lakes. More details on individual sites are included below.

Like Daimiel, the so-called 'La Mancha Húmeda' is but a ghost of its former self, having lost much of the ornithological importance it had in the 1950s and 1960s, but it is still of international importance. The lagoons are now isolated in a sea of cereals, vines and irrigated sunflowers in a huge area of intensive cultivation. As a result the future of at least some of the lakes seems precarious since the area is subject to excessive groundwater abstraction. It must be hoped that a solution will be found to this problem, reconciling agricultural needs with those of wildlife, although any climate warming may exacerbate the situation.

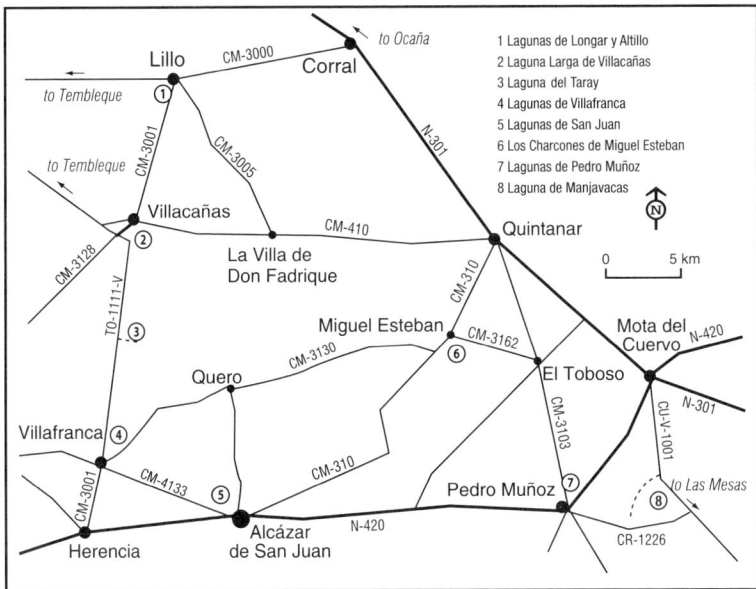

Species

The lagoons still support internationally important populations of breeding Black-necked Grebes, with one of the largest breeding colonies in Europe. Other species occurring in significant numbers include Common

Shelduck, Red-crested Pochard, White-headed Duck, Marsh Harrier, Collared Pratincole, Gull-billed and Whiskered Terns, Savi's and Moustached Warblers and Bearded Tit. The list of breeding species also includes Gadwall, Little Bittern, Night Heron, Cattle Egret, Water Rail, Black-winged Stilt, Yellow Wagtail, Penduline Tit and Great Reed Warbler. The Great Bittern has nested in some recent seasons. Lagoons that still hold water in summer, such as (usually) Manjavacas, can attract considerable concentrations of Black-necked Grebes and Gull-billed Terns in July. Greater Flamingos often visit the lakes and have nested at Manjavacas.

Grey Herons, Cormorants, Cranes and a diversity of wildfowl are present in winter. The migration periods, particularly the autumn passage, see many waders on the salty and muddy shores such as those existing near Alcázar, Lillo and Pedro Muñoz and at Manjavacas. Migration can be especially good in late March and April in some years with frequent records of 'rarities'.

The surrounding agricultural land is also important for steppe birds such as Great and Little Bustards, Stone-curlews and many Pin-tailed Sandgrouse. Indeed the western part of this area is one of the best areas in Castilla–La Mancha for Great Bustards.

Timing
Between June and October there is little or no water but outside this period the area can be outstanding. The region can be very cold in winter and heat haze can be a problem in spring when temperatures begin to pick up. The seasonality of many of the lagoons means they are dependent on weather and rainfall: in drought years they may hold little or no water for extended periods.

Access
The general area where most of the lagoons are located is around the town of Alcázar de San Juan, around 30km east on the CM-42 from the A-4 motorway at Madridejos, between Madrid and Manzanares. You will probably want to visit a number of the sites in turn. The lakes are listed below in one of a number of possible visiting orders, and numbered accordingly on the map.

Penduline Tit

1. *Lagunas de El Longar y Altillo* These seasonal lagoons occur in a steppe habitat to the south of the village of Lillo, although the Laguna de El Longar receives waste water from the village and so is relatively permanent. The margins of the lake have well-developed salt-influenced vegetation and some areas also show signs of enrichment from the waste waters. As the site is near the village there is a certain amount of disturbance. Steppe and scrub occur around the lakes and the vegetation is dominated by Albardine, a rush-like grass. Although the main focus of interest is at the lakes: especially the Gull-billed Terns, the steppe area can produce many species typical of this habitat and including Great Bustard and Dupont's Lark.

From Tembleque on the A-4, take the CM-3000 to Lillo (16km). In Lillo take the CM-3001 Villacañas road southwards and turn right after 2km on to a track to the lagoon. It is possible to get good views from the track and the area can be walked in a relatively short time. There are also a number of other smaller seasonal lagoons nearby, such as El Altillo: almost opposite the El Longar turn-off.

2. *Laguna Larga de Villacañas* The largest of a complex of saline lakes with surrounding halophytic vegetation. Collared Pratincoles and Gull-billed Terns have nesting colonies here and the lake regularly attracts Flamingoes and waterfowl, including White-headed Ducks. Dupont's Lark is a possibility in the surrounding area.

From Lillo take the CM-3001 south to Villacañas and turn east on the CM-410 towards La Villa de Don Fadrique. At km-95.7 a signposted track on the right leads to a hide (Observatorio del Flamenco). Another track from the CM-410, at km-94, leads to another hide (Observatorio de La Canastera).

3. *Laguna del Taray, Quero* A brackish seasonal lagoon (120ha) with small islands, reedbeds, tamarisks and saltflats. White-headed Ducks and Bearded Tits are regular here. On private land and being developed for birding; there are hides. Take the TO-1111-V south from Villacañas and turn east (left) after some 9km on to a dirt track (Camino de los Tinajeros) that passes just north of the saline Laguna de Peñahueca: this is always worth a look. Continue until you reach a triangular junction (3km from the TO-1111-V) and bear left here on to another track that soon skirts the western margin of the Laguna del Taray, offering good views of the lake.

4. *Lagunas de Villafranca* Two interconnected lakes, the Laguna Grande and the Laguna Chica, have been linked to the Río Cigüela and tend to have permanent water as well as a fringe of emergent vegetation. Tracks lead to and surround the wetlands but the area suffers from disturbance and development. Typical key species include Gull-billed Tern, but the area is favoured by other species that prefer cover, including Purple Heron. Surrounding land has Little Bustards and Pin-tailed Sandgrouse. There is a hide at the Laguna Grande.

From Villafranca de los Caballeros drive north-east on the CM-3130 towards Quero; the lagoons are visible on the west side of the road.

5. *Lagunas de San Juan* The Lagunas de Las Yeguas, del Camino de Villafranca and de La Veguilla are just west of Alcázar de San Juan. The last of these is less saline than the others and tends to retain permanent water and considerable fringing emergent vegetation. The other two are very salty and shallow, with muddy edges and only a sparse halophytic flora. Breeding birds include White-headed Ducks, Red-crested Pochards, Black-necked Grebes, Purple Swamphens, Black-winged Stilts, Avocets and Gull-billed Terns. The site also attracts passage waders and other migrants, such as Black Terns.

Take the CM-4133 north-west from Alcázar de San Juan. A track on the north side of the road, at km-89.5, leads to La Veguilla, where there is a car park and one of several hides overlooking the lagunar complex. Explore on foot.

6. *Los Charcones de Miguel Esteban* Formerly a natural lagoon that now serves as reservoirs but with an overspill that floods in winter. The reservoirs have permanent water and reedbeds and other emergent vegetation. Breeding birds include White-headed Ducks, Black-necked Grebes, Avocets, Black-winged Stilts, Whiskered Terns and Gull-billed Terns. Steppe birds such as sandgrouse, Little Bustards and Greater Short-toed Larks occur on the adjoining land, with Yellow Wagtails and waders on the wetter ground.

From Alcázar de San Juan take the CM-310 north-west to Miguel Esteban. Turn right here towards El Toboso on the CM-3162 and at km-2.3 a signposted track on the right leads to the lake, where there is a car park and field centre. Explore on foot or on the drivable marginal tracks (5km), returning the same way. There are several hides.

7. *Laguna del Pueblo, Pedro Muñoz* The Laguna del Pueblo is one of the most sizeable in this wetland complex and is semi-permanent. There is an information centre (Centro de Interpretación El Humedal de Don Quijote) and two hides. A track along the eastern shoreline offers good views. Breeding species include Red-crested Pochard, White-headed Duck, Black-necked Grebe and Whiskered Tern. Flamingos are usually present. The site is very good for passage migrants, which include Ospreys, Glossy Ibises and waders and occasionally Ferruginous Ducks, among many others.

The information centre is on the CM-3103, just north of Pedro Muñoz, a village about 25km east of Alcázar de San Juan on the N-420. The trail on the opposite bank is reached by returning to Pedro Muñoz and turning left to return to the lake; the path is on the left 500m from the village.

8. *Laguna de Manjavacas* A very important, large (200ha), seasonal lagoon. There are reedbeds but much of the perimeter is sparsely vegetated. The muddy margins and shallows attract diverse waders on passage, including Temminck's Stints, Ruffs and Spotted Redshanks. Breeding species include Black-necked Grebe, Red-crested Pochard, Whiskered Tern, and Gull-billed Terns, Savi's Warbler and Bearded Tit. Flamingos are often present and over 1,000 pairs nested successfully in 2010. In winter there are roosts of Cranes and both Marsh and Hen Harriers.Take the N-420 east from Alcázar de San Juan to the roundabout just north of Pedro Muñoz, and take the minor road for Las Mesas. Alternatively continue on the N-420 to Mota del Cuervo and then take the CUV-1001 southwards towards Las Mesas. The lagoon is near the hermitage of Manjavacas, at km-6 on the CU-V-1001. A track runs for some 600m from the C-UV-1001 south of the hermitage to the lagoon.

CALENDAR

All year: Common Shelduck, Gadwall, Red-crested Pochard, White-headed Duck; Black-necked, Little and Great Crested Grebes, Little and Cattle Egrets, Greater Flamingo, Marsh Harrier, Water Rail, Kentish Plover, Little and Great Bustards, Stone-curlew, Black-bellied and Pin-tailed Sandgrouse, Black-headed Gull, Little Owl, Hoopoe; Dupont's, Calandra and Thekla Larks, Bearded Tit, Cetti's Warbler, Rock Sparrow, Corn Bunting.

Breeding season: Teal, Shoveler, Common Pochard, Night and Purple Herons, Little Bittern, Black Kite, Spotted Crake, Black-winged Stilt, Avocet, Little Ringed Plover, Lapwing, Common Redshank, Common Sandpiper, Collared Pratincole; Gull-billed,

Little and Whiskered, Bee-eater, Great Spotted Cuckoo, Greater Short-toed Lark, Tawny Pipit, Yellow Wagtail, Black-eared Wheatear; Savi's, Reed and Great Reed Warblers.

Winter: Greylag Goose, Wigeon, Teal, Shoveler, Common Pochard, Ferruginous Duck, Hen Harrier, Merlin, Peregrine Falcon, Crane, Common Sandpiper, Curlew, Lesser Short-toed Lark, Penduline Tit.

Passage periods: Pintail, Garganey, Osprey, Crane, Ringed Plover, Grey Plover, Knot, Little Stint, Dunlin, Ruff, Temminck's Stint, Black-tailed Godwit, Spotted Redshank, Greenshank, Whiskered and Black Terns.

LAS TABLAS DE DAIMIEL (Ciudad Real)   CLM12

Status: Parque Nacional, UNESCO Biosphere Reserve, Ramsar site and ZEPA (1,928ha).

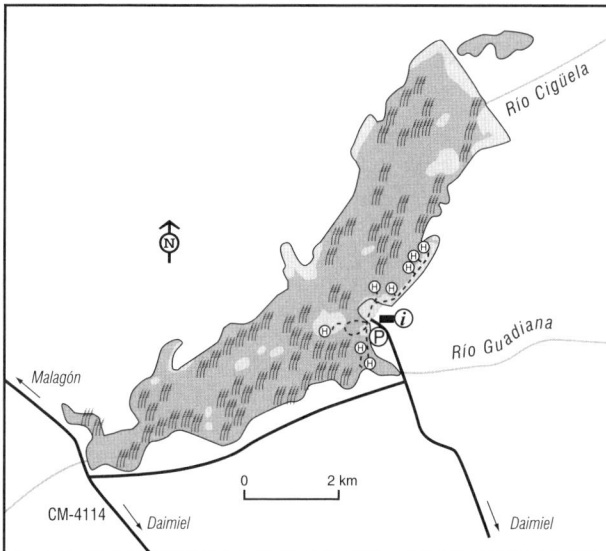

Site description

Las Tablas de Daimiel, the smallest of Spain's National Parks, lies at the heart of La Mancha Húmeda, an extensive area peppered with inland lagoons and flooded areas and crossed by Castilian rivers. Las Tablas is only one of a diversity of wetlands in this zone: see also CLM11.

The 'tablas' of La Mancha are the (formerly) extensive floods or washes along some rivers that remain inundated for much of the year. They result from the flatness of the landscape, which leads to rivers overflowing across large areas during the rainy season. Las Tablas de Daimiel lies at the confluence of the brackish and seasonal Río Cigüela and the more permanent Río Guadiana. The region has a water-saturated calciferous aquifer that sustains the wetlands. Unfortunately, the very abundance of water led to unregulated over-abstraction for crop irrigation during the 1970s, not long after the park's designation in 1973. This over-exploitation coincided with a period of severe drought in the late 1970s which together all but drained the aquifer and came close to the complete destruction of the National Park. A wetland restoration plan, which involves diverting water via an aqueduct from the Río Tajo, sustains the National Park but the extent of Las Tablas has been reduced from over 30,000ha in the 1960s to the 2,000ha which survive today. Much of what was former wetland is now cultivated land. The unfortunate history of the National Park should not distract from the fact that it remains a large, very interesting and important wetland. The protected area is a maze of islands, channels, loops and flooded land: 'the Venice of La Mancha', as it has often been called.

The Laguna de Navaseca, a very recently restored wetland just north of Daimiel town, has become an essential destination for visitors to the area, offering a large diversity of species that may be viewed at close range.

Species

The ancestral wetlands were a happy hunting ground for wildfowlers from as far afield as Madrid and Valencia, attracted by the many thousands of wintering ducks. Up to 10,000 ducks now benefit from protection in winter. The majority are Mallard, Teal and Shoveler but there are also numbers of Wigeon, Gadwall, Pintail and Common Pochards. Cranes fly in to roost in the park in spectacular and clamorous formations on winter evenings. The Red-crested Pochard is a symbol of the Park and is present all year round, with a significant breeding population. Marbled Ducks occur occasionally and have bred. Mallard and Gadwall breed commonly and both Garganey and White-headed Ducks do so in some years.

Daimiel is noted for its breeding herons, including over 100 pairs of Purple Herons alongside breeding Cattle, Little and Great White Egrets; Grey, Squacco and Night Herons and Little Bitterns. Great Bitterns also occur and have bred in some years. Cormorants and Greylag Geese are recent additions to the breeding list and both Glossy Ibises and Spoonbills have also nested recently. Black-necked Grebes, Black-headed Gulls and Whiskered Terns also breed locally.

The breeding passerine community is interesting. A visit in spring is invariably accompanied by the pleasing clamour of Nightingales and Cetti's, Great Reed and Reed Warblers, among many others. Daimiel still retains significant breeding populations of much less widespread passerines, including Savi's and Moustached Warblers, Bearded and Penduline Tits and Reed Buntings. Passage periods also see an attractive diversity of species, including passerines in the fringing tamarisks.

Timing

There is much to see at Las Tablas at any time of year. However, the summer months are the least rewarding because of the intense drought, when there is little open water and waterfowl numbers are lowest. Mosquitoes can be a problem in spring and summer, so bring insect repellent. Weekends and public holidays can be busy and are best avoided. It can be very cold in winter so be prepared. The early mornings and late afternoons tend to be the most productive times.

Access

The National Park is around 140km from Madrid and about 40km from Ciudad Real. Leave the A-4 Madrid/Andalucía motorway at Manzanares and take the A-43 22km west to Daimiel. From Ciudad Real take the A-43 east to Daimiel (28km). The park and its information centre are signposted from the Daimiel bypass road and there is no need to go into Daimiel town. The park is some 11km from the bypass along a tarmac road that leads to the Visitors' Centre (Tel. 926 693 118). The park website (lastablasdedamiel. com) is informative. The park and centre are open daily all year round from 09.00–19.00 hours in winter and 09.00–21.00 hours in summer.

Three colour-coded trails provide easy access along footpaths and boardwalks to some of the most interesting parts of the reserve, which are overlooked by a number of hides. Visit them all in turn. The hides offer views of the mixed heronries and the boardwalks cross large tracts of reedbed and open water. Guided tours, including by 4WD vehicle, are available in spring but need to be pre-booked with the Centre. A layby on the left just north of the bridge across the Guadiana offers close views of riverside vegetation often used by numbers of herons.

The unmissable **Laguna de Navaseca** straddles the road to the water purification works (Depuradora) just 2km from the N-420 bypass road immediately north of Daimiel village. It is viewable from the road and the perimeter footpath. There are hides. This is an excellent location for seeing White-headed Ducks, Black-necked Grebes and Collared Pratincoles, among a host of other species. Those in the know have recently ranked it superior to Daimiel itself – it is certainly birder-friendly.

Red-crested Pochard and Teal

CALENDAR

All year: Greylag Goose, Gadwall, Mallard, Red-crested Pochard, Common Pochard, Cormorant; Great Crested, Little and Black-necked Grebes, Grey Heron, Glossy Ibis, Marsh Harrier, Moorhen, Purple Swamphen, Common Coot, Hoopoe, Cetti's and Moustached Warblers, Zitting Cisticola, Bearded and Penduline Tits, Reed Bunting.

Breeding season: Garganey, White-headed Duck, Little Bittern, Night, Squacco and Purple Herons, Little Egret, Great White Egret, White Stork, Black Kite, Montagu's Harrier, Short-toed and Booted Eagles, Lesser Kestrel, Hobby, Water Rail, Black-winged Stilt, Collared Pratincole, Whiskered

Tern, Great Spotted Cuckoo, Bee-eater, Roller, Red-rumped Swallow, Nightingale; Savi's, Reed, Great Reed and Melodious Warblers.

Winter: Pintail, Wigeon, Teal, Shoveler, Marbled Duck (rare), Merlin, Hen Harrier, Crane, Lapwing (sometimes breeds), Common Snipe, Short-eared Owl, Bluethroat.

Passage periods: Ferruginous Duck, Garganey, Black Stork, Black-tailed Godwit, Wood Sandpiper; Gull-billed, Whiskered and Black Terns, Wryneck, Sand Martin, Garden and Willow Warblers, Pied Flycatcher, Ortolan Bunting.

CABAÑEROS   CLM13
(Toledo/Ciudad Real)

Status: Parque Nacional (41,805ha), part of the ZEPA 'Montes de Toledo' (117,191ha).

Site description

Cabañeros National Park lies within the Montes de Toledo, the low sierras in the south of Toledo province bordering Ciudad Real. The region is dominated by huge estates dedicated to livestock rearing, forestry and hunting. Until recently Cabañeros was the largest such estate in Europe, revered by hunters as 'The Cathedral' because of its high density of Red Deer. The area is thinly populated and mainly covered in mature Mediterranean forest, one of the best examples of this habitat in Spain.

Most of Cabañeros comprises low sierras lying between the valleys of the Ríos Estena and Bullaque. Much of the area, including the Sierra del Chorito, Sierra de Valdefuentes and the isolated ridge of El Rostro, is densely vegetated with Mediterranean forest of evergreen oaks: including Cork Oaks, Lusitanian Oaks and Iberian Holm Oaks mixed with Strawberry Trees, Mastic Trees, Turpentine Trees, Honeysuckles, Myrtles, wild Olives and dense areas of *Cistus* scrub. In the south, between these hills, is the Raña, a large plain dotted with very old evergreen oaks, and where each morning and evening large concentrations of deer gather to graze. The Raña has more than a passing resemblance to the *Acacia*-studded plains of East Africa, with their herds of herbivores, so that Cabañeros is frequently called the 'Spanish Serengeti'.

The banks of the Río Bullaque have riverine woodland, an uncommon habitat in Europe. The Río Estena passes through a rocky gorge in the north-west of the park, an area that is freely open to public access, unlike the core of

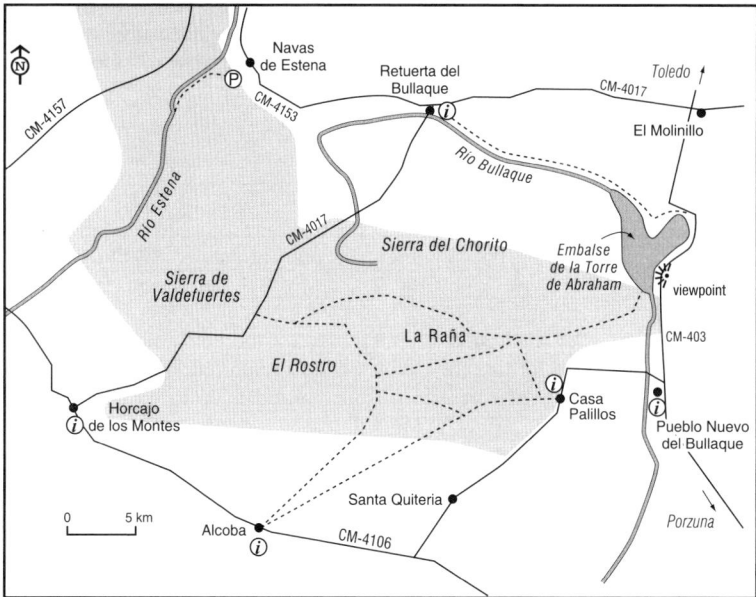

the reserve. The Torre de Abraham reservoir holds some numbers of common wildfowl and waders, particularly during passage periods.

Species

Cabañeros offers an opportunity to see the Mediterranean bird community of inland Spain in peaceful, near-pristine surroundings. The highlights among the 200 or so bird species that have been recorded within the Park are undoubtedly the raptors. Cabañeros boasts a breeding population of over 160 pairs of Black Vultures, one of the largest concentrations in Spain. Their massive nests adorn tree-tops in the Sierra del Chorito. Several pairs of Spanish Imperial Eagles also breed in and near the park, as well as Short-toed, Golden and Booted Eagles and Egyptian Vultures. Several pairs of Black-shouldered Kites and Montagu's Harriers occur in La Raña, where there are other birds of open country: including resident Little Bustards and Stone-curlews, and Cranes in winter. Black Storks also breed in the Park and Griffon Vultures are frequent visitors. Among the smaller breeding birds, Woodchat Shrikes are particularly obvious alongside Azure-winged Magpies, Southern Grey Shrikes, Thekla Larks, warblers, Golden Orioles and Spanish Sparrows. The rocky course of the Río Estena has Eagle Owls, Crag Martins and Dippers, with Subalpine Warblers in the fringing scrub. Ospreys occur from time to time at the reservoir, both on passage and in winter.

The mammal populations are noteworthy. The numerous Red Deer are accompanied by Roe Deer and also Wild Boar. Iberian Lynx are being reintroduced in the Montes de Toledo: 21 were released in 2015–16, and rabbit populations in the Park are being reinforced to support this project. Commoner carnivores include Otters and Egyptian Mongooses.

Timing

The Spanish Imperial Eagles are most noticeable when they display, during February and March. Late April to June is the best time for most of the breeding birds, while winter is good for Cranes and the resident raptors. Deer watchers will be most successful in autumn, during the rut.

Access

There are a number of walking trails, some of which are freely accessible. However, access to most of the Park is strictly controlled and the key sectors can really only be visited by booking a trip on seven-seater 4WD tour buses which will take you to the best areas. The cost is 23€ per person. It is best to avoid public holidays and weekends, however, when you might have to share your bus with a 'less-dedicated' clientele. By far the best arrangement is to book a private guided birding tour, which takes a minimum of three hours and costs 138€ per vehicle. The vehicle will accommodate up to six persons. The pace is leisurely and the driver/guide will stop on demand. The tour can be extended at an additional cost of 40€ per hour (2016 prices). For more information and to make reservations for guided tours contact Cabañeros National Park, Pueblo Nuevo del Bullaque, Ciudad Real (Tel. 926 783 297) and check the website (visitacabaneros.es) for current visiting arrangements and opening hours. For private birding tours, which we recommend, it is best to telephone the company directly to make arrangements: Tel. 926 850 371; English and French are spoken, as well as Spanish. Tour reservations should be made as much in advance as possible.

A useful starting point is the Casa Palillos Centre near Pueblo Nuevo del Bullaque. From Ciudad Real take the CM-412 and then the CM-403 north-west towards Porzuna and then on to Pueblo Nuevo del Bullaque. From the north and Toledo take the CM-401 until it joins the CM-403 and continue south to El Bullaque. The Casa Palillos centre and park entrance are 5km from Bullaque on the local road between there and Santa Quiteria. The Park is signposted at the north end of Bullaque but the entrance to Casa Palillos has a small sign and is easily missed. Casa Palillos, and another Centre at Horcajo de los Montes at the south-western corner of the park, 30km west of Quiteria, are the starting points for guided tours.

Independent birding is also possible along the roads on the Park periphery, for example the former drove road (CM-4153) from Navas de Estena to Retuerta del Bullaque and the CM-4017 from Retuerta del Bullaque to Cabañeros and Horcajo de los Montes. The CM-4106 crosses the rocky course of the Río Estena (in Extremadura) 14km north-west of Horcajo, where there is access to the river. A little further north it is also worth driving the scenic road (CM-4157) across the north end of the Park, stopping frequently to search for woodland passerines and raptors.

There are seven self-guided and marked walking trails of various lengths within the Park boundary, offering access to woodland and riparian habitats especially. The Centres provide an informative leaflet and map for each trail. For example, a 3.2km trail leads from Navas de Estena along the picturesque valley of the Río Estena passing through a gorge, the Garganta de El Boquerón: follow the road south-west just south of Navas to the car park at the start of the trail.

The reservoir of the Torre de Abraham is overlooked from a signposted *mirador* on the CM-403 above the east shore. A telescope is essential here. Access to the shoreline is possible from a minor road that follows the north shore.

CALENDAR

All year: Black Stork, Black-shouldered and Red Kites, Griffon and Black Vultures, Goshawk, Sparrowhawk, Common Buzzard, Golden and Spanish Imperial Eagles, Little Bustard, Stone-curlew, Eagle and Long-eared Owls, Hoopoe, Thekla and Wood Larks, Green Woodpecker, Crag Martin, Dipper, Blue Rock Thrush, Dartford and Sardinian Warblers, Firecrest, Crested Tit, Southern Grey Shrike, Azure-winged Magpie, Spanish Sparrow, Cirl Bunting.

Breeding season: White Stork, Honey-buzzard, Black Kite, Egyptian Vulture, Montagu's Harrier, Short-toed and Booted Eagles, Hobby, Turtle Dove, Great Spotted Cuckoo, Scops Owl, Bee-eater, Roller, Black-eared Wheatear; Melodious, Spectacled, Subalpine, Orphean and Bonelli's Warblers, Golden Oriole, Woodchat Shrike.

Winter: Shoveler, Great Crested Grebe, Cormorant, Grey Heron, Hen Harrier, Osprey, Peregrine, Merlin, Crane.

SIERRA DE LOS CANALIZOS CLM14 (Ciudad Real)

Status: ZEPA (24,135ha).

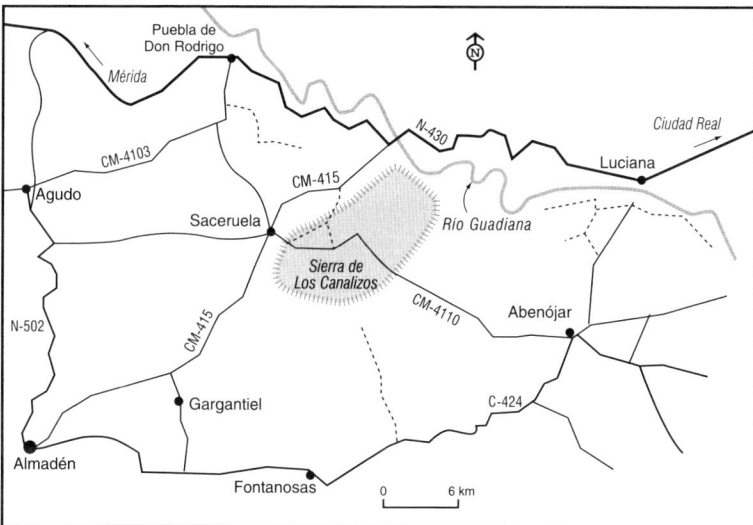

Site description

The area to the south of the Montes de Toledo and immediately north of the Valle de Alcudia offers isolated ridges rising to around 800m. These are clothed

Tree Sparrow

in Mediterranean woodland, chiefly of evergreen oaks: Cork Oaks, Lusitanian Oaks and Encinas, but also including Pedunculate and Pyrenean Oaks and Narrow-leaved Ash and large areas of low scrub-heath. The mountains, which include the Sierra de Los Canalizos to the east of Saceruela, are interspersed with dehesas of Cork Oaks and Encinas and grassland, the latter given over to sheep and cattle grazing. The whole area is sparsely populated.

Species
Up to 100 pairs of Black Vultures breed in the area, alongside several pairs of Spanish Imperial Eagles. Golden, Short-toed and Booted Eagles also breed as well as Eagle Owls and both Black and White Storks. This is an excellent area for dehesa and open-country birds, which include Quail, Black-shouldered Kites, Red-rumped Swallows, Azure-winged Magpies and Tree Sparrows. Little Bustards and Black-bellied Sandgrouse occur on the grasslands.

Timing
Late winter and early spring are best for displaying raptors. Spring visits are generally most productive but the area is relatively little studied and would probably repay exploration at other times.

Access
Take the N-430 west out of Ciudad Real through Piedrabuena to Luciana, which is north-east of the Sierra de Los Canalizos. The area of interest is delimited in the north by the N-430 between Luciana and Puebla de Don Rodrigo, in the west by the CM-4103 and the N-502 to Almadén and in the south and east by the C-424 returning to Luciana. Small estate roads and tracks penetrate the area from these encircling roads. The roads radiating from Saceruela, at the centre of the area, are also worth exploring.

CALENDAR

All year: Black-shouldered and Red Kites, Black Vulture, Common Buzzard, Spanish Imperial and Golden Eagles, Stock Dove, Eagle and Little Owls, Little Bustard, Black-bellied Sandgrouse, Green Woodpecker, Hoopoe; Crested, Thekla, Wood and Sky Larks, Azure-winged Magpie, Tree Sparrow.

Breeding season: Quail, Black Stork, White Stork, Black Kite, Egyptian Vulture, Short-toed and Booted Eagles, Lesser Kestrel, Turtle Dove, Great Spotted Cuckoo, Bee-eater, Greater Short-toed Lark, Red-rumped Swallow, Woodchat Shrike.

VALLE DE ALCUDIA (Ciudad Real)   CLM15

Status: Part of the Parque Natural Valle de Alcudia y Sierra Madrona and of the ZEPA 'Sierra Morena' (26,000ha).

Site description

This is a broad, sparsely-vegetated valley largely given over to sheep pasture. It occupies a large depression surrounded by hills, to the north of the main ranges of the Sierra Morena. The valley is a traditional wintering ground for sheep flocks and is mostly treeless apart from areas of dehesa on the hillsides. There are many abandoned lead mines and the area is now sparsely populated.

Species

The valley supports a good diversity of breeding steppeland birds, notably Little Bustards, Black-bellied and Pin-tailed Sandgrouse and Stone-curlews, as well as Montagu's Harriers and White Storks. Many of the latter nest on the ruined lead mines in the valleys, which are also used by Common Kestrels and

Red-billed Choughs. Lesser Kestrels nest locally.

Raptors from the adjoining sierras (see CLM16) visit the area. They include Black and Egyptian Vultures and Spanish Imperial, Golden and Bonelli's Eagles. The area supports winter flocks not just of sheep but also of Little Bustards, Cranes and Golden Plovers.

Timing
Spring and winter visits are recommended.

Access
Take the N-420 south from Ciudad Real to Puertollano and continue south for 30km before turning right on to the CM-4202 minor road to La Bienvenida and Alamillo. This road can be particularly good for scanning the steppe and takes you west along the valley across the broad plains which have good populations of Little Bustards and Stone-curlews. The CM-4201 will bring you into the Sierra de la Umbría de Alcudia, to the south.

CALENDAR

All year: Black-shouldered and Red Kites, Goshawk, Eagle Owl, Little Bustard, Stone-curlew; Calandra, Thekla and Wood Larks, Black Wheatear, Mistle Thrush, Southern Grey Shrike, Azure-winged Magpie, Hawfinch.

Breeding season: White Stork, Black Stork, Short-toed and Booted Eagles, Red-necked

Nightjar, Bee-eater, Roller, Greater Short-toed Lark, Red-rumped Swallow, Common Redstart; Melodious, Subalpine and Orphean Warblers, Golden Oriole, Woodchat Shrike.

Winter: Merlin, Crane, Golden Plover, Lapwing, Redwing, Fieldfare.

SIERRA MADRONA (Ciudad Real)　　　　CLM16

Status: Part of the Parque Natural Valle de Alcudia y Sierra Madrona. Within the ZEPA 'Sierra Morena' (97,528ha).

Site description
The Sierra Madrona is an extensive sector, some 75km long, of the Sierra Morena: the long west/east mountain chain which separates Extremadura and Castilla–La Mancha from Andalucía. Together with the Sierra de Andújar in Córdoba province to the south, the Sierra Madrona harbours some of the best preserved examples of Mediterranean woodland ecosystems in Spain. Large areas are covered in mixed scrub and low woodland of wild Olives, Strawberry Trees, Lentiscs, *Cistus*, junipers and heaths. There are also mature woodlands of Encinas, Lusitanian Oaks and Pyrenean Oaks, the taller and denser formations occurring on the northern slopes. Riparian vegetation along the streams and rivers is very well developed. The generally gentle relief is enlivened by a series of steep river gorges and cliffs.

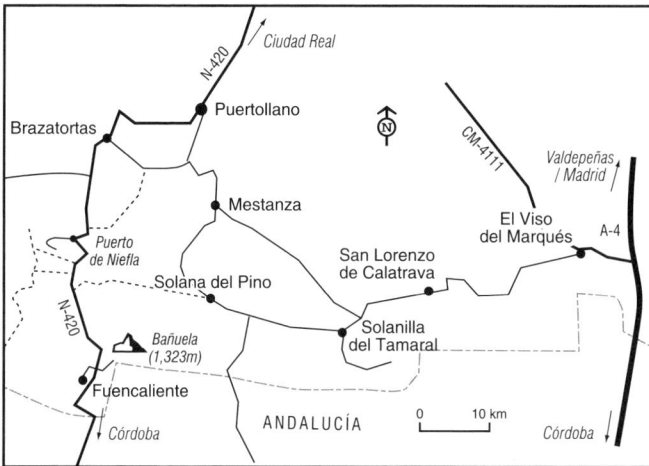

Species

The region, but especially the Andalucían sector, is a core site for the Iberian Lynx. It is noteworthy for breeding raptors, with significant populations of Black Vultures, all five eagles and Eagle Owls, as well as Black Storks. Other interesting breeding birds include Subalpine and Orphean Warblers, Black Wheatears, Rock Sparrows and Rock Buntings.

Timing

Spring and early summer visits are recommended, early spring being best for seeing displaying raptors.

Access

Take the N-420 south from Ciudad Real through Puertollano and continue towards Fuencaliente. A diversity of forest tracks and minor roads penetrate the woods either side of Puerto de Niefla. There are cave paintings at Peña Escrita near Fuencaliente. A good way to get to know the area is to take the picturesque road from Puertollano towards Andújar (Córdoba), via Mestanza and Solana del Pino.

CALENDAR

All year: Griffon and Black Vultures, Goshawk; Spanish Imperial, Golden and Bonelli's Eagles, Peregrine Falcon, Eagle Owl, Crag Martin, Blue Rock Thrush, Black Wheatear, Nuthatch, Jay, Red-billed Chough, Raven, Rock Sparrow, Rock Bunting.

Breeding season: Black Stork, Egyptian Vulture, Short-toed and Booted Eagles, Common Redstart, Black-eared Wheatear; Melodious, Subalpine, Orphean and Bonelli's Warblers, Golden Oriole.

OTHER SITES WORTH VISITING

CLM17 MONTES DE TOLEDO (TOLEDO/CIUDAD REAL)
These are the mountains south-west of Toledo, a region that includes Cabañeros Natural Park (CLM13). The whole range is excellent for raptors including Spanish Imperial and Golden Eagles and Black Vultures, as well as Black Storks. From Toledo take the CM-401 south-westwards.

CLM18 LAGUNA DE POZUELO DE CALATRAVA (CIUDAD REAL)
A small, shallow, seasonal lagoon with hides. This wetland has Black-winged Stilts, Avocets and Kentish Plovers as well as breeding Little Terns. From Ciudad Real, take the CM-412 towards Valdepeñas until you reach Pozuelo de Calatrava (12km). The lagoon is just north of the town, off the CR-5112.

CLM19 LA GUARDIA/TEMBLEQUE/ROMERAL (TOLEDO)
A triangular route east of the A-4 through steppe habitat with Great and Little Bustards and Pin-tailed Sandgrouse. A small marshy area at the Dehesa de Monreal alongside the River Cedrón also has breeding Gull-billed Terns and Marsh Harriers, with wintering Red-crested Pochards. Leave the A4 at La Guardia, 19km south of Ocaña, or at Tembleque.

CLM20 EMBALSE DE ALMOGUERA (GUADALAJARA)
A small, long, thin reservoir with an extensive reedbed situated south of the village of Almoguera. It offers breeding Red-crested Pochards and Purple Herons, with Ospreys and Cranes on passage. From Guadalajara take the N-320 towards Sacedón. After 18km turn left onto the CM-2006 to Pastrana and then take the CM-200 and CM-2029 south towards Almoguera. Bear left to reach the dam before you reach the village.

CLM21 PARAMERA DE MARANCHÓN, EMBID Y MOLINA DE ARAGÓN (GUADALAJARA)
A highland 'páramo' or plateau at an altitude of 1,000–1,200m in the far north-east of the region between Guadalajara and Zaragoza (Aragón). The N-211 forms its southern boundary. The habitat is mainly grassland, cereal cultivation, some scrub and Spanish Juniper woodlands. It is important for its steppe birds including Montagu's Harriers, Stone-curlews, Black-bellied Sandgrouse and Dupont's Larks. Take the N-211 at Alcolea del Pinar (off the A-2) for 22km to Maranchón. The plateau is between Maranchón and Mazarete. Similar areas also occur further east around Embid and Molina de Aragón.

CLM22 LAGUNA DE EL HITO (CUENCA)
A large seasonal lagoon near the village of Montalbo just south of the A-3 at km-115, south-east of Madrid. Large numbers of Cranes use the lake when on passage in late autumn and early spring. A diversity of waterfowl and waders occur in winter and on passage. The general area is also important for steppe birds, including Great Bustards.

CLM23 LLANOS DE VALDELOBOS (CUENCA/ALBACETE)
An upland plateau steppe area between the towns of Villarrobledo and San Clemente, with Great and Little Bustards, Stone-curlews and sandgrouse. The region is 71km north of Albacete, on either side of the N-301.

CLM24 VALERIA, GUADAZAÓN AND MOYA (CUENCA)
These three separate areas comprise plateau land at around 1,000m, totalling some 6,000ha. They are particularly important for Dupont's Larks. All three areas are devoted to cereals, although there are tracts of *Genista*, lavender and thyme scrub. The first area is south of Cuenca along the CM-2100 to Valeria; the second around 40km east of Cuenca, south of the N-420 around Carboneras de Guadazaón; and the third in the far east on the borders with Aragón and the Comunidad Valenciana. Take the N-420/CM-215/N-330 east from Cuenca to Santa Cruz de Moya.

CLM25 LAS HOCES DEL CABRIEL (CUENCA)
These gorges are south-east of Cuenca and upstream of the Embalse de Contreras. There are also other riverine habitats with meanders, and surrounding pinewoods. The area is good for raptors, including Egyptian Vultures, Golden Eagles and Eagle Owls. Turn south off the N-420 at Carboneras de Guadazaón, about 40km from Cuenca, and take the CM-2109 towards the reservoir and headwaters.

CLM26 LLANOS DE MONTIEL (CIUDAD REAL)
A succession of stony plains dotted with Evergreen oaks and junipers. Steppe birds here include Montagu's Harriers, Lesser Kestrels, Great Bustards, Stone-curlews and Dupont's Larks. The area lies around 50km east of Valdepeñas, south of the CM-412. Turn right at Villahermosa.

CLM27 SIERRA DE ALCARAZ Y ALTO SEGURA (ALBACETE)
A landscape of impressive gorges and steep-sided mountains with some of the highest peaks in Castilla–La Mancha. There are also extensive forests and riverside woodland. The area is good for Griffon and Egyptian Vultures, Goshawks and Short-toed and Bonelli's Eagles. Take the N-322 south-west of Albacete to Alcaraz and then the CM-3216 south-east into the Sierra towards and beyond Cortijo de Tortas.

CLM28 HOCES DEL RÍO MUNDO Y EL RÍO SEGURA (ALBACETE)
The limestone gorges along these two rivers have Golden and Bonelli's Eagles, Eagle Owls and Red-billed Choughs. They are around 60km south of Albacete along the CM-3203 towards Ayna.

CLM29 SALADARES DE CORDOVILLA (ALBACETE)
An area of salt-steppe habitat of great botanical interest. Breeding birds include Dupont's Lark, Red-necked Nightjar and Stone-curlew. A small lake, the Laguna de Alboraj, has concentrations of wintering and passage waterfowl and waders. The area is immediately east of Tobarra, 51km south of Albacete off the N-301.

CLM30 LLANOS DE CHINCILLA/ALMANSA (ALBACETE)

A large undulating plain with extensive cereal and vine cultivation. It stretches east of Albacete to Almansa along the A-31 and to the borders with Valencia and Murcia. Contiguous with site MU5. Side roads from the A-31, including the CM-3261 to Pétrola at km-125 and the CM-3220 Almansa/Yecla road from Almansa, provide access. Open-country species occur, including Great and Little Bustards, Stone-curlews and Black-bellied Sandgrouse.

CLM31 LAGUNAS DE PÉTROLA AND SALOBRALEJO (ALBACETE)

Saline lagoons that sometimes attract White-headed Ducks in the breeding season as well as Red-crested Pochards, Kentish Plovers and Gull-billed Terns. Flamingos have nested in recent years at Pétrola. For Pétrola lagoon take the CM-3211 southwards from the A-31 at km-112. Turn right at the roundabout immediately below Pétrola village and after 100m turn right on to the signposted track to the lake. Park by the buildings (abandoned saltworks) and explore on foot. For Salobralejo lagoon turn north towards Higueruela at km-112; the lagoon is on the right next to the railway line.

CASTILLA Y LEÓN

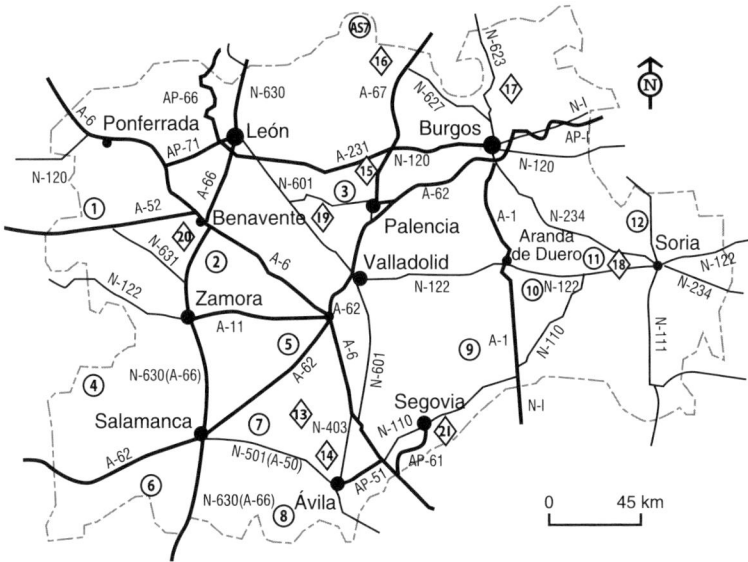

Main sites

CyL1   Lago de Sanabria
CyL2   Estepas y Lagunas de Villafáfila
CyL3   Laguna de La Nava
CyL4   Arribes del Duero
CyL5   Riberas de Castronuño
CyL6   Las Batuecas and Sierra de la
        Peña de Francia
CyL7   Azud de Riolobos
CyL8   Sierra de Gredos
CyL9   Hoces del Río Duratón
CyL10   Montejo Raptor Refuge (Hoces
        del Río Riaza)
CyL11   Cañón del Río Lobos
CyL12   Sierra de Urbión

Other sites worth visiting

CyL13   Estepas de Madrigal
CyL14   Laguna del Oso
CyL15   Río Carrión y Canal de Castilla
CyL16   Fuentes Carrionas
CyL17   Hoces de los Ríos Ebro y
        Rudrón
CyL18   Sabinar de Calatañazor
CyL19   Laguna de Boada
CyL20   Sierra de La Culebra
CyL21   La Granja de San Ildefonso
CyL22   Segovia city

A huge area, so huge (nearly 94,000km²) that it is the largest single autonomous region in the European Union and 70% of the size of England. It is dominated by the Meseta Norte; a great, flat, semi-arid plain, 700–1,000m above sea level. The Meseta is fringed in the north by the Cantabrian mountains and in the south by the mountains of the Sistema Central, which include the Sierra de Gredos. The Río Duero and its gorges are the most significant feature of the western boundary, which borders Portugal. The mountains of the Sistema Ibérico mark the eastern limits of the region. Castilla y León is full of history from the Christian reconquest, with a landscape that is dominated by castles and by the romantic legends that spawned the Christian hero El Cid. There is much to occupy the birder here, along with plenty of distractions in the architecture, bars, impressive squares and history of the region's towns and cities, notably the provincial capitals: Ávila, Segovia, Salamanca, Burgos, Valladolid, Palencia, Zamora and León itself.

The Meseta Norte is vast, with cereals as far as the eye can see, broken up by vines, extensive pastures devoted to sheep rearing and, increasingly often, a diversity of irrigated crops such as sunflowers. Covering over two-thirds of the region and still extremely important for its steppe birds, the north Meseta is one of the best areas in Spain to see Great Bustards, one of the most rewarding sites being the Estepas de Villafáfila (CyL2). Here you can also find Little Bustards, Black-bellied Sandgrouse, Stone-curlews, Montagu's Harriers, Lesser Kestrels, Short-toed and Calandra Larks and Tawny Pipits. These and other 'steppe' species are widespread in the cereal belt and on the arid pastures. Pintailed Sandgrouse occur sparsely, chiefly in the provinces of Ávila, Salamanca and Valladolid, for example in the Estepas de Madrigal (CyL13). Dupont's Larks also occur locally, especially in the eastern Meseta, as in the arid steppe around the Hoces del Río Duratón (CyL9).

Wetlands are at a premium in Castilla y León, which is unsurprising given the increasing demand for water for crop irrigation. Nevertheless, there are some outstanding wetland sites, some of them recently restored and all attracting great numbers of waterfowl in winter especially, as well as an impressive diversity of passage and wintering waders. The best sites include the Lagunas de Villafáfila (CyL2), the Laguna de la Nava (CyL3), the Azud de Riolobos (CyL7) and the Laguna del Oso (CyL14).

Riverine woodlands are also noteworthy. The best examples occur on the banks of the River Duero: for example the Riberas de Castronuño (CyL5), and along the Río Carrión and Canal de Castilla (CyL15). They offer mixed heronries, including Night, Purple and Grey Herons as well as Little Bitterns, Little Egrets and, very locally, Cattle Egrets: this last species being a relatively recent colonist of the region. The woodlands also attract a diversity of passerines including Golden Orioles and Penduline Tits.

To the south of Zamora and between Salamanca and the western border the predominant landscape is the dehesa, an open grazing woodland of Iberian Holm Oaks: an extension of the similar habitat found in neighbouring Extremadura. Breeding birds here include both White and Black Storks, Black-shouldered and Black Kites, Great Spotted Cuckoos, Rollers, Azurewinged Magpies, Red-rumped Swallows and Spanish Sparrows. All of these species can be found at the Arribes del Duero (CyL4) but this landscape is widespread and extends well beyond the river valley.

The Río Duero (CyL4) along the Portuguese border has eroded a spectacular landscape of towering river cliffs, where Golden and Bonelli's Eagles, Griffon and Egyptian Vultures, Peregrines, Eagle Owls, Alpine Swifts, Redbilled Choughs and Crag Martins all vie for places on the rock faces. Indeed riverine gorges, '*hoces*', are widespread in Castilla y León: other outstanding examples, supporting similar bird communities, include the Hoces del Río Duratón (CyL9), del Río Riaza (CyL10) and del Ebro y Rudrón (CyL17), and the Cañón del Rio Lobos (CyL11).

The mountain ranges bordering Castilla y León rise to significant altitudes, all with peaks well above 2,000m. The most interesting ornithologically is the Cordillera Cantábrica, which houses an important montane bird community including the Capercaillie, Grey Partridge, Wallcreeper, Alpine Accentor, Ring Ouzel, Yellow-billed Chough, Snowfinch and Citril Finch. The forests here have good populations of both Black and Middle Spotted Woodpeckers, together with a diversity of passerines which in Spain occur chiefly or only in north: they include the Goldcrest, Marsh Tit, Eurasian Treecreeper, Bullfinch and Yellowhammer. The Picos de Europa (AS7), which has a large sector within Castilla y León, is a good site to look for all these species. The community is also well represented at Fuentes Carrionas (CyL16).

The Sistema Ibérico in the east lacks most of the high mountain species, but breeding Grey Partridges, Hen Harriers, Woodcock, Eurasian Treecreepers, Red-backed Shrikes, Bullfinches and Yellowhammers are present, for example at the Sierra de Urbión (CyL12). The Sistema Central mountains in the south also lack most of the northern high-altitude species, but you can still find breeding Alpine Accentors and Citril Finches here, and this is one of the easiest regions in which to see Bluethroats in Spain. The key sites here are the Sierra de Gredos (CyL8) and the Sierra de Guadarrama (M1). The lower mountains that are a westward extension of the Sistema Central, such as the Sierra de la Peña de Francia (CyL6), are also interesting. Their avifauna has a distinctly Mediterranean flavour, including a large resident population of Black Vultures, a diversity of other raptors including all five eagles, Black Wheatears and Pallid Swifts.

Finally, Castilla y León is the Spanish stronghold for two particular species, the Short-eared Owl and the Rook. The Short-eared Owl only nested sporadically in Spain until the early 1990s but since then a population that exceeded 300 pairs in the mid-1990s has settled in the northern Meseta, exploiting the cyclical plagues of Common Voles which now occur there. The owls may be sought around Villafáfila (CyL2) where they are most evident in plague years. They are more widespread in winter. The Rook is not a species that will quicken the pulse of most birders from more northern countries but it is now almost unknown in Spain. A breeding population was discovered around the city of León in the early 1950s and remains there today, with some now nesting in the parks in the city itself. The current population of about 2,000 pairs represents a 25% increase since the 1970s but their range is becoming more restricted. The birds are a little more widespread across the northern Meseta in winter.

LAGO DE SANABRIA (León)   CyL1

Status: Parque Natural (22,365 ha).

Site description

The park is in the far west of Castilla y León bordering Galicia. Its centrepiece, and the focus of attraction for most visitors, is the Lago de Sanabria itself, the largest glacial lake (5,027ha) in the Iberian peninsula. The protected area encompasses a large expanse of mountain including the Sierra Segundeira and the Sierra de la Cabrera Baja. It displays a striking range of glacial features, including a diversity of smaller glacial lakes, glacial valleys, gorges and moraines. The altitude ranges from around 1,000m to 2,127m at Peña Trevinca, the highest peak in the sierras to the north. The rivers that flow down to Sanabria lake have carved deep ravines. The mountain slopes are a mosaic of woods of Pyrenean Oak, Chestnut, Holly and Yew, together with scrub and meadows. Springs and streams abound and feed a number of peat bogs.

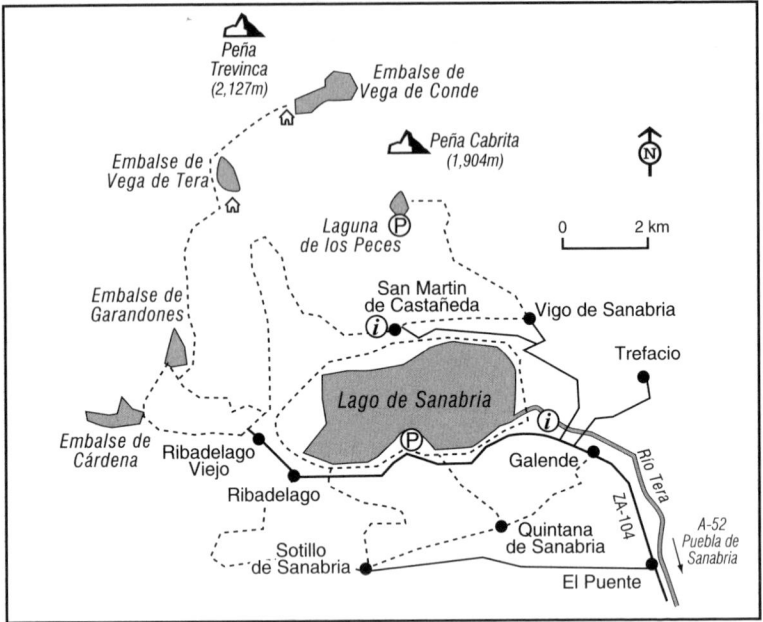

Species

The lake is not of particular ornithological interest, attracting nothing more than the odd Mallard and Common Sandpiper. The mountains, however, support a diversity of montane species, including a significant population of Grey Partridges in the scrub on the high tops. Citril Finches, Water Pipits, Rufous-tailed Rock Thrushes, Bluethroats and Ortolan Buntings also occur at the higher levels. Breeding raptors include Golden, Booted and Short-toed Eagles, Goshawks and Eagle Owls. The woodlands and scrub have a good range of passerines including Red-backed Shrikes.

Wolves are relatively numerous in the area and the other local mammals include Pyrenean Desmans.

Timing

Spring and summer visits are recommended.

Access

From the north take the A-52 west from the A-6 at km-205, north of Benavente. From the south take the N-630/N-631 north-west from Zamora, to the A-52. Head west along the A-52 as far as Puebla de Sanabria, then take the ZA-104 to El Puente and the lake. You can drive along both the southern and northern shores and also up to the Laguna de los Peces (1,707m) to the north, where there is parking. Walking from here offers good chances of finding the mountain-top species. There is also a well-marked track up to this lake from the village of Vigo de Sanabria and another route to another lake (the Embalse de Cárdena) at the western end of Sanabria, from the village of Ribadelago. Other possibilities include the link between the two villages of San Martín de Castañeda and Ribadelago. An information centre in a restored monastery at San Martín can supply more detailed information on routes within the park. It is open daily in summer but only at weekends in winter. Another information centre near Galende, at km-4.5 on the ZA-104, is chiefly open at weekends.

CALENDAR

All year: Red-legged and Grey Partridges, Mallard, Hen Harrier, Goshawk, Sparrowhawk, Common Buzzard, Golden Eagle, Tawny and Eagle Owls, Kingfisher, Wood Lark, Crag Martin, Water Pipit, Grey Wagtail, Dipper, Dunnock, Black Redstart, Blue Rock Thrush, Dartford Warbler, Bullfinch, Citril Finch, Cirl Bunting.

Breeding season: Black Kite, Montagu's Harrier, Short-toed and Booted Eagles, Hobby, Common Sandpiper, Bee-eater, Wryneck, Nightingale, Bluethroat, Common Redstart, Rufous-tailed Rock Thrush, Melodious and Bonelli's Warblers, Spotted Flycatcher, Red-backed Shrike, Ortolan Bunting.

ESTEPAS Y LAGUNAS DE VILLAFÁFILA (Zamora)   CyL2

Status: Espacio Nacional, Reserva Nacional de Caza and ZEPA (32,541 ha). Ramsar site (2,854 ha). Special conservation area for Great Bustards and Lesser Kestrels under the EU 'Life' programme.

Site description

An open steppe landscape, farmed and famous for its cereals, being on the edge of the so-called Tierra del Pan or 'Bread Land'. The gently undulating relief is broken by isolated clumps of trees and the scattered multistorey pigeon lofts which are typical of the area. Some of these have been adapted to provide accommodation for Lesser Kestrels, to help their population recovery. Villafáfila village is fringed by a complex of seasonal lagoons, comprising three relatively large lakes: the Laguna de Barillos, Laguna Grande and Laguna de Las Salinas, and a scattering of smaller pools. The information centre has three artificial pools.

Species

This is an extremely important site all year round, whose location and range of habitats makes it attractive to a wide range of species, including rarities. It harbours the densest population of Great Bustards in Spain, well over 2,000 birds in recent years. It also supports a large Lesser Kestrel population (300 pairs) and good numbers of other steppe birds, including Little Bustards, Stone-curlews and Black-bellied Sandgrouse. The area comes into its own especially during the wetter months when the lagunar complex floods and attracts great numbers of waterfowl, most notably thousands of Greylag Geese. The Greylags often exceed 10,000 birds and counts as high as 40,000 are on record. The Greylag flocks forage on the fields surrounding the lagoons and fly to roost on reservoirs further south. The feeding geese sometimes mingle with transient Cranes and with the resident Great Bustards: you can sometimes see all three species at once in your telescope's field of view. It is always worth scanning the goose flocks for other species: Bean Geese occur with some regularity as well as occasional White-fronted and Barnacle Geese. Canada, Pink-footed, Lesser White-fronted, Snow and Bar-headed Geese have been recorded as vagrants. The lagoons support large numbers of ducks in winter.

Although most of the lagoons dry up completely in summer, water is pumped into the easternmost pool and small numbers of waterfowl remain to breed. They are chiefly Mallard, Gadwall and Shoveler, these last being very local nesters in Spain. Greylag Geese also now breed in small numbers.

The area attracts good numbers of raptors, especially in winter when there is a significant wintering population of Red Kites, Common Buzzards and both Marsh and Hen Harriers. Occasional vole 'plagues' are a recent local feature in autumn and winter and result in considerable concentrations of predators, including Short-eared Owls. Wintering waders include flocks of Lapwings and Golden Plovers. A variety of passage waders also occur and Black-winged Stilts and Avocets breed as do some Common Redshanks and Lapwings.

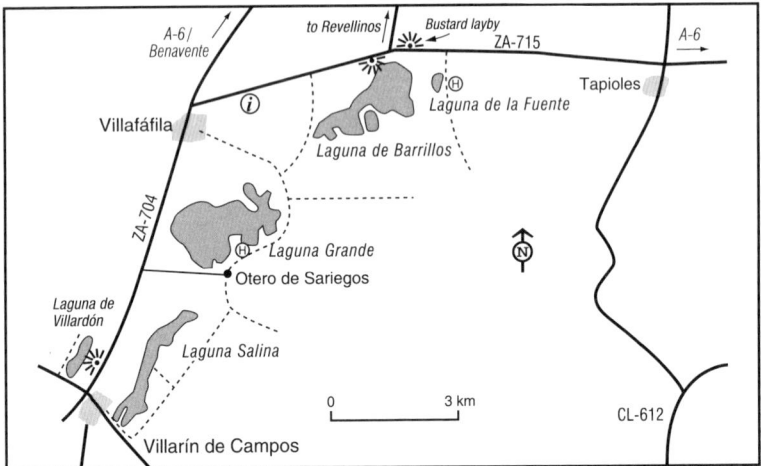

Timing
The site is of interest all year round. Winter sees most birds, with great numbers of geese and ducks reinforcing the local populations of steppe birds and other resident species. Spring and autumn passage can bring a variety of waders and other species. Spring and early summer have considerable breeding bird interest associated with the steppe bird community especially.

Great Bustards

Access

The Villafáfila area is to the east of the main León–Zamora road (N-630) and south of the A-6 motorway near Benavente. From Benavente take the A-6 south-east towards Tordesillas, turning left after 13km at San Esteban del Molar, passing over the main road on to the ZA-704 and continuing for 12km to Villafáfila. If you approach from the south-east you can leave the A-6 2km past Villalpando, taking the ZA-715 to Villafáfila past Tapioles.

A good starting point is the information centre (Tel. 980 586 046. Open Fridays and weekends: 11.00–14.00 and 16.00–19.30 hours) on the south side of the Villafáfila/Tapioles road, 1km east of Villafáfila. There is a nature trail here (1.5km) and hides from which to view the adjacent lagoons. The website (villafafila.com) is very informative and includes details of recent sightings. The Laguna de la Fuente generally has water pumped into it in summer, when most of the lagoons are dry, and is then thronged with waterbirds. The pumping station is in a conspicuous ochre and red brick building topped by a hide. Both Stone-curlews and Black-bellied Sandgrouse sometimes come to drink near the hide. Access is from the short road leading south from the ZA-715, 5km east of Villafáfila.

The lagoons and surrounding fields are readily viewable from the main roads, where there are hides/viewpoints. A purpose-built lay-by at km-8 on the ZA-715 could be termed the 'bustard lay-by' since Great Bustards can usually be seen very well from here. The minor road to Revellinos, just west of the bustard lay-by is also good for steppe birds. A hide at the abandoned village of Otero de Sariegos gives excellent elevated views of the Salina Grande; the quiet tarmacked access road to this hide offers good views of pools and wet pastures on both sides; stop frequently. The principal lagoons are also skirted by a network of tracks, originating just east of the information centre and beyond Otero de Sariegos. You may need to walk along parts of these if they are too muddy for vehicles; they are very slippery when wet. These same tracks are useful in summer since they also give access to the arable land, where bustards and other steppe species can be watched at close quarters, especially if you use your car as a hide.

CALENDAR

All year: Gadwall, Mallard, Shoveler, Marsh Harrier, Common Buzzard, Little and Great Bustards, Stone-curlew, Lapwing, Common Redshank, Black-bellied Sandgrouse; Barn, Little and Short-eared Owls, Zitting Cisticola, Calandra Lark, Southern Grey Shrike.

Winter: Bean Goose (rare), Greylag Goose, Common Shelduck, Wigeon, Mallard, Teal, Pintail, Common Pochard, Red Kite, Hen Harrier, Peregrine Falcon, Merlin, Golden Plover, Dunlin, Ruff, Common Snipe, Reed Bunting.

Breeding season: White Stork, Black Kite, Montagu's Harrier, Lesser Kestrel, Black-winged Stilt, Avocet, Little Ringed Plover, Black-headed Gull, Gull-billed Tern, Red-necked Nightjar, Bee-eater, Roller, Hoopoe, Greater Short-toed Lark, Tawny Pipit, Yellow Wagtail, Spectacled Warbler, Northern Wheatear.

Passage periods: Garganey, Spoonbill, Crane, Ringed and Kentish Plovers, Little and Temminck's Stints, Black-tailed Godwit (has bred), Whimbrel, Spotted Redshank, Greenshank; Green, Wood and Common Sandpipers, Black Tern, Whiskered Tern (has bred), Whinchat.

LAGUNA DE LA NAVA (Palencia)   CyL3

Status: Within the ZEPA 'Nava-Campos Norte' (54,936ha). Ramsar site.

Site description

The meseta to the north-west of Palencia was once occupied by an immense wetland (2,500ha), an inland sea, appropriately named 'Mar de Campos'. This was drained by the late 1960s but more enlightened times, and EU funding, enabled the restoration of some 10% of the original lake in the 1990s. La Laguna de la Nava is a shallow lake of some 300ha, split in two by the P-940 which links the villages of Mazariegos and Fuentes de Nava. The northern half is a nature reserve and the southern half, which is largely wet grassland, is used by livestock. There are extensive reed and sedge beds, expanses of open water and fringing willows. The water level is maintained artificially between October and May, the lake then being permitted to dry up partly as it would do naturally. The surrounding farmland includes large areas of pasture and cereals. Another shallow lake, the Laguna de Güera, is between La Nava and Mazariegos, alongside the Río Valdeginate.

Species

This is once again one of the most important wetlands in Castilla y Léon and one of the few where Garganey, Black-necked Grebes, Purple Herons, Black-headed Gulls and Whiskered Terns breed, alongside a diversity of other more widespread waterbirds. The site list now stands at over 240 species and increases annually. Spoonbills have lingered late in recent springs and may colonise the site. La Nava is well known as a regular staging post of Aquatic Warblers in August–September. It is also excellent for wintering and passage waders, with over 40 species recorded. Waterfowl numbers are especially significant in winter, when over 20,000 birds may be present. Greylag Geese and dabbling ducks predominate. There is a large winter roost of Marsh Harriers, attracting over 100 birds but sometimes many more: a census in November 2006 found 270 Marsh Harriers and 178 Hen Harriers, a local record and no doubt the result of the vole 'plague' which then affected the region. This well-watched lake produces sightings of scarce and vagrant species annually: recent records have included Pink-footed, Greater White-fronted, Lesser White-fronted, Eastern Greylag, Bar-headed, Canada, Barnacle and Red-breasted Geese, Ruddy Shelduck, American Wigeon, Ring-necked Duck, White-headed Duck, Great White Egret, Yellow-billed Stork, Long-billed Dowitcher and Red-throated Pipit. The surrounding farmland has a good population of Great Bustards and other steppe species but they are thinly spread and hence elusive. Passage waders find the shallow Laguna de Güera attractive.

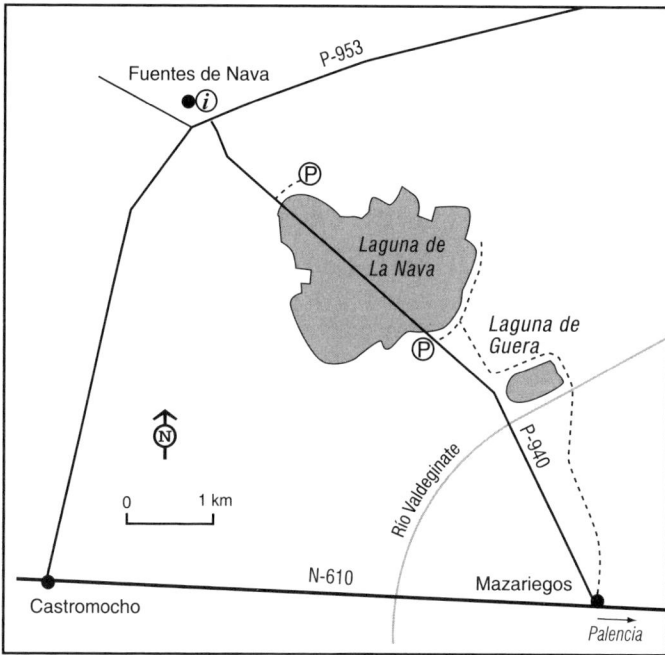

Timing
The lake is interesting all year round but particularly during passage periods and in winter.

Access
Easily accessible. Take the N-610 west from Palencia and turn north-west at km-17 on to the P-940, which crosses the lake. Car parks are available at both ends of the lake and footpaths, with hides and viewpoints allowing closer inspection of the basins. A good track leads east from the main eastern footpath to the Laguna de Güera, where there is also a hide, and on to Mazariegos. The Visitors' Centre, at Fuentes de Nava, is open Wednesday–Friday in the afternoons and all day at weekends.

CALENDAR

All year: Mallard, Gadwall, Shoveler, Common Pochard, Black-necked Grebe, White Stork, Marsh Harrier, Water Rail, Great Bustard, Lapwing, Common Redshank, Black-headed Gull, Black-bellied Sandgrouse, Calandra Lark.

Breeding season: Garganey, Purple Heron, Montagu's Harrier, Spotted and Baillon's Crakes (occasional), Black-winged Stilt, Avocet, Little Ringed and Kentish Plovers, Whiskered Tern, Common Cuckoo, Nightingale, Yellow Wagtail; Savi's, Reed and Great Reed Warblers.

Winter: Greylag Goose, Teal, Wigeon, Pintail, Red Kite, Hen Harrier, Merlin, Peregrine Falcon, Golden Plover, Dunlin, Common Snipe, Water Pipit, Bluethroat, Penduline Tit, Reed Bunting.

Passage periods: Spoonbill, Crane, waders: including Ringed Plover, Little Stint, Curlew Sandpiper, Temminck's Stint, Ruff, Black-tailed and Bar-tailed Godwits, Whimbrel, Curlew, Spotted and Common Redshanks, Greenshank; Green, Wood and Common Sandpipers, Black Tern, Bluethroat; Grasshopper, Aquatic and Sedge Warblers.

ARRIBES DEL DUERO (Zamora/Salamanca)   CyL4

Status: ZEPA (86,000 ha).

Site description

The Río Duero and its main tributaries: the ríos Águeda, Huebra and Tormes, have eroded deep gorges for over 100km across this otherwise rather flat area. The rivers themselves have long been tamed by dams, which generate hydro-electricity, but the spectacular river cliffs and rock faces remain and are of great ornithological interest. The hinterland is given over to traditional farming, with expanses of pasture, cereal and vineyards and many drystone walls. The numerous streams have associated riverine woodland. The vegetation includes important areas of Pyrenean and Iberian Holm Oak woodland as well as patches of *Cistus* and broom scrub and Lusitanian and Cork Oaks. Several large reservoirs are conspicuous in the north of the region but they attract little wildlife. The Duero itself here marks the border with Portugal.

Species

The Duero river and its tributaries are distinguished by their significant populations of cliff-breeding species. They offer some ten pairs of Bonelli's Eagles, the largest population in Castilla y León, as well as outstanding breeding concentrations of Egyptian and Griffon Vultures, Golden Eagles, Black Storks, Peregrines, Eagle Owls, Alpine Swifts, Crag Martins and Red-billed Choughs. The scrub and open countryside are good for Spectacled Warblers and other scrub warblers, as well as Red Kites, Short-toed Eagles, both European and Red-necked Nightjars, Great Spotted Cuckoos, Hoopoes and Azure-winged Magpies. Dupont's Larks have a very small and elusive population in the region, which was first detected in 1993.

Red Kite

The old bridge on the Río Huebra has breeding Rock Doves, Crag Martins, Spotless Starlings and Rock Sparrows. Golden Orioles occur and Common Sandpipers may nest locally. Black Storks visit the river.

Timing

Visits in spring and summer, when the cliff species are breeding, are most productive, but the hinterland of the gorges is interesting all year round.

Access

There are various alternatives for exploring the River Duero, its tributaries and its cliffs depending on your itinerary and where you are based. The approaches to the Duero include some very scenic tracts along peaceful roads, ideal for stopping and viewing raptors as well as woodland and scrub species.

Southern sector Take the SA-324 north from Ciudad Rodrigo or the CL-517 west from Salamanca to Lumbrales from where you can continue towards the Portuguese border at the wharf of Vega de Terrón or take the SA-330 north from Lumbrales to explore the hinterland of Salto de Saucelle, Saucelle and Vilvestre. The approaches to the dam (Presa) at Salto de Saucelle offer a good vantage point.

The CL-517 between Lumbrales and Vitigudino is also good, especially where it crosses the Río Huebra between the villages of Cerralbo and Picones. It is well worth descending to the old bridge here to look for riparian and woodland species; the sole entrance is on the south side of the road, 0.9km west of the new bridge, where the old road descends to the bridge and continues for a further 1.5km.

Central sector This part of the area is best visited from Vitigudino, which is 67km west of Salamanca on the CL-517. The key area is around the dammed sector of the Duero below Aldeadávila. Follow the signs to the Salto de Aldeadávila and continue upriver towards the Presa (dam). The road rises to the Presa gate, from where you can scan the area. You can also continue all the way upwards to the Salida de Lineas (where the powerlines originate), where you can park and a viewpoint gives spectacular views of the dam and the reservoir. The Duero is particularly hemmed in by rock walls here and close views of raptors, including Bonelli's Eagle, and other rupestral species, including Alpine Swift and Red-billed Chough, are available. Take the SA-320 north-west from Vitigudino for 23km and then turn north to Aldeadávila via La Zarza.

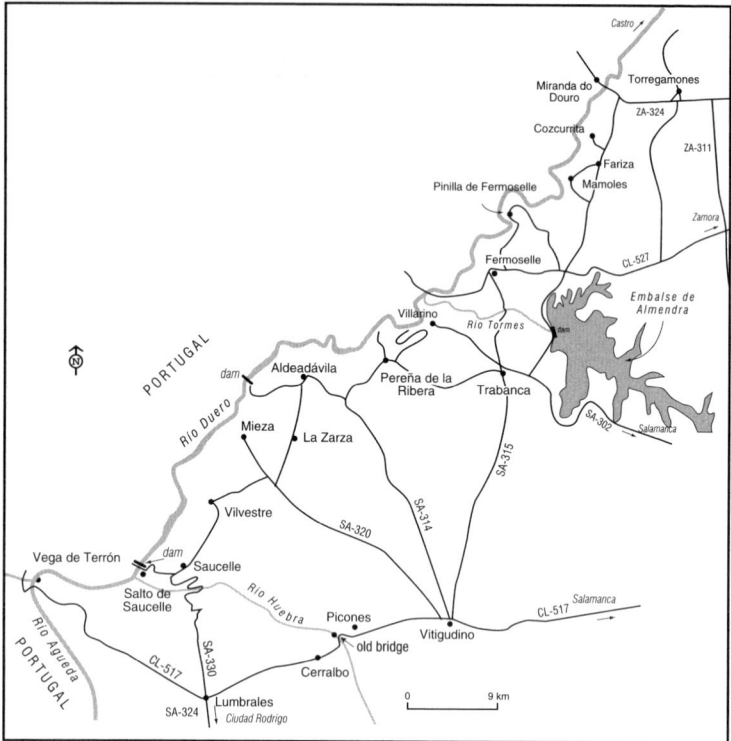

Northern sector   This is readily accessible from both Salamanca on the SA-302 and Zamora on the CL-527.The imposing dam of the Embalse de Almendra offers a good if vertiginous viewpoint down the valley of the Río Tormes. The CL-527 from Fermoselle to the Portuguese border is quiet and scenic and there is a good view of the riverside cliffs just before the road descends to the crossing. The river is also accessible north of Fermoselle from the villages of Pinilla de Fermoselle, Mámoles and Cozcurrita and also where the ZA-324 crosses the border west of Torregamones.

An interesting way to view a large tract of the upper Duero, including some very good bird cliffs, may be to take a boat trip along the river. A service runs at least once daily between Miranda do Douro and Castro. The operators are the Estación/Estação Biológica Internacional Douro/Duero. (Tel. 980 557 557, website europarques.es). We haven't tried this trip ourselves but it is probably best to avoid weekends and public holidays, when numbers of noisy day-trippers may be a problem.

CALENDAR

All year: Great Crested Grebe, Grey Heron, Black-shouldered Kite and Red Kites, Griffon Vulture, Goshawk, Sparrowhawk, Common Buzzard, Golden and Bonelli's Eagles, Common Kestrel, Peregrine Falcon, Stone-curlew, Lesser Spotted Woodpecker, Rock Dove, Eagle Owl, Hoopoe, Kingfisher; Calandra, Dupont's, Thekla and Wood Larks, Crag Martin, Dipper, Black Redstart, Black Wheatear, Blue Rock Thrush, Dartford Warbler, Southern Grey Shrike, Azure-winged Magpie, Red-billed Chough, Raven, Rock Sparrow, Hawfinch, Rock Bunting.

Breeding season: White and Black Storks, Black Kite, Egyptian Vulture, Montagu's Harrier, Short-toed and Booted Eagles, Lesser Kestrel, Great Spotted and Common Cuckoos, European and Red-necked Nightjars, Alpine Swift, Bee-eater, Roller, Tawny Pipit, Red-rumped Swallow, Northern and Black-eared Wheatears; Spectacled, Subalpine, Sardinian and Orphean Warblers, Golden Oriole.

Winter: Cormorant, Black Vulture, Spanish Imperial Eagle (occasional), Hen Harrier, Wallcreeper (rare).

RIBERAS DE CASTRONUÑO (Valladolid) CyL5

Status: ZEPA (8,420ha).

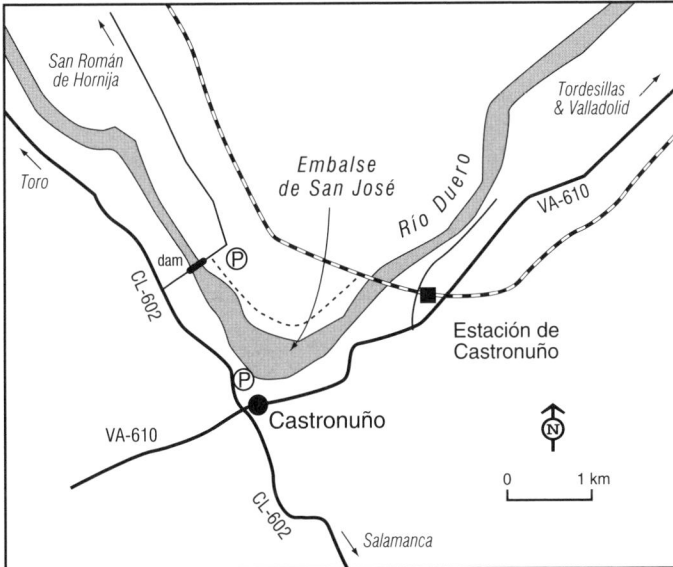

Site description
Riverine woodland alongside the banks of the River Duero, which has been dammed here to produce a small, relatively shallow reservoir, the Embalse de

San José. The reservoir has extensive reedbeds and fringing woods of willows and poplars. Nearby there are large poplar plantations and Holm Oak woodland.

Species

The riverine woods support one of the largest mixed heronries in Castilla y León, including up to 100 pairs of Grey Herons. Several pairs of Little Egrets, Night and Purple Herons and sometimes Little Bitterns also nest here. Black Kites and Marsh Harriers are characteristic breeding raptors and up to 80 of the latter roost here in winter. The reservoir attracts Cormorants and a diversity of other wildfowl, especially in winter. The adjacent countryside includes both dry and irrigated arable land and offers a number of steppe and open-country birds including Pin-tailed Sandgrouse and Rollers. Rooks, a regional speciality, occur occasionally in winter.

Timing

Interesting species are present all year round.

Access

The site is almost equidistant between Salamanca and Valladolid. From the south leave the A-62 at Alaejos taking the CL-602 to Castronuño and the Río Duero. From the north-east take the A-62 south-west from Tordesillas, leaving after 7km at the first exit and heading west to Castronuño along the VA-610. From the north-west take the A-11 towards Tordesillas for 33km to Toro, taking the CL-602 south from there to Castronuño. Head for the dam just north of Castronuño and explore the area on the inner bend of the river, where a footpath follows the north bank. The arable land along the CL-602 north-west of Castronuño should be scanned for open-country birds. It is also worth exploring the countryside around the minor road to San Román de Hornija and the road past the railway station (Estación) that leads to the riverside. There is a visitors' centre in Castronuño (Tel. 983 866 107).

CALENDAR

All year: Little, Great Crested and Black-necked Grebes, Cormorant, Grey Heron, Marsh Harrier, Peregrine Falcon, Stone-curlew, Tawny and Long-eared Owls, Kingfisher, Lesser Spotted Woodpecker, Zitting Cisticola, Cetti's Warbler, Azure-winged Magpie.

Breeding season: Little Bittern, Little Egret, Night and Purple Herons, White Stork, Black Kite, Montagu's Harrier, Booted Eagle, Hobby, Little Bustard, Black-bellied and Pin-tailed Sandgrouse, Great Spotted Cuckoo, European Nightjar, Bee-eater, Roller, Hoopoe; Great Reed, Reed, Savi's and Melodious Warblers, Penduline Tit, Golden Oriole.

Winter: Greylag Goose, Common Pochard, Shoveler, Wigeon, Hen Harrier, Merlin, Avocet, Golden Plover, Rook.

LAS BATUECAS AND SIERRA DE   CyL6
LA PEÑA DE FRANCIA (Salamanca)

Status: Parque Natural (30,182 ha), Reserva Nacional de Caza. Includes the ZEPAs 'Las Batuecas' and 'Arca y Buitrera'.

Site description

Las Batuecas is a sector of the Sistema Central in the extreme south of Salamanca province, bordering the region of Las Hurdes in Extremadura. These sierras came to be called the 'French mountains', having been populated with settlers from France in the 11th century after the Christian reconquest. This remains a very quiet part of Spain with vast areas covered in forest, mountain pastures and scrub. The terrain is very broken in places, with frequent rocky outcrops and cliffs. The Peña de Francia (1,732m) is the highest peak in the sierra but you can drive to the top and enjoy spectacular views north to Salamanca city, west into Portugal, east to the Sierra de Gredos and south into Extremadura. Much of the woodland in this area is natural with a variety of oak species and Sweet Chestnut on the north-facing slopes particularly. The southern-facing slopes have more of a Mediterranean character with Strawberry Tree, Mastic Tree, Yew, Tree Heaths and Cistus. Some areas have been planted with pines.

Species

An important area for raptors, including breeding Black, Griffon and Egyptian Vultures and Golden Eagles. Spanish Imperial Eagles occur and nested in the province in 2015. Black Storks also nest here. The region is a meeting place for certain species of generally northerly distribution, such as Dunnocks and Ortolan Buntings and those, such as Pallid Swifts and Black Wheatears, whose range is mainly in the south. The other fauna includes Spanish Ibex, which are sometimes visible on the ridges, and an endemic lizard, as well as good populations of Red and Roe Deer and Wild Boar.

Timing
The area is most productive in spring and early summer. Autumn colours on the northern slopes are pleasing.

Access
The region is situated about halfway between Plasencia, Extremadura, to the south and Salamanca to the north. From the north take the A-62 south-west from Salamanca towards Ciudad Rodrigo and turn left after some 46km on to the SA-215 towards Tamames. Alternatively, take the CL-512 and SA-210 direct from Salamanca to Tamames. Take the SA-201 south from Tamames to the area of interest. From the south and Plasencia take the A-66 to Béjar and follow the SA-220 north-west to join the SA-201 at El Cabaco.

The area offers many quiet roads and a diversity of signposted footpaths. However, the best region for an initial visit is in the south, where a key site to aim for is the monastery at the peak of Peña de Francia. Drive to the top and scan the area for raptors. It is also worth walking east from the point opposite the start of the final access road to the monastery, following the stony ridge through heathland with scattered pines. Black and Griffon Vultures are often overhead and wheatears and other passerines inhabit the scrub. The SA-203 west of the monastery pinnacle is very quiet and also good for passerines.

A second particularly worthwhile area to explore is the col and viewpoint above the picturesque village of La Alberca on the SA-201. Stop and scan here and then follow the very winding road down to the monastery at Las Batuecas. A footpath leads west from the monastery. An information centre in La Alberca (Tel. 923 415 421) is open daily except Mondays during July–September; on Fridays–Sundays otherwise. You may then continue south towards Las Mestas, passing a small cliff with a Griffon Vulture colony on the right just over the border with Extremadura.

CALENDAR

All year: Griffon and Black Vultures, Goshawk, Common Buzzard, Spanish Imperial Eagle (occasional), Golden Eagle, Peregrine Falcon, Lesser Spotted Woodpecker, Thekla Lark, Grey Wagtail, Dipper, Dunnock, Black Wheatear, Blue Rock Thrush, Dartford Warbler, Crested Tit, Nuthatch, Short-toed Treecreeper, Red-billed Chough.

Breeding season: White and Black Storks, Black Kite, Egyptian Vulture, Short-toed Eagle, Montagu's Harrier, Lesser Kestrel, Hobby, Quail, Great Spotted Cuckoo, Alpine and Pallid Swifts, Bee-eater, Crag Martin, Red-rumped Swallow, Black-eared Wheatear, Rufous-tailed Rock Thrush, Ortolan Bunting.

AZUD DE RIOLOBOS (Salamanca)   CyL7

Status: Inadequately protected. Zona Húmeda Catalogada, part of the ZEPA 'Campos de Alba' (15,637ha).

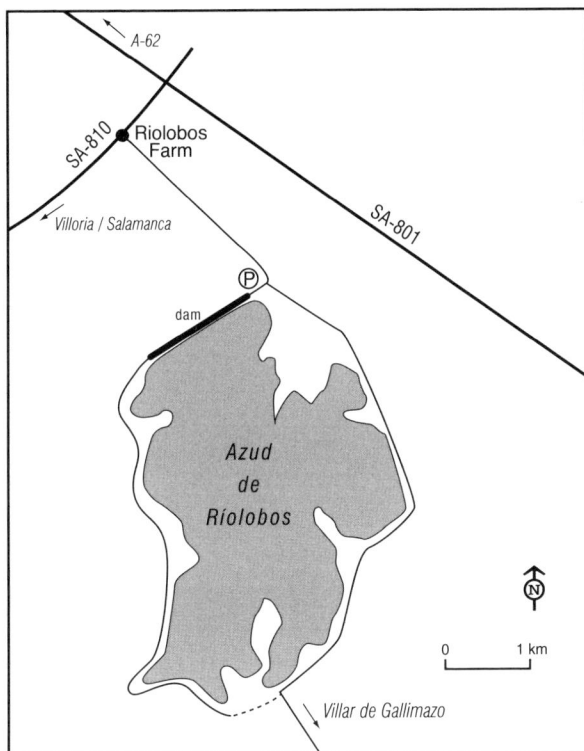

Site description
The Azud is a reservoir (476ha) occupying a shallow basin in the cereal crop-lands in the north-east of Salamanca province. It was created in 1998 but soon came to be one of the premier wetlands of Castilla y León, despite the lack of waterside vegetation until recently. Some small islands are important to nesting waders especially. The lake has been seriously affected by low water levels, poor water quality and excessive disturbance by fishermen in recent years, reducing wildfowl and wader numbers, but measures are in hand to rectify these problems. Water levels were excellent in 2016.

Species
This is an especially important site for passage waders both in spring and autumn, with over 30 species recorded, including such species as Oystercatcher,

Grey Plover, Knot, Sanderling and Turnstone which are uncommon inland. Up to 10,000 waterfowl are present in winter in some years; chiefly Greylag Geese and dabbling ducks, mainly Mallards. Other duck species have included autumn gatherings of up to 200 White-headed Ducks. Up to 400 Cranes roost at the lake in winter.

Breeding species include Black-winged Stilts as well as both Little Ringed and Kentish Plovers. Several Lesser Kestrel colonies occupy buildings nearby. Spoonbills and Ospreys are among other species which occur regularly on passage. The site has acquired a reputation for attracting rarities, which have included such a diverse mixture as African Spoonbill, Ruddy Shelduck, Smew, Pectoral Sandpiper, Lesser Yellowlegs and Long-tailed Skua.

The surrounding croplands have a good population of steppe birds, including both bustards, both sandgrouse, Montagu's and Hen Harriers and Stone-curlews.

Timing

The site is interesting all year round but passage periods and winter see the largest numbers of birds.

Access

The site is some 30km north-east of Salamanca, to the north of the A-50 Salamanca/Ávila motorway. Leave the A-50/N-501 some 14km east of Salamanca at Encinas de Abajo and take the SA-810 to Villoria. Continue on this road for 7km and turn right at a farm 1km south of the SA-801/SA-810 crossroads, where the lake is signposted. The lake may be viewed from the perimeter road, nearly all of which is good tarmac, and especially from the dam itself. The road is a little distant from the lake at most points but it is possible to approach more closely on foot. The minor roads throughout the area provide opportunities for viewing the steppe species.

CALENDAR

All year: Mallard, Great Crested and Little Grebes, White Stork, Hen Harrier, Great and Little Bustards, Stone-curlew, Black-bellied and Pin-tailed Sandgrouse, Lapwing, Barn and Long-eared Owls, Calandra Lark, Southern Grey Shrike.

Breeding season: Black Kite, Montagu's Harrier, Lesser Kestrel, Quail, Black-winged Stilt, Little and Kentish Plovers, Hoopoe, Bee-eater, Tawny Pipit, Yellow Wagtail, Northern Wheatear.

Winter: Greylag Goose, Wigeon, Gadwall, Teal, Pintail, Shoveler, Common Pochard, Tufted Duck, White-headed Duck, Black-necked Grebe, Cormorant, Little and Great White Egrets, Red Kite, Marsh Harrier, Merlin, Common Coot, Golden Plover, Crane, Short-eared Owl, Sky Lark, Meadow Pipit, rarities.

Passage periods: Garganey (spring), Spoonbill, Osprey, Hobby, Avocet, Ringed Plover, Little Stint, Curlew Sandpiper, Dunlin, Temminck's Stint, Ruff, Common Snipe, Black-tailed and Bar-tailed Godwits, Whimbrel, Curlew, Spotted and Common Redshanks, Greenshank, Green, Wood and Common Sandpipers; Gull-billed, Little, Black and Whiskered Terns, rarities.

SIERRA DE GREDOS (Ávila)   CyL8

Status: Parque Regional (86,236ha).

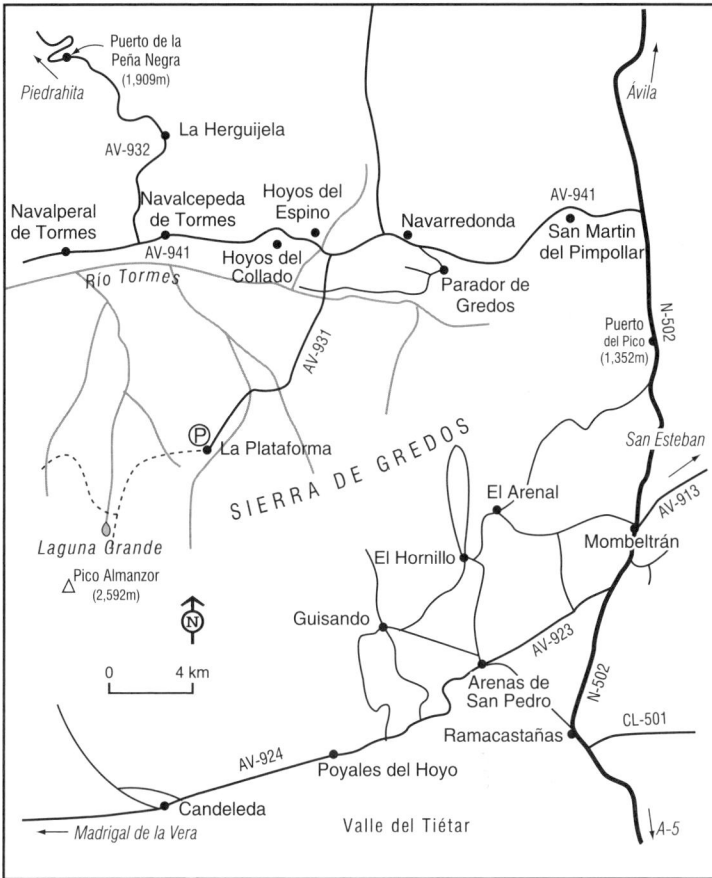

Site description
The Sierra de Gredos and the Sierra de Guadarrama (M1) are the major and
highest components of the Sistema Central, the mountainous barrier separating
Castilla y León to the north from western Castilla–La Mancha, Madrid and
Extremadura to the south. The Sierra de Gredos is a granitic outcrop whose
highest peaks remain snow-capped well into the spring. The high tops include
many glacial lakes set in alpine meadows. The northern slopes are relatively
gentle and are well forested with Pyrenean Oaks and Maritime Pines. The
southern aspect is much more abrupt, the mountains rising steeply from the
Tiétar valley. The vegetation here includes such Mediterranean components as
the Cork Oak and Gum Cistus.

The Sierra extends roughly east/west for some 140km but it is the highest, central sector which is of greatest interest. This lies between the Puerto de Tornavacas (1,275m) at the head of the Valle del Jerte in the west and the Puerto del Pico (1,352m) in the east. The peaks in this sector extend above 2,000m, the highest summit being Pico Almanzor (2,592m).

This central part was once a royal hunting reserve, the Coto Real de Gredos, which was established by Alfonso XIII in 1905 to save the Spanish Ibex from extinction. His initiative was highly successful. The Iberian population now exceeds 35,000 individuals and herds have been successfully reintroduced to several other mountain areas in Spain. In 1928 he also established the Parador de Gredos, the first of this now extensive chain of distinguished hotels.

Species
The Sierra de Gredos is a superb area for birds, particularly when a visit to the high mountain habitats is combined with trips to the northern and southern valleys; with their riverine habitats, reservoirs, steppe and dehesas. The sierra itself is one of the best places to see Bluethroats in Spain and provides one of the few opportunities outside the Pyrenees and Cordillera Cantábrica for seeing breeding Alpine Accentors. The upper reaches also have nesting populations of Water Pipits, Rufous-tailed Rock Thrushes, Goldcrests, Citril Finches and Ortolan Buntings. A diversity of raptors include visiting Spanish Imperial Eagles and nesting Black Vultures, on the southern slopes particularly.

Timing
Spring and summer are necessary for birding on the high tops, which disappear under heavy snow cover and become largely birdless in winter. The weather in the mountains can still be very cold in late spring. Avoid weekends and the summer when visiting some of the more accessible areas and villages, including the Hoyos del Espino road. The whole area can still be very quiet then on weekdays and outside holiday periods.

Blue Rock Thrush

Access

The N-110 Ávila/Plasencia road crosses the range in the west at the Puerto de Tornavacas: turn east at El Barco de Ávila to follow the AV-941 along the Tormes valley. The N-502 from Ávila crosses the range in the east at the Puerto del Pico and you can join the AV-941 westwards 11km north of the pass. The N-502 links up with the A-5 motorway from Madrid near Talavera, providing access from Madrid and the south. There are many high-level signposted trails throughout the range and numerous more casual paths around the villages and from some of the roads. There are also a good number of mountain refuges if you are a keen walker. However, the key montane species can be found quite easily around the Plataforma and along its access road (see below) without needing to walk too far.

The Northern slopes and the Tormes valley   The AV-941 follows the Tormes valley along the northern side of the central massif. From here a detour northwards along the AV-932 to Piedrahita is worthwhile: it is good for woodland birds and also for upland species around the Puerto de la Peña Negra (1,909m).

Access to the highest reaches, in the shadow of Pico Almanzor, is readily available from Hoyos del Espino. The Pinos Cimeros Park information centre (Tel. 920 349 046; open daily except Mondays from 16 June to 31 August, otherwise only on Fridays–Sundays) is at km-0.5 on the AV-931 here. The Centre offers maps of the region. The road climbs for 12km to a car park, known as La Plataforma: where you can find Ortolan and Rock Buntings, Northern Wheatears, perhaps a Rufous-tailed Rock Thrush and Spanish Ibexes. A small charge per vehicle for access to the Plataforma is payable at a barrier on the access road. It is well worth walking on from La Plataforma to the Laguna Grande, the largest glacial lake in the range. The trail takes some two hours each way so you will need food, water and weatherproof clothing. It crosses meadows favoured by Water Pipits and low scrub inhabited by Bluethroats. Bear right to approach the lake, which is signposted. The trail continues west to areas of scree and rocky outcrops where you can search for Rufous-tailed Rock Thrushes and Alpine Accentors. Red-billed Choughs are frequent and the area is visited by Golden Eagles and both Griffon and Black Vultures.

The Puerto del Pico, the pass on the ridge on the N-502, is used as a flyway by migrants and merits a stay of a few hours during passage periods. Such species as the Cormorant and Spoonbill have been seen crossing here, together with a range of raptors.

The pinewoods in the vicinity of the Parador de Gredos hold a representative selection of woodland species. Here you can find both Firecrests and Goldcrests, as well as Crested Tits, Crossbills, Serins and Citril Finches. Red Squirrels are common. Follow the signs to the Parador (an excellent place to stay: Tel. 920 348 048), which is at km-10 on the AV-941, east of Navarredonda. A number of trails lead through the woods from the western end of the Parador car park.

The scenic Iruelas valley, in the far north-east of the Gredos, is well worth a visit. Black Vultures have a very large colony here and Spanish Imperial Eagles and other raptors may also be found. Access is from near the village of El Tiemblo. The 'Valle de Iruelas' is signposted from the N-403 at km-93 and km-97.

The Southern slopes and the Tiétar Valley The eastern section of the range is accessible from the AV-913 which leads eastwards from the N-502 at Mombeltrán, 9km south of the Puerto del Pico, continuing to San Esteban and beyond. To visit the south-eastern part of the central massif take the AV-923 or AV-924 westward from the N-502 to Arenas de San Pedro, from where a network of minor roads serves the villages higher up. There is an information centre 'El Risquillo' (Tel. 920 374 055) at Guisando, 6km north-west of Arenas.

Signposted walks are possible from El Arenal: from where you can walk over the top of Gredos via the Puerto de Cabrilla, and the village of El Hornillo: the recognised start of the Circo de Gredos. Other walking routes are possible from the villages, or you can just explore the general area.

Follow the AV-924 westwards from Arenas for further opportunities to explore Gredos from the southern side. This will take you to Candeleda and on to Madrigal de la Vera and Jarandilla in Extremadura. The possibilities from the Extremaduran sector include trails starting from Madrigal, and from Guijo de Santa Barbara: which is above Jarandilla. You can also visit the southern part of the eastern sector by taking the CL-501 east from Ramacastañas and then exploring the area along the minor roads leading higher into the mountains.

The southern slopes have more of a Mediterranean character than the northern side and offer a wide range of woodland and scrub species, such as the Short-toed and Booted Eagles, Bee-eater, Woodchat and Southern Grey Shrikes, Dartford Warbler and Golden Oriole.

CALENDAR

All year: Red Kite, Griffon and Black Vultures, Goshawk, Sparrowhawk, Common Buzzard, Spanish Imperial and Golden Eagles, Peregrine Falcon, Common Kestrel, Rock Dove, Eagle and Long-eared Owls, Lesser Spotted Woodpecker, Dipper, Alpine Accentor, Black Redstart, Blue Rock Thrush, Dartford Warbler, Goldcrest, Firecrest, Crested Tit, Southern Grey Shrike, Azure-winged Magpie, Red-billed Chough, Raven, Rock Sparrow, Citril Finch, Crossbill, Hawfinch, Rock Bunting.

Breeding season: White and Black Storks, Black Kite, Honey-buzzard, Egyptian Vulture, Short-toed and Booted Eagles, Common Snipe (rare), Great Spotted Cuckoo, Bee-eater, Hoopoe, Red-rumped Swallow, Water Pipit, Bluethroat, Common Redstart, Northern and Black-eared Wheatears, Rufous-tailed Rock Thrush; Melodious, Orphean and Bonelli's Warblers, Pied Flycatcher, Golden Oriole, Woodchat Shrike, Ortolan Bunting.

Winter: Fieldfare, Song Thrush, Redwing, Brambling, Siskin.

HOCES DEL RÍO DURATÓN (Segovia) CyL9

Status: Parque Natural and ZEPA (5,037 ha).

Site description
The Hoces del Río Duratón is just north of the Sierra de Guadarrama. The river runs for 25km downstream from the town of Sepúlveda in the east to the

Burgomillodo dam through a deep gorge with spectacular cliffs up to 100m high. The gorge also has caves and riverine woodland of willow and poplar, which contrasts sharply with that of the surrounding 'barren' plain, the '*paramera*'. This open terrain is dotted with clumps of juniper and other low scrub. There are some areas of pinewood within the park's boundaries and the sides of the gorge have scrub vegetation.

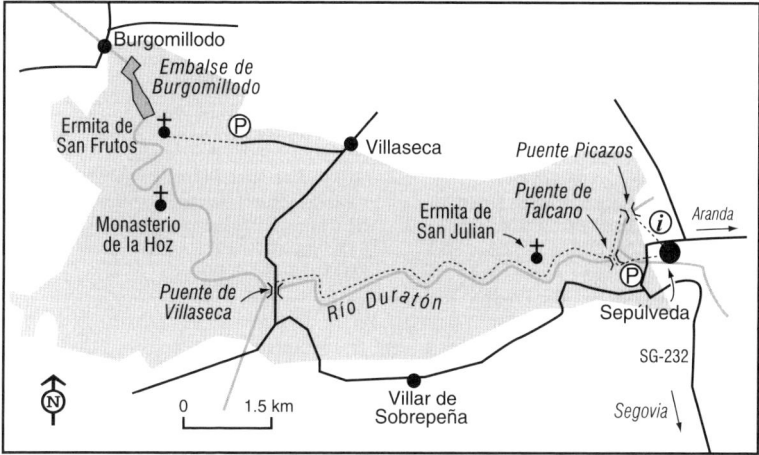

Species

The site is renowned for its large colonies of Griffon Vultures, totalling over 500 pairs. They share the cliffs with several pairs of Egyptian Vultures, Peregrines and Eagle Owls, and at least one pair of Golden Eagles. The park is also very good for other raptors including Red and Black Kites, Goshawks and Booted and Short-toed Eagles. Red-billed Choughs are characteristic. Both Blue and Rufous-tailed Rock Thrushes breed, alongside Rock Sparrows, Rock Buntings and Black, Black-eared and Northern Wheatears. The *paramera* supports an outpost population of Dupont's Larks.

Timing

Spring and early summer are most productive, especially if you are looking for the Dupont's Larks, which are most vocal then. It can get very hot here later in the summer.

Access

The best starting point for a visit is Sepúlveda, where there is a visitors' centre 'Casa del Parque' (Tel. 921 540 322; open daily). From Segovia take the CL-601 northwards for around 10km then turn right on to the C-603, and then the SG-231 to Sepúlveda. From Madrid or the north take the A-1 and then the SG-232/SG-234 to Sepúlveda. Paths in Sepúlveda lead to the bridges (Puentes de Talcano and Picazos) over the Ríos Duratón and Caslilla, where there are good views down into the gorge. A trail follows the northern bank of the Duratón downstream from the Puente de Talcano for over 12km to the Puente de Villaseca. Access to this trail is restricted to a maximum of 75 persons per day during the first half of the year, to reduce disturbance of the nesting raptors: ask for permission at the visitors' centre. You can also walk upstream along a shorter trail from the Puente de Talcano.

Another main vantage point down into the gorge is at the Ermita de San Frutos. Take the road out of Sepúlveda to Villar de Sobrepeña and across the river to Villaseca. From Villaseca a track leads to the ruined hermitage and you can park about 1km from there. The road and track cross a very good area for Dupont's Larks.

CALENDAR

All year: Great Crested Grebe, Cormorant, Grey Heron, Red Kite, Griffon Vulture, Goshawk, Sparrowhawk, Common Buzzard, Golden and Bonelli's Eagles, Peregrine Falcon, Stone-curlew; Tawny, Eagle and Long-eared Owls, Hoopoe, Green Woodpecker; Dupont's, Calandra and Thekla Larks, Grey Wagtail, Black Redstart, Blue Rock Thrush, Dartford Warbler, Long-tailed and Crested Tits, Southern Grey Shrike, Azure-winged Magpie, Red-billed Chough, Rock Sparrow, Rock Bunting,

Breeding season: White Stork, Black Kite, Egyptian Vulture, Montagu's Harrier, Short-toed and Booted Eagles, Hobby, Lesser Kestrel, Common Sandpiper, Great Spotted Cuckoo, Bee-eater, Roller, Greater Short-toed Lark, Crag Martin, Tawny Pipit, Nightingale, Northern and Black-eared Wheatears, Rufous-tailed Rock Thrush, Spectacled Warbler, Golden Oriole.

MONTEJO RAPTOR REFUGE.   CyL10
HOCES DEL RÍO RIAZA (Segovia)

Status: Parque Natural (6,470ha). Includes the ZEPA Refugio de Rapaces de Montejo de la Vega (2,100ha), administered by WWF España.

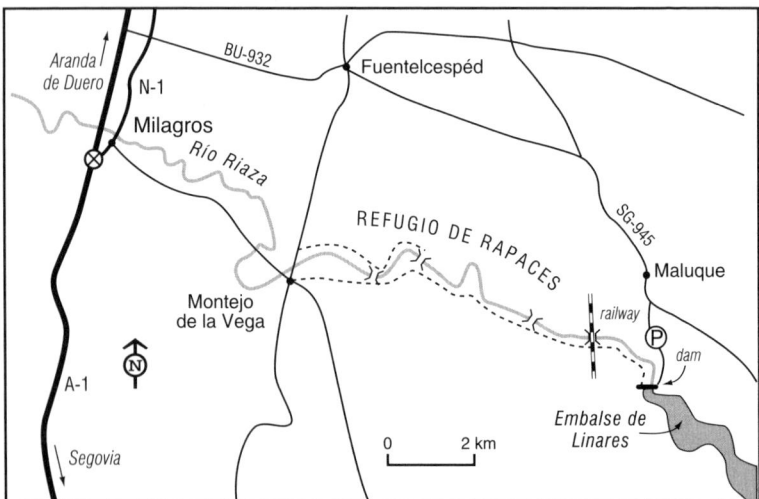

Site description

The Río Riaza, a tributary of the Duero, has carved a deep limestone ravine through a region of dry scrub, the '*paramera*'. The river has been dammed upstream of the ravine, forming the Embalse de Linares. The gorge downstream of the reservoir, between the dam and the town of Montejo de la Vega, has steep cliffs some 150m high. The area is interesting botanically, with attractive mixed riverine woodland along the channel. The slopes have important stands of Spanish Junipers well as clumps of stunted Holm Oaks and other shrubs.

Species

The interest is centred around cliff-nesting species, especially the colony of Griffon Vultures (544 pairs in 2014), one of the largest in Spain. Several pairs of Egyptian Vultures, Peregrines and Eagle Owls also nest here, as well as a pair of Golden Eagles. The cliffs also have Alpine Swifts, Crag Martins, Red-billed Choughs and Rock Sparrows. Warblers and thrushes, including Ring Ouzels, are attracted to the fruiting junipers in winter. The surrounding steppe has a resident population of Dupont's Larks and Black-bellied Sandgrouse.

Timing

Spring and early summer for the cliff-nesting species.

Access

The site is in the extreme north of Segovia province, 12km south of Aranda de Duero along the A-1/N-I motorway: take the minor roads from the motorway at km-133.6 or km-146.4 to Montejo de la Vega, where there is an information centre, 'Casa del Parque' (Tel. 921 532 459, open daily for most of the year).

Three contiguous signposted trails can be followed along the gorge from Montejo. Two of them follow the southern bank and then cross over to return to Montejo along the opposite side. The shortest trail, crossing the first bridge, is only 3km long and comfortably covered in an hour. The second trail is 6.5km and the third continues all the way to the dam at the end of the gorge, a distance of 11.5km.

Access is also available at the reservoir end. Drive north from Montejo to Fuentelcésped and take the SG-945 eastwards for 10km, turning right at the sign for the Embalse de Linares. Park where indicated above the dam and walk down the road to the reservoir. Cross here to the southern bank and follow the trail as far as inclination, energy or time permit.

CALENDAR

All year: Griffon Vulture, Golden Eagle, Peregrine Falcon, Black-bellied Sandgrouse, Rock Dove; Barn, Eagle and Little Owls, Kingfisher, Green and Great Spotted Woodpeckers, Hoopoe, Dupont's and Thekla Larks, Black Wheatear, Blue Rock Thrush, Azure-winged Magpie, Red-billed Chough, Southern Grey Shrike, Spotless Starling, Rock Sparrow, Rock Bunting.

Breeding season: Egyptian Vulture, Booted and Short-toed Eagles, Hobby, Scops Owl, Alpine Swift, Bee-eater, Wryneck, Crag and House Martins, Tawny Pipit, Northern and Black-eared Wheatears, Rufous-tailed Rock Thrush; Spectacled, Subalpine and Bonelli's Warblers, Whitethroat, Woodchat and Red-backed Shrikes, Golden Oriole.

Winter: Red Kite, Alpine Accentor, Ring Ouzel, Fieldfare, Song Thrush, Redwing, Mistle Thrush.

CAÑÓN DEL RÍO LOBOS (Soria)   CyL11

Status: Parque Natural and ZEPA (9,580ha).

Site description

This park protects over 20km of the valley of the Río Lobos (Wolf River) and in particular the 14km-long *cañón*, a deep gorge with sheer, cave-riddled walls as high as 200m. There is some riverine woodland: chiefly willows and poplars, along parts of the watercourse and clumps of Spanish Juniper and Holm Oak on the slopes, with Scots and Maritime Pines on the steeper gradients.

Species

The gorge supports a typical cliff-nesting community including colonies of Griffon Vultures, as well as Egyptian Vultures, Peregrines and Eagle Owls, alongside Alpine Swifts, Red-billed Choughs, Rock Sparrows and Rock Buntings. Golden Eagles nest in some years. Citril Finches are a possibility and there is a chance of a Wallcreeper in winter.

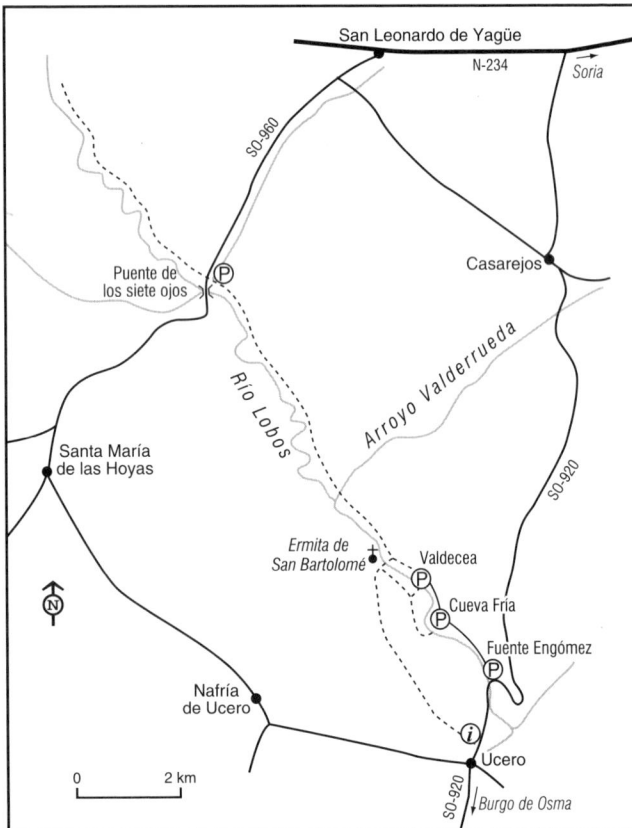

Timing

Spring and early summer. This is a very popular picnic site and can get crowded at weekends, on public holidays and during the summer months, so these times are best avoided. Indeed disturbance of nesting raptors by visitors has caused problems in some years. Most visitors enter the park from the south, so if you want the park to yourself, come in the morning – and from the northern end. Access roads and car parking are subject to restrictions at popular periods.

Access

You can approach either end of this gorge, although it is a little ambitious to walk the whole length, unless you have two vehicles and can leave one at each end. For the northern end, take the N-234 from Soria westwards towards Burgos, and turn left after 48km at San Leonardo de Yagüe on to the SO-960 towards Santa María de las Hoyas. This road goes over the river, where there is parking at Seven-eye bridge, the Puente de los Siete Ojos. A trail leads upstream into the gorge from here.

For the southern end take the N-122 out of Soria for 57km far as El Burgo de Osma and turn north on to the SO-920 to Ucero. From there a forestry road takes you to the southern entrance to the gorge where there is parking and an information centre (Tel. 975 363 507; open mainly Thursdays–Sundays, daily in summer) in an old mill. The popular 3km trail downstream to the Ermita de San Bartolomé is recommended, and is also accessible from the car parks at Fuente Engómez, Cueva Fría and Valdecea. The trail continues beyond the hermitage, the next 8km or so being particularly spectacular.

CALENDAR

All year: Griffon Vulture, Goshawk, Golden Eagle, Peregrine Falcon, Rock Dove, Eagle Owl, Kingfisher, Wood Lark, Dipper, Black Redstart, Black Wheatear, Azure-winged Magpie, Red-billed Chough, Jackdaw, Rock Sparrow, Citril Finch, Serin, Cirl and Rock Buntings.

Breeding season: Egyptian Vulture, Short-toed Eagle, Scops Owl, Alpine Swift, Crag and House Martins, Black-eared Wheatear, Subalpine Warbler, Whitethroat, Golden Oriole, Ortolan Bunting.

Winter: Merlin, Goldcrest, Wallcreeper.

SIERRA DE URBIÓN (Soria)   CyL12

Status: ZEPA. Part of the 'Picos de Urbión' Reserva Nacional de Caza (100,023ha).

Site description

An attractive sector of the central Sistema Ibérico, bordering La Rioja and near the Sierra de la Demanda (R1). These are high mountains, with several peaks above 2,000m including Urbión itself (2,229m). The area is clothed with extensive forests of Scots Pine, with smaller amounts of beech and Pyrenean Oak. The unforested tracts offer a mixture of steep rocky slopes, high meadows and heath. There are also a number of mountain lakes, the most famous being the Laguna Negra, which lies at 1,700m in the heart of the Sierra. The area forms part of the watershed between the Ebro and Duero basins and includes the source of the Duero itself at 2,100m, from where the river starts its journey westwards through Castilla y León and then across Portugal to the Atlantic.

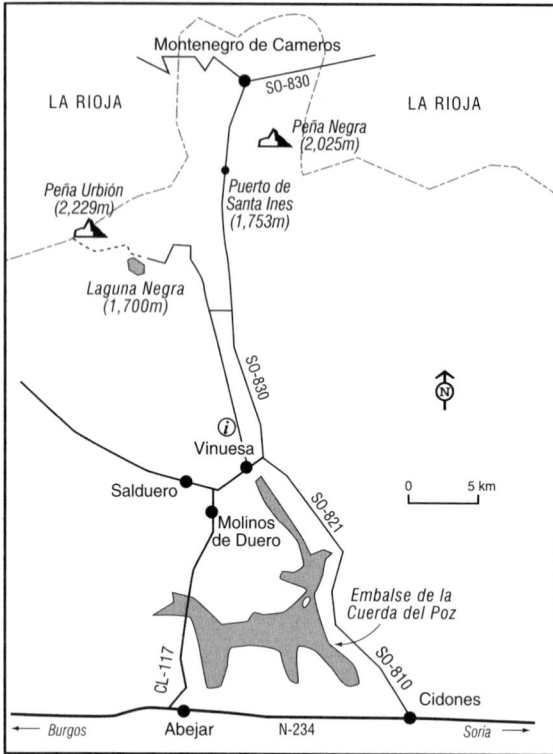

Species
The mountains and forests support a varied avifauna, including a number of species: Grey Partridge, Marsh Tit, Eurasian Treecreeper, Bullfinch and Yellowhammer which are at or near the southernmost limit of their Spanish breeding ranges here. Breeding raptors include Honey-buzzards and Hen Harriers among other more widespread species. Woodcock, Alpine Accentors and Citril Finches also breed.

Timing
Spring and summer visits are best. It may be difficult to reach the lake and the pass during cold springs when snow lies deep.

Access
Most visitors to the sierra drive up to the Laguna Negra. There is an information centre (Tel. 975 377 490) on the access road. The lake is of no significant birding interest but from here you can explore higher along the footpath to the

Laguna Larga and beyond. Look for Citril Finches on the woodland fringes, Water Pipits on the meadows and Alpine Accentors on the rocky slopes.

From Soria take the N-234 westwards for 13km to Cidones. Turn right here on to the SO-810 to Vinuesa and continue onwards on the SO-830, taking the minor road on the left after 7km, signposted to the Laguna Negra. It is also worth continuing further up the SO-830 to the pass of Puerto de Santa Ines (1,753m), where you can search for Alpine Accentors on the scree and Grey Partridges in the scrub.

CALENDAR

All year: Grey Partridge, Griffon Vulture, Goshawk, Common Buzzard, Golden Eagle, Woodcock, Tawny and Long-eared Owls, Wood and Sky Larks, Water Pipit, Dipper, Alpine Accentor, Blackcap, Goldcrest, Crested and Marsh Tits, Eurasian Treecreeper, Citril Finch, Crossbill, Bullfinch, Yellowhammer.

Breeding season: White Stork, Honey-buzzard, Egyptian Vulture, Hen Harrier, Short-toed and Booted Eagles, Hobby, Common Cuckoo, Bee-eater, Tree Pipit, Northern Wheatear, Rufous-tailed Rock Thrush, Song Thrush, Whitethroat, Garden and Bonelli's Warblers, Pied Flycatcher.

OTHER SITES WORTH VISITING

CYL13 ESTEPAS DE MADRIGAL (SALAMANCA/ÁVILA)

Largely a cereal growing area where much steppe habitat has been lost to irrigation schemes. Steppe species present include both bustards and both sand-grouse, as well as Montagu's Harriers and Lesser Kestrels. The main interest is between Madrigal de las Altas Torres and Peñaranda de Bracamonte, on the CL-610 and farmland to the east of this, which is crossed by many minor roads. Leave the A-50 Salamanca/Ávila motorway at Peñaranda (km-50) and head north towards Madrigal on the CL-610. Explore the minor roads through the general area. Possibilities include the roads to and around Horcajo de las Torres to the west of the CL-610 and those south and east of Rasueros.

CYL14 LAGUNA DEL OSO (ÁVILA)

A small lake (16ha) with reed and sedge beds some 23km north of Ávila city. It is a SEO/Birdlife reserve. There are winter roosts of Red Kites and hundreds of Cranes and large numbers of Greylag Geese and other waterfowl also occur on passage and in winter. A diversity of wintering and passage waders are recorded. There are steppe species in the adjacent cereal lands, including Pin-tailed and Black-bellied Sandgrouse: which drink at the lake in summer. Take the AV-804 north from Ávila to Las Berlanas and then the minor road north from there for 5km to El Oso village. The lake is reached along a 1km sandy track opposite and just north of the village, alongside a tyre depot. Park by the hide and view from the trackside. The hide is usually locked but the key is available on request at the bar in El Oso.

CYL15 RÍO CARRIÓN AND CANAL DE CASTILLA (PALENCIA)

Riverine woodland of poplar, Alder, willow and elm. Breeding birds include Night and Purple Herons, Little Bitterns, Penduline Tits, Great Reed Warblers and Golden Orioles. Take the N-611 north out of Palencia and after 15km turn left along the P-984 to Ribas de Campos. Continue through the village for 1km until you reach the canal. The river is on your left. Footpaths follow both waterways.

CYL16 FUENTES CARRIONAS (PALENCIA)

A mountainous area bordering Cantabria, with peaks up to 2,500m and much oak and beech forest. Black Woodpeckers occur as well as Alpine Accentors, Wallcreepers, Yellow-billed Choughs and Snowfinches at the highest elevations. Take the A-67/N-611 to Aguilar de Campóo and head westwards on the CL-626 to Cervera de Pisuerga. From here either take the CL-627 29km north to Puerto de Piedraslenguas or the P-210 34km west to Cardaño de Abajo and Cardaño de Arriba.

CYL17 HOCES DE LOS RÍOS EBRO Y RUDRÓN (BURGOS)

Gorges along the confluence of the Rudrón and Ebro rivers. Cliff-nesters including Griffon Vultures, Golden Eagles, Peregrine Falcons, Eagle Owls and Alpine Swifts occur. Yellow-billed Choughs may be present among the Red-billed Choughs. Take the N-623 north from Burgos towards Santander. Turn off around km-60 to Valdelateja to explore Rudrón Gorge. Continue northward on the N-623 to Quintanilla-Escalada a few kilometres further on for the Ebro gorge.

CYL18 SABINAR DE CALATAÑAZOR (SORIA)

Venerable Spanish Juniper woodland with scrub and small river gorges. Egyptian Vultures, Subalpine Warblers and Ortolan Buntings all breed. Take the N-122 south-west out of Soria towards Burgo de Osma and turn north at km-188 for Calatañazor and continue towards Muriel de la Fuente to reach the woodland. Footpaths at Calatañazor also follow the banks of the Río Avión to and from Aldehuela de Calatañazor.

CYL 19 LAGUNA DE BOADA (PALENCIA)

A small lake that attracts similar birds to the Laguna de La Nava, including large numbers of Greylag Geese in winter. Take the N-610 west from Palencia (33km) and follow the P-992 for 4km to Boada de Campos. Park in the village and follow the signposted 1.2km access track to where a hide overlooks the lake.

CYL 20 SIERRA DE LA CULEBRA (ZAMORA)

An extensive hilly region south-west of Sanabria (CyL1). The region is a mosaic of broom scrub, heathland, pine plantations and oak woods. It is renowned for its Iberian Wolf population, although these are ever-elusive and best sought with the aid of a guide. A visitors' centre, the 'Centro del Lobo Ibérico' (centrodellobo.es/) at Robledo, some 12km south-east of the A-52 at Puebla de Zanabria offers information (and captive wolves). The region may also be accessed from the many minor roads leading west from the N-631 to the east. The breeding bird species include Black-shouldered Kites, Honeybuzzards, European Nightjars, Bonelli's Warblers and Southern Grey Shrikes.

CYL 21 LA GRANJA DE SAN ILDEFONSO (SEGOVIA)

A former royal summer palace. The extensive grounds attract woodland species including Goldcrest, Crested Tit, Azure-winged Magpie and Crossbill. Citril Finches sometimes occur. The surrounding area, on the approaches to the Sierra de Guadarrama at the Puerto de Navacerrada (M1), is excellent for overflying raptors, including Black Vultures and Spanish Imperial Eagles. The palace is on the CL-601, 10km from Segovia.

CYL 22 SEGOVIA CITY

The scenic city is renowned for the Roman aqueduct and other historical artefacts but it also has noteworthy populations of Red-billed Choughs, White Storks and Common Swifts.

CATALUÑA (Catalunya)

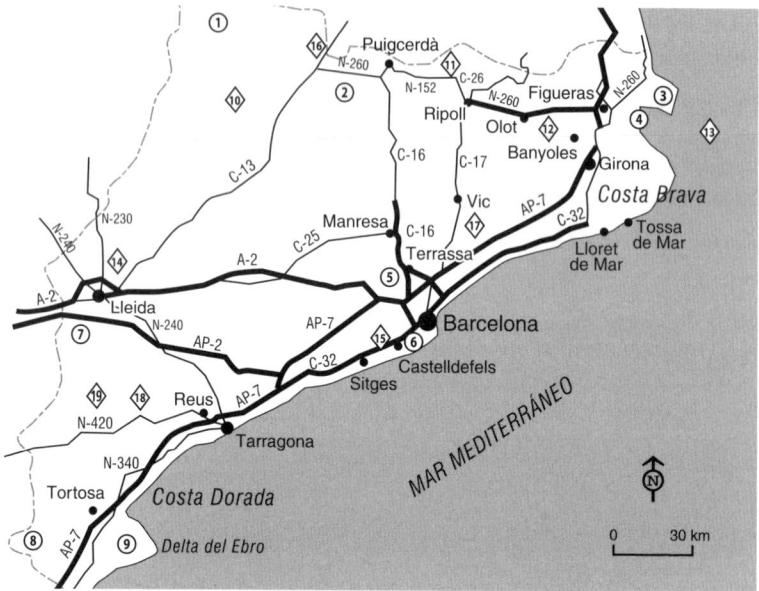

Main sites

CAT1	Parc Nacional d'Aigüestortes i Estany de Sant Maurici
CAT2	Cadí–Moixeró
CAT3	Cap de Creus (Cabo de Creus)
CAT4	Aiguamolls de L'Empordà
CAT5	Muntanya de Montserrat
CAT6	Delta del Llobregat
CAT7	Estepas de Lleida y Embalse de Utxesa
CAT8	Els Ports de Tortosa–Beseit
CAT9	Delta de l'Ebre (Ebro delta)

Other sites worth visiting

CAT10	Serra de Boumort (Sierra del Boumort)
CAT11	La Vall de Núria
CAT12	Parc Natural de la Zona Volcanica de la Garrotxa
CAT13	Illes Medes (Islas Medes)
CAT14	Estepas de Algerri
CAT15	Parc Natural de Garraf
CAT16	L'Alt Pirineu
CAT17	Montseny
CAT18	Montsant
CAT19	Reserva Natural de Sebes

The Catalan region is one of the most distinctive in Spain. It has its own language, Catalán, and its own special customs and culture, reflected in a firm assertion of regional autonomy. The capital, Barcelona, has for many become the top Spanish city, a lively energetic metropolis famous for Las Ramblas and its Modernist buildings – and which sums up the vibrancy of this dynamic entity in the north-east corner of Spain.

The diversity of Cataluña extends to its landscape, habitats and birds: all of which are immensely varied. In a relatively compact area we have the high mountains of the Pyrenees, the Mediterranean coastal mountains, the rocky coast of the north (Costa Brava), the sandy coast to the south (Costa Dorada), the remarkable Ebro Delta: one of the most important coastal sites in Europe, the inland steppes of the Ebro valley around Lleida and the wooded volcanic plugs of Garrotxa: a region that recalls temperate Europe despite being in the Mediterranean.

The Catalan coast was one of the first stretches of the Spanish littoral to be developed for mass tourism but, in the main, any excesses have been confined to the south. However, the Aiguamolls (CAT4), potentially one of the finest coastal wetlands in the country, has lost much of its importance as a result of recent indifferent management, although it remains well worth visiting.

The Llobregat delta (CAT6) is a must if you are staying in or visiting Barcelona. The nearby airport ensures that the backdrop is not as pleasant as at the Aiguamolls but this site, as well as being handy for the city, is another important coastal wetland with breeding Little Bitterns, Audouin's Gulls and Purple Swamphens among others and huge numbers of wintering Mediterranean Gulls. The delta also seems to pick up quite a number of rarities among the many passage migrants.

The Ebro Delta (CAT9) is unlike any other site in Spain. What it lacks in the compactness and ease of observation that the Aiguamolls offers, it makes up for in scale: not merely in the extent of the delta but also of the number of species likely to be encountered and the size of the breeding and wintering populations. It is impossible to do the delta justice in a few lines or even adequately to describe its interest, but with over 6,000 pairs in total of breeding terns of five species, 4,000 pairs of Red-crested Pochards, 70 pairs of Collared Pratincoles, some 5,000 pairs of Audouin's Gulls and several hundred pairs of Slender-billed Gulls its importance is easy to grasp. Come the winter and there could be approaching 100,000 wildfowl around and many thousands of herons, Glossy Ibises and egrets!

The Catalan sector of the Pyrenees includes one of the most beautiful parts of the mountain chain, the Aigüestortes National Park (CAT1), sometimes described as the Spanish equivalent of the Swiss Alps, with a landscape dotted with lakes and surrounded by huge peaks, pastures and forest. Cadí-Moixeró (CAT2) is another excellent area and this, the most easterly part of the Pyrenees, still has all the high-altitude specialities: Lammergeier, Ptarmigan, Alpine Accentor, Wallcreeper, Yellow-billed Chough, Snowfinch and Ring Ouzel. Move into the forested parts and given luck and patience you should see Capercaillie, Black Woodpeckers, Citril Finches and Siskins. But perhaps the species most emblematic of the high-altitude forests is the Boreal (Tengmalm's) Owl; Cataluña has the bulk of the Spanish population, around 150 pairs.

The lower sierras and the valleys, woods and pastures of the Pyrenean foothills are not often given the attention they deserve when you pass through on the way up to the peaks. One good example is the Sierra de Boumort (CAT10). Grey Partridges, Griffon and Egyptian Vultures, Honey-buzzards, Woodcock, Red-backed Shrikes, Tree Pipits, Whinchats, Bullfinches and Yellowhammers all make time here well spent: some of these species are also relatively widespread in the UK and northern Europe but they are at or near their southern limits in Europe here.

Finally there is that forgotten part of Cataluña, its steppes around Lleida (CAT7), where the eastern part of the Ebro Valley and Los Monegros sneak into the region. A visit here is increasingly becoming an important part of any birding itinerary with the attractions of White Storks, Black Kites, Montagu's

Harriers, Little Bustards, Stone-curlews, Pin-tailed Sandgrouse, Dupont's and Calandra Larks and Rollers. And if you do have a day or two left at the end of your holidays, then why not travel to la Zona Volcanica de la Garrotxa (CAT12) with its 30 extinct volcanoes!

We have used Catalan names for all the sites in this chapter, since these are the ones you will meet most widely on signposts.

PARC NACIONAL D'AIGÜESTORTES i ESTANY DE SANT MAURICI (Lérida)   CAT1

Status: Parque Nacional (39,797ha, with a core area of 13,900ha and 26,079ha of peripheral protection), ZEPA (10,230ha). Ramsar site.

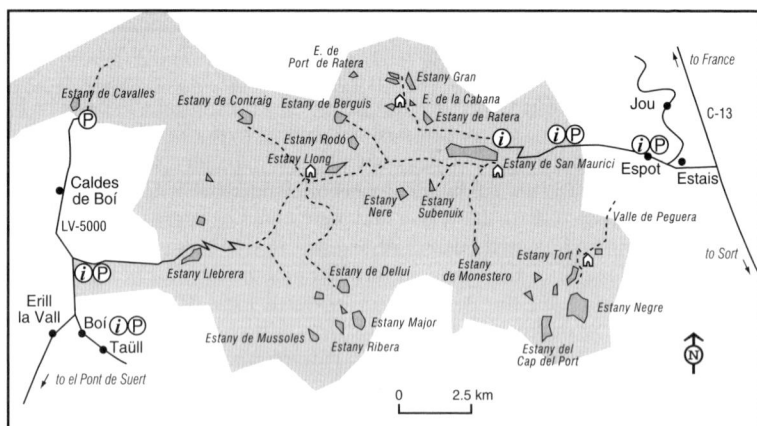

Site description

The Parque Nacional de Aigüestortes i Estany de Sant Maurici is in the high Pyrenees, in Lleida province. Another National Park in the high Pyrenees – Ordesa and Monte Perdido (AR4) – adjoins it in Aragón. The Park comprises two distinct halves – Aigüestortes (Catalan for 'winding or twisted waters') in the west: accessible from the Boi Valley, and Sant Maurici in the eastern half: accessible from the Espot valley.

The Park has some of the most beautiful scenery in the whole of the Pyrenees, including around 200 lakes, along with many streams, waterfalls and marshes. With forests, meadows, and jagged snow-capped peaks to complement its wetland features it is often referred to as the 'jewel of the Catalan Pyrenees'. Few places in Europe can match the beauty of Estany de Sant Maurici in particular, a large lake completely encircled by trees and mountains. Comaloforno, at 3,030m, is the highest peak in the Park.

The valleys are a mixture of pasturelands with woodlands of Black Pine, Silver Fir, beech and birch. At Caldes de Boi there are many hot springs and a spa.

Wallcreeper

Species

Like much of the Pyrenees this area is especially important for raptors, particularly Lammergeiers and Golden Eagles. Key forest species, including
Capercaillie and Black Woodpeckers, are scattered throughout and Boreal
Owls are found further up the mountain slopes in the high-altitude woods
around the lakes. Overall it has a very rich woodland bird fauna.

Another sought-after group of birds is composed of those that breed at the
highest altitudes. They include Ptarmigan, Alpine Accentors, Wallcreepers,
Ring Ouzels, Yellow-billed Choughs, Snowfinches, Rufous-tailed Rock
Thrushes and Water Pipits. Citril Finches are relatively widespread within
the park, around the margins of forests in open glades (and at car parks and
picnic sites). Other species occurring at lower altitudes in the valleys include
Whinchat, Red-backed Shrike and Yellowhammer.

Otters are found in some of the lakes and Chamois breed in the park, but
are seen more easily in the winter when they come down for shelter. Alpine
Marmots occur at high elevations.

Timing

May through to early July is recommended. Weekends can be very busy and
some roads are blocked by snow in winter.

Access

There are two main access points to the Park, via the Boí and the Espot valleys,
but private vehicles are not allowed into the core area. Arrangements can be
made with recognised official 4x4 taxis to take you further and higher into the
Park. Ask at the information centres at Boí (Tel. 973 696 189) or Espot (Tel.
973 624 036) for details. Information on the many trails is also available there.

Aigüestortes   The western part of the National Park. Take the N-230 north
out of Lleida towards the French border and 3km after El Pont de Suert, turn
right on the L-500 to Caldes de Boí. The turning into the National Park, some
2km before you reach this spa, is well signposted to the right and there is car
parking (La Palanca de la Molina) at the Park entrance. The main trail from

the car park, La Ribera de Sant Nicolau, takes you to the Estany Llong and the refuge with a 650m climb. You will need to take water and food with you as the walk takes around 3½ hours each way but it is well worth the effort. The trail follows the Sant Nicolau Valley past the Estany de Llebreta to the Sant Esperit waterfall, passing through woodland and meadows to the Planell d' Aigüestortes, one of the most picturesque and best known places in the whole of the National Park. The trail continues up the Sant Nicolau valley to Estany Llong and on to the Estany Llong refuge, about ten minutes further along. From here you can see El Portarró d'Espot, the pass to the Escrita valley. It is quite feasible to cross the pass to Sant Maurici, given the right conditions, but you must be a relatively experienced walker.

Instead of turning into the National Park, an alternative is to continue on to Caldes de Boí. A road continues past the spa as far as the dam at Cavallers lake, where there is a car park. A track follows the right-hand side of the lake as far as the other end, the Pleta del Riu Malo.

Estany de Sant Maurici Access to the eastern side of the National Park is via the Espot valley. Take the N-260 to Sort and head north on the C-13. Turn left on to LV-5004 to Espot, about 3km after Escaló. From Espot carry on to the National Park entrance, where car parking is available. From here tracks lead to the Estany de Sant Maurici, and beyond to the lakes of Ratera, the Amitges and a refuge beside the lakes at 2,400m; the high-altitude species may be expected here.

Puerto de La Bonaigua and Pla de Beret These passes are north of the Park proper. From Espot return to the C-13 and continue north to Esterri d'Aneu, where it becomes the C-28 and continues to the ski slopes and Vielha. The forests between Esterri and the Puerto de La Bonaigua offer a good chance of finding the Black Woodpecker. Further on it is worth turning north at Baquèira on to a minor road that leads above the treeline, where high-altitude species may be located around the Beret pass. In general, there are many opportunities for birding along this route and it enables you to do a round trip taking the N-230 back to Lleida from Vielha.

CALENDAR

All year: Ptarmigan, Capercaillie, Grey Partridge, Lammergeier, Griffon Vulture, Goshawk, Golden Eagle, Common Kestrel, Peregrine Falcon, Boreal Owl, Black Woodpecker, Dipper, Black Redstart, Blue Rock and Mistle Thrushes, Marsh Tit (rare), Crested Tit, Goldcrest, Firecrest, Eurasian and Short-toed Treecreepers, Yellow-billed and Red-billed Choughs, Raven, Rock Sparrow, Snowfinch, Citril Finch, Siskin, Bullfinch, Crossbill, Yellowhammer.

Breeding season: Honey-buzzard, Red Kite, Short-toed Eagle, Woodcock, Crag Martin, Water Pipit, Grey Wagtail, Alpine Accentor, Whinchat, Rufous-tailed Rock Thrush, Ring Ouzel, Nuthatch, Wallcreeper, Garden and Bonelli's Warblers, Common Chiffchaff, Golden Oriole, Red-backed Shrike, Rock Bunting.

CADÍ–MOIXERÓ
(Lérida/Gerona/Barcelona)

CAT2

Status: Parque Natural and ZEPA (41,342ha).

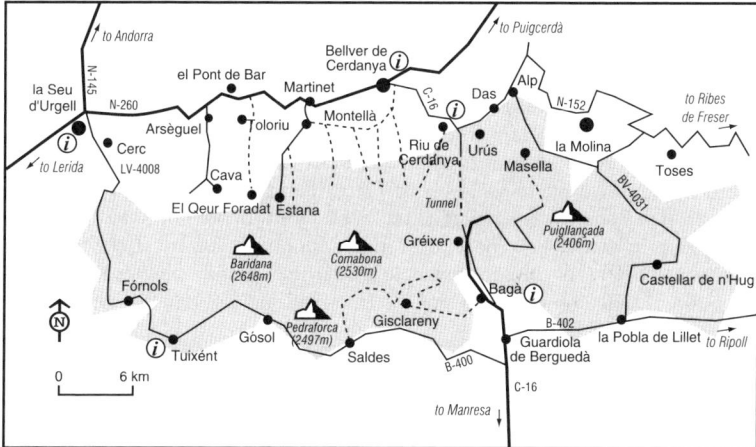

Site description

A high pre-Pyrenean mountain range comprising the Cadí and Moixeró ridges, running east/west for over 30km and covering over 41,000ha. It is renowned for its sheer and imposing cliffs. This is a very wild and remarkably diverse area, with peaks, valleys, meadows, pastures and forests. Altitudes range from 800m on the valley floors to the 2,648m Puig de la Canal Baridana. Pedraforca (2,497m) is one of the most attractive mountains, particularly popular with Catalan mountaineers. Alpine meadows are typical above the tree line, at around 2,000m. The lower slopes are covered with forests of Black and Scots Pine and Silver Fir, as well as beechwoods and oakwoods.

Species

The location and range of altitude make for a diverse bird community. There is considerable bird interest, in particular Capercaillies, Lammergeiers, Boreal Owls, Alpine Accentors, Wallcreepers and Black Woodpeckers. These last are the symbol of the park and are relatively common. The higher pastures and forest edges have Grey Partridges, Rufous-tailed Rock Thrushes, Ring Ouzels, Water Pipits and Citril Finches. In addition, the forests and woodlands have Goshawks, Short-toed Eagles, Honey-buzzards, both Eurasian and Short-toed Treecreepers, Coal Tits and Crossbills. Lower down, the meadows, hedgerows and scrub have Wrynecks, Bee-eaters, Sky Larks, Subalpine Warblers, Red-backed Shrikes and Yellowhammers.

Timing

Spring and summer are the best months. Snow is less of a problem in early spring than in the Pyrenees.

Access

The park is best approached along the C-16, directly north of Manresa and Barcelona. The first stop could be at Bagà where the main Information Centre for the park (Tel. 938 244 151; open daily) is sited. There are smaller Visitors' Centres in Saldes, Bellver de Cerdanya and Martinet. Many forest tracks and walks throughout the park enable you to spend time in all the main habitats: forest, pastures, cliffs and mountain peaks. The centres can provide leaflets on walking and cycling trails, including the 'Ruta del Trencapinyes' – the Crossbill Trail.

The southern areas of the park can be explored by taking roads west or east of the main C-16. Westwards take the B-400 left before you reach Guardiola de Berguedá and Bagà. Various forest tracks and walks can be taken off this road.

For the eastern route turn right at Guardiola de Berguedá on to the B-402, another stunning drive to La Pobla de Lillet, then turn left on the BV-4031 to Castellar de n'Hug, where a marked trail (2km) leads to the Fonts del Llobregat, the source of that river. There are various options to follow tracks that lead southwards off the N-260, for example at Martinet, but you are recommended to get the detailed trail guides from the Information Centre beforehand.

CALENDAR

All year: Ptarmigan, Capercaillie, Grey Partridge, Lammergeier, Griffon Vulture, Goshawk, Golden and Bonelli's Eagles, Peregrine Falcon, Rock Dove, Eagle and Boreal Owls, Black and Great Spotted Woodpeckers, Crag Martin, Sky Lark, Water Pipit, Dipper, Alpine Accentor, Stonechat, Black Redstart, Blue Rock Thrush, Goldcrest, Firecrest, Crested Tit, Nuthatch, Wallcreeper, Short-toed and Eurasian Treecreepers, Yellow-billed and Red-billed Choughs, Raven, Rock Sparrow, Snowfinch, Citril Finch, Crossbill, Yellowhammer, Rock Bunting.

Breeding season: Honey-buzzard, Black Kite, Short-toed Eagle, Alpine Swift, Hoopoe, Wryneck, Rufous-tailed Rock Thrush, Ring Ouzel; Subalpine, Melodious and Bonelli's Warblers, Red-backed Shrike.

Winter: Snowfinch.

CAP DE CREUS (Cabo de Creus)   CAT3 (Gerona)

Status: Parque Natural (13,886ha:10,813ha on land and 3,073ha offshore).

Site description

This rocky headland at the eastern end of the Pyrenees is also the easternmost point of the Spanish mainland. Lying just south of the French border it is part of the Costa Brava but the rocky coastline has kept it mainly unspoilt by tourist developments. The area is made up of many headlands, bays, small islets and low coastal mountains which are found between the small coastal towns of Llançà, El Port de la Selva, Cadaqués and Roses (Rosas). Inland the ground rises to around 670m above sea level at its highest point, Sant Salvador. The windswept peninsula supports a mixture of vegetation on its poor thin soils, including maquis scrub, small pine plantations, Holm and Cork Oaks, vines and olive groves.

In addition to its biological interest it is also very important for its geology and archaeological interest, including the San Pere de Rodes monastery and numerous *dolmens* (megalithic tombs).

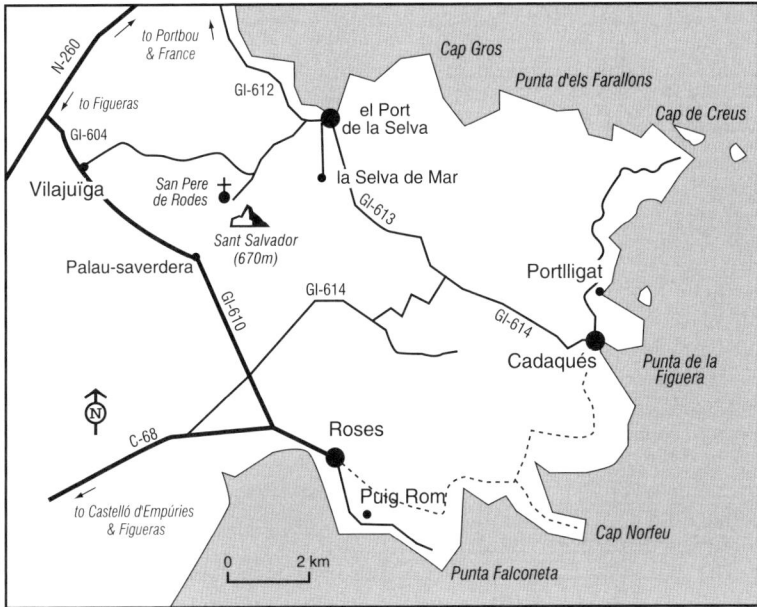

Species

The low scrub supports breeding Sardinian, Subalpine and Spectacled Warblers. More open ground favours Black-eared Wheatears, Thekla Larks and Ortolan Buntings. Orphean Warblers occur in some of the small wooded areas, particularly where there are scattered Holm Oaks. Both the open and vegetated areas are often productive during passage periods, sheltering spring and autumn falls of migrants. Spring migrants especially quite often include species of more easterly breeding distribution, such as Icterine Warblers, that are seldom encountered further west in Spain.

The sea cliffs and those inland are home to Bonelli's Eagles, Peregrine Falcons, Eagle Owls, Pallid Swifts, Crag Martins, Blue Rock Thrushes and Black Redstarts. Both Rufous-tailed and Blue Rock Thrushes occur at Sant Salvador castle. Pallid Swifts and Red-rumped Swallows also occur in and around Cadaqués and Port de la Selva.

Some high-altitude species occur on the headland from early winter onwards. Alpine Accentors are found then on Sant Salvador castle and also around the monastery on rocks and boulders, while Wallcreepers regularly winter at Cap de Creus and Cap de Norfeu and have even been seen on the monastery walls.

The Cape is one of the best seawatching sites in the Mediterranean, offering a range of both passage and wintering gulls, shearwaters and skuas, among others. It is a reliable site for seeing Levantine (Yelkouan) Shearwaters, mainly in winter (December–January), when thousands gather to feed on shoaling anchovies. Balearic Shearwaters occur all year round and Cory's (Scopoli's) Shearwaters are present in summer and early autumn.

Timing

The Cape is particularly rewarding during the migration periods: March–May and August–October, although early summer can also be very productive since there is a good range of breeding species. Early winter is best to look for Alpine Accentors and Wallcreepers that may have descended from the Pyrenees. Winter is also the best season for seeing Levantine Shearwaters.

Access

Cap de Creus is east of Figueres, which is 24km south of the French border and 32km north of Girona. The whole peninsula is worth exploring and there are numerous trails along the clifftops and inland as well, many of them medieval routes. There are also the GR-11 and GR-92 long distance routes. Details of these routes can be found at the Park Office/Information Centre in the Palau de l'Abat at the Monastery of Sant Pere de Rodes (Tel. 972 193 191).

Two major roads, the AP-7 motorway and the N-11, run parallel north/south past the area. Leave at Figueras and take the N-260 towards Portbou and France. After about 12km turn right on to the GI-610 for Vilajuïga and turn left at the village for the monastery, El Port de la Selva and Cadaqués. Take the signposted minor road north from Cadaques (8km) to reach the viewpoint and lighthouse at the Cape. The general area can also be approached from the south via the C-68 and Roses.

The streamside at Port de la Selva is also worth checking during migration time for waders and herons, as are the sheltered parts of the coastline. From here take a minor road to Sant Pere de Rodes monastery, where there is a car park. There is a short walk to the monastery and a path up to the peak of Sant Salvador.

CALENDAR

All year: Red-legged Partridge; Cory's (Scopoli's), Balearic and Levantine Shearwaters, Shag, Common Buzzard, Bonelli's Eagle, Common Kestrel, Peregrine Falcon; Barn, Little and Eagle Owls, Crested and Thekla Larks, Crag Martin, Stonechat, Blue Rock Thrush, Zitting Cisticola, Dartford and Sardinian Warblers, Firecrest, Raven, Rock Sparrow, Serin, Goldfinch; Cirl, Rock and Corn Buntings.

Breeding season: Hobby, Turtle Dove, Alpine and Pallid Swifts, Red-rumped Swallow, Tawny Pipit, Nightingale, Black-eared Wheatear, Rufous-tailed Rock Thrush; Spectacled, Subalpine and Orphean Warblers, Woodchat Shrike, Ortolan Bunting.

Winter: Gannet, Great Skua, Razorbill, Alpine Accentor, Wallcreeper.

Passage periods: Gannet, Purple Heron, Arctic Skua, Little Gull, Kittiwake; Sandwich, Whiskered and Black Terns, Great Spotted Cuckoo, Short-eared Owl, Common Redstart; Melodious, Icterine and Wood Warblers.

AIGUAMOLLS DE L'EMPORDÀ   CAT4 (Gerona)

Status: Parque Natural (4,730ha), Ramsar site and ZEPA (867ha).

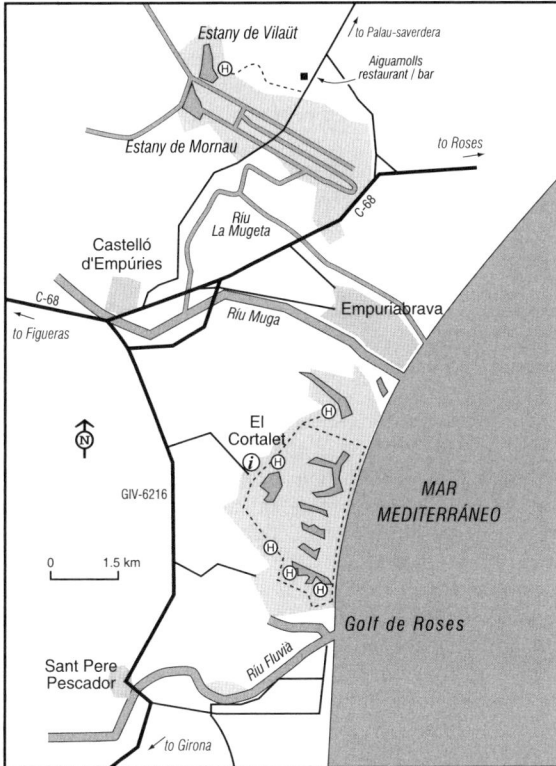

Site description

The Aiguamolls is what remains of a much more extensive coastal wetland system in Roses bay and most if not all interest is focused on the area between the Fluvià and Muga rivers. There is a huge variety of habitats in what is a relatively compact space, including coastal brackish lagoons, freshwater lagoons, reedbeds, sand dunes, periodically flooded meadows (*closes*), riverine woodland and ricefields. Some areas of former ricefields are now reverting to meadows and are grazed by cattle and Camargue horses.

This has been one of the best coastal wetland sites for birds in the whole of Spain. Around 330 species have been recorded and over 80 species have bred here. Unfortunately, poor management in recent years has considerably reduced its value. In particular, breeding birds have been badly affected by the uncontrolled depredations of American Mink and Wild Boar. It is to be hoped that this problem will be remedied. Nevertheless, the Aiguamolls is still well worth visiting, especially during passage periods.

The reserve comprises three main areas, listed from north to south:

Els Estanys   Freshwater marshes and freshwater lagoons and surrounding pastures and scrub. The main focus of attention here is the hide overlooking the Estany de Vilaüt. This section is physically separated from the main area by the Empuriabrava holiday complex.

Les Llaunes/El Cortalet   Freshwater and saltwater lagoons at El Cortalet. This is the core area, offering a visitors' centre, many paths and hides and the greatest variety of species. It holds the areas of brackish lagoons, although a freshwater lagoon has been created next to the visitors' centre.

Río Fluvià   The river Fluvià and its riparian woodland of willows, White and Black Poplars, Alder, Smooth-leaved Elm, Ash and tamarisk, near Sant Pere Pescador.

Species
The flooded meadows and old rice paddies can be excellent for waders, such as Black-winged Stilts, and waterfowl and are also good for occasional Glossy Ibises, Whiskered Terns and Gull-billed Terns on passage. Garganey have bred here in wet years.

The lagoons with reedbeds have Purple Herons, a very small and fluctuating nesting population of Great Bitterns, Little Bitterns and a few Moustached Warblers. Bearded Tits are seen here occasionally, although they no longer breed locally. Marsh Harriers breed and are seen regularly quartering the wetland. Saline lagoons are important throughout the year for various duck species, Greater Flamingos which occur all year round but do not breed, waders and terns during the passage periods. Look out for crakes in the spring: this is perhaps the best place in Spain for Little Crakes but Spotted Crakes and the scarcer Baillon's Crakes are also regular.

The coast (Roses Bay) can be good for seawatching in winter: the Bay is one of the few Spanish locations where the Black-throated Diver winters with some regularity.

Passage migrants are often obvious in spring – especially when strong northerly winds *(tramuntana)* blow down from the Pyrenees making migration difficult – and autumn. These regularly include some species, such as the Red-footed Falcon, Red-throated Pipit and the Aquatic, Icterine and Wood Warblers, that are very scarce or local in Spain. This well-watched site has produced a long list of rarities; including such diverse species as Bewick's Swan, Smew, White-tailed Eagle, Rough-legged Buzzard, Citrine Wagtail, Desert Wheatear and Hooded Crow, and the list grows annually.

Non-avian species include Polecats, Painted Frogs, Marbled Newts, Mediterranean Terrapins and the rare Three-toed Skink. Both Otters and Fallow Deer have been reintroduced.

Timing
This site can be visited all year round and is rewarding at any time of year, although quietest at the peak of the summer in July. Heat haze can be a problem for viewing during the hottest parts of the day.

Access

Take the AP-7 motorway or N-II to Figueras and then the C-68 towards Castelló d'Empúries, where you turn south on to the GI-6216 towards Sant Pere Pescador. The 'Aiguamolls' is signposted on the left about 3km along this road, where you reach the main part of the reserve, the visitors' centre and car parking. It is better to start in this central portion to get your bearings and make use of the information at the centre. Most of the interest is also found here. Well-signposted trails guide you through the reserve and there are paths and hides scattered throughout the site. It is possible to do a circuit, although some coast sections may be closed off in the breeding season: check at the visitors' centre before starting. The information centre, El Cortalet (Tel. 972 454 222), is open daily.

Access to the lagoons and hide in the northern part of the site is from the GIV-6103 minor road between Castelló and Palau-Saverdera. After 4–5km from Castelló you cross over three channels and a signposted track leads off left (before the Aiguamolls restaurant and Bar) to the Estany de Vilaüt and the hide. Good views can be had along this road and across other minor roads which cross the area to the east and west. The first part of the track is drivable weather-permitting: otherwise it is a walk of around 1.5km. This sector of the reserve has lost much of its interest in recent years other than in winter, when some wildfowl and the occasional Great Bittern occur.

The third area of interest is along the Riu Fluvià to the south. From the main part of the reserve, turn left on to the main road to Sant Pere Pescador. Go through Sant Pere across the river and then immediately left towards the coast and a campsite. Again various tracks lead along the coast and back to the river.

CALENDAR

All year: Gadwall, Shoveler, Red-legged Partridge, Little and Great Crested Grebes, Great Bittern; Cattle, Little and Great White Egrets, Grey Heron, Greater Flamingo, Marsh Harrier, Water Rail, Purple Swamphen, Common Coot, Common Snipe, Stone-curlew, Rose-ringed and Monk Parakeets, Kingfisher, Hoopoe, Lesser Spotted Woodpecker; Cetti's, Moustached and Sardinian Warblers, Zitting Cisticola, Penduline Tit.

Breeding season: Little Bittern, Night and Purple Herons, White Stork, Black Kite, Short-toed Eagle, Baillon's Crake, Black-winged Stilt, Kentish Plover, Whiskered Tern, Great Spotted Cuckoo, Bee-eater, Roller, Greater Short-toed Lark, Yellow Wagtail, Nightingale; Savi's, Reed, Great Reed, Melodious and Subalpine Warblers, Golden Oriole, Woodchat Shrike.

Winter: Greylag Goose, Wigeon, Teal, Mallard, Pintail, Common Pochard, Tufted Duck, Black-throated Diver, Great Crested Grebe, Gannet, Cormorant, Hen Harrier, Golden Plover, Lapwing, Common Snipe, Curlew, Sandwich Tern, Razorbill, Short-eared Owl, Common Chiffchaff, Reed Bunting.

Passage periods: Garganey, Squacco Heron, Black Stork, Glossy Ibis, Spoonbill, Marsh Harrier, Red-footed and Eleanora's Falcons, Hobby, Spotted and Little Crakes, Common Crane, Collared Pratincole, Dotterel, Knot, Little Stint, Curlew Sandpiper, Dunlin, Ruff, Wood and Marsh Sandpipers, Common Redshank, Audouin's Gull, Gull-billed, White-winged Black and Black Terns, Red-throated Pipit, Bluethroat, Northern Wheatear; Aquatic, Icterine and Wood Warblers.

MUNTANYA DE MONTSERRAT   CAT5 (Barcelona)

Status: Parque Natural (c.7,700ha, including the protection zone). Includes a Reserva Natural (1,981ha).

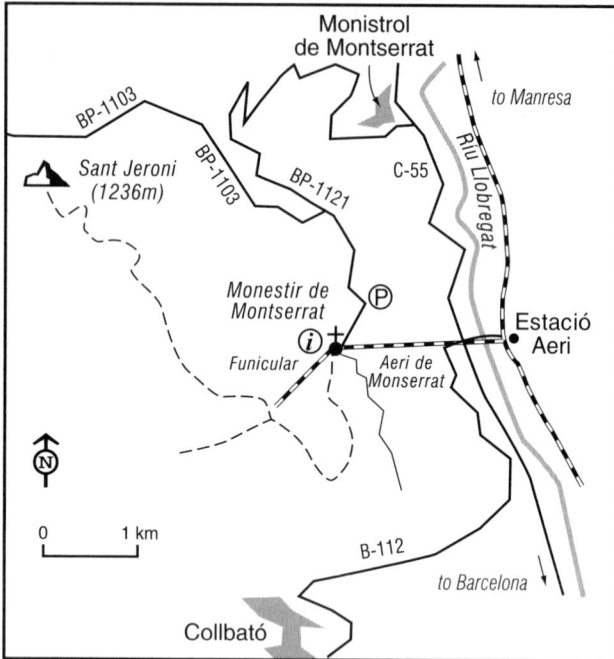

Site description

This site is only 50km from Barcelona and famous for its 9th-century monastery and shrine of the Black Madonna, and its spectacular jagged peaks and pinnacles. The highest peak is Sant Jeróni at 1,236m. It also offers a good opportunity to mix history and sightseeing with birding.

The slopes of the massif are clothed in pine and oak forests, although the southern aspect has a more Mediterranean influence with fewer trees, more scrub oak and aromatic shrubs and herbs. The massif is around 10km long and 5km wide. Scenically it is best viewed from the north where the origin of its name Montserrat, 'sawn-off mountain', is plain to see. It is frequently compared by many visitors to a cathedral.

Species

The site is especially good for a mixture of species that favour mid-altitude rocky ground, and for cliff-nesters, including in particular Bonelli's Eagle, Peregrine Falcon, Eagle Owl, Alpine Swift, Crag Martin and Blue Rock Thrush. The Egyptian Vulture has recently colonised the area. Sardinian, Dartford and

Subalpine Warblers also breed, as do Rock Buntings and Rock Sparrows. Alpine Accentors, Ring Ouzels and Wallcreepers occur in the winter and are seen regularly at Sant Jeróni; the accentors even appear at the monastery car park.

Timing
Spring and early summer are best but the monastery and the whole area can be extremely busy at weekends and during holiday periods. The mountains are also very popular with climbers.

Access
The C-55 follows the base of the eastern boundary of the Natural Park. Follow signs to Monistrol de Montserrat. From there turn left on to a minor road signposted to the monastery, Monestir de Montserrat. Some way up the road splits, with the left hand arm taking you to the monastery where there is a pay-car park. There are also souvenir shops, a restaurant and cafe and an hotel.

There is a regular hourly train service (R5) from Plaça Espanya station Barcelona, which presents two options, apart form walking, to reach the monastery. There is the Cremallera (rack railway) which runs every 20 minutes from the railway station at Monistrol or you can reach the monastery by the cable car (Montserrat Aeri station) which departs every 15 minutes. Car parking is free at both stations.

The top of the plateau can be reached from the monastery by tracks or on the Sant Joan funicular railway. Once on top there are numerous tracks that take you across the massif, although the most popular takes you towards the highest point, Sant Jeróni. Many of the routes are marked and there are also various options from the monastery itself. The lower ground below the monastery is also of interest.

An information centre (Tel. 938 777 701) at the monastery is open all day Monday to Saturday. There is also a nature centre (Tel. 938 284 007) in the building at the head of the Sant Joan Funicular Railway. Maps are available giving details of the many trails and walks.

CALENDAR

All year: Red-legged Partridge, Sparrowhawk, Common Buzzard, Bonelli's Eagle, Peregrine Falcon, Rock and Collared Doves, Barn and Eagle Owls, Crested and Wood Larks, Crag Martin, Black Redstart, Blue Rock Thrush, Sardinian and Dartford Warblers, Crested Tit, Raven, Common Starling, Rock Sparrow, Serin, Cirl and Rock Buntings.

Breeding season: Egyptian Vulture, Turtle Dove, Common Cuckoo, Scops Owl, Alpine Swift, Bee-eater, Wryneck, Rufous-tailed Rock Thrush; Melodious, Subalpine and Bonelli's Warblers, Golden Oriole, Woodchat Shrike, Ortolan Bunting.

Winter: Alpine Accentor, Ring Ouzel, Wallcreeper.

DELTA DEL LLOBREGAT   CAT6
(Barcelona)

Status: Reserva Natural & ZEPA (573ha).

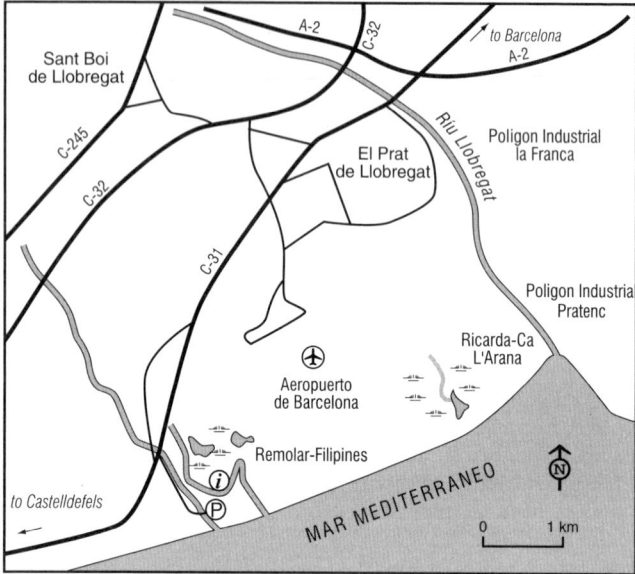

Site description

This wetland is made up of two reserves, Ricarda-Ca L'Arana and the more accessible Remolar-Filipines. They are separated by Barcelona airport, although still linked by the beach. Their formal designation has saved them from further development, despite the expansion of the airport. They protect a coastal wetland of considerable importance and are well worth a visit if you are visiting Barcelona and do not mind the surrounding backdrop of urban and industrial land use.

The reserve is centred around the Llobregat river as it enters the Mediterranean immediately south of Barcelona city. It is a coastal floodplain with small saline lagoons, fields that flood at certain times of year, dense reed-beds, pinewoods, saltmarsh and dunes.

Species

The site offers a very broad selection of coastal and wetland species year-round. It is very well watched by some of the region's most experienced birders, which partly explains why it is a national hotspot for migrants and rarities, although its strategic coastal location is a major factor. The breeding species include Little Bitterns; Night, Squacco, Purple and Grey Herons, Marsh Harriers and Water Rails, as well as Great Reed and Cetti's Warblers and Penduline Tits. Audouin's Gulls have established a nesting colony in recent seasons. Northern

Shovelers, Gadwall and Red-crested Pochards are also known to breed. The flooded fields have Yellow Wagtails, Black-winged Stilts and Cattle Egrets.

The area comes into its own during passage periods. The regular migrants include all the east coast spring specialities, such as the Red-footed Falcon, Red-throated Pipit and the Wood and Icterine Warblers, although the numbers of these rarer species recorded vary greatly between seasons. Spotted and Little Crakes are regular on passage and Baillon's Crake is recorded at least annually. Many commoner migrants occur annually and these include large numbers of Black Terns, with a few White-winged Black Terns appearing as well. The many national rarities found by the cognoscenti in recent years have included Lesser Scaup, Semipalmated Sandpiper, Franklin's Gull, Royal and Elegant Terns, Blue-cheeked Bee-eater, Red-flanked Bluetail, Siberian Stonechat, Marmora's and Greenish Warblers and Siberian Chiffchaff, so this is a place to expect the unexpected.

The coastal waters offer a good range of seabirds, especially on passage and in winter. In particular, very large numbers of Mediterranean Gulls occur in winter, counts sometimes exceeding 10,000 birds.

Timing
Spring and winter visits are especially productive. Weekends can be very busy.

Access
Take the C-31 out of Barcelona towards El Prat de Llobregat and Castelldefels. Take the next exit, Remolar-Filipines', following the last exit to the Airport T-1, and follow directions to the reserve car parks. There is weekday car parking adjacent to the reserve and a more distant car park (1km) is open only at weekends.

The reserve and its small information centre (Tel. 936 586 761) are open daily except Mondays. There are a number of routes around the site and hides overlook the lagoons. Access to the beach areas is partly restricted during the Kentish Plover breeding season. A watchtower at the beach is useful for sea-watching.

CALENDAR

All year: Shelduck, Little Grebe, Little and Cattle Egrets, Night Heron, Marsh Harrier, Purple Swamphen, Water Rail, Kentish Plover, Audouin's Gull, Monk Parakeet, Cetti's and Sardinian Warblers, Zitting Cisticola, Short-toed Treecreeper, Penduline Tit, Common Waxbill. Levantine Shearwaters, Gannet, Cormorant; Great White Egret, Common Buzzard, Golden Plover, Common and Jack Snipes, Mediterranean Gull, Sandwich Tern, Razorbill, Kingfisher, Water Pipit, Bluethroat, Moustached Warbler, Reed Bunting.

Breeding season: Red-crested Pochard, Little Bittern, Purple Heron, Black-winged Stilt, Little Ringed Plover, Great Spotted Cuckoo, Scops Owl, Greater Short-toed Lark, Yellow Wagtail, Great Reed and Reed Warblers.

Winter: Ferruginous Duck, Balearic and

Passage periods: Glossy Ibis, Spoonbill, Greater Flamingo, Hen Harrier; Red-footed Falcon; Baillon's, Little and Spotted Crakes, Sanderling, Temminck's Stint, Spotted Redshank, Marsh and Wood Sandpipers, Slender-billed and Little Gulls; Gull-billed, Whiskered, White-winged Black and Black Terns, Red-throated Pipit, Icterine and Wood Warblers.

ESTEPAS DE LLEIDA Y EMBALSE   CAT7
DE UTXESA (Lérida)

Status: Mostly unprotected but an SPA under the European Birds Directive. Includes the Reserves Natural de Mas de Melons (1,140ha) and Utxesa (240ha).

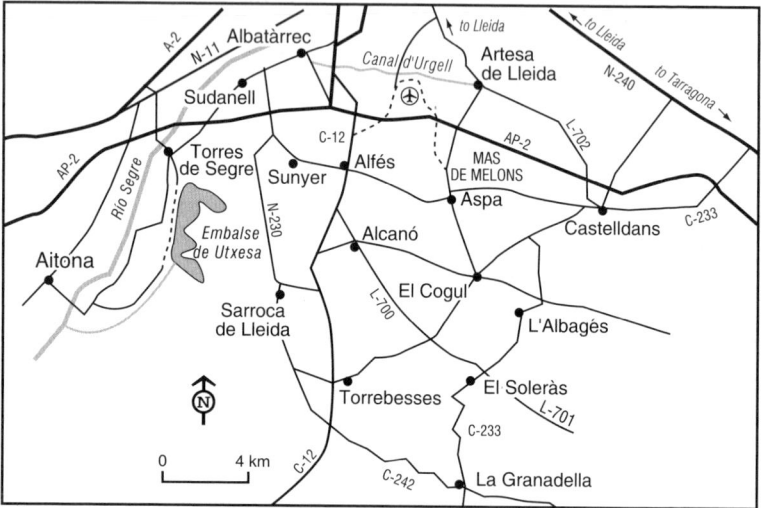

Site description

These are the best areas of grassland and 'steppe' in Cataluña, although they are now very fragmented and much land has been lost to agricultural intensification, as in other parts of Spain. Much of the region is given over to cereal production with only remnant natural steppe vegetation, with a mixture of some pasture and occasional fallow areas. The area is an eastward extension of Los Monegros in Aragón (AR13). Utxesa reservoir is to the west within the steppe area. Although relatively small, it is also important with an impressive reedbed, the largest in Cataluña.

Species

The whole area has a very rich and varied bird fauna and it is easily possible to get a very respectable list from a day's birding here. It is the best site in Cataluña for steppe birds with good numbers of Little Bustards, Stone-curlews and Pin-tailed Sandgrouse, and smaller numbers of other key species such as Montagu's Harrier. Seven lark species occur, including Dupont's Lark near Alfés; where it was 'rediscovered' in 2015 after having apparently disappeared some years before.

While the steppe area is most definitely worth visiting in its own right, the reservoir is a welcome bonus and makes an excellent day's birding with Purple Herons, Little Egrets, Little Bitterns, Black Kites, Marsh Harriers, Water Rails, Cetti's Warblers and Great Reed Warblers. A few Moustached Warblers breed and the reservoir holds a population of Witherby's Reed Bunting, the endemic subspecies of north-east Spain. Bearded Tits have a sizeable nesting population here and are relatively easy to encounter.

The open country south of Lleida can also be productive for birds of open country, with White Storks, Lesser Kestrels, Hobbies, Rollers, Great Spotted Cuckoos, Scops Owls, Black-eared Wheatears and Red-necked Nightjars all breeding. The gullies have Black Wheatears and Eagle Owls. The area held a remnant outpost population of Lesser Grey Shrikes, here at the western edge of their European range, but these have declined virtually to extinction, although attempts to boost the population with released captive-bred birds have had some limited success.

Timing
Spring is the best season at all steppe areas. The Utxesa reservoir is also interesting in autumn and winter.

Access
Much of the steppe interest is found directly south and south-west of Lleida, to the east of the C-12 and across to the C-233. One of the largest fragments of steppe is immediately north of the AP-2 motorway around a small former aerodrome lying between the Canal d'Urgell and the motorway. Access is from the L-702 to the north: heading south along a 3km tarmacked track 4km west of Artesa de Lleida, or along a track off the C-12 north of Alfés. Lesser Grey Shrikes used to nest here but other typical steppe species, including Dupont's Lark, remain. Please view only from the tracks, to avoid disturbance. Other areas of steppe occur around Aspa and the minor road between Aspa and Castelldans passes through the Mas de Melons area, part of which is a Reserva Natural.

For Utxesa reservoir take the A-2 south out of Lleida towards Zaragoza. About 2km out of Alcarrás take the left exit at a roundabout for Torres de Segre. A road leads to the reservoir immediately outside Torres de Segre and follows its western margins and the canal to the south. There are also footpaths and observation points, giving views over the extensive reedbeds.

CALENDAR

All year: Red-legged Partridge, White Stork, Marsh Harrier, Common Buzzard, Peregrine Falcon, Water Rail, Little Bustard, Pin-tailed Sandgrouse, Little and Long-eared Owls, Green Woodpecker; Dupont's, Calandra, Lesser Short-toed, Crested and Thekla Larks, Black Wheatear, Blue Rock Thrush; Cetti's, Moustached and Sardinian Warblers, Penduline Tit, Southern Grey Shrike, Red-billed Chough, Raven, Common and Spotless Starlings, Rock Sparrow, Cirl Bunting.

Breeding season: Quail, Little Bittern, Purple Heron, Egyptian Vulture, Montagu's Harrier, Short-toed Eagle, Hobby, Lesser Kestrel, Stone-curlew, Great Spotted Cuckoo, Scops Owl, Red-necked Nightjar, Bee-eater, Roller, Red-rumped Swallow, Tawny Pipit, Greater Short-toed Lark, Black-eared Wheatear; Great Reed, Reed, Spectacled, Subalpine and Savi's Warblers, Lesser Grey Shrike (very rare), Woodchat Shrike, Golden Oriole.

Passage: Great White Egret, Red-footed Falcon, Dotterel and other waders.

Winter: Ferruginous Duck (has bred), Hen Harrier, Merlin, Lapwing, Redwing, Common Chiffchaff, finches.

ELS PORTS DE TORTOSA – BESEIT CAT8 (Tarragona)

Status: Parque Natural and Reserva Nacional de Caza (30,000ha).

Site description

A range of mountains that runs parallel to the popular coasts of Cataluña and Valencia immediately behind the town of Tortosa and the Ebro Delta. Els Ports de Tortosa-Beseit massif is an area of complex relief. Its limestone mountains are deeply dissected by gullies, particularly in the west where there are spectacular gorges. There is an impressive karst system and an extensive cave system, making the area very popular with potholers.

There are large areas of pine and oak woodland. The south, near La Sénia, boasts one of the southernmost beechwoods in Europe, climbing high up the mountain slopes and including trees of considerable age and size. The highest peak in the range is Mont Caro (1,447m).

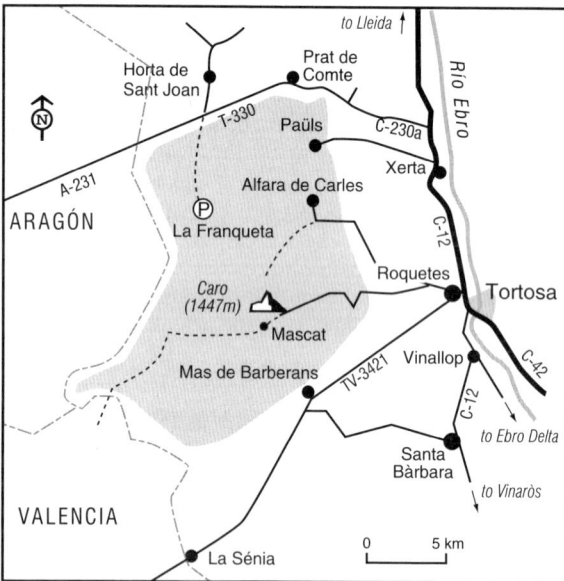

Species

The limestone cliffs are excellent for Griffon Vultures, Egyptian Vultures, Golden and Bonelli's Eagles and Red-billed Choughs, with Black Redstarts, Blue Rock Thrushes and Rock Sparrows all relatively common. The woodlands have breeding Short-toed Eagles, Goshawks, Nuthatches, Crossbills and Bonelli's Warblers, and Dippers in the river gorges. The lower slopes of the mountain are also worth exploring, with the lower valleys, orchards and olive groves good for Hoopoes, Wrynecks and Orphean and Melodious Warblers.

Wryneck

There is a large population of Spanish Ibex which is managed by the National Hunting Reserve. Over 20 bat species comprise one of the most important bat communities in Spain.

Timing
Spring and summer visits are recommended.

Access
The information centre for Els Ports Natural Park in Roquetes (Tel. 977 504 012) is open daily and offers details of the many routes through this very large park. The towns of Mas de Barberans and Alfara de Carles are the starting point of popular trails. Ready access is available from the coastal AP-7 motorway, coming off at either exit 40 (l'Aldea–Tortosa) and then on to the C-42 for Tortosa, or exit 41 (Amposta – Sant Carles de la Ràpita) and on to the C-12 for Tortosa. A particularly recommended route gives access from the north, turning south off the T-330 shortly after the turning (north) to Horta de Sant Joan, along a tarmac road signposted 'Els Ports'. This leads to La Franqueta picnic area (9.5km), where there are information boards indicating walking routes. A drivable forest track leads off to the left 5km from the start of the tarmac road, to the base of the imposing Roques de Benet, a massive rocky 'molar' that is a local landmark. The whole of this area offers a mix of woodland and impressive rocky outcrops, and all the typical bird species.

CALENDAR

All year: Red-legged Partridge, Griffon Vulture, Goshawk, Golden and Bonelli's Eagles, Common Kestrel, Peregrine Falcon, Rock Dove; Barn, Eagle and Little Owls, Green Woodpecker, Wood Lark, Crag Martin, Dipper, Black Redstart, Blue Rock Thrush; Cetti's, Sardinian and Dartford Warblers, Jay, Red-billed Chough, Raven, Spotless Starling, Rock Sparrow, Crossbill, Cirl Bunting.

Breeding season: Short-toed and Booted Eagles, Egyptian Vulture, Turtle Dove, Common Cuckoo, Alpine and Common Swifts, Bee-eater, Hoopoe, Wryneck, Nightingale, Barn Swallow, House Martin, Northern Wheatear, Orphean, Melodious and Bonelli's Warblers, Citril Finch.

Winter: Alpine Accentor, Wallcreeper.

Passage periods: White Stork, Honey-buzzard, Black Kite, Ring Ouzel.

DELTA DE L'EBRE/EBRO DELTA   CAT9 (Tarragona)

Status: Parque Natural, Ramsar Site and ZEPA (7,736ha). Incorporates two Reservas Naturales (including the SEO/Birdlife Riet Vell reserve) and seven Reservas de Fauna.

Site description

The Delta del Ebro is the largest coastal wetland in Cataluña and the second largest in Spain after the Coto Doñana, covering an area of around 320km². It is arguably the most important wetland in the western Mediterranean after the Camargue. This internationally important area for birds was recognised formally by its designation as a Parque Natural in 1986.

The Ebro Delta is a massive triangular deposit of sediment sustained by the mighty Río Ebro, which drains much of north-east Spain, including the southern slopes of the Pyrenees. The delta extends into the Mediterranean Sea for around 20km, attracting birds by the tens of thousands, and is one of the most extensive rice-growing areas in Spain. While much of the natural vegetation has disappeared under rice – over half of the delta – the paddies are fortunately very attractive to a range of birds: including herons, ducks, terns and waders, providing large areas of open water for the greater part of the year. SEO/Birdlife has established a large area of organic rice cultivation and is working to encourage other rice farmers to adopt eco-friendly practices (see Riet-Vell below).

The management of the rice paddies through manipulation of water levels, and the movement of water between areas through the myriad of canals and channels is crucial to maintaining the interest of the area. However, the value and importance of the natural features: including the lagoons, reedbeds, woods, sand dunes and saline steppes, should not be disregarded. In addition to the rice paddies, fruit and vegetables are grown on the inland side of the delta. Nearer to the coast, there are large lagoons bordered by reeds and other emergent plants, wide expanses of sandy ground with halophyte vegetation and long sandy beaches featuring sand dunes with Marram Grass. The salty zones often include sand dunes and are known locally as *tores*. Reedbeds are common and sedges and reed mace occur in deeper water. Small freshwater ponds, the *ullals,* are also frequent, these often choked by waterlilies. Riverside woods of poplars, willows, Alder, eucalyptus and planes fringe the banks of the Ebro, giving way to Oleanders and tamarisks to seaward.

There are two information centres, one in Deltebre and one next to the largest lagoon, L'Encanyissada, and there are many hides/observation platforms scattered throughout the delta. The main thing to bear in mind is that, despite the improved signposting, it can be easy to get lost in this huge expanse and you will need to focus your visit on particular sites if time is short. The Delta offers some unusual opportunities to get to know your birds really well: EG visited a restaurant there whose menu featured Braised Moorhen and Coot Risotto – he had the fish!

Species

Birds are an obvious feature of the Delta all year round but the great numbers involved are perhaps most apparent in October and November when the rice has been harvested and the paddies remain flooded and attract thousands of passage and wintering birds, many of them seeking spilt rice. Duck numbers then and in winter can reach over 75,000 and, along with over 30,000 Common Coots, represent over 90% of the waterfowl wintering in Cataluña. Mallards predominate but Shoveler and Teal are also abundant. Some 5,000 Red-crested Pochards winter here alongside smaller numbers of a range of other species including Wigeon, Pintail, Common Shelduck, Gadwall and Common Pochards.

Thousands of waders use the Delta on passage and in winter. The wintering waders include very large numbers of Little Stints and Dunlin and significant gatherings of such species as Grey Plover, Ruff, Spotted Redshank, Greenshank, Wood Sandpiper and Turnstone, that are otherwise uncommon then on the Mediterranean coast. Other notable wintering species include the Osprey, Booted Eagle, Whiskered Tern and Moustached Warbler. In winter too there are hundreds of Slender-billed Gulls and thousands of Mediterranean Gulls. The Marsh Harrier does not nest in the Delta but several hundred winter there.

The delta supports breeding concentrations of a number of key species. It is especially attractive to gulls and terns. The former included some two-thirds of the global population of Audouin's Gull, around 14,000 pairs, but numbers have declined to around 5,000 pairs as birds have moved away to establish colonies elsewhere, for example at the Llobregat Delta (CAT6) and at Torrevieja (V11). Several hundred pairs of Slender-billed Gulls nest during most years. There is a small outpost population of up to a hundred pairs of Lesser Black-backed Gulls. Five tern species breed here annually, including some 2,000 pairs of Common Terns, 1,500 pairs of Sandwich Terns, 1,000 pairs of Whiskered Terns, 300 pairs of Little Terns and 700 pairs of Gull-billed Terns. Lesser Crested Terns have bred in the past. Non-breeding Caspian Terns are frequent in spring, summer and autumn.

Gull-billed tern

Herons and egrets are also well represented. Great Bitterns only occur in winter but bred formerly and may return. There is a very large breeding population of Little Bitterns, however, perhaps as many as 1,000 pairs, alongside several hundred pairs of Night Herons, up to 1,000 pairs of Squacco Herons, 100+ pairs of Grey Herons and an increasing population of Purple Herons, numbering at least 500 pairs. Cattle and Little Egrets are abundant all year round. Great White Egrets are widespread in winter, when several hundred are present, and have bred in small numbers since 1997: these were the first breeding records for Spain of this increasingly widespread species. The Delta has housed an increasing population of Glossy Ibises since 1996, now totalling a few thousand pairs, and flocks of thousands frequent the ricefields in autumn especially. Greater Flamingos also nest in some years but several thousand are present year-round.

Breeding waterfowl include some 4,000 pairs of Red-crested Pochards and the largest Spanish population of Common Shelducks: some 60 pairs. Rallids are represented by abundant Water Rails, Moorhens and Common Coots and a thriving population of Purple Swamphens. Red-knobbed Coots have reached the Delta from reintroduced populations further south but are very scarce.

Several wader species have important breeding concentrations at the Delta. There are over 1,500 pairs of Kentish Plovers and 30 pairs of Oystercatchers, the largest populations of these species in Spain. Other breeding waders include 70 pairs of Collared Pratincoles, over 2,000 pairs of Black-winged Stilts and 400 pairs of Avocets.

The smaller birds also include many interesting species, notably breeding Savi's Warblers and a small population of the endemic race *witherbyi* of the Reed Bunting. Moustached Warblers have declined in recent years to just a few pairs, if any, but are more abundant in winter when migrants arrive from southern France and elsewhere. Bearded Tits used to breed commonly until the 1990s but are now only seen rarely in winter.

Almost any species may turn up here during passage periods and the Delta is a happy hunting ground for birders seeking rarities. Since 1980, for example, records have included Bewick's and Whooper Swans, King Eider, Long-tailed Duck, Smew, Western Reef Egret, African Spoonbill, Lesser Flamingo, Long-legged and Rough-legged Buzzards, Greater Spotted Eagle, Lanner Falcon, Greater Sand Plover, Pacific Golden Plover, Great Knot; Least, White-rumped, Baird's, Pectoral, Broad-billed, Buff-breasted, Terek and Spotted Sandpipers, Great Snipe, Lesser Yellowlegs, Wilson's Phalarope, Laughing and Ring-billed Gulls; Elegant, Bridled and Sooty Terns, Little Auk, Black-headed and Citrine Wagtails, Siberian Blue Robin, Moussier's Redstart, Siberian Stonechat, Naumann's Thrush; Paddyfield, Dusky and Yellow-browed Warblers, Collared Flycatcher and Black-headed Bunting.

Timing
The ricefields are driest in the first part of the year between January and March, when most of the interest is focused on the natural lagoons and the saltpans. The Delta is brilliant throughout the year, often literally – so that heat haze needs to be taken into account in warm weather. Mosquitoes are a minor hazard in the evenings, particularly in September, so be prepared. A few of the beaches can be busy at weekends, particularly in summer.

Access

The Ebro Delta is seaward of the main coastal roads, the AP-7 motorway and the N-340, between Tarragona to the north and Vinaròs in Valencia region to the south. From the AP-7 take the km-41 exit for Amposta/Sant Carles de la Ràpita. There are also exits at km-40 and km-39. From the N-340 turn west at Amposta for Els Muntells/Platja Eucaliptus. The AP-7 and N-340 bridge the Ebro and a new bridge connecting Deltebe and Sant Jaume d'Enveja enables north/south crossings within the Delta proper.

The road network on the Delta is complex and many areas and places of interest are poorly signposted. It is a good idea to start at the main information centre at the northern side of Deltebre (Tel. 977 482 181; open daily) on C/ Doctor Martí Buera 22, where there is detailed information on species present and areas to visit, and free maps are available. There is another visitors' centre, Casa de Fusta Information Centre (Tel. 977 261 022), on the southern part of the Delta on the northern side of L'Encanyissada lagoon, where there is an elevated viewpoint and access to the lagoon.

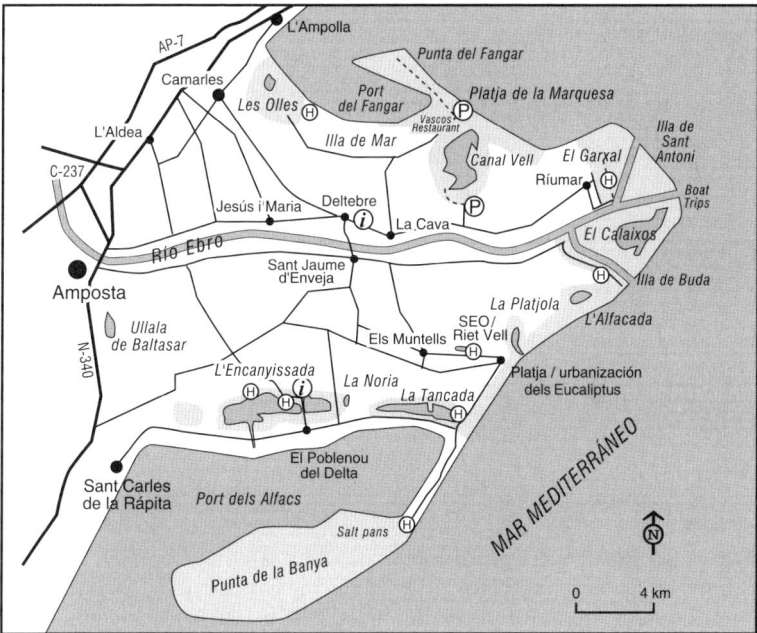

A. Ricefields and canals everywhere

Attract Purple Herons, Little Bitterns, Cattle and Little Egrets, terns: especially Whiskered Terns, Stilts, Avocets and many other waders on passage, including Temminck's Stints. Audouin's Gulls have taken to foraging for crayfish in the rice paddies.

B. North side of Delta

Les Olles A small lagoon with a good variety of waterfowl and herons. Also Whiskered and Caspian Terns and Slender-billed Gulls. El Fangar Bay may also be viewed from here.

Punta del Fangar   Sandspit and dunes, with a breeding colony of Slender-billed Gulls and Sandwich, Common, Little and Gull-billed Terns. Lesser Crested Terns have bred here. Gulls and coastal waders, including Grey Plovers and Curlews, occur on passage and in winter: when numbers of Mediterranean Gulls and waders roost here. The Bay itself has Great Crested and Black-necked Grebes, Red-breasted Mergansers and Common Scoters in winter, when both Velvet Scoters and Eiders are recorded occasionally.

El Canal Vell   A large lagoon with a hide on the southern shore. Good for Marsh Harriers, Greater Flamingos, Little Bitterns and Whiskered Terns.

El Garxal   A shallow sea lagoon at the mouth of the Ebro. Red-crested Pochards gather here, and Audouin's and Slender-billed Gulls are relatively easy to see. It is a key place to head for during migration seasons when it can be outstanding for waders, ducks, gulls and terns. Lesser Short-toed Larks occur in the coastal dunes. Accessible on foot from the Riumar resort.

C. South side of Delta

Illa de Buda/El Calaixos   This is specially protected, with restricted access. It consists of a lagoon and coastal sands and scrub. Breeding birds include Little Bitterns, Squacco Herons, Great White Egrets, Glossy Ibises, Little Terns and Whiskered Terns. It is also excellent in winter and during passage periods; attracting non-breeding Spoonbills and passage waders. It is viewable from an elevated hide on the south side.

L'Alfacada   A shallow lagoon and saltmarshes attracting a good variety of ducks, waders, gulls and terns, and large numbers of Purple Swamphens.

La Tancada   A lagoon next to the adjacent Sant Antoni saltflats. It is excellent for Flamingos and for waders: including Kentish and Little Ringed Plovers, Avocets and Black-winged Stilts, all of which are relatively common, and good for passage waders such as Grey Plovers, Ruffs, Spotted Redshanks and Little Stints. Both Greater and Lesser Short-toed Larks also breed and it is one of the best areas for breeding Collared Pratincoles. Slender-billed Gulls sometimes breed here and it is also good for terns: Caspian Terns occur relatively frequently.

L'Encanyissada   The largest lagoon on the delta, attracting numbers of ducks, cormorants, grebes and gulls. A track follows the northern shore west from the information centre, where there are hides. Marsh Harriers occur in autumn and winter. Excellent views of herons are often possible: they include breeding Great White Egrets, Purple Herons and Little Bitterns and overwintering Great Bitterns. This is also a good site for Squacco and Night Herons. Other breeding species include Red-crested Pochard, Glossy Ibis, Whiskered Tern and warblers in the reedbeds: notably including Savi's Warbler. Little Crakes are recorded regularly. Vast numbers of hirundines roost in the reedbeds in autumn; 1.5 million Barn Swallows were estimated in early October 2012. SEO/Birdlife have a small reserve, El Clot, at the eastern end of the lagoon.

Punta de la Banya   This is the large sandy spit marking the southernmost coast of the Delta. A long (5km) narrow causeway links the spit proper to the mainland. Access to the spit itself is normally restricted but a hide allows viewing. Saltpans are a feature on the north side of the spit. The main colonies of Audouin's and Slender-billed Gulls are here, alongside breeding Sandwich and Gull-billed Terns. The saltpans attract Greater Flamingos and numerous waders, including Avocets.

Riet Vell   An essential destination. This is the SEO/Birdlife organic rice enterprise and is west of Els Muntells on the north side of the road to Platja/ Urbanicación dels Eucaliptus at km-18.5. The 50ha of organic paddies really do seem to hold larger numbers of birds than the conventional ones elsewhere in the Delta. Purple Swamphens are particularly in evidence here. There is also an 11ha freshwater lagoon, with reedbeds, overlooked by a hide. There is an information centre and a shop selling the particularly good homegrown shortgrain rice varieties, excellent for paellas: as well as 'organic' pasta from Belchite. The multilingual website (rietvell.org) is interesting and informative. The centre is open daily: guided visits are available.

CALENDAR

All year: Common Shelduck, Gadwall, Teal, Red-crested Pochard, Black-necked Grebe, Night Heron; Cattle, Little and Great White Egrets, Glossy Ibis, Greater Flamingo, Marsh Harrier, Water Rail, Common and Red-knobbed Coots, Purple Swamphen, Avocet, Kentish Plover; Slender-billed, Lesser Black-backed and Yellow-legged Gulls, Sandwich and Whiskered Terns, Hoopoe, Lesser Short-toed and Crested Larks, Cetti's Warbler, Moustached Warbler (few), Zitting Cisticola, Penduline Tit, Reed Bunting.

Breeding season: Garganey, Little Bittern; Night, Squacco and Purple Herons, Cory's (Scopoli's) Shearwater (offshore), Oystercatcher, Black-winged Stilt, Collared Pratincole, Little Ringed Plover, Common Redshank, Audouin's Gull; Gull-billed, Lesser Crested, Common and Little Terns, Bee-eater, Short-toed Lark; Savi's, Reed and Great Reed Warblers, Woodchat Shrike.

Winter: Huge numbers of duck (up to 100,000); sea-duck occasionally including Eider, Common and Velvet Scoters and Red-breasted Merganser, Great Northern Diver, large numbers of herons and egrets, Great Bittern, Spoonbill, Marsh and Hen Harriers, Merlin, Peregrine Falcon, Great Skua, Mediterranean Gull, Short-eared Owl, Meadow and Water Pipits, Bluethroat, Moustached Warbler.

Passage periods: Balearic Shearwater (offshore), Gannet, Hobby, Eleonora's Falcon, Osprey, Spotted, Little and Baillon's Crakes, Grey Plover, Lapwing, Knot, Sanderling, Little and Temminck's Stints, Dunlin, Ruff, Common Snipe, Black-tailed and Bar-tailed Godwits, Whimbrel, Curlew, Spotted Redshank, Greenshank; Pectoral, Curlew, Marsh, Green, Wood and Common Sandpipers, Turnstone, Great Skua, Kittiwake; Caspian, Black and White-winged Black Terns, Razorbill, Red-throated Pipit, Aquatic and Icterine Warblers.

OTHER SITES WORTH VISITING

CAT10 SERRA DE BOUMORT (SIERRA DEL BOUMORT) (LÉRIDA)

A limestone massif with a large Griffon Vulture colony and other cliff-nesting birds including Alpine Swifts; also nesting Lammergeiers. Take the C-13 north from Lleida to Tremp (85km) and continue for 16km to La Pobla de Segur, then turn right on to a minor road to El Pont de Claverol and follow signs to St Martí and Pessonada. A track leads from this last village on to the massif. Also try Collegats Gorge on the main N-260 north of La Pobla, where there is car parking: good for views of vultures, other raptors and Red-billed Choughs.

CAT11 LA VALL DE NÚRIA (GERONA)
Part of the Reserva Nacional de Freser i Setcases. A high mountain area with Ptarmigan, Alpine Accentors, Ring Ouzels, Citril Finches and Chamois. Take the C-17 north from Barcelona to Ripoll and then on the N-260 north-west to Ribes de Freser. From here take the GIV-5217 minor road to the village of Queralbs, where a funicular railway takes you up to the sanctuary and ski resort at Núria. Explore along the marked paths from there.

CAT12 PARC NATURAL DE LA ZONA VOLCANICA DE LA GARROTXA (GERONA)
The best volcanic landscape in Spain and one of the finest in Europe, with some 30 dormant volcanic cones. These are now mostly covered in woodland, with some scrub and meadows, but the craters are unmistakable. The breeding birds include Goshawks, Short-toed Eagles, Hobbies, Dartford Warblers, Marsh Tits and Red-backed Shrikes. Leave the AP-7 at junction 6 (Girona N.) and take the C-66 north towards Banyoles. Turn west there along the GI-524 to Olot, which traverses much of the area of interest.

CAT13 ILLES MEDES (GERONA)
These small islands, a Marine Nature Reserve, are close to the coast off L'Estartit in the north of Cataluña and feature a coral reef, among other attractions. There is a large colony of Yellow-legged Gulls: some 8,000 pairs, as well as a few pairs of Shags. There is also a small heronry with Cattle, Little and Night Herons and the odd pair of Squacco Herons as well. Other breeding birds include Peregrine Falcons and Pallid and Alpine Swifts. Seabirds offshore include European Storm-petrels and Cory's (Scopoli's), Balearic and Levantine Shearwaters. Leave the AP-7 at junction 6 (Girona N.) and take the C-66 and GI-643 east to Torroella. Continue beyond for 7km to the coast at L'Estartit. Cruises to the islands are available from L'Estartit, some using glass-bottomed boats for viewing the coral reef and its fish. The Ter Vell lagoon, on the beach at L'Estartit itself, attracts ducks and warblers, as well as Great Bitterns in winter and Otters at dusk; it merits a look.

CAT14 ESTEPAS DE ALGERRI (LÉRIDA)
Fragments of steppe north of Lleida with Montagu's Harriers, Little Bustards, Red-necked Nightjars, Quails, Calandra Larks, Rollers and Tree Sparrows. Take the C-12 or C-13 north-east out of Lleida towards Balaguer, then turn left on to the C-26 towards Algerri and the plains.

CAT15 PARC NATURAL DE GARRAF (BARCELONA)
A stony and rocky limestone massif to the west of Barcelona city with ravines and coastal cliffs. Bonelli's Eagles are a particular attraction. The open scrub landscape also supports Tawny Pipits, Black and Black-eared Wheatears, Blue Rock Thrushes; Spectacled, Subalpine and Dartford Warblers, Southern Grey

Shrikes and Ortolan Buntings. Leave the C-32 at junction 42 (Casteld. O.) just west of Casteldefels and take the minor road inland to Olivella. Various minor roads cross the centre and north of the park.

CAT16 L'ALT PIRINEU (LÉRIDA)

The largest Natural Park in Cataluña: 70,000ha, and including some of the highest ground in the Pyrenees. Has similar species to sites CAT1 and CAT2: including Lammergeier, Ptarmigan and Boreal Owl. Situated between CAT1 and CAT2, largely to the north-east of the C-13. Good access is available along the L-504 ascending the Cardos valley, and the L-510 to Alins; leave the C-13 at Llavorsí (where there is an information centre), 16km north of Sort, for both routes.

CAT17 MONTSENY (BARCELONA)

Another large mountain area, over 30,000ha of mixed forest and Mediterranean scrub. A Parque Natural and Biosphere Reserve with a large diversity of bird species reflecting its geographical position relatively close to the coast; its variety of forest, cliff, scrub and open ground habitats and its altitudinal range: accessible by car up to 1,713m. The park office is at Fogars de Monclús (Tel. 938 475 290). The BV-5301 crosses the park through Montseny village from the C-35, 2km south of junction 11 (St. Celoni) of the AP-7 between Barcelona and Girona.

CAT18 MONTSANT (TARRAGONA)

A rocky limestone massif with a very good mixture of habitats, including cliff faces, forest, scrub and grassland. Residents include Bonelli's and Golden Eagles, Peregrine Falcons, Eagle Owls, Thekla Larks, Black Wheatears, Blue Rock Thrushes, Dippers, Rock Sparrows and Cirl Buntings. Wallcreepers occur in winter. Take the Reus exits (34 or 35) off the AP-7 motorway and then the N-240/C242 towards Ulldemolins. The Park Centre is at La Morera de Montsant (Tel. 977 827 310). Parque Natural.

CAT19 RESERVA NATURAL DE SEBES (TARRAGONA)

A compact (206ha) wetland reserve on the Ebro at Flix, comprising a long strip of riverine woodland, wet meadows and reedbeds on the north (left) bank, upstream from the Flix bridge. There are hides, a boardwalk and a good information centre (Mas del Director). Breeding birds include Little Bitterns, Purple Herons and Marsh Harriers, as well as White Storks; which have been successfully introduced here. Kingfishers are often conspicuous. Access is along a track leading west from the C-12 immediately north of the bridge.

GALICIA

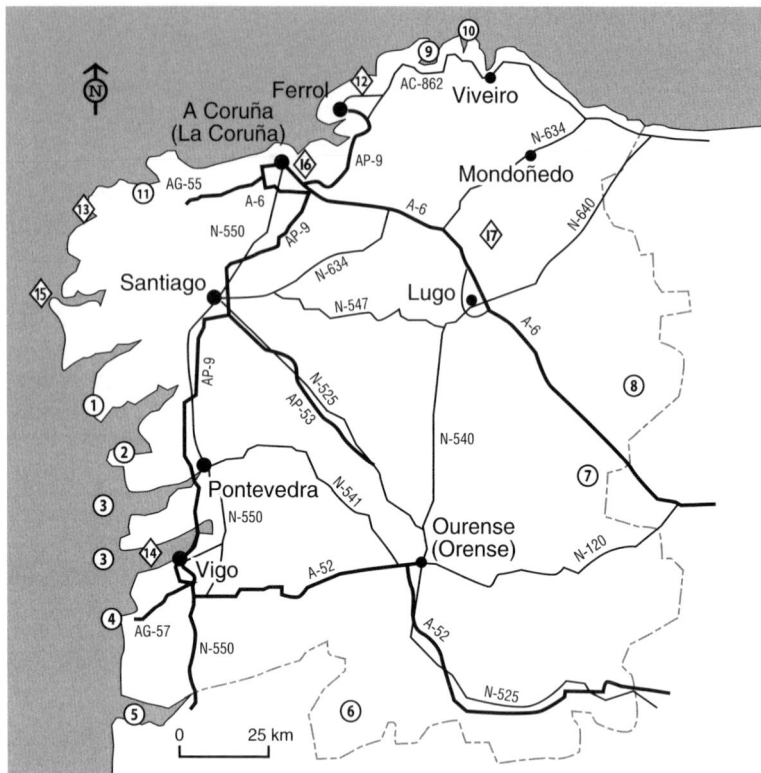

Main sites

GA1	Dunas de Corrubedo
GA2	O Grove Peninsula
GA3	Galician Islands National Park
GA4	Baiona Coast
GA5	Río Miño estuary
GA6	Baixa Limia–Sierra de Xurés
GA7	Sierra de Caurel
GA8	Sierra de Os Ancares
GA9	Ría de Ortigueira
GA10	Estaca de Bares
GA11	Ensenada de A Insua and Laguna de Traba

Other sites worth visiting

GA12	Laguna de A Frouxeira
GA13	Cabo Vilán
GA14	Ría de Vigo
GA15	Cabo Touriñán
GA16	Ría do Burgo
GA17	Terra Chá

The region of Galicia contrasts sharply with the image typically held of the Spanish countryside: of dusty plains and craggy mountains shimmering through the heat haze. On the contrary, it has more in common with the landscape and climate of Ireland than with Andalucía or Castilla–La Mancha. Its location in the north-westernmost corner of Iberia ensures that it is greener and wetter than anywhere else in the peninsula. Galicia shares more than the weather with Ireland (or Brittany): the national musical instrument is the 'gaita', which is very similar to Irish bagpipes. Moreover, its people are Celtic in origin and a large percentage speak Galego, the regional language. While not as militant as the Basques and the Catalans, there is a strong nationalist movement here which has championed the use of Galego and road signs and maps these days tend to be in that language. Our site accounts use Castillian but give the names in Galego as well where they may prove helpful.

The countryside and the rightly famous coast are picturesque but the main reason why large numbers of tourists visit the region is the shrine at Santiago de Compostela, the greatest goal for pilgrims in medieval Europe and still popular to this day. Countless people have gone to Compostela on pilgrimage since Saint James's tomb was identified there in the early 9th century: many travel on foot along the Camino de Santiago, which you will see signposted throughout northern Spain. Even if you have come to Galicia on a coastal or birdwatching holiday it would be a great pity not to spend a day in this splendid and historic city.

The Galician coast is spectacular, never more so than when it is receiving the full force of the winter storms which drive in from the west and north across the Atlantic or which descend from the equally stormy Bay of Biscay. It is deeply indented with a succession of estuaries, the fjord-like *rías*.There are dramatic sea cliffs, especially on the northern coast, where the Sierra de A Capelada is cut off sheer into the sea at the cliffs of Vixía Herbeira, the highest in Europe at 612m. The coastline from A Coruña (La Coruña) to Cabo Fisterra (Cabo Finisterre), the Spanish equivalent of Land's End, is known as the Costa da Morte (the death coast), its rocks having claimed numerous lives of fishermen and other mariners over the years.

Collectively the estuaries are known as the Rías Gallegas: the Rías Altas (upper inlets) lying on the north coast, with the Rías Bajas (lower inlets) on the western coast south of Cabo Fisterra. These *rías* are an important interconnected system of feeding and resting grounds for a rich variety of wildfowl and waders that breed in northern Europe, Russia and the high Arctic and winter in Spain or pass through to winter in Africa. Its position on the western edge of Europe makes Galicia a hotspot for vagrants from North America, especially in late summer and autumn when American waders occur with some regularity, particularly after westerly gales. Vagrant waterfowl and gulls also occur in autumn and these may linger to winter in the region. Rarities may turn up anywhere but the Ensenada de A Insua and the Laguna de Traba (GA11) have a remarkable reputation for attracting such strays. They should also be looked for in season among the very large numbers of waders and waterfowl which regularly use all the many other wetlands of the Galician coast, among which we have highlighted the Dunas de Corrubedo (GA1), the O Grove peninsula (GA2), the Baiona coast (GA4), the Río Miño estuary (GA5) and the Ría de Ortigueira (GA9). The more abundant wintering waders include Oystercatchers, Ringed Plovers, Knot, Sanderlings, Dunlins, Bar-tailed Godwits, Curlews and Common Redshanks. Turnstones are common on rocky shores along with Purple Sandpipers, a north coast speciality in winter in Iberia. A comprehensive range of other waders occur regularly on passage.

The Rías also shelter a diversity of marine and coastal waterfowl in winter, especially when the weather is stormy. These include Common Scoters, Black-necked Grebes, Great Northern Divers and Razorbills. Wigeon and other dabbling ducks are also numerous in winter in the coastal marshlands, which are often at the top of the Rías. Galicia has what is unarguably the best seawatching site in Iberia (and one of the best in Europe) at Estaca de Bares (GA10) but offers excellent seabirding opportunities at many other of its abundant headlands. 'Autumn' (August–October) is the best season, offering good chances of seeing at least five shearwater species, Sabine's Gulls, Long-tailed Skuas and many others, some of them in impressive numbers.

Galicia has significant breeding populations of Yellow-legged Gulls and, more importantly, of Shags. The 2,000 pairs of breeding Shags on the Islas Cíes and Isla de Ons (GA3) comprise the largest colonies in Iberia and about two-thirds of the Iberian Atlantic population of this species. Many smaller Shag colonies are a feature of most of the Galician coast. European Storm-petrels nest on offshore islands in small colonies. A few pairs of Lesser Black-backed Gulls nest in the region, chiefly on the Islas Sisargas west of A Coruña, with smaller groups breeding as far south as the Islas Cíes.

Galicia also had outpost populations of Kittiwakes and Guillemots until very recently but both have declined to extinction and neither species bred in 2016. The Kittiwakes were first reported as recently as 1975 and the population peaked at 200 pairs in the early 1980s but thereafter declined rapidly. Most nested at Cabo Vilán (GA13). The Guillemot population was of far longer standing. They numbered at least 3,000 pairs in eight colonies in 1960 but their story since then is a sad tale of decline: in 2016 none at all appeared at their last Iberian breeding colony, at Cabo Vilán.

Galicia is lush and heavily wooded inland, the valleys a patchwork of tiny fields where every bit of cultivable land is farmed. The scale of farming is small and not intensive and so provides much variety of bird habitat. Here species characteristic of northern Spain, such as the Bullfinch, Red-backed Shrike and Yellowhammer, occur alongside more typically southern species, such as the Hoopoe, Sardinian Warbler and Golden Oriole. The Sierra de Xurés (GA6) is typical of southern Galicia.

Move further east and you reach the far western edge of the Cordillera Cantábrica, where the high peaks reach 1,800–1,900m in the massifs of O Courel (GA7) and Os Ancares (GA8). Grey Partridges, Black and Middle Spotted Woodpeckers and Marsh Tits have their westernmost outposts here.

No description of Galicia is complete without relating how much the region has suffered at human hands. Enormous tracts of land, especially on the coastal hills, have disappeared under eucalyptus plantations – you won't fail to notice them. *Eucalyptus globulus* does very well here and is grown to feed a thriving papermill industry. Large plantations of the Maritime Pine have also displaced much native forest. These monocultures of resinous trees have proved all too susceptible to forest fires, which have plagued Galicia in summer for many years, reducing thousands of hectares to cinders. Fortunately, the worst fires have affected the plantations but the Eucalyptus soon regenerates and re-establishes what is largely a bird-poor habitat.

The coast has suffered from the usual proliferation of tourist developments in many places. Even more seriously, the marine ecosystem has been damaged by a succession of shipwrecks of oil tankers. The wreck of the *Prestige* off the

Costa da Morte in November 2002 was only one of the most recent and news-worthy of a series of such events, all of which produced large scale pollution of coastal habitats and killed many birds.

The continuing attractiveness and biodiversity of Galicia, in the face of all these ravages, is a tribute both to the resilience of nature and to the efforts of local and international conservation associations. It remains a most interest-ing and rewarding region to visit. An informative English-language website (turismo.gal/que-facer/birding-in-galicia/os-mellores-lugares) describing many of the best sites is highly recommended.

Records of Galician birds are welcomed by the compilers of the Galician bird report (Anuario das Aves de Galicia). Email to Sociedade Galega de Ornitología (anuario@sgosgo.org).

DUNAS DE CORRUBEDO   GA1
(A Coruña)

Status: Parque Natural 'Complexo Dunar de Corrubedo y Lagunas de Carregal y Vixán' (996ha). Ramsar site. ZEPA.

Site description

The natural park fringes a wide bay south of Corrubedo, on the Ribeira pen-insula at the northern entrance to the Ría de Arousa. The outstanding feature is the active dune system, including dunes up to 1km long, 250m wide and 12–15m high. The largest dunes are in the north of the reserve. Marshy areas are associated with the three small rivers; the Ríos Longo, Sirves and Artes, which combine in an estuary at the north end of the site. Further south there are two lagoons, both with hides: the saline Lago de Carregal and the fresh-water Laguna de Vixán, with marshland, reedbeds and damp meadows as well as pinewoods and the inevitable eucalyptus plantations. The lighthouse at Cabo Corrubedo provides a good vantage point for watching seabird migration.

Species

The varied habitats support a diversity of breeding birds, including Stone-curlews in the dunes, Kentish Plovers on the beach and Gadwall, Water Rails and Great Reed Warblers in the reedbeds. Passage and wintering waders, including Oystercatchers, Curlews, Dunlin, Grey Plovers and Bar-tailed Godwits frequent the beach and marshes. Nearctic waders, such as Pectoral Sandpipers, occur with some regularity in autumn. Marsh Harriers are present in winter when Reed Buntings occur in the marsh and Richard's Pipits may be present in grassy areas. Wintering waterfowl include Common Scoters and the occasional Greater Scaup offshore, alongside Great Northern Divers and sometimes other divers.

The reserve has an interesting flora and the dunes boast no fewer than 10 amphibian and 14 reptile species.

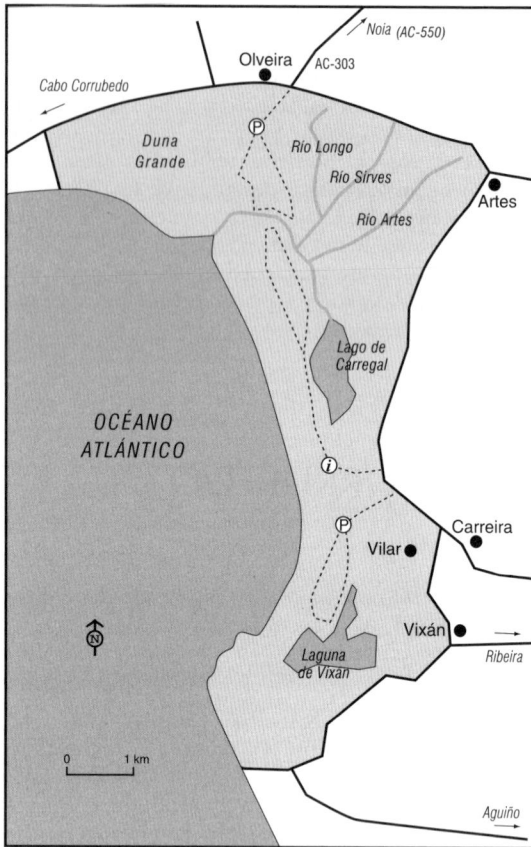

Timing

Interesting species are present all year but passage periods provide the greatest diversity of waders and winter is best for divers and seaduck. Seawatching from Cabo Corrubedo is most productive during onshore (westerly) winds.

Access

From Santiago take the N-550 or the AP-9 motorway south to Padrón, and then the AG-11 to Ribeira. Alternatively take the AC-543 west from Santiago to Noia and continue on the AC-550 to Ribeira. From Ribeira take the road to Carreira and Vilar and, having passed these villages, take a track left to the centre, where you can park. The visitors' centre at the park (Centro de Interpretación del Ecosistema Litoral de Galicia) is a good place to start. From here you can walk to the south and Vixán lagoon (2km round trip), or north to the dunes and marshes and Carregal lagoon (4km round trip). Otherwise, to visit the northern part of the site, return to the main road and turn left to Olveira and Corrubedo. Near Olveira, and almost opposite the AC-303 road that returns you to the AC-550, a track to the left leads to the dunes where there is another car park. Continue west to and beyond Corrubedo to reach the seawatching site at the lighthouse on the cape (Cabo Corrubedo).

CALENDAR

All year: Goshawk, Water Rail, Kentish Plover, Stone-curlew, Barn Owl, Kingfisher, Stonechat, Zitting Cisticola, Cetti's Warbler, Serin.

Breeding season: Hobby, Common Cuckoo, Hoopoe, Tree Pipit; Great Reed, Reed and Melodious Warblers.

Winter: Mallard, Teal, Gadwall, Shoveler, Pochard, Tufted Duck, Scaup, Common Scoter; Red-throated, Black-throated and Great Northern Divers, Great Crested and Black-necked Grebes, Cormorant, Grey Heron, Merlin, Common Coot, Oystercatcher, Grey Plover, Knot, Sanderling, Dunlin,

Common and Jack Snipe, Bar-tailed Godwit, Curlew, Common Redshank, Greenshank, Common Sandpiper, Great Black-backed Gull, Razorbill, Richard's Pipit, Reed Bunting.

Passage periods: Cory's, Great (autumn only), Sooty (autumn only), Manx and Balearic Shearwaters, Gannet, Little Bittern, Purple Heron, Spotted Crake, Marsh Harrier, Whimbrel; Pomarine, Arctic, Long-tailed and Great Skuas; Mediterranean, Little and Sabine's Gulls, Kittiwake; Sandwich, Common, Arctic, Little and Black Terns, Guillemot, Razorbill, Puffin, Yellow Wagtail, Nightingale, Whinchat.

O GROVE PENINSULA   GA2
(Pontevedra)

Status: Espacio Natural en Régimen de Protección General, ZEPA and Ramsar site (2,561ha). SEO/Birdlife Reserve (7,500ha).

Site description

This small peninsula marks the southern side of the entrance to the Ría de Arousa. It encloses a sheltered shallow inlet with extensive areas of intertidal sands and muds, saltmarsh and a number of small islands. The largest island, La Toja (A Toxa), is at the head of the inlet to the north and connected to the peninsula by a causeway. The Río Umia has its estuary in the north-east of the inlet. The peninsula itself is linked to the mainland by a sandy isthmus, with the beach of A Lanzada to seaward. The isthmus, most of the coastal areas of the peninsula and the mudflats offshore comprise a SEO/Birdlife reserve.

Species

This is one of the most important sites in Galicia for wintering waders with many species using the intertidal areas for feeding and roosting. The Ría de Arousa as a whole holds nationally important numbers of several species in winter, including over 5,000 Dunlins, over 1,000 Grey Plovers, over 500 Oystercatchers and some 200 Turnstones. It is also important for waders and terns on passage. Spoonbills occur regularly on passage and over 100 may be present in winter. Numbers of waterfowl occur in winter especially, when there are also concentrations of gulls. Great Northern and other divers, grebes and Razorbills occur to seaward in winter. Balearic Shearwaters may be numerous offshore in summer and autumn.

Timing

The largest concentrations of waders and waterfowl occur in winter. Passage periods are also rewarding, especially in autumn. The area is a popular resort and can be very busy in summer. Waders are best observed on a rising tide and mornings are preferable on the western side of the inlet on bright days.

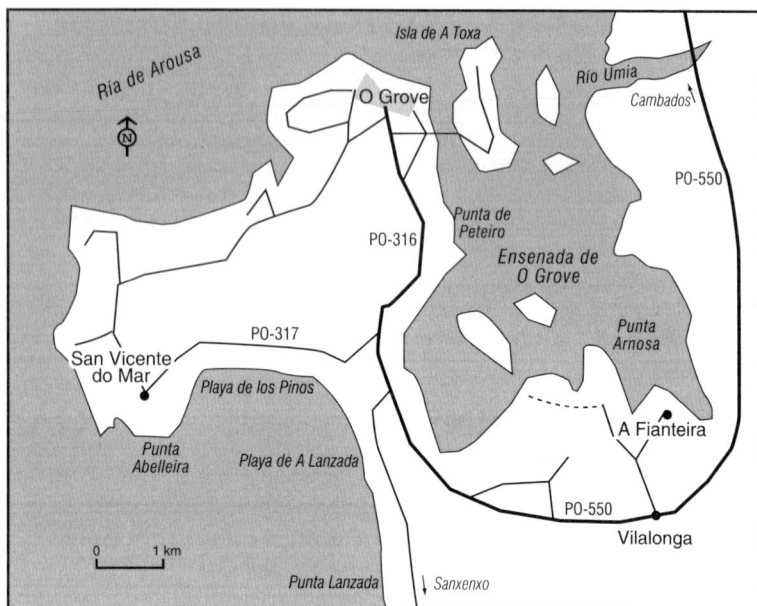

Access

The most pleasant approach is to leave the AP-9 motorway at the Pontevedra Norte exit to take the scenic drive along the coast on the PO-308 to Sanxenxo and on to O Grove. There are many opportunities to stop and birdwatch with views across the Ría de Pontevedra and across to the Isla de Ons. The road leads to the isthmus and out to the peninsula along the Playa de A Lanzada. The beach is good for divers, grebes and ducks in winter and for waders and terns on passage. If it looks promising it is worth following the PO-317 around to the north side of the bay towards San Vicente do Mar, to scan from the beaches there.

The O Grove inlet (Ensenada) is the key area for wintering and passage waders. Excellent views of the inner reaches are available across the marisma de O Bao on the eastern side of the isthmus from the PO-550 roadside: the light and state of tide are critical here, low tide being best avoided. Continue on to the peninsula and take the PO-316 towards the resort of O Grove, which skirts the eastern side of the inlet and offers good views. You can then continue across the bridge on to the Isla de A Toxa. The island has a spa and hotel, both of which can attract the crowds at popular periods, but it offers excellent views into the inlet. Returning to the mainland, it is worth following the PO-550 for 5km around to the bottom of the inlet. Take the road north opposite the petrol station at Vilalonga. This road forks after 1km. Drive to the end of each branch in turn for access to the southern shore of the inlet, at Punta Arnosa to the west and at A Fianteira to the east, where good views are possible at high tide especially.

CALENDAR

All year: Mallard, Common Buzzard, Common Kestrel, Peregrine Falcon, Crested Lark, Zitting Cisticola, Dartford and Sardinian Warblers, Serin, Cirl Bunting.

Breeding season: Kentish Plover, Common Redshank, Common Sandpiper, European Nightjar, Alpine and Common Swifts, Hoopoe, Melodious Warbler, Whitethroat.

Winter: Shelduck, Wigeon, Gadwall, Teal, Pintail, Shoveler, Pochard, Tufted Duck, Scaup, Common Scoter, Eider, Black-throated and Great Northern Divers, Great Crested Grebe, Cormorant, Shag, Little Egret, Grey

Heron, Spoonbill, Marsh and Hen Harriers, Merlin, Oystercatcher, Ringed and Grey Plovers, Dunlin, Bar-tailed and Black-tailed Godwits, Jack and Common Snipe, Curlew, Common Redshank, Greenshank, Turnstone; Mediterranean, Little, Black-headed, Common and Great Black-backed Gulls, Sandwich Tern, Razorbill, Guillemot.

Passage periods: Cory's and Balearic Shearwaters, Gannet, Spoonbill, Montagu's Harrier, Hobby, Sanderling, Bar-tailed Godwit, Whimbrel, Spotted Redshank; Sandwich, Common, Little and Black Terns.

GALICIAN ISLANDS NATIONAL PARK (Pontevedra)   GA3

Status: Parque Nacional 'Marítimo-Terrestre de las Islas Atlánticas de Galicia' and ZEPA (2,272ha).

Site description

This National Park, designated in 2002, includes the Islas Cíes and the archipelagos of Ons and Sálvora and their surrounding waters. These small but very attractive islands lie just 3–8km off the west coast. They are all accessible to private vessels but the Islas Cíes and the Isla de Ons also have regular ferry links to the mainland.

The Islas Cíes are off the mouth of the Ría de Vigo. The three main islands; Monte Agudo, Faro and San Martiño, have steep faces to the Atlantic but the eastern shores are gentler, with dunes and sandy beaches. Pine and eucalyptus plantations have taken over much of the interior of the islands but the understorey is largely natural and can provide welcome shelter for birds on migration. Monte Agudo and Faro are linked by a road across a sand bar.

The Isla de Ons is the largest in the Park, at 5.5km long and up to 0.8km wide. The relief is less abrupt than in the Islas Cíes and the island supports several small farms. There are large expanses of coastal heath. The archipelago, which is north of the Cíes and off the Ría de Pontevedra, also includes the uninhabited islet of Onza and a number of rocks and stacks.

The wrecking of the oil tanker *Prestige* occurred just a few months after the Park was designated and the islands were all badly affected by oil. The visible damage at least has largely disappeared since, although longer term effects on the ecosystem may remain.

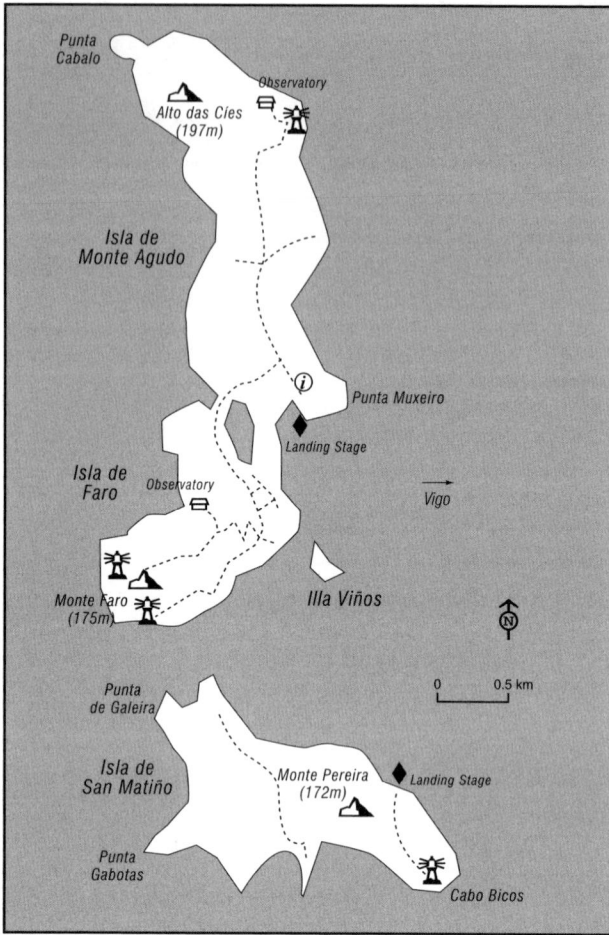

Species

The Islas Cíes and Ons have the largest Shag colonies in Spain, with over 1,000 breeding pairs in total, although these are declining, partly as a result of birds drowning in fishing nets. A small colony of Lesser Black-backed Gulls nests on Sálvora where the birds are vastly outnumbered by the large colonies of Yellow-legged Gulls which occur on all the islands. A few European Storm-petrels and, latterly, Cory's Shearwaters, also breed in the Park. The Guillemot used to be a key attraction. Some 400 pairs bred on the Islas Cíes in the early 1960s but these had declined to just a few pairs by the mid-1970s and are now extinct locally both here and in the Ons islands, where they also used to breed.

A diversity of seabirds frequent these waters, particularly in winter and during the autumn passage period, but there are always some interesting species around. Gannets; Cory's, Manx and Balearic Shearwaters, gulls and terns may

Cory's Shearwaters

be expected during your boat trips and may be looked for from watchpoints on the islands themselves. Breeding landbirds on the islands include Sardinian and Dartford Warblers in the scrub, with Peregrines, Red-billed Choughs and Alpine Swifts on the cliffs.

Timing
Visits are most feasible in spring and summer, when the boats run regularly. Autumn and winter visits can be interesting nonetheless.

Access
Islas Cíes   A number of companies now offer services to these and other islands, from Vigo, Baiona and Cangas de Morrazo. A well-established service is offered by 'Naviera Mar de Ons', who claim to have the highest hourly crossing frequency. See their website for full details (mardeons.es; Tel. 986 225 272). Weather permitting, boats run to Monte Agudo from about late May to the end of September, at Easter and sometimes during fine weekends in spring and autumn. The crossing takes up to 45 minutes. Adult fares at peak periods from Vigo are €18.50 return (2016). It is also possible to arrange private trips for groups of up to 10 at any time of year. A number of trails allow exploration of Monte Agudo and the linked island of Faro: a popular option is to walk north on Monte Agudo to the lighthouse, where there is a bird observatory (Observatorio del Faro do Peito). Faro also has an observatory (Observatorio de La Campana) and a summer campsite, as well as the information centre for the Park.

Isla de Ons   Boat services operated by 'Naviera Mar de Ons' (mardeons.es; Tel. 986 225 272) run from Bueu in the Ría de Pontevedra to the island from June to September and irregularly at other times, again weather permitting. The crossing takes 30 minutes. Services also operate from Marín and Sanxenxo. A circular trail (11.5km) follows the island periphery.

CALENDAR

All year: Shag, Peregrine Falcon, Kentish Plover, Yellow-legged Gull, Rock Dove, Stonechat, Black Redstart, Blackbird, Dartford and Sardinian Warblers, Red-billed Chough, Raven.

Breeding season: Cory's Shearwater, European Storm-petrel, Lesser Black-backed Gull, European Nightjar, Alpine Swift.

Winter: Red-throated, Black-throated and Great Northern Divers, Gannet, Cormorant, Great Skua, Kittiwake, Sandwich Tern, Razorbill, Puffin.

Passage periods: Common and Velvet Scoters; Cory's, Great (autumn), Sooty (autumn), Manx and Balearic Shearwaters, Gannet; Pomarine, Arctic, Long-tailed and Great Skuas; Mediterranean, Little and Sabine's Gulls, Kittiwake; Sandwich, Common, Arctic, Little and Black Terns, Guillemot, Razorbill, Puffin, Turtle Dove, Nightingale, Common Redstart, Whinchat, Northern Wheatear.

BAIONA COAST (Pontevedra)   GA4

Status: Part of the Galician network of protected spaces: 'Zona de Especial Conservación dos Valores Naturais'.

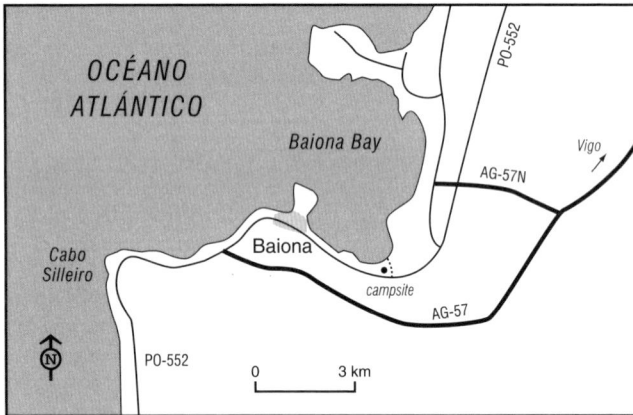

Site description

The fishing village and resort of Baiona lies within a shallow bay, including a sandy beach and a marshy estuary in the south-eastern corner. The Islas Cíes (GA3) provide an attractive backdrop to the north-west. The coastline south from Baiona is rocky but gently sloping, providing a substantial intertidal zone. The slopes fronting the shoreline are covered in dense coastal heath.

Species

The area offers good opportunities for seawatching and such remarkable species as a Frigatebird and Black Guillemot have been recorded here. The rocky shoreline is attractive to numbers of Purple Sandpipers and Turnstones in winter. Yellow-legged Gulls and Shags are always present. Wintering seabirds include Mediterranean, Common and Great Black-backed Gulls, Sandwich Terns and Razorbills. Small numbers of waders frequent Baiona Bay which has attracted a number of Nearctic rarities in autumn, including at least two Buff-breasted Sandpipers, an American Golden Plover and a Killdeer. The coastal scrub is attractive to the resident Sardinian and Dartford Warblers and Cirl Buntings and should be searched for passerine migrants in spring and autumn.

Timing
The most productive periods occur in autumn, from late August onwards, and also in winter. Spring migration may also be interesting. Seabird watching from the west-facing coastline can be difficult in the afternoons and evenings on sunny days. The area is fairly quiet except in summer, when it gets many visitors.

Access
Take the A-9/AP-9 motorway south past Vigo and take the AG-57 and then the AG-57N to bring you to the PO-552, where you should turn left for Baiona. The marshy estuary in Baiona Bay is behind the campsite on the right as you reach the Bay. Park here and follow a track around the back of the campsite and round to the beach.

Seabird watching is best from the disused lighthouse at Cabo Silleiro, which is to seaward just off the PO-552 as it follows the shoreline south from Baiona. The site is lower down and further from the sea than ideal but good views of seabirds may be had provided you use a telescope. A track on the landward side of the road opposite the old lighthouse provides useful access to the coastal scrub.

CALENDAR

All year: Shag, Yellow-legged Gull, Kentish Plover, Black Redstart, Stonechat, Blue Rock Thrush, Sardinian and Dartford Warblers, Cirl Bunting.

Winter: Common Scoter, Great Northern Diver, Gannet, Cormorant, Oystercatcher, Grey Plover, Sanderling, Purple Sandpiper, Dunlin, Turnstone; Mediterranean, Common and Great Black-backed Gulls, Sandwich Tern, Razorbill, Common Chiffchaff.

Passage periods: Cory's, Great (autumn), Sooty (autumn), Manx and Balearic Shearwaters, Gannet, Knot, Curlew Sandpiper, Bar-tailed Godwit, Whimbrel; Pomarine, Arctic, Long-tailed and Great Skuas; Mediterranean, Little and Sabine's Gulls, Kittiwake; Sandwich, Common, Arctic, Little and Black Terns, Guillemot, Razorbill, Puffin, Common Redstart, Whinchat, Northern Wheatear, Willow Warbler, Blackcap, rarities.

RÍO MIÑO ESTUARY (Pontevedra)   GA5

Status: ZEPA. The valley upstream is a UNESCO Biosphere Reserve.

Site description
The Río Miño, in the extreme south-west of Galicia and marking the border

with Portugal, is the principal river in Galicia. The estuary is broad and has a good variety of habitats: with sandbanks, mudflats, saltmarshes, reedbeds, bankside woodlands and a number of riverine islands.

Species

A diversity of species breed around the estuary. These include Little Bittern, Kentish Plover, Zitting Cisticola, Great Reed and Sardinian Warblers and Golden Oriole. Common Waxbills have colonised the area and the Yellow-crowned Bishop may be doing so. The site is most interesting for passage and wintering species, however. Large numbers of waterfowl, including Wigeon and Teal, are present in winter on the river. Great Northern Divers, Black-necked Grebes, Red-breasted Mergansers and Razorbills also enter the estuary, particularly to shelter from rough weather.

A variety of waders occur on passage and in winter. Oystercatchers, Grey and Ringed Plovers, Sanderlings, Bar-tailed Godwits and Whimbrels occur among many others, which include occasional Nearctic rarities. Ospreys are regular on passage and in winter and Marsh Harriers are often present in winter.

Passerine migrants occur at times in the dunes, scrub and woodland on both sides of the estuary. Both Bluethroats and Aquatic Warblers are regularly found in the reedbeds in early September. Seabirds are frequently visible off the river mouth, with cormorants, gulls and terns often entering the estuary.

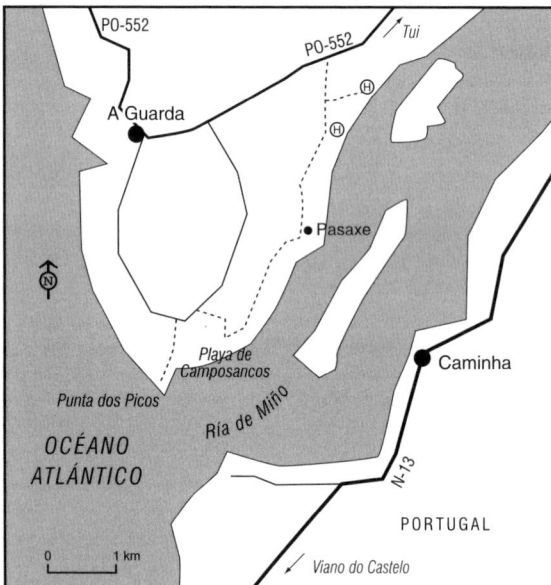

Timing

The best periods for migrants are September–October and April–May. Wintering birds are present mainly during November–March. Summer can be particularly busy on the river, and parts of the estuary are also affected by shooting interests at certain times of the year, at weekends and on public holidays.

Access

Rapid access is available from Vigo by taking the AP-9 motorway south to the border at Tui and then following the north bank of the river on the PO-552 to A Guarda. A more pleasant drive is to take the PO-552 from Vigo through Baiona and down to A Guarda along the coast, taking the opportunity for seabirding along the way (GA4).

Once at A Guarda follow the coast road south, keeping the hill (Monte de Santa Tegra) to your left. The road here is a loop, which eventually returns to A Guarda. However, as it reaches the estuary you should take the track to the Playa de Camposancos. Park here and walk to the rocky point, Punta dos Picos, from where you can watch for seabirds and waterfowl in and off the estuary. Return to the road and continue upstream. The jetty at Pasaxe also gives views of the river. Some 250m further along, a track off to the right takes you close to the riverbank and a campsite (Camping Santa Tecla). Two large hides on stilts give good views over the shoreline and shallows and across to several large reedy islands. The best views of waders especially are generally to be had from here. You can return along the PO-552 to A Guarda from here.

Depending on the distribution of the birds in the estuary and available time, it can be worth making a special detour to the Portuguese side, either by driving across at the head of the estuary through Tui or by taking the ferry across the Miño from Goián (almost halfway from A Guarda to Tui) across to Vila Nova de Cerveira. Then take the N-13 south-west towards Caminha and the mouth of the river, and a large pinewood and dune system.

CALENDAR

All year: Mallard, Cormorant, Shag, Red Kite, Goshawk, Sparrowhawk, Common Buzzard, Peregrine Falcon, Water Rail, Kentish Plover, Crested Lark, Zitting Cisticola, Sardinian Warbler, Crested Tit, Red-billed Chough, Tree Sparrow, Common Waxbill, Yellow-crowned Bishop, Reed Bunting.

Breeding season: Little Bittern, Quail, Hobby, Common Cuckoo, Turtle Dove, Scops Owl, European Nightjar, Common Swift, Hoopoe, Yellow Wagtail, Great Reed Warbler, Golden Oriole.

Winter: Wigeon, Gadwall, Teal, Tufted Duck, Red-breasted Merganser, Common Scoter, Great Northern Diver, Black-necked Grebe, Gannet, Little Egret, Marsh Harrier, Oystercatcher, Ringed Plover, Dunlin, Jack and Common Snipe, Black-tailed Godwit, Curlew, Purple Sandpiper, Turnstone, Razorbill, Guillemot, Great Skua, Mediterranean and Great Black-backed Gulls, Sandwich Tern, Common Chiffchaff.

Passage periods: Cory's, Great (autumn), Sooty (autumn), Manx and Balearic Shearwaters, Gannet, Spoonbill, Osprey, Marsh Harrier, Avocet, Curlew Sandpiper, Ringed Plover, Bar-tailed Godwit, Common Redshank, Greenshank, Wood Sandpiper; Pomarine, Arctic and Great Skuas, Mediterranean and Little Gulls, Kittiwake; Sandwich, Common, Arctic, Little and Black Terns, Guillemot, Razorbill, Whinchat, Willow Warbler, Bluethroat, Spotted and Pied Flycatchers.

BAIXA LIMIA–SERRA (SIERRA)   GA6
DE XURÉS (Ourense)

Status: Parque Natural (20,920ha). ZEPA.

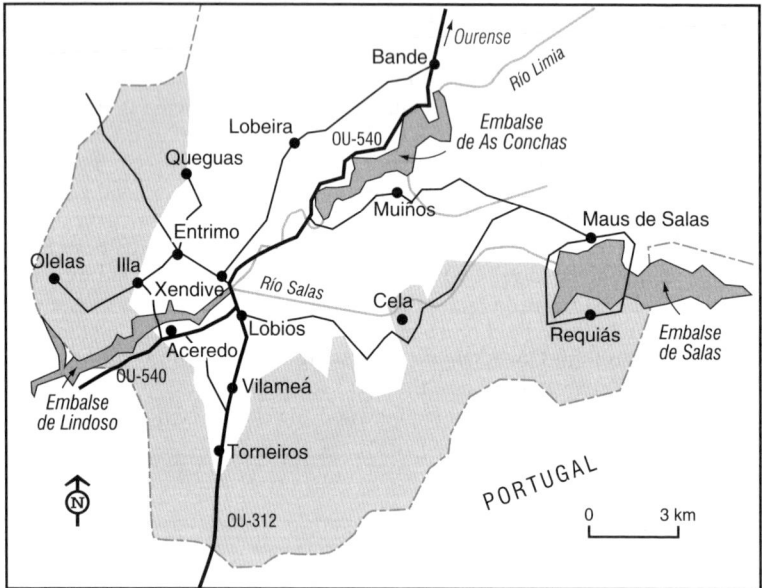

Site description

The Natural Park of Baixa Limia–Serra Xurés is in south-west Galicia bordering Portugal. This is a huge area of contrasting landscape and scenery, with a corresponding variety of bird habitats. The massif is mainly granite, and one of the park's most obvious features is the '*bolos*', granitic rock deposits left behind after glacial erosion. Two main river systems, the Río Limia and the Río Salas, drain the area although many other streams and rivers feed into these two rivers. Three reservoirs: the Embalses de Salas, de As Conchas and de Lindoso, also add to the interest although they do not all fall entirely within the park's boundaries.

The Atlantic forests typical of the humid north-west meet Mediterranean forest in this region, with areas of Pedunculate Oaks and other deciduous species alternating with a maquis of Cork Oaks and Strawberry Trees. Farming is generally small scale, of low intensity and mainly pasture-based, with parts of the park terraced for agricultural use. The reservoirs have limited marginal vegetation although there are some reedbeds. There are good riverine woods along some river sections. The area is also of considerable archaeological interest, including many ancient burial sites scattered through the valley of the Río Salas and adjoining mountains.

Species
Over 140 bird species have been recorded here, including at least 14 breeding warblers and three shrike species. A few pairs of Common Snipe breed in the Río Salas valley, one of the very few places in Spain where they nest, alongside Lapwings and Little Ringed Plovers.

Timing
Spring through to summer.

Access
Take the OU-540 south out of Ourense, through Celanova and Bande, and continue south-west. This road takes you through the centre of the park. The Park Information Centre is in Lobios. Many side roads off the OU-540 take you higher up into the sierra and are worth exploring. There are also a number of trails throughout the area: try the one from the village of Queguas, a round walk of around 6–7km, through some Oak and Sweet Chestnut woods, scrub and farmland.

CALENDAR

All year: Red-legged Partridge, Little and Great Crested Grebes, Goshawk, Sparrowhawk, Common Buzzard, Golden Eagle, Stock Dove; Barn, Little and, Tawny Owls, Green Woodpecker, Grey and White Wagtails, Dipper, Black Redstart, Blue Rock Thrush, Zitting Cisticola; Cetti's, Dartford and Sardinian Warblers, Blackcap, Common Chiffchaff, Goldcrest, Firecrest, Crested Tit, Southern Grey Shrike, Red-billed Chough, Tree Sparrow; Cirl, Rock and Corn Buntings.

Breeding season: White Stork, Black Kite, Short-toed Eagle, Quail, Little Ringed Plover, Lapwing, Common Snipe, Common Sandpiper, Turtle Dove, Common Cuckoo, Common Swift, Hoopoe, Wood Lark, Sand and House Martins, Yellow Wagtail, Nightingale, Whinchat; Melodious, Subalpine, Garden and Bonelli's Warblers, Whitethroat, Iberian Chiffchaff, Golden Oriole, Red-backed and Woodchat Shrikes.

Winter: Golden Plover, Redwing, Fieldfare.

SIERRA DE CAUREL   GA7
(SERRA DO COUREL) (Lugo)

Status: Part of the Galician network of protected spaces: Zona de Especial Conservación dos Valores Naturais (102,562ha).

Site description
This is another very quiet mountainous area in the far eastern hinterland of Galicia on the western fringes of the Cordillera Cantábrica, south-west of the Sierra de Os Ancares (GA8). While similar to Os Ancares with its steep wooded valleys and cliff faces it has more of a Mediterranean character, especially in the valleys where there are woods of Cork Oak, Iberian Holm Oak and Chestnut with associated *Cistus* and Strawberry Tree scrub. Above 1,000m

there are the beech, oak and birch forests, typical of the humid north-west. The highest point of the Caurel range is Pico Formigueiros (1,654m).

Species

Grey Partridges have their westernmost outpost here in the mountain-top heaths but they are scarce. Hen Harriers also breed sparsely on the high tops. The woodland avifauna is very rich as in the Sierra de Os Ancares, with a similar list of breeding birds, including Honey-buzzards, Short-toed Eagles, Woodcocks, Common Redstarts and Iberian Chiffchaffs.

Timing

Spring and early summer.

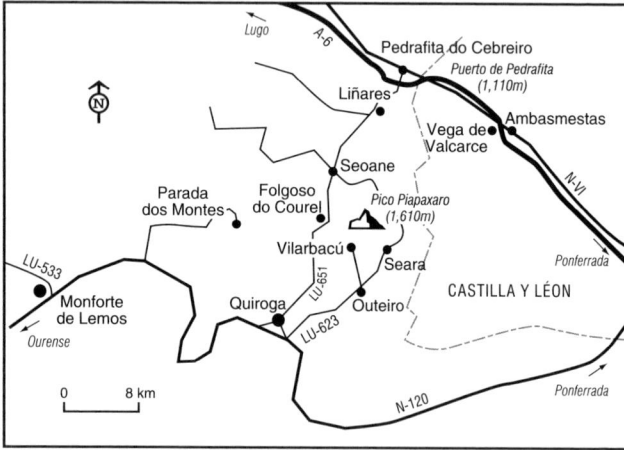

Access

From the north leave the A-6 Lugo/Ponferrada motorway at Pedrafita do Cebreiro (km-433) and take the LU-633 south-west for 8km, past Linares, to head south to Seoane do Courel, to join the very scenic LU-651. This road crosses the best area for birds and eventually (35km) joins the N-120 at the southern end of the area near Quiroga. From Ourense take the N-120 to Monforte and continue to Quiroga (km-490) where you head north on the LU-651. A number of walking trails originate from Seoane do Courel. A minor road loops south from the LU-651 at Seoane for 31km to Quiroga, offering the chance of a circular route through the region. Both roads offer plenty of opportunities to stop and explore the countryside and woodlands.

CALENDAR

All year: Grey Partridge, Hen Harrier, Goshawk, Sparrowhawk, Golden Eagle, Woodcock, Great Spotted Woodpecker, Crag Martin, Dipper, Blue Rock Thrush, Dartford Warbler, Firecrest, Goldcrest, Crested Tit, Nuthatch, Bullfinch, Cirl and Rock Buntings.

Breeding season: Honey-buzzard, Short-toed Eagle, Montagu's Harrier, Hobby, Rufous-tailed Rock Thrush; Subalpine, Melodious and Bonelli's Warblers, Iberian Chiffchaff, Spotted Flycatcher, Red-backed Shrike.

SIERRA DE OS ANCARES   GA8
(SERRA DOS ANCARES) (Lugo)

Status: Part of the Galician network of protected spaces: Zona de Especial Conservación dos Valores Naturais. ZEPA. Prospective Parque Natural. Contiguous with the Reserva Nacional de los Ancares Leoneses in Castilla y León. UNESCO Biosphere Reserve.

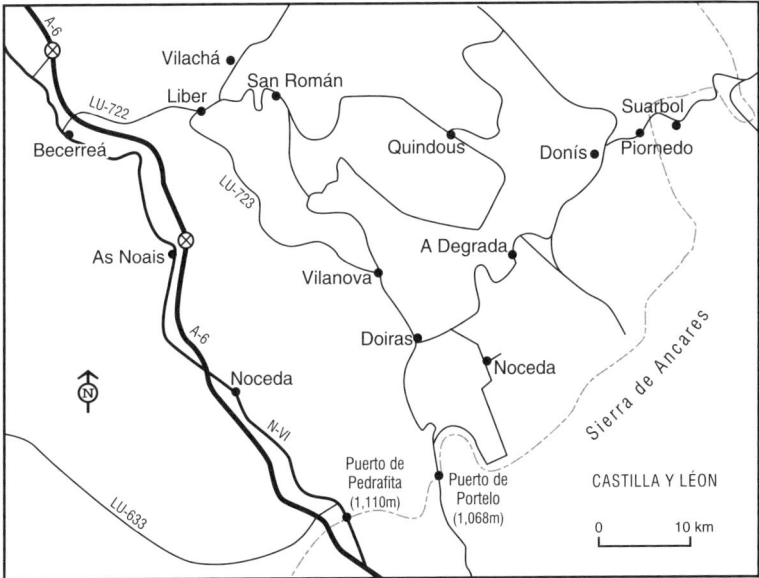

Site description

A sparsely populated and wooded mountainous area in the far eastern part of Galicia, bordering Asturias and Castilla y León and comprising the far western end of the Cordillera Cantábrica. There is some difference between the north- and south-facing slopes, with a more Atlantic woodland community: mainly Pedunculate Oak, Silver Birch and Sweet Chestnut on the northern slopes and Mediterranean scrub on the warmer southern ones.

Species

Much of the attraction of the area is the presence of those montane species of the Cordillera that have their westernmost outposts here. Grey Partridges, Black Woodpeckers and Marsh Tits occur but are scarce. The Capercaillie has declined to extinction in the Galician sector of Os Ancares, a sad consequence of its general demise in Spain, although a diminished population survives in adjacent parts of Castilla y Léon and Asturias. The diverse woodland avifauna includes Woodcocks, Honey-buzzards, Short-toed Eagles and Iberian Chiffchaffs. Rufous-tailed Rock Thrushes and Alpine Accentors occur on the rocky peaks.

Resident mammals include Wild Cats, Wild Boars, Beech Martens and Red Squirrels.

Timing

Spring and early summer visits are recommended.

Access

Leave the A-6 Lugo/Ponferrada motorway at km-448 near Becerreá and take the LU-722 east towards Liber. Scenic access to the best of the area is provided by taking the right turn to San Román 1km north of Liber and continuing to Vilanova via Quindous (31km). From Vilanova take the road to A Degrada via Doiras and continue to Donís and Piornedo in the heart of the sierra (18km). There are many places to stop and take short walks across the range or through the woodlands. A trail leading south-east from Piornedo, giving access to some of the higher reaches, is one of numerous marked paths in the region. You can also drive for some 10km beyond Piornedo via Suarbol to reach the pass, the Puerto de Ancares (1,648m) and explore that area on foot.

CALENDAR

All year: Grey Partridge, Hen Harrier, Goshawk, Sparrowhawk, Common Buzzard, Golden Eagle, Woodcock, Tawny Owl, Black and Great Spotted Woodpeckers, Water Pipit, Dunnock, Alpine Accentor, Goldcrest, Firecrest, Marsh Tit, Bullfinch.

Breeding season: Honey-buzzard, Short-toed Eagle, Wryneck, Common Redstart, Rufous-tailed Rock Thrush, Blackcap, Bonelli's Warbler, Iberian Chiffchaff, Long-tailed Tit, Short-toed Treecreeper, Jay, Red-backed Shrike.

RÍA DE ORTIGUEIRA (A Coruña)   GA9

Status: ZEPA and Ramsar site (2,940ha).

Site description

Spectacular scenery on the north-westernmost point of Spain provides the backdrop for this wide tidal estuary situated between the headlands of Cabo Ortegal to the west and Cabo de Estaca de Bares in the east. The outer part of the estuary is deep, with a rocky coastline and cliffs, whereas the inner two arms to either side of the town of Ortigueira are sheltered and much shallower. There are large areas of intertidal mud and sand, expanses of saltmarsh and sand dunes, and some pine and eucalyptus plantations.

Species

The inner estuary is the main focus of attention since it attracts large numbers of wintering and passage ducks and waders. The former include Wigeon, Teal, Common Pochards, Mallard, Pintail and Shoveler. The regular waders include Oystercatchers, Grey Plovers, Sanderlings, Dunlins, Curlews, Bar-tailed Godwits and Turnstones. Slavonian Grebes occur with some regularity in winter. Rare gulls are a frequent attraction at Cariño beach and harbour; they include Glaucous and Iceland Gulls and sometimes much rarer species such as Bonaparte's and American Herring Gulls.

Seabird passage is often spectacular at Cabo Ortegal but most watchers prefer to visit Cabo de Bares (GA10) nearby, which extends just a little further north. The bay between the two, which becomes the mouth of the Ría, attracts fishing Gannets at times, as well as seaduck and occasional Great Northern Divers in winter. Shags and Yellow-legged Gulls nest on the coastline and on the offshore islets. Peregrines, Ravens and Red-billed Choughs also frequent the cliffs.

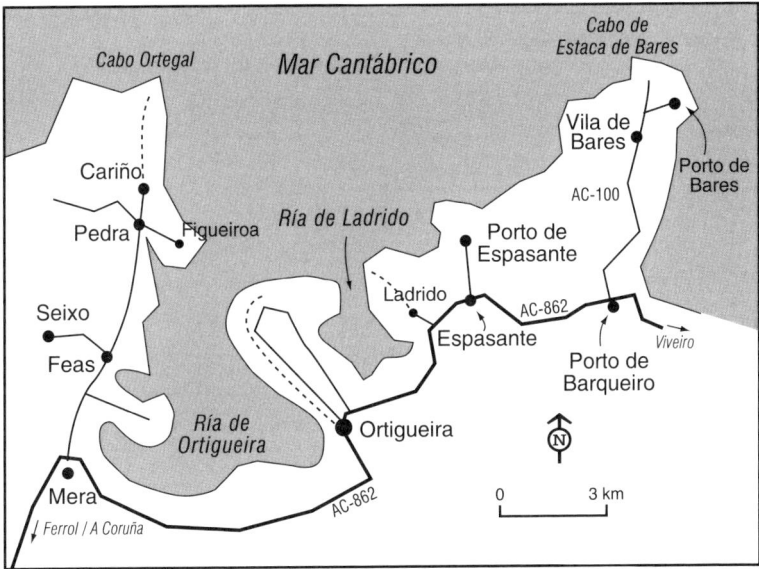

Timing
Worth visiting throughout the year, with winter important for wintering ducks and waders and for rare gulls. Spring and autumn are good for passage waders and autumn is best for seabirds.

Access
The AC-862 skirts the estuary and provides a direct link with Ferrol to the west and with the LU-862 for coastal points further east and the N-634 to Asturias. The deeper areas of the outer estuary are best viewed from the western bank from the port at the village of Cariño. The road leading north from Cariño will bring you to the lighthouse at Cabo Ortegal, which is well placed for seawatching. On the eastern side the Ría may be viewed from the shoreline at Porto de Espasante and at Ladrido, both just north of the AC-862. The sheltered shallow areas with mudflats and saltmarsh are easily accessed at Ortigueira itself, from where a footpath follows the shoreline around the headland to the north-west, giving excellent views at any state of the tide. They may also be viewed from the western side from the Cariño road.

CALENDAR

All year: Shag, Common Buzzard, Peregrine Falcon, Common Kestrel, Yellow-legged Gull, Barn Owl, Black Redstart, Blue Rock Thrush, Zitting Cisticola, Cetti's and Dartford Warblers, Firecrest, Crested Tit, Red-billed Chough, Raven, Spotless Starling, Tree Sparrow, Serin, Cirl and Rock Buntings.

Breeding season: Hobby, Common Cuckoo, Yellow Wagtail, Melodious Warbler.

Winter: Red-breasted Merganser, Wigeon, Teal, Mallard, Pintail, Shoveler, Common Pochard, Common Scoter, Red-throated and Great Northern Divers, Slavonian Grebe, Merlin, Oystercatcher, Ringed and Grey

Plovers, Knot, Purple Sandpiper, Dunlin, Curlew, Whimbrel, Bar-tailed Godwit, Common Redshank, Greenshank, Turnstone, Common and Great Black-backed Gulls, Sandwich Tern, Razorbill, Guillemot, rarities.

Passage periods: Cory's, Great (autumn), Sooty (autumn), Manx and Balearic Shearwaters, Leach's Storm-petrel, Gannet, Grey Heron, Spotted Redshank, Common Sandpiper; Pomarine, Arctic, Long-tailed and Great Skuas, Mediterranean, Little and Sabine's Gulls, Kittiwake; Sandwich, Common, Arctic, Little and Black Terns, Guillemot, Razorbill, Puffin, rarities.

ESTACA DE BARES (A Coruña)   GA10

Status: Part of the Galician network of protected spaces: Zona de Especial Conservación dos Valores Naturais. ZEPA.

Site description

Cabo de Bares (Cape Bares) is the northernmost point of Iberia, a precipitous headland jutting out into the southern approaches to the Bay of Biscay. The Estaca (stacks) comprises the rocky islets just offshore. The cape is fringed by tall cliffs and there are pastures and expanses of coastal heath inland.

Species

This is unarguably the best site in Spain for seabird migration. Seabirds pass offshore in very large numbers, notably in autumn, when the species diversity is greatest and includes species such as Long-tailed Skuas and Sabine's Gulls which are rare elsewhere in Spain. Wilson's Storm-petrels are regular in late summer and autumn, usually well offshore but occasionally visible from land. Petrels of the Fea's/Zino's complex have been recorded annually in recent autumns, most often in August and September: there were 11 sightings here in 2011; at least one has been identified as a Fea's Petrel. Even rarer seabirds may turn up: there are recent records of Black-browed Albatross, Brown Booby, Red-billed Tropicbird and South Polar Skua. The site remains excellent for seabirds in winter and spring. Regular seabird migrants include Cory's, Great, Sooty, Manx and Balearic Shearwaters, Common Scoters; Great, Pomarine, and Arctic Skuas, Little Gulls and Kittiwakes, terns and auks. Gannets can be especially numerous, with peak counts regularly exceeding 1,000 birds per hour in autumn and reaching 8,000 per hour on some days. Visible migration of other species, including seaduck and waders, is often prominent and grounded migrant passerines enliven the surrounding coastal scrub during fall conditions. An English language website (seawatchingestaca.com) provides frequent reports of observations from the Cape during passage periods as well as more general information.

Timing

The site comes into its own following westerly and north-westerly gales, which force seabirds into the Bay of Biscay, from which they follow the coast westwards again, passing close around the Cape. Such conditions are most frequent in late autumn and winter. October and November produce the greatest numbers of species but August and September are also very rewarding months for seawatching. Calm days, and those with offshore winds, may prove disappointing. Spring passage here is usually very poor.

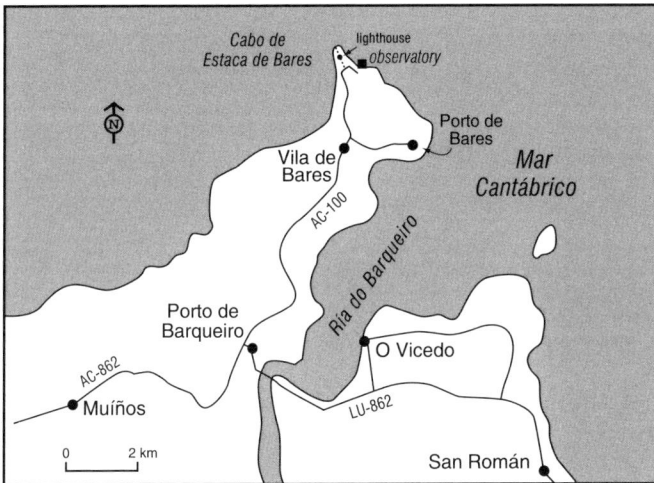

Access

Take the AC-862/LU-862 north coast road to Porto do Barqueiro and turn north for 5km on the AC-100 to Vila de Bares. Take the left turn here sign-posted for the Faro (lighthouse). The best watchpoint, where you will only be in the company of other birders (if any), is the balcony of the bird observatory, which is east of the lighthouse. Turn right on arrival at the lighthouse and continue past the abandoned weather station. Park here and walk down a sandy track to the bird observatory, the small building on the cliff edge. The observatory may be closed but it is still possible to watch from the balcony or from the slopes nearby. A telescope is essential.

An alternative but more exposed site, which is lower down and is closer to the stack itself is also available. In this case park in the car park on the left just before the lighthouse. Follow the path up to and beyond the lighthouse, descending as far as you can go to a sandy platform just opposite the stack. This provides an excellent and comfortable viewpoint despite being on the tourist beat, since only the more intrepid visitors venture that far. Take care; the access path is perfectly safe but there are severe drops alongside at two points, which would upset those prone to vertigo. The platform is some 65m above the sea and a telescope is all but essential.

The village of Porto de Bares, in the sheltered Bay west of the Cape, has a pleasant restaurant for those wishing to emulate the fish-eating birds. The Hotel Semaforo de Bares (hotelsemaforodebares.com), which sponsors the birding website, has an ideal position on the Cape itself and offers both food and accommodation.

CALENDAR

All year: Shag, Common Buzzard, Peregrine Falcon; Great Black-backed Lesser Black-backed and Yellow-legged Gulls, Stonechat, Zitting Cisticola, Dartford Warbler, Red-billed Chough, Raven.

Breeding season: European Storm-petrel, Whitethroat.

Winter: Common Scoter, Velvet Scoter (occasional); Red-throated, Black-throated and Great Northern Divers, Red-necked Grebe, Gannet, Cormorant, Common Gull (scarce), Little Gull, Kittiwake, Guillemot,

Razorbill, Puffin, Little Auk (occasional).

Passage periods: Red-breasted Merganser (occasional), Common Scoter, Velvet Scoter (occasional); Cory's, Great (summer/autumn only), Sooty (summer/autumn only), Manx and Balearic Shearwaters, Fea's/Zino's Petrel (summer/autumn only), Wilson's Storm-petrel (autumn: rare), Leach's Storm-petrel, Gannet, Grey Heron; Pomarine, Arctic, Long-tailed and Great Skuas; Mediterranean, Little and Sabine's Gulls, Kittiwake; Sandwich, Common, Arctic, Little and Black Terns, Guillemot, Razorbill, Puffin, rarities.

ENSENADA DE A ÍNSUA AND LAGUNA DE TRABA (A Coruña)   GA11

Status: Part of the Galician network of protected spaces: Zona de Especial Conservación dos Valores Naturais. ZEPAs.

Site description

These two sites are considered together because they share an enviable reputation for attracting Nearctic rarities. Both lie in westernmost Galicia, ideally placed to welcome stray birds from across the Atlantic.

The Ensenada de A Ínsua is the narrow estuary: with areas of sand and pebbles, mudflats and saltmarsh, at the foot of the Ría de Corme y Laxe. The northern side is a broad sandy spit. The Laguna de Traba is a small coastal lagoon, fringed by reeds and bulrushes, separated by sand dunes from the adjacent beach. Cabo Laxe, which lies between the two sites, is a vantage point across the mouth of the Ría on its southern side.

Species

These two sites could well be named the 'rarity hotspots' of western Galicia thanks largely to the meticulous observations over many years of local ornithologist José Luís Rabuñal Patiño (who served with EG on the Iberian Peninsula Rarities Committee in the 1990s). Both localities continue to receive a succession of transatlantic avian visitors annually, most especially in autumn, although some years are much better than others. The majority are waders and indeed the species list almost resembles the index of a North American wader guide. Accepted rare wader records from these two sites include Semipalmated and American Golden Plovers; Semipalmated, Western, Least, White-rumped, Baird's, Pectoral, Buff-breasted and Spotted Sandpipers, Long-billed Dowitcher, Greater Yellowlegs and Lesser Yellowlegs.

The sites also continue to attract rare waterfowl and other wetland birds, with records of Red-breasted Goose, American Wigeon, Falcated Duck, Green-winged Teal, Blue-winged Teal, Ring-necked duck, Lesser Scaup, King Eider, Black Scoter, Surf Scoter, Bufflehead, Barrow's Goldeneye, Smew, Goosander, American Bittern, Pied-billed Grebe and Sora Crake. A good variety of rare gulls and terns have also been reported here: Laughing, Bonaparte's, Ring-billed, Iceland and Glaucous Gulls and Forster's Tern, among others. Other rarities that have appeared here include Rufous Turtle Dove, Siberian Stonechat and Yellow-rumped Warbler.

Rarities apart, Reed Buntings and both Great Reed and Reed Warblers breed at Laguna de Traba. The Ría attracts the usual diversity of wintering and passage waders, notably Oystercatchers, Knots, Dunlins, Curlews and Bar-tailed Godwits and waterfowl, notably Wigeon. A few divers, chiefly Great Northern Divers, and grebes occur in the Ría in winter. Good seawatching is possible at Cabo Laxe. Wintering passerines include Richard's Pipit, which is fairly regular.

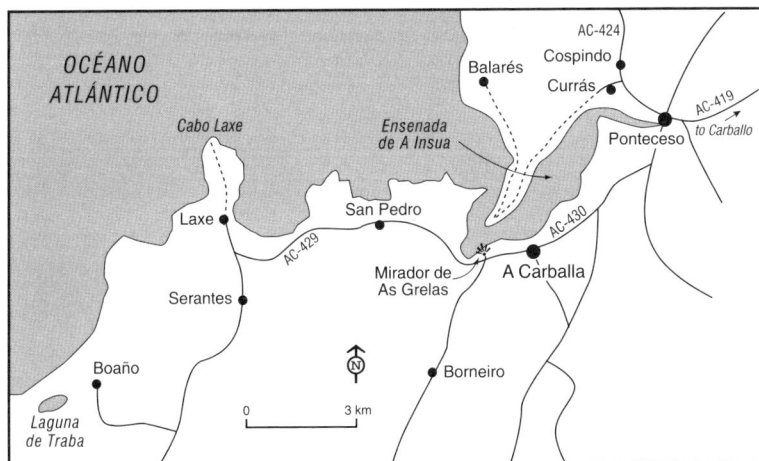

Timing

By definition, rarities cannot be guaranteed. However, both these sites are well worth a visit in autumn, from August onwards, particularly if there have been any westerly gales or spent hurricanes blowing in from the Atlantic. Seawatching at Cabo Laxe is also best in autumn. Winter can also be good, especially for rare waterfowl, which tend to linger longer than many waders. The 'regular' birds make both places worth visiting at all times of year.

Access

Take the AG-55 south-west from A Coruña and leave the motorway at Carballo to follow the AC-414 and then the AC-419 to Ponteceso, at the foot of the Ensenada de A Ínsua. To visit the north side of the Estuary take the AC-424 northwards towards Cospindo and turn left after 1km on to a minor road to the shoreline at Currás. You can walk around the sand spit which comprises the northern bank from here. To view the estuary from the south take the AC-430 west from Ponteceso. The road soon crosses a bridge, offering views of the saltmarsh. Continue west for about 4km and scan the mouth of the Ensenada from the viewpoint on the right (Mirador de As Grelas). To visit Cabo Laxe bear right on to the AC-429 which takes you to Laxe village, from where a track by the cemetery leads out to the cape.

The Laguna de Traba is reached by heading south from the AC-429 1km before Laxe and turning right on the minor road to Boaño, from where a track at the end of the road leads to the lagoon and beach.

CALENDAR

All year: Water Rail, Stone-curlew, Kentish Plover, Zitting Cisticola, Reed Bunting.

Breeding: Great Reed and Reed Warblers.

Winter: Wigeon, Common Pochard, Tufted Duck, Common Scoter, Great Northern Diver, Oystercatcher, Ringed and Grey Plovers, Knot, Sanderling, Dunlin, Curlew, Common Snipe, Bar-tailed Godwit, Turnstone, Common and Great Black-backed Gulls, Sandwich Tern, Razorbill, Richard's Pipit, rarities.

Passage periods: Cory's Shearwater, Great (autumn), Sooty (autumn), Manx and Balearic Shearwaters, Leach's Storm-petrel, Gannet, Spoonbill, waders: including Pectoral Sandpiper, Lesser Yellowlegs and other rarities; Pomarine, Arctic, Long-tailed and Great Skuas; Mediterranean, Little and Sabine's Gulls, Kittiwake; Sandwich, Common, Arctic, Little and Black Terns, Guillemot, Razorbill, Puffin.

OTHER SITES WORTH VISITING

GA12 LAGUNA DE FROUXEIRA (VALDOVIÑO) (A CORUÑA)

A shallow lagoon with reedbeds, linked to the sea on the north coast. It is good for waterfowl and waders in winter, and for Marsh Harriers and passerine species on passage. Take the AC-566 north from Ferrol and the lagoon lies to the left of the road at Valdoviño.

GA13 CABO VILÁN (A CORUÑA)

A rocky west coast headland, good for seabirds but best known as the last breeding location in Iberia of Kittiwakes and Guillemots. These both nested on the rocky stacks just off the Cape, alongside Shags and Yellow-legged Gulls. Neither was present in 2016, unfortunately. Take the road north-west for 4km to the Faro (lighthouse) from the village of Camariñas, reached from the AC-552 coast road at Vimianzo (km-67) via the AC-432 (20km).

GA14 RÍA DE VIGO (PONTEVEDRA)

A wide estuary, one of the largest in Galicia and in Spain. The whole of the estuary can be interesting, although the area around Vigo is developed and some others are heavily disturbed. Take the PO-551 for views at the mouth of the estuary, closest to the Islas Cíes (GA3) offshore. The innermost section, the Ensenada de San Simón, is the best preserved and there are several good view-points available from the N-554 which follows the shore along the western side and off the N-550 along the eastern side. The birds are similar to those of the Ría de Miño (GA5).

GA15 CABO TOURIÑÁN (A CORUÑA)

Another rocky west coast headland and the westernmost point of Spain. It is relatively undisturbed and offers excellent prospects for seawatching from the cliff top alongside the small lighthouse. The Cape itself is covered with low coastal scrub and grassy areas that attract passerine and other migrants. The site is little watched but has great potential. Leave the AC-552 coast road around km-87 and head west to the Cape via A Pereiriña, Frixe and Touriñán.

GA16 RÍA DO BURGO (A CORUÑA)

The small estuary just south-west of A Coruña city. It attracts a diversity of gulls, waders and others; as many as 75 species have been found in a 2–3 hour walk here in winter. A waterside trail (Paseo da Ría do Burgo) follows much of the west bank.

GA17 TERRA CHÁ (LUGO)

An extensive plain north of Lugo city, criss-crossed by numerous minor roads. It lies mainly south of the N-634 and north of the A-6 and N-640. The towns of A Feira de Monte (Cospeito; where there are interesting lagoons) and Castro do Rei are centrally located. See turismo.gal/que-facer/birding-in-galicia/os-mellores-lugares for recommended routes. There is a relict breeding population of Little Bustards as well as abundant nesting White Storks. Montagu's Harriers are characteristic and the Black-shouldered Kite occurs and may breed.

Lesser Grey Shrike

MADRID

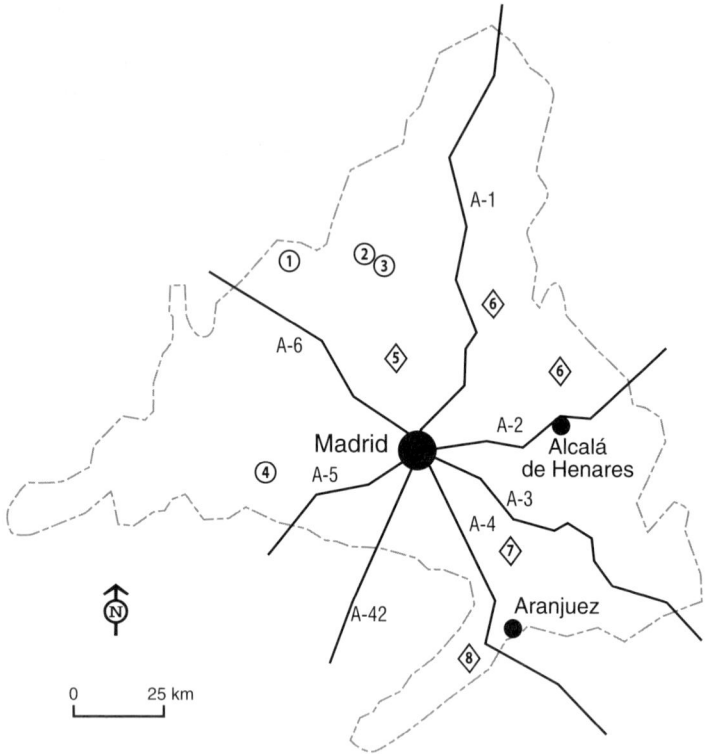

Main sites

M1	Sierra de Guadarrama
M2	La Pedriza del Manzanares
M3	Embalse de Santillana
M4	South-western woodlands

Other sites worth visiting

M5	El Pardo
M6	Estepas Cerealistas de los Ríos Jarama y Henares
M7	Parque Regional del Sureste
M8	Río Tajo at Aranjuez

It will come as no surprise that the Spanish capital dominates the 8,000km² comprising the Madrid autonomous region. The city itself is somewhat less distinguished than some of its neighbours, lacking as it does the charm, history and splendour of Segovia, Toledo, Ávila and Cuenca, not to mention the nearby palaces of Aranjuez. What Madrid does have though are wide boulevards, some great museums, a superb selection of tapas bars and a vibrant nightlife – the locals claiming very proudly that their city stays up later than any other in Europe!

Many visitors to Spain coming in search of birds, mountains and wild flowers, and flying in to Madrid as the gateway to the country, neglect the city and its environs completely and head directly east or south in search of the birds offered by Extremadura or Andalucía. However, we strongly recommend that you stay awhile sampling the late nights, the food and the surrounding countryside, where you can see a remarkable diversity of birds, including Black Storks, Black Vultures, Spanish Imperial Eagles, Purple Swamphens, Great and Little Bustards, Black-bellied Sandgrouse, Bluethroats, Alpine Accentors and Citril Finches, all nearby.

The high biodiversity of the Madrid region springs from the great range of habitats that it offers within rapid and easy reach of the city. The Sierra de Guadarrama dominates the skyline to the north, its often snowy peaks providing a splendid backdrop to the city itself. These are high mountains, with many peaks over 2,000m, providing a cool environment quite different from that of the lowlands, which have a distinctly Mediterranean character. Holm Oak dehesas are prominent to the west of the city and rolling expanses of cereal steppe predominate in the east and south. The rivers descending from the Guadarrama feed a number of interesting wetlands, most of them man-made.

The Sierra de Guadarrama (M1) has breeding Alpine Accentors, one of only three populations outside the Pyrenees and Cantabria: the other two being in the Sierra de Gredos and Sierra Nevada. However, such montane specialities as Wallcreepers and Alpine Choughs do not breed this far south, although the former at least are a possibility in winter. The community does include Griffon Vultures, Golden Eagles, Water Pipits, Bluethroats, Black Redstarts, Rufous-tailed Rock Thrushes and Red-billed Choughs. The Sierra is densely forested with Scots Pines, with deciduous woodlands on the lower reaches; supporting nesting Honey-buzzards, Goshawks, Booted Eagles, Bonelli's Warblers and Pied Flycatchers, with Citril Finches at the higher levels. Black Vultures have an important colony in the central pinewoods.

Lower down and towards the city there is the strikingly located colony of Griffon Vultures at La Pedriza del Manzanares (M2), where such Mediterranean birds as Thekla Larks, Bee-eaters, Red-rumped Swallows, Blue Rock Thrushes, Sardinian Warblers and Subalpine Warblers may also be found.

The grazing woodlands or dehesas of Holm Oaks are an important habitat west of the city (M4) and have a notable extension into the north-west of the urban area in the medieval hunting reserve of El Pardo (M3). These woodlands have an important breeding population of Spanish Imperial Eagles. There are years when a pair at the nest in El Pardo is close enough to the city to be visible by telescope from the university in central Madrid. They share their habitat with nesting Black Vultures, Red-necked Nightjars, Great Spotted Cuckoos, Azure-winged Magpies and Orphean Warblers. Black Storks nest on rocky outcrops also west of the city.

The extensive areas of cereal cultivation east of the city have been designated a ZEPA, the Estepas Cerealistas de los Ríos Jarama y Henares (M6). The habitat has been damaged by the construction of new motorways and is threatened by the spread of urbanisation but it still supports an excellent steppe bird community on the city's doorstep. Here you see numbers of Great and Little Bustards as well as Black-bellied Sandgrouse, Stone Curlews, Greater Short-toed and Calandra Larks and Spanish Sparrows. The steppes attract a diversity of raptors, especially in winter, and have nesting Montagu's and Hen Harriers and Lesser Kestrels.

The wetland interest is centred on the rivers and some of the reservoirs and gravel pits. All the main rivers, including the Ríos Henares and Jarama (M7) in the south-east and the Tajo (M8) in the extreme south, are of note with their riparian woods (sotos) and river cliffs. Some stretches have Night Heron and Cattle Egret colonies, and such additional attractions as Little Bitterns, Purple Herons, Cetti's Warblers, Penduline Tits and Golden Orioles are widespread. Waterfowl are numerous on the gravel pits (M7) in winter. The reservoirs are especially important in winter and during passage periods. One of the best is the Embalse de Santillana (M3), below the Sierra de Guadarrama, which is good for wintering ducks and for passage waders and terns.

SIERRA DE GUADARRAMA   M1
(Madrid/Segovia)

Status: Parque Nacional (33,960ha plus 62,687ha protected peripheral zone). UNESCO Biosphere Reserve and ZEPA in part.

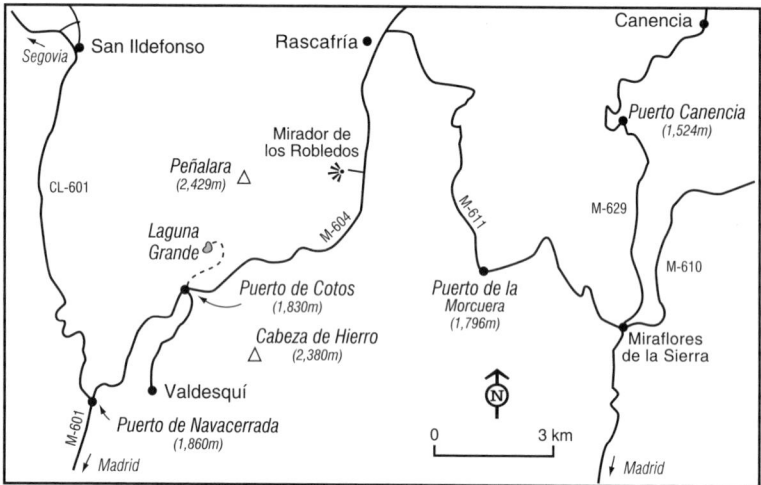

Site description

The Sierra de Guadarrama is the east-central sector of the Sistema Central, extending for over 80km south-west/north-east along the northern boundary between Madrid and Castilla y León. Some two-thirds of the National Park, designated in 2013, is in Madrid, the remainder being in Segovia, Castilla y León. These are rounded granitic mountains, with 15 peaks above 2,000m, most of them, including the highest (Peñalara, 2,430m), in the central part of the range. The south slopes of Peñalara particularly offer a number of impressive glacial cirques and some small lakes. Throughout the range, the higher slopes have mature forests of Scot's Pine with Pyrenean Oaks at middle elevations. The montane grasslands and the pastures around the summits are fringed with juniper and Spanish Broom scrub. The vegetation in the western, lower sector of the range has a more Mediterranean character, with Stone Pines and Holm Oaks. The Guadarrama watershed drains into the Tagus to the south and the Duero to the north, via numerous streams and rivers. The river valley floors have extensive deciduous woods, especially of Narrow-leaved Ash, as well as pastures and crops. Snowfall is significant and lies late into the spring on the uppermost slopes, providing skiing for the Madrileños at several resorts.

Species
The Sistema Central is too far south to offer all the montane species of northern Iberia but the mountains still support a varied and pleasing bird community. The Guadarrama has a significant nesting population of Black Vultures and its forests attract breeding woodland raptors, such as Honey-buzzards, Red Kites and Goshawks. The pine forest community includes Goldcrests, Crested Tits and Crossbills, with Citril Finches on the upper forest margins, where there are also Ortolan Buntings and, locally, Tree Pipits. Bluethroats nest in the juniper scrub. The mountain pastures have Tawny and Water Pipits and Northern Wheatears, with Rufous-tailed Rock Thrushes on the rocky outcrops. Alpine Accentors nest on broken ground around the highest tops but are more widespread at lower altitudes in winter. Clearings in the valley floors have Whinchats and Red-backed Shrikes.

Timing
The mountains are very popular with the Madrileños and so weekends are best avoided. Spring and summer are the most productive seasons. The mountain passes are sometimes closed by snow and, if so, this is indicated on the approach roads.

Access
From Madrid, take the M-607 motorway north out of the city to Colmenar Viejo.

Eastern sector. From Colmenar take the M-609 north and the M-608 east for 12km to the M-611, north to Miraflores de La Sierra. At Miraflores turn left on the M-611 towards the pass (Puerto de la Morcuera, 1,796m). A number of trails allow exploration of the mountain heaths and woodland around the pass. It is also worth driving on down on the M-629 from Miraflores to Puerto Canencia (1,524m): park here and explore the surrounding pinewoods on foot.

Western sector. Take the M-607 past Colmenar to Cerceda and Navacerrada and there take the M-601 north to the pass (Puerto de Navacerrada, 1,860m). Alternatively take the A-6 north-west from Madrid to Collado Villalba and head north on the M-601 from there. Once at the Pass take the M-604 north-east for 4km to reach the Puerto de Cotos (1,830m). It is also worth taking the trail north from the pass to the Laguna Grande, passing through woodlands and pastures. You may also drive for 3km south up to the ski resort of Valdesquí, from where you can explore the high-altitude meadows for grassland and scrub species.

Various scenic viewpoints around the mountains are additionally useful for scanning for raptors. The Mirador de Los Robledos, on the left 10km north of Puerto de Cotos on the M-604, is particularly well placed. The whole region is amply provided with marked trails and refuges for serious walkers.

CALENDAR

All year: Red Kite, Griffon and Black Vultures, Goshawk, Sparrowhawk. Common Buzzard, Golden Eagle, Peregrine Falcon, Rock Dove; Barn, Eagle, Little, Tawny and Long-eared Owls, Alpine Accentor, Dunnock, Black Redstart, Blue Rock Thrush, Dartford Warbler, Goldcrest, Crested Tit, Nuthatch, Southern Grey Shrike, Red-billed Chough, Raven, Rock Sparrow, Citril Finch, Crossbill, Cirl and Rock Buntings.

Breeding season: Honey-buzzard, Black Kite, Short-toed and Booted Eagles, Hobby, Scops Owl, Hoopoe, Wryneck, Crag Martin, Sky Lark; Tawny, Tree and Water Pipits, Bluethroat, Common Redstart, Whinchat, Northern Wheatear, Rufous-tailed Rock Thrush, Melodious and Bonelli's Warblers, Pied Flycatcher, Red-backed Shrike, Ortolan Bunting.

Winter: Fieldfare, Redwing.

LA PEDRIZA DEL MANZANARES   M2

Status: Within the Parque Nacional 'Sierra de Guadarrama' (M1) and the Parque Natural 'La Cuenca Alta del Manzanares' (4,000 ha).

Site description

The Pedriza is a remarkable boulder field of strangely eroded granitic outcrops, on the lower southern slopes of the Sierra de Guadarrama. The vegetation is sparse but there are some stunted trees and areas of *Cistus* scrub on the lower reaches and some juniper and planted pines on the upper slopes. However, this is one of those sites where the geology steals the show. The rock formations have been compared to an open-air art gallery, which has not deterred Griffon Vultures from building their nests on the massive columnar 'exhibits' and anointing them liberally with their 'guano'. One of the visitors' centres of the National Park is at the entrance (Tel. 918 539 978; open Wednesdays–Sundays).

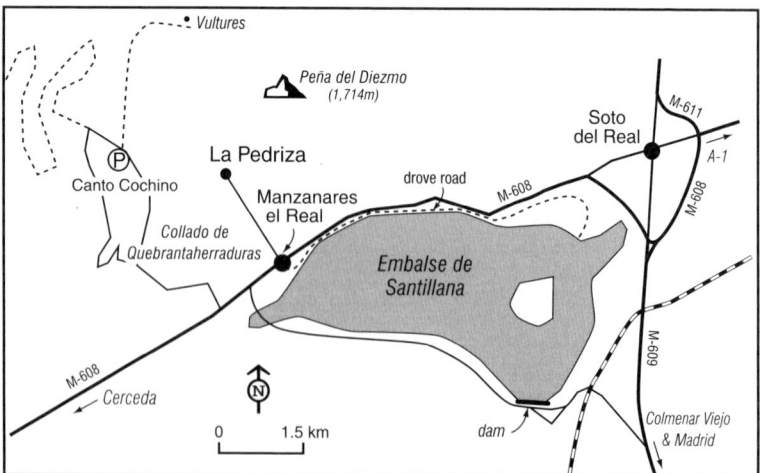

Species

The Griffon Vultures nesting on the craggy outcrops are a key attraction: the colony of over 100 pairs is the largest in Madrid. Other rock-loving species which nest in the area include Eagle Owls, Crag Martins, both Blue Rock and Rufous-tailed Rock Thrushes, Northern and Black-eared Wheatears and Red-billed Choughs. Bluethroats nest in the junipers and Melodious and Subalpine Warblers breed in the scrubby areas. Alpine Accentors may be present in winter.

Scops Owl

Timing

Spring and early summer are the best seasons, although early spring can still be very cold. The site is very popular and best avoided at weekends and on public holidays, when access may be restricted at peak periods.

Access

Take the M-607 north to Comenar Viejo and continue on the M-609 to the M-608, heading west towards Manzanares el Real, along the north shore of the Embalse de Santillana (M3). About 1km beyond Manzanares a signposted road on the right leads to the control post at the gates of La Pedriza and up through the mountain pass of Collado de Quebrantaherraduras (horseshoe-break pass). You can park at the pass and have a panoramic view over the area from the nearby *mirador*, as well as explore the pinewoods of the adjacent Sierra de los Porrones. Thereafter drive on to the parking area of Canto Cochino next to the river. A diversity of well-worn trails allow further exploration from here.

CALENDAR

All year: Red Kite, Griffon Vulture, Common Buzzard, Golden Eagle, Peregrine Falcon, Rock Dove; Barn, Eagle, Little and Long-eared Owls; Crested, Thekla Lark and Wood Larks, Crag Martin, Dipper, Blue Rock Thrush, Dartford and Sardinian Warblers, Azure-winged Magpie, Red-billed Chough, Raven, Rock Bunting.

Breeding season: Black Kite, Booted Eagle, Hobby, Cuckoo, Scops Owl, Bee-eater, Hoopoe, Red-rumped Swallow, Tawny Pipit, Bluethroat, Northern and Black-eared Wheatears, Rufous-tailed Rock Thrush, Melodious and Subalpine Warblers, Woodchat Shrike, Ortolan Bunting.

Winter: Alpine Accentor.

EMBALSE DE SANTILLANA   M3

*Status: Within the Parque Regional 'Cuenca Alta del Manzanares'
(101,300ha).*

Site description

This large reservoir, extending over 1,000ha when full, receives water from
the Río Manzanares and a couple of seasonal streams. The water levels vary
considerably and the site attracts the greatest diversity of birds when the lake
is half-full, producing shallow areas and exposed margins. The western end
is more gently shelving and particularly attractive to ducks, waders, herons
and storks. The surrounding farmland; with small stands of trees, scrub and
well-developed bankside vegetation along the watercourses, is also of interest.

Species

The lake holds abundant waterfowl in winter, when thousands of Black-headed
and Lesser Black-backed Gulls also roost there. The margins attract feeding
herons and egrets as well as passage waders. White Storks breed nearby and
form very large post-breeding congregations on the shore. This well-watched
site has produced a number of records of scarce or rare species, including Bean,
Barnacle and Egyptian Geese and several observations of Ruddy Shelducks.

The surrounding area has breeding Thekla Larks, Spectacled Warblers
and Azure-winged Magpies. The farmland east of the reservoir attracts Little
Bustards in the latter part of the summer.

Timing

The site is worth visiting all year round, although winter sees the largest
bird numbers. A visit here can readily be combined with one to the adjacent
Pedriza (M2).

Access

See map for M2. Take the M-607 and then the M-609 north from Madrid to
Soto del Real. From here take the M-608 west towards Manzanares el Real,
along the north shore of the reservoir, where there are lay-bys from which you
can scan the lake and its margins. A former drove-road (Vía Pecuaria) between
the M-608 and the reservoir follows the entire length (4km) of the northern
shore, offering many good viewpoints. It is accessible from various points but
a good option is to park opposite the castle in Manzanares and walk east from
there. It is also worth driving around the lake to the dam, to view grebes and
other diving species on the deeper water.

CALENDAR

All year: Gadwall, Mallard, Shoveler, Common Pochard, Little and Great Crested Grebes, White Stork, Little Egret, Common Coot, Moorhen, Water Rail, Thekla Lark, Zitting Cisticola, Dartford and Sardinian Warblers, Southern Grey Shrike, Azure-winged Magpie.

Breeding season: Little Bustard, Cattle Egret, Black-winged Stilt, Stone-curlew, Great Spotted Cuckoo, Red-necked Nightjar, Bee-eater, Short-toed Lark, Yellow Wagtail; Melodious, Subalpine and Spectacled Warblers, Woodchat Shrike.

Winter: Wigeon, Teal, Pintail, Red-crested Pochard, Black-necked Grebe, Cormorant, Grey Heron, Black-headed and Lesser Black-backed Gulls.

Passage periods: Purple and Night Herons, Black Stork, Montagu's Harrier, Osprey, Hobby, Little Bustard, Avocet, Black-tailed and Bar-tailed Godwits, Common Redshank, Greenshank, Common Sandpiper, Black and Whiskered Terns.

SOUTH-WESTERN WOODLANDS   M4

Status: Zepa 'Encinares del Río Alberche y Río Cofio' (82,938ha).

Site description
The south-western hinterland of Madrid city, where the western foothills of the Sierra de Guadarrama meet the eastern fringes of the Sierra de Gredos, is hilly terrain with a number of rocky outcrops. There are large areas of Iberian Holm Oak woodland and plantations of Maritime Pines, as well as expanses of pasture and scrub. The whole region has a Mediterranean character. The principal rivers, the Ríos Alberche and Cofio, drain into a small reservoir, the Embalse de San Juan. An information centre in the village of Chapinería features the Spanish Imperial Eagle: with an impressive tableau of life-size model eagles at the nest, and has a viewing terrace from which you have a good chance of seeing the real thing.

Species
This is a particularly good site for Spanish Imperial Eagles, with over 15 breeding pairs. Scanning for these will turn up a diversity of other raptors, most often Griffon Vultures, Black Kites and Short-toed and Booted Eagles. Black Vultures, Goshawks and Golden Eagles are also present and there is a chance of finding a Black-shouldered Kite. The other interesting breeding species include Black Storks and a thriving population of Great Spotted Cuckoos. The nesting community of Mediterranean species also includes Red-necked Nightjars, Black-eared Wheatears and Orphean and Subalpine Warblers.

Timing
The Spanish Imperial Eagles are resident and may be found at any time of year. The area is nonetheless at its most attractive and productive in spring and early summer.

Access

The M-501 passes across the southern part of the ZEPA. The information centre (Centro de Educación Ambiental El Águila) in the village of Chapinería, just south of the M-501 and about 35km west of Madrid city, is a good place to start. Guided tours through the adjacent woodlands are offered here but birding from the terrace offers a good opportunity for seeing Spanish Imperial Eagles, other raptors and such woodland birds as Great Spotted Cuckoos: these last sometimes pursued by their indignant Magpie hosts.

The principal habitats are accessed from the M-512. Turn north on to this road from the M-501 5km west of Chapinería and just north-west of Navas del Rey. The M-512 is undulating and offers several obvious vantage points from where you should scan the area. Turn left after 11km at Robledo de Chavela and continue west on the M-537 for 6km to Valdemaqueda. A signposted broad footpath leads north from here for 3km through open woodlands, along the foot of a long, rocky outcrop, to a small hermitage. This is a pleasant stroll though a good area for Spanish Imperial Eagles and other raptors, and for passerines. You can also follow a trail south from Valdemaqueda to the Río Cofio.

CALENDAR

All year: Griffon and Black Vultures, Goshawk, Common Buzzard, Spanish Imperial and Golden Eagles, Peregrine Falcon, Eagle Owl, Thekla Lark, Blue Rock Thrush, Crested Tit, Azure-winged Magpie, Common Magpie, Rock Sparrow, Hawfinch, Rock Bunting.

Breeding season: Black and White Storks, Black Kite, Short-toed and Booted Eagles, Great Spotted Cuckoo, Red-necked Nightjar, Red-rumped Swallow, Black-eared Wheatear, Orphean and Subalpine Warblers.

OTHER SITES WORTH VISITING

M5 EL PARDO
A royal hunting reserve just north-west of the city that still houses the Royal Palace and is accordingly of restricted access. Principally Holm Oak dehesa. Raptors overhead often include Black Vultures and Spanish Imperial Eagles. Melodious, Orphean and Subalpine Warblers, Azure-winged Magpies and Cirl Buntings breed. Take the M-605 off the M-40 outer ring-road at km-51 to El Pardo. There are car parks on the left just before the town, with trails along the course of the Río Manzanares, where breeding birds include Little Bitterns, Golden Orioles and Penduline Tits.

M6 ESTEPAS CEREALISTAS DE LOS RÍOS JARAMA Y HENARES
Cereal-growing areas to the north and east of the city, with hills and some Holm Oak woodland. The area is good for steppe birds including Montagu's Harriers, Lesser Kestrels, Great and Little Bustards, Black-bellied Sandgrouse, Rollers and larks. For the Jarama valley take the A-I Burgos motorway from the M-40 ring-road at km-1 and exit after 11km on the M-106 to Algete, where you take the M-103 north to the cereal steppe between Valdetorres de Jarama and Talamanca de Jarama: farm tracks allow good access on foot. For the Henares valley take A-2 west from the M-40 ring-road at km-1 to Alcalá de Henares and then the M-119 through the best area, which is north of Camarma de Esteruelas.

M7 PARQUE REGIONAL DEL SUROESTE
A complex of over 120 lagoons, most of them flooded gravelpits, and associated riverine vegetation along the course of the Río Jarama, south-east of Madrid. The lakes attract numbers of waterfowl in winter. Breeding birds include Red-crested Pochards, Black-necked Grebes, Little Bitterns, Purple Swamphens, Savi's Warblers and Penduline Tits. Many of the lakes are accessible from footpaths and some have hides.

For a representative sample take the A-3 south-east, exiting at km-20 to Rivas-Vaciamadrid. Follow the Metro line south from the town to reach the Laguna El Campillo, which can be viewed from a circular path (4km) around the boundary. Return to the A-3 and continue south, leaving at La Poveda, where you turn north on the M-208 to Velilla de San Antonio. Drive west through Velilla towards the river, where a footpath follows the east bank northwards skirting several lagoons. Return to the M-208 and continue north past Mejorada del Campo, turning right here on to the M-203. Stop at the picnic site (Area Recreativa Las Islillas) on the left shortly after this junction, from where there is access to the Henares/Jarama confluence, with good riverine vegetation.

An alternative site further south is the municipal reserve of Los Albardales, established with the cooperation of SEO/Birdlife. Take the A-4 south for 20km and then the M-506 east to San Martín de la Vega. The reserve comprises a lagoon and reedbeds just north of the village.

M8 RÍO TAJO AT ARANJUEZ

A stretch of river and floodplains between Aranjuez and Toledo, offering a mixed habitat including the river itself, reedbeds, riverine woodlands, cliffs, farmland and parkland. The considerable range of species includes Pin-tailed Sandgrouse, Penduline Tit, Little Bittern, Roller and Night Heron. The best area is at the Aranjuez end, sandwiched between the CM-4001 to the north and the N-400. A small reservoir south of Aranjuez, the Mar de Ontígola, is also worth visiting.

Spotless Starlings

MURCIA

Main sites

MU1   Sierra de Espuña
MU2   Mar Menor and Salinas de San
       Pedro del Pinatar

Other sites worth visiting

MU3   Parque Regional de Calblanque
       and Sierra de la Fausilla
MU4   Embalse de Alfonso XIII
MU5   Estepas de Yecla

Murcia is a small region comprising part of the arid south-east of the Iberian Peninsula. It boasts 320 sunny days per year and correspondingly low rainfall. The Murcian coast, the Costa Cálida (warm coast), has its share of holiday-makers, many of whom are concentrated around the semi-inland sea, the Mar Menor, whose high-rise hotels dominate the seaward horizon.

There was a time when Cartagena was the major city of the Carthaginians in Spain and it had an important silver- and gold-mining industry. Murcia's history tends to be overlooked by modern sun worshippers and most also do not look twice at its countryside nor are put off by the austerity of its appearance. The land lies in a rain shadow of the Betic mountains and looks uncompromisingly arid with its dry, rugged, bare mountain slopes and its gullies with expanses of False Esparto Grass. However, even here, significant expanses of important bird habitat have been lost to golf courses and other development.

The coast is where the rugged landscape of the mountains reaches the sea's edge, and with it comes an horizon of Oleander, Prickly Pear and Fan Palm, and the occasional ruined watchtower, a relic of the distant days when pirates were a real danger.

The higher sierras were typically covered in pinewoods, but deforestation and forest fires have largely restricted these to the far north-west of the region. These forests disappear at lower altitudes and closer to the coast to be replaced by scrub. In many parts not even scrub is present and the ground is mostly bare and eroded. Those areas with a covering of trees have respectable woodland bird communities with birds of prey represented by Short-toed and Booted Eagles, Goshawks, Sparrowhawks, Common Buzzards and Hobbies. Other breeding birds include Crested Tits, Crossbills and Bonelli's Warblers. A good example, but perhaps atypical, is the Sierra de Espuña (MU1): an upland area that was systematically cleared of its trees and subsequently suffered horrendous erosion, but which has been successfully reforested.

The more widely distributed bare and eroded areas of countryside, with rocks, gullies and gorges are, however, certainly not without their bird interest. Murcia has good populations of both Golden and Bonelli's Eagles. You do not have to travel far to see these species as they are not restricted to the higher sierras but found widely in the region and at low levels. Griffon Vultures colonised west Murcia in the 1990s although the breeding population is very small. In addition, Alpine Swifts, Crag Martins, Black Wheatears, Black-eared Wheatears, Blue Rock Thrushes, Red-billed Choughs and Ravens, along with Rock Sparrows and Rock Buntings, are also likely to be encountered. Warblers can be well represented where there is at least some vegetation and scrub. They include Sardinian, Subalpine, Spectacled and Dartford Warblers, and Common Whitethroats, with Orphean Warblers in taller scrub or young pine plantations and Olivaceous Warblers in the tamarisks along watercourses.

Steppe areas in Murcia are now few and far between, most lost to development or cultivation of cereals and irrigated crops: including almonds, fruit orchards and vines. Most of the typical bird species of steppe occur although Great Bustards are mainly scarce winter visitors to the far north-east of the region (MU5) and Pin-tailed Sandgrouse are rare. However, Montagu's Harriers, Little Bustards, Stone-curlews, Black-bellied Sandgrouse and six lark species can still be found in the ever decreasing area of suitable habitat: a seventh, Dupont's Lark, formerly inhabited the Sierra de Espuña (MU1) but is now probably extinct in the region. There are good populations of Lesser Short-toed and Thekla Larks found for example on the remaining area of salt steppes of Los Solares de Río Guadalentín (south of the A-7 but very fragmented by development) and in the farmland around the Alfonso XIII reservoir (MU4). Other open-country birds such as Lesser Kestrels, Rollers, Great Spotted Cuckoos and Red-rumped Swallows all occur while Spanish Sparrows may be found in the far north-west.

Murcia also has many 'typical' Mediterranean species, such as Hoopoe, Bee-eater, Nightingale, Golden Oriole and Woodchat Shrike, especially along the often dry watercourses and on the cultivated and irrigated land between the sierras and the coast. These areas should also be checked for Rufous-tailed Scrub-robins and Olivaceous Warblers.

Wetlands are at a premium in Murcia given the low rainfall and the region's predeliction for irrigation. Most of the rivers have suffered as a consequence, although there are some reservoirs of interest, the best being the Embalse de Alfonso XIII (MU4): offering such birds as Water Rails, Great Reed Warblers, and some waders, particularly Black-winged Stilts. However, the region is dominated by one site, the Mar Menor (MU2), the largest coastal lagoon in Spain, which supports a comprehensive range of waterbird species: breeding, wintering and on passage.

Pallid Swifts breed along the coast and European Storm-petrels have small colonies on offshore islets, notably on Isla Grosa off the Mar Menor, which also supports a pair or two of Shags. Good views can be had of passing Cory's (Scopoli's) Shearwaters, Audouin's Gulls and migrant and wintering seabirds generally from rocky headlands, such as Cabo Cope, Cabo Tiñoso and Cabo de Palos.

SIERRA DE ESPUÑA   MU1

Status: Parque Natural (13,855ha) and Reserva Nacional de Caza (14,181ha).

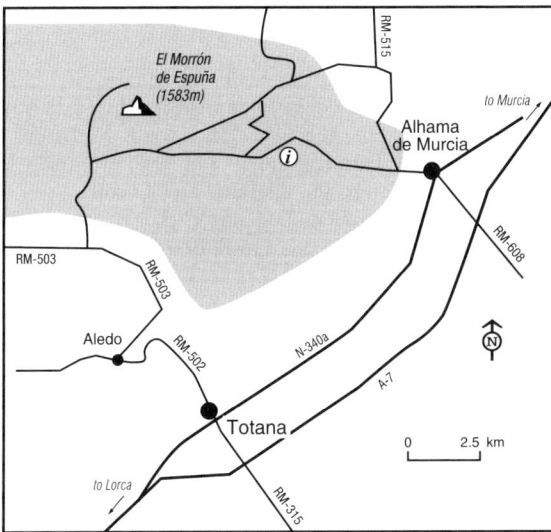

Site description

Part of the eastern section of the Andalucían mountain chain (Cordillera Subbética), which stretches from Cádiz Bay to Cabo La Nao in Alicante. Its highest point here is El Morrón de Espuña (1,583m), with another two peaks surpassing 1,500m, and it regularly receives at least some snow each year despite its southerly position. The area consists of four distinct mountain blocks separated by flood valleys and ravines. There is a considerable extent of pine forest on the slopes with areas of scrub. Indeed, much of the area is now covered with replanted pines, chiefly Aleppo Pines. Elsewhere large rocky limestone formations dominate the scenery. The Río Espuña and the river flowing through the Enmiedo Ravine are the most important watercourses. The former has its origin in Collado Bermejo (1,207m) and flows into the Guadalentín 100m above sea level, after only 19km, which gives some idea of the steepness of the watercourse.

Species

Three main habitats in the park need to be explored to find a wide range of species. Cliffs and rocky faces hold large birds of prey including Golden and Bonelli's Eagles, Peregrines and Eagle Owls, and also Blue Rock Thrushes. Typical forest species such as Goshawk, Booted Eagle, Bonelli's Warbler and Crossbill, can be found in the pinewoods. Black Wheatears occur on the lower slopes and larks, including Thekla and Lesser Short-toed Larks, frequent the grassland and open country habitats, especially of semi-arid ground, The scrub areas can also be good for Subalpine, Dartford and Spectacled Warblers.

One of the most interesting mammals in the park is a particularly large and pale-coloured variant of the Red Squirrel. There is also a thriving introduced population of the Arruí, or Barbary Sheep *Ammotragus lervia*.

Timing

April through to June. Weekends can be busy and the area is popular with climbers.

Access

The Sierra is within easy reach of the coast and Murcia city. Take the A-7 south-west out of Murcia and leave the main road at Alhama de Murcia. From Alhama de Murcia initially take the RM-515 towards Mula, but after three kilometres turn left into the Parque Natural. This road eventually loops south to the village of Aledo and on to the RM-502 and Totana.

The Ricardo Codorníu Interpretation Centre (Tel. 968 228 937) is open daily year round except Mondays. Follow signs to El Berro and then the Centre from a point seven kilometres from Alhama.There are many tracks through the sierra, although most of these are unmarked, as well as a number of mountain refuges. The Interpretation Centre can provide further details. The lower slopes are less forested and you should look out for grassland and open-country species there.

CALENDAR

All year: Goshawk, Sparrowhawk, Common Buzzard, Golden and Bonelli's Eagles, Peregrine Falcon, Tawny Owl; Lesser Short-toed, Thekla and Wood Larks, Crag Martin, Black Wheatear, Blue Rock Thrush, Dartford and Sardinian Warblers, Red-billed Chough, Crossbill, Rock Bunting.

Breeding season: Short-toed and Booted Eagles, Great Spotted Cuckoo, Alpine Swift, Bee-eater, Red-rumped Swallow; Subalpine, Spectacled, Orphean and Bonelli's Warblers.

MAR MENOR AND SALINAS DE SAN PEDRO DEL PINATAR   MU2

Status: Ramsar site (14,933ha), ZEPA and Parque Regional.

Site description

The largest coastal lagoon in Spain and one of the largest in the Mediterranean, 21km long and up to 10km wide. It is separated from the Mediterranean by a long coastal sand spit known as La Manga (The Sleeve) which is 24km long and 900m wide at its broadest point. The Mar Menor was originally a bay but La Manga began progressively to close it off to the point where today only a system of canals and sluices keep the Mar in direct contact with the open sea.

The waters used to be incredibly salty but 'improvement' of the connections with the sea has made the lagoon less saline and somewhat cooler. At the same time there has been a tendency towards eutrophication resulting from run-off of agricultural fertilisers. All these changes have had important, ongoing and mainly negative repercussions for birds: especially wintering ducks, other fauna and the algal community. While much of the immediate surrounds to the lagoon has been developed, there are areas of saltpans, most especially to the north at San Pedro del Pinatar – also known as the Salinas de Coterillo. Together with a line of sand dunes – separating them from the Mediterranean, they cover an area of 800ha. There are also relatively small areas of saltpans to the south at Marchamalo. In addition, there are sandy areas and dunes, some saltflats and areas of reedbed, irrigation ponds, farmland and a number of islands, mainly within the lagoon but also beyond: the largest being Isla Perdiguera and Isla Mayor. Cabo de Palos headland marks the south-eastern corner of the area.

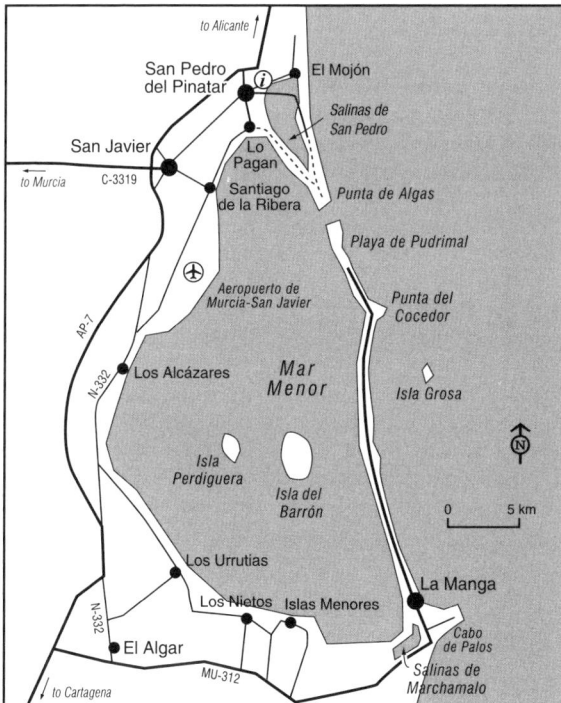

Species

The Mar Menor is a well-known wintering site for waterfowl, attracting nationally important numbers of Black-necked Grebes and Red-breasted Mergansers, although the latter have declined and have averaged around 50 birds in recent years. There are winter concentrations of other ducks, Great Crested Grebes, Cormorants and Common Coots. Large numbers of waders, gulls and terns use the saltpans on passage and in winter. Greater Flamingos may be seen here all year but do not breed.

The breeding birds of the lagoons and associated habitats include Black-winged Stilts, Avocets, Kentish Plovers, Stone-curlews and a good array of larks: notably Calandra, Greater Short-toed and Lesser Short-toed Larks. Collared Pratincoles have nested recently and there is also a colony of Black-headed Gulls. There are small breeding colonies of Sandwich, Gull-billed, Common and Little Terns in the northern saltpans and at various sites around the Mar Menor. European Storm-petrels breed on the islands off the seaward side of the Mar Menor, notably on Isla Grosa, along with Audouin's Gulls and one or two pairs of Shags. The saltpans can have large roosts of Audouin's Gulls, especially post-breeding but some are present all year. Slender-billed Gulls are also regular on passage and in winter.

The Mar Menor has something of a reputation for attracting most unexpected species. In recent years these have included a King Eider and an Egyptian Plover, these perhaps of uncertain origin, a putative Short-billed Dowitcher and the only Belted Kingfisher as yet recorded in Spain. The lagoons are also renowned for the presence of an endangered small fish, an Iberian endemic endearingly called the Fartet *Lebias ibera*.

Timing
Well worth visiting throughout the year, although high summer can be very busy and heat haze is a problem during the hottest parts of the day in spring and summer. Windsurfers can cause disturbance from time to time.

Access
The site lies immediately south of the border with Valencia. From Murcia take the A-30 south towards Cartagena, but turn left near Baños y Mendigo on to the RM-19 to San Javier. From Alicante take the AP-7 south and exit at km-774 to San Pedro del Pinatar and beyond.

For the northern saltpans (the most important and user-friendly site) head for San Pedro del Pinatar and then take the road signposted for the port and saltpans (Puerto y Salinas). An information centre 'Las Salinas' (Tel. 968 178 139) is on the left at the roundabout immediately before the causeway across the saltpans; open year-round except Mondays and weekend afternoons. Follow the road across the saltpans and on to the port, where you can view the sea. Two car parks and a hide along this road allow good views over some of the best saltpans. There are two interesting circular trails. The shorter of the two, 'El Coterillo' (3.8km, 1+ hours) includes both car parks and leads to a viewpoint over more saltpans and visits saltflats, dune vegetation and the sandy shoreline. The longer trail, 'Las Encañizadas' (11.9km, 3+ hours) encircles the main saltpan area and includes the end of the spit at Punta de Algas and the channel connecting the Mar Menor to the sea. This channel can be good for seeing feeding gulls, terns, herons and waders.

Further views across the Mar Menor, the adjoining saltmarsh and associated habitats can be obtained from the coast road in the south where it follows the boundary of the lagoon closely. Continue south past the airport, 'Aeropuerto de San Javier', and onwards through Los Alcázares, Los Urrutias and beyond, stopping every so often to view any flooded grassland and pools. This road eventually joins the RM-12 if you want to view the southern saltpans at Marchamalo, which can be scanned from the road. Another road follows the seaward spit that almost encloses the lagoon and offers further views right across the Mar Menor as well as to seaward; it can be particularly good in winter. The road runs along almost the entire length of the spit, some 21km. It is thronged with high-rise holiday developments but these thin out towards the north.

CALENDAR

All year: Common Shelduck, Little Grebe, Greater Flamingo, Little Egret, Black-winged Stilt, Avocet, Stone-curlew, Kentish Plover; Black-headed, Audouin's and Slender-billed Gulls, Sandwich Tern, Kingfisher; Calandra, Lesser Short-toed and Crested Larks, Black Wheatear, Zitting Cisticola, Dartford Warbler, Rock Sparrow.

Breeding season: Storm Petrel, Shag; Little, Common and Gull-billed Terns, Pallid Swift, Greater Short-toed Lark, Spanish Sparrow, Spectacled Warbler.

Winter: Red-breasted Merganser, Great Crested and Black-necked Grebes, Cormorant, Great White Egret, Grey Heron; Ringed, Grey and Golden Plovers.

Passage periods: Quail, Grey Heron, Baillon's Crake, Knot, Little and Temminck's Stints, Ruff, Spotted and Common Redshanks, Green and Common Sandpipers, Red-necked Phalarope, Whiskered and Black Terns, Great Spotted Cuckoo, Wryneck, Red-rumped Swallow.

OTHER SITES WORTH VISITING

MU3 PARQUE REGIONAL DE CALBLANQUE AND SIERRA DE LA FAUSILLA

Low coastal hills and steppe-like expanses, with some ephemeral pools and saltflats. Trumpeter Finches, Golden and Bonelli's Eagles and Eagle Owls are present and seawatching is possible from the headlands, Cabo del Agua and Cabo Negrete. The areas are immediately south of the RM-314 (Calblanque) and the RM-320 (Sierra de la Fausilla), which is further west along the coast. There is an information centre in the village of Las Cobaticas (Tel. 649 227 582).

MU4 EMBALSE DE ALFONSO XIII

A reservoir in rocky terrain with adjacent farmed but arid areas. Red-crested Pochards, Water Rails and Marsh Harriers are found alongside Black-bellied Sandgrouse, Montagu's Harriers and Thekla Larks. Take the A-30 north-west from Murcia city to Cieza. The area of interest is the minor road that skirts the reservoir. This road is accessed from the RM-532 3km south-west of Cieza or the RM-552 6km south-east of Calasparra.

MU5 ESTEPAS DE YECLA

An area of steppe-like open country with cereal crops and fallows. The most likely site in Murcia for Great Bustards. Little Bustards, both sandgrouse, Stone-curlews and Calandra and Greater Short-toed Larks also occur. View from minor roads leading off the RM-426 leading north from Yecla to Almansa (Albacete) (CLM30).

NAVARRA

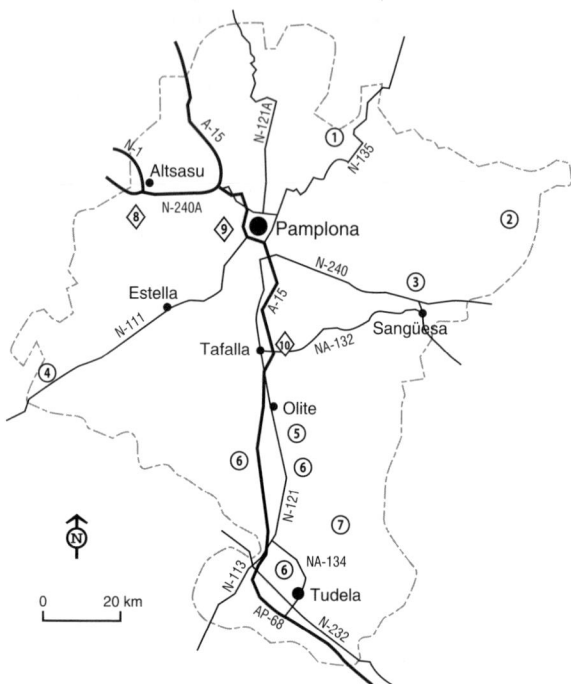

Main sites

N1	Western Pyrenees
N2	Valle de Roncal
N3	Foz de Arbayún and Foz de Lumbier
N4	Embalse de las Cañas
N5	Laguna de Pitillas
N6	Sotos del Río Aragón y Río Ebro
N7	Las Bardenas Reales

Other sites worth visiting

N8	Sierra de Urbasa
N9	Peñas de Echauri
N10	Monte del Conde
N11	Señorío de Bertiz

Navarra comes tumbling down from the Pyrenees; moist, misty, full of legends and influenced by the proximity of the Bay of Biscay. The vast beech and Silver Fir forests of Irati, spreading out into the foothills and lower sierras, give way to the strange, semi-arid landscapes of the Bardenas 'desert'. Navarra has few large towns or cities and the regional capital, Pamplona, dominates the scene. Pamplona is most famous for Los Sanfermines, a manic festival in July where there is much celebration and partying, in which the celebrated bull-running through the streets plays only a small part.

The Pyrenees stand as the natural border with France along a 163km stretch, but the mountains of Navarra are gentler, less rugged, and do not reach such great heights – at least in the west – as further east in the range. They are also far less developed but, although there are no ski resorts in the region, there are wind turbines: a worrying development given the importance of Navarra's mountain passes for bird migration.

The higher Pyrenees, with peaks over 2,000m, are in the far east, at the head of the Roncal valley (N2), and this is by far the most rugged part of Navarra. Lammergeiers, Yellow-billed Choughs and Citril Finches are fairly widely distributed in the Navarran mountains, but many high-altitude birds are restricted to this far-eastern corner of the region. Come here if you want the chance of finding Grey Partridges, Boreal Owls, Alpine Accentors, Wallcreepers and Snowfinches. Ptarmigan and Capercaillie also occur but they have only a relict declining population in Navarra and you should seek them in Aragón or Cataluña.

What the western end of the Navarran Pyrenees lacks in alpine species is made up for by its importance as a migration route. The Ibañeta and Lindux mountain passes (N1) are among the best places to observe migration in Western Europe and there is a bird migration study centre at the Collado de Ibañeta. In addition to some of the commoner birds, such as Woodpigeons, large numbers of Black Storks, Common Cranes, Honey-buzzards, Black Kites, Red Kites, Short-toed Eagles and Booted Eagles can be seen here on their post-breeding migration in the autumn.

Another feature of the Navarran Pyrenees are the woodlands, a hugely important wildlife habitat. Most are dominated by beech and, locally, Silver Fir. The most extensive forests are at Quinto Real and at Irati, the largest ancient forest in the Pyrenees at around 6,250ha (N1). If you are lucky it is possible to see all seven Iberian woodpecker species here, including strong populations of both Black Woodpeckers and White-backed Woodpeckers. Navarra is the key region for White-backed Woodpeckers, holding almost all of the 60–70 pairs thought to breed in Spain: undoubtedly it is *the* bird of Navarra. The woods and forests have much more besides, with good populations of Honey-buzzards, Goshawks, Booted Eagles and Hobbies, and a diversity of passerines.

Moving south, down the picturesque valleys of Salazar and Roncal (N2) and into the sierras there are some very impressive gorges or *foces*, especially in the east of the region. Large Griffon Vulture colonies are a particular feature, notably at the Foz de Burgui: part of the Roncal valley (N2), and at the Foces de Arbayún (Arbaiun) and Lumbier: part of the Sierra de Leyre (N3). Egyptian Vultures, Peregrine Falcons and Red-billed Choughs also vie for attention here, alongside Crag Martins, Blue Rock Thrushes and Rock Sparrows. Other sierras with their gorges, rivers and woodlands are also worth seeking out: they include the Monte del Conde (N10) and the Sierra de Urbasa in the west of the region (N8).

The country changes rapidly south of Pamplona. The mountains and wooded hills are left behind and the 'monotonous plain' so characteristic of central Spain begins to open out. This area is extremely important for its steppe species and is dominated by the open expanse of Las Bardenas Reales (N7), where sandgrouse, larks and wheatears inhabit the eerie, eroded, lunar-like landscape. Most of the typical steppe species are present: Montagu's Harrier, Little Bustard, Stone-curlew and Black-bellied and Pin-tailed Sandgrouse. Great Bustards occurred formerly but are no longer present. The larks are well represented with good numbers of Dupont's, Calandra, Thekla and both Greater and Lesser Short-toed Larks. Lesser Kestrels and Black-eared

Wheatears are also characteristic.

If the arid landscape of the Bardenas gets too much for you then you do not have far to look for some wetland interest. Although open water is relatively rare in Navarra, the riverine woodlands of the Aragón and Ebro valleys (N6) have Night and Purple Herons, Nightingales, Penduline Tits and Golden Orioles. Such riparian woodlands are a very rare and threatened habitat across the whole of Europe, with few extensive areas now remaining. Rivers apart, the two most important wetlands are the Embalse de Las Cañas (N4) and the Laguna de Pitillas (N5). Both have extensive reedbeds, especially at Pitillas, with breeding Great Bitterns, Night Herons, Purple Herons, Red-crested Pochards, Savi's Warblers, Bearded Tits and Reed Buntings. Little Bitterns and Garganey breed here too at least occasionally.

Further information on the birds and birding sites of Navarra can be found on the excellent website birding.navarra.es, which has both Spanish and English versions.

WESTERN PYRENEES   N1

Status: Coto Nacional de Caza and Reservas Naturales in part. Includes the ZEPAs 'Aritzakun-Urrizate-Gorramendi' (5,909ha) and Selva de Irati–Roncesvalles (18,684ha).

Site description

This area includes the far western end of the Pyrenees where most of the highest peaks are between 1,000m and 1,500m. Some, however, reach 2,000m and above at the eastern end of Irati Forest and the Sierra de Abodi, but this is not typical. There are three distinct areas in this part of the Pyrenees, gradually increasing in altitude from west to east. What they do share, apart from their altitude, mountain peaks, rocky gorges and cliffs, are the extensive forests, which cover considerable areas of the slopes on both the French and Spanish sides. Quinto Real and the Selva de Irati have the largest forest tracts.

Pico Gorramendi The area nearest to the coast, a mountainous region topping 1,000m and close to the French border. Here cliffs, rocky bluffs and wet pasture intermingle with small beechwoods, with scattered farms and sheep and goat grazing.

Kintoa/Quinto Real Further south and slightly east is the Coto Nacional Kintoa/Quinto Real, an extensive and mature beech woodland. This is at the western fringe of the vast Irati Forest but is more open, with more pasture, heather and scrub. It is centred around the peak of Monte Adi (1,458m) covering some 5,982ha of relatively gentle mountain slopes just south of the frontier with France.

Roncesvalles/Selva de Irati/Sierra de Abodi This area is further east still and is perhaps the most important, stretching from around Roncesvalles east to the

Selva (Bosque) de Irati and the Sierra de Abodi. This sparsely populated mountainous region, rising up to the peak of Orhi (2,017m) on the French border, has further extensive areas of mixed beech and Silver Fir woods. Indeed, the forest at Monte de la Cuestión, part of the Selva de Irati, is the largest beech forest in Spain. Irati is supposedly haunted by the ghost of Jeanne d'Albret, the queen of Navarra and mother of Henri IV, who was poisoned in 1572 and who reputedly revisits her old 'haunts' on windy nights.

This vast forest extends over the border into France where it becomes known as the Forêt d'Iraty. The historic battlefield at Roncesvalles is part of this area, and is where the rearguard of Charlemagne's army was massacred by the Basques in 778 AD while retreating into France. There is another important forest near here, this time of oak, at Garralda.

The centre at the Collado de Ibañeta, north of Roncevalles, monitors bird migration across the Pyrenees, notably during the post-breeding season.

Black Woodpecker

Species

The beech and Silver Fir forests are the most important habitat. They comprise the only area in Spain where, luck permitting, you can find all seven woodpecker species: the Wryneck and the Green, Black, Great Spotted, Lesser Spotted, Middle Spotted and White-backed Woodpeckers. Some are easier to find than others. In particular, the White-backed Woodpecker can be elusive given its small population. This is nonetheless the main area in Spain for White-backed Woodpeckers: virtually all of the 60–70 pairs in Spain are in Navarra, although one or two pairs may still occur in westernmost Aragón. The Lesser Spotted Woodpecker is regarded as very rare locally but may be encountered at Quinto Real. It is not just woodpeckers that make the forests important, although they are indicators of the ecological health and conservation value of the area. Other notable breeding birds include Honey-buzzards, Goshawks, Woodcocks, Common Redstarts, Marsh Tits, Eurasian Treecreepers, Pied Flycatchers and Hawfinches.

There are plenty of interesting birds outside the forests, including Lammergeiers, Egyptian and Griffon Vultures, Golden Eagles and Yellow-billed Choughs, with Water Pipits and Citril Finches on the higher pastures.

The westernmost section, however, lacks some of the species that you will begin to find as you go further east. These latter include the Spanish race of the Grey Partridge and the Wallcreeper but, unfortunately, not the Capercaillie and Ptarmigan: both of which have declined to near-extinction in this part of the Pyrenees. It is possible to find both Alpine Accentors and Snowfinches in the easternmost part of the Sierra de Abodi, where the altitude increases.

Timing

Winters are milder and spring begins earlier than elsewhere in the Pyrenees since the mountains do not reach such great heights here and the nearby Bay of Biscay has an ameliorating effect on temperatures. Mid-April to late June is the best time, although some of the raptors are obvious earlier in the year. February onwards can also be a good time to track down woodpeckers as they are very vocal from February to April and are far easier to see before the deciduous trees are in leaf. Spring and autumn can be good for passage, the autumn especially so for the migration of many species including raptors, Common Cranes and Black Storks.

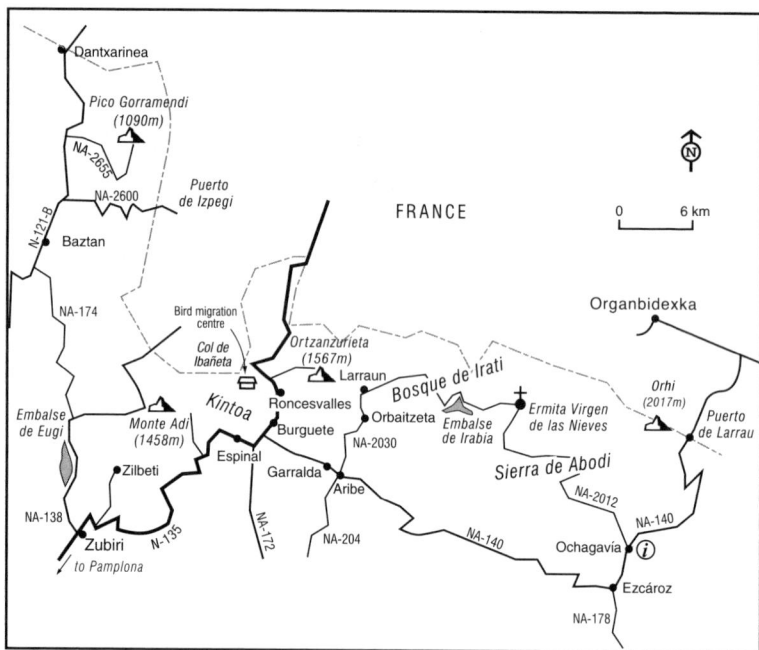

Access

Pico Gorramendi This area is to the east of the crossing into France at Dantxarinea, on the N-121-B. From Pamplona take the N-121-A north for around 34km, passing through a couple of tunnels and turning right around 7km after Almándoz on to the N-121-B. The NA-2600 to the right 16km beyond Erratzu and leading for 9km to the border at Puerto de Izpegi can be good for Golden Eagles and other raptors. The NA-2655, another right turning 7km further north along the N-121-B, leads for 10km along the southern flank of Pico Gorramendi (1,081m). Both these roads have stunning scenery.

Kintoa/Quinto Real From Pamplona take the N-135 to Zubiri and just north of the town turn left on to the NA-138. This road goes through Eugi and along the east side of the Eugi reservoir climbing up to the Collada de Urquiaga: the mountain pass that takes you into France. It is possible to explore the woods and pastures here from tracks going into and through the forest along the ridge.

Roncevalles/Selva de Irati/Sierra de Abodi The Selva de Irati, the main forest area, lies east of Roncesvalles. There are a large number of alternatives for exploring this vast forest and the lower mountain slopes. We recommend the following:

The west side of Irati and the Arrazola area above Orbaitzeta Take the N-135 north from Pamplona and turn right on to the NA-140 about 4km past Espinal. Continue for 10km to Aribe and there take the NA-2030 north to Orbaitzeta. Continue for 3km and then take a track to the right at Larraun to enter the forest. This brings you to the car park and reception area at Arrazola and also to the Embalse de Irabia (see below).

The east side of Irati From Pamplona take the above route to Aribe and continue on the NA-140 for 21km to Ochagavía. In Ochagavía take the NA-2012 for another 19km to the Ermita de La Virgen de las Nieves. Park here and follow the riverside track through the forest to the Embalse de Irabia: both Black and White-backed Woodpeckers are present. The picturesque village of Ochagavía has a Nature Interpretation Centre (Tel. 948 890 680) on the Carretera de Izalzu, next to the tourist office, which has information on the wildlife of the Salazar valley and the Irati forest.

Further east, the NA-140 leads from Ochagavía to the border with France again and the Puerto de Larrau, where it is possible to see Alpine Accentors and Snowfinches at their westernmost location in the Pyrenees. Park just before the tunnel and follow the path to the left of the road up to the summit of Orhi. Migration watchers may wish to pass through the tunnel into France, turning right at Larrau to reach the col of **Organbidexka**, the principal migration watchpoint in the French Pyrenees (see migraction.net).

The Lindux col and migration watchpoint The Ibañeta pass and Lindux col are some of the best places to see bird migration in Western Europe, notably in 'autumn'. However, the massive passage of Woodpigeons in late autumn is met by numerous hunters, complicating observation from October onwards. The Bird Migration Centre and Observatory (Tel. 948 151 077) is at 1,057m at the Collado de Ibañeta, north of Roncevalles off the N-135, which leads north from Pamplona. The centre is open from July to November to study the post-breeding migration of birds across the Pyrenees and is run by the non-governmental organisation Gurelur (gurelur.org). The Lindux col, a traditional vantage point for migration watchers, is reached via the road that runs west through beech forest for 3km from the centre. The forest itself has both White-backed and Black Woodpeckers, and Citril Finches occur on the margins.

CALENDAR

All year: Red Kite, Lammergeier, Griffon Vulture, Goshawk, Sparrowhawk, Common Buzzard, Golden Eagle, Peregrine Falcon; Tawny, Eagle and Long-eared Owls, Woodcock; Green, Black, Middle Spotted, White-backed, Great Spotted and Lesser Spotted Woodpeckers; Wood Lark, Crag Martin, Water Pipit, Grey Wagtail, Dipper, Alpine Accentor, Blue Rock and Song Thrushes, Blackcap, Goldcrest, Firecrest, Marsh and Crested Tits, Nuthatch, Eurasian Treecreeper, Jay, Yellow-billed and Red-billed Choughs, Raven, Snowfinch, Citril Finch, Bullfinch, Cirl and Rock Buntings.

Breeding season: Black Kite, Honey-buzzard, Egyptian Vulture, Short-toed Eagle, Hen Harrier, Wryneck, European Nightjar, Hoopoe, Tree Pipit, Common Redstart, Rufous-tailed Rock Thrush; Melodious, Garden and Bonelli's Warblers, Red-backed Shrike.

Passage periods: Greylag Goose, Cormorant, Black and White Storks, Honey-buzzard, Black Kite, Short-toed Eagle and Booted Eagles, Marsh and Montagu's Harriers, Osprey, Crane, Stock Dove, Wood Pigeon, Mistle Thrush, Ortolan Bunting.

VALLE DE RONCAL   N2

Status: Includes the Reserva Natural 'Foz de Burgui' (424ha) and the ZEPAs 'Sierra de Illón- Foz de Burgui' (4,619ha), 'Larra-Aztaparreta' (3,767ha) and 'Sierra de San Miguel' (2,987ha).

Site description

The Roncal valley is easternmost in Navarra and includes the most 'alpine' area in the region, the head of the valley being the western extremity of what is known as the high Pyrenees. It has much in common with its adjoining valleys in Aragón: the Valle de Ansó (AR1) and the Valle de Hecho (AR17). The lower parts of the valley have pastures, hay meadows, small woods and the river itself, the Río Esca, with side tributaries, rocky outcrops and deep limestone gorges. The most famous of these gorges is the Foz de Burgui, on the border between Navarra and Aragón, but there are others: Sigüés, Roncal and Urzainqui. The pastures gradually become more alpine as you reach the higher parts of the valley, containing many botanically–rich wet flushes. There are also extensive woods and forest of Mountain Pine, beech and Silver Fir amid the high peaks and rocky crags.

Species

This is a very rich valley for birds, from the Embalse de Yesa right up to the French border. The pastures, hayfields and small woods of the lower and middle valley have a pleasant, varied avifauna including Quail, Wrynecks, Green Woodpeckers, Dippers, Tree Pipits, Common Redstarts, Dartford Warblers, Firecrests, Eurasian Treecreepers, Red-backed and Woodchat Shrikes, Bullfinches, Yellowhammers and Cirl Buntings.

The Burgui gorge has one of the biggest Griffon Vulture colonies in Navarra as well as nesting Egyptian Vultures, Golden Eagles, Peregrine Falcons, Eagle Owls, Red-billed Choughs and Blue Rock Thrushes. Alpine Accentors,

Yellow-billed Choughs and Wallcreepers occur in winter.

The forests of the Belagua refuge provide a scenic mixture of open and wooded habitats with a very rich flora. The breeding birds here include Grey Partridges, Woodcocks, European Nightjars, Water Pipits, Black Woodpeckers, White-backed Woodpeckers, Goldcrests, Eurasian Treecreepers, Yellow-billed Choughs, Citril Finches and Common Crossbills. Boreal Owls have their most westerly site here.

The uppermost reaches, at the Collado de la Piedra de San Martín and the French border, have alpine pastures with coniferous forest in places, alongside rocky outcrops and crags. Lammergeiers, Water Pipits, Alpine Accentors, Ring Ouzels, Wallcreepers, Yellow-billed Choughs and Snowfinches may be seen here.

Timing
Best in late spring and summer, between May and August. However, some of the alpine species can be seen at lower altitudes in winter.

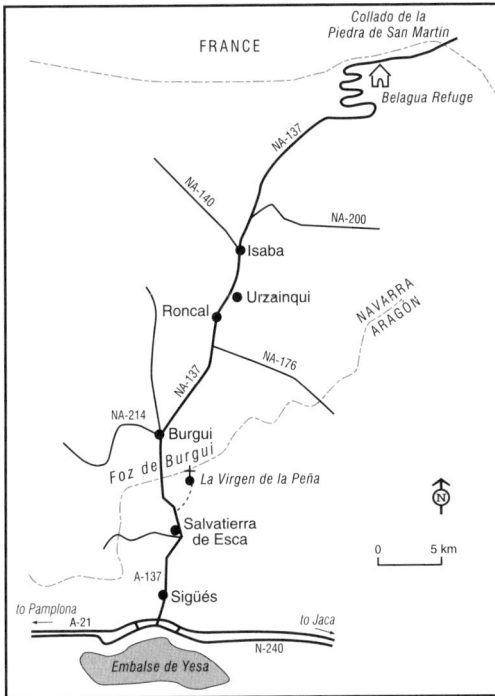

Access
From Pamplona take the A-21/N-240 eastwards up to the Embalse de Yesa, and its abandoned hilltop villages. You are now in Aragón. Turn left into the Roncal Valley along the A-137 at the eastern end of the reservoir. This road becomes the NA-137 as you enter Navarra once more. There is a Nature Interpretation Centre at Roncal (Tel. 948 475 317) which shares a building with the tourist office.

Foz de Burgui The NA-137 follows the gorge and provides a good opportunity for birding from one of a number of stopping points. Views are also possible from the chapel of La Virgen de la Peña above the gorge, which is reached by a track to the right about 1km before you enter the gorge.

Belagua Continue on the NA-137 through the Foz de Burgui and past Roncal to Isaba, where the road bears right and ascends into the highest parts of the valley. A disused mountain refuge is about 18km from Isaba after a series of hairpin bends. There is plenty of car parking at the refuge and you can walk from here into rich pasture and forest.

Collado de la Piedra de San Martín (International Border) Continue on the NA-137 from Belagua up to the pass at 1,760m and into France. There are plenty of opportunities for exploration around the border, although some of the paths across the Sierra de Añalara and up to the peaks are only suitable for experienced mountain walkers. If you continue over the border you reach the Forêt d'Isseaux, which is also very beautiful and good for woodpeckers.

CALENDAR

All year: Red-legged and Grey Partridges, Red Kite, Lammergeier, Griffon Vulture, Goshawk, Sparrowhawk, Common Buzzard, Golden Eagle, Common Kestrel, Peregrine Falcon, Woodcock; Tawny, Eagle and Boreal Owls, Kingfisher; Green, Black, Great Spotted and White-backed Woodpeckers, Crag Martin, Water Pipit, Grey Wagtail, Dipper, Dunnock, Alpine Accentor, Black Redstart, Stonechat, Blue Rock Thrush, Dartford Warbler, Goldcrest, Firecrest, Wallcreeper, Eurasian Treecreeper, Yellow-billed and Red-billed Choughs, Snowfinch, Serin, Citril Finch, Common Crossbill, Bullfinch, Yellowhammer, Cirl Bunting.

Breeding season: Quail, Black Kite, Egyptian Vulture, Hen Harrier, Short-toed and Booted Eagles, Common Sandpiper, European Nightjar, Wryneck, Alpine Swift, House Martin, Tawny and Tree Pipits, Rufous-tailed Rock Thrush, Ring Ouzel, Bonelli's Warbler, Spotted Flycatcher, Red-backed and Woodchat Shrikes.

Passage periods: Black Stork, Black Kite, Honey-buzzard, Woodpigeon.

FOZ DE ARBAYÚN and FOZ DE LUMBIER   N3

Status: Comprised by the Reservas Naturales 'Foz de Arbayún' (1,164ha) and 'Foz de Lumbier' (30ha). Also the ZEPA 'Sierra de Leyre-Foz de Arbayún' (9,020ha).

Site description
Two impressively deep and unspoilt limestone river gorges in the Sierra de Leyre, a small range of mountains rising to 1,356m, in the Pyrenean foothills. Both are nature reserves and famed for their vulture colonies.

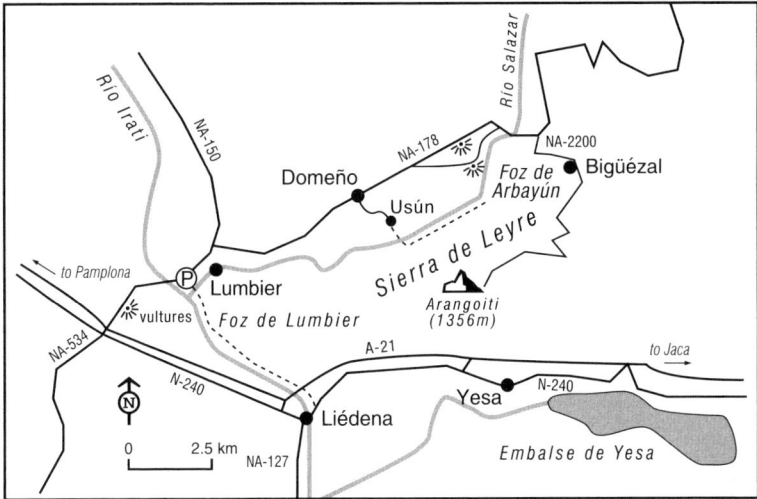

The Foz de Arbayún is one of the most dramatic gorges in Spain. It is almost 6km long, the longest of all the Navarran gorges, with vertical walls over 200m down to the Río Salazar. The valley floor has a covering of scrub and mixed woodland of oaks, beech, Maple, Ash, Willow, Hazel and Box.

The Foz de Lumbier is a shorter, narrower gorge, around 1,300m long, near the village from which it takes its name. However, it is no less dramatic, especially as it possible to walk along the gorge floor alongside the Río Irati beneath the 150m vertical walls. The vegetation here has more of a Mediterranean character.

Species
The general area has very large numbers of breeding Griffon Vultures, up to 1,000 pairs in the recent past. The colony at the Foz de Arbayún is particularly notable, with up to 250 nests. Both gorges are extremely important for other cliff-nesting birds including Egyptian Vultures, Golden Eagles, Peregrine Falcons, Eagle Owls, Alpine Swifts, Blue Rock Thrushes, Red-billed Choughs, Jackdaws and Ravens.

Timing
Visitors from April through to late June will find immature vultures at the nest sites. Come earlier in the year for displaying raptors and vultures. Vulture activity depends on the time of day and the weather: there is most activity around the colonies in the mornings, before the birds drift off in search of food, and when they return in the late afternoons.

Access
Take the A-21/N-240 for 30km east from Pamplona, turning left on to the NA-150 towards Lumbier and continue beyond on the NA-178. Soon after turning off the N-240 (0.5km) a viewpoint on the right overlooks a vulture 'restaurant' that attracts large numbers of these and other scavengers at times.

Egyptian and Griffon Vultures

Foz de Lumbier   Carry on up towards Lumbier and turn right just before the village, which takes you to the start of the gorge and a car park. It is then possible to walk along a disused railway line alongside the river and on the floor of the gorge. Vultures sometimes drift past at low levels here. Take a torch with you to go through the now disused railway tunnels. The old track continues along a very interesting valley with Nightingales and Bee-eaters and eventually takes you down to the next village of Liédena. The gorge Information Centre (Tel. 948 880 874) in the Plaza Major in Lumbier is open Fridays–Sundays except from mid-June to mid-September when it is open daily, generally from 10.00–14.00hrs. It provides information on additional walks around both gorges.

Foz de Arbayún   Carry on past Lumbier village and take the right fork on to the NA-178, continuing past Domeño towards Navascués. Around 6km on from Domeño on the right-hand side of the road is the Iso *mirador* above the gorge. An alternative viewpoint, closer to the river, is on the NA-2160 minor road, below the Iso watchpoint. Amazing views are possible from these viewpoints down into this spectacular chasm. Remember to bring a telescope for close views into the nests. The scrub around the platform can be good for warblers. Another option for the energetic with a good head for heights is a footpath along the east side of the gorge, accessible from Usún, below Domeño.

If you carry on past the mirador and continue along the NA-178 you come to a right turning (NA-2200) to Bigüezal immediately after a bridge over the Río Salazar. Bear right after the village up a steep narrow road through Scots Pine forest to the Arangoiti peak (1,356m), the highest point of the Sierra de Leyre. From here you get tremendous views across the Pyrenees and of vultures flying to and from the nearby gorges.

CALENDAR

All year: Lammergeier, Griffon Vulture, Goshawk, Sparrowhawk, Golden Eagle, Peregrine Falcon, Rock Dove, Long-eared and Eagle Owls, Grey Wagtail, Dipper, Wren, Stonechat, Black Redstart, Blue Rock Thrush, Dartford and Sardinian Warblers, Southern Grey Shrike, Crested Tit, Red-billed Chough, Jackdaw, Raven, Rock Sparrow, Crossbill, Cirl and Rock Buntings.

Breeding season: Red Kite, Black Kite,

Honey-buzzard, Egyptian Vulture, Short-toed and Booted Eagles, Alpine Swift, Hoopoe, Crag and House Martins, Tawny Pipit, Red-backed Shrike; Melodious, Orphean and Subalpine Warblers, Golden Oriole, Ortolan Bunting.

Winter: Woodcock, Alpine Accentor, Wallcreeper, Yellow-billed Chough, Siskin, Hawfinch.

EMBALSE DE LAS CAÑAS   N4

Status: Reserva Natural, ZEPA and Ramsar site (101ha).

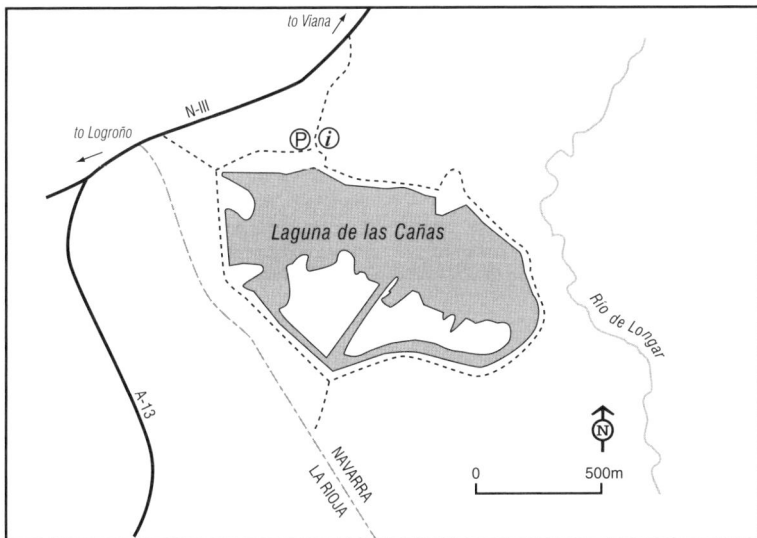

Site description

One of the best wetland sites in Navarra, providing water for irrigation of the surrounding farmland. It is near the Río Ebro close to Logroño, in an area of cereal and vine cultivation, horticulture and some industry on the periphery of the city. There is permanent water although levels fluctuate. The lake has a well-developed fringe of emergent vegetation, including reedbeds, and surrounding trees and scrub including Willow, Black Poplar and Tamarisk. A central causeway splits the lake into two.

Species

The reservoir houses one of the few heronries in Navarra, offering nesting Grey and Purple Herons, a few pairs of Night Herons and also Little and Cattle Egrets. Great Bitterns occur regularly on passage and in winter and have bred in the past. Other notable breeding species include Savi's Warbler, Bearded Tit and Reed Bunting. The site attracts good numbers of wintering and passage waders and waterfowl. More unusual sightings here have included Pink-backed Pelican, White-tailed Eagle, Marbled Duck and Purple Swamphen.

Timing

Spring and autumn are the best times of year but there is always something to see here.

Access

The reservoir is in the extreme north-west of Navarra, only 3km from Logroño (in La Rioja). From Logroño take the N-111 towards Viana. An access track on the right, shortly after you pass the regional boundary into Navarra, leads to a parking area, El Bordón Information Centre (Tel. 696 830 898: open mainly at weekends) and the lake. There are paths and tracks around the lake margin.

CALENDAR

All year: Gadwall, Mallard, Little and Great Crested Grebes, Little Egret, Grey Heron, Marsh Harrier, Water Rail, Moorhen, Common Coot, Kingfisher, Cetti's Warbler, Zitting Cisticola, Bearded and Penduline Tits, Tree Sparrow.

Breeding season: Red-crested Pochard (has bred), Night and Purple Herons, Cattle and Little Egrets, White Stork, Black Kite, Little Ringed Plover, Bee-eater; Savi's, Reed, Great Reed and Melodious Warblers, Golden Oriole.

Winter: Common Shelduck, Wigeon, Teal, Pintail, Shoveler, Common Pochard, Tufted Duck, Cormorant, Great Bittern, Hen Harrier, Jack Snipe, Reed Bunting.

Passage periods: Greylag Goose, Garganey, Ferruginous Duck, Great and Little Bitterns, Black Stork, Red Kite, Osprey, Little Crake (rare), Black-winged Stilt, Avocet, Ringed Plover, Ruff, Common Snipe, Black-tailed Godwit, Whimbrel, Curlew, Greenshank, Green Sandpiper, Black-headed Gull, Whiskered and Black Terns.

LAGUNA DE PITILLAS   N5

Status: Reserva Natural (300ha), ZEPA and Ramsar site (215ha).

Site description

The Laguna de Pitillas, the best natural wetland in Navarra, is in a cereal-growing area in the valley of a tributary of the Río Cidacos, itself a tributary of the Río Aragón. Most of the very shallow lake is covered by reedbeds but there are areas of open water. Management has included the maintenance of water levels and the planting of a variety of trees and shrubs on the site periphery to serve as both a nesting habitat and a screen.

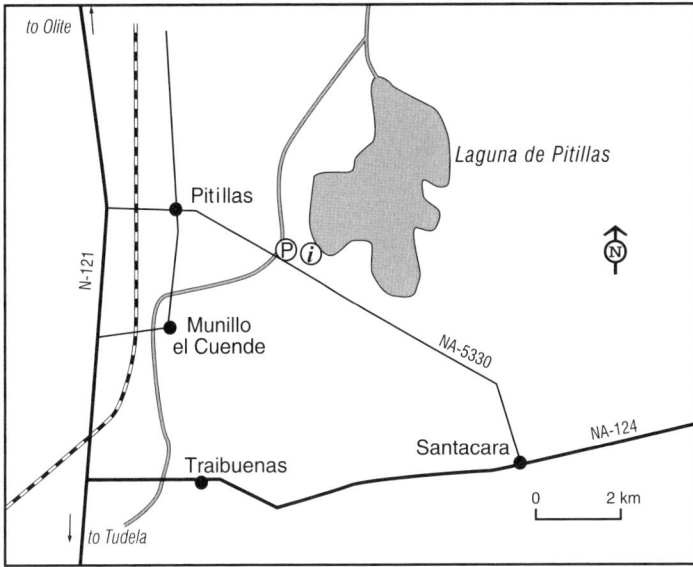

Species

Pitillas is renowned as a breeding site of the Great Bittern, a rare and very local breeding species in Spain; several pairs nest here. There are also colonies of both Grey and Purple Herons and Little Bitterns nest at least occasionally. Other noteworthy breeding birds include Black-necked Grebes and Bearded Tits. The Purple Swamphen is recorded occasionally and may yet become established here. This is a prime site for Marsh Harriers, with a breeding population of over 30 pairs, sometimes more, and a large winter roost. A diversity of wildfowl, waders and other species occur on passage and in winter.

The fields around the lagoon have breeding Montagu's Harriers, Stone-curlews, Calandra Larks and Tawny Pipits. Black-bellied Sandgrouse are seen here occasionally.

Timing

The lake is interesting throughout the year.

Access

From Pamplona and Tafalla take the N-121 south towards Tudela. Around 6km south of Olite turn left on to the local road, the NA-5330, for the village of Pitillas. Continue past the village on the NA-5330 towards Santacara. After some 3km you reach a car park and an observatory/information centre (Tel. 619 463 450): open at weekends, see lagunadepitillas.org) on the left, on a hill overlooking the lake. A wire fence marks the boundary of the protected area, to which access is not allowed. It is possible to walk around the periphery of the lake except during the breeding season.

CALENDAR

All year: Mallard, Red-crested Pochard; Little, Great Crested and Black-necked Grebes, Great Bittern, Little Egret, Grey Heron, Marsh Harrier, Water Rail, Cetti's Warbler, Bearded Tit.

Breeding season: Garganey, Little Bittern (occasional), Purple Heron, Black Kite, Black-winged Stilt, Lapwing, Common Redshank, Common Sandpiper, Sand Martin; Reed, Great Reed and Melodious Warblers.

Winter: Wigeon, Gadwall, Teal, Pintail, Shoveler, Common Pochard, Tufted Duck, Penduline Tit, Reed Bunting.

Passage periods: Greylag Goose, Common Shelduck, Garganey, Black Stork, Glossy Ibis, Osprey, Crane, Common Snipe, Green Sandpiper, Whiskered Tern.

SOTOS DEL RÍO ARAGÓN Y RÍO EBRO   N6

Status: Six sotos are Reservas Naturales and a further 20 are protected as Enclaves Naturales de Navarra.

Site description

The *sotos* are riparian woodlands, notably of Willow and Black Poplar, with Narrow-leaved Ash, Elm, Alder and Tamarisk, here along the courses of the Río Ebro and the Río Aragón and its tributaries: the Ríos Cidacos and Arga. Such woodlands were once far more widespread but they have largely disappeared from many parts of Europe. Where they do occur they support a rich bird community. The *sotos* differ slightly from site to site: for example on the Ebro the woodland tends to be a little more mature with a more varied mix of trees and shrubs, and is more extensive. *Cortados,* or sandbanks, also occur along some sections of the rivers. In addition to the *sotos*, there are also a number of other reserves, mainly small woods or lagoons, in the general area.

Species

The *sotos* are especially important for nesting Penduline Tits and Golden Orioles, both closely associated with poplars, and for small colonies of Night and Purple Herons. The trees are also used by roosting herons and egrets, and in autumn by Barn Swallows. Nightingales and Cetti's Warblers are typically abundant, and their songs can be almost deafening at times. The sandbanks have strong colonies of Sand Martins and Bee-eaters. The ricefields around Arguedas attract passage and wintering herons, waders and waterfowl; breeding species include a sizeable colony of Black-winged Stilts.

Timing

Spring visits are recommended, especially from late March through into June.

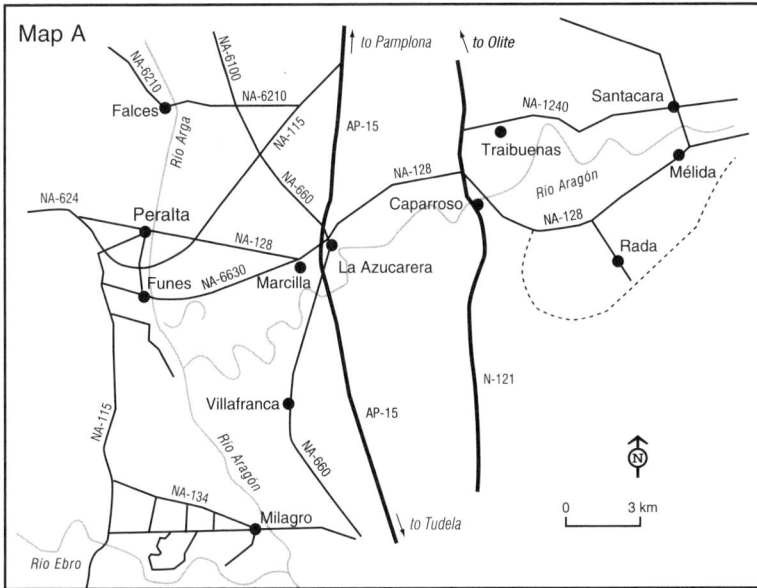

Map A

to Pamplona to Olite

NA-6210 NA-6100 NA-6210 AP-15 NA-1240 Santacara
Falces NA-115 Traibuenas
Río Arga NA-660 NA-128 Mélida
NA-624 Río Aragón
Peralta Caparroso NA-128
NA-128 La Azucarera Rada
Funes NA-6630 Marcilla
Villafranca AP-15 N-121
NA-115 NA-660
Río Aragón
NA-134 N
Milagro 0 3 km
Río Ebro to Tudela

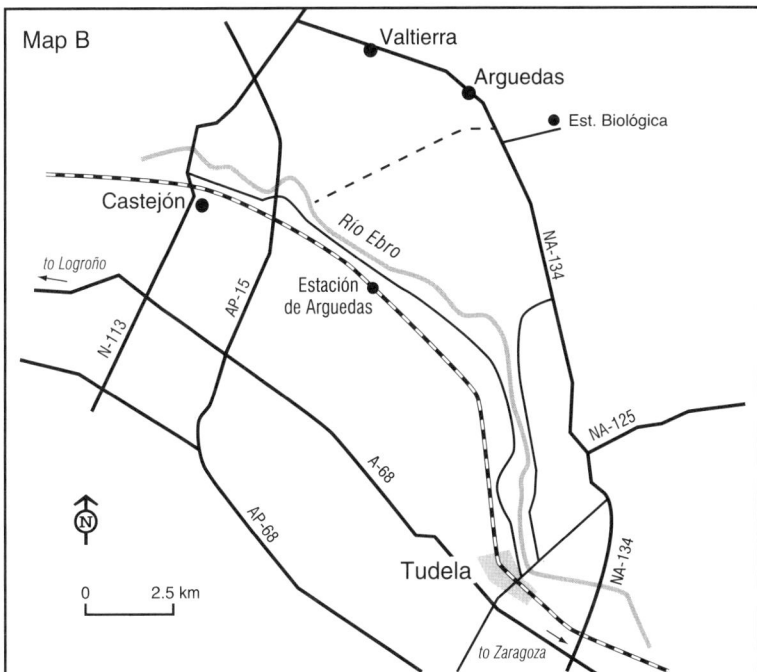

Map B

Valtierra
Arguedas
Est. Biológica
Castejón
to Logroño Río Ebro NA-134
AP-15 Estación
de Arguedas
N-113
NA-125
A-68
N AP-68 NA-134
0 2.5 km Tudela
to Zaragoza

Access

There are *sotos* especially along the courses of the Ríos Aragón and Ebro, and also on the Río Cidacos, along the stretch of river south of Olite flanking the minor roads through Beire, Pitillas and Murillo el Cuende. See R5 for the Sotos de Alfaro on the Ebro in La Rioja. From Pamplona take the N-121 south towards Tudela. The *sotos* occur on either side of this road along the Aragón and its tributaries, south of the town of Olite. The main concentration of *sotos* on the Ebro is further south, near Tudela. We suggest visits to any of the following:

Sotos and cortados between Falces and Peralta (Map A) Turn west from the NA-121 12km south of Olite and follow the NA-128 to Peralta. The nearby village of Falces is north of Peralta along minor roads, but can more easily be found by turning right off the NA-115 south of Tafalla. View the *sotos* where this road crosses over the Río Arga, immediately before you reach Falces. Minor roads follow both banks of the river between Falces and Peralta, giving views of the sotos between the two towns.

Sotos de Funes (Map A) Take the NA-128 towards Peralta and turn left at Marcilla on to the NA-6630 to the village of Funes. The *sotos* are on the east bank of the Río Arga at Funes.

Sotos and cortados at Caparroso (Map A) Turn off the N-121 13km south of Olite to the village of Caparroso. Paths in Caparroso lead into the *sotos*, on both banks of the Río Aragón.

Sotos on the Río Aragón from Mélida to Caparroso (Map A) Turn off to the east from the N-121 10km south of Olite on to the NA-1240 to Santacara. A track in the first village, Traibuenas, leads south to the river. Return to the N-1240 and continue to Santacara and then south to Mélida to get good views and explore the area from both sides of the river. Access to the river is also available between the villages of Murillo El Fruto and Carcastillo, east of Santacara and Mélida.

Sotos and cortados around Milagro (Map A) Take the NA-115 south from Peralta for about 10km and turn east at km-40 on to the NA-134 towards Milagro. Minor roads leading south of this road lead to the river.

Sotos on the Río Ebro above Tudela (Map B) Take the N-121 south from Olite and then turn left on to the NA-134 towards Tudela. Approaching Tudela, and immediately after crossing the bridge over the Ebro to enter the town, turn north on to a minor road that follows the river. There are plenty of opportunities to explore the river and its woodland off this route. Alternatively you can explore the minor road on the east bank, accessible just before you cross the bridge.

Estación Biológica de Arguedas (Map B) An ornithological and educational centre (Tel. 948 151 077), run by Gurelur, a non-governmental organisation, just south of Arguedas east of the NA-134 to Tudela around km-15. As well as providing information on Las Bardenas Reales (N7), it also gives information on the sotos nearby and offers opportunities for birding on the adjoining rice fields. See gurelur.org

Hoopoe

CALENDAR

All year: Little and Great Crested Grebes, Little Egret, Red Kite, Sparrowhawk, Common Sandpiper, Barn Owl, Kingfisher, Green and Great Spotted Woodpeckers, White Wagtail, Cetti's Warbler, Zitting Cisticola, Long-tailed Tit, Tree Sparrow, Cirl Bunting.

Breeding season: Night and Purple Herons, White Stork, Black Kite, Egyptian Vulture, Booted Eagle, Hobby, Little Ringed Plover, Turtle Dove, Scops Owl, Bee-eater, Wryneck, Hoopoe, Sand Martin, Yellow Wagtail, Nightingale; Reed, Great Reed and Melodious Warblers, Penduline Tit, Golden Oriole, Woodchat Shrike.

LAS BARDENAS REALES   N7

Status: Parque Natural, ZEPA and Biosphere Reserve (39,273ha). Also includes the Reservas Naturales 'Rincón del Bú' (460ha) and Caídas de la Negra' (1,926ha) and borders on the Reserva Natural 'Vedado de Eguaras' (500ha) and the Enclave Natural 'Pinar de Santa Águeda'.

Site description

A huge, spectacular, desert-like area of over 40,000ha with a large number of ravines and cliffs cutting though a flat-topped plateau or *mesa*. It represents one of the most important steppe areas in the Ebro Valley and in Spain. The gypsum, marl and clay landscape is a very strange one, with what appear to be stranded eroded islands standing in a semi-arid desert sea. Within this 'desert' of dry grassland and scrub of Albardine, Rosemary, Thyme and Kermes Oak there are extensive areas of cereals and other crops, and also stands of pine. Water bodies are scattered through the site. The area is uninhabited but has traditionally been used for transhumance, with up to 90,000 sheep being brought down from the Pyrenees in the winter months. There are more than 250 archaeological sites within the Biosphere Reserve.

The landscape is also home to a sprinkling of castles, now mostly ruined, which add to the atmosphere of the plain. The north of the Bardenas Reales is normally referred to as La Gran Meseta or El Plano de Bardenas. The central area is La Bardena Blanca: two of the reserves are here, as well as a military zone used by the Air Force. The southern section, La Bardena Negra, houses the Caídas de la Negra reserve.

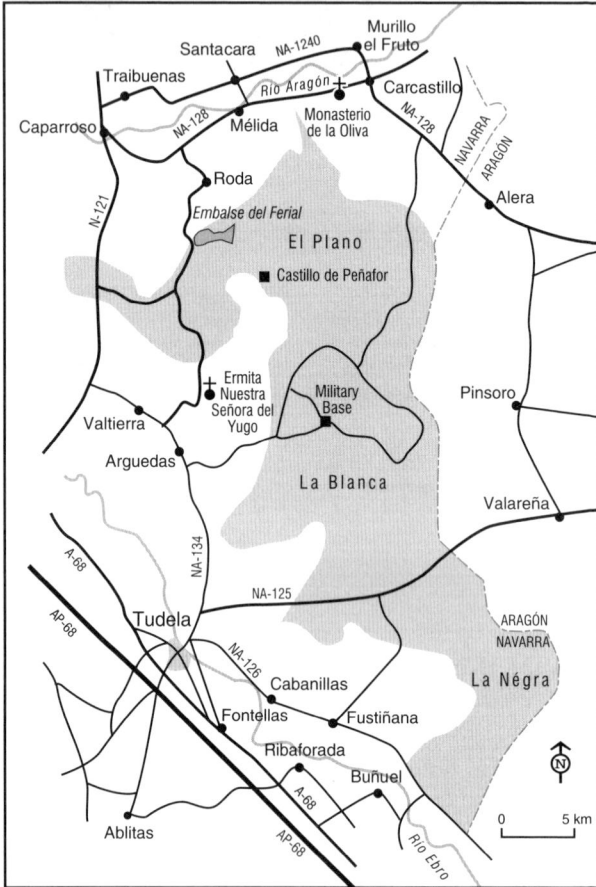

Species

The Bardenas Reales are very important for steppe birds, although Little Bustards are scarce and Great Bustards no longer occur here. There is a notable concentration of Dupont's Larks, perhaps over 100 pairs, as well as large numbers of breeding Calandra and Lesser Short-toed Larks. There are also populations of both Black-bellied and Pin-tailed Sandgrouse and Stone-curlews. Red-necked Nightjars are present, typically on the open ground fringing the pinewoods.

The cliffs are home to Egyptian and Griffon Vultures and Golden Eagles. Eagle Owls are also resident and Alpine Swifts breed. Short-toed Eagles nest in the more wooded parts, such as at Caídas de la Negra. Here there is also a sizeable summer roost – mainly in pines – of Egyptian Vultures, attracting up to 200 birds in July–August.

Timing
Spring is best. Visiting in the height of the summer will not be very rewarding since it gets very hot here. Black-bellied and Pin-tailed Sandgrouse can often be found flying in small flocks in the evenings, heading for some of the many small lagoons that dot the landscape. Winter is cold but not usually as frosty as in other parts of the Ebro Valley. By mid-April the warmer weather and summer visitors have arrived.

Access
The Bardenas Reales are extensive but the area is not well served with roads. In general, access to the protected areas is restricted and you need to remain on the roads or marked tracks, shown on the map. Access is only allowed from 08.00 hours until dusk. Walks and cycle routes are also available (see bardenasreales.es/turismo). Among these, the GR13 long-distance path crosses the central sector from the Hermitage of La Virgen del Yugo.

From Pamplona, take the N-121/NA-134 (or the AP-15) south towards Tudela. From Zaragoza head north-west on the A/NA-126 to Tudela.

Northern sector Take the NA-128 east from the N-121 at km-55 to Carcastillo. From Carcastillo take the NA-128 south-east and turn south at km-6 on to a track that crosses the northern sector to the central area.

Central sector Take the NA-134 towards Arguedas. About 1km south of Arguedas turn left after the petrol station on to a narrow road. The information centre for the Bardenas is at km-6 on this road, which leads to the military base. A 25km circular route takes you around the periphery of the military zone, passing through some of the most representative habitats.

Another minor road leads north out of Arguedas, past the Nuestra Señora del Yugo chapel (4km). Turn right after around 8km and explore the plains here. This road leads to the Castillo de Peñafor, within the Vedado de Eguaros reserve, after a further 6km.

Southern sector From Tudela take the NA-134 towards Arguedas and after 2km head east on the NA-125. This road enters Las Bardenas after about 7km and crosses a good part of the area, although it is busy. To the north of this road is the reserve of Rincon del Bú with a number of tracks off to the left. The reserve of Caídas de la Negra is south of the road. Alternatively, take the NA-134 north from Tudela, cross the bridge over the Ebro and turn off to the right on to the NA-126 immediately afterwards. Continue through Cabanillas and Fustiñana to the south entrance at around km-22.

CALENDAR

All year: Griffon Vulture, Golden Eagle, Peregrine Falcon, Little Bustard, Stone-curlew, Black-bellied and Pin-tailed Sandgrouse; Dupont's, Calandra, Lesser Short-toed, Crested and Thekla Larks, Black Wheatear, Blue Rock Thrush, Dartford Warbler, Red-billed Chough, Rock Sparrow.

Breeding season: White Stork, Egyptian

Vulture, Montagu's Harrier, Lesser Kestrel, Great Spotted Cuckoo, Red-necked Nightjar, Alpine Swift, Bee-eater, Greater Short-toed Lark, Tawny Pipit, Northern and Black-eared Wheatears, Spectacled Warbler.

Winter: Red Kite, Hen Harrier, Merlin, Short-eared Owl.

OTHER SITES WORTH VISITING

N8 SIERRA DE URBASA Y ANDÍA

A sierra with deep gorges and limestone cliffs, woods, fast flowing streams and cultivated land. The attractions are Griffon Vultures and other raptors, Eagle Owls, Red-billed Choughs and Dippers. The sierra is just south of A-10 motorway at km-30, between Vitoria-Gasteiz and Pamplona. The NA-718 and NA-120 cross the area southwards towards Estella. Parque Natural.

N9 PEÑAS DE ECHAURI

A small sierra with a 200m-high escarpment and limestone cliffs with scrub and oak woodland. An important area for Griffon and Egyptian Vultures, Yellow-billed Choughs, Blue Rock Thrushes and Crag Martins. Wallcreepers occur in winter. From Pamplona take the NA-700 west towards Arazuri, Ororbia and Echauri (Etxauri). The cliffs begin 2–3km outside the village of Echauri.

N10 MONTE DEL CONDE

Mediterranean oak woodland. Breeding birds include Goshawks, Short-toed and Booted Eagles and a good range of other woodland species. Take the N-121/AP-15 south from Pamplona for some 30km. Turn left on to the NA-5110 to Olleta. Tracks lead through the woodland. Reserva natural.

N11 SEÑORÍO DE BERTIZ

Oak and beech woods in the Baztán valley. Breeding birds include Goshawks, Honey-buzzards, Hobbies, Black Woodpeckers, Firecrests and Melodious Warblers. Take the N121-A from Pamplona in the south (44km) or Irun in the north. Turn off on to the N-121-B at Oronoz-Mugaire. The entrance to the park is in Oieregi, next to the petrol station, where you cross the bridge over the Río Bidasoa. Reserva natural.

PAÍS VASCO (EUSKADI)

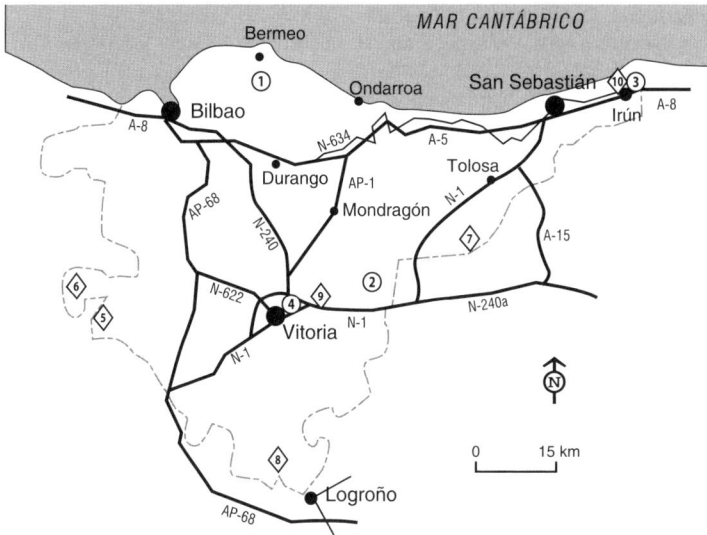

Main sites
PV1   Urdaibai
PV2   Aitzgorri
PV3   Plaiaundi Ecological Park
PV4   Salburúa Wetlands

Other sites worth visiting
PV5   Hoz de Sobrón
PV6   Valderejo
PV7   Sierra de Aralar
PV8   Laguardia Lagoons
PV9   Mendixur Ornithological Park
PV10   Cabo Higer

The País Vasco, the Basque Country at the western end of the Pyrenees, is known in the somewhat impenetrable Basque language as Euskadi, literally 'collection of Basques'. Euskadi, strictly-speaking, encompasses people and territory in the neighbouring regions, including south-west France, as well as the Basque Country proper. Euskadi has much in common with Cataluña, at the eastern end of the Pyrenees, in that both have their own language, history and customs. If you have come to Spain to enjoy a relaxed and slower pace of life for a week or two, then perhaps the Basque country is not for you. Take care if you dare to chance your arm at pelota – a game invented by the Basques and thought to be the 'fastest game on earth'!

For its relatively small size the País Vasco has a long, attractive, rocky coastline, the Costa Vasca, on the Bay of Biscay. It stretches from the border with France westwards to Cantabria, passing through the elegant resort of San Sebastián (Donostia) and the industrial port of Bilbao (Bilbo): the arrival point for many visitors on their way to the Pyrenees or the Picos de Europa. The coast has numerous small inlets and harbours and also the Ría de Gernika in the west, the site of the large Urdaibai reserve (PV1). The highest point on the

Basque coast, Cabo Ogoño (280m) is part of that Reserve and has breeding European Storm-petrels, Peregrine Falcons, Ravens and Blue Rock Thrushes.

While there is much to interest the visiting birder all year on the coast, it is during migration periods and winter that birding can become very exciting. Anything can turn up on passage, and during the winter months you are likely to encounter a good range of 'seabirds' such as Common and Velvet Scoters, Great Northern, Black-throated and Red-throated Divers, Slavonian Grebes, Great Skuas and auks: especially Razorbills. Cabo Matxitxako (PV1) and Cabo Higer (PV10) are excellent locations for seawatching.

The coast is not without interest during the breeding season, being important for European Storm-petrels, Shags and Grasshopper Warblers. The Basque region, and not just the coast, is a key area for the Grasshopper Warbler in Spain, with some 1,500 breeding pairs.

There is much more to the coast than Urdaibai (PV1) but this site more than any other dominates the region, not only because of its bird and natural history attractions but also because of its sad history during Spain's civil war. The destruction of Gernika in April 1937 killed thousands of local people. Eighty years on memories are still strong but the town is now the core of the Urdaibai Biosphere reserve. Around 250 species are recorded annually at this reserve, which extends considerably beyond the shores of the estuary and is well placed for passage migrants, given its geographical position between the Bay of Biscay and the Pyrenees. Even Wallcreepers are a possibility in winter.

Mediterranean species are largely missing from the coastal areas, although Zitting Cisticolas are common and Sardinian Warblers have colonised the coast since the 1980s. However, you do not need to travel too far inland before encountering Black Kites, Eagle Owls, Golden Orioles and Spotless Starlings, with White Storks, Bee-eaters and Black-eared Wheatears occurring further south, towards La Rioja.

The hinterland of the Basque Country is fairly intensively cultivated but it is also well wooded in parts, especially as the ground rises. Here there is a good population of Honey-buzzards and a notable diversity of woodpeckers: Green, Great Spotted, Middle Spotted, Lesser Spotted and Black Woodpeckers breed, as well as Wrynecks. Lesser Spotted Woodpeckers, always elusive in Iberia, have one of their denser Spanish populations here in the mixed oakwoods, numbering at least 150 pairs. Middle Spotted Woodpeckers breed in similar habitat in the south-east of the region, where a very few Black Woodpeckers also occur.

There are relatively few wetlands away from the coastal marshes and rivers (PV1, PV3) but the reservoirs to the north of Vitoria-Gasteiz: the Embalses de Urrunga and de Ullibarri-Gamboa (PV9) have breeding Shovelers and attract a wide range of wintering waterfowl. The Salburúa Wetlands (PV4) are another interesting inland site, with a breeding colony of Black-winged Stilts. The Laguardia Lagoons (PV8) are also worth visiting.

In the west, the Ebro gorges, such as the Hoz de Sobrón (PV5), have important breeding numbers of Griffon Vultures in addition to Egyptian Vultures and Golden Eagles. The main mountain ranges to the east of the region, in which Aitzgorri (PV2) and the Sierra de Aralar (PV7) are located, link the Pyrenees to the east with the Cordillera Cantábrica to the west. Their upper reaches have breeding Alpine Accentors, Rufous-tailed Rock Thrushes, Yellow-billed Choughs and Citril Finches. Prospecting Lammergeiers are occasional but increasingly frequent visitors from the Pyrenees.

URDAIBAI (Vizcaya) PV1

Status: UNESCO Biosphere reserve (22,041ha), Ramsar site (945ha) and ZEPA (23,000ha).

Site description

Urdaibai, also known as the Riá de Gernika, comprises a deep estuary, with one of the most important saltmarshes in northern Spain, and a stretch of rocky coastline. It is some 30km north-east of Bilbao between the Matxitxako and Ogoño headlands, extending eastwards to Arbolitx point. It includes the small island of Ízaro at the mouth of the estuary. The Ría itself is the principal focus of birding interest but the reserve extends well away from the estuary both eastwards and westwards, and also inland well beyond the town of Gernika-Lumo to include 12 towns and villages and parts of another 10! This is because the reserve boundaries are fixed by the river catchments and so it includes the immediate areas around the Río Oka and its feeder streams.

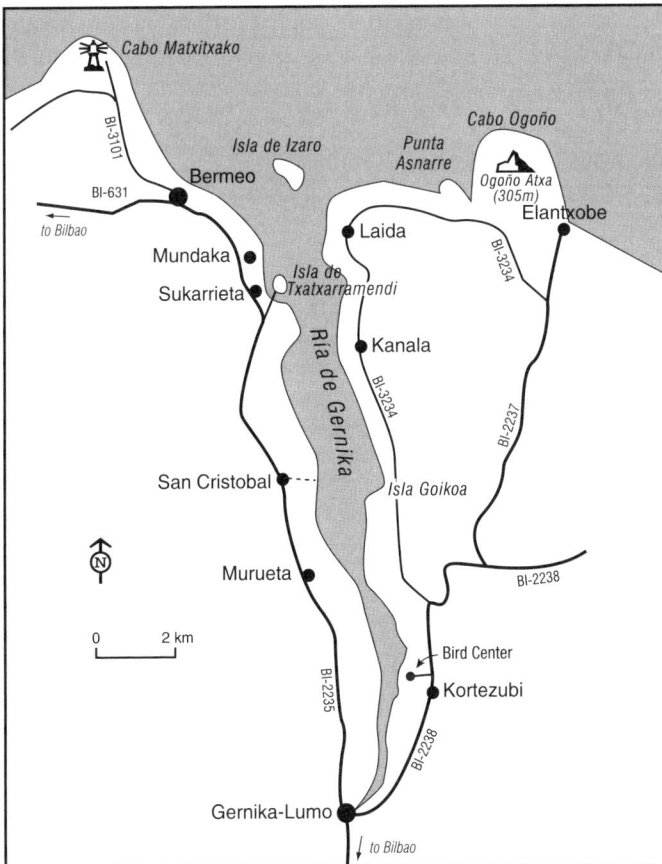

The Oka river, which forms the axis of the valley, has its source on the slopes of Mount Oiz. From Gernika seawards it opens out to form the estuary, extending for about 12km from the town to the coast. The reserve is a complex mosaic of sandbanks, mudflats, saltmarsh, rocky coast and cliff faces, wet pasture, arable land, Holm Oak woodland and other deciduous and coniferous woodland.

Species

Over 250 species are recorded at the reserve annually. Breeding birds include Little Bitterns, Water Rails, Little Ringed Plovers, Zitting Cisticolas and Grasshopper, Reed, Great Reed and Cetti's Warblers. Short-toed Eagles, Peregrine Falcons, Hobbies, Barn Owls, Lesser Spotted Woodpeckers, Red-rumped Swallows, Sardinian Warblers, Red-backed Shrikes and Bullfinches also nest in the hinterland. The rocky coastline, particularly the Isla de Ízaro and other offshore islets, has large colonies of Yellow-legged Gulls as well as smaller numbers of Shags and European Storm-petrels. The Urdaibai Bird Center (see below) is helping to conduct a project to establish nesting Ospreys, by releasing young birds obtained elsewhere.

The reserve also offers excellent opportunities to watch seabird movements, especially from Cabo Matxitxako in autumn, when onshore winds may produce large numbers of Gannets, shearwaters, seaducks, skuas, gulls, terns and auks, most of them coasting westwards. The aftermath of north-westerly gales is most productive. Wintering seabirds are also an attraction both within the estuary and offshore. They regularly include Great Northern Divers, Common Gulls, Guillemots and Razorbills.

The diversity of wintering and passage waders is considerable. The estuary is a good site for wintering Curlews and Purple Sandpipers winter on the rocky coastline. Spoonbills occur regularly on passage.

The reserve regularly sees such scarcer waterfowl as Barnacle and Brent Geese, Long-tailed Ducks, Velvet Scoters and Eiders, which tend to be elusive in Spain. Wallcreepers occur occasionally in winter at Cabo Ogoño.

Timing

Interesting birding is available throughout the year. However, the area is very popular in summer when the beaches on the eastern side, Laiga and Laga, can get crowded occasionally.

Access

From Bilbao travel east along the AP-8/N-634 to Amorebieta-Etxano and then take the BI-365 north to Gernika-Lumo. From here the BI-2235 gives access to the west side of the Ría and continues to Bermeo and Cabo Matxitxako. The BI-3234 offers access to the east side from Gernika. In the west the BI-631 connects Bilbao to Bermeo via Bilbao Airport and Mungia. Many other roads cross the area. The following viewpoints are particularly recommended.

Urdaibai Bird Center A good starting point and an excellent source of current information. Open daily, except Mondays. See their trilingual website (birdcenter.org), which includes a live webcam. A trail from the centre leads to two hides overlooking marshland and the Orueta lagoon. The centre is on the east side, west of the BI-2238, 4.5km north of Gernika. It is signposted 700m north of Kortezubi.

Cabo Matxitxako The most northerly point of the Basque Country and ideal for seawatching. Take the BI-3101 north for 4km from Bermeo and continue for 2km on the access road to the Cape.

Isla de Txatxarramendi Especially good for observing waders and seabirds on autumn and winter afternoons. Many species roost here and around the island of Ízaro at the mouth of the estuary. Take the BI-2235 Gernika-Bermeo road, for around 7km from Gernika.

Bermeo Harbour A good site for finding wintering seabirds. Bermeo is on the BI-2235 at the western entrance to the Ría.

San Cristobal saltmarshes The most productive site for birding the saltmarshes and intertidal areas, and good for spoonbills and waders. The marshes are off the BI-2235 Gernika-Bermeo road, around 5km from Gernika. Park at the station. A hide overlooks the marshes and estuary.

Isla Goikoa This provides elevated ground with views across the estuary from the eastern side. It is on the road from Gernika to Laida beach.

Punta Asnarre and Cabo Ogoño A good place to see the cliffs of Urdaibai and the highest point on the Basque coast at 280m. Take the BI-2238 and then the BI-2237 from Gernika for around 12km towards Elantxobe and follow the BI-3234 coast road to Punta Asnarre.

Elantxobe Harbour East of Cabo Ogoño and also good for wintering seabirds.

CALENDAR

All year: Shag, Little Egret, Grey Heron, Peregrine Falcon, Water Rail, Common Sandpiper, Yellow-legged Gull; Barn, Little and Tawny Owls, Great Spotted and Lesser Spotted Woodpeckers, Crag Martin, White and Grey Wagtails, Blue Rock Thrush, Cetti's Warbler, Zitting Cisticola, Sardinian Warbler, Blackcap, Crested Tit, Serin, Bullfinch, Yellowhammer, Reed and Corn Buntings.

Breeding season: European Storm-petrel, Little Bittern, Short-toed Eagle, Osprey (introduction project), Hobby, Little Ringed Plover, Red-rumped Swallow, Tawny Pipit, Yellow Wagtail, Northern Wheatear; Grasshopper, Reed, Great Reed and Melodious Warblers, Spotted Flycatcher, Red-backed Shrike.

Winter: Barnacle and Brent Geese, Eider, Long-tailed Duck, Common and Velvet Scoters; Red-throated, Black-throated and Great Northern Divers, Slavonian Grebe, Cormorant, Ringed Plover, Sanderling, Purple Sandpiper, Dunlin, Black-tailed and Bar-tailed Godwits, Curlew, Common Redshank, Greenshank, Turnstone, Great Skua; Black-headed, Common and Great Black-backed Gulls, Razorbill, Guillemot, Wallcreeper, Southern Grey Shrike.

Passage periods: Cory's, Sooty (summer/autumn only), Great (summer/autumn only), Manx and Balearic Shearwaters, Gannet; Great, Pomarine and Arctic Skuas, Purple Heron, Spoonbill, Red Kite, Osprey, Whimbrel, Little Stint, Spotted Redshank; Sandwich, Common and Arctic Terns, Wryneck, Sand Martin, Willow Warbler, Pied Flycatcher.

AITZGORRI (Alava/Guipúzcoa)   PV2

Status: Parque Natural (18,000ha).

Site description
A limestone massif, the highest in the Basque Country reaching an altitude of just over 1,500m. It comprises the Sierras de Aitzgorri, Elgea and Urkilla and the mountains of Altzania. These are undulating rocky outcrops with rounded peaks and deep gullies, and limestone gorges at Arantzazu and Araotz. The slopes are covered in large areas of beech forest, particularly in the north of the area. There are also some oak woodlands and peat bogs: a rarity in Spain. The mountain pastures are home to the traditional '*latxa*' sheep.

Species
Water Pipits, Alpine Accentors, Yellow-billed Choughs and Citril Finches occur at the higher levels. Griffon and Egyptian Vultures nest in the gorges. The woodlands have breeding Booted Eagles, Goshawks and a few Black Woodpeckers.

Timing
Spring and summer visits are recommended.

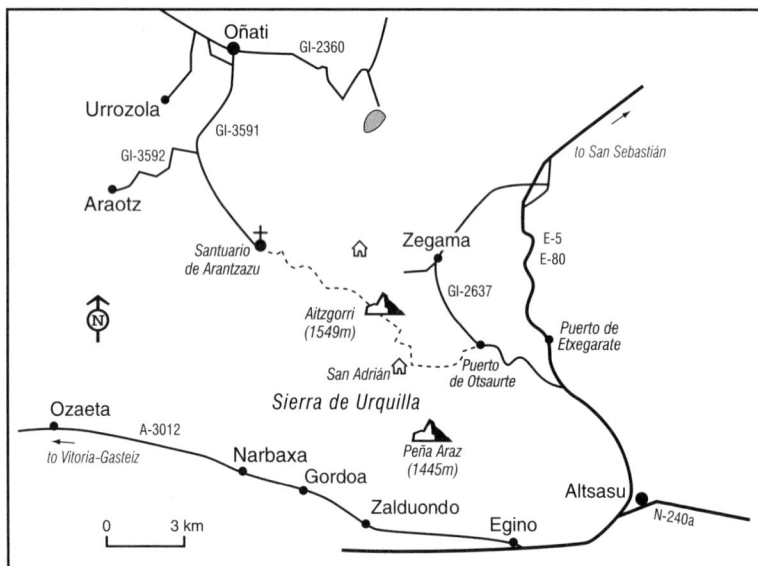

Access
From Vitoria-Gasteiz take the N-240/AP-1 north for about 10km and then follow the GI-627 north. Turn right at km-39 and take the GI-2630 to Oñati. The Santuario de Arantzazu is signposted from Oñati. Tracks lead up into the mountains, meadows and woodland from the Santuario.

Access is also possible from the eastern end but it is not so easy. Take the A-I out of Vitoria-Gasteiz towards San Sebastián and go past Altsasu towards the Puerto de Etxegárate. Before reaching the pass turn left on to the GI-2637 towards Zegama. After 3km you reach another pass, Puerto Otsaurte, from where a forestry road on the left leads to the mountain refuge of San Adrián. There is a mountain route to the top of Aitzgorri from here. Alternatively, there is much to explore lower down, including Saint Adrian's cave.

CALENDAR

All year: Griffon Vulture, Sparrowhawk, Common Buzzard, Tawny Owl, Black Woodpecker, Crag Martin, Stonechat, Black Redstart, Mistle Thrush, Common Chiffchaff, Firecrest, Spotted Flycatcher, Nuthatch, Short-toed and Eurasian Treecreepers, Jay, Red-billed and Yellow-billed Choughs, Common Starling, Tree and Rock Sparrows, Citril Finch, Bullfinch, Yellowhammer, Cirl and Rock Buntings.

Breeding season: Egyptian Vulture, Booted Eagle, Wryneck, Water Pipit, Alpine Accentor, Northern Wheatear, Rufous-tailed Rock Thrush, Whitethroat, Garden and Bonelli's Warblers, Pied Flycatcher, Red-backed Shrike.

PLAIAUNDI ECOLOGICAL PARK   PV3 (Guipúzcoa)

Status: Part (24ha) of the much larger Txingudi ZEPA and Ramsar site.

Site description

A reserve reclaimed and created from a former industrial and agricultural area at the mouth of the Ría de Bidasoa in the far east of the País Vasco next to the town of Irún and close to the border with France. The 'park' consists of two saline pools connected by sluices to the tidal river and a freshwater pond, along with islets, reedbeds and intertidal beach. In addition to wildlife habitats the park has been designed with the visitor in mind with good infrastructure for birders, general visitors and school parties.

A nearby larger area of marshland, the Marismas de Jaitzubia, has more recently been restored and is served by footpaths.

Species

A variety of coastal and wetland birds provide interest throughout the year, although the breeding species are generally eclipsed by migrants and winter visitors. The reedbeds and shoreline are worth searching during passage periods, and can be especially interesting during the autumn migration: Spoonbills occur regularly at this season. The avifauna is similar to that of Urdaibai. Natterjack Toads inhabit the reserve.

Timing

Interesting all year round but especially in winter and during passage periods.

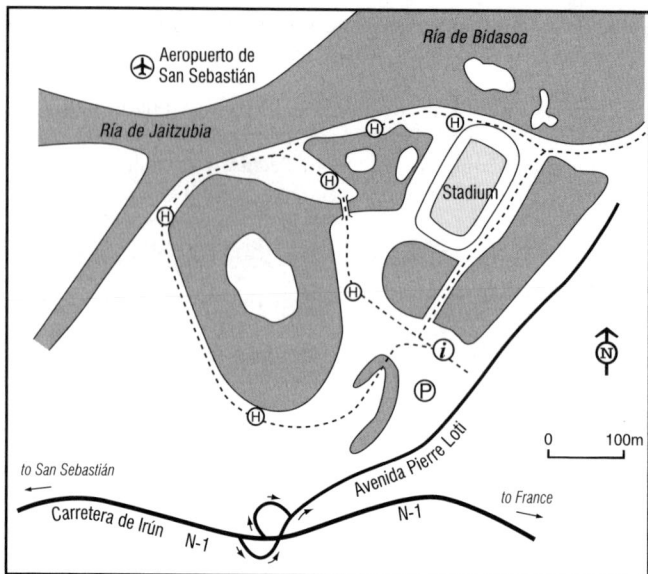

Access

Plaiaundi is in Txingudi Bay in the Bidasoa River estuary, very close to the town centre of Irún, from where you can walk to the park in ten minutes. When arriving by car from San Sebastián follow the N-I to the north of the centre of Irun, from where the Ecological Park is signposted at km-478.

A number of hides, tracks, many interpretation panels and the Txingudi Ekoetxea Interpretation Centre (Tel. 943 619 389) are at the entrance on Avenida Pierre Loti. The Centre is open daily except Mondays. Car parking is available next to the Centre.

The Marismas de Jaitzubia are immediately west of the N-638 airport approach road. They may be reached on foot from Plaiundi but it is best to take the N-638 and turn left after crossing the Ría de Jaitzubia: there are designated car parks on the northern side and footpaths around the marshes.

CALENDAR

All year: Little Grebe, Shag, Little Egret, Grey Heron, Peregrine Falcon, Water Rail, Common Coot, Common Sandpiper, Yellow-legged Gull, Kingfisher.

Breeding season: Hobby, Little Ringed Plover, Yellow Wagtail; Grasshopper, Reed and Great Reed Warblers, Red-backed Shrike.

Winter: Red-throated, Black-throated and Great Northern Divers; Slavonian and Black-necked Grebes, Cormorant, Ringed Plover, Sanderling, Dunlin, Black-tailed and Bar-tailed Godwits, Curlew, Common Redshank, Greenshank, Turnstone, Southern Grey Shrike, Reed Bunting.

Passage periods: Purple Heron, Black Stork, Spoonbill, Red Kite, Osprey, Whimbrel, Little Stint, Spotted Redshank; Mediterranean, Little and Great Black-backed Gulls; Sandwich, Common and Black Terns, Wryneck, Sand Martin, Sedge and Willow Warblers, Bluethroat, Penduline Tit.

BALSAS DE SALBURÚA (Álava)   PV4

Status: Part of a Ramsar site (203ha).

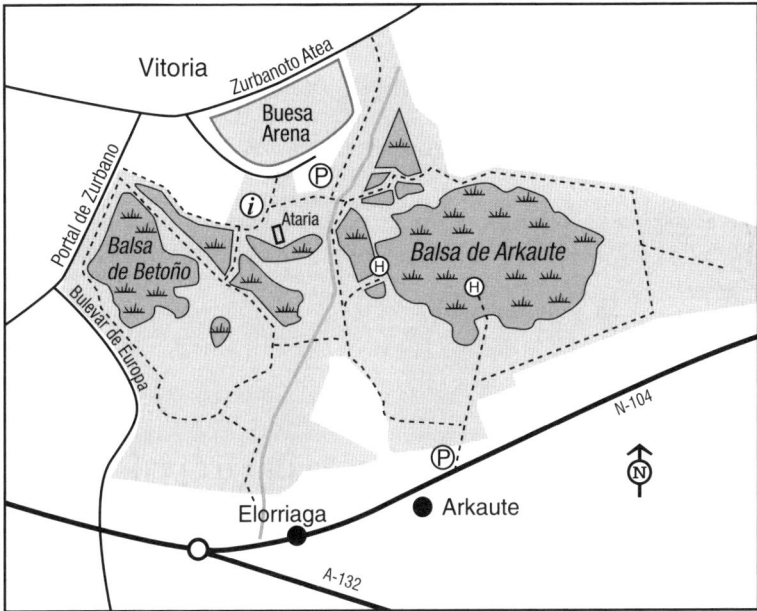

Site description
This wetland is only 5km from the centre of the Basque capital, Vitoria-Gasteiz, in the middle of the Álava plain. It is a key element of the Anillo Verde (Green Ring), a verdant corridor of restored and reclaimed habitat encircling the city, which earned the title of 'European Green Capital' in 2012. There are two principal lagoons at Salburúa, the Balsa de Betoño (21ha) and the Balsa de Arkaute (40ha). Both are shallow basins that were restored from farmland in the mid-1990s and, as well as providing open water, they are part of a complex of pools, ditches, sedge beds, damp pasture and reedbeds. A relict oak grove (8ha) of considerable historic importance is by the Arkaute lagoon. There are also poplar plantations.

Species
This is the principal breeding site in the País Vasco for breeding Black-winged Stilts. Both Garganey and Little Bitterns have nested here. Breeding waterfowl also include Shovelers and Tufted Ducks. Little Ringed Plovers breed and other waders occur on passage. Waterfowl numbers increase in winter, when the site attracts Greylag Geese.

Timing
The lakes are interesting all year round.

Access

The principal entrance, and the futuristic visitors' centre of Ataria (Tel. 945 254 759), is north of the site and is most easily reached by public transport. The L3 bus to the Buesa Arena serves Ataria from the city centre. The centre is open daily except Mondays.

Access by car from the south is from the N-104 Pamplona road, where there is a roadside carpark just east of the village of Arkaute. Marked trails, with hides, give access to the areas of interest.

CALENDAR

All year: Shoveler, Common Pochard, Tufted Duck, Little Grebe, Grey Heron, Water Rail.

Breeding: Garganey, Little Bittern, Black-winged Stilt, Little Ringed Plover.

Winter: Greylag Goose, Teal, Black-necked Grebe, Cormorant, Marsh Harrier, Common Snipe, Curlew, Kingfisher.

Passage: Purple Heron, Black Stork, White Stork, Spoonbill, Avocet, Spotted and Baillon's Crakes, Whiskered and Black Terns, Turtle Dove, Kingfisher, Sand Martin, Sedge Warbler.

OTHER SITES WORTH VISITING

PV5 HOZ DE SOBRÓN (ÁLAVA/BURGOS)

A thickly wooded gorge along the Río Ebro, on the border with Castilla y León. It accommodates a very large Griffon Vulture colony as well as breeding Egyptian Vultures, Red-billed Choughs and other birds of rocky terrain. Take the N-102 for 7km west from Vitoria-Gasteiz and then the A-2622 as far as the T-junction 6km west of Añana. Turn south here on to the A-2625 and continue for 4km to the Río Ebro. Take a left turn here on to the A-2122, leading west along the north bank to the gorge.

PV6 VALDEREJO (ÁLAVA)

A beautiful, sparsely populated valley with limestone crags, pine forest and beechwoods. There is a large Griffon Vulture colony at Vallegrull. Golden Eagles, Peregrine Falcons, Crossbills and Crested Tits are also characteristic. Take the A-2622 west from Vitoria-Gasteiz (see PV5) towards Valdegovia and turn south just before San Millán, where minor roads take you into the heart of the area. There is an Interpretative Centre at Lalastra.

PV7 SIERRA DE ARALAR (GUIPÚZCOA)

A high massif with huge limestone outcrops, upland pastures and beech, Holm Oak and mixed oak woods. It is right in the heart of 'Goierri': which means 'highlands' in Basque. Breeding birds include Booted Eagles, Black Woodpeckers, Citril Finches and Yellow-billed Choughs. Take the N-I south out of San Sebastián towards Vitoria-Gasteiz. Come off at Ordizia for Zaldibia and the sierra along the GI-2133, or at Beasain for Ataun and beyond along the GI-120. There is an information centre at the Puerto de Lizarrusti on the GI-120 at the border with Navarra.

PV8 LAGUARDIA LAGOONS (ÁLAVA)

Four lakes, three of which, Carravalseca, Carralogrone and Musco, are natural waterbodies, whereas the fourth: Prao de Paul, was created by a dam on formerly marshy ground. The three natural water bodies are markedly seasonal, salty and mainly dry in summer. Breeding species include grebes and ducks with Night and Purple Herons and a good variety of waders. The lakes are close to Laguardia, which is on the A-124, 18km north-west of Logroño: the nearest lake, Prao de Paul is about 500m from the village centre whereas Carravalseca is about 2km away.

PV9 MENDIXUR ORNITHOLOGICAL PARK (ÁLAVA)

An important wetland, in the south-eastern tail of the massive Ullibarri-Gamboa Reservoir. It attracts a good range of breeding birds, including several, such as Gadwall and Purple Heron, that are rare in the País Vasco. It is also good for wintering species, which include Black-necked Grebe, Red-crested Pochard and a diversity of other waterfowl. One or more Great Northern Divers may be present in winter. Take N-104 from Vitoria crossing under the main road north (N-1) and then the A-3012 towards Ozaeta. Turn left on the A-4012 to Garaio (where there is information and parking) before you reach Maturana.

PV10 CABO HIGER (GUIPÚZCOA)

A headland on the Spanish/French border at the western extremity of the Bahía de Txingudi (PV3). It offers good seawatching opportunities, especially in autumn and winter, with similar species to those encountered at Cabo Matxitxako (PV1). Take the GI-2261 for 5km northwards from Hondarribia to the lighthouse at the Cape.

LA RIOJA

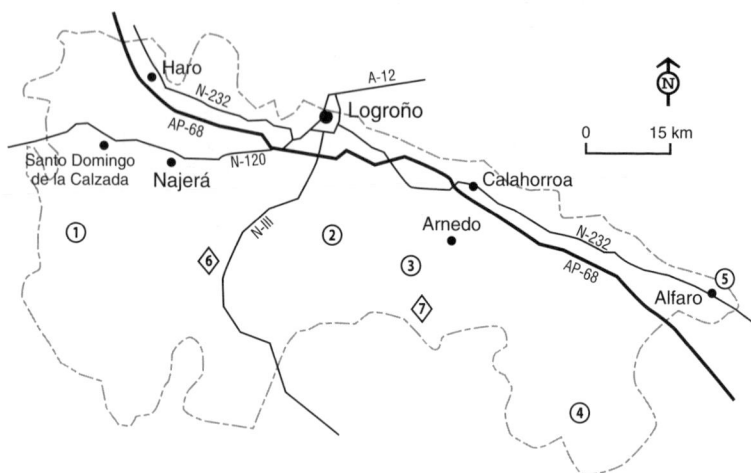

Main sites

R1   Sierra de la Demanda
R2   Peñas de Iregua, Leza y Jubera
R3   Peñas de Arnedillo, Isasa y Turruncún
R4   Sierra de Alcarama and Río Alhama
R5   Sotos de Alfaro

Other sites worth visiting

R6   Obarenes–Sierra de Cantabria
R7   Enciso: La Ruta de los Dinosaurios

The smallest autonomous region in Spain and named after the Río Oja, one of the Ebro tributaries. The Ebro itself forms its northern boundary. For most people however 'Rioja' is synonymous with the very well-known Spanish wines that originate here.

Wine is at the very heart of La Rioja's identity but the region played a key part in the evolution of the modern Castilian language. Some of the earliest words in Castilian Spanish, the modern language of much of Spain, are lines of verse written by a monk, Gonzalo de Berceo, from a Riojan monastery where he appreciated '*un vaso de bon vino*' (a glass of good wine)! Viniculture and winemaking were certainly practised before the Romans arrived. Today the industry is as strong as ever with the main centre of production focused on the area around Haro, a town some 40km north of Logroño, the regional capital. Most wine comes from three zones: Rioja Alta, Rioja Alavesa and Rioja Baja.

With good wine all around, this seems an ideal region in Spain to combine an interest in birds and grapes. Although small, the region does have its wide plains, gorges, the northern mountains of the Sistema Ibérico and riverine woodlands, all on an agreeably accessible scale. La Rioja, despite being much more compact than its neighbours, still offers many opportunities to see a wide diversity of species. The mountainous areas that form part of the Sistema

Ibérico Norte, rising to over 2,000m, include the Sierra de la Demanda (R1), contiguous with the Sierra de Urbíon (CyL12) and other ranges in Castilla y León. Although not as rich in species as the Pyrenees, they do hold Grey Partridge, Alpine Swift, Water Pipit, Citril Finch and, more rarely, Alpine Accentor. The geographical position of La Rioja and its wooded hill landscapes mean that a number of species occur here near or at the southern edge of their breeding range in Spain. If you are heading for Castilla–La Mancha, or further south still, this may be your last chance for Hen Harrier, Woodcock, Marsh Tit, Red-backed Shrike and Yellowhammer, at least during the breeding season.

Wine apart, the greatest interest for birdwatchers in La Rioja is the wooded terrain with its occasional deep ravines, gorges and cliffs. These last hold important populations of Griffon and Egyptian Vultures as at the Iregua, Leza y Jubera gorges (R2). The Peñas de Arnedillo, Isasa y Turruncún (R3) and the Sierra de Alcarama y Río Alhama (R4) also have vulture colonies, along with many other cliff-nesting birds including Bonelli's Eagles, Eagle Owls, Crag Martins, Blue Rock Thrushes, Red-billed Choughs and Rock Sparrows.

La Rioja lacks extensive plains but there are pockets of suitable habitat in the east of the region, in the Ebro Valley, where Montagu's Harriers, Black-bellied Sandgrouse, Stone-curlews and Great Spotted Cuckoos may be found. Bustards are rare here though and, in general, steppe birds are best sought in the adjacent Navarran region of Las Bardenas Reales (N7). Semi-arid rocky areas, such as the Sierra de Alcarama y Río Alhama (R4), also occur in the east and should be visited for Thekla Larks, Tawny Pipits, Black and Black-eared Wheatears and Spectacled Warblers.

Wetland interest is very definitely limited in La Rioja, with most of what there is confined to the rivers and the Río Ebro itself, especially the *sotos*, the riverine woodlands of poplars and willows found along its banks. The best example is the Sotos de Alfaro (R5), in the far north-eastern corner close to the border with Navarra. These woodlands offer Night and Purple Herons and Penduline Tits. La Rioja may be small but it is also famous for something rather large, the dinosaur footprints in the gullies of the Rioja Baja, near Enciso (R7). This site, La Ruta de los Dinosaurios, should not be missed and it also offers a good range of such widespread species as White Stork, Black Kite, Quail, Hoopoe, Dartford and Melodious Warblers and Woodchat Shrike.

Subalpine Warbler

SIERRA DE LA DEMANDA   R1

Status: Reserva Natural. Part of ZEPA 'Sierras de Urbión, Cebollera y Cameros' (139,000ha) that also includes sites R6 and CyL12.

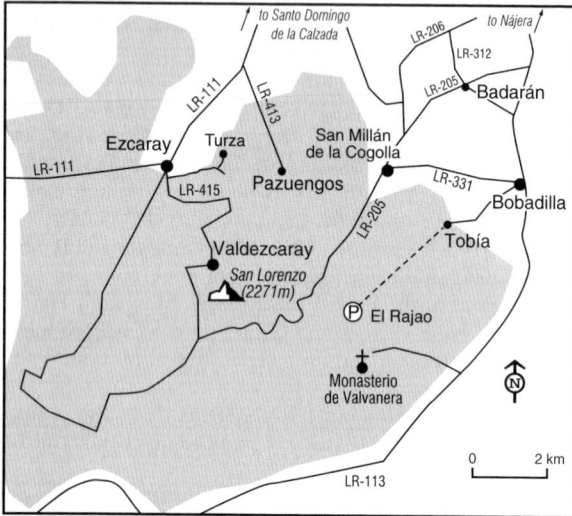

Site description

A mountainous area, part of the Sistema Ibérico Norte, with extensive deciduous woodland of Pyrenean Oak and beech, areas of maquis scrub, alpine pasture and river valleys. Afforestation with Scots Pine has taken place locally. The whole site is very imposing with its high peaks of San Lorenzo (2,271m) and San Millán (2,131m). There is a ski resort at Valdezcaray.

Species

The highest levels have a complement of montane species, including the Alpine Accentor, Water Pipit and Citril Finch. Woodland raptors are another principal attraction, these including Honey-buzzards, Short-toed Eagles, Goshawks, Sparrowhawks and Booted Eagles. Hen Harriers also breed here as do Egyptian Vultures. This area is particularly interesting as it holds southern outliers of the Spanish populations of the Grey Partridge, Woodcock, Marsh Tit, Eurasian Treecreeper and Bullfinch, plus a considerable population of Pied Flycatchers: a local species in Spain. The Sierra sees significant passage, particularly in autumn, of Honey-buzzards, Red Kites, Cranes and, especially, Woodpigeons.

The road along the Turza and Tobía valleys can produce considerable diversity including Egyptian Vultures, Short-toed Eagles, Woodcocks, Rufous-tailed Rock Thrushes, Red-backed Shrikes, Bullfinches and both treecreeper species.

Timing

May and June are the best times to visit.

Access

From Logroño take the A-12 west towards Burgos. There are two main entry points off this road.

Around 25km out of Logroño turn left at Nájera on to the LR-113 southbound. This road follows the eastern and southern boundaries of the reserve, so you need to take one of a number of right turns into the core of the area, for example at Bobadilla to San Millán de la Cogolla (Cárdenas Valley), or again at Bobadilla to Tobía (Tobía Valley) or, 15km further south from Bobadilla on the LR-113, another right turn to Monasterio de Valvanera (Valvanera Valley). Roads, tracks and paths lead you higher up the respective valleys from each of these destinations. An easy circular route (9.8km) through magnificent beechwoods starts from El Rajao recreation area, at the top of the Tobía valley, 8km beyond the village. It is good for Honey-buzzards, Woodcock and Eurasian Treecreepers.

The other main entry point in the area has equally stunning views. Turn left off the N-120 at Santo Domingo de la Calzada and continue on the LR-111 to Ezcaray. From here it is possible to drive around the sierra on a circular route with many opportunities for birding. This is also the route to the ski resort at Valdezcaray. From this resort a path leads up to the peak of San Lorenzo (2,271m), providing the best opportunity for finding such high altitude birds as Water Pipits and Alpine Accentors.

At Ezcaray there is an established walk along the old road to the village of Turza, which starts near the old railway station.

CALENDAR

All year: Grey and Red-legged Partridges, Hen Harrier, Goshawk, Sparrowhawk, Common Buzzard, Golden Eagle, Peregrine Falcon, Woodcock, Tawny and Eagle Owls, Green and Great Spotted Woodpeckers, Sky Lark, Crag Martin, Water Pipit, Alpine Accentor, Blue Rock Thrush, Dartford Warbler, Marsh and Crested Tits, Nuthatch, Eurasian and Short-toed Treecreepers, Red-billed Chough, Citril Finch, Bullfinch, Yellowhammer, Cirl and Rock Buntings.

Breeding season: White Stork, Honey-buzzard, Black Kite, Egyptian Vulture, Short-toed and Booted Eagles, Tree Pipit, Common Redstart, Northern Wheatear, Subalpine, Melodious and Bonelli's Warblers, Pied Flycatcher, Red-backed Shrike.

Passage periods: Red Kite, Honey-buzzard, Crane, Woodpigeon.

PEÑAS DE IREGUA, LEZA Y JUBERA   R2

Status: ZEPA (7,840ha). Part of the 'Valles del Jubera, Leza, Cidacos y Alhama' Biosphere Reserve (117,000ha) which also includes site R3.

Site description

Precipitous gorges that have been cut into the limestone by tributaries of the River Ebro. They are south of Logroño, where the Ebro flows through the mountains of the Sistema Ibérico Norte. The site includes sectors of the rivers Iregua, Leza and Jubera. Deciduous woodland and open country occur between the three gorges.

Species

Griffon Vultures (over 100 pairs), Golden Eagles and Eagle Owls are the main reasons for its designation as a ZEPA and these valleys comprise the best site in La Rioja for raptors. Bonelli's Eagle occurs at least occasionally and has nested. There are occasional sightings of Lammergeiers and Black Vultures. Other cliff-nesters in the gorges include Common Kestrels, Crag and House Martins, Black Redstarts, Rufous-tailed and Blue Rock Thrushes, Red-billed Choughs, Jackdaws, Ravens and Rock Sparrows. The woodlands between the gorges should not be overlooked and have Short-toed and Booted Eagles, Tawny Owls, Great Spotted Woodpeckers and many passerines.

Timing

Spring and summer are most productive.

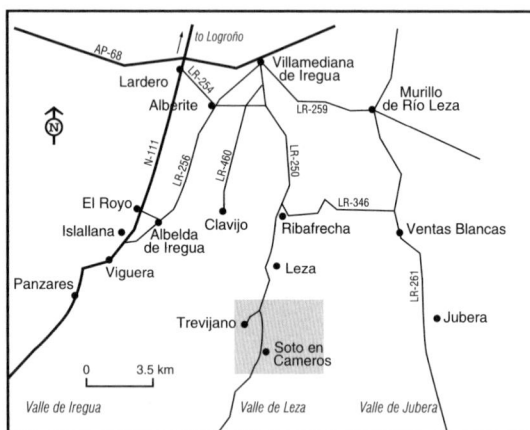

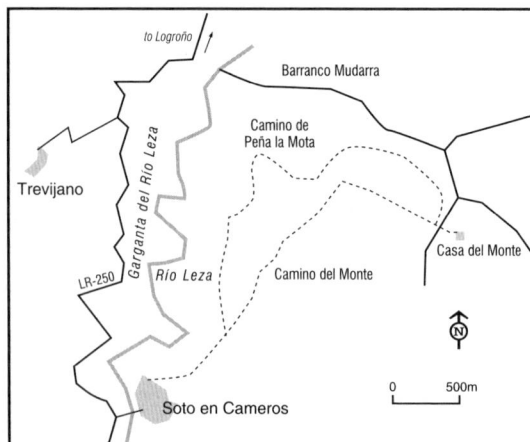

Access

Peña Iregua For Iregua Gorge take the N-111 south out of Logroño down the valley. The gorge is deepest between the villages of Islallana, Viguera and Panzares. A footpath to Viguera (3km) along the right bank follows the river southwards from the bridge at Islallana.

Peña Leza For Leza Gorge take the LR-250, south of Villamediana de Legua towards Laguna de Cameros. The gorge is between the villages of Leza and Soto en Cameros. There are great views from the road along the Río Leza. From Soto en Cameros you can walk from the hermitage along the top of the gorge along the Camino de Peña la Mota.

Peña Jubera For Jubera Gorge, use the same local road out of Logroño but at Villamediana de Iregua take the LR-259 to Murillo de Río Leza. From here take the LR-261, which follows the river south: the gorge can be seen from the village of Jubera itself.

The country around is most easily explored by taking one of the many minor roads that run off the N-111, LR-250 or LR-259.

CALENDAR

All year: Red-legged Partridge, Lammergeier (occasional), Griffon Vulture, Black Vulture (occasional), Golden and Bonelli's Eagles, Common Kestrel, Peregrine Falcon, Rock Dove, Tawny and Eagle Owls, Great Spotted Woodpecker, Thekla Lark, Crag Martin, Black Redstart, Blue Rock Thrush, Dartford Warbler, Zitting Cisticola, Red-billed Chough, Spotless Starling, Jackdaw, Raven, Rock Sparrow, Serin, Cirl and Rock Buntings.

Breeding season: Egyptian Vulture, Short-toed and Booted Eagles, Scops Owl, Alpine Swift, Bee-eater, House Martin, Tawny Pipit, Rufous-tailed Rock Thrush, Melodious and Bonelli's Warblers.

Winter: Alpine Accentor, Wallcreeper.

PEÑAS DE ARNEDILLO, ISASA Y TURRUNCÚN   R3

Status: ZEPA (2,400 ha). Part of the 'Valles del Jubera, Leza, Cidacos y Alhama' Biosphere Reserve (117,000ha) which also includes site R2.

Site description
An area of chiefly limestone cliffs and rocky outcrops in a region of extensively deforested rugged hills. The vegetation now consists largely of Mediterranean scrub with vineyards, orchards and small copses on some slopes.

Species
The cliffs and rocky areas have breeding Griffon and Egyptian Vultures,

Bonelli's Eagles, Peregrines, Eagle Owls, Alpine Swifts, Crag Martins and Blue Rock Thrushes.

Exploration of the countryside around, both open ground and scrub, can be rewarding. Typical species include Bee-eater, Tawny Pipit, Black and Black-eared Wheatears, Dartford and Subalpine Warblers and Ortolan Bunting.

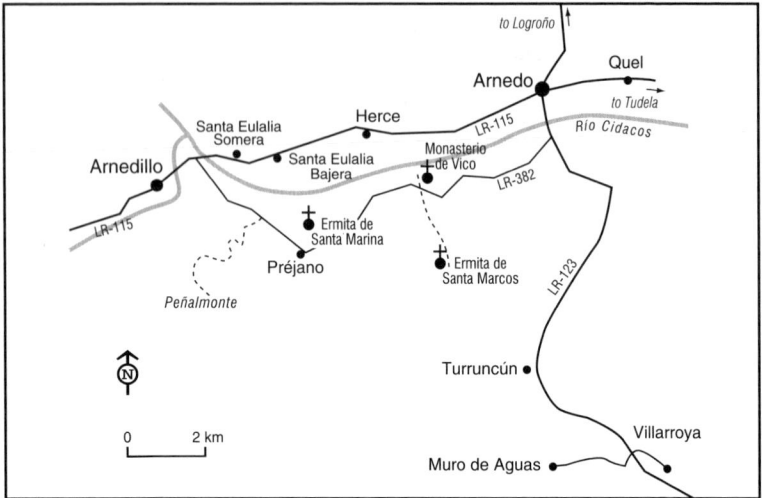

Timing
Spring and early summer are the most productive.

Access
From Logroño take the N-232 east some 35km to El Vilar de Arnedo and then follow the LR-123 southwards for 10km to the town of Arnedo. The area of interest lies in the triangle between Arnedo in the east, Arnedillo in the west: along the LR-115, and Préjano in the south. The minor road from Préjano to Arnedillo takes you to the Peñalmonte cliffs which have both Egyptian and Griffon Vultures. A track following an old railway line runs between the village of Herce and Arnedillo, and a vulture viewing area and Interpretation Centre (Mirador del Buitre) is signposted from the LR-115 800m east of Arnedillo.

A track from the Monasterio de Vico near the Río Cidacos, through pines and groves to the Ermita de San Marcos, allows you to see many of the scrub and open-country species.

CALENDAR

All year: Red-legged Partridge, Griffon Vulture, Bonelli's Eagle, Peregrine Falcon, Rock Dove, Little and Eagle Owls, Thekla Lark, Crag Martin, Black Redstart, Black Wheatear, Blue Rock Thrush, Dartford Warbler, Zitting Cisticola, Red-billed Chough, Jackdaw, Carrion Crow, Spotless Starling, Rock Sparrow; Cirl, Rock and Corn Buntings.

Breeding season: Egyptian Vulture, Short-toed Eagle, Scops Owl, Alpine Swift, Bee-eater, Hoopoe, House Martin, Tawny Pipit, Nightingale, Black-eared Wheatear, Rufous-tailed Rock Thrush, Subalpine Warbler, Woodchat Shrike, Ortolan Bunting.

SIERRA DE ALCARAMA AND RÍO ALHAMA   R4

Status: ZEPA (8,780ha).

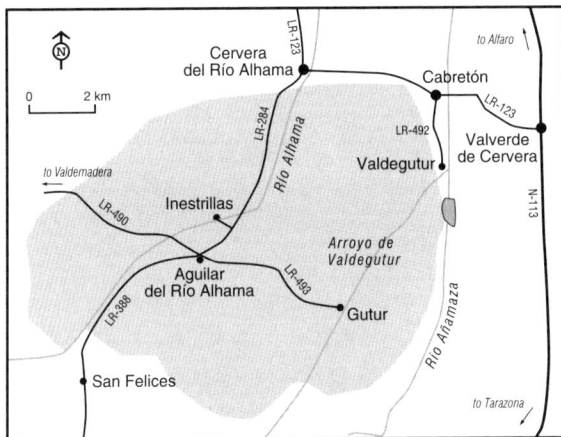

Site description

An area of open country with Mediterranean scrub of Rosemary, genista, juniper, thyme, Kermes Oaks and scattered trees, tucked away in the south-east corner of La Rioja. Willows and poplars flank the rivers. Gullies and cliffs are important features. The impressive river gorge below the village of Valdegutur houses a notable array of rupestral species and is a must when visiting the area.

Species

Another important area for vultures and raptors, with a sizeable colony of Griffon Vultures. It also has breeding Egyptian Vultures, Short-toed Eagles, Peregrines and Eagle Owls. Bonelli's Eagle occurs at least occasionally and may breed. Other birds associated with the rocks and cliff faces include Common Kestrels, Rock Doves, Crag Martins, Black Redstarts, Black-eared and Black Wheatears, Rufous-tailed and Blue Rock Thrushes, Red-billed Choughs and Rock Sparrows.

The cultivated areas in the valleys and riverine woodlands are also of interest, and support Nightingales, Cetti's and Sardinian Warblers and Serins. The scrub areas have Tawny Pipits, Dartford and Spectacled Warblers and Ortolan Buntings.

Timing

Spring and early summer are the most productive.

Access

The area of interest is west of the N-113 at Valverde de Cervera. It can be reached from the AP-68 Logroño/Zaragoza motorway: leave at exit 16

(Alfaro) and head south past Citruénigo to the N-113. Turn west at Valverde de Cervera on the LR-123 to Cabretón and Cervera del Río Alhama. No specific walks are recommended but much of the area is easily explored by investigating the many local tracks in the countryside. It is worth driving to Valdemadera, and also to the main gorge at Valdegutur: 2km south of Cabretón on the LR-492. A track from Valdegutur leads to the gorge.

CALENDAR

All year: Red-legged Partridge, Griffon Vulture, Bonelli's Eagle, Common Kestrel, Peregrine Falcon, Eagle Owl, Rock Dove, Great Spotted Woodpecker, Thekla Lark, Black Redstart, Black Wheatear, Blue Rock Thrush, Cetti's, Sardinian and Dartford Warblers, Red-billed Chough, Raven, Rock Sparrow, Serin, Rock Bunting.

Breeding season: Egyptian Vulture, Short-toed Eagle, Alpine Swift, Bee-eater, Wryneck, Crag Martin, Tawny Pipit, Black-eared Wheatear, Rufous-tailed Rock Thrush, Spectacled and Subalpine Warblers, Nightingale, Golden Oriole, Red-backed Shrike, Ortolan Bunting.

SOTOS DE ALFARO   R5

Status: Reserva Natural 'Sotos del Ebro en Alfaro' (933ha).

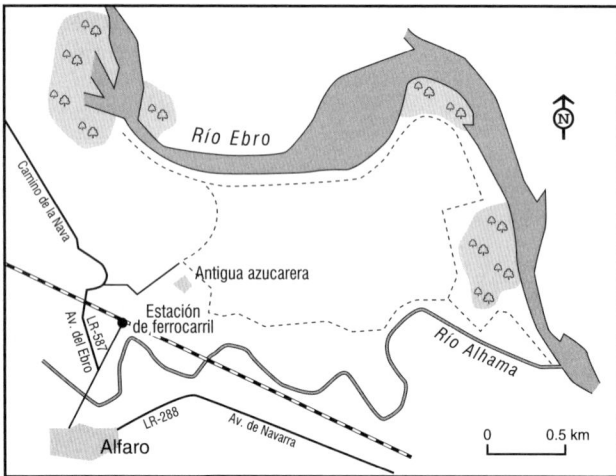

Site description

Riverine woodland on the banks of the River Ebro, mainly of Black Poplar but also other species including willows and tamarisks. Such woodlands were much more extensive in the past but are now restricted to small pockets along the Ebro. Unfortunately, and despite its protected status, this site was severely affected by channel-management works in 2015–16, which included felling many trees. It remains to be seen whether the site will retain its interest in future.

White Stork

Species

Despite its small size this riverine woodland has (or had) an interesting breeding community, including Purple and Night Herons, Melodious Warblers and Penduline Tits. Lesser Spotted Woodpeckers, associated with riparian woodland in Spain, occur here.

The village of Alfaro is well worth a visit in its own right for its spectacular colony of White Storks, with over 190 breeding pairs. Most of them are on the roof of a church, the Colegiata de San Miguel, probably a world record for a single building!

Timing

Late spring visits are recommended.

Access

Take the N-232 south-eastwards out of Logroño and follow the Río Ebro to the town of Alfaro, where there is a visitors' centre (Tel. 941 182 999) in the Plaza de España. Full details of the site and directions can be obtained at the centre but basically you need to head for the railway station and cross the railway line, from where a track to the right takes you towards the *sotos* and the river.

CALENDAR

All year: Red Kite, Common Sandpiper, Barn Owl, Kingfisher, Green and Lesser Spotted Woodpeckers, Cetti's Warbler, Zitting Cisticola, Firecrest, Short-toed Treecreeper, Penduline Tit, Spotless Starling, Serin, Cirl Bunting.

Breeding season: White Stork, Purple and Night Herons, Black Kite, Hobby, Turtle Dove, Scops Owl, Bee-eater, Hoopoe, Wryneck, Sand Martin, Nightingale, Great Reed and Melodious Warblers, Woodchat Shrike, Golden Oriole.

OTHER SITES WORTH VISITING

R6   OBARENES–SIERRA DE CANTABRIA

A mid-altitude sierra, partly deforested but with mixed maquis scrub and some remnant forest. Cliffs and ravines have nesting Griffon and Egyptian Vultures. Take the N-232 west from Logroño past Haro to Tirgo and then north on the LR-202 for an introduction to the area.

R7   ENCISO: LA RUTA DE LOS DINOSAURIOS

An exciting site with dinosaur fossils and footprints in rocks. There is plenty to see in the way of living birds as well, with Bee-eaters, Golden Orioles and Melodious Warblers. It is in the south of the region, starting from the village of Enciso on the LR-115 between Arnedo and Soria. Enciso has a dinosaur museum, on the LR-286 just south of the river. The track begins on the opposite side of the Río Cidacos between two hermitages.

Serin

VALENCIA (Comunidad Valenciana)

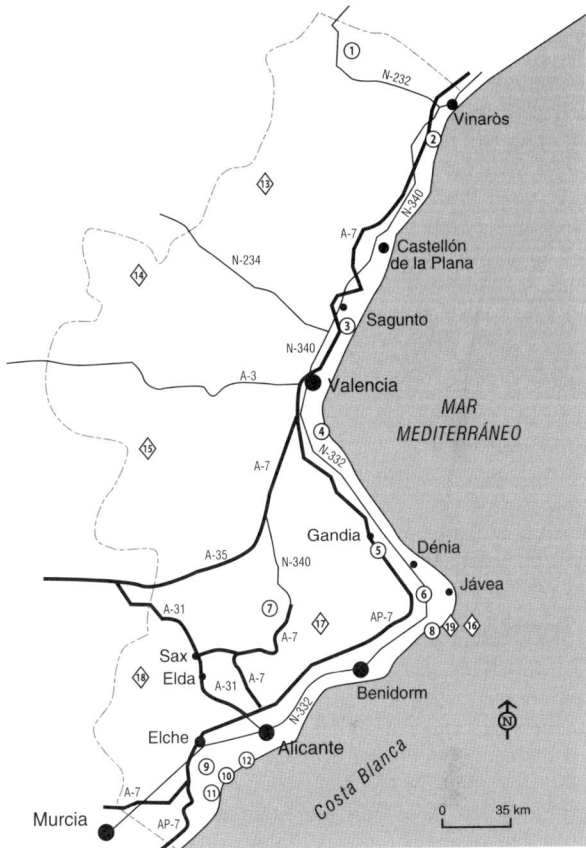

Main sites
V1   Els Ports–Maestrat
V2   Prat de Cabanes–Torreblanca
V3   Marjal de Moros
V4   Albufera de Valencia
V5   Marjal de Pego-Oliva
V6   Sierra de Montgó–Cabo de San Antoni
V7   Carrascal de la Fuente Roja
V8   Peñón de Ifach and Salinas de Calpe
V9   El Hondo de Elche
V10   Salinas de Santa Pola
V11   Lagunas de la Mata and Torrevieja
V12   Clot de Galvany

Other sites worth visiting
V13   Peñagolosa
V14   Alto Turia
V15   Hoces del Río Cabriel
V16   Isla de Tabarca
V17   Sierra de Aitana
V18   Laguna de Salinas
V19   Cabo de la Nao

This long but relatively narrow coastal region stretches for over 300km from its border with Murcia in the south up to Cataluña in the north. The Comunidad Valenciana comprises three provinces: Castellón in the north, Valencia in the centre and Alicante in the south. It is one of the most fertile areas in Europe, the 'land of oranges and rice', although water availability is a growing problem. It is also the original home of one of Spain's best known dishes, paella. Despite intensification of agriculture and the continuing ravages of the tourist industry, particularly on the Costa Blanca, there is much to interest birders in its nationally important coastal wetlands.

The inland sierras have escaped the fate of the coastline and are a million miles away from the excesses of package holidays. Many of the hills and mountains are limestone, with peaks and gorges, and most are also well clothed in a variety of woodland and scrub. As a result, they are home to a diverse range of species with raptors well represented: they include both Golden and Bonelli's Eagles, along with Eagle Owls. The uplands of the south and north of the region differ, with some species mainly restricted to the north. These include Griffon and Egyptian Vultures, Dipper, Great Spotted Woodpecker, Dunnock, Common Redstart, Rufous-tailed Rock Thrush, Nuthatch, Citril Finch and Ortolan Bunting. European Nightjars also have a strong population in the north.

It is, however, to the coast that the majority of birders will be drawn, both as a base for their holiday perhaps and also because Valencia still, perhaps surprisingly, has some very fine coastal marshes, lagoons and saltpans. These wetlands are much smaller and more heavily fragmented than they once were, and some have suffered further from urban encroachment in recent years, but they are still of immense value to birds. There are wetlands along the whole coastal strip but the most famous is La Albufera de Valencia (V4). One of the most important sites in Spain for wintering wildfowl, especially Shovelers and Red-crested Pochards, it also supports a huge range of other species throughout the year. There are good numbers of herons and egrets in particular, the large breeding population of Squacco Herons being especially noteworthy. It is also important for breeding terns and Collared Pratincoles. Other wetlands in the northern half of the region are not as extensive as La Albufera but still hold a similar range of species. Among these, the Prat de Cabanes–Torreblanca (V2) and the Marjal de Pego-Oliva (V5), are particularly good sites for seeing the Moustached Warbler.

The southern wetlands, in Alicante province, include some very interesting sites. Perhaps the best of these is El Hondo (V9), now well known as a regular wintering site for one or more Greater Spotted Eagles and also for the regular presence of both Marbled and White-headed Ducks. These are among the highlights of a very diverse avifauna that includes other wildfowl, waders, terns and passerines. El Hondo never fails to produce one or more national rarities each year. The other principal southern wetlands; the Santa Pola saltpans (V10), the Laguna de La Mata (V11) and the Clot de Galvany (V12) are all highly recommended for the diverse and ever-changing communities of wetland species.

Cliffs are lacking from most of the coastline except in the northern half of Alicante, including the area around the Parque Natural de Montgó (V6), Cabo de La Nao (V19) and the Peñón de Ifach (V8). These areas are good for migrants and offer seawatching opportunities. The breeding birds include

Pallid Swifts and, locally, Bonelli's Eagles and Peregrines.

While the south of Valencia is semi-arid in nature, it lacks the steppe habitats and the birds that go with them. Certain species typical of steppe, such as Greater and Lesser Short-toed Larks and Stone-curlew, can be found associated with areas of saltpans. The typical species of the wider countryside include Little Owl, Hoopoe, Red-rumped Swallow, Black Wheatear and Woodchat Shrike.

The Western Olivaceous Warbler and Rufous-tailed Scrub-robin, two sought-after species, occur in Valencia, most often outside the 'listed' sites included here. Olivaceous Warblers favour low scrub, notably tamarisks along water courses: unfortunately they are scarce and declining in the region. The Scrub-robins are typical of orchards and olive groves throughout Alicante province. It is important to bear in mind that both these species are among the latest summer visitors to arrive in Spain and you would be lucky to see them before May – or later than August.

ELS PORTS–MAESTRAT (Castellón)   V1

Status: No special protection.

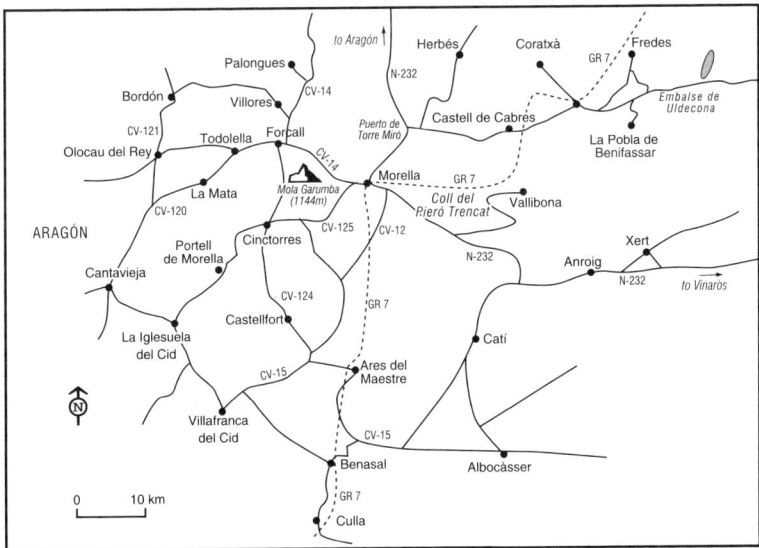

Site description

The Els Ports and Maestrat districts comprise a very attractive low mountain range (700–1,400m) in the northernmost corner of Valencia. They are contiguous with El Maestrazo in Aragón (AR25). Forestry and sheep production are the main land uses. The area has a relatively good infrastructure but there are only scattered villages and the population density is fairly low. The hillsides and mountain slopes are clothed in Aleppo Pine, small mixed oak woods and smaller amounts of beech, Box, Holly and juniper with large expanses of Holm Oak scrub. Riverside woodland is also well represented. Within the forest complex is a complicated mosaic of pasture, craggy peaks and frequent cliffs and river gorges, with occasional hermitages and sleepy mountain villages.

The numerous religious monuments reflect the historical importance of these towns and villages in medieval times. The Tinença de Benifassár area in particular has been appreciated for its natural beauty for centuries and is little changed in many ways. The celebrated local botanist and naturalist Cavanilles described the Tinença as an area 'surrounded and closed in on all sides by tall calcareous mountains, snow-covered in winter, which penetrate to the midst of it, alternating with deep gorges...'

Species

Given the great variety of land-form, altitude, land management and habitat, it is easy to appreciate that the whole area offers a correspondingly wide range of bird species. El Ports–Maestrat is a very good upland area for raptors with several resident pairs of Bonelli's and Golden Eagles and Eagle Owls. The woodlands add to this diversity with breeding Goshawks, Booted and Short-toed Eagles and passerines such as Bonelli's Warblers. The more open woodland areas support Wrynecks and Scops Owls, while the scrub holds Dartford and Spectacled Warblers. Cliff faces and gorges criss-cross the area, attracting Alpine Swifts and Crag Martins, with Dippers along the rivers. This is one of the few areas in Valencia with breeding Egyptian Vultures, along with a number of other birds not found in the southern sierras of the region. They include Griffon Vultures, Rufous-tailed Rock Thrushes, Nuthatches, Common Redstarts and Ortolan Buntings. Golden Orioles, Red-backed Shrikes, Great Spotted Cuckoos and Bee-eaters frequent the lower reaches.

The area is noted for its population of Spanish Ibexes, and also has Wild Cats and Wild Boars.

Timing

An interesting region throughout the year but best in spring, from April onwards into June. Some of the tracks through the forests and alongside gorges can get a little tricky when wet, in early spring and autumn particularly.

Ortolan Bunting

Access

From the coast take the N-232 from Vinaròs towards Zaragoza for 64km to Morella, at the heart of the region. If travelling south along the coastal AP-7 motorway leave at exit 42 for Vinaròs. There are various points of access once within the area but Morella can be used as the focal point, as a number of good roads and tracks that radiate from there. Morella, the capital of the Els Ports district, dominates the horizon for miles around, with 'cubist' houses clinging to its steep slopes and crowned by a rocky summit bearing the remains of the town's castle.

Tinença de Benifassár can easily be reached from Morella. Continue along the N-232 towards the Aragón border and more specifically the Puerto de Torré Miró, where you turn right along the CV-105 to Castell de Cabres, El Boixar, Fredes and La Pobla de Benifassár.

In addition to the many roads across the area, there are also numerous forest and mountain trails suitable for mountain bikes, and both long-distance and short-distance walking routes. The GR7 long-distance trail, indicated by red and white painted posts, crosses the district and links various towns such as Fredes, El Boixar, Vallibona, Morella, Ares del Maestre, Benesal and Culla. The section between Morella and Ares del Maestre runs through terrain that is fairly easy to cover and with a great variety of habitat and bird species. The section between Morella and the Coll del Peiró Trencat, towards Vallibona, is also worth trying, with both open and wooded areas including a section alongside the Río Cérvol.

The GR7 branches off into a series of shorter routes signposted as PRs and indicated by yellow and white painted posts. For example, the PR-V-2 from Morella descends along the Costa del Nogueral and crosses the River Bergantes to climb the Mola de la Garumba (1,144m), winding to the top of the summit and offering impressive views over Morella, an area good for birds of prey, and then descends to the town of Forcall. Another short-distance route, connects Fredes to the Ulldecona Reservoir and then passes through the spectacular Portell de l'Inferno ('hell pass'): this route offers particularly scenic views and climbs up and down throughout its length.

CALENDAR

All year: Griffon Vulture, Goshawk, Sparrowhawk, Golden and Bonelli's Eagles, Peregrine Falcon, Rock Dove; Tawny, Long-eared and Eagle Owls, Kingfisher, Dipper, Blue Rock Thrush; Dartford, Spectacled and Sardinian Warblers, Firecrest, Nuthatch, Red-billed Chough, Rock Sparrow, Rock Bunting.

Breeding season: Egyptian Vulture, Short-toed and Booted Eagles, Hobby, Great Spotted Cuckoo, Scops Owl, Red-necked Nightjar, Alpine Swift, Bee-eater, Wryneck, Greater Short-toed Lark, Crag Martin, Common Redstart, Black-eared Wheatear, Rufous-tailed Rock Thrush; Olivaceous, Subalpine and Orphean Warblers, Ortolan Bunting.

PRAT DE CABANES–TORREBLANCA   V2
(Castellón)

Status: Parque Natural, ZEPA and Ramsar site (812ha).

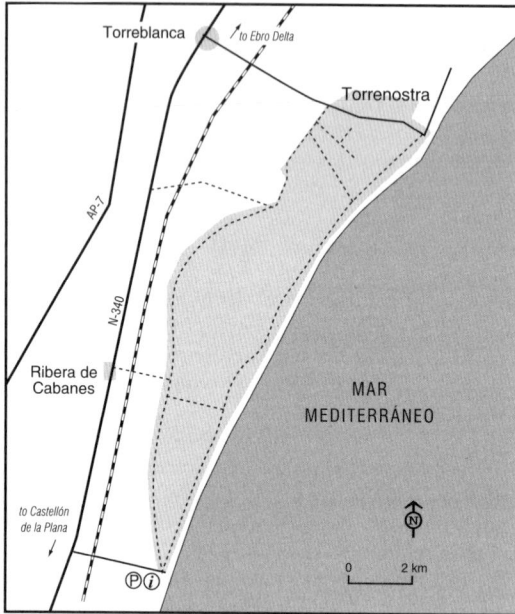

Site description

The marshland of the Prat de Cabanes–Torreblanca extends south from Torreblanca for 7km. It is only separated from the sea by a narrow stretch of shingle and sand dunes. This important brackish coastal lagoon or *albufera* has gradually silted up and the area has developed into a rich mixture of wetland habitats. Most of it is now wet fen, sedgebeds and reedbeds with pockets of open water, scrub and saltflats along the seaward boundary. Much of the remaining open water is at the northern end and includes lagoons created from peat workings The scrubby areas are towards the south. The site is flooded in winter and some parts retain open water into the summer.

Species

This coastal marsh is important for many wetland birds. Some 50 pairs of Moustached Warblers nest here, a considerable reduction from the several hundred that occurred formerly. It is also a good site for seeing Collared Pratincoles: around 30 pairs regularly breed here, with up to 100 pairs in some years. Good views can be had of these colonial breeders both on and around their nesting sites as they feed on insects over open water, reeds, scrub and the nearby rice fields.

El Prat de Cabanes is very important for breeding Montagu's Harriers. Marsh Harriers have bred here but are common in winter. There are good breeding populations of Red-crested Pochards, Little Bitterns, Black-winged Stilts and Kentish Plovers. The reeds also support numbers of Zitting Cisticolas, Reed and Great Reed Warblers, and Reed Buntings. This stretch of the coast can give good views of Audouin's Gulls in summer. The area is good for passage migrants in spring and autumn, especially at the southern end of the site.

Timing
The site is interesting all year round, although in high summer there is little open water and the beach is generally much busier. April and May are the most productive months when a visit combines the interest and excitement of birds on passage with those species that have begun to breed. The autumn can also be interesting but the site can be disturbed during the duck hunting season (October–January).

Access
The wetland is on the coast north of Castellón de la Plana, off the N-340 coast road at Ribera de Cabanes at km-92 towards the Torre de la Sal Aquaculture Centre, where the Information Centre (open Wednesday–Friday and on the first weekend of each month; Tel. 964 319 777) is located at the southern end of the site. Take the Oropesa exit from the AP-7 to join the N-340 northwards. From Torreblanca you can get to the reserve from Torrenostra beach. Some car parking is available at both the northern and southern access points and there are marked trails at both ends.

CALENDAR

All year: Marbled Duck, Red-crested Pochard, Little and Great Crested Grebes, Cattle and Little Egrets, Water Rail, Common Coot; Little Ringed and Kentish Plovers, Zitting Cisticola, Cetti's and Moustached Warblers, Reed Bunting.

Breeding season: Little Bittern, Purple Heron, Montagu's Harrier, Black-winged Stilt, Avocet, Collared Pratincole, Audouin's Gull; Sandwich and Little Terns, Greater Short-toed Lark, Nightingale; Savi's, Reed and Great Reed Warblers, Woodchat Shrike.

Winter: Black-necked Grebe, Marsh Harrier, Wigeon, Gadwall, Teal, Avocet, Audouin's and Mediterranean Gulls, Grey Plover, Little Stint, Kingfisher, Penduline Tit, Bluethroat.

Passage periods: Greylag Goose, Garganey, Greater Flamingo, Osprey, Black-tailed Godwit, Curlew Sandpiper, Alpine Swift, Northern Wheatear, Bluethroat, Olivaceous Warbler.

MARJAL DE MOROS (Valencia)   V3

Status: ZEPA (620ha).

Site description
In addition to the well-known wetlands, Valencia has a number of smaller coastal marshes between Castellón de la Plana and Valencia city. The most

important of these, the Marjal de Moros, is a regional nature reserve. It is relatively small but has a good variety of habitats including coastal shingle scrub, saltflats, open water lagoons, disused ricefields and reedbeds, as well as a Mediterranean woodland garden around the information centre.

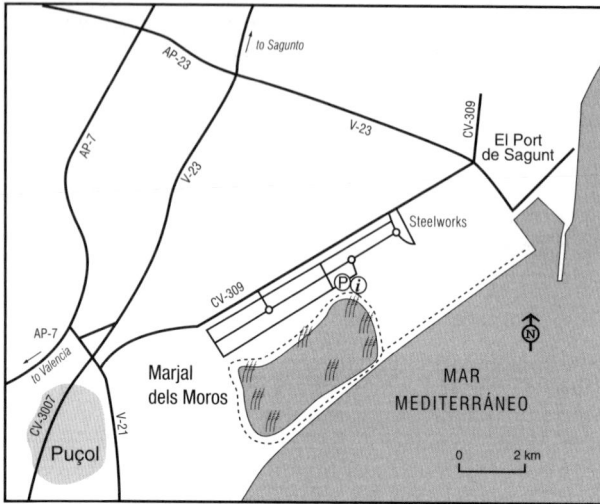

Species
A few pairs of Marbled Ducks and Red-crested Pochards breed in some years. Other attractions include breeding Little Bitterns, Purple Herons and Purple Swamphens and small colonies of Collared Pratincoles and Black-winged Stilts as well as of Common, Little and Whiskered Terns. The breeding warbler community includes Moustached and Savi's Warblers. Aquatic Warblers occur on passage, particularly in April. In addition the area attracts a remarkable range of passage waders and waterfowl. Red-knobbed Coots have been introduced here.

Timing
The site is worth visiting throughout the year, including the winter, but is especially good in spring and during passage periods.

Access
The site is south of Sagunto (Sagunt) off the CV-309. The easiest access route is via the V-23 coastal motorway, which may be reached from exits 50 or 51 of the AP-7 motorway. Follow the V-23 towards El Port de Sagunt and exit at the second roundabout on to the CV-309. After around 2km a network of service roads on the left marks the location of an industrial estate, as yet unbuilt in 2015. Follow these along their coastward edge to a signposted track that leads to the site and the visitors' centre (Tel. 962 680 000): which is open mornings and afternoons on Mondays to Thursdays, and mornings only on Fridays and weekends. Park outside the centre if you visit or plan to stay when it is closed. Follow signs to the wetland through the gardens and adjacent fields. A circular trail (allow three hours) follows the wetland boundary, where there are several hides and viewing platforms.

CALENDAR

All year: Mallard, Red-crested Pochard, Little Grebe, Water Rail, Purple Swamphen, Red-knobbed Coot, Kentish Plover, Common Redshank, Zitting Cisticola; Cetti's and Moustached Warblers.

Breeding season: Marbled Duck, Little Bittern, Night and Purple Herons, Black-winged Stilt, Collared Pratincole, Little Ringed Plover; Common, Little and Whiskered Terns, Scops Owl, Lesser Short-toed Lark, Yellow Wagtail; Savi's, Reed and Great Reed Warblers.

Winter: Greylag Goose, Common Shelduck,

Wigeon, Gadwall, Pintail, Teal (has bred), Red-crested and Common Pochards, Ferruginous Duck (has bred), Tufted Duck, Great Crested and Black-necked Grebes, Cattle and Little Egrets, Grey Heron, Marsh Harrier, Common Coot, Avocet; Ringed, Golden and Grey Plovers, Little Stint, Dunlin, Ruff, Jack and Common Snipe, Curlew, Greenshank, Common Sandpiper, Sandwich Tern, Kingfisher, Bluethroat, Reed Bunting.

Passage periods: Garganey (has bred), White Stork, Glossy Ibis, Squacco Heron, Marsh Harrier, Osprey, Black-tailed Godwit, Little Gull, Aquatic Warbler.

LA ALBUFERA DE VALENCIA (Valencia)   V4

Status: Parque Natural, ZEPA and Ramsar site (21,120ha).

Site description

This vast lagoon and its fringing ricefields, extending to the immediate south of the city of Valencia, comprise one of the largest remaining wetland areas and one of the most important ornithological sites in Spain. Its designation as a natural park in 1986 has played a major part in protecting the area from further development and pollution.

Around 8,000 years ago a 30km-long sandbar, including what is now the Playa de La Devesa, cut off a portion of the sea, forming the Albufera. The lagoon originally covered some 30,000ha but has progressively shrunk, partly as a result of natural sedimentation but also through land reclamation for agriculture; rice has been cultivated here since the 15th century. The lagoon now covers only 2,800ha, including reedbeds and the islands known as matas, although an additional 18,200ha of marsh, ricefields and sand dunes are also included within the natural park. The lake itself is very shallow, typically 0.5m deep and only 2.5m at its deepest. Industrial, urban and tourist developments are responsible for more recent peripheral losses to the wetland.

A narrow strip of sand protects the wetland area from the sea. Aleppo Pine woodland and dense scrub have developed on the dunes, giving way to more open low vegetation to seaward where the dune slacks provide damp hollows. Four canals with sluices, the *golas*, connect the lagoon and surrounding wet-lands with the sea and each has its own characteristic flora and fauna. The ricefields are flooded with water from the lagoon via irrigation ditches.

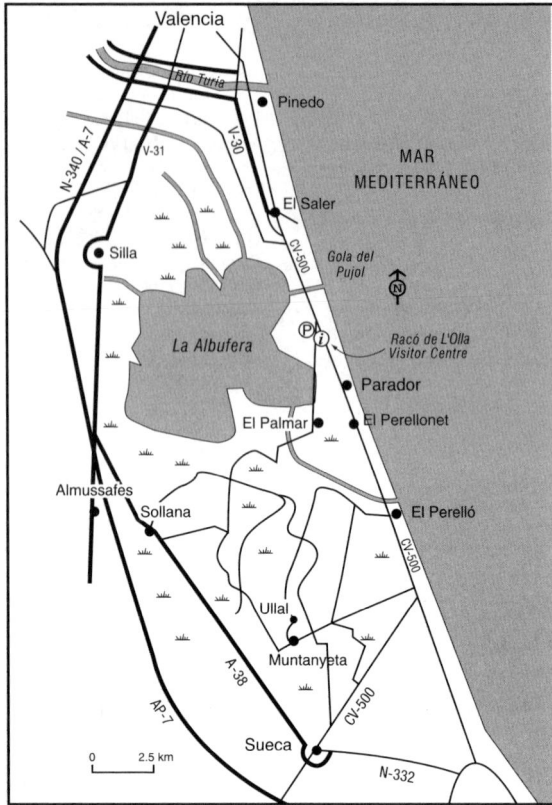

Species

The Albufera and its surrounding ricefields comprise one of the most important wetlands in Spain, attracting a great diversity of breeding, migrant and
wintering species. Almost anything can turn up here. This is despite an
historical decline in water quality through eutrophication, a consequence of
agricultural fertiliser run-off, that has in turn led to a decline in the submerged
macrophytes that formerly sustained large populations of Coots in particular.
Nevertheless, over 250 species have been recorded here and about 100 species
breed or have bred within the reserve.

Breeding and wintering herons are very well represented. There are around
250 pairs of Little Bitterns, 100–150 pairs of Night Herons, 1,000+ pairs of
Cattle Egrets, 1,500 pairs of Little Egrets, 100 pairs of Squacco Herons, up to
1,000 pairs of Grey Herons and up to 100 pairs of Purple Herons. The Great
White Egret has bred and is now an obvious presence on the ricefields in
winter. Another relative newcomer is the Glossy Ibis which has also nested
and which seems ever more abundant on the ricefields in autumn and winter;
flocks totalling over 3,000 have been present in recent years. Other noteworthy
breeding waterbirds include the Common Shelduck, Red-crested Pochard and
a few Marbled Ducks. Purple Swamphens and Red-knobbed Coots have been
introduced to the lagoon; the former are common and often quite obvious on

the fringes of reedmace and reedbeds but the latter are represented by just a few individuals and are elusive. There is a significant resident population of the Moustached Warbler and a few breeding pairs of Bearded Tits.

Breeding waterbird numbers are eclipsed by the much larger concentrations of waterfowl that winter at the Albufera. Numbers fluctuate from year to year and within seasons but wintering duck counts range from 10,000–40,000 birds. The most abundant wintering ducks are Mallards, Shovelers and Red-crested Pochards. Gadwalls, Teals, Pintails and Common Pochards are also numerous. This is the principal wintering location in Spain of the Cormorant; several thousand occur.

The Albufera is also noted for its gull and tern colonies. There are recently established colonies, each of several hundred pairs, of Slender-billed, Mediterranean and Audouin's Gulls. The breeding terns include around 600 pairs of Gull-billed Terns, over 4,000 pairs of Sandwich Terns, over 2,000 pairs of Common Terns and 200 pairs of Little Terns. Lesser Crested and Elegant Terns have bred among the Sandwich Terns, in some cases forming mixed pairs with that species.

Waders occur in large numbers on the ricefields, especially on passage and in winter. The characteristic breeding species include some 1,000 pairs of Black-winged Stilts, a small colony of Collared Pratincoles and over 50 pairs of Kentish Plovers. Up to 3,000 Black-tailed Godwits occur on passage and are joined in winter by large numbers of Lapwings and smaller numbers of Golden Plovers, Common Snipe, Common and Green Sandpipers and Common Redshanks, among others. Rare waders are recorded annually and in recent years have included both American and Pacific Golden Plovers; White-rumped, Baird's, Pectoral, Sharp-tailed, Broad-billed, Buff-breasted and Terek Sandpipers, Lesser Yellowlegs and Red-necked Phalarope.

Raptors are most evident in winter when many Marsh Harriers are present together with a few Booted Eagles and Ospreys, among others.

Timing

Worth visiting at any time of year but the ricefields are usually drained during March–April and October, which greatly reduces their attractiveness to water-birds then. Hunters on the ricefields at weekends during November–February can cause some disturbance. Gates generally close-off areas when hunting is in progress. Winter visits see the most spectacular waterbird concentrations.

Access

The lagoon proper is 10km south of Valencia city. An obvious place to start and get your bearings is the Racó de l'Olla Visitors' Centre (Tel. 961 627 345). Access is off the CV-500 coast road. Take the turn-off signposted to the village of El Palmar and the Centre itself, which is immediately on the left just after the turn-off. The Centre has leaflets, details of current bird interest and suggestions for routes. It also includes an observation tower with good but somewhat distant views of a large reed-fringed inlet of the main lagoon (La Mata de Fang); a tele-scope is all but essential here. A nature trail through Mediterranean woodland leads from the Centre to a small artificial lagoon with hides; an island in this lagoon is the site of the principal ternery of the Albufera and of great interest when the terns are nesting. The CV-500 itself between El Perolló and Sueca crosses ricefields and can be very good in the winter; it tends to be busy but there are a few obvious places where you can turn off. Boat trips on the lagoon are available, from El Palmar for example, but are probably not ideal for birding.

There are numerous points of access to the ricefields and fringing wetlands, via broad tracks. Most of the route recommended here, through the southern ricefields, is tarmacked but there are sandy stretches and other tracks that are easily drivable except during the wettest conditions. The suggested route (25km) begins from El Palmar, a short distance beyond the Racó de l'Olla centre. Most of the route crosses ricefields and you will want to stop frequently wherever birds are feeding. Drive right through El Palmar and turn right towards Sollana, crossing a small bridge. After 3.1km there is a crossroads and a gate, which will be closed if hunting is in progress. Turn left at the crossroads and follow the road for 5.1km until you reach the road leading to the Muntanyeta dels Sants, where you turn right and continue for 4.6km to the Muntanyeta itself. The Muntanyeta is a low rocky hill, the only one for miles, topped by a Chapel and offering panoramic views of the ricefields. Descend from the chapel car park on the hill. There is now the option to head directly from here to the CV-500; follow the main tracks in the direction of the villages and other buildings visible to the east. The alternative is to remain within the ricefields; turn right from the Muntanyeta and then right again at a T junction, to reach the Ullal (spring) de Baldovi/Na Molins nature reserve (500m) along a short dirt track. The Ullal comprises 5.8ha of reedbeds and spring-fed pools accessed by boardwalks. To return through ricefields to El Palmar continue past the T junction for 1km to a crossroads. Turn right and follow this road northwards to reach the gate encountered earlier and continue from there to El Palmar. The bars and restaurants of El Palmar may prove welcome at this stage. The entire route may be followed in the opposite direction.

The Parador de El Saler is by the CV-500 on the seaward side of La

CALENDAR

All year: Common Shelduck, Marbled Duck (rare), Red-crested Pochard, Great Crested and Little Grebes, Night Heron, Cattle and Little Egrets, Grey Heron, Greater Flamingo, Purple Swamphen, Red-knobbed Coot (rare), Kentish Plover, Black-headed Gull, Sandwich Tern, Kingfisher, Hoopoe, Long-eared Owl, Lesser Short-toed Lark, Zitting Cisticola; Cetti's, Moustached and Sardinian Warblers, Bearded Tit.

Breeding season: Little Bittern, Squacco and Purple Herons, Black-winged Stilt, Collared Pratincole; Slender-billed, Mediterranean and Audouin's Gulls, Gull-billed, Common and Little Terns, Bee-eater, Greater Short-toed Lark, Nightingale; Savi's, Reed and Great Reed Warblers, Golden Oriole, Woodchat Shrike.

Winter: Common Shelduck, Gadwall, Teal (has bred), Mallard, Pintail, Shoveler (has

bred), Red-crested and Common Pochards, Ferruginous Duck (has bred), Black-necked Grebe, Cormorant, Great White Egret (has bred), Glossy Ibis (has bred), Marsh Harrier, Booted Eagle, Osprey, Avocet, Little Ringed Plover, Golden Plover, Lapwing, Sanderling, Common and Jack Snipes, Green Sandpiper, Common Redshank, Great Skua, Mediterranean and Little Gulls, Short-eared Owl, Bluethroat, Penduline Tit, Reed Bunting. Also Common Scoter, Balearic and Levantine Shearwaters, Gannet, Great Skua, gulls, Sandwich Tern and Razorbill on the sea.

Passage periods: Garganey (has bred), Little and Temminck's Stints, Curlew Sandpiper, Dunlin, Ruff, Spotted Redshank, Greenshank; Green, Marsh and Wood Sandpipers; Whiskered, Black and White-winged Black Terns, European Nightjar, Pallid Swift, Water Pipit, Melodious Warbler.

Albufera, 3km south of the Racó de l'Olla/El Palmar turn-off. It is a handy place to stay and offers access to the beach, the dune scrub and the coastal pine-woods. These and the adjacent golf course may hold many passerine migrants at times. Seabirds and waders may be seen from the shore.

MARJAL DE PEGO-OLIVA   V5
(Valencia/Alicante)

Status: Parque Natural, ZEPA and Ramsar site (1,290ha).

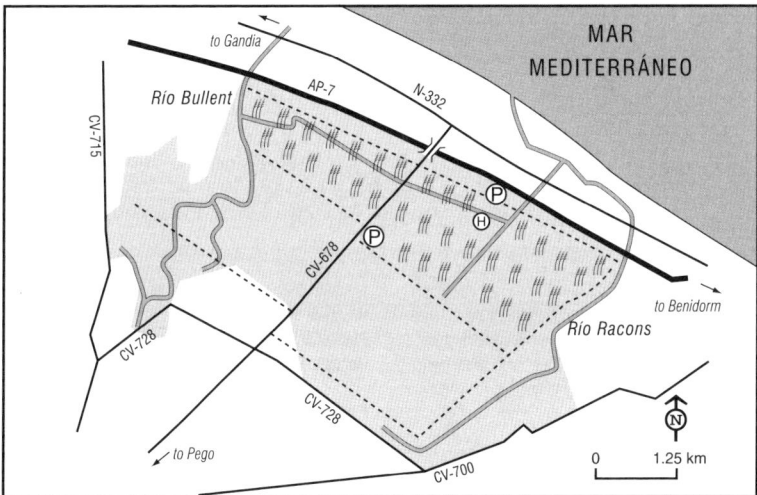

Site description
Another of Valencia's coastal marshes and one of the best of its wetland sites. The marshes occupy a sizeable area, once a lagoon but now chiefly large expanses of reedbed providing a very rich habitat for many species. The Ríos Bullent and Racons, numerous small springs and a complicated network of drainage channels and irrigation ditches lying between the two rivers together form an interweaving matrix of watercourses that quarter and break up the site. Ricefields comprise the western fringe of the site.

Species
The Marjal de Pego-Oliva is especially important for Moustached Warblers, which have a sizeable resident breeding population here; some 150 pairs. They frequent the wetter areas of reed where they especially favour the reed mats near the water. Breeding herons and egrets include some 70 breeding pairs of Little Bitterns, 20 pairs of Purple Herons and a colony of Cattle Egrets. Night Herons and Squacco Herons occur regularly on passage and Great Bitterns occur

occasionally on passage and in winter. Introduced Red-knobbed Coots have nested here. Marbled Ducks have bred occasionally, attracted by the shallow water with extensive emergent and submerged vegetation. Around 20 pairs of Red-crested Pochards also breed here and there is a small nesting population of Whiskered Terns. Common Pratincoles breed occasionally. Purple Swamphens are characteristic of the area. The marsh has also proved attractive to Common Waxbills, which can often be found around the western part of the site.

The site is very good for passage and wintering species. Both Bluethroats and Penduline Tits are regular visitors in winter.

Timing
The site is of interest year-round.

Access
This marsh is approximately halfway between Alicante and Valencia, and also midway between Gandia and Dénia. The easiest approach is from the N-332. Take the CV-678 off the N-332, which takes you through the middle of the site and offers some off-road parking. The road first takes you over the AP-7 motorway immediately after which a track on the right leads to a boardwalk, observation platform and hide. There are further tracks across the marsh to both left and right of the CV-678 that are worth exploring. Stands of the Giant Reed obscure the view in places but there are obvious gaps allowing closer inspection. The ricefields beyond the marsh can also be viewed from the innermost tracks.

CALENDAR

All year: Mallard, Marbled Duck (few), Red-crested Pochard, Little and Great Crested Grebes, Cattle Egret, Water Rail, Moorhen, Purple Swamphen, Common Coot, Kingfisher, Zitting Cisticola, Cetti's and Moustached Warblers, Common Waxbill.

Breeding season: Little Bittern, Purple Heron, Black-winged Stilt, Little Ringed and Kentish Plovers, Whiskered and Little Terns, Greater Short-toed Lark; Savi's, Reed and Great Reed Warblers.

Winter: Wigeon, Teal, Shoveler, Common Pochard, Little Egret, Grey Heron, Marsh Harrier, Bluethroat, Penduline Tit.

Passage periods: Garganey, Great Bittern, Night and Squacco Herons, Spoonbill, Osprey, Ringed Plover, Spotted and Little Crakes, Grey Plover, Little Stint, Curlew Sandpiper, Black-tailed Godwit, Ruff, Spotted Redshank, Caspian and Black Terns, Sand Martin.

SIERRA DE MONTGÓ–CABO DE SAN ANTONIO (Alicante)   V6

Status: Parque Natural (825ha) and Reserva Natural (110ha).

Site description
The Sierra de Montgó is a hilly coastal area rising to an impressive rocky outcrop (753m) dominating the local landscape. As it reaches the coast on its

north-west side it eventually ends at the Cabo de San Antonio (Cap de San Antoni), a rocky promontory with a lighthouse. Montgó has sheer cliffs on either side and areas of shrubby vegetation. The maquis has Rosemary, heathers, Lavender and Kermes Oak together with some stands of juniper and Holm Oak and planted Aleppo Pine woodland. The prominent position of the site makes it important for migration and the headland allows seawatching but Cabo de la Nao (V19) to the south is better for this purpose.

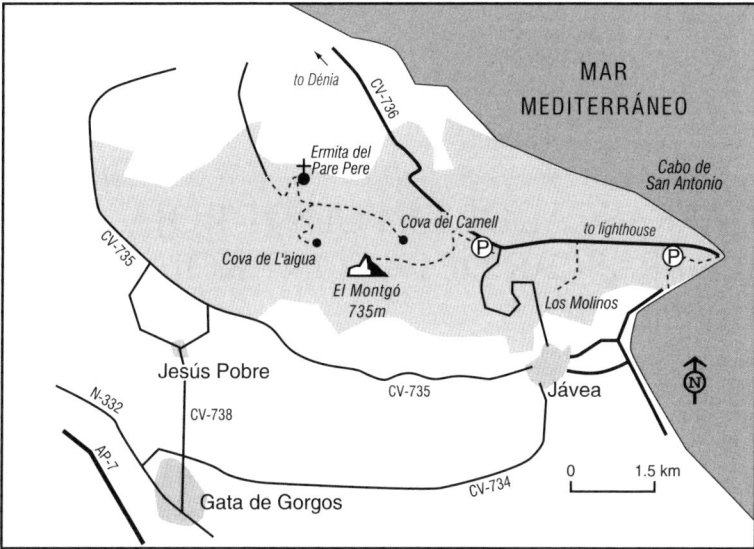

Species
Cliff- and rock-nesting species are the principal interest here but the area has a wide range of habitats and so offers a diversity of species, especially in spring. Bonelli's Eagles, Peregrine Falcons, Eagle Owls, Black Wheatears, Blue Rock Thrushes, Red-billed Choughs and Rock Buntings are all resident. The general area is also good for Barn, Scops, Tawny and Little Owls, and for passage migrants.

The sea cliffs have Pallid Swifts, a typical species of the Mediterranean coast. The rocky coastal areas also have Black Redstarts, with Dartford Warblers in the scrub. Eleonora's Falcons occur occasionally.

Timing
Interesting all year and good for migration in spring and autumn.

Access
The site is 75km north-west of Alicante and reached via the AP-7 motorway (exit 22 Ondara) or the parallel coastal road, the N-332. Take one of the turnings off the N-332 for Jávea, Dénia or Benitatxell. You can walk up to the mountain summit along marked paths from the nearby towns of Dénia and Jávea and various nature trails can be followed in the park itself. The CV-736 between Jávea and Dénia crosses the park and a road leads to the lighthouse at the cape.

CALENDAR

All year: Bonelli's Eagle, Peregrine Falcon, Common Kestrel, Rock Dove; Barn, Scops, Little, Tawny and Eagle Owls, Hoopoe, Thekla Lark, Crag Martin, Black Redstart, Stonechat, Black Wheatear, Dartford and Sardinian Warblers, Blue Rock Thrush, Firecrest, Long-tailed and Crested Tits, Short-toed Treecreeper, Southern Grey Shrike, Red-billed Chough, Raven, Spotless Starling, Serin, Crossbill, Rock Bunting.

Breeding season: Cory's (Scopoli's) and Balearic Shearwaters, Turtle Dove, Pallid Swift.

Winter: Northern Gannet, Great Skua, Mediterranean Gull, Sandwich Tern, Razorbill.

Passage periods: Eleonora's Falcon, Arctic Skua, Audouin's Gull, Tree Pipit, Common Redstart, Black-eared Wheatear, Willow Warbler, Spotted Flycatcher.

CARRASCAL DE LA FUENTE ROJA   V7 (CARRASCAR DE LA FONT ROJA) (Alicante)

Status: Parque Natural (2,450ha).

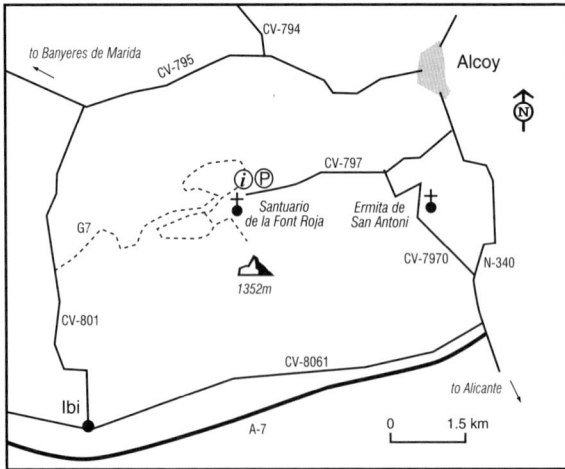

Site description

This park, occupying the Sierra Monejador, has some of the best preserved Mediterranean forest remaining in Valencia. The range runs east/west, reaching a maximum height of 1,352m. The southern slopes are relatively gentle but the northern ones are much steeper, with gorges and screes. The vegetation on the southern slopes consists of Rosemary, broom and occasional stands of pine, while on the northern slopes above 1,000m there is mixed woodland of Holm and Lusitanian Oaks and other broadleaves. The lower slopes are covered in dense Aleppo Pine plantations.

Species
The interesting resident birds include Bonelli's Eagles, Blue Rock Thrushes and Cirl and Rock Buntings. The woodlands also have a diverse avifauna including Goshawks, Great Spotted Woodpeckers, Bonelli's Warblers, Firecrests, Crossbills and Serins. The lower levels have Nightingales and Golden Orioles, with Hoopoes and Woodchat Shrikes in the more open areas.

Timing
Spring and early summer, from early April through to June, are the best times.

Access
From Alicante take the A-7 towards Alcoy. Leave at junction 45 (46 if travelling south) on to the N-340. About 3km before reaching Alcoy, turn left on the CV-7970/797 to the Santuario de la Font Roja and the Parque Natural, where there is also a car park and information centre. Various tracks and paths start around the information centre (Tel. 965 337 620). The G7 long-distance trail goes through the site. There are signposted routes providing a good range of walks through the full range of habitats, including woodland, scrub and open ground.

CALENDAR

All year: Bonelli's Eagle, Goshawk, Sparrowhawk, Little and Eagle Owls, Great Spotted Woodpecker, Crag Martin, Robin, Stonechat, Black Wheatear, Blue Rock Thrush, Dartford Warbler, Firecrest, Crested Tit, Short-toed Treecreeper, Rock Sparrow, Serin, Crossbill, Cirl and Rock Buntings.

Breeding season: European Nightjar, Hoopoe, Nightingale, Black-eared Wheatear, Subalpine Warbler, Blackcap, Bonelli's Warbler, Spotted Flycatcher, Golden Oriole, Red-backed and Woodchat Shrikes.

PEÑÓN DE IFACH AND SALINAS DE CALPE (Alicante) V8

Status: Parque Natural 'Peñón de Ifach' (45ha).

Site description
Joined to land via a narrow isthmus, the limestone rock of Ifach (Penyal d'Ifac) towers 332m over the surrounding sea near Calpe (Calp), dominating the scenery all around. It strongly recalls the Rock of Gibraltar, although rather smaller. The gentler rock faces are covered in scrub including Lavender, Fan Palm and juniper. The long-disused saltpans of Calpe, once just a small fishing port, are situated beneath the rock and alongside the main coastal road. Calpe itself has grown inexorably and is a sizeable residential area and holiday resort, whose high-rise buildings now ring the saltpans, which now resemble a large park lake, and extend to the very foot of the rock.

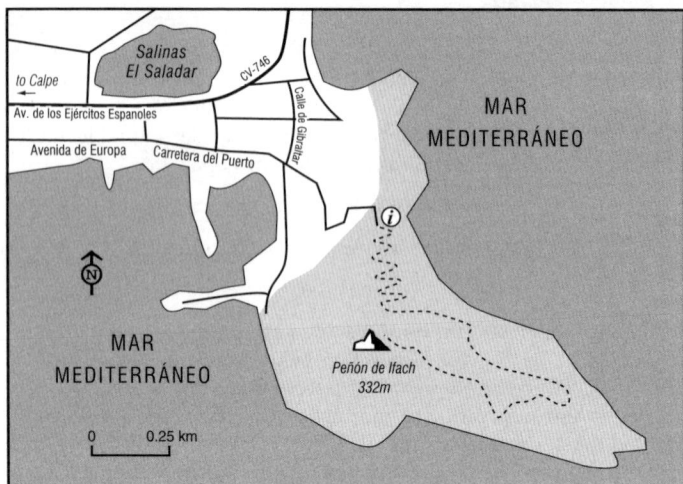

Species

The Peñon is right next to a highly developed part of the coast, including that temple to mass tourism, the one-time village of Benidorm. Nevertheless, over 170 bird species have been recorded here or at the nearby saltpans. It offers an opportunity for seawatching, especially in winter when numbers of Gannets may feed off the coast. The rock itself has a pair of sea-cliff nesting Peregrine Falcons and the inevitable colony of Yellow-legged Gulls. A walk up the rock in spring and summer will also find breeding Pallid Swifts, Blue Rock Thrushes, Black Redstarts, Crag Martins, Stonechats, Dartford Warblers and Ravens. It is worth checking the scrub on the way up for migrants such as Northern Wheatears.

The saltpans still retain considerable ornithological interest despite their novel semi-urban location. Audouin's Gulls can readily be seen here. In addition to breeding Avocets, Black-winged Stilts and Kentish Plovers, the area attracts Greater Flamingos and a good mixture of terns and waders on passage.

Timing

Spring and autumn are the best seasons but winter seawatching can be productive.

Access

Calpe is 21km north-east of Benidorm. The CV-746 through road skirts the saltpans. Park alongside the road on the southern side of the saltpans (Avenida de las Fuerzas Armadas) and view the lagoon, the causeways of the former salt workings and the fringing scrubby areas from the footpath that follows their margin. The Peñón de Ifach is a short walk away. Alternatively head for Calpe port and follow the road past the harbour and up to the information centre (Tel. 965 972 015). From here a track and tunnel lead to the summit; the track is paved and easy going at first but the upper stretches are much rougher. Robust footwear and a reasonable degree of fitness are advisable for the ascent, which takes some two hours.

CALENDAR

All year: Grey Heron, Little Egret, Greater Flamingo, Peregrine Falcon, Common Coot, Moorhen, Black-headed and Yellow-legged Gulls, Crested Lark, Crag Martin, Stonechat, Black Redstart, Blue Rock Thrush, Dartford and Sardinian Warblers, Raven, Serin.

Breeding season: Avocet, Black-winged Stilt, Kentish Plover, Pallid Swift, Reed Warbler, Spectacled Warbler.

Winter: Balearic Shearwater, Gannet, Cormorant, Sandwich Tern.

Passage periods: Black-necked Grebe, Hobby, Eleonora's Falcon, Common Sandpiper, Audouin's Gull; Sandwich, Common, Little, Whiskered and Black Terns, Northern Wheatear.

EL HONDO DE ELCHE (ELX) (Alicante)   V9

Status: Parque Natural, ZEPA and Ramsar site (2,378ha).

Site description

Arguably the flagship site of Alicante province and one of the most important wetlands in eastern Spain. Two irrigation reservoirs were constructed on the site of a former marshy lagoon, and large stands of reedbed and other emergent vegetation, including reedmace and saltmarsh, have become established here. A number of other smaller brackish and freshwater waterbodies are also present as well as areas of saltflats. The adjacent fields, viewed from the Vistabella Road, are often interesting in wet winters. The two principal waterbodies are quite sizeable: the Embalse de Levante being 450ha and the Embalse de Poniente 650ha. Unfortunately, and despite its protected status, this wetland is severely affected by drought, particularly since water is extracted to irrigate crops over a large area. As a result it is prone to drying out completely in summer.

Species

The bird interest of the site is very substantial, with around 200 species recorded. El Hondo is one of the more important sites in Europe for Marbled Ducks: up to 30 pairs breed in some seasons. Small numbers of White-headed Ducks, another globally threatened species, also breed. El Hondo is a major wintering site for White-headed Ducks, with over 1,000 present in good years. Common Shelducks nest in small numbers and are much more numerous in winter, when recent counts have exceeded 1,700 birds. In general, as might be expected, waterbird numbers vary greatly with water availability.

In recent years El Hondo has also become renowned for the regular presence of Spotted Eagles in winter, including one individual of Estonian origin that returned for its eighth consecutive season in autumn 2015. Up to four individuals have been present at a time, making this the best and most reliable site to see what is a rare species anywhere in Iberia. Booted Eagles, a few Ospreys and numerous Marsh Harriers are among the other regular wintering raptors.

Breeding herons include numerous Little Bitterns, a few pairs of Squacco, Night and Purple Herons and several hundred pairs of Cattle and Little Egrets. Other regular breeding species include Red-crested Pochard, Purple Swamphen, Avocet, Black-winged Stilt, Collared Pratincole, Kentish Plover, Little Tern, Moustached Warbler and Bearded Tit. Several hundred pairs of Black-necked Grebes nest here, making El Hondo one of the most important sites for this species in Spain. The colony of Whiskered Terns; 500+ pairs in some seasons, is the largest in the Valencian community. The drier areas support such species as Montagu's Harrier; Greater Short-toed, Lesser Short-toed and Crested Larks, Bee-eater and Black-eared Wheatear.

White-headed Ducks apart, the site is also very important for passage and wintering waterfowl, notably Red-crested Pochards and Shovelers in good numbers. Scarcer wintering waterfowl sometimes include Ferruginous Ducks. Other winterers include Bluethroats and Penduline Tits, and Common Starlings which roost in the reedbeds.

The site attracts a diversity of passage and wintering waders: the former occasionally include Dotterels, that may appear on the Vistabella road fields in autumn. Large roosts of Barn Swallows and other hirundines are also a feature in autumn.

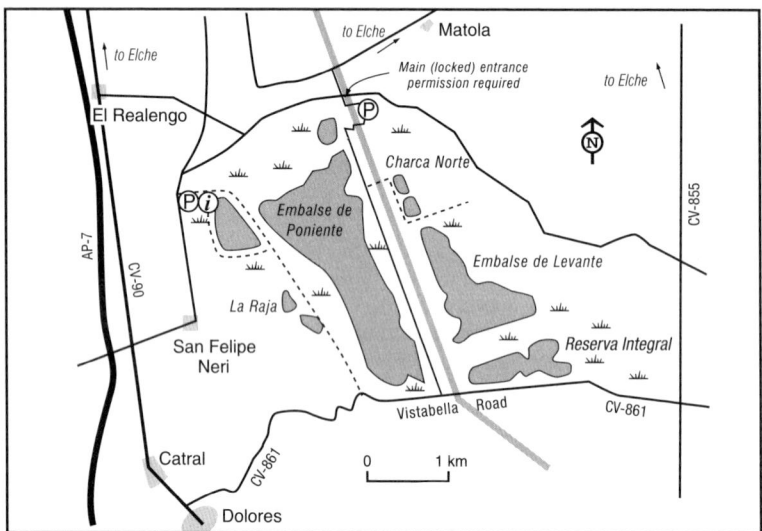

Timing
El Hondo is of great interest at any time of year except in years when it is totally dry in summer and early autumn. As with many wetland sites, heat haze can make viewing difficult during the middle of the day at the height of summer.

Access
El Hondo is just south of Elche and just over 40km from Alicante. It is best approached from the Elche/Torrevieja stretch of the AP-7. From the Elche direction (north) take the exit at km-730 signposted Catral; at the first round-about take the Catral exit and at the second roundabout, the San Felipe Neri

exit. From the Torrevieja direction (south) take the exit also at km-730 sign-posted Catral-Crevillent (Crevillente railway station) and take the turn-off to San Felipe Neri at the roundabout. Turn left to drive through San Felipe Neri village and after 2km turn right into a signposted road that leads to the reserve entrance and information centre (Tel. 966 678 515).

Two circular routes originate from the centre and offer hides over lagoons and other representative habitats. There is usually plenty to see and the longer of these circular routes will take up to two hours. A much longer diversion (allow four hours return on foot) from the outer circular route skirts a large lagoon and leads to the reserve margin at the Vistabella Road (CV-861) where it turns northward parallel to the road to reach another lagoon, the Reserva Integral, overlooked by three hides; best visited in the morning on sunny days. The fields flanking the reserve may hold waders, and even Cranes, especially in winter and during passage periods. The Vistabella road can also be visited by car – return to Catral and take the CV-9218 towards Dolores, turning left on to the CV-861 shortly before Dolores. In addition, a guided route is avail-able that runs between the two main reservoirs of the reserve, the Embalse de Poniente and the Embalse de Levante, which are overlooked by a number of hides; visits here are by prior arrangement with the visitors' centre.

CALENDAR

All year: Common Shelduck, Marbled and White-headed Ducks, Red-crested and Common Pochards; Little, Great Crested and Black-necked Grebes, Cattle and Little Egrets, Greater Flamingo, Marsh Harrier, Water Rail, Moorhen, Purple Swamphen, Common Coot, Black-winged Stilt, Avocet, Kentish Plover, Kingfisher, Lesser Short-toed Lark, Zitting Cisticola, Moustached Warbler, Bearded Tit.

Breeding season: Little Bittern; Night, Squacco and Purple Herons, Spotted Crake, Montagu's Harrier, Collared Pratincole, Whiskered Tern, Yellow Wagtail; Savi's, Reed, Great Reed and Spectacled Warblers.

Winter: Greylag Goose, Wigeon, Teal, Pintail, Shoveler, Ferruginous Duck, Cormorant, Grey Heron, Glossy Ibis, Marsh Harrier, Greater Spotted and Booted Eagles, Osprey, Crane, Golden Plover, Crag Martin, Water Pipit, Bluethroat, Penduline Tit.

Passage periods: Garganey, Gadwall, Glossy Ibis, Crane, Hobby, Dotterel, Golden Plover, Lapwing, Temminck's Stint, Dunlin, Black-tailed Godwit, Spotted Redshank, Marsh Sandpiper, Mediterranean and Little Gulls, Common and Black Terns, Barn Swallow, European Nightjar, Grasshopper Warbler, Common Starling.

SALINAS DE SANTA POLA (Alicante)   V10

Status: Parque Natural, ZEPA and Ramsar site (2,496ha).

Site description

These saltpans are at the former Albufera de Elche, a lagoon at the mouth of the River Vinalopó. The lagoon was drained at the end of the 19th century and the area now consists of saltpans, freshwater marshes with reedbeds, extensive saltflats, sand dunes and a 5km beach. Several channels cross the landscape, draining through the original outlet of the lagoon into the sea. The dunes in the Pinet area also form part of the park. Areas of the saltpans are still in use and these are also of value to birds, but the degree to which they are attractive depends on their current state of working.

Species
This coastal wetland was designated a Ramsar site for its wintering populations of Greater Flamingos and Avocets and breeding Common Shelducks, Marbled Ducks, Red-crested Pochards, Black-winged Stilts, Avocets, Kentish Plovers and Little Terns. The very obvious Flamingos are present throughout the year and have nested occasionally: up to 8,000 have been recorded on the saltpans but it is more normal for hundreds to use the site in the winter, with numbers peaking at a few thousand in late summer.

There is sufficient cover of reedbeds to support breeding Little Bitterns and Night, Squacco and Purple Herons and there are resident populations there of both Moustached Warblers and Bearded Tits. Marbled Ducks occur and nest with some regularity but usually in very small numbers. The saltpans have significant breeding populations of Avocets, Black-winged Stilts and Kentish Plovers. A few hundred pairs of Common and Little Terns breed as well as small numbers of Whiskered and Gull-billed Terns. This is an important location for Slender-billed Gulls, which are present all year and usually nest alongside Black-headed Gulls. Large winter flocks of Common Coots, sometimes over 10,000 birds, occur. Up to 2,000 Black-tailed Godwits have been recorded on the Salinas de Bonmati, with small numbers of Spoonbills. The diversity of passage and wintering waders is high and this is a good site for such regionally scarce species as Marsh Sandpiper and Red-necked Phalarope, especially in autumn. Ospreys occur regularly on passage and in winter.

Timing
The site is rewarding throughout the year but species diversity is probably greatest during migration periods.

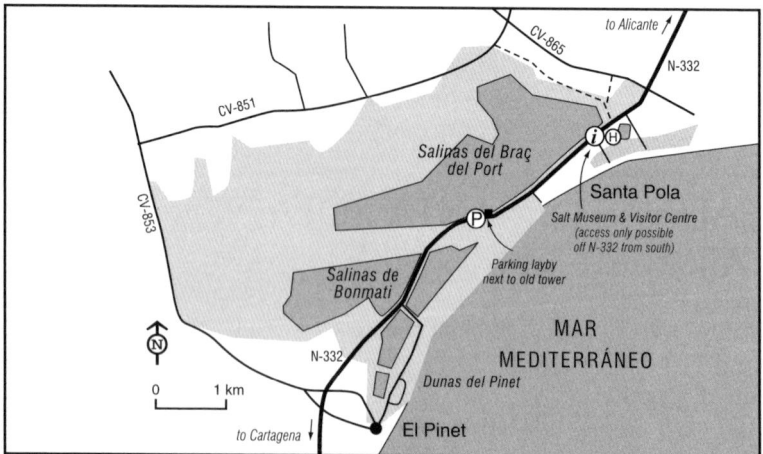

Access

The salinas are south of Alicante. This is a large site and some birds may be far off so a telescope will be very useful. Take the N-332 and after approximately 20km you come to the small resort of Santa Pola: the saltpans are immediately south of the town. The N-332 crosses through the saltpans but there are a few obvious places to pull off this very busy road to get good views over the area. It is often unwise to cross the road with the car and great caution is needed to cross on foot; much of the traffic is dangerously fast. Hence the turn-offs on the landward (western) side are best accessed when travelling south; at km-86.6 a turning on the right leads to a track that passes between disused saltpans, some overlooked by a hide. Another obvious stopping place is at km-83 where there is a large lay-by adjacent to a very obvious white tower. Another rougher lay-by is accessible at km-82.5.

Northbound a trail on the right at El Pinet, at the southern end of the saltpans, runs between the sea and saltpans across saltflats and dunes. The trail is well marked and includes some boardwalks, viewing platforms, hides and information panels. Follow the signs to the beach (Playa de Pinet) and after 1km park next to the Hostal Galicia. From the N-332 there is a good place to pull off at the entrance to the Salinas de Bonmati 1km north of El Pinet. A visitors' centre (Tel. 966 693 546) at km-87.4 on the southern outskirts of Santa Pola on Avenida Zaragoza also houses a salt museum. The Centre is open daily, 09.00–14.00 hrs. It is best approached when travelling north via an exit road on the right-hand side immediately before you reach Santa Pola. A trail from the Centre leads to three small lagoons overlooked by a hide and areas of saltflats and dune scrub.

CALENDAR

All year: Common Shelduck, Red-crested Pochard, Marbled Duck, Great Crested Grebe, Little Egret, Glossy Ibis, Greater Flamingo, Purple Swamphen, Avocet, Kentish Plover; Black-headed, Slender-billed and Yellow-legged Gulls, Lesser Short-toed Lark, Zitting Cisticola, Cetti's and Moustached Warblers, Bearded Tit.

Breeding season: Little Bittern; Night, Squacco and Purple Herons, Montagu's Harrier, Black-winged Stilt, Collared Pratincole; Little, Common, Gull-billed and Whiskered Terns, Savi's and Great Reed Warblers.

Winter: Wigeon, Teal, Pintail, Shoveler, Common Pochard, Black-necked Grebe, Cormorant, Spoonbill, Great White Egret, Grey Heron, Marsh Harrier, Osprey, Ringed and Golden Plovers, Little Stint, Curlew, Spotted Redshank, Sandwich Tern, Crag Martin, Water Pipit, larks, Reed Bunting.

Passage periods: Garganey, Spotted Crake, Grey Plover, Little and Temminck's Stints, Curlew and Marsh Sandpipers, Dunlin; Ruff, Black-tailed and Bar-tailed Godwits, Red-necked Phalarope, Little and Audouin's Gulls, Caspian and Black Terns, Kingfisher, Sand Martin.

LAGUNAS DE LA MATA AND TORREVIEJA (Alicante)   V11

Status: Parque Natural, ZEPA and Ramsar site (3,693ha).

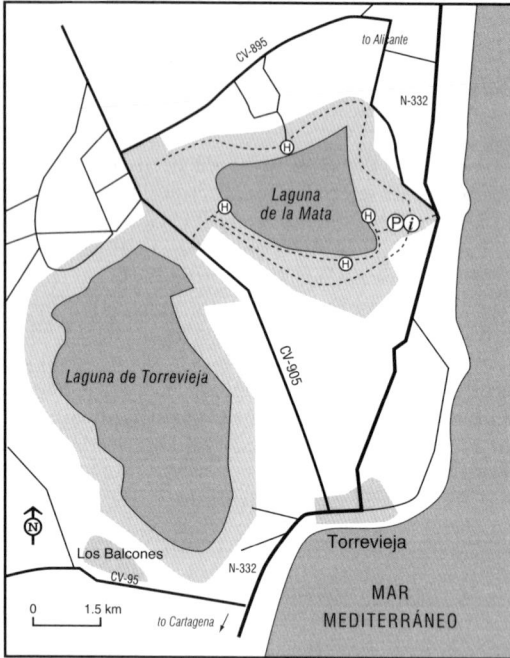

Site description

The Lagunas de la Mata and Torrevieja comprise two large coastal lagoons that have been exploited for salt extraction, with a permanent salt water supply from the sea. The two interconnected wetlands are still used for salt extraction, as they have been for centuries. The Laguna de la Mata (700ha) is used to regulate the water levels in the larger lagoon, the Laguna de Torrevieja (1,400ha). Salt water is drawn from the Cabeç de la Sal in Pinoso and left to evaporate at the Laguna de Torrevieja, which is where salt is harvested. The waters of Torrevieja consequently have a higher salinity than those of La Mata, and this has a direct influence on the use of the two sites by birds. The shores of the lagoons range from muddy beaches to reedbeds and saltflats. The surrounding area is a patchwork of woodland, Aleppo Pine plantations, vineyards and irrigated farmland.

Species

The site is currently most important for the breeding colony of Audouin's Gulls at the Laguna de Torrevieja. This colony was only established in 2004 when there were just a few pairs but these had increased to over 3,000 pairs by 2010. Audouin's Gulls are present all year round, chiefly at the Laguna de Torrevieja but they can also be seen regularly at La Mata. Both Black-headed and Slender-billed Gulls also often nest here.

There is a small colony and recently established colony of Iberian Azure-winged Magpies south of the Laguna de Torrevieja; some 25 birds in 2014. These are over 100km from the current range of the species. However, several of the 'pioneers' were colour-ringed and it seems highly likely that the birds were introduced to the area.

The lagoons also have a small number of breeding Common Shelducks but over 1,000 may be present in winter. The lakes also attract remarkable numbers of Black-necked Grebes; small numbers nest but there are post-breeding concentrations of up to 3,000 birds and hundreds remain in winter. The grebes may form dense rafts that resemble low-lying islands from a distance. There are significant breeding populations of Black-winged Stilts, Kentish Plovers and Common and Little Terns. Whiskered Terns nest in some years. The surrounding fields and vineyards attract such species as Montagu's Harrier and Stone-curlew as well as many passerines.

Timing
The site can be rewarding throughout the year although low water levels in summer can mean that the birds are then distant and heat haze can make viewing very difficult. Wildfowl numbers can be particularly impressive in winter.

Access
The lagoons are on the landward side of the N-332 coastal road at Torrelamata/Torrevieja. You can also take the CV-95 or CV-905 turn-offs to Torrevieja from the AP-7 motorway. All visits are centred on La Mata: La Laguna de Torrevieja is not easily accessible. An information centre (Centro de Información), La Casa Forestal de la Mata (Tel: 966 920 404) is signposted at the roundabout on the N-332 at Torrelamata. The Centre is 200m from the roundabout on a rise overlooking La Mata lake. It is open daily except Sundays, generally 09.00–14.00 hours, but its car park and trail are always accessible. A sandy walking route descends from the Centre to the lake margin around which a number of hides or observation points overlook the site.

The Azure-winged Magpies are on the fringes of the Urbanization Los Balcones, immediately south of La Laguna de Torrevieja, where the housing gives way to farmland, citrus groves and the lake margin.

CALENDAR

All year: Common Shelduck, Red-crested Pochard, Black-necked and Great Crested Grebes, Greater Flamingo, Avocet, Stone-curlew, Kentish Plover, Audouin's Gull, Lesser Short-toed Lark, Cetti's Warbler, Zitting Cisticola, Azure-winged Magpie.

Breeding season: Montagu's Harrier, Black-winged Stilt, Black-headed and Slender-billed Gulls, Common and Little Terns, Yellow Wagtail, Rufous-tailed Scrub-robin, Spectacled, Reed and Great Reed Warblers, Black-eared Wheatear, Reed Bunting.

Winter: Wigeon, Mallard, Pintail, Shoveler, Common Pochard, Marsh Harrier, Glossy Ibis, Reed Bunting.

Passage periods: Garganey, Golden Plover, Little Stint, Lapwing, Marsh Sandpiper, Little Gull, Sedge Warbler.

EL CLOT DE GALVANY (Alicante)   V12

Status: Paraje Natural Municipal (180ha)

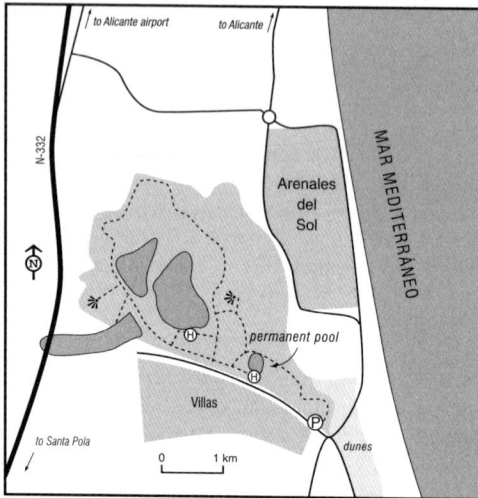

Site description

This compact wetland is a veritable natural oasis in the 'villa steppe' of the Alicante coast, just north of the headland and town of Santa Pola. The site preserves a fragment of the natural habitats of the coastline, from beachside sand dunes to stands of Aleppo Pines to sparsely-vegetated low sandy hillsides: with clumps of Tamarisks, False Esparto Grass and scattered Olives, Lentiscs, Carobs and other low shrubs. Three natural shallow brackish lagoons are the key attraction, although they dry up in summer. A smaller artificial pool provides a refuge for waterfowl at other times. The water levels of the main lagoons fluctuate considerably between years, according to rainfall. The whole site is served by a number of marked trails and there are hides at the main lagoons.

Species

The key attractions here are the few breeding pairs of White-headed and Marbled Ducks, which nest in most years. White-headed Ducks are most numerous when water levels are high but, in contrast, Marbled Ducks favour shallower waters. Ferruginous Ducks have nested here. Breeding waders include Avocets and Black-winged Stilts but these too do best when water levels are not too high. Conversely, Common and Red-crested Pochards and Little and Black-necked Grebes are most numerous when the rains have been more generous and the lagoons are deepest. A mixed colony of Black-headed Gulls and Common Terns nests in some seasons. Whiskered and Little Terns also breed occasionally. The reedbeds have breeding Purple Swamphens. Other interesting breeding birds of the reserve include Red-necked Nightjars, Rufous-tail Scrub-robins and both Black-eared and Black Wheatears.

A wide diversity of wetland and passerine species occur on passage and also in winter. The variability in water availability and the small size of the site both mean that not all of the typical species are present every year but, on the positive side, the Clot is well placed to attract migrants and vagrants and 'anything' may turn up here.

Timing

The permanent lagoon, although very small, maintains the wetland interest of the site year-round but the Clot is at its best in spring and early summer in years when rainfall has been adequate. The area is popular with walkers from the adjacent villa developments and attracts picnickers in quantity at weekends, so early morning visits are recommended.

Access

The easiest access is from the north. Take the N-332 south for 10km from Alicante and then the signposted coast-side road to Arenales del Sol, 2km after the second (N-338) turn-off for Alicante airport. Drive through the village to the waterfront and continue (southwards) along the coastline. The car park for El Clot is indicated on the right but it is best to drive past it and park about 1km further along the service road below the villas where there is an entrance to the reserve proper. Follow the trails from here to visit the nearby permanent lagoon, which you should view both from the hide on the southern side and from the elevated viewpoint on the north side, in order to see the birds on both sides of the central reed islands. Further trails lead around the periphery of the reserve, a walk of an hour or so for non-birders. It is worth ascending the hillsides to overlook the reserve, especially at the western end where you can scan a sometimes marshy watercourse.

CALENDAR

All year: Mallard, Marbled and White-headed Ducks, Red-crested Pochard, Red-legged Partridge, Little Grebe, Cattle and Little Egrets, Water Rail, Purple Swamphen, Barn and Little Owls, Hoopoe, Green Woodpecker, Crested Lark, Zitting Cisticola, Southern Grey Shrike.

Breeding season: Common Quail, Little Bittern, Common Shelduck, Montagu's Harrier, Black-winged Stilt, Avocet, Kentish Plover; Common, Little and Whiskered Terns, Common Cuckoo, Red-necked Nightjar, Red-rumped Swallow, Rufous-tailed Scrub-robin, Black-eared Wheatear, Black Wheatear, Blue Rock Thrush, Great Reed and Reed Warblers, Woodchat Shrike.

Winter: Teal, Common Pochard, Grey Heron, Marsh Harrier, Stone-curlew, Common Snipe, Water Pipit, Bluethroat, Cetti's and Moustached Warblers, Common Chiffchaff, Penduline Tit, Reed Bunting.

Passage periods: Garganey, Shoveler, Night and Purple Herons, Little Ringed Plover, Little Stint, Ruff, Black-tailed Godwit, Common Redshank, Greenshank; Green, Wood and Common Sandpipers, Turtle Dove, Great Spotted Cuckoo, Bee-eater, Wryneck, Yellow Wagtail, Whinchat, Common Wheatear, Spectacled and Subalpine Warblers, Whitethroat.

OTHER SITES WORTH VISITING

V13 PEÑAGOLOSA (PENYAGOLOSA) (CASTELLÓN)
A limestone mountain area rising to 1,815m with gorges and extensive pine forests. Breeding species include Golden and Short-toed Eagles, Eagle Owls, Red-billed Choughs and Crossbills. Take the CV-10/CV-15 north-west from Castellón and then the CV-170 towards Aragón. A minor road 1km west of Vistabella del Maestrazo leads south into the heart of the area.

V14 EL ALTO TURIA (VALENCIA)
A mountain area with gorges and extensive pinewoods and scrub. Griffon Vultures, other raptors and woodland species occur. Take the CV-35 north-west from Valencia towards Chelva. Continue past Chelva for 6km and take the CV-390 south to Tuéjar (1km), where there is an information centre.

V15 HOCES DEL CABRIEL (VALENCIA)
Riverine gorges with riparian woodland and scrub, offering a diversity of passerines and others. Raptors include Golden, Bonelli's and Short-toed Eagles. Take the A-3 west from Valencia to Requena and then the N-322 south from Requena for 30km to the Río Cabriel.

V16 ISLA DE TABARCA (ALICANTE)
A small, inhabited island and marine reserve 4km off Santa Pola. Breeding species include Pallid Swifts and European Storm-petrels. The island is sometimes good for migration. It is accessible by boat from Alicante and Santa Pola.

V17 SIERRA DE AITANA (ALICANTE)
A limestone mountain area with pine and oak woods. Golden and Bonelli's Eagles, Crested Tits, Red-billed Choughs and Cirl Buntings are characteristic. Take the N-332 south from Benidorm to Villajoyosa and head inland on the CV-770 to Sella (15km). Continue for 3km past Sella and then turn north and continue for another 3km to the top of the Sierra.

V18 LAGUNA DE SALINAS (ALICANTE)
A natural lagoon with saltmarsh vegetation. Breeders include Avocets, Black-winged Stilts, larks and Stone-curlews. Take the A-31 north from Alicante towards Elda. Continue for 7km to Sax and take the CV-830 to Salinas (8km). The lagoon is on the left before Salinas.

V19 CABO DE LA NAO (CAP DE LA NAU) (ALICANTE)
A suitable location for seawatching, offering views from a good height (120m). The Balearic island of Ibiza is sometimes visible from here. Follow signs to the Cape from the CV-742, heading southwards from Javea.

STATUS LIST OF THE BIRDS OF NORTHERN AND EASTERN SPAIN

This list provides a brief outline of the status of all the species that have been recorded in northern and eastern Spain, including those which are vagrants or occur very rarely. The taxonomy is that of the most recent Western Palearctic List of the Association of European Records and Rarities Committees (Crochet & Joynt 2015). Spanish names are those approved by SEO/Birdlife.

A well-planned trip, visiting the full range of available habitats, will produce 170–200 species in most parts of our area. The list will allow you to separate the commonplace from the more unusual since we hope that you will submit your more interesting records to local organisations. The area is covered by the Spanish Ornithological Society's Rarities Committee (CR-SEO: Comité de Rarezas de la Sociedad Española de Ornitología). Only those species whose records have been ratified by the Committee, with the exception of some very recent sightings that are pending scrutiny, have been included. Record totals for rarities are given for northern and eastern Spain only and are the number of records (not individuals) **accepted up to 2013**; the totals serve to give an idea of the degree of rarity. Species that have only occurred outside our area (i.e. in Andalucía or Extremadura) are excluded.

A detailed account of all Iberian birds is available in *The Birds of the Iberian Peninsula*, by Eduardo de Juana and Ernest Garcia, published by Bloomsbury in 2015. That book covers rarities accepted up to 2011 as well as records that pre-date the Committee. The Rarities Committee's reports for 2012 and 2013 are published in the SEO/Birdlife journal *Ardeola* 62(2), 2015, 453–508 and subsequent rarity reports are published there annually.

Frequent updates on news of rarities from throughout Spain are available on the highly-recommended web site **Rare Birds in Spain** (rarebirdspain.net/home). If you are lucky enough to come across any rare birds we strongly urge you to submit the details. Records to CR-SEO may be submitted in English: send an email to rarezas@seo.org attaching your description.

Descriptions are only required by the Spanish Rarities Committee for species that are rarities in Spain as a whole. Such species are denoted below by an asterisk (*) and the full list, together with the Rarity Record Submission Form, is available on the SEO/Birdlife website (seo.org) or may be downloaded from the 'Rare birds in Spain' site. Records of other scarce species are also welcomed and should be sent to noticiario@seo.org. Annual reports of rare birds, and other interesting records from around Spain, are published in the Spanish ornithological society's journal *Ardeola* or in its newsletter *Aves y Naturaleza*, as well in provincial and regional bird reports. All published records are acknowledged.

Black Swan *Cygnus atratus* Cisne Negro
Birds of feral origin occur annually, mainly in the north.

Mute Swan *Cygnus olor* Cisne Vulgar
Vagrant. Also introduced but scarce. Wandering individuals may occur any-where.

Bewick's (Tundra) Swan* *Cygnus columbianus* Cisne Chico
Vagrant. Eight records, most from Catalonia.

Whooper Swan* *Cygnus cygnus* Cisne Cantor
Vagrant. 40 records, some of family groups, chiefly from the Atlantic coast.

Bean Goose* *Anser fabalis* Ánsar Campestre
Rare winter visitor, formerly numerous in the north.

Pink-footed Goose *Anser brachyrhynchus* Ánsar Piquicorto
Rare winter visitor, chiefly in the north.

White-fronted Goose *Anser albifrons* Ánsar Careto Grande
Rare winter visitor, chiefly in the northern Meseta.

Lesser White-fronted Goose* *Anser erythropus* Ánsar Careto Chico
Vagrant. Seven records from the North and Meseta.

Greylag Goose *Anser anser* Ánsar Común
Widespread in winter, when locally abundant on the Meseta (Villafáfila).
Breeds locally.

Bar-headed Goose *Anser indicus* Ánsar Indio
Rare winter visitor of feral (Scandinavian) origin.

Canada Goose* *Branta canadensis* Barnacla Canadiense
Vagrant of feral origin, chiefly in winter in the north and the Meseta.

Barnacle Goose *Branta leucopsis* Barnacla Cariblanca
Rare winter visitor, some at least originating from feral populations.

Brent Goose *Branta bernicla* Barnacla Carinegra
Scarce but annual in winter on the north coast. Dark-bellied *B.b.bernicla* is
the most frequent with Pale-bellied* *B.b.hrota* occurring mainly on western
Atlantic coasts. There is one record of a Black Brant* *B.b.nigricans* from
Villafáfila, Castilla y Léon.

Red-breasted Goose* *Branta ruficollis* Barnacla Cuellirroja
Vagrant in winter. Eight records.

Egyptian Goose *Alopochen aegyptiaca* Ganso del Nilo
Escapes and birds from feral European populations may be colonising the
region. Has bred in Catalonia.

Ruddy Shelduck *Tadorna ferruginea* Tarro Canelo
Scarce visitor. Some may originate from feral populations. Has bred.

Common Shelduck *Tadorna tadorna* Tarro Blanco
Breeds locally. More numerous in winter.

Mandarin Duck* *Aix galericulata* Pato Mandarín
Rare, chiefly in winter.

Eurasian Wigeon *Anas penelope* Silbón Europeo
Widespread in winter and on passage: present October–March. Locally abundant.

American Wigeon* *Anas americana* Silbón Americano
Vagrant, chiefly in winter on the north coast; 33 records.

Falcated Duck* *Anas falcata* Cerceta de Alfanjes
Vagrant. Three records.

Gadwall *Anas strepera* Ánade Friso
Small numbers breed widely. Common locally in winter.

Baikal Teal* *Anas formosa* Cerceta del Baikal
Vagrant. Two records.

Eurasian Teal *Anas crecca* Cerceta Común
Widespread and common in winter and on passage. Locally abundant. Rare breeder.

Green-winged Teal *Anas carolinensis* Cerceta Americana
Very rare, chiefly in winter. At least 48 records, most from Galicia.

Mallard *Anas platyrhynchos* Ánade Azulón
Widespread and common as a breeding species. Locally abundant in winter.

American Black Duck* *Anas rubripes* Ánade Sombrío
Vagrant. 12 records.

Northern Pintail *Anas acuta* Ánade Rabudo
Widespread and locally numerous on passage and in winter. Rare local breeder.

Garganey *Anas querquedula* Cerceta Carretona
Frequent on passage, especially in spring, and occasional in winter. Breeds sporadically.

Blue-winged Teal* *Anas discors* Cerceta Aliazul
Very rare, chiefly in winter and spring. Twenty-nine records.

Northern Shoveler *Anas clypeata* Cuchara Común
Common and locally numerous on passage and in winter. Scarce local breeder.

Marbled Duck *Marmaronetta angustirostris* Cerceta Pardilla
A very scarce breeding species in the south-east. Rare elsewhere.

Red-crested Pochard   *Netta rufina*   Pato Colorado
Widespread but local as a breeding species. Flocks of several hundred form locally in winter.

Common Pochard   *Aythya ferina*   Porrón Europeo
Widespread but local as a breeding species. Locally abundant in winter.

Ring-necked Duck   *Aythya collaris*   Porrón de Collar
Very rare, chiefly in winter. Over 75 records of single birds and flocks of up to eight, mainly from Atlantic coasts and the Meseta.

Ferruginous Duck   *Aythya nyroca*   Porrón Pardo
A very scarce and sporadic breeding species in the east. Rare elsewhere.

Tufted Duck   *Aythya fuligula*   Porrón Moñudo
Widespread in winter in small numbers. Breeds locally in the north.

Greater Scaup   *Aythya marila*   Porrón Bastardo
A very scarce winter visitor, chiefly to the north coast.

Lesser Scaup*   *Aythya affinis*   Porrón Bola
Very rare. Mainly in the north-west in winter. At least 18 records, including a flock of four.

Common Eider   *Somateria mollissima*   Eider
A very scarce and irregular winter visitor to Atlantic coasts and in Catalonia.

King Eider*   *Somateria spectabilis*   Eider Real
Vagrant. Five records.

Long-tailed Duck   *Clangula hyemalis*   Havelda
A rare winter visitor to Atlantic coasts and Catalonia. Vagrant elsewhere.

Common Scoter   *Melanitta nigra*   Negrón Común
Common on passage and in winter off Atlantic coasts, scarcer in the Mediterranean.

Black Scoter*   *Melanitta americana*   Negrón Americano
Vagrant to northern coasts. Three records.

Siberian Scoter*   *Melanitta stejnegeri*   Negrón Siberiano
Vagrant. One record from Galicia.

Surf Scoter*   *Melanitta perspicillata*   Negrón Careto
Very rare, recorded in winter on Atlantic coasts. Nineteen-plus records.

Velvet Scoter   *Melanitta fusca*   Negrón Especulado
Scarce winter visitor to Atlantic coasts. Rare in the Mediterranean.

White-winged Scoter*   *Melanitta deglandi*   Negrón Aliblanco
Vagrant. One record from Galicia.

Bufflehead*   *Bucephala albeola*   Porrón Albeola
Vagrant. Three records.

Barrow's Goldeneye* *Bucephala islandica* Porrón Islándico
Vagrant. One record from Galicia.

Common Goldeneye *Bucephala clangula* Porrón Osculado
Scarce winter visitor in the north and Catalonia. Rare elsewhere.

Smew* *Mergellus albellus* Serreta Chica
Very rare, in winter, chiefly on the north coast and in Catalonia. Twenty-six records.

Hooded Merganser* *Mergus cucullatus* Serreta Capuchona
Vagrant. One record from León.

Red-breasted Merganser *Mergus serrator* Serreta Mediana
Common on passage and in winter off Atlantic coasts, scarcer in the Mediterranean.

Goosander* *Mergus merganser* Serreta Grande
Vagrant in winter, chiefly on the north coast and in Catalonia. Fifty-one records.

Ruddy Duck* *Oxyura jamaicensis* Malvasía Canela
Strays, probably of feral origin, appear increasingly seldom, following culls.

White-headed Duck *Oxyura leucocephala* Malvasía Cabeciblanca
Breeds very locally in Valencia and on the southern Meseta. Rare elsewhere.

Common Quail *Coturnix coturnix* Codorníz Común
Widespread and locally numerous breeding species. Present mainly March–October.

Red-legged Partridge *Alectoris rufa* Perdiz Roja
Widespread and abundant. Very large numbers are released locally as hunting quarry.

Hazel Grouse *Bonasa bonasia* Grevól Común
A reintroduction project is underway in the Catalan Pyrenees (Arán valley).

Rock Ptarmigan *Lagopus muta* Lagópodo Alpino
Scarce resident in the Pyrenees, mainly in Aragón and Catalonia, generally above 2,000m.

Western Capercaillie *Tetrao urogallus* Urogallo Común
Scarce resident in the central Cordillera Cantábrica and the Pyrenees. Declining.

Grey Partridge *Perdix perdix* Perdiz Pardilla
Resident in open montane scrub in the Pyrenees, Cordillera Cantábrica and Sistema Ibérico.

Common Pheasant *Phasianus colchicus* Faisán Vulgar
Scattered feral populations derived from released birds occur.

Red-throated Diver (Loon) *Gavia stellata* Colimbo Chico
Regular but very scarce in winter: November–March, along the Atlantic coast. Rarer in the Mediterranean.

Black-throated Diver (Loon) *Gavia arctica* Colimbo Ártico
Very scarce, in winter: November–March, along the Atlantic coast and in
northern Catalonia (Roses bay). Rare elsewhere.

Pacific Diver (Loon)* *Gavia pacifica* Colimbo del Pacífico
Vagrant. One record (Santoña).

Great Northern Diver (Common Loon) *Gavia immer* Colimbo Grande
Regular in winter: November–March on the Atlantic coast. Scarcer in the
Mediterranean.

Pied-billed Grebe* *Podilymbus podiceps* Zampullín Picogrueso
Vagrant. Six-plus records.

Little Grebe *Tachybaptus ruficollis* Zampullín Común
Common on reed-fringed lakes. Mainly resident.

Great Crested Grebe *Podiceps cristatus* Somormujo Lavanco
Breeds commonly on larger lakes and on reservoirs. More widespread in
winter.

Red-necked Grebe *Podiceps grisegena* Somormujo Cuellirojo
Scarce but regular in winter on Atlantic coasts. Rare elsewhere.

Slavonian (Horned) Grebe *Podiceps auritus* Zampullín Cuellirrojo
Scarce but regular in winter on Atlantic coasts. Rare elsewhere.

Black-necked Grebe *Podiceps nigricollis* Zampullín Cuellinegro
Breeds very locally, chiefly in Castilla–La Mancha. Widespread and locally
abundant post-breeding and in winter, especially at Levant wetlands.

Black-browed Albatross* *Thalassarche melanophris* Albatros Ojeroso
Vagrant. Five records from the Atlantic coast plus several of albatross
species.

Northern Fulmar *Fulmarus glacialis* Northern Fulmar
Regular off Biscay coasts, especially August–September. Vagrant in the
Mediterranean.

Fea's/Zino's Petrel* *Pterodroma feae/madeira* Petrel Freira/Gongon
Annual in recent years off Galicia, especially Estaca de Bares, in June–
December but chiefly mid August–September. One has been identified as a
Fea's Petrel.

Black-capped Petrel* *Pterodroma hasitata* Petrel Antillano
Vagrant. One record 120km off Galicia.

Bulwer's Petrel* *Bulweria bulwerii* Petrel de Bulwer
Recorded far off western Galicia, mainly in summer and autumn. Very rare
inshore.

Cory's Shearwater *Calonectris diomedea* Pardela Cenicienta
Present and sometimes numerous off all coasts: mainly March–October.
Mediterranean form is Scopoli's Shearwater.

Great Shearwater   *Puffinus gravis*   Pardela Capirotada
Present off Atlantic coasts, mainly August–November. Exceptional in the
Mediterranean.

Sooty Shearwater   *Puffinus griseus*   Pardela Sombría
Present off Atlantic coasts, mainly August–November. Exceptional in the
Mediterranean.

Manx Shearwater   *Puffinus puffinus*   Pardela Pichoneta
Present off Atlantic coasts, mainly July–December.

Levantine (Yelkouan) Shearwater   *Puffinus yelkouan*   Pardela Mediterránea
Present and sometimes numerous off Mediterranean coasts, especially off
Catalonia in winter.

Balearic Shearwater   *Puffinus mauretanicus*   Pardela Balear
Present offshore all year round.

Macaronesian (Barolo's) Shearwater*   *Puffinus baroli*   Pardela Chica
Scarce but regular in late summer and autumn off Atlantic coasts.

Wilson's Storm-petrel*   *Oceanites oceanicus*   Paíño de Wilson
Scarce but regular in summer and autumn off Atlantic coasts.

European Storm-petrel   *Hydrobates pelagicus*   Paíño Europeo
Breeds locally on rocky islets off the north and south-east coasts.
Widespread offshore, mainly May–November.

Leach's Storm-petrel   *Oceanodroma leucorhoa*   Paíño de Leach
Present off Atlantic coasts in autumn and winter. Very rare in the
Mediterranean.

Swinhoe's Storm-petrel*   *Oceanodroma monorhis*   Paíño de Swinhoe
Vagrant. One record from Benidorm islet.

Band-rumped (Madeiran) Storm-petrel*   *Oceanodroma castro*   Paíño de
Madeira
Very rare inshore. Eleven records, nearly all off Galicia.

Red-billed Tropicbird*   *Phaeton aethereus*   Rabijunco Etéreo
Vagrant off Galicia. At least two pending records.

Red-footed Booby*   *Sula sula*   Piquero Patirrojo
Vagrant. One Mediterranean record.

Masked Booby*   *Sula dactylatra*   Piquero Enmascarado
Vagrant. One Biscay record.

Brown Booby*   *Sula leucogaster*   Piquero Pardo
Vagrant. Four records from Galicia.

Northern Gannet   *Morus bassanus*   Alcatraz Común
Abundant migrant and in winter off Atlantic coasts. Also common in the
Mediterranean.

Great Cormorant *Phalacrocorax carbo* Cormorán Grande
Common in winter on lakes, reservoirs and along coasts. Breeds locally inland.

European Shag *Phalacrocorax aristotelis* Cormorán Moñudo
Common resident on Atlantic coasts. Also more locally in the Mediterranean.

Pygmy Cormorant* *Phalacrocorax pygmeus* Cormorán Pigmeo
Vagrant. One pending record from Catalonia.

Great White Pelican* *Pelecanus onocrotalus* Pelícano Vulgar
Vagrant. Eleven records: origin unknown.

Pink-backed Pelican* *Pelecanus rufescens* Pelícano Rosado
Vagrant. Nine records: origin unknown.

Magnificent Frigatebird* *Fregata magnificens* Rabihorcado Magnífico
Vagrant. One record from Cantabria. Also three records of unidentified frigatebirds.

Great (Eurasian) Bittern *Botaurus stellaris* Avetoro Común
Scarce local breeder. Scarce but more widespread in winter.

American Bittern* *Botaurus lentiginosus* Avetoro Lentiginoso
Vagrant. Four records, three of them from Galicia.

Little Bittern *Ixobrychus minutus* Avetorillo Común
Widespread April–September, nesting in reedbeds. A few remain in winter.

Black-crowned Night Heron *Nycticorax nycticorax* Martinete Común
Widespread but local in the east and centre April–September. Some remain in winter.

Squacco Heron *Ardeola ralloides* Garcilla Cangrejera
Locally numerous on the east coast and also very locally inland. Mainly April–September.

Cattle Egret *Bubulcus ibis* Garcilla Bueyera
Resident. Locally numerous in the east and centre. Recent colonist on the north coast.

Western Reef Heron (Egret)* *Egretta gularis* Garceta Dimorfa
Vagrant. At least 24 records of 'pure' birds, in our region chiefly from the east coast.

Little Egret *Egretta garzetta* Garceta Común
Breeds locally. Common, especially along coasts, all year round.

Great White Egret *Egretta alba* Garceta Grande
Breeds locally at large wetlands. Increasingly widespread and numerous in winter: mainly October–March.

Grey Heron *Ardea cinerea* Garza Real
Numerous and widespread in winter and on passage. Breeds locally.

Purple Heron   *Ardea purpurea*   Garza Imperial
Breeds locally, in the Ebro valley, the east coast and Castilla–La Mancha especially. Widespread on passage. Present April–October mainly.

Black Stork   *Ciconia nigra*   Cigüeña Negra
Scarce breeder in the west. Increasing. Migrants cross the Pyrenees and east.

White Stork   *Ciconia ciconia*   Cigüeña Blanca
Widespread breeder in the west and centre, very local or absent in the northern coastlands and in the east, except in the Ebro valley. Partial migrant.

Marabou Stork*   *Leptoptilos crumenifer*   Marabú Africano
Vagrant. Thirteen records.

Glossy Ibis   *Plegadis falcinellus*   Morito Común
Breeds in the Ebro Delta and occasionally elsewhere on the east coast. Also nests at Daimiel. Numerous in winter on eastern ricefields especially. Scarce and irregular elsewhere but there have been small influxes in the north.

Sacred Ibis*   *Threskiornis aethiopicus*   Ibis Sagrado
Occasional records, all believed to be of feral or captive origin.

Eurasian Spoonbill   *Platalea leucorodia*   Espátula Común
Regular on passage at Santoña and locally elsewhere. Some winter.

Greater Flamingo   *Phoenicopterus roseus*   Flamenco Común
Breeds in the Ebro Delta and often at El Hondo; irregularly in Castilla–La Mancha. Frequent along the east coast. Very rare in the north.

Lesser Flamingo*   *Phoenicopterus minor*   Flamenco Enano
Vagrant. At least 25 records: of single birds and groups of up to four. Has bred in Cuenca.

European Honey Buzzard (Honey-buzzard)   *Pernis apivorus*   Abejero Europeo
Widespread breeder in the north and west. Large numbers cross the east and Pyrenees on passage. Occurs mainly May–September.

Black-shouldered (Black-winged) Kite   *Elanus caeruleus*   Elanio Común
Scarce but increasing resident on the Meseta. Local elsewhere.

Black Kite   *Milvus migrans*   Milano Negro
Common breeder in the north and west, scarce elsewhere. Large numbers cross the east and Pyrenees on passage. Occurs mainly March–September.

Red Kite   *Milvus milvus*   Milano Real
Breeds mainly in Castilla y Léon, Aragón and Navarra, scarce or absent elsewhere. Large numbers winter on the Meseta.

White-tailed Eagle*   *Haliaetus albicilla*   Pigargo Europeo
Vagrant. Eight records of wintering birds, most in the north-east.

Lammergeier (Bearded Vulture)   *Gypaetus barbatus*   Quebrantahuesos
Scarce resident in the Pyrenees. Reintroduction underway in Cantabria. Rare elsewhere.

Egyptian Vulture *Neophron percnopterus* Alimoche Común
A widespread breeding species, especially in the north and north-east. Mainly present March–September.

Griffon Vulture *Gyps fulvus* Buitre Leonado
Widespread and locally abundant breeding species. Resident, but immatures dispersive.

Rüppell's Vulture *Gyps rueppellii* Buitre Moteado
Vagrant, but regular in SW Iberia. At least ten records from the meseta.

Lappet-faced Vulture* *Torgos tracheliotus* Buitre Orejudo
Vagrant. One 1940 Pyrenean record.

Black (Cinereous) Vulture *Aegypius monachus* Buitre Negro
Locally common as a breeding species in central Spain. Rare elsewhere.

Short-toed (Short-toed Snake) Eagle *Circaetus gallicus* Culebrera Europea
Widespread and locally common breeding species. Chiefly present March–October.

Western Marsh Harrier *Circus aeruginosus* Aguilucho Lagunero
Locally common breeding species. Widespread on passage and in winter.

Hen (Northern) Harrier *Circus cyaneus* Aguilucho Pálido
Scarce breeder, chiefly in the north. Widespread on passage and in winter.

Pallid Harrier *Circus macrourus* Aguilucho Papialbo
Rare, on passage and in winter. Over 40 records, mainly of single birds but including a group of three. Reported increasingly regularly on the east coast especially and has wintered there.

Montagu's Harrier *Circus pygargus* Aguilucho Cenizo
A common breeder in cereal crops and steppe. Mainly present April–September.

Northern Goshawk *Accipiter gentilis* Azor Común
Widespread in forested areas. Largely resident.

Eurasian Sparrowhawk *Accipiter nisus* Gavilán Común
Widespread in forested areas. Many occur on passage and in winter.

Common Buzzard *Buteo buteo* Busardo Ratonero
Widespread and common breeder. Migrants from the north increase numbers in winter.

Long-legged Buzzard* *Buteo rufinus* Busardo Moro
Regular in SW Iberia and has bred. At least ten records from the north and east.

Rough-legged Buzzard* *Buteo lagopus* Ratonero Calzado
Vagrant. Seven records, all in Catalonia October–March.

Greater Spotted Eagle* *Aquila clanga* Águila Moteada
Very scarce but regular in winter, especially at Levant wetlands, notably El Hondo.

Lesser Spotted Eagle* *Aquila pomarina* Águila Pomerana
Very rare migrant. May have nested in the Pyrenees in 2011.

Booted Eagle *Aquila pennata* Aguililla Calzada
A widespread and locally common breeder. Present mainly March–October.
Some winter on the east coast.

Golden Eagle *Aquila chrysaetos* Águila Real
Present in some numbers in all mountain ranges. Mainly resident.

Bonelli's Eagle *Aquila fasciata* Águila-azor Perdicera
Widespread and characteristic of cliffs and broken country. Declining in the
north. Largely resident but disperses more widely in winter, when some
occur in steppes and cultivated areas.

Spanish Imperial Eagle *Aquila adalberti* Águila Imperial Ibérica
A scarce and vulnerable species. The world population was only 131 pairs
in 1999 but increased under protection to 365+ pairs by 2012. Most are in
central and south-west Spain. Generally resident but juveniles especially disperse more widely in winter.

Eastern Imperial Eagle* *Aquila heliaca* Águila Imperial Oriental
Vagrant. One 2010 ringing recovery from Alicante and two old records from
the north-east.

Osprey *Pandion haliaetus* Águila Pescadora
Widespread on passage: March–May and August–October. Some winter
locally.

Lesser Kestrel *Falco naumanni* Cernícalo Primilla
Locally common on the Meseta and in the Ebro valley. Present mainly
February–October.

Common Kestrel *Falco tinnunculus* Cernícalo Vulgar
Widespread and common. Resident, but numbers are increased by migrants
in winter.

Red-footed Falcon* *Falco vespertinus* Cernícalo Patirrojo
Rare migrant. Most frequent in Catalonia, where occasional irruptions occur
in spring.

Merlin *Falco columbarius* Esmerejón
Scarce but regular and widespread in winter. Present October–April.

Hobby *Falco subbuteo* Alcotán Europeo
Widespread, most abundant in the north. Present April–October.

Eleonora's Falcon *Falco eleonorae* Halcón de Eleonora
Occasional in summer on the meseta and on the Mediterranean coast. Rare
in the north.

Lanner Falcon* *Falco biarmicus* Halcón Borni
Vagrant to the region but regular in south-western Spain and Gibraltar.

Saker Falcon* *Falco cherrug* Halcón Sacre
Vagrant. At least one record; a radio-tracked bird from Hungary crossed the region.

Gyr Falcon *Falco rusticolus* Halcón Gerifalte
Vagrant. One record of an overwintering bird in Asturias.

Peregrine Falcon *Falco peregrinus* Halcón Peregrino
Widespread, nesting on coastal and inland cliffs and locally on tall buildings. Some northern European birds occur in winter.

Water Rail *Rallus aquaticus* Rascón Europeo
Locally common resident in suitable habitat. More widespread in winter.

Spotted Crake *Porzana porzana* Polluela Pintoja
Small numbers cross the region on passage and some winter. Rare breeder.

Sora Crake* *Porzana carolina* Polluela de Carolina
Vagrant. One record from Galicia.

Little Crake *Porzana parva* Polluela Bastarda
Rare migrant. Most often at east coast wetlands.

Baillon's Crake *Porzana pusilla* Polluela Chica
Scarce and very local breeder. Chiefly a trans-Saharan migrant.

Corn Crake *Crex crex* Guión de Codornices
Crosses the region on passage but very rarely recorded.

Common Moorhen *Gallinula chloropus* Gallineta Común
A common and widespread breeding species. Mainly resident.

Allen's Gallinule* *Porphyrula alleni* Calamón de Allen
Vagrant. Four records.

Purple Swamphen *Porphyrio porphyrio* Calamón Común
Locally common at wetlands in south-central Spain and along the east coast.

Common (Eurasian) Coot *Fulica atra* Focha Común
A common and widespread breeder. Large numbers of migrants are also present in winter.

American Coot* *Fulica americana* Focha Común
Vagrant. Three records.

Red-knobbed Coot *Fulica cristata* Focha Moruna
A very scarce local resident on the east coast. These populations derive from reintroductions.

Common Crane *Grus grus* Grulla Común
Abundant in winter in south-central Spain. Frequent on passage in the northeast, notably at Gallocanta. Present mainly from late-October to early March.

Sandhill Crane* *Grus canadensis* Grulla Canadiense
Vagrant. One record.

Demoiselle Crane* *Grus virgo*   Grulla Damisela
Vagrant. Two records.

Little Bustard *Tetrax tetrax* Sisón Común
Mainly resident. Widespread and locally common on the Meseta, scarce or absent elsewhere. Large flocks, of a few hundred birds, form outside the breeding season. Declining.

Great Bustard *Otis tarda* Avutarda Común
Resident. Locally common on the Meseta but scarce or absent elsewhere. Range contracting.

Eurasian Stone-curlew *Burhinus oedicnemus* Alcaraván Común
A common breeding species in steppe habitats. Some winter, mainly in the south.

Black-winged Stilt *Himantopus himantopus* Cigüeñuela Común
Widespread and locally numerous, breeding commonly along the Mediterranean coast and more locally at inland wetlands. Mainly present March–October, but some winter.

Pied Avocet *Recurvirostra avosetta* Avoceta Común
Breeds at major east coast wetlands and locally inland. Mainly present March–October, but some winter.

Eurasian Oystercatcher *Haematopus ostralegus* Ostrero Euroasiatico
Scarce breeder in the Ebro delta and locally on the north coast. Common on passage and in winter on the north coast, scarcer in the Mediterranean. Exceptional inland.

Pacific Golden Plover* *Pluvialis fulva* Chorlito Dorado Siberiano
Vagrant. Nine records, including five from the east coast.

American Golden Plover* *Pluvialis dominica* Chorlito Dorado Americano
Vagrant. Twenty-six records, including 16 from Galicia.

European Golden Plover *Pluvialis apricaria* Chorlito Dorado
Locally numerous in winter. Mainly present November–March.

Grey Plover *Pluvialis squatarola* Chorlito Gris
Common in winter and on passage in coastal habitats, rarely inland.

Sociable Lapwing* *Vanellus gregarius* Avefría Social
Very rare, mainly in winter. At least 33 records.

White-tailed Lapwing* *Vanellus leucurus* Avefría Culiblanca
Vagrant. One record from Asturias.

Northern Lapwing *Vanellus vanellus* Avefría Europea
Small numbers nest, chiefly on the Meseta. Common and often abundant in winter, especially when harsh conditions occur further north in Europe. Mainly present November–March.

Little Ringed Plover *Charadrius dubius* Chorlitejo Chico
Small numbers breed, especially on stony river beds. Mainly present March–October. Widespread on passage. Small numbers remain in winter.

Common Ringed Plover   *Charadrius hiaticula*   Chorlitejo Grande
Common on coasts on passage and in winter. Scarce inland.

Semipalmated Plover*   *Charadrius semipalmatus*   Chorlitejo Semipalmeado
Vagrant. Four records from Galicia.

Killdeer*   *Charadrius vociferus*   Chorlitejo Culirrojo
Vagrant. Four records from Galicia.

Kittlitz's Plover*   *Charadrius pecuarius*   Chorlitejo Pecuario
Vagrant. One record.

Kentish Plover   *Charadrius alexandrinus*   Chorlitejo Patinegro
Widespread and common on sandy coasts and saltpans in the east and north-west. Some nest locally inland. Residents are augmented by migrants on passage and in winter.

Lesser Sand Plover*   *Charadrius mongolus*   Chorlitejo Mongol Chico.
Vagrant. One record.

Greater Sand Plover*   *Charadrius leschenaultii*   Chorlitejo Mongol Grande.
Vagrant. Two records from the Ebro delta and one from Galicia.

Eurasian Dotterel   *Charadrius morinellus*   Chorlito Carambolo
Has bred in the Pyrenees in Catalonia. Usually recorded very locally on passage in March–April and August–October and occasionally in winter. Most sightings are of small groups.

Upland Sandpiper*   *Bartramia longicauda*   Correlimos Batitú
Vagrant. Three records from the north-west.

Hudsonian Whimbrel   *Numenius (phaeopus) hudsonicus*   Zarapito de Hudson
Vagrant. Two records from the north-west.

Eurasian Whimbrel   *Numenius phaeopus*   Zarapito Trinador
Common on passage, chiefly on the coast. Small numbers winter.

Slender-billed Curlew*   *Numenius tenuirostris*   Zarapito Fino
Formerly a very rare passage migrant and winter visitor. No recent reports.

Eurasian Curlew   *Numenius arquata*   Zarapito Real
Common on passage: July–October and March–April, and in winter on Atlantic coasts. Scarce in the Mediterranean and rare inland.

Black-tailed Godwit   *Limosa limosa*   Aguja Colinegra
Common on passage: in February–April and July–September, and in winter, chiefly on the coast but also at favoured inland localities.

Bar-tailed Godwit   *Limosa lapponica*   Aguja Colipinta
Common on passage, in March and September–October, and in winter in coastal habitats.

Ruddy Turnstone   *Arenaria interpres*   Vuelvepiedras
Common in small numbers on passage and in winter on Atlantic coasts. Scarcer in the Mediterranean. Chiefly on rocky coasts.

Great Knot* *Calidris tenuirostris* Correlimos Grande
Vagrant. One record from the Ebro delta.

Red Knot *Calidris canutus* Correlimos Gordo
Scarce but regular on passage and in winter on the north coast. Uncommon
in the Mediterranean.

Ruff *Calidris pugnax* Combatiente
Common on passage; mainly March–April and August–September, and locally
in winter, at both coastal and inland wetlands.

Sharp-tailed Sandpiper* *Calidris acuminata* Correlimos Acuminado
Vagrant. Three records.

Broad-billed Sandpiper* *Calidris falcinellus* Correlimos Falcinelo
Vagrant. Thirty-plus records, including 22 from Catalonia.

Curlew Sandpiper *Calidris ferruginea* Correlimos Zarapitín
Common on passage, both along coasts and inland. Mainly in May and
August–September but some winter on the east coast.

Red-necked Stint* *Calidris ruficollis* Correlimos Cuellirojo
Vagrant. One record from Valencia.

Temminck's Stint *Calidris temminckii* Correlimos de Temminck
Scarce migrant and winter resident, both inland and on the coast.

Sanderling *Calidris alba* Correlimos Tridáctilo
Common on passage and in winter on sandy coasts. Rare inland.

Dunlin *Calidris alpina* Correlimos Común
Abundant on passage; mainly in April and September, and in winter. Chiefly in
coastal habitats but locally common inland. Small numbers of non-breeders
remain in summer.

Purple Sandpiper *Calidris maritima* Correlimos Oscuro
Regular but scarce on the north coast in winter. Exceptional in the
Mediterranean.

Baird's Sandpiper* *Calidris bairdii* Correlimos de Baird
Vagrant. Eleven records, eight from Galicia.

Little Stint *Calidris minuta* Correlimos Menudo
Common on passage on coasts and inland. Small numbers are present in
winter.

White-rumped Sandpiper* *Calidris fuscicollis* Correlimos de Bonaparte
Vagrant. Twenty records, including ten from Galicia.

Least Sandpiper* *Calidris minutilla* Correlimos Menudillo
Vagrant. Three records.

Buff-breasted Sandpiper *Tryngites subruficollis* Correlimos Canelo
Vagrant. Sixty-plus records, including 25 from Galicia. Occurs chiefly in
September–October.

Pectoral Sandpiper *Calidris melanotos* Correlimos Pectoral
Rare but annual on all coasts, mainly at coastal wetlands in August–October.
Very rare in spring, April–May. Exceptional inland.

Western Sandpiper* *Calidris mauri* Correlimos de Alaska
Vagrant. Three records from Galicia.

Semipalmated Sandpiper* *Calidris pusilla* Correlimos Semipalmeado
Vagrant. Twelve records, including eight from Galicia.

Wilson's Phalarope* *Phalaropus tricolor* Falaropo Tricolor
Rare vagrant. Fifteen-plus records, chiefly in spring and autumn. Has overwintered.

Red-necked Phalarope *Phalaropus lobatus* Falaropo Picofino
Occasional individuals are reported on passage, most frequently on the east
coast.

Grey (Red) Phalarope *Phalaropus fulicarius* Falaropo Picogrueso
Regular off north-west coasts on autumn passage and occasionally in winter.

Terek Sandpiper* *Xenus cinereus* Andarríos del Terek
Very rare migrant and has wintered. At least 35 records, including 19 from
Catalonia.

Common Sandpiper *Actitis hypoleucos* Andarríos Chico
Breeds locally, especially along streams in the northern mountains. Common
on passage both inland and on coasts: July–November and March–May. A few
winter.

Spotted Sandpiper* *Actitis macularius* Andarríos Maculado
Vagrant. Seventeen records, including seven from Galicia.

Green Sandpiper *Tringa ochropus* Andarríos Grande
Widespread and common on passage and in winter, generally by fresh water.

Solitary Sandpiper* *Tringa solitaria* Andarríos Solitario
Vagrant. One record.

Spotted Redshank *Tringa erythropus* Archibebe Oscuro
Common on passage inland and on coasts, and locally at coastal sites in
winter.

Greater Yellowlegs* *Tringa melanoleuca* Archibebe Patigualdo Grande
Vagrant. Five records from Galicia.

Greenshank *Tringa nebularia* Archibebe Claro
Widespread and common on passage; July–October and March–May, mainly
on coasts but also at inland wetlands. Locally common in winter at coastal
wetlands.

Lesser Yellowlegs* *Tringa flavipes* Archibebe Patigualdo Chico
Vagrant. Fifty-plus records, including 22 from Galicia.

Marsh Sandpiper *Tringa stagnatilis* Archibebe Fino
Very scarce but regular on passage and in winter, especially on the east
coast.

Wood Sandpiper *Tringa glareola* Andarríos Bastardo
Common on passage along the east coast, where some also winter. Scarce elsewhere. Generally by fresh water.

Common Redshank *Tringa totanus* Archibebe Común
Scarce breeder on the east coast and locally inland. Common on coasts on passage and in winter.

Jack Snipe *Lymnocryptes minimus* Agachadiza Chica
Present on passage and in winter, chiefly on inland wetlands, from October–April.

Short-billed Dowitcher* *Limnodromus griseus* Agujeta Gris
Vagrant. One record from the Mar Menor, Murcia.

Long-billed Dowitcher* *Limnodromus scolopaceus* Agujeta Escolopácea
Vagrant. At least 16 records.

Eurasian Woodcock *Scolopax rusticola* Chocha Perdiz
Scarce breeder in the north. Widespread in winter, most abundant in the north.

Common Snipe *Gallinago gallinago* Agachadiza Común
Common on passage and in winter, chiefly on inland wetlands. Very rare local breeder.

Great Snipe *Gallinago media* Agachadiza Real
Very rare, mainly on passage. Twenty-plus records, including 17 from Catalonia.

Cream-coloured Courser* *Cursorius cursor* Corredor Sahariano
Vagrant. Five records: but has bred in eastern Andalucía.

Collared Pratincole *Glareola pratincola* Canastera Común
Locally common on the east coast and in Castilla–La Mancha. Rare elsewhere. Mainly present April–August.

Black-winged Pratincole *Glareola nordmanni* Canastera Alinegra
Vagrant. One record from Valencia.

Pomarine Skua *Stercorarius pomarinus* Págalo Pomarino
Regular on autumn passage along northern coasts, scarcer in spring. Scarce in the Mediterranean, where recorded mainly in spring.

Arctic Skua (Parasitic Jaeger) *Stercorarius parasiticus* Págalo Parásito
Regular on autumn passage along northern coasts, scarcer in spring. Scarcer in the Mediterranean. Some remain in winter. Occasional in summer.

Long-tailed Skua (Jaeger) *Stercorarius longicaudus* Págalo Rabero
Regular on autumn passage off north-west coasts, mainly August–September. There are at least ten records from the Mediterranean coast and several inland.

Great Skua *Stercorarius skua* Págalo Grande
Regular on passage and in winter off all coasts, but more numerous in the Atlantic. Occasional in summer.

South Polar Skua* *Stercorarius maccormicki* Págalo Polar
Vagrant. One autumn record from Estaca de Bares and others pending.

Common Guillemot (Murre) *Uria aalge* Arao Común
Recently extinct as a breeding species in Galicia. Common on passage and in winter off Atlantic coasts. Rare in the Mediterranean.

Brünnich's Guillemot (Thick-billed Murre)* *Uria lomvia* Arao de Brünnich
Vagrant. One record from Galicia.

Razorbill *Alca torda* Alca Común
Common on passage and in winter along coasts. Often seen fishing inshore. Present October–May.

Black Guillemot* *Cepphus grylle* Arao Aliblanco
Vagrant. Four north coast records in winter.

Little Auk *Alle alle* Mérgulo Marino
Rare winter visitor. Most records are of beached birds found after winter storms along the Atlantic coast. Vagrant in the Mediterranean.

Atlantic Puffin *Fratercula arctica* Frailecillo Común
Common on passage and in winter off Atlantic coasts. Present November–May in the Mediterranean but seldom seen from shore.

Sooty Tern* *Onychoprion fuscata* Charrán Sombrío
Vagrant. Three records, two of them from Galicia.

Bridled Tern* *Onychoprion anaethetus* Charrán Embridado
Vagrant. One record from the Ebro delta.

Little Tern *Sternula albifrons* Charrancito
Breeds locally on sandy Mediterranean coasts and at scattered inland wetlands. Widespread on passage. Present April–October.

Gull-billed Tern *Gelochelidon nilotica* Pagaza Piconegra
Mainly small colonies breed locally, notably at the Ebro delta, elsewhere on the east coast and at scattered inland wetlands. Absent from the north. Mainly present April–October.

Caspian Tern *Hydroprogne caspia* Pagaza Piquirroja
Scarce migrant on the Mediterranean coast, where a few winter. Rare on the north coast.

Whiskered Tern *Chlidonias hybrida* Fumarel Cariblanco
Up to 1,000 pairs nest at the Ebro delta and there are other much smaller colonies on the east coast and at scattered inland localities. Common on passage on the east coast but scarce in the Atlantic. Chiefly present March–October but small numbers winter at the delta.

Black Tern *Chlidonias niger* Fumarel Común
Breeds very sporadically at inland wetlands, chiefly in Castilla–La Mancha. Widespread on passage, especially in May and August–September, when large numbers sometimes occur along coasts. Present April–October. Occasional in winter.

White-winged Black Tern *Chlidonias leucopterus* Fumarel Aliblanco
A very scarce passage migrant on the Mediterranean coast in late April and May, more frequent but still rare during August–mid October. Has wintered. Exceptional in the north.

Sandwich Tern *Sterna sandvicensis* Charrán Patinegro
Breeds very locally on the Mediterranean coast, with over 1,000 pairs at the Ebro delta and the Albufera de Valencia. Common on passage and in winter along all coasts. Present mainly August–April but some non-breeders occur in summer.

Elegant Tern* *Sterna elegans* Charrán Elegante
Vagrant. One accepted record and others pending. Has bred at the Albufera.

Royal Tern* *Sterna maxima* Charrán Real
Vagrant. Four records from Catalonia.

Lesser Crested Tern *Sterna bengalensis* Charrán Bengalí
Rare on passage on the Mediterranean coast. Exceptional elsewhere. Has bred at the Ebro delta and the Albufera de Valencia.

Forster's Tern* *Sterna forsteri* Charrán de Forster
Vagrant. Two records from Galicia.

Common Tern *Sterna hirundo* Charrán Común
Common on passage, especially along coasts, in August–October and March–May. Breeds locally on the Mediterranean coast and also in Santander Bay, and occasionally inland. A few winter.

Roseate Tern *Sterna dougallii* Charrán Rosado
Occurs on passage off Atlantic coasts but rarely seen onshore. Rare in the Mediterranean but has nested at the Ebro delta.

Arctic Tern *Sterna paradisaea* Charrán Ártico
Occurs on passage off Atlantic coasts but scarce onshore. Vagrant in the Mediterranean.

Little Gull *Hydrocoleus minutus* Gaviota Enana
Regular but usually scarce on passage on all coasts: August–October and March–May. Common in some winters, especially offshore in the Mediterranean.

Ross's Gull* *Rhodostethia rosea* Gaviota Rosada
Vagrant. Three records.

Sabine's Gull *Xema sabini* Gaviota de Sabine
Regular on passage off northern coasts, especially in autumn. Very rare in the Mediterranean.

Black-legged Kittiwake *Rissa tridactyla* Gaviota Tridáctila
Common October–April off Atlantic coasts. Recently extinct as a breeder in Galicia. Scarce and irregular in the Mediterranean. Occasionally storm-blown inland.

Slender-billed Gull *Larus genei* Gaviota Picofina
Breeds in the Ebro delta and locally elsewhere on the east coast. Mainly
present March–September but some remain in winter. Exceptional inland and
on the north coast.

Bonaparte's Gull* *Larus philadelphia* Gaviota de Bonaparte
Vagrant. At least 35 records, half of them from Galicia.

Black-headed Gull *Larus ridibundus* Gaviota Reidora
Small breeding colonies occur on the east coast and locally inland.
Widespread and abundant in winter both inland and on the coast.

Laughing Gull* *Larus atricilla* Gaviota Guanaguanare
Vagrant. At least 33 records, 24 from Galicia or the Biscay Coast.

Franklin's Gull* *Larus pipixcan* Gaviota de Franklin
Vagrant. Ten records.

Audouin's Gull *Larus audouinii* Gaviota de Audouin
Breeds in the Ebro delta (up to 15,000 pairs in the past, now fewer)
and locally elsewhere on the east coast. Common on passage along
Mediterranean coasts, mainly February–April and August–October. Small
numbers winter in the Mediterranean. Exceptional inland and on the north
coast.

Mediterranean Gull *Larus melanocephalus* Gaviota Cabecinegra
Common on passage and numerous in winter on the Mediterranean coast and
has bred there. Less numerous but still common on passage and in winter
on Atlantic coasts. Occasional inland but becoming more frequent and has
nested at Black-headed Gull colonies there.

Common (Mew) Gull *Larus canus* Gaviota Cana
Regular on the north coast in small numbers, chiefly in winter. Scarcer in the
Mediterranean.

Ring-billed Gull *Larus delawarensis* Gaviota de Delaware
Rare but formerly regular on the north coast, chiefly in winter. Vagrant in the
Mediterranean.

Lesser Black-backed Gull *Larus fuscus* Gaviota Sombría
Small numbers breed in Galicia and the Ebro delta. Common on coasts on
passage and in winter. Very large numbers winter inland, notably along the
Guadiana River and in Madrid.

European Herring Gull *Larus argentatus* Gaviota Argéntea
Regular on the north coast in small numbers, chiefly in winter. Rare in the
Mediterranean.

Caspian Gull *Larus cachinnans* Gaviota Caspia
Rare. Over 70 records, since the first in 2005: from Catalonia, the Atlantic
coast and rubbish dumps in Madrid. Mainly in winter.

Yellow-legged Gull *Larus michahellis* Gaviota Patiamarilla
Locally abundant, with large nesting colonies on all coasts. Mainly resident
but disperses widely along coasts. Scarce inland.

American Herring Gull* *Larus smithsonianus* Gaviota Argéntea Americana
Vagrant. Five records.

Thayer's Gull *Larus thayeri* Gaviota Esquimal
Vagrant. One record from Galicia.

Iceland Gull *Larus glaucoides* Gaviota Groenlandesa
Rare. Over 70 records, mainly from the north coast, chiefly immature birds in winter. Annual in recent years, sometimes in twos and threes.

Glaucous Gull *Larus hyperboreus* Gavión Hiperbóreo
Rare but over 100 records all from the north coast, chiefly immature birds in winter. Annual in recent years. Has summered.

Great Black-backed Gull *Larus marinus* Gavión Atlántico
Regular on the north coast in small numbers, chiefly in winter but some nest. Rare in the Mediterranean.

Black-bellied Sandgrouse *Pterocles orientalis* Ganga Ortega
Locally common resident in stony steppe habitats, chiefly on the Meseta and in the Ebro valley.

Pin-tailed Sandgrouse *Pterocles alchata* Ganga Común
Locally common resident in steppe habitats. Most abundant in Castilla–La Mancha but also occurs in the Ebro valley and Castilla y Léon.

Pallas's Sandgrouse* *Syrrhaptes paradoxus* Ganga de Pallas.
Vagrant. One 19th-century record from Valencia.

Rock Dove *Columba livia* Paloma Bravía
Feral birds are common. Wild-type birds occur on rocky coasts and on inland cliffs.

Stock Dove *Columba oenas* Paloma Zurita
Breeds commonly in the north-east, more sparsely elsewhere. More widespread in winter.

Common Wood Pigeon (Woodpigeon) *Columba palumbus* Paloma Torcaz
An increasingly widespread and common resident. Migrants from the north greatly increase numbers in winter, when large flocks occur – and are hunted as they cross mountain passes.

African Collared Dove *Streptopelia risoria* Tórtola Rosigrís
A small feral population exists in coastal Valencia and Alicante.

Eurasian Collared Dove *Streptopelia decaocto* Tórtola Turca
Widespread and locally common, particularly frequenting town parks and farms.

European Turtle Dove *Streptopelia turtur* Tórtola Común
Widespread and common April–October. Declining.

Rufous (Oriental) Turtle Dove* *Streptopelia orientalis* Tórtola Oriental
Vagrant. Two records.

Laughing Dove* *Streptopelia senegalensis* Tórtola Senegalesa
Vagrant. Six records.

Rose-ringed Parakeet *Psittacula krameri* Cotorra de Kramer
Feral populations occur, mainly along the east coast, in Asturias and in Madrid.

Monk Parakeet *Myopsitta monachus* Cotorra Monje
Feral populations occur, along the east coast and in Madrid.

Great Spotted Cuckoo *Clamator glandarius* Críalo Europeo
Widespread in the breeding season, except in the far north and Pyrenees: confined to areas where its customary host, the Common Magpie breeds. Widespread on passage. Some arrive very early, November–February, departing July–August: with juveniles lingering through September.

Common Cuckoo *Cuculus canorus* Cuco Común
Widespread and common on passage, especially in spring, and in the breeding season. Adults present March–July, some juveniles lingering into September.

Barn Owl *Tyto alba* Lechuza Común
A widespread and common resident.

Eurasian Scops Owl *Otus scops* Autillo
Widespread and common in open woodlands and often in parks and gardens. Chiefly present March–October. Some remain in winter in Mediterranean coastlands.

Eurasian Eagle Owl (Eagle-Owl) *Bubo bubo* Búo Real
A widespread and locally common resident, mainly in rocky hilly or mountainous terrain, with scrub and open woodland. Absent from the highest elevations and scarce in the north-west.

Little Owl *Athene noctua* Mochuelo Común
A widespread and common resident, especially in open habitats including cultivated land.

Tawny Owl *Strix aluco* Cárabo Común
A widespread and locally common resident in wooded habitats.

Long-eared Owl *Asio otus* Búho Chico
A widespread but scarce resident in pinewoods, riparian woodlands and forested edges. Some occur on passage and in winter.

Short-eared Owl *Asio flammeus* Lechuza Campestre
Small numbers widespread on passage and in winter: October–April. Scarce breeder in Castilla y Léon.

Boreal (Tengmalm's) Owl *Aegolius funereus* Mochuelo Boreal
A scarce resident in the Pyrenees, especially in Catalonia.

European Nightjar *Caprimulgus europaeus* Chotacabras Gris
Locally common in summer in open heathland, nesting at higher altitudes than the next species. Scarce in the south-east. Widespread on passage. Present April–October.

Red-necked Nightjar *Caprimulgus ruficollis* Chotacabras Pardo
Widespread and locally common breeder in central Spain and in the east.
Associated with open pinewoods and other areas with scattered trees.
Present April–October.

Chimney Swift* *Chaetura pelagica* Vencejo de Chimenea
Vagrant. Four records from Galicia.

Common Swift *Apus apus* Vencejo Común
Abundant on passage and numerous in most towns and villages. A trans-Sa-
haran migrant: arriving from late March and departing by the end of
September.

Pallid Swift *Apus pallidus* Vencejo Pálido
Locally common in south-central Spain and along the east coast, with col-
onies in most coastal towns. Also nests in Santander, Gijón and coastal
Galicia. Mainly present March–October. Rare migrant in the north.

Alpine Swift *Apus melba* Vencejo Real
Widespread and locally common, small colonies inhabiting mountains and
coastal cliffs. Mainly present March–October.

White-rumped Swift *Apus caffer* Vencejo Cafre
Rarely recorded. Strays into the area from further south and has nested in
Castilla–La Mancha and Madrid.

Little Swift *Apus affinis* Vencejo Moro
Has recently colonised Andalucía and may spread northwards. Five records,
including three from Murcia.

Common Kingfisher *Alcedo atthis* Martín Pescador Común
Frequent on passage and in winter, occurring both inland and on rocky
coasts. Breeds locally.

Belted Kingfisher* *Megaceryle alcyon* Martín Gigante Norteamericano
Vagrant. One record from the Mar Menor, Murcia.

European Bee-eater *Merops apiaster* Abejaruco Europeo
Widespread breeder, except in the far north and Pyrenees. Mainly present
April–September.

Blue-cheeked Bee-eater* *Merops persicus* Abejaruco Papirrojo
Vagrant. Two records.

European Roller *Coracias garrulus* Carraca Europea
Breeds mainly in the southern Meseta, the lower Ebro valley and locally on
the east coast. Mainly present April–September.

Hoopoe *Upupa epops* Abubilla
A widespread and common breeder, except on the north coast. Mainly
present March–September but significant numbers winter, especially along
the east coast.

Eurasian Wryneck   *Jynx torquilla*   Torcecuello
A scarce but widespread breeding species, most numerous in northern
Castilla y Léon and the north-east. Mainly present March–September but
small numbers winter locally.

European Green Woodpecker   *Picus viridis*   Pito Real
A widespread and locally common resident. The Iberian race *P.v.sharpei* is
very distinctive.

Black Woodpecker   *Dryocopus martius*   Picamaderos Negro
Scarce but increasing resident in the Pyrenees and Cordillera Cantábrica.
Favours pine and pine/beech forests in the Pyrenees and beeches in the
Cordillera Cantábrica.

Great Spotted Woodpecker   *Dendrocopus major*   Pico Picapinos
A common and widespread resident, particularly associated with conifers in
mountain areas.

Middle Spotted Woodpecker   *Dendrocopus medius*   Pico Mediano
Scarce resident in the Cordillera Cantábrica and western Pyrenees. In mixed
sessile oak/birch/chestnut woodlands.

White-backed Woodpecker   *Dendrocopus leucotos*   Pico Dorsiblanco
Rare resident in the western Pyrenees, almost entirely in Navarra. Confined
to old-growth beech and beech/birch/pine forests, offering mature trees and
abundant dead wood.

Lesser Spotted Woodpecker   *Dendrocopus minor*   Pico Menor
A very local resident. Most likely to be encountered in lusher, often river-
ine woodlands in south-western Castilla y Léon, the eastern Cordillera
Cantábrica, the upper Ebro valley and Catalonia.

Bar-tailed Desert Lark*   *Ammomanes cinctura*   Terrera Colinegra
Vagrant. Two east coast records.

Dupont's Lark   *Chersophilus duponti*   Alondra Ricotí
Mainly resident. Largely confined to steppes in the Ebro valley and the high
grasslands of the Sistema Ibérico, occurring very locally elsewhere. Most
populations are declining.

Calandra Lark   *Melanocorypha calandra*   Calandria Común
Locally abundant on the Meseta and in the Ebro valley. Rare or absent elsewhere. Characteristic of cereal crops and steppe habitats. Forms large winter
flocks.

Greater Short-toed Lark   *Calandrella brachydactyla*   Terrera Común
Widespread and common in pastures, steppes and fallow areas. Absent
north of the Cordillera Cantábrica and in the Pyrenees. Mainly present April–
September.

Lesser Short-toed Lark   *Calandrella rufescens*   Terrera Marismeña
Locally common but largely confined to salt flats and arid steppe in the
south-east and the Ebro delta and valley. Mainly resident.

Crested Lark *Galerida cristata* Cogujada Común
Widespread and common, but largely absent from the northern coastlands.
Found generally in lower-lying and more open, often cultivated, country than
the Thekla Lark. Mainly resident.

Thekla Lark *Galerida theklae* Cogujada Montesina
Common in open bushy country, typically in hilly terrain. Absent from the
northern coastlands. Mainly resident.

Wood Lark (Woodlark) *Lullula arborea* Alondra Totovía
Common in open woodlands, especially dehesas. Local birds are resident but
others occur on passage and in winter.

Sky Lark (Eurasian Skylark) *Alauda arvensis* Alondra Común
Breeds widely and commonly in the northern half of the region but a mountain bird further south. Widespread and abundant on passage and in winter.

Horned Lark* *Eremophila alpestris* Alondra Cornuda
Vagrant. Four accepted records, three of them from Asturias.

Sand Martin *Riparia riparia* Avión Zapador
Large breeding colonies occur locally, most commonly in the north, often
along major river valleys. Widespread and common on passage. Mainly
present March–October.

Eurasian Crag Martin *Ptyonoprogne rupestris* Avión Roquero
Widespread and common wherever there are cliffs or rocky areas. Largely
coastal in winter, forming large roosts locally.

Barn Swallow *Hirundo rustica* Golondrina Común
Abundant breeder and passage migrant. Mainly present February–October.

Common House Martin *Delichon urbicum* Avión Común
Abundant breeder and passage migrant. Most nest on buildings but also on
dams and cliffs. Mainly present February–October.

Red-rumped Swallow *Cecropis daurica* Golondrina Dáurica
Widespread and locally common in the southern half of the region, more
local or absent in the north. Nests on rocks and under bridges especially.
Mainly present February–October.

Richard's Pipit *Anthus richardi* Bisbita de Richard
Very scarce on passage and in winter, when annual in the northern coastlands, especially Galicia and Asturias. Also recorded from the Mediterranean
coast.

Blyth's Pipit* *Anthus godlewskii* Bisbita Estepario
Vagrant. One record from Asturias.

Tawny Pipit *Anthus campestris* Bisbita Campestre
Common breeder in the northern Meseta and Ebro valley, more local elsewhere. Widespread on passage. Mainly present April–September.

Olive-backed Pipit* *Anthus hodgsoni* Bisbita de Hodgson
Vagrant. One record from Galicia.

Tree Pipit   *Anthus trivialis*   Bisbita Arbóreo
Breeds in the northern third of the region. Widespread and common on
passage, chiefly March–May and September–October.

Meadow Pipit   *Anthus pratensis*   Bisbita Común
Widespread and common on passage and in winter. Present September–April
mainly but a few nest in the Cantabrian range.

Red-throated Pipit   *Anthus cervinus*   Bisbita Gorgirrojo
Very scarce on passage, predominantly in spring in April–early May.
Occasional in winter, Noted mainly in the eastern coastlands.

Water Pipit   *Anthus spinoletta*   Bisbita Alpino
Characteristic of high mountain pastures, breeding in all the major ranges.
Widespread and locally common in winter, in waterside habitats at low eleva-
tions.

Eurasian Rock Pipit   *Anthus petrosus*   Bisbita Costero
Scarce winterer on northern coasts. Very rare elsewhere.

Yellow Wagtail   *Motacilla flava*   Lavandera Boyera
The Iberian race *M. f. iberiae* breeds commonly on the north and east coasts,
in the northern Meseta and locally elsewhere. Mainly present March–October.
Widespread and common on passage, when races *flava, thunbergi* and
flavissima are regular. There are six accepted records of the distinctive black-
headed race, *feldegg*, chiefly from the east coast.

Citrine Wagtail   *Motacilla citreola*   Lavandera Cetrina
Rare migrant but annual, chiefly on the east coast in autumn, reports peaking
in September.

Grey Wagtail   *Motacilla cinerea*   Lavandera Cascadeña
A common resident along rocky watercourses. More widespread on passage
and in winter.

White Wagtail   *Motacilla alba*   Lavandera Blanca
Common and widespread resident. Common on passage and abundant in
winter, when large winter roosts occur in cities. The Pied Wagtail *M.a.yarrellii*
occurs in very small numbers in winter and on passage.

Bohemian Waxwing*   *Bombycilla garrulus*   Ampelis Europeo.
Vagrant in winter. Fourteen recent records, of groups of up to six, chiefly in
the north.

White-throated Dipper   *Cinclus cinclus*   Mirlo Acuático
Common in the northern mountains and more locally along boulder-strewn,
fast-flowing streams elsewhere. Resident.

Winter Wren   *Troglodytes troglodytes*   Chochín Común
A widespread and common resident, absent only from steppes and agricultural lands.

Dunnock   *Prunella modularis*   Acentor Común
Common in northern Spain, especially in the Cordillera Cantábrica and
Pyrenees, and in high mountain areas elsewhere. More widespread but
inconspicuous in winter, occurring in scrub.

Alpine Accentor   *Prunella collaris*   Acentor Alpino
Breeds on the high tops of the Cordillera Cantábrica, Pyrenees, Sistema
Central and Sistema Iberico. Occurs more widely at lower levels in winter,
always in rocky terrain.

Rufous-tailed Scrub-robin   *Cercotrichas galactotes*   Alzacola Rojizo
Locally common in the arid south-east and locally on the southern Meseta,
frequenting low scrub along watercourses as well as vineyards and olive and
citrus groves. Mainly present April–September.

European Robin   *Erithacus rubecula*   Petirrojo Europeo
A common resident in the more humid woodlands. Most widespread in the
north. Migrants occur widely on passage and it is abundant in winter.

Siberian Blue Robin*   *Larvivora cyane*   Ruiseñor Azul
Vagrant. One record from the Ebro delta.

Common Nightingale   *Luscinia megarhynchos*   Ruiseñor Común
Widespread and abundant, although scarce in the northern coastlands. Nests
in dense vegetation especially along watercourses. Common on passage.
Present March–October.

Bluethroat   *Luscinia svecica*   Ruiseñor Pechiazul
Breeds in montane scrub in the Sistema Central and western Cordillera
Cantábrica. More widespread on passage and a few winter, generally near
water, especially on the east coast.

Red-flanked Bluetail*   *Tarsiger cyanurus*   Ruiseñor Coliazul
Vagrant. Five records.

Black Redstart   *Phoenicurus ochruros*   Colirrojo Tizón
Locally common in rocky hills and mountains. Widespread and abundant on
passage and in winter.

Common Redstart   *Phoenicurus phoenicurus*   Colirrojo Real
Very local in well-wooded, humid mountainous areas. Numerous only in the
Cordillera Cantábrica, most of Asturias and in the Sistema Ibérico. Mainly
present April–September. Widespread and common on passage.

Moussier's Redstart*   *Phoenicurus moussieri*   Colirrojo Diademado
Vagrant. One accepted record.

Whinchat   *Saxicola rubetra*   Tarabilla Norteña
Breeds in the northern Meseta, Cordillera Cantábrica and Pyrenees. Common
on passage, crossing the area in numbers in April–May and August–October.

Siberian Stonechat   *Saxicola maurus*   Tarabilla Siberiana
Vagrant. At least six records from northern coastal sites.

European Stonechat   *Saxicola rubicola*   Tarabilla Común
Abundant, widespread and characteristic of the region. The large resident
population is greatly increased by migrants in winter.

Isabelline Wheatear   *Oenanthe isabellina*   Collalba Isabel
Vagrant. Five records from Galicia.

Northern Wheatear   *Oenanthe oenanthe*   Collalba Gris
Breeds commonly in the north, generally above 300m, and more locally
further south, where it is a montane species. Widespread and common on
passage. Mainly present March–October.

Black-eared Wheatear   *Oenanthe hispanica*   Collalba Rubia
Common and widespread, especially in the east, inhabiting dry, open habitats.
Absent from the north coast and high mountains. Mainly present March–
October.

Desert Wheatear*   *Oenanthe deserti*   Collalba Desértica
Vagrant. Nine records. Most appear in late autumn and may overwinter.

Black Wheatear   *Oenanthe leucura*   Collalba Negra
Resident. Common in rocky areas in the east and occurs more locally on the
Meseta.

Rufous-tailed (Common) Rock Thrush   *Monticola saxatilis*   Roquero Rojo
Widespread but local breeder in all the major mountain ranges. Present April
to October.

Blue Rock Thrush   *Monticola solitarius*   Roquero Solitario
A widespread and common resident, inhabiting coastal and inland cliffs,
generally below 1,700m. Also often on castles, churches, ruins and other
buildings. Commonest in the east.

Ring Ouzel   *Turdus torquatus*   Mirlo Capiblanco
Breeds in open Black Pine woodlands above 1,700m in the Pyrenees, and very
locally in the Cordillera Cantábrica and Sistema Ibérico. Scarce but widespread on passage, in March–April and October–November. Small numbers
winter in all mountain ranges.

Common Blackbird   *Turdus merula*   Mirlo Común
An abundant and widespread resident species. Numbers increased by
migrants in winter.

Eyebrowed Thrush*   *Turdus obscurus*   Zorzal Rojigrís
Vagrant. One pending record.

Naumann's Thrush*   *Turdus naumanni*   Zorzal de Naumann
Vagrant. One record from the Ebro delta.

Fieldfare   *Turdus pilaris*   Zorzal Real
Regular in winter in montane juniper woods. Scarcer elsewhere.

Song Thrush   *Turdus philomelos*   Zorzal Común
Breeds commonly in forests of the northern third of Iberia, more locally and
usually in mountains further south. Widespread and abundant on passage
and in winter.

Redwing   *Turdus iliacus*   Zorzal Alirrojo
Common on passage and in winter. Most abundant in montane juniper woods.

Mistle Thrush   *Turdus viscivorus*   Zorzal Charlo
Widespread and common. Mainly resident.

American Robin* *Turdus migratorius* Zorzal Robín
Vagrant. One record from the Basque country.

Cetti's Warbler *Cettia cetti* Ruiseñor Bastardo
Widespread and common, especially in the dense vegetation of watercourses.
Resident.

Zitting Cisticola (Fan-tailed Warbler) *Cisticola juncidis* Buitrón
Common in open grassy habitats, on coasts and in river valleys. Mainly resident.

Common Grasshopper Warbler *Locustella naevia* Buscarla Pintoja
Scarce breeder in the northern coastlands. Widespread on passage. Occurs
April-October.

River Warbler* *Locustella fluviatilis* Buscarla Fluvial
Vagrant. One record from Galicia.

Savi's Warbler *Locustella luscinoides* Buscarla Unicolor
Very local, most widespread along the east coast and in Castilla–La Mancha,
nesting in reedbeds. Mainly present April–September.

Booted Warbler* *Iduna caligata* Zarcero Escita
Vagrant. Two records.

Western Olivaceous Warbler *Iduna opaca* Zarcero Pálido
Breeds very locally in the east, in Valencia and Castilla–La Mancha. Typical of
hot, low-lying areas. May–September.

Icterine Warbler *Hippolais icterina* Zarcero Icterino
Scarce migrant, mainly in the east and most numerous in spring, late April–
May.

Melodious Warbler *Hippolais polyglotta* Zarcero Común
Widespread and common, occurring especially in scrub with scattered trees,
often near water. Often numerous on passage. April–October.

Moustached Warbler *Acrocephalus melanopogon* Carricerín Real
Very local, largely confined to reedbeds at east coast wetlands and on the
southern meseta. Mainly resident but joined by migrants from France in
winter.

Aquatic Warbler *Acrocephalus paludicola* Carricerín Cejudo
Extremely scarce but regular on passage in autumn. August–October. Also in
spring (April) on the east coast. Chiefly recorded by ringers.

Sedge Warbler *Acrocephalus schoenobaenus* Carricerín Común
Widespread on passage: March–May and August–October.

Paddyfield Warbler* *Acrocephalus agricola* Carricero Agricola
Vagrant. At least ten records from the east coast, chiefly caught by ringers in
winter.

Marsh Warbler* *Acrocephalus palustris* Carricero Políglota
Rare passage migrant. Three accepted records from the east coast.

Eurasian Reed Warbler *Acrocephalus scirpaceus* Carricero Común
Nests commonly in reedbeds. Widespread on passage. April–October.

Great Reed Warbler *Acrocephalus arundinaceus* Carricero Tordal
Nests commonly in reedbeds. Widespread on passage. April–October.

Marmora's Warbler* *Sylvia sarda* Curruca Sarda
Vagrant. Two records.

Dartford Warbler *Sylvia undata* Curruca Rabilarga
Widespread and common in low scrub. Mainly resident.

Spectacled Warbler *Sylvia conspicillata* Curruca Tomillera
Locally common in extremely low scrub in the Mediterranean coastlands and
arid inland regions. Also in steppe habitats, as in the Ebro basin, sometimes
at considerable altitude. Mainly present March–October.

Subalpine Warbler *Sylvia cantillans* Curruca Carrasqueña
Common breeder in tall scrub and the understorey of open woodlands, chiefly
in hilly or mountainous terrain. Mainly absent from the northern coastlands.
February–October.

Sardinian Warbler *Sylvia melanocephala* Curruca Cabecinegra
Widespread and abundant resident in the southern meseta, the east and the
Ebro valley. Occurs locally in the northern coastlands. In scrub and dry wood-
land. Mainly resident.

Asian Desert Warbler* *Sylvia nana* Curruca del Turquestán
Vagrant. One record from Cantabria.

African Desert Warbler* *Sylvia deserti* Curruca Sahariana
Vagrant. One record from Alicante.

Western Orphean Warbler *Sylvia hortensis* Curruca Mirlona
Widespread breeder in open woodlands. Absent from the northern coastlands. April–October.

Barred Warbler* *Sylvia nisoria* Curruca Gavilana
Vagrant. Two records.

Lesser Whitethroat* *Sylvia curruca* Curruca Zarcerilla
Very rare migrant, chiefly in the east.

Common Whitethroat *Sylvia communis* Curruca Zarcera
Widespread breeder in the north but more local in the south and east.
Common on passage. Mainly present March–October.

Garden Warbler *Sylvia borin* Curruca Mosquitera
Breeds commonly in the northern half of the region, very locally elsewhere.
Widespread and common on passage: April–May and August–October.

Blackcap *Sylvia atricapilla* Curruca Capirotada
Widespread and common, nesting in scrub, gardens and open broadleaved
woodlands. Confined in drier regions to riverine woodlands. Local birds are
joined by large numbers of migrants in winter, when it is particularly abundant in olive groves.

Greenish Warbler* *Phylloscopus trochiloides* Mosquitero Verdoso
Vagrant. One accepted record.

Pallas's Warbler* *Phylloscopus proregulus* Mosquitero de Pallas
Vagrant. Seven records.

Yellow-browed Warbler *Phylloscopus inornatus* Mosquitero Bilistado
Rare migrant, now reported annually in autumn, chiefly in October. Several
winter records.

Hume's Leaf Warbler* Phylloscopus humei Mosquitero de Hume
Vagrant. One record from Galicia.

Radde's Warbler* *Phylloscopus schwarzi* Mosquitero de Schwarz
Vagrant. Three records.

Dusky Warbler* *Phylloscopus fuscatus* Mosquitero Sombrío
Vagrant. Five records.

Western Bonelli's Warbler *Phylloscopus bonelli* Mosquitero Papialbo
Nests commonly in open mixed woodlands but more local in the northern
coastlands and the south-east. Widespread on passage. Mainly present April–
September.

Wood Warbler *Phylloscopus sibilatrix* Mosquitero Silbador
Rare or sporadic breeder in the Cordillera Cantábrica and Pyrenees. Very
scarce but widespread on passage in April–May. Rare in autumn.

Common Chiffchaff *Phylloscopus collybita* Mosquitero Común
Breeds in the Pyrenees and locally elsewhere. Common on passage and
abundant in winter, then often occurring in open country far from any trees.

Iberian Chiffchaff *Phylloscopus ibericus* Mosquitero Ibérico
Breeds commonly in the north and north-west of the area, typically in humid
woodlands. It is best located by its 'chiff chiff' song; a monotonous but
distinctive repetition of one syllable. A trans-Saharan migrant, present April–
August mainly.

Willow Warbler *Phylloscopus trochilus* Mosquitero Musical
Rare breeder in the Cordillera Cantábrica and País Vasco. A trans-Saharan
migrant, crossing the region in large numbers from March–May and August–
October.

Goldcrest *Regulus regulus* Reyezuelo Sencillo
Common breeder in coniferous forests in high mountains. More widespread
at lower altitudes in winter.

Common Firecrest *Regulus ignicapilla* Reyezuelo Listado
Common breeder in forests and woodlands in the north, more local in the
south. The resident population is increased by migrants in winter, when it is
more widespread.

Spotted Flycatcher *Muscicapa striata* Papamoscas Gris
Widespread breeder, commonest in the east. Present April–September.
Common on passage.

Red-breasted Flycatcher* *Ficedula parva* Papamoscas Papirrojo
Very rare migrant. Twenty-seven records, mainly from the east coast and in autumn.

Collared Flycatcher* *Ficedula albicollis* Papamoscas Collarino
Very rare migrant. Twenty-plus records, mainly from Catalonia in April–May.

European Pied Flycatcher *Ficedula hypoleuca* Papamoscas Cerrojillo
Breeds in the Sistema Ibérico, Sistema Central, the central and eastern Cordillera Cantábrica and the western Pyrenees, very locally elsewhere. Common and widespread on passage. Present April–October.

Bearded Reedling (Tit) *Panurus biarmicus* Bigotudo
Breeds very locally in large reedbeds, especially in Castilla–La Mancha and on the east coast. Mainly resident but irruptive and may appear elsewhere.

Red-billed Leiothrix *Leiothrix lutea* Leotrix Piquirrojo
A naturalised population is resident in forests near Barcelona.

Long-tailed Tit *Aegithalos caudatus* Mito
Locally common in mixed and oak woodlands. Resident.

Blue Tit *Cyanistes caeruleus* Herrerillo Común
A widespread and common resident. Typically in woodlands, parks and gardens.

Great Tit *Parus major* Carbonero Común
A widespread and common resident. Typically in woodlands, parks and gardens.

Coal Tit *Periparus ater* Carbonero Garrapinos
Widespread and common in coniferous woodlands. Resident.

European Crested Tit *Lophophanes cristatus* Herrerillo Capuchino
Widespread and common in open evergreen woodlands. Resident.

Marsh Tit *Poecile palustris* Carbonero Palustre
Confined to deciduous woodlands in the Cordillera Cantábrica, the Pyrenees and Sistema Ibérico. Resident.

Eurasian Nuthatch *Sitta europaea* Trepador Azul
Widespread in open deciduous woodlands and in montane conifers. Resident.

Wallcreeper *Tichodroma muraria* Treparriscos
Breeds locally at altitude in the central Cordillera Cantábrica and in the Pyrenees: chiefly in Aragón and Catalonia. Occurs more widely in winter, sometimes down to sea level in the north, generally favouring limestone cliffs.

Eurasian Treecreeper *Certhia familiaris* Agateador Norteño
Confined to deciduous forests generally above 1,000m in the Cordillera Cantábrica, Pyrenees and Sistema Ibérico.

Short-toed Treecreeper *Certhia brachydactyla* Agateador Común
Widespread and common in all woodland types but favouring mature trees. Mainly resident but more widely dispersed in winter, when many descend from higher altitudes.

Eurasian Penduline Tit *Remiz pendulinus* Pajaro Moscón
An increasing population frequents riverine vegetation in the Ebro, Duero and Tajo valleys and locally elsewhere. More widespread in winter in reedbeds and along watercourses.

Eurasian Golden Oriole *Oriolus oriolus* Oropéndola
Nests commonly in mature open and, especially, riverine woodland, as well as in poplar plantations. Widespread on migration. Mainly present April–September.

Brown Shrike* *Lanius cristatus* Alcaudón Pardo
Vagrant. One record from the Ebro delta.

Isabelline Shrike* *Lanius isabellinus* Alcaudón Isabel
Vagrant. Two records.

Red-backed Shrike *Lanius collurio* Alcaudón Dorsirrojo
Breeds commonly in the northern coastlands, the Cordillera Cantábrica, Pyrenees and northern Sistema Ibérico. Present April–September. Scarce elsewhere on passage.

Lesser Grey Shrike* *Lanius minor* Alcaudón Chico
Formerly bred in the north-east, in the provinces of Gerona, Lleida and Huesca, but close to extinction in Spain, despite releases of captive-bred birds. Present April–September.

Great Grey Shrike* *Lanius excubitor* Alcaudón Norteño
Occasional individuals occur in winter, chiefly in the northern coastlands.

Southern Grey Shrike *Lanius meridionalis* Alcaudón Reál
Widespread and common in open woodlands and in scrub with scattered trees. Rare or absent in the northern coastlands, the Cordillera Cantábrica and Pyrenees. Mainly resident.

Woodchat Shrike *Lanius senator* Alcaudón Común
Widespread and common, absent chiefly from closed forests and mountains above 1,500m and from the northern coastlands. Present mid-March–October.

Eurasian Jay *Garrulus glandarius* Arrendajo
Widespread and common in woodlands, especially where oaks are present. Resident.

Iberian Azure-winged Magpie *Cyanopica cooki* Rabilargo Ibérico
Common in evergreen oak and pine woodlands and olive groves in the south-west, extending north-west to Madrid and central Castilla y Léon. Rare elsewhere. Resident.

Common Magpie *Pica pica* Urraca
Widespread and common. Resident.

Spotted Nutcracker* *Nucifraga caryocatactes* Cascanueces
Vagrant. Has irrupted occasionally, chiefly to the north-east. Only one recent record.

Yellow-billed (Alpine) Chough *Pyrrhocorax graculus* Chova Piquigualda
Breeds commonly in the Cordillera Cantábrica and Pyrenees, generally above 1,000m. Flocks frequent pastures. Descends lower in winter, sometimes to sea level in the northern coastlands. Resident.

Red-billed Chough *Pyrrhocorax pyrrhocorax* Chova Piquirroja
Widespread and locally common, principally on cliffs in mountainous country and on the northern coast and also in river gorges. Resident.

Western Jackdaw *Corvus monedula* Grajilla
Widespread and locally common, although scarce in Galicia and the northern coastlands. Colonies favour bridges, ruined castles and similar buildings as well as cliffs. Resident.

Rook *Corvus frugilegus* Graja
An isolated population of up to 2,000 pairs, the only one in Spain, breeds in León province. Rare elsewhere, chiefly in winter, when the resident birds disperse more widely in the north.

Carrion Crow *Corvus corone* Corneja Negra
Common in the northern half of the area but largely absent from the east coast and south-western Castilla–La Mancha. Mainly resident but occasional individuals wander in winter.

Hooded Crow* *Corvus (corone) cornix* Corneja Cenicienta
Vagrant. Ten-plus records, chiefly from Catalonia.

Northern Raven *Corvus corax* Cuervo
Widespread and common, nesting on cliffs but also on pylons and tall trees. Large flocks form on farmland in winter. Resident.

Spotless Starling *Sturnus unicolor* Estornino Negro
Widespread and common, nesting in holes in trees and on buildings. Mainly resident.

Common Starling *Sturnus vulgaris* Estornino Pinto
Common breeder in Catalonia and in the northern coastlands from central Asturias eastwards. Migrant, wintering throughout in the area. Present October–April. Numbers vary greatly between winters.

Rosy Starling* *Sturnus roseus* Estornino Rosado
Vagrant. Twenty-six records, nine of them from Catalonia.

House Sparrow *Passer domesticus* Gorrión Común
Widespread and common, nesting colonially in trees in open country as well as in towns and villages, where holes in buildings are used. Resident.

Spanish Sparrow *Passer hispaniolensis* Gorrión Moruno
Locally abundant in the south-west of the region, very local in central areas and largely absent from the east. Large colonies in isolated clumps of trees are typical. Mainly resident.

Eurasian Tree Sparrow *Passer montanus* Gorrión Molinero
Widespread and common in open habitats, especially on the Meseta. Mainly resident.

Rock Sparrow *Petronia petronia* Gorrión Chillón
Widespread and locally common, but absent from the northern coastlands.
Frequents rocky terrain and open woodlands nearby, generally above 500m.
Resident.

White-winged Snowfinch *Montifringilla nivalis* Gorrión Alpino
Breeds locally above 1,800m in the central Cordillera Cantábrica and in the
Pyrenees: chiefly in Aragón. Resident. Favours mountain pastures, scree and
the edges of snowfields.

Common Waxbill *Estrilda astrild* Pico de Coral Común
An introduced and naturalised species. Breeds in western Galicia and at
scattered wetlands along the east coast. Often reported in small groups in
reedbeds.

Red Avadavat *Amandava amandava* Bengalí Rojo
An introduced and naturalised species. Breeds along the Tagus and Jarama
valleys in Madrid and has nested at scattered wetlands along the east coast.

Red-eyed Vireo* *Vireo olivaceus* Vireo Olirrojo
Vagrant. Three east coast records.

Common Chaffinch *Fringilla coelebs* Pinzón Vulgar
A widespread and common resident in all types of woodland. Large numbers
also occur on passage and in winter.

Brambling *Fringilla montifringilla* Pinzón Real
Scarce but regular on passage and in winter. Numbers vary considerably
from year to year. Occurs chiefly November–March.

European Serin *Serinus serinus* Verdecillo
Widespread and common. Absent only from treeless areas although winter
flocks occur in open country. Southern birds are resident but many northern
and central birds winter further south.

Citril Finch *Serinus citrinella* Verderón Serrano
Locally common in all the principal high mountain ranges, descending lower
in winter. Associated with montane conifers.

European Greenfinch *Carduelis chloris* Verderón Común
A widespread and common resident. Numbers are increased by migrants in
winter.

European Goldfinch *Carduelis carduelis* Jilguero
A widespread and common resident. Numbers are increased by migrants in
winter.

Eurasian Siskin *Carduelis spinus* Lúgano
Breeds locally and sporadically in mountain pinewoods, chiefly in the
Pyrenees. Widespread and common in winter, when associated with alders.
Occurs chiefly November–March.

Common Linnet *Carduelis cannabina* Pardillo Común
Widespread and common. Many are resident but others move south to winter.
Numbers are increased by migrants in winter.

Twite* *Carduelis flavirostris*   Pardillo Piquigualdo
Vagrant in winter. Five records, including a flock of 19 in Asturias.

Common Redpoll* *Carduelis flammea*   Pardillo Sizerín
Vagrant to the north in winter. At least six recent records.

Red Crossbill *Loxia curvirostra*   Piquituerto Común
A local breeding species, inhabiting pine forests. Most widespread in irruption
years.

Trumpeter Finch *Bucanetes githagineus*   Camachuelo Trompetero
Nests in the driest parts of Murcia and Alicante. Mainly resident.

Common Rosefinch* *Carpodacus erythrinus*   Camachuelo Carminoso
Vagrant. Twelve records, mainly juveniles found in autumn.

Eurasian Bullfinch *Pyrrhula pyrrhula*   Camachuelo Común
Breeds commonly in the northern coastlands, the Cordillera Cantábrica and
Pyrenees, and also in the northern Sistema Ibérico. Individuals and small
groups occur more widely in winter.

Hawfinch *Coccothraustes coccothraustes*   Picogordo
Locally common breeder in open deciduous woodland in Castilla y Léon and
Castilla–La Mancha and very locally elsewhere. More widespread in winter.

Yellow-rumped Warbler *Dendroica coronata*   Reinita Coronada
Vagrant. One record from Galicia.

Lapland Bunting (Longspur)* *Calcarius lapponicus*   Escribano Lapón
Rare. September–January. Single birds and flocks of up to four are reported,
chiefly from the north coast, where it may occur more regularly in winter.

Snow Bunting *Plectrophenax nivalis*   Escribano Nival
Scarce but fairly regular on north-west coasts, October–March. Vagrant elsewhere.

Pine Bunting* *Emberiza leucocephalos*   Escribano de Gmelin
Vagrant. Four records.

Yellowhammer *Emberiza citrinella*   Escribano Cerillo
Breeds in the humid north and the Pyrenees, south to northernmost Castilla y
Léon. More widespread in winter but rare in the south.

Cirl Bunting *Emberiza cirlus*   Escribano Soteño
Widespread and common, mainly in open bushy country near woodland in the
lower sierras.

Rock Bunting *Emberiza cia*   Escribano Montesino
Widespread and common in rocky areas, notably in all the main sierras.
Mainly resident but some descend to lower levels in winter.

Ortolan Bunting *Emberiza hortulana*   Escribano Hortelano
Breeds in the northern half of the region, north to the south-facing slopes
of the Cordillera Cantábrica and Pyrenees. Favours open woodlands at
moderate altitudes, higher in the southern mountains. Mainly present April–
September. Widespread on passage.

Rustic Bunting* *Emberiza rustica*   Escribano Rustico
Vagrant. Three records.

Little Bunting* *Emberiza pusilla*   Escribano Pigmeo
Vagrant. Thirty-seven records, chiefly in autumn and winter.

Yellow-breasted Bunting* *Emberiza aureola*   Escribano Aureolado
Vagrant. One record from Belchite, Aragón.

Common Reed Bunting *Emberiza schoeniclus*   Escribano Palustre
Breeds locally, chiefly in Galicia and the northern coastlands, the Ebro delta
and some wetlands of Castilla–La Mancha. Immigrants are widespread and
common in winter, especially in the east.

Red-headed Bunting* *Emberiza bruniceps*   Escribano Carirrojo
Vagrant. Three records from Catalonia.

Black-headed Bunting* *Emberiza melanocephala*   Escribano Cabecinegro
Vagrant. Four records from Catalonia.

Corn Bunting *Emberiza calandra*   Triguero
A typical and abundant species of open country and farmland, but scarce in
the northern coastlands. Mainly resident but flocks wander in winter and
Galician birds winter further south.

APPENDICES

1 SCIENTIFIC NAMES OF PLANT SPECIES MENTIONED

Albardine	*Lygeum spartum*	Kermes Oak	*Quercus coccifera*
Aleppo Pine	*Pinus halepensis*	Lavender	*Lavandula spp.*
Alder	*Alnus glutinosa*	Lentisc	*Pistachia lentiscus*
Almond	*Prunus dulcis*	Lime	*Tilia spp.*
Ash	*Fraxinus excelsior*	Lusitanian Oak	*Quercus faginea*
Black Pine	*Pinus nigra*	Maritime Pine	*Pinus pinaster*
Agave	*Agave americana*	Maple	*Acer opalus*
Asphodel	*Asphodelus albus*	Mountain Pine	*Pinus uncinata*
Black Poplar	*Populus nigra*	Myrtle	*Myrtus communis*
Beech	*Fagus sylvatica*	Narrow-leaved Ash	*Fraxinus angustifolia*
Birch	*Betula spp.*	Oleander	*Nerium oleander*
Box	*Buxus sempervirens*	Olive	*Olea europaea*
Blackthorn	*Prunus spinosa*	Orache	*Atriplex halimus*
Buckthorn	*Rhamnus alaternus*	Pedunculate Oak	*Quercus robur*
Canarian Oak	*Quercus canariensis*	Prickly Pear	*Opuntia ficus-indica*
Carob	*Ceratonia siliquae*	Pyrenean Oak	*Quercus pyrenaica*
Chamomile	*Chamaemelum spp.*	Retama	*Lygos sphaerocarpa*
Chestnut	*Castanea sativa*	Rhododendron	*Rhododendron ponticum*
Cistus (Sun-rose)	*Cistus spp.*		
Common Gorse	*Ulex europaeus*	Rosemary	*Rosmarinus officinalis*
Common Reed	*Phragmites communis*	Rowan	*Sorbus acuparia*
Cork Oak	*Quercus suber*	Scots Pine	*Pinus sylvestris*
Eelgrass	*Zostera marina/ Z. noltii*	Sea Daffodil	*Pancratium maritimum*
Eucalyptus	*Eucalyptus globulus etc*	Sessile Oak	*Quercus petraea*
		Silver Fir	*Abies alba*
Encina	*Quercus rotundifolia*	Smooth-leaved Elm	*Ulmus minor*
False Esparto Grass	*Stipa tenacissima*	Spanish Juniper	*Juniperus thurifera*
Fan Palm	*Chamaerops humilis*	Spiny Broom	*Calicotome villosa*
Genista	*Genista spp.*	Strawberry Tree	*Arbutus unedo*
Giant Reed	*Arundo donax*	Stone Pine	*Pinus pinea*
Glasswort	*Salicornia spp.*	Sweet Chestnut	*Castanea sativa*
Gum Cistus	*Cistus ladanifer*	Tamarisk	*Tamarix africana*
Hawthorn	*Crataegus monogyna*	Thyme	*Thymus spp.*
Hazel	*Corylus avellana*	Tree Heath	*Erica arborea*
Halimium	*Halimium halmifolium*	Willow	*Salix spp.*
Holly	*Ilex aquifolium*	White Poplar	*Populus albus*
Holm Oak	*Quercus rotundifolia*	Yew	*Taxus baccata*
Juniper	*Juniperus phoenicea etc*		

2   GLOSSARY OF LOCAL GEOGRAPHICAL TERMS

Albufera	Coastal lagoon	Hayedo	Beechwood
Alcornocál	Cork Oak wood	Laguna	Lake
Azúd	Dam	Marismas	Tidal flats
Bahía	Bay	Mirador	View Point
Braña	Upland pasture	Montaña	Mountain
Brezal	Heathland, moorland	Peñon	Rock
Cabo	Cape	Piornal	*Cytisus* Broom scrub
Cañón	Canyon, gorge	Playa	Beach
Cascada	Waterfall	Prat	Meadow
Clot	A hollow	Porreo	Wet meadow
Dehesa	Grazing woodland	Presa	Dam
Desembocadura	Estuary	Puente	Bridge
Desfiladero	Gorge	Puerto	Mountain pass (also seaport)
Desierto	Desert		
Embalse	Reservoir	Punta	Headland
Encinar	Holm Oak wood	Ría	Tidal inlet
Enebral	Juniper scrub	Ribera	River valley
Ensenada	Inlet, Cove	Río	River
Ermita	Hermitage	Salada	Saline lagoon
Estany	Lagoon	Salina	Salt Pan
Estepa	Steppe	Santuario	Shrine
Estuario	Estuary	Serranía	Mountain range
Faro	Lighthouse	Sierra	Mountain
Galacho	Oxbow lake	Soto	Riverine woodland

FURTHER READING

Blondel, J. & Aronson, J. 1999. *Biology and wildlife of the Mediterranean region.* OUP, Oxford.

Crochet P.-A. & Joynt G. (2015). AERC list of Western Palearctic birds. July 2015 version. Available at aerc.eu/tac

del Hoyo, J. & Collar, N. 2014. *Handbook of the Birds of the World/Birdlife International Illustrated checklist of the birds of the World.* Volume 1. Non-passerines. Lynx Edicions, Barcelona.

del Hoyo, J. & Collar, N. 2016. *Handbook of the Birds of the World/Birdlife International Illustrated checklist of the birds of the World.* Volume 2. Passerines. Lynx Edicions, Barcelona.

de Juana, E. & Garcia, E. 2015. *The Birds of the Iberian Peninsula.* Christopher Helm, London.

Garcia, E. & Paterson, A. 2008. *Where to watch birds in Southern and Western Spain.* Third edition. Christopher Helm, London.

Gutiérrez, R., de Juana, E. & Lorenzo, J. A. 2012. *Lista de las aves de España.* Sociedad Española de Ornitología, Madrid.

Montero, J.A. *et al. 2005. Where to watch birds in Spain. The 100 best sites.* Lynx Edicions, Barcelona.

Thorogood, C. 2016. *Field guide to the wild flowers of the Western Mediterranean.* Kew Publishing, Richmond, UK.

SITE INDEX

INDEX OF SPECIES BY SITE NUMBER

AR = Aragón; AS = Asturias; CAN = Cantabria; CAT = Cataluña; CLM = Castilla–La Mancha; CyL = Castilla y León; GA = Galicia; M = Madrid; MU = Murcia; N = Navarra; PV = País Vasco (Euskadi); R = La Rioja; V = Valencia (Comunidad Valenciana)